AF571782

TIME *and* TRANSFORMATION *in Seventeenth-Century Dutch Art*

TIME *and* TRANSFORMATION

in Seventeenth-Century Dutch Art

SUSAN DONAHUE KURETSKY

With contributions by

WALTER S. GIBSON, CATHERINE LEVESQUE, ERIK P. LÖFFLER,

LYNN FEDERLE ORR, AND ARTHUR K. WHEELOCK JR.

THE FRANCES LEHMAN LOEB ART CENTER

Vassar College · Poughkeepsie, New York

This catalogue is published in conjunction with the exhibition
Time and Transformation in Seventeenth-Century Dutch Art

EXHIBITION SCHEDULE:

Frances Lehman Loeb Art Center, Vassar College, Poughkeepsie
April 8 – June 19, 2005

John and Mable Ringling Museum of Art, Sarasota
August 20 – October 30, 2005

The Speed Art Museum, Louisville
January 10 – March 26, 2006

The exhibition and its catalogue have been supported by generous contributions from the Samuel H. Kress Foundation, Inc., the Smart Family Foundation, Inc., and the Agnes Rindge Claflin Fund.

Editor: Maya Hoptman
Design & Typography: Howard I. Gralla
Printed by Thames Printing Company, Inc., Norwich, Connecticut

Distributed by the University of Washington Press, Seattle, Washington
ISBN 0-9644263-7-4

COVER ILLUSTRATION:

Daniel Vosmaer, *View of a Dutch Village with a Ruined Wall*, c. 1660–65 (oil on panel, 64.1 × 53 cm)
Frances Lehman Loeb Art Center, Vassar College, 1962.2 (Cat. 44)

Contents

Foreword

The power of time to transform all things is one of the given conditions of existence. Everything, inanimate or animate, changes with the passage of time. Paradoxically, paintings and other works of representational art capture moments of time and freeze them as long as the support and materials of the art work continue to exist—for those materials are also subject to the immutable laws of change with time. The only things that do not change are the physical laws of time and transformation. The exhibition documented by this catalogue focuses on Dutch visual culture of the seventeenth century and its fascination with the locations and objects that evince the inevitable metamorphoses created by the passage of time.

The exhibition *Time and Transformation in Seventeenth-Century Dutch Art* is the intellectual creation of Susan Donahue Kuretsky, Sarah Gibson Blanding Professor of Art at Vassar College. In the best possible sense of the role colleges and universities play in the research and development of new ideas, the inspiration for this exhibition grew out of many years of classroom teaching and thinking, often using works in the Frances Lehman Loeb Art Center, six of which are in this exhibition. It is the type of exhibition that college museums do best, where the idea leads and the quality of execution follows in the spirit of pure research with little thought for the "marketability" of the results. While comprising a lovely group of paintings, drawings, and prints, the legacy of *Time and Transformation* is found between the covers of this publication. Professor Kuretsky's rigorous examination of the material, her perceptive choice of works to complement the various conceptual chapters, and her selection of a truly gifted team of collaborators have been a pleasure to behold. Her work does great honor to Vassar College as a place where the classical phases of learning are never out of date or style. Professor Kuretsky's exacting scholarship is a strong testimonial to this principle. It is a great pleasure to share this work with a broader public.

It is also a pleasure for me to acknowledge the significant financial support of the Samuel H. Kress Foundation, Inc., the Agnes Rindge Claflin Fund, and the Smart Family Foundation, Inc., in bringing this exhibition and its publication to fruition. The exhibition would not have been able to achieve its broad selection of the finest Dutch art from American collections without the support of our two institutional partners in Sarasota and Louisville and their directors, John Wetenhall, executive director, John and Mable Ringling Museum of Art, and Peter Morrin, director, The Speed Art Museum. In addition to hosting *Time and Transformation* at their museums, they also lent important paintings to the cause. I would also like to express appreciation to all the lenders of works to the exhibition. Their cooperation has been remarkable and is, I believe, an expression of their collegial respect for Professor Kuretsky. Finally, I would like to acknowledge the University of Washington Press and its director, Pat Soden, for their support in distributing the catalogue to a wider audience.

James Mundy
The Anne Hendricks Bass Director
The Frances Lehman Loeb Art Center

Acknowledgments

The beginnings of this project (not fully recognized until quite recently) go all the way back to my earliest encounters with art history as a Vassar undergraduate. In 1962 the Frances Lehman Loeb Art Center, then known as the Vassar College Art Gallery, purchased Daniel Vosmaer's *View of a Dutch Village with a Ruined Wall* (Cat. 44). I wrote a term paper on this painting, which subsequently made its way into a college publication called *The Vassar Journal of Undergraduate Studies*. That Vosmaer's painting now appears on the cover of the present volume testifies to the profound and cumulative effect of exposure to original objects in a college art museum. A Vassar seminar on Old Master drawings, taught in 1963 by visiting scholar and collector Curtis O. Baer, was an introduction to the joys of communing with works on paper, which Mr. Baer brought with him each week from his house in New Rochelle. One of the sheets that emerged from his black travel case was Jacob van Ruisdael's unforgettable *Ruined Cottage* (Cat. 30). These encounters with original works of art continued in the Ph.D. program at the Fogg Art Museum at Harvard University, where Rembrandt's etching of *St. Jerome with the Pollard Willow* (Cat. 73) became the subject of a paper under the inspirational guidance of Seymour Slive. These three works—a painting, a drawing, and a print—would unexpectedly emerge again many years later to become cornerstones of this project.

A powerful impetus to build upon them has been the pleasure of working, now on the other side of the desk, with Vassar's lively and creative undergraduates, especially the participants in several recent seminars: Northern European Landscape, Dutch Ruins, Master Printmakers, and Art and Science in the Age of Vermeer. The discussions in these courses have stimulated reflection in and beyond class meetings, proving again and again that the best way to find out about something you don't know (or to delve more deeply into something you do) is to try teaching it. My students have been responsive in their looking, resourceful in their research, and often original in their thinking. My gratitude to them is boundless and heartfelt.

To teach a topic in the classroom and to form an exhibition around it in the museum are very different matters, however. One does not undertake the latter alone and never without substantial support, both collegial and financial. My profound thanks are offered to the small but dedicated staff of the Frances Lehman Loeb Art Center at Vassar College: James Mundy, director, who welcomed a colleague from the departmental side of our enterprise and found funding to get the project underway and to see that it developed into a more ambitious and wide-ranging exhibition and catalogue than originally envisioned; Joann Potter, registrar, for careful organizational overview, constant practical assistance, and encouragement at all stages of this project; Karen Casey Hines, assistant registrar, for devoted attention to photographic orders and documentation; and Francine Brown, assistant to the director, for additional help with photographs. Advice and assistance have also been generously offered by curators Patricia Phagan and Joel Smith and by Bruce Bundock, the museum's preparator. Faithful and enthusiastic student assistants and interns over the past three years deserve highest praise for their assistance with the many tasks involved in catalogue preparation: Josi Ward, Margaret Horn, Lara Yaeger, Jason Schreiber, Brittany Prieto, Adam Tessier, Anna Gutman, Rebecca Worthington, and Tara Pyle.

My colleagues in the Art Department have been unfailingly generous in their support, and for special counsel, I thank Karen Lucic, Eve d'Ambra, Brian Lukacher, Jessica Winston, Nicholas Adams, and Peter Huenink. Thomas Hill, Vassar's art librarian, and his assistant Ellie Davies have provided frequent bibliographical assistance, as has Ronald Patkus, special collections librarian. Beyond my own institution, I have greatly benefited from access to the resources of the New York Public Library and the Frick Art Reference Library in New York and the Koninklijke Bibliotheek and the Rijksbureau voor Kunsthistorische Documentatie in The Hague.

The five scholars who contributed essays to this volume (Catherine Levesque, Walter Gibson, Arthur Wheelock, Lynn Orr, and Erik Löffler) brought their expertise and creative thinking to the table while also serving as project consultants. I am indebted to all of them and particularly thank Erik Löffler of the Rijksbureau voor Kunsthistorische Documentatie for his consultation on historical and bibliographical matters and for patiently correcting my translations of Dutch inscriptions and other texts. Professor Robert Brown of Vassar's Department of Classical Studies has provided important assistance with Latin terms and inscriptions. Maya Hoptman, the meticulous editor of this volume, has worked closely and patiently with all contributors, while the book's handsome design is the creation of Howard Gralla, whose participation in this project is also deeply appreciated. George Laws, publications manager at Vassar College, has generously consulted during all phases of this project.

Numerous colleagues from other museums and libraries have shared information and offered assistance, for which I express warm thanks: Carol Clausen of the National Library of Medicine, Bethesda, Maryland; Clifford Ackley, Thomas Rassieur, Sue Reed, and Ronni Baer of the Museum of Fine Arts, Boston; Katy Kline of the Bowdoin College Museum of Art, Brunswick, Maine; Marjorie Cohn, William Robinson, and Miriam Stewart of the Fogg Art Museum, Harvard University, Cambridge, Massachusetts; Hope Mayo and Thomas Ford of The Houghton Library, Harvard University; Suzanne McCullagh and Martha Wolfe of the Art Institute of Chicago; Timothy Rub, Kristin Spangenberg, and Betsy Wieseman of the Cincinnati Art Museum; Katharine Lee Reid and Heather Lemonedes of the Cleveland Museum of Art; George Keyes of the Detroit Institute of Arts; Eric Zafran of the Wadsworth Atheneum, Hartford, Connecticut; James Clifton and Leslie Scattone of the Sarah Campbell Blaffer Foundation, Houston; Erika Franek of the Museum of Fine Arts, Houston; Franklin Robinson of the Johnson Museum of Art, Cornell University, Ithaca, New York; Peter Morrin of the Speed Museum, Louisville, Kentucky; Stephanie Wiles of the Davison Art Center, Wesleyan University, Middletown, Connecticut; Evan M. Maurer and Erika Holmquist-Wall of the Minneapolis Institute of Arts; Walter Liedtke, George Goldner, Nadine Orenstein, Michiel Plomp, and Constance McPhee of the Metropolitan Museum of Art, New York; Margaret Glover and Roberta Waddell of the New York Public Library; Charles Pierce, Rhoda Eitel-Porter, and Jennifer Tonkovich of the Pierpont Morgan Library, New York; Katherine Solender of the Allen Memorial Art Museum, Oberlin College, Oberlin, Ohio; Lynn Orr of the Fine Arts Museums of San Francisco; Lloyd deWitt, Innes Shoemaker, and Joseph Rishel of the Philadelphia Museum of Art; John Wetenhall of the John and Mable Ringling Museum of Art, Sarasota, Florida; Larry Nichols of the Toledo Museum of Art; Arthur Wheelock, Neal Turtell, Lamia Doumato, and Molli Kuenstner of the National Gallery of Art, Washington, D.C.; Elizabeth Wyckoff of the Davis Museum and Cultural Center, Wellesley College, Wellesley, Massachusetts; James Welu of the Worcester Art Museum, Worcester, Massachusetts; and several private collectors who wish to remain anonymous.

I am no less grateful to the following individuals for help and advice along the way: George Abrams, Ann Jensen Adams, Liesbeth Brenninkmeyer-van Boven, Diane Cearfoss-Mankin, Susan Dackerman, Beth Darlington, Alice Davies, Judith Dolkert, Ali Can Ertug, John Feroe, Dorothy Glass, Mary Gibbons-Landor, Christine Havelock, Egbert Haverkamp-Begemann, Willem Jan Hoogsteder, Caroline Houser, Joy Kenseth, Marni Kessler, León Krempel, Rebecca Lawton, David Levine, Michael Lewin, Michael McCarthy, Mary McLaughlin, Mia Mochizuki, J. Michael Montias, Otto Naumann, Elizabeth Nogrady, Gary Schwartz, Herman Shickman, Seymour Slive, David Smith, Eric Jan Sluijter, Nicolette Sluijter-Seijffert, Peter Sutton, Jane Shoaf Turner, Eunice Williams, and Douglas Winblad.

Finally and most deeply, I offer thanks to my husband, Robert, for being a constant sounding board, reader of drafts, and provider of perspective, encouragement, and unfailing humor over the entire course of this endeavor.

Susan Donahue Kuretsky
Sarah Gibson Blanding Professor of Art
Vassar College

Lenders to the Exhibition

George Abrams, Boston

Allen Memorial Art Museum,
Oberlin College, Oberlin

The Art Institute of Chicago

The Sarah Campbell Blaffer Foundation,
Houston

Bowdoin College Museum of Art, Brunswick

Cincinnati Art Museum

The Cleveland Museum of Art

Davison Art Center,
Wesleyan University, Middletown

The Detroit Institute of Arts

Fine Arts Museums of San Francisco,
California Palace of the Legion of Honor

Fogg Art Museum,
Harvard University Art Museums, Cambridge

Houghton Library, Harvard University, Cambridge

Herbert F. Johnson Museum of Art,
Cornell University, Ithaca

The Frances Lehman Loeb Art Center,
Vassar College, Poughkeepsie

The Metropolitan Museum of Art, New York

The Minneapolis Institute of Arts

The Pierpont Morgan Library, New York

Museum of Fine Arts, Boston

National Gallery of Art, Washington, D.C.

National Library of Medicine, Bethesda

The New York Public Library

Philadelphia Museum of Art

John and Mable Ringling Museum of Art,
Sarasota

Herman and Lila Shickman, New York

The Speed Art Museum, Louisville

E. V. Thaw & Co. Inc., New York

The Toledo Museum of Art

Wadsworth Atheneum Museum of Art, Hartford

Worcester Art Museum

Private Collections

Notes to the Reader

For dimensions of works in the catalogue, height precedes width in centimeters (millimeters for works on paper) and in inches.

Frequently used terms and abbreviations:

Dictionary of Art
J. S. Turner, ed., *The Dictionary of Art*, 34 vols., New York, 1996.

Hofstede de Groot
C. Hofstede de Groot, *Beschreibendes und kritisches Verzeichnis der Werke der hervorragendsten holländischen Maler des XVII. Jahrhunderts*, 10 vols., Esslingen/Paris, 1907–28 (Hofstede de Groot assigned numbers to the paintings of most major Dutch artists by which the works are still identified today).

Hollstein
F. W. H. Hollstein, *Dutch and Flemish Etchings, Engravings and Woodcuts, ca. 1450–1700*, Amsterdam: [1949]– (The counterpart to Hofstede de Groot, this multi-volume series, assigns numbers to Netherlandish prints).

Van Mander
K. van Mander, *Het Schilder-boeck*, Haarlem, 1604 (The earliest theoretical treatise on Dutch art, which includes the author's advice on painting as well as artist biographies. Modern reprints and translations are listed in the bibliography).

q.v.
quod vide (which see). Replaces an artist's dates when the artist is represented in the catalogue with a full biography.

Rembrandt Corpus
J. Bruyn et. al., *A Corpus of Rembrandt Paintings*, 3 vols. to date, The Hague, Boston, and London, 1982–.

RKD
Rijksbureau voor Kunsthistorische Documentatie, The Hague.

RDMZ
Rijksdienst voor de Monumentenzorg, Zeist.

Schulte et al.
A. G. Schulte et al., *Ruïnes in Nederland: Rijksdienst voor de Monumentenzorg, Zeist*, with contributions by M. J. Kuipers-Verbuijs, H. Klomp, N. C. M. Maes, J. Michaels, A. G. Schulte, A. de Vries, and R. J. Wielinga, Zwolle, 1997. (A catalogue of all ruin sites in the Netherlands with photographs, ground plans, and discussions of their history and conservation).

State
States of prints (impressions displaying an artist's successive revisions to the plate) are indicated by lower-case Roman numerals, along with the total number of known states, i/iii, ii/iv, etc.

Thieme-Becker
U. Thieme and F. Becker, *Allgemeines Lexikon der bildenden Künstler*, 37 vols., Leipzig, 1907–50.

TIME *and* TRANSFORMATION *in Seventeenth-Century Dutch Art*

Dutch Ruins: Time and Transformation

Susan Donahue Kuretsky

The vivid presence of seventeenth-century Dutch art, often linked to the tastes of a practical, middle-class society, lies in its ability to evoke perceptions and experiences that still seem familiar today.[1] This distinctive specificity is revealed not only in artists' close scrutiny of local places and people, but also in their down-to-earth renderings of biblical and historical narratives. More abstract and less readily definable is the sharp awareness of time that pervades the art of this period. The popular vanitas still lifes, whose skulls and ticking timepieces warn viewers of their mortality (Cats. 77–79), are only the most obvious examples of a consciousness of time that emerges even in works that would appear to have other aims. No paintings, for example, celebrate aliveness with more conviction than the portraits of Frans Hals (1581/85–1666) (Fig. 1). Yet even as his flickering brushstrokes capture (and fix for posterity) the faint quirk of a mouth, the turn of a glance that characterizes an individual face, or subtle implications of age, the artist seems to imply that his sitters are mortal beings who exist within an ongoing temporal process. Hals's people look alive within the moment because the moment itself appears so specific: both instantaneous and fleeting.

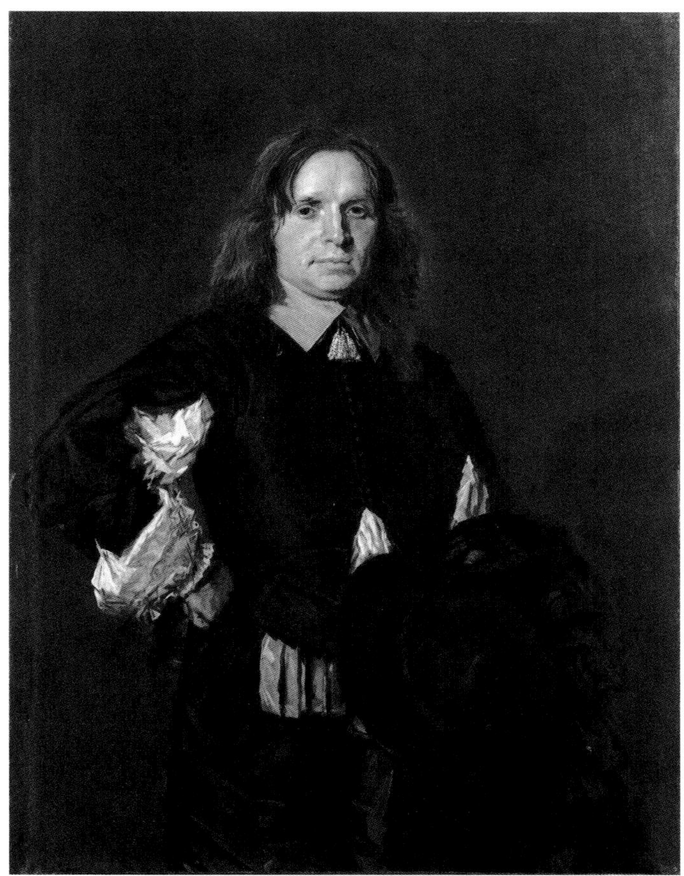

FIGURE 1. Frans Hals, *Portrait of a Man*, c. 1650–52, oil on canvas. The Metropolitan Museum of Art, New York.

As this study will suggest, the definition and understanding of time, which became a central preoccupation of the seventeenth century, was explored most directly in a category of subject matter to which Dutch painters, draftsmen, and printmakers were frequently drawn: ruins and related images of transformation. Through such themes they depicted the world around them not as a static accretion of matter, however precisely rendered, but as a realm both subject to and created by the workings of time. Most often Dutch artists combined ruins with landscapes, illustrating the era's intense interest in nature, but they also described ruins in their own right and within a variety of contexts from biblical narratives to contemporary events. These representations remain among the most powerful expressions of Dutch art, revealing the dynamic processes of time and circumstance that have always shaped the physical world.

Reflections on Ruins

A small etching (Cat. 2a), made in 1616 by the Haarlem printmaker Willem Buytewech, shows the vestiges of Brederode, the most frequently depicted of the ruined medieval castles in the Dutch countryside. Working in a pictorial field of less than three by five inches, the artist has managed to encapsulate the most basic characteristics of ruins, silhouetting this monumental structure's irregular shape against land and sky while evoking its weathered surfaces with firmly hatched, yet subtly quavering lines. Studying the print, one is reminded that only something once intact can be a ruin, which may be defined as the fragment or extensively damaged state of a larger totality that no longer exists, whose wholeness can only be inferred or remembered.[2] As this image of Brederode demonstrates, voids create the character of ruins as much as solids do, and their interplay encourages the observer to reflect upon disparities between what is and what was. Yet the spell cast both by actual sites and by artists' representations of them involves more than notions of *memento mori*, for ruins are not simply the remains of lost wholes. The transformation that divests a structure of its original appearance and purpose produces a new entity with equal—or even greater—resonance and meaning.

Ruins are the creations of time and circumstance, for the very processes that erode or destroy a physical structure are those that remake it on different terms. With their evocative irregularities, unexpected disclosures, and juxtapositions of shapes and surfaces, they inspire thoughts about the tenacity of human works and nature's creations as well as their evanescence. Subversions of planning and order, ruins are arrestingly uneven presences, scattering, softening, or sharpening what was once whole. Because their appearance can shift so radically from different vantage points, they are often more difficult to recognize or identify than intact structures are. Yet they allow the observer to understand the physical world more deeply by revealing how various kinds of matter respond to external forces or conditions. Indeed, matter itself—wood, stone, brick, or any other material—may appear more characteristically and distinctively itself when it no longer functions within an intact structure. When architectural ruins are depicted within landscapes, their affective possibilities are multiplied, for now they encourage consideration of the reciprocal interactions between human works and the processes of nature.

While ruins are usually assumed to be the monumental remains of buildings or cities, the material world encompasses both man-made and natural structures that are subject to transformation: trees, land formations, and even the human body itself. In all cases, ruins may be said to embody time as well as symbolize it, for they are seen to have been acted upon by it, revealing their own history by manifesting the processes or events that brought them to their present state of being. The older they are, the more they may appear to have absorbed time.

Ruins may express different kinds of temporality, however, and artists have interpreted them in many ways. Most examples display the tendency of physical structures to weather, crumble, and collapse gradually over the course of years or even centuries, fusing with nature like the pleasantly derelict Dutch farmhouse in a memorable chalk drawing by Jacob van Ruisdael of about 1655 (Cat. 30) or the remains of the soaring Roman aqueduct in Adriaen van de Velde's Italianate landscape of 1664 (Cat. 69). Instantaneous ruins, on the other hand, are the results of the rapid, disastrous invasion of wind, water, or fire, which can make even the most familiar places turn suddenly strange. The aftermath of the Delft gunpowder explosion of 1654, as depicted by Herman Saftleven (Cat. 41) and Daniel Vosmaer (Cat. 42), is a city transformed into starkly jagged shapes, eviscerated from within and disconnected from the ongoing processes of nature. Time here appears stopped—or perhaps mislaid—as the moment of the explosion has passed, yet the scene has been so altered by the event that it seems cut off from past and future alike. By contrast, depictions of floods or fires in progress (Cats. 37, 38, 40, 45, and 46) have the opposite effect, showing dramatically heightened moments within a continuing process of destruction. In both cases, the almost universal human attraction to scenes of disasters and their aftermath is that they make life more vivid by reminding the observer of its fragility.

In their depictions of ruins, Dutch artists exploited oil paint's fluidity and range of color to recreate the tones and textures of damaged or time-worn surfaces (Cats. 10, 11, 24, and 25). Significantly, however, they chose various graphic media even more frequently than painting, perhaps because prints and drawings on paper are smaller and more fragile objects that call for the kind of close, patient scrutiny elicited by visually complex forms (Cats. 2a, 2b, 5, 18, 29, 30, and 48). In addition, visible touch in the form of line, stippling, or wash is well suited to describing processes of fragmentation. Following the shape, density, and direction of such marks is one of the greatest pleasures offered by graphic images (of any subject), where one witnesses the accumulated gestures of the hand that made them. Thus, a drawing by Jan Lievens of about 1655–65 that shows another view of the ruins of Brederode Castle (Cat. 8) not only illustrates the effects of time in its subject, but tracks the temporal process of its creation in visible shifts of line and tone: from the deeper, more irregular strokes in the foreground that define shadowed underbrush, to paler, more structural diagonal hatchings that capture the irregular shapes of the ruin, to the freer touches that evoke shimmering leaves beyond. The form and content of this image—what it represents and *how* it represents—are so intriguingly analogous that in his drawing, Lievens appears to be literally marking time.

Before and after the Seventeenth Century

Interest in the depiction of ruins in Netherlandish art can be traced to early Renaissance paintings and manuscript illuminations in which scenes of Christ's Nativity were staged within a dilapidated wooden shed or a crumbling stone edifice—decrepit settings that express both the humility of the Holy Family and the deterioration of the Old Order with the coming of Christianity.[3] A late fifteenth-century Adoration of the Magi by the Master of the Legend of St. Lucy (Fig. 2) accordingly features a ruined Romanesque building that divides the scene in triptych-like fashion in order to emphasize the approach of each magus with his offering.[4] As E. Panofsky was the first to observe, Netherlandish painters also employed the additional archi-

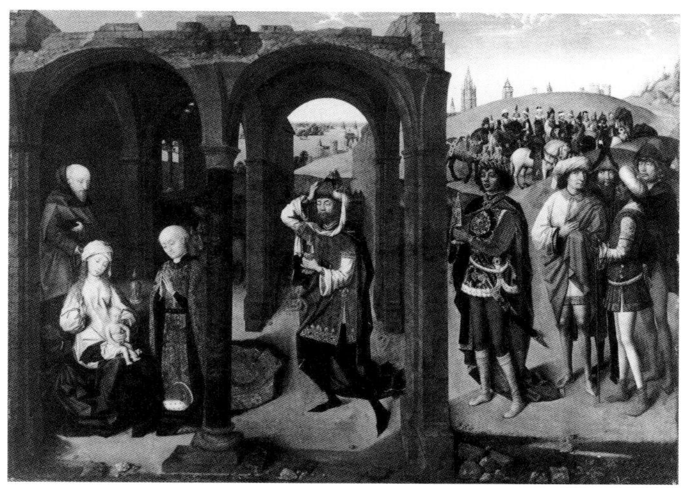

FIGURE 2. Master of the Legend of St. Lucy, *The Adoration of the Magi*, c. 1480–85, oil on panel. Cincinnati Art Museum.

tectural symbolism of juxtaposing Romanesque with the relatively newer Gothic style in order to indicate the temporal shift to the Christian era.[5] In this example, the dark Romanesque ruin at left strongly contrasts with intact Gothic towers rising in the sunlight behind the hill at right, although the two sides of the scene remain linked by the repetition of the round arches in the curving contour of the distant hill. In later depictions of the Nativity (Cats. 15 and 50), artists would continue to set their scenes in or near ruins to summon up an aura of the distant past, even though the medieval or Roman structures they chose to represent may not have existed in Bethlehem in the time of Christ.

With the Renaissance revival of interest in classical antiquity came a new awareness and appreciation of the ancient ruins of Italy, as these solid, measurable vestiges of the past began to be recorded and classified by architects and depicted by artists. Among the latter were the many Netherlandish draftsmen and painters who made the long, often hazardous, journey from northern Europe to Rome, "drawn to warmth," as P. Schatborn titled a recent exhibition, and by the lure of experiencing a world new to them in climate, terrain, and in its capacity to connect them with a great age of the distant past.[6] Beginning with Jan Gossaert (c. 1478–1532), who accompanied his patron Philip of Burgundy to Rome in 1508–9 to record the remains of ancient buildings and sculptures, artists from both the Southern and Northern Netherlands arrived by land and sea, some remaining in Italy for a decade or more.[7] Many produced drawings and prints, either for sale or as repositories of imagery they could consult for their own work or use for teaching students after their return home to northern Europe. There was much for these visitors to see, for in the sixteenth century, the ruins of uninhabitable ancient structures constituted at least two-thirds of the area within the city walls.[8]

One of the most important figures of this period was the Antwerp print publisher Hieronymus Cock (c. 1510–70), whose shop, Aux Quatre Vents (At the Sign of the Four Winds), became a meeting place for intellectuals, writers, and artists, including Pieter Bruegel the Elder (c. 1525–69). Cock issued two influential suites of etchings: *Praecipuae aliquot Romanae antiquitatis ruinarum* of 1551 (Some outstanding representations of the Roman ruins of antiquity; known today as *Views of Roman Ruins*), followed by *Operum antiquorum Romanorum reliquiae* of 1562 (Remains of ancient Roman buildings; now known as *The Small Book of Roman Ruins*).[9] As indicated in one of the ten views of the Colosseum (Fig. 3) in the earlier cycle of twenty-five prints, Cock established many of the fundamental tactics that would remain operative in seventeenth-century depictions of the theme, such as Bartholomeus Breenbergh's series of Roman etchings of 1639–40 (Cats. 55a–f). Taking a low viewpoint, Cock silhouettes the irregular profiles of the shattered structure against the sky, using deep pockets of shadow to model its mass, tightly framing and cropping it to evoke its monumental scale. Sprouting foliage and fallen shards of masonry indicate that the ruin has come to its current state over a long temporal process that will continue. Clouds, birds in flight, and visitors and sightseers—including an artist sketching the damaged structure—also set the scene within a believable moment in the present, allowing the observer of the image to feel equally like an observer of the monument itself.

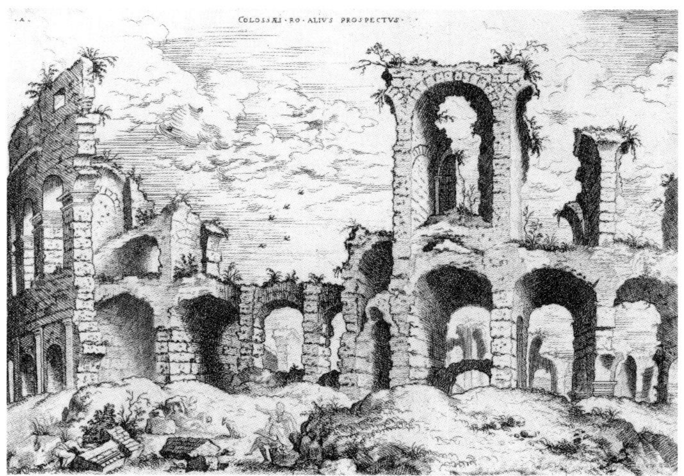

FIGURE 3. Hieronymus Cock, *Fifth View of the Colosseum*, etching, from *Praecipuae aliquot Romanae antiquitatis ruinarum*, 1551. Museum of Fine Arts, Boston.

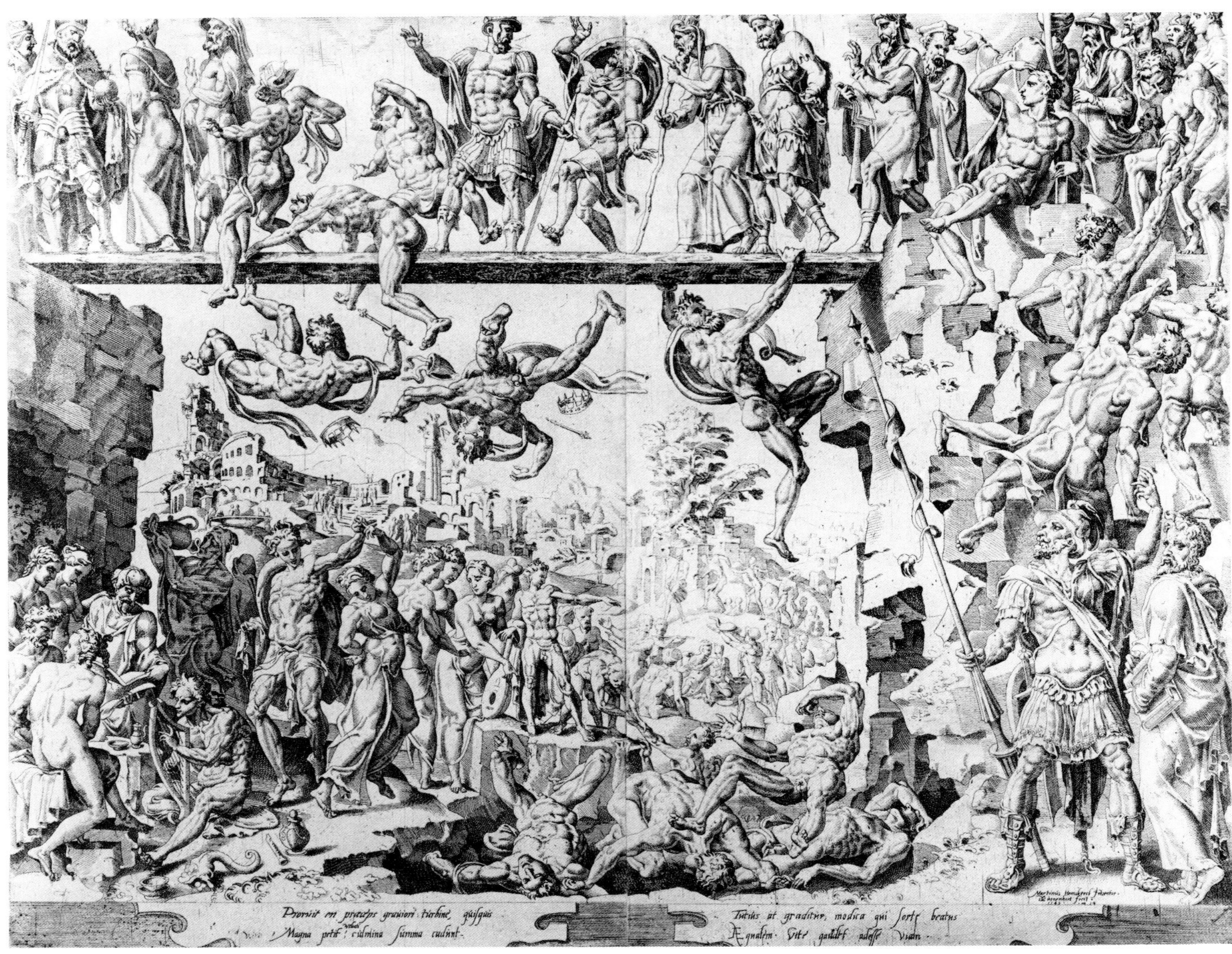

FIGURE 4. Maerten van Heemskerck, etched by Dirck Volkertz. Coornhert, *Allegory of Human Ambition*, 1549. Museum Boijmans Van Beuningen, Rotterdam.

Even beyond their aesthetic and archaeological interest in the remains of ancient Rome, sixteenth-century artists, especially those from the Northern Netherlands, were attracted to ruins for their moralizing and allegorical potential, as illustrated in the prints of Maerten van Heemskerck (1498–1574) of Haarlem and Cornelis Anthonisz. (c. 1505–53) of Amsterdam. Heemskerck's large *Allegory of Human Ambition* of 1549, etched by Dirck Volkertz. Coornhert (Fig. 4), illustrates the folly of lofty ambition by showing popes, kings, generals, and scholars falling from a high plank into a pit below, as those of modest ambition remain safely at ground level, enjoying music and wine at left.[10] In the background, Roman ruins, among which is featured the Colosseum, make the same point. Indeed, both artists and writers commonly used variations on the term *vervallen gebouwen* (fallen buildings) to designate ruins, for the word ruin derives from the Latin *ruina*, meaning "that which has collapsed or fallen."[11] Fallen architecture as a symbol of pride would continue to appear in more contemporary guise in seventeenth-century Dutch prints, as in an emblem in Roemer Visscher's *Sinnepoppen* of 1614—a collapsing church tower under the motto in Latin and Dutch: "Finis ad alta levatis" and (on the facing page) "Hoe hoogher gheklommen, hoe zwaerder val" (The higher they rise, the harder they fall) (Fig. 5).[12]

One of the most popular narratives of the sixteenth century concerning the penalties of pride was that of the Tower of Babel (Genesis 11:1–9), the story of humanity's arrogant attempt to build a tower to heaven and God's punishment: dispersing people across the earth with different languages ("babel," or confusion of tongues) so they could never again

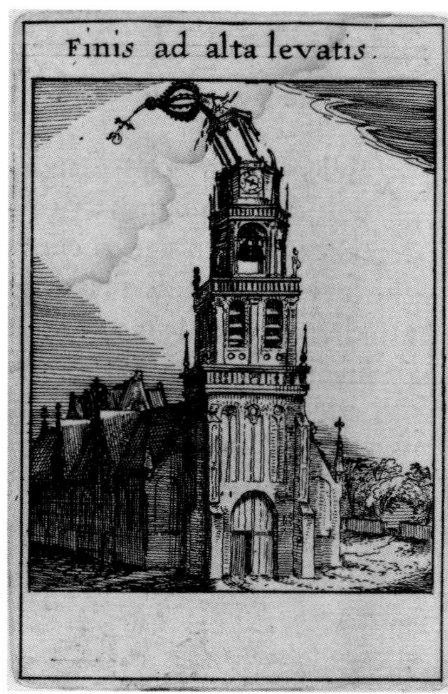

FIGURE 5. Roemer Visscher, "Finis ad alta levatis," from Roemer Visscher, *Sinnepoppen*, Amsterdam, 1614. Department of Rare Books, The Houghton Library, Harvard College Library, Cambridge, Massachusetts.

communicate. Best known from Pieter Bruegel the Elder's painting of the tower as a huge construction site (1563, Kunsthistorisches Museum, Vienna), this narrative was also the subject of a large (324 × 384 mm) etching by Cornelis Anthonisz. of 1547, which shows it tumbling into fragments (Fig. 6).[13] Like Bruegel, Anthonisz. based his tower on the ruined Colosseum, the most familiar manifestation of a great civilization's fall. Multiplying the famous monument's curving tiers and repetitions of encircling colonnades, he added two inscriptions to his print. At the upper left are the words "Alst op thoechste was / most het doen niet vallen" (When it was highest, must it not then fall?) and at the upper right: "Babelon / Genesis 14" beside the artist's monogram.[14] As C. M. Armstrong has discussed, the conflation of Babel with Babylon, another great ancient city that collapsed into ruin, had particular significance during the time of the Protestant Reformation in northern Europe, when papal Rome was often described as a sinful Babylon or "babel" of different religious orders and devotions, while the corruption and fall of ancient Rome were invoked in relation to the contemporary Catholic city.[15] Thus, even as Netherlandish artists were admiring the grandeur of the monuments of ancient Rome, those ruins were freighted with certain moralizing implications for religious dissidents and reformers of the same period—a time of iconoclasm that also saw the widespread destruction of devotional art and architecture in northern Europe.[16]

In the wake of this religious and political upheaval, seventeenth-century Dutch artists, who inherited an era of peace and growing prosperity, produced many more representations of ruins (Roman and otherwise), both as subjects of interest in themselves and as accessory motifs within the new, non-devotional narratives, landscapes, and portraits of the officially Protestant Dutch Republic. Indeed, the Dutch were the first to make ruins a significant and widespread focus of artistic attention.

Making sense of this material within its own time remains a challenge, however, for the appearance and meaning of images may be inflected by past precedents but not by any future thematic evolution. Nonetheless, today's scholars and museum viewers find themselves looking back through an intervening screen of what has been broadly classified as the Romantic period, which began in the late eighteenth century and continued into the nineteenth and which saw an explosive proliferation of "ruin pictures" in Europe and America. These later works and the extensive scholarly attention they have attracted reveal attitudes toward ruins that must be acknowledged before one considers the very different world of the seventeenth century.[17]

During the Romantic period, political and social revolution and the rapid growth of technology and industry accelerated the human experience of time while challenging traditional values and attitudes about the past. Ruins became popular during this period both as objects of antiquarian documentation and as stimuli for the emotion and imagination. Depictions of such subjects, which involved attempts to retrieve the past both historically and nostalgically, often suggest how the individual, and the physical world as a whole,

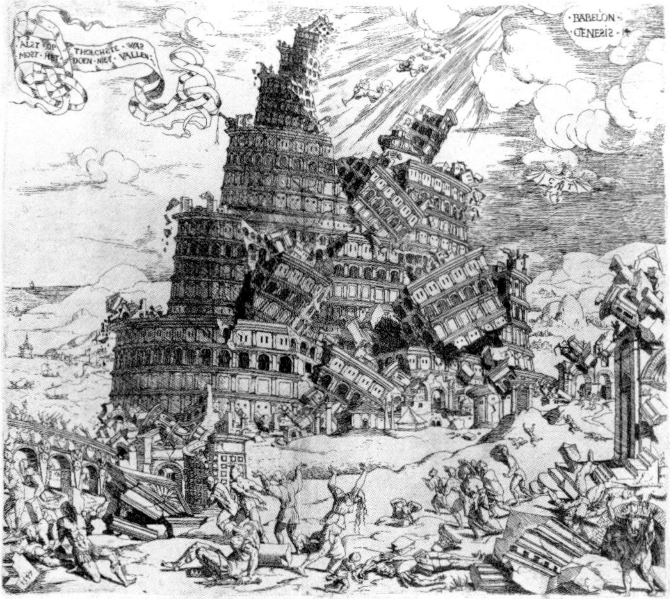

FIGURE 6. Cornelis Anthonisz., *The Fall of the Tower of Babel*, 1547, etching. Kupferstichkabinett, Staatliche Museen, Berlin.

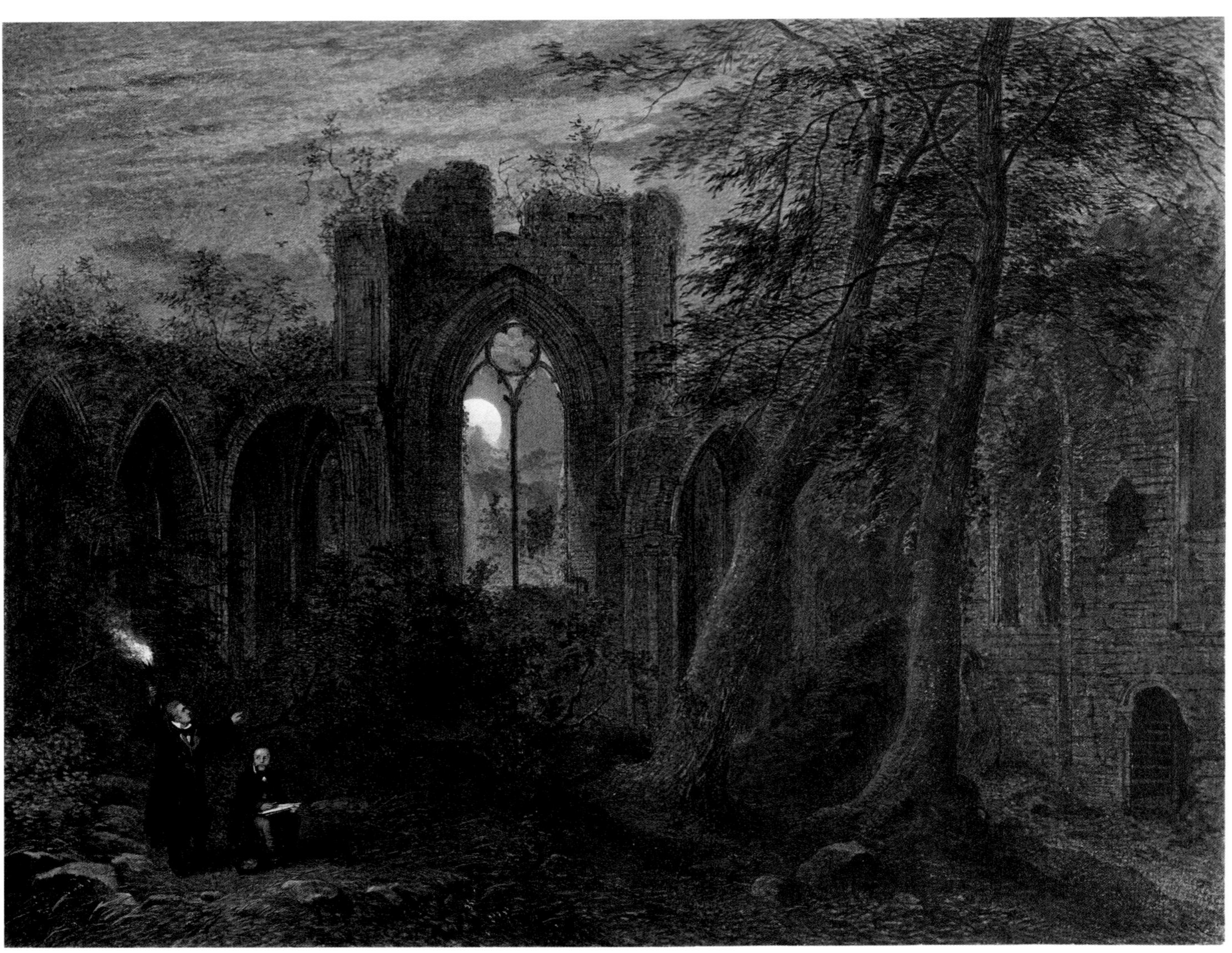

FIGURE 7. James F. Buckley, *Netley Abbey by Torchlight*, 1854 or 1856, watercolor on paper. Frances Lehman Loeb Art Center, Vassar College, Poughkeepsie, New York.

are at the mercy of larger forces beyond reason or control. While romantic images of ruins were commonly used for violent, irrational, or fantastic subjects, their appeal to individual sentiment and sensation remains obvious even in relatively down-to-earth scenes that recall seventeenth-century precedents. One is reminded, for example, of Hercules Segers's richly evocative prints of medieval ruins (Cat. 5) in works such as *Netley Abbey by Torchlight* (Fig. 7), a watercolor by the nineteenth-century British artist James F. Buckley (active 1843–73).[18]

Buckley's painting, staged to elicit an intensely emotional response, depicts the shell of a ruined Gothic abbey by night, a scene doubly illuminated—and in a sense doubly observed—by the rising moon in the background, framed in the lancet of a Gothic window, and by the figures at the lower left foreground. The standing man (probably representing the artist's patron) holds a flaming torch aloft, gesturing dramatically toward the ruin as if instructing the draftsman seated beside him, who balances his sketchbook on his lap. While a specific building has been represented here, the ruin appears mysterious and strange, evoking pleasurable melancholy and a shiver of disquiet. One senses something of a disjunction between these shadowy vestiges of the past, with their implications of mortality and loss, and the modern visitors in their fashionable cravats and tailcoats. Buckley's landscape implies that even when tangible relics of history are examined and recorded, the past itself remains elusive and out of reach except to the imagination. Past and present exist here in distinctly different realms, for these onlookers are seen to be confronting an earlier time from a vantage point outside it. Thus, the subject of the painting is not simply the ruin itself but the experience of viewing it.

Segers's etching of Rijnsburg Abbey (Cat. 5), made more than two centuries earlier, uses similarly deep tones and rough surface textures to convey the complex character of a shattered, weathered structure of great age. Yet here the anonymous figure at the center foreground sinks into the scene and merges with it, just as the ruin itself appears overgrown by and fused with its natural setting. In this image, the present does not seem separated from the past but is its direct continuation. Time's steady accumulation through ongoing processes is evident in the solid shapes and tangibly corroded brickwork of Rijnsburg. Both Segers and Buckley were clearly drawn to ruined abbeys for their capacity to generate intensely atmospheric effects, but to the Dutch in the seventeenth century, images of this kind were addressed more to a collective public consciousness than to individual sentiment. Ruins—particularly those of local structures—were more directly tied to common, everyday experience and frequently to actual events within people's recent memory and present awareness.

Monumental Ruins in the Local Landscape

Such connections between past and present are powerfully evident in the innovative depictions of their native landscape that Dutch printmakers began to produce in the city of Haarlem during the first decades of the seventeenth century, as discussed in C. Levesque's essay (pp. 49–62). With the signing of the Twelve Year Truce with the Spanish (1609–21), images of the local countryside began to appear, expressing peace and prosperity after decades of conflict and upheaval. These early landscape prints often feature the large medieval castles that had been destroyed during the late sixteenth century, such as those lost in the devastating siege of Haarlem of 1572–73 (Cats. 1, 2a–b, and 4). Jan van de Velde II's (q.v.) *Wide View of Haarlem* (Fig. 8) of 1621, etched on three plates after a design by Pieter Molijn (q.v.), praises the virtue and courage of the city in inscribed cartouches and allegorical figures, beyond which appear quiet fields and the city skyline. Darkly silhouetted against the light at the far left rise the shattered remains of a large building: the Huis ter Kleef, former headquarters of the Spanish garrison at Haarlem (Cats. 2b and 4). Reminiscent of earlier prints of Roman sites (Fig. 3), the diminutive draftsman sketching the ruin from his position at the center foreground acts as a surrogate-witness for those who visit the site by examining the print. That he has turned his attention to the destroyed building rather than the intact and flourishing city beyond it suggests that such monuments were valued not only for their inherent visual interest but also as reminders of historical events that had brought the world of the present into being.

Because of the upheavals of the Eighty Years' War, dilapidated and ruined buildings were rather common sights in the Dutch countryside, especially the castles dating from the medieval period that had been put to military use in the late sixteenth century. During the 1570s, some were demolished by the Spanish invaders, others by the Dutch themselves to prevent them from being captured. In both cases, the fact that artists depicted the remains of such monuments so frequently, and continued to do so throughout the century, raises intriguing questions about what their own local ruins meant to the Dutch people of the seventeenth century. Major sites probably had considerable patriotic significance, especially in the years immediately preceding or following the Twelve Year Truce or the Treaty of Münster, which established the official independence of the seven Dutch provinces in 1648. Haarlem's historian, Samuel Ampzing, made this point earlier in 1628 in his verses on the Huis ter Kleef, again illustrated by Jan van de Velde II (Cat. 4), in which he laments the building's loss, reminding his readers how it came to be destroyed. Similarly, Gerrit Gouw's etching of the ruins of Brederode of about 1600–1610 (Cat. 1) bears a caption tying the remains of the castle to its earlier history.

As E. P. Löffler notes in his essay (pp. 96–110), large structures such as Brederode that had suffered extensive damage were often prohibitively costly to reconstruct or remove. Thus, many remained in their fallen state within the Dutch landscape, visible for decades or even centuries unless their materials were quarried and carted away for other construction projects. One cannot therefore suppose that ruined abbeys and castles were deliberately left around the countryside as loci for patriotic remembrance. Yet the frequency of their depiction suggests how deeply they captured the interest of artists and of a public who apparently enjoyed visiting these sites either by making excursions to them or by examining pictorial representations. Depictions of recognizable local scenery also offered ways of eulogizing and promoting the beauty, peace, and prosperity of the countryside, especially in the province of Holland, which rapidly became one of the most densely populated and highly urbanized areas in western Europe.[19]

Early in the century, images of local ruins in prints (inexpensive images that could be circulated in multiples to a broad audience) certainly fostered awareness and appreciation of the actual sites. Significantly, these landscape etchings often show visitors wandering about, quietly discussing the

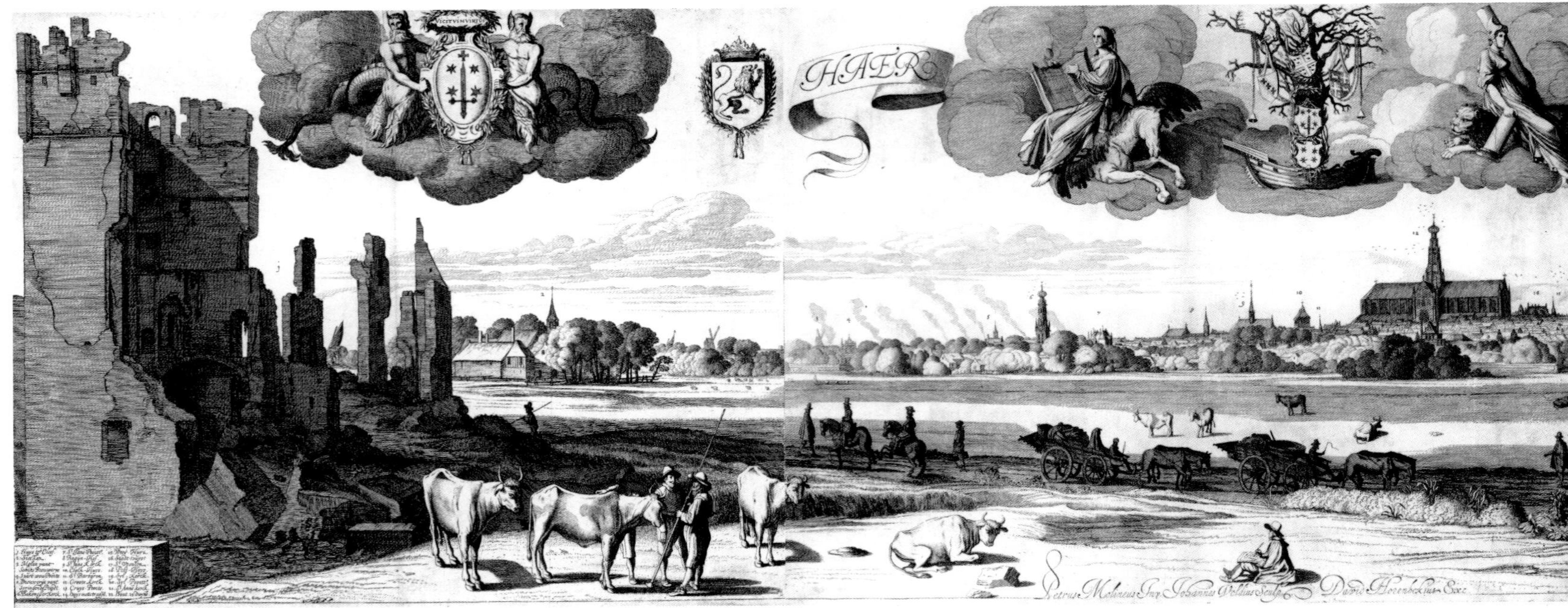

FIGURE 8. Jan van de Velde II, after Pieter Molijn, *Wide View of Haarlem*, 1621, etching. Rijksprentenkabinet, Rijksmuseum, Amsterdam.

ruin, or even sketching it (Cats. 1, 4, and 5). Important evidence of the popularity of this imagery, from the beginning of the century on, has recently emerged in J. M. Montias's investigations of the terminology used in Dutch notarial citations. Among the various subject categories devised by auction assistants and notaries for the classification of works of art, the term *ruijnken* or *ruwijntie* appears repeatedly.[20] The use of the diminutive suffix is especially telling here, for it was usually meant to suggest not the small size of the object, but rather the familiarity and frequency of the subject.[21] That such *ruijntjes* were purchased for display on the walls of Dutch homes is illustrated by a painting of a domestic interior in the style of Pieter Janssens Elinga (active c. 1653–before 1682) (Fig. 9), which includes a large view of a ruined castle among a selection of other Dutch landscapes.[22]

While most depictions of local ruins dating from the early years of the century were the work of draftsmen and printmakers, by 1650 the theme had been enthusiastically taken up by major landscape painters such as Jan van Goyen (Cat. 10), Aelbert Cuyp (Cats. 11–13), and especially Jacob van Ruisdael (Cats. 30–32), who featured ruined buildings in approximately thirty paintings and more than a dozen drawings.[23] An important example is the majestic *Landscape with the Ruins of Egmond Castle at Egmond aan den Hoef* of about 1653 (Fig. 10), which depicts the remains of the seat of the counts of Egmond near Alkmaar. This strategically located castle, also discussed in Löffler's essay, was destroyed in 1574 at the order of Prince William of Orange (William the Silent) to prevent the Spanish troops, who had occupied it between 1573 and 1574, from returning to retake it.[24] As S. Slive has observed, Ruisdael was first drawn to the site during the early 1650s, when monumental structural forms were beginning to play an important role in his landscapes.[25]

In this view of the southeast corner tower of Egmond's central structure, a great shard of masonry rises near the center of the scene above fallen walls and a broken arcade, its size emphasized by the miniature scale of the shepherd with his flock on the bank of the moat at right.[26] Touched by soft sunlight and transparent shadow, the ruined castle has comfortably settled into its surroundings, overlapping the falling diagonal of the hillside behind it and standing at the intersection of land, water, and sky. Its ancient bricks are mirrored in the quiet water in the foreground, while the tower is framed by masses of cloud that move counter to the slope of the hillside. As in many of Ruisdael's landscapes (Cat. 32), time is evoked here not merely as an accumulation of physical changes exemplified by the ruined castle, but also as a dynamic process that is seen to be happening and continuing.

In this painting, Ruisdael dramatized Egmond Castle by placing it within terrain that is much hillier and more irregular than the building's actual setting. His most famous (and most unusual) ruin landscape takes imaginative invention still further. *The Jewish Cemetery* (versions in the Detroit Institute of Arts of c. 1653–55, Fig. 11; and in the Staatliche

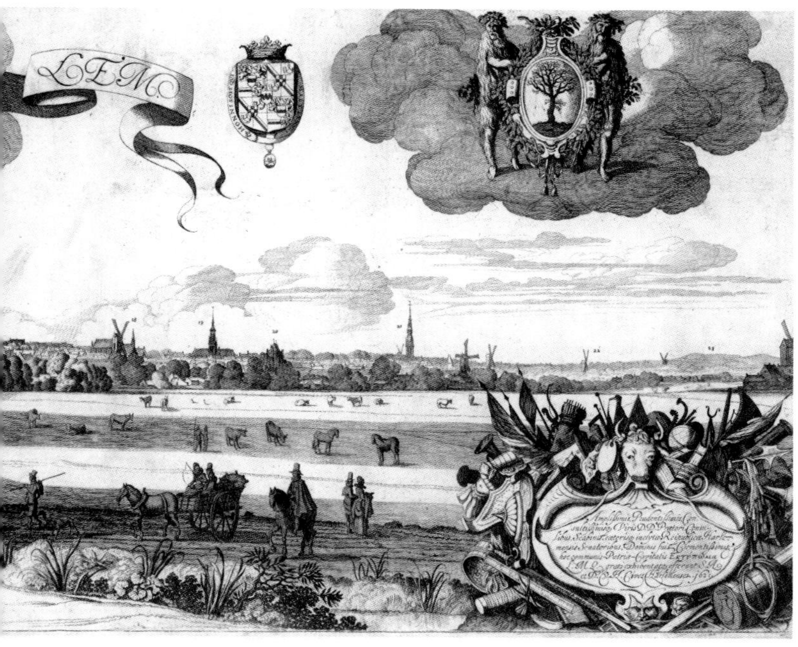

Kunstsammlungen, Dresden, of c. 1660–65)[27] is a transparently allegorical scene that belongs to the category of imagery for which the Dutch coined the term "vanitas": a pictorial meditation on mortality and transience (Cats. 77–79). On a hill in the background of this scene is a ruined abbey loosely based upon the architecture of Egmond Castle, while the tombs at the right foreground derive from those in the Jewish burial ground (the Beth Haim, or House of Life, cemetery) at Ouderkerk near Amsterdam.[28] Here a somewhat brooding effect is created by deeper, more sonorous colors and a darker, stormier sky, while dead trees and a flowing stream (an obvious anomaly at a cemetery site) add further implications of time's passing. Yet the rainbow at the left, as well as contrasts of dead trees and living foliage, underline the cyclical processes of existence, implying that death and decay can lead to regeneration and rebirth and indeed are their necessary preconditions. A seventeenth-century viewer, accustomed to thinking in allegorical terms, may well have found in this landscape parallels to human mortality and resurrection.[29]

Ruisdael has often been compared to landscapists of the late eighteenth and early nineteenth centuries, whom he strongly influenced, such as John Constable (1776–1837), who delivered an appreciative lecture on the Dutch artist at the British Institution in London in 1835. Yet in contrast to his admiration for many of Ruisdael's works, Constable spoke disparagingly about a painting that he claimed was entitled in its own time "An Allegory of the Life of Man" (very likely the Detroit version of *The Jewish Cemetery*), complaining that the artist "... failed because he attempted to tell that which is outside the reach of art."[30] While it is true that Dutch landscape painters of the seventeenth century rarely employed such overtly symbolic imagery, there is reason to believe that during this period, many familiar motifs, including ruins, carried associations beyond their purely visual effects.

Moralizing emblem books, which draw didactic parallels between words and images, make clear that to a seventeenth-century audience, images with ruins could offer not only practical advice (Fig. 5) but also spiritual counsel (Figs. 12 and 13). Among the stunningly naturalistic prints in a emblem book of 1624 by the Calvinist moralist Johan de Brune (1588–1658) is a landscape featuring a Ruisdael-like ruin overgrown with plant life (Fig. 12) under the motto "'t Gheloof zich voedt door teghen-spoed" (Faith nourishes itself on adversity).[31] The accompanying text and image draw a parallel between the human capacity to have faith in difficult circumstances and the ability of small plants to eke out nourishment from the brickwork of old ruins as they reach up toward the light. A later emblem from Jan Luyken's (1649–1712) compendium entitled *De bykorf des gemoeds* (The beehive of the mind), published in 1711 (Fig. 13), shows people contemplating a ruin that evokes thoughts of those who have gone before them and are no longer alive. The motto above reads: "Het Oud Gebouw. Zy zynder geweest" (The old building. They have been there), while the text below is taken from the first epistle of the Apostle Peter: "All flesh is as grass, and all the glory of man like the flower of grass.

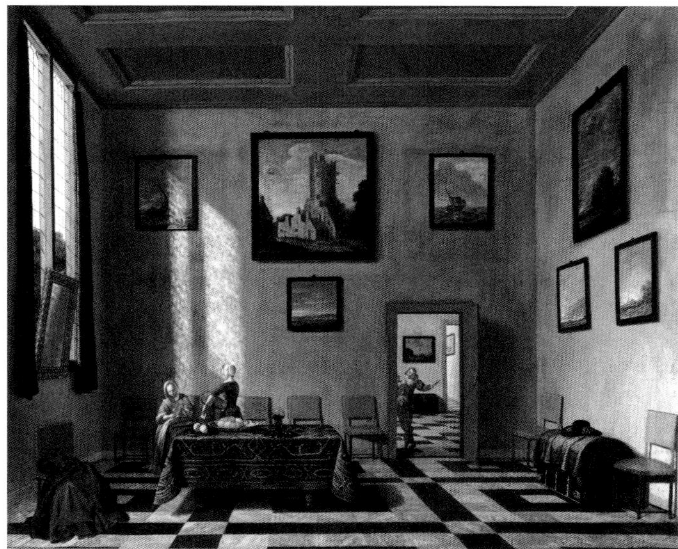

FIGURE 9. Style of Pieter Janssens Elinga, *Interior with a Lady Reading a Letter*, eighteenth-century copy, oil on canvas. Wadsworth Atheneum Museum of Art, Hartford, Connecticut.

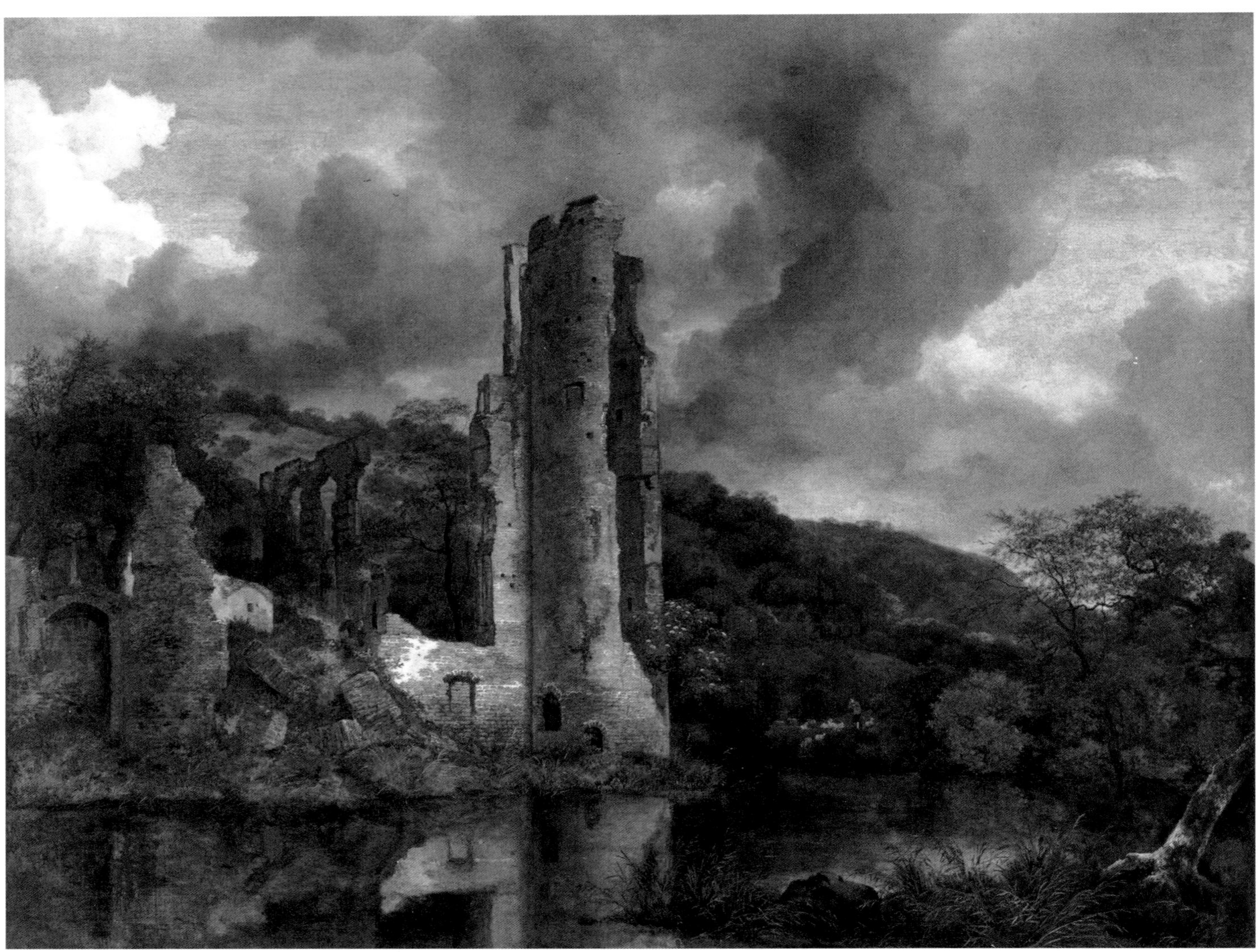

FIGURE 10. Jacob van Ruisdael, *Landscape with the Ruins of Egmond Castle at Egmond aan den Hoef*, c. 1653, oil on canvas. The Art Institute of Chicago.

The grass withers, and the flower falls, but the word of the Lord abides forever" (1 Peter 1:24–25).[32]

As mentioned above, castles such as Egmond and Brederode were destroyed in the 1570s under the most violent and traumatic circumstances during the Spanish occupation of the Dutch provinces. Yet by the time artists had begun to depict these sites, decades had passed, and the shattered buildings had begun to weather and mellow into a fusion with the surrounding landscape. What they might have looked like at the moment of their destruction can be inferred only through comparisons with representations of other monumental structures lost in contemporary local disasters caused by fire, flood, weather, or war. As A. K. Wheelock Jr. discusses in his essay (pp. 73–82), Dutch artists rarely represented the catastrophic events of their own time. Nonetheless, accidents and disasters offered opportunities to instruct, as in Jan van der Heyden's demonstrations of the most efficient ways to fight a fire (Cat. 46). They also elicited moralizing reflection about human fallibility or virtue, as in Romeyn de Hooghe's dramatic depictions of events from the "Rampjaar," or Year of Disaster, of 1672–73, when the armies of Louis XIV invaded the Netherlands (Cats. 38 and 39). Equally important, such scenes encouraged artists to expand their understanding of the world around them by examining the instantaneous physical transformations that can occur when destructive forces—natural or human—are suddenly unleashed.

Like Haarlem a century earlier, the small town of Grave on the Maas River in Brabant between Arnhem and 's-Hertogenbosch was besieged and extensively damaged in

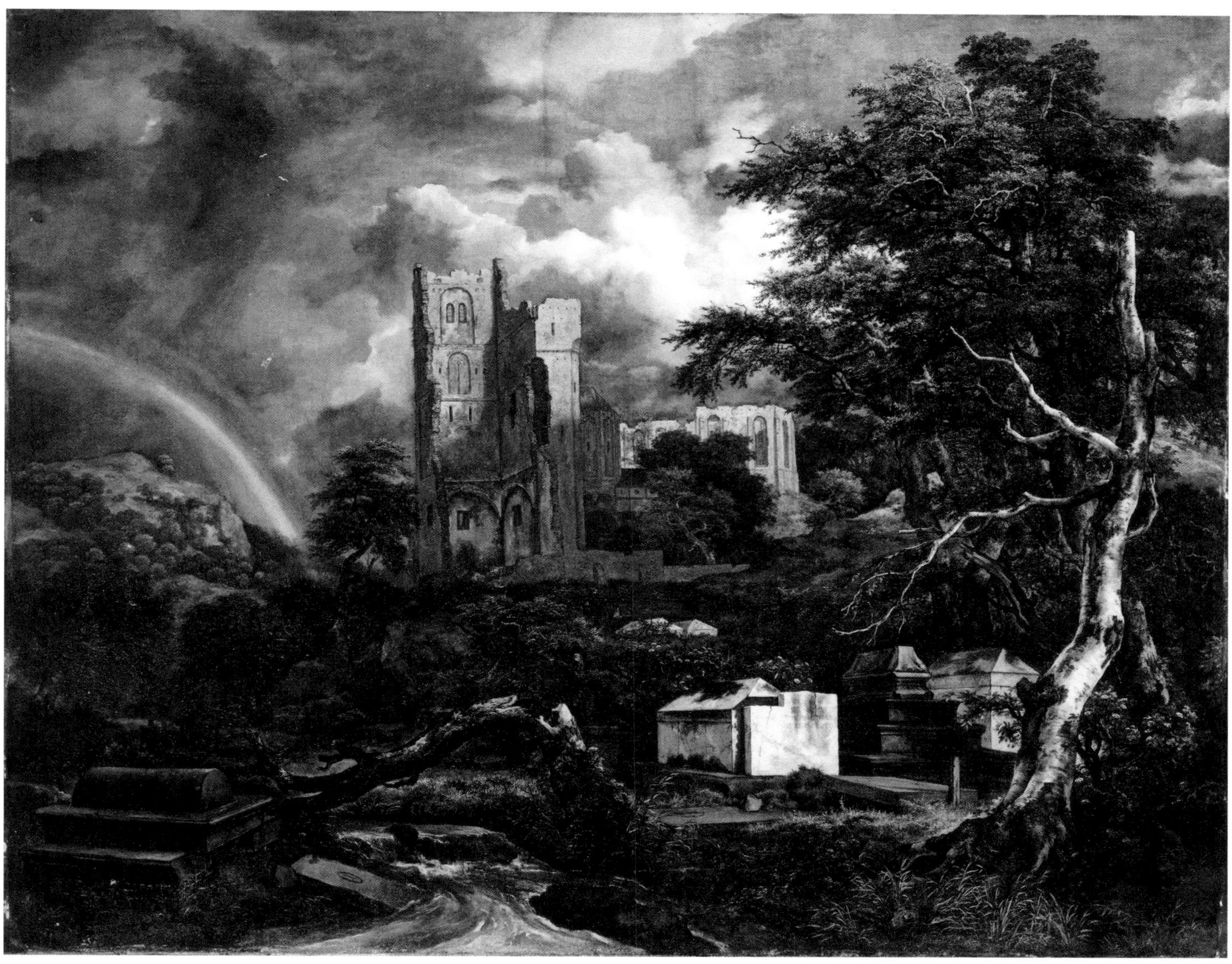

FIGURE 11. Jacob van Ruisdael, *The Jewish Cemetery*, c. 1653–55, oil on canvas. The Detroit Institute of Arts.

1674. From 1604 to 1672 it had remained under Dutch control, but it was then taken by the invading armies of Louis XIV, who used it as a storage depot for captured war materials. After a siege that lasted from 25 July to 27 October 1674, the town surrendered to William III of Orange, but not before mortar fire had almost destroyed it. Valentijn Klotz (c. 1648–after 1716), a Dutch military engineer who was also a talented amateur draftsman, recorded the immediate and devastating effects of the shelling in at least eighteen drawings that recall depictions of the famous gunpowder explosion in Delft of 1654 (Cats. 41 and 42).[33] Avoiding the anecdotal—there are no people present—Klotz shows Grave as a kind of cemetery of itself, with the large Church of St. Elizabeth and the smaller damaged cloister tower presiding over an area that is utterly devastated and empty of life (Fig. 14). Yet if the scene depicted is static, the image itself is saturated with visual energy in the nervously quivering pen lines, heightened by delicate brown-gray wash, that delineate these fractured, sharp-edged structures with an eerie beauty.

During the same period, an illustrated account of the French invasion was published in two volumes in 1674–76 by Tobias van Domselaer with illustrations by Johan Horions.[34] *Het ontroerde Nederlandt* (The Netherlands in turmoil) was written, as was Abraham de Wicquefort's *Advis fidelle aux veritables hollandois* of 1673 (Cat. 39), to celebrate Dutch heroism in the face of French atrocities. Along with scenes of burning villages, it includes depictions of country estates on the river Vecht near Utrecht that were looted and burned by French troops. As D. Cearfoss Mankin's research has revealed, these summer houses, many of which belonged to prosperous

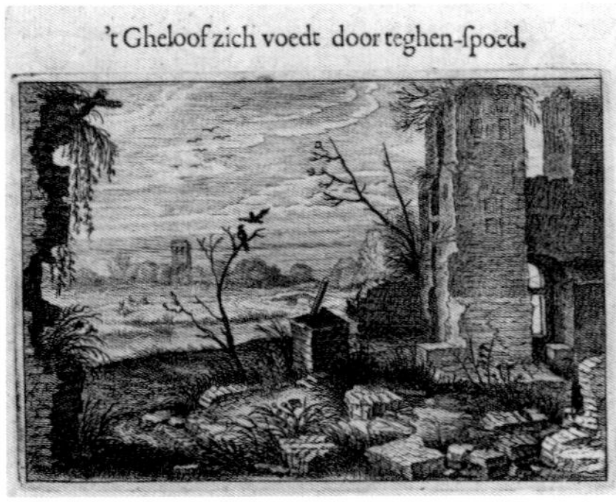

FIGURE 12. Johan de Brune, "'t Gheloof zich voedt door teghen-spoed," from *Emblemata of zinne-werck*, Amsterdam, 1624, page 139, no. XVIII. Department of Printing and Graphic Arts, The Houghton Library, Harvard College Library, Cambridge, Massachusetts.

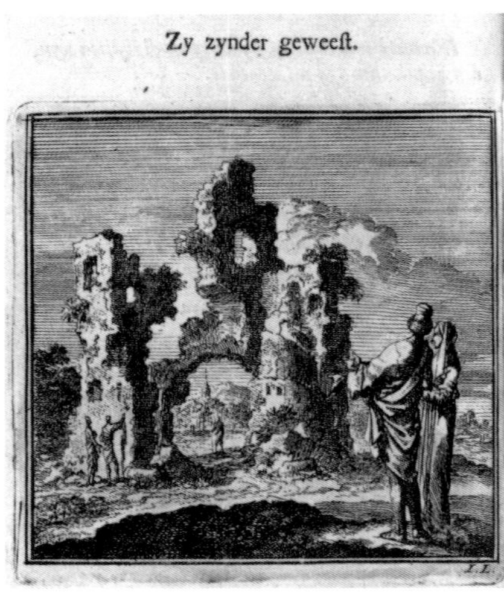

FIGURE 13. Jan Luyken, "Zy zynder geweest," from *De bykorf des gemoeds*, Amsterdam, 1711, page 6. Department of Rare Books, The Houghton Library, Harvard College Library, Cambridge, Massachusetts.

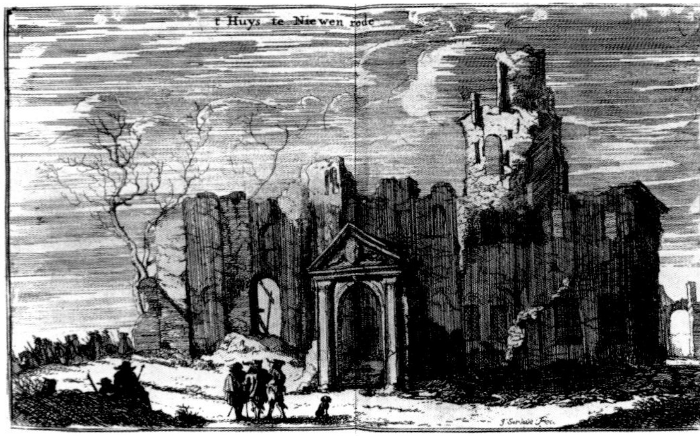

FIGURE 15. Johan Horions, "Nijenrode in Ruins," from Tobias van Domselaer, *Het ontroerde Nederlandt*, Amsterdam, 1674/76, vol. 2, no. 626. Utrecht University, Special Collections.

Amsterdam burghers, consisted of both late medieval castles and classicizing villas of more recent vintage—apparently destroyed in both cases because their patriotic owners refused to pay the taxes demanded by the foreign invaders.[35] Nijenrode, a thirteenth-century *ridderhofstad*, or knight's estate, that was one of the most frequently depicted of all Dutch country houses, appears as a drastically ruined structure in Horions's print (Fig. 15), only identifiable by its entrance gate in the "modern" classical style of its period.[36]

Rustic Ruins: Cottages and Trees

The difference between ruins created by violent acts of destruction and those that come into being slowly and organically over time becomes obvious when one turns to images of more modest, tumble-down rural structures by artists such as Abraham Bloemaert (Cat. 18), Jan de Bisschop (Cat. 29), and Ruisdael (Cat. 30). The Dutch depicted ruined residential dwellings rather rarely, perhaps because this intensely domestic society so valued the meticulous household maintenance that is on display in the spotless interiors of Johannes Vermeer (1632–75) and other Dutch genre painters. Among the most powerful of all evocations of ruin, scenes of domestic dilapidation include houses that have lost their intended function of enclosing and protecting their inhabitants (Cats. 18, 22a, 26, and 30) but also the more frequent representations of shabby structures that have simply been marked or reshaped by weather or hard use (Cats. 16, 17, 20, 23, and 24). Surveying this group of images offers a lesson in the importance of flexible iconographic interpretation, as the meaning of very similar motifs often shifts radically according to their

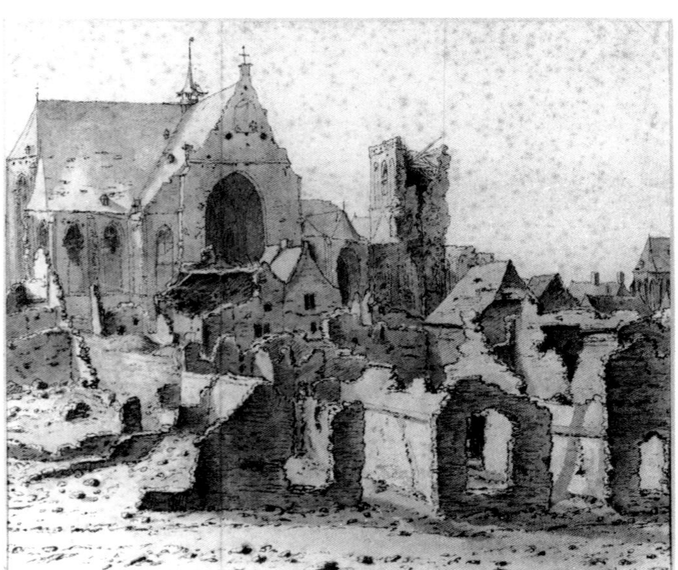

FIGURE 14. Valentijn Klotz, *View of Grave*, 1675, graphite, ink and wash drawing. The Courtauld Institute of Art Gallery, London.

context. Some examples, such as the alarmingly ill-cared-for farmhouse in a print after Jacques de Gheyn II (Cat. 20) or the ramshackle inns in prints by Pieter Molijn (Cat. 22b) and Gerrit de Heer (Cat. 27), probably had moralizing intentions, commenting on derelictions of domestic duty or the consequences of sloth and other vices. Others seem to express, in a more positive way, the pleasures of living a simple life close to nature (Cats. 24 and 28). As W. S. Gibson points out in his essay (pp. 63–72), the virtues of poverty and humility are also suggested in scenes that show ordinary people in decrepit surroundings, as well as depictions of the Holy Family in the ruins (Cat. 15) or devout hermits in the company of ancient trees (Cats. 72–74).

Nature's own ruins are the decaying or fallen trees that appear so often in Dutch art. Familiar features of almost every landscape, trees vary in configuration according to their type, location, age, and life history. Most experience transformation through time in a double sense. Healthy deciduous varieties pass through an annual cycle that strips them of their foliage for part of every year, while all species are subject to the consequences of weathering and age. Surely no aspect of landscape has acquired a richer or more complex symbolism—both religious and secular—for trees join earth and sky and have often been understood as symbols of rebirth and regeneration because of their yearly renewal of foliage and because of their capacity to sprout again when pruned or cut down (Cat. 73).[37] While the bent and twisted stumps in depictions of St. Jerome and other holy hermits evoke associations between the tree and the cross as instruments of mortality and Christian redemption (Cats. 72–74), most of the ruined trees in Dutch art illustrate nature's cycle of life and death in a more open-ended way (Cats. 19, 21, 31, 32, and 33).[38] Even while responding to them in visual or aesthetic terms, one senses an affinity with these beings that, like ourselves, are subject to metamorphosis through time—beginning as small sprouts, growing to stand upright and reach out into the world around them, eventually thinning in their crowns and branches, and finally falling back to earth.

A vanitas print of 1599 by Jacob Matham (q.v.) after Karel van Mander (1548–1606; Fig. 16) makes this association clear, for among its diverse allegorical imagery and inscriptions the artist has paralleled the stages of human life with the life cycle of the tree. Flanking a large vase of fragile flowers in the center are a young child at left, behind whom is a fully foliated tree, and, at right, a skeleton in a coffin, behind which is a tree that has lost almost all of its leaves. Above the bare tree is inscribed, "The world is like a tree, you, man, are like the leaf that grows and falls and vanishes." The slate held by the skeleton exhorts the viewer: "Mend the roof of your house for the sake of virtue."[39]

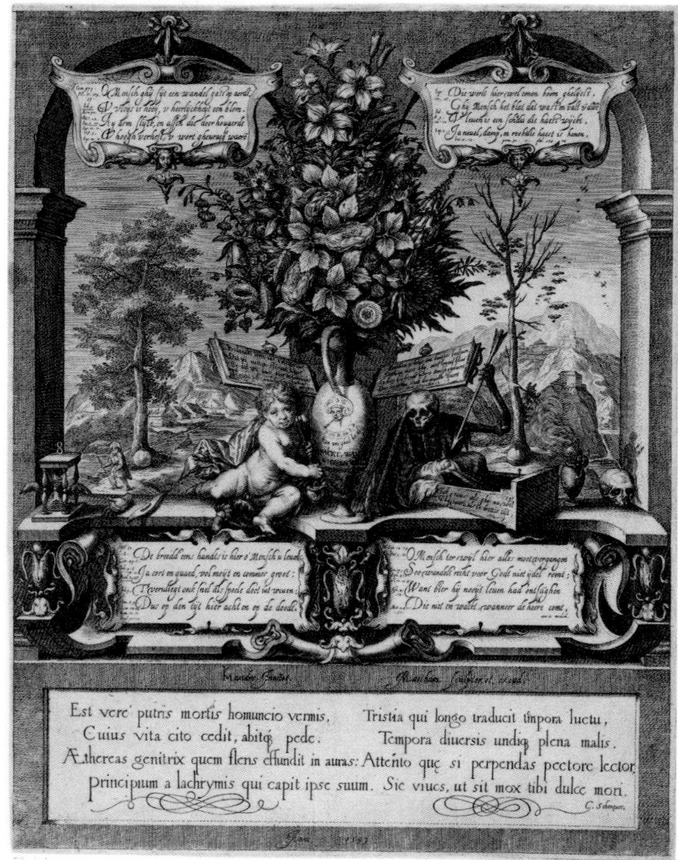

FIGURE 16. Jacob Matham, after Karel van Mander, *Vanitas Allegory on the Transience of Human Life*, 1599, engraving. Rijksprentenkabinet, Rijksmuseum, Amsterdam.

Gibson, who coined the term "rustic ruin," has suggested that the taste for dilapidated rural scenery that developed during the first half of the century cannot be explained merely by the Dutch tendency to symbolize and moralize or even by these artists' empirical involvement with nature. An aesthetic preference, he argues, was also in play, for even though such lowly imagery was ignored in poems and literary descriptions of the period, it was praised by early seventeenth-century writers on art including Van Mander, whose influential treatise *Het schilder-boeck* (The book of painting) was published in Haarlem in 1604.[40] What might be called an aesthetic of the irregular can already be recognized at the beginning of the century in the works of mannerist artists whose primary concern was to display their grace and sophistication of style, or *maniera* (Cats. 15, 16, and 17). In their works, one encounters visually complicated scenes rendered with an exceptionally high degree of technical finish, employed even for forms that are, in effect, incomplete. The ruined cottages in Abraham Bloemaert's incomparable drawings (Cat. 18) or the well-worn farmhouses engraved after his designs by other artists (Cats. 16 and 17) present unexpected polarities in their display of extreme linear refinement as applied to barnyard motifs that are anything but elegant. No less technically impressive are works made closer to mid-century (Cats. 21, 25, 31, and 32), in which a freer, rougher touch was employed to capture the surfaces and textures of decrepit or collapsing structures. Dutch theorists from Van Mander on recognized a distinction between two kinds of artistic virtuosity: *net* (a neat or polished approach in which the artist's touch is hidden) and *rouw* (a rough technique that emphasizes it).[41] Ruins appealed to both kinds of artists because they present intricate, irregular outlines that may encourage a fine touch but also uneven surfaces that are well served by a rough one.

The taste for classicizing art that emerged in the Dutch Republic during the 1660s and '70s was clearly inimical to homely (versus Italianate) ruins, for it opposed images of the decaying and derelict, even representations of unidealized human beings. Although artists such as Ruisdael (Cats. 30–32), Adam Pynacker (Cat. 33), and Adriaen van de Venne (Cat. 75) continued to depict this kind of subject matter after mid-century, later art theorists promoted a very different aesthetic: one that was sharply critical of what they considered ugly and distasteful. De Bisschop, whose drawing of a derelict windmill (Cat. 29) can be counted among the most poignant of all rustic ruins, nonetheless produced the two-volume *Signorum veterum icones* (Images of ancient sculptures) in 1668–69, followed by *Paradigmata graphics variorum artificum* (Examples of the drawings of various artists), published posthumously in 1671. In them he praised idealized classical art and criticized what he called "the unsightly in nature."[42] Significantly, De Bisschop's large, panoramic drawing of Rome (Cat. 62), so wide that it had to be made on two sheets, deemphasizes ruins, for the city's most celebrated monuments appear, mostly as intact structures, far in the distance, while only a few small, anonymous fragments of buildings emerge from the dense foreground foliage.

Gerard de Lairesse's (q.v.) *Het groot schilderboek* (The great book of painting), published in 1707, articulates an even sharper aversion to rustic motifs such as twisted trees, collapsing cottages, and storm-damaged landscapes, expressing particular dislike of ruins: "things deformed and broken, falsely called Painter-like."[43] Interestingly, both De Bisschop and De Lairesse invoked the term *schilderachtig* (roughly, "painter-like" or "suitable for artistic depiction"), challenging Van Mander's earlier endorsement of visual diversity and irregularity and claiming that only idealized and elevated scenes are properly *schilderachtig*.[44] De Lairesse did advocate that artists study classical ruins, but not because he found them interesting in their own right. Rather, he saw them as sources of knowledge about the architecture of antiquity and reminders of the beautiful temples and amphitheaters they once were, advising artists "… to learn the ancient state of old structures in order to know perfectly what they were in their best condition."[45]

Time and Travel

As noted above, Netherlandish artists had been traveling to Italy since the beginning of the sixteenth century to record the remains of ancient Roman civilization. By the later seventeenth century, this artistic tourism had become so widespread that Samuel van Hoogstraten, writing in 1678, was poking fun at the spectacle of so many of his countrymen returning from Italy with great bundles of sketches of broken walls and corroded stones ("de gebroke mueren en uitgegeete steenen") but without any knowledge of the monuments to which they belonged.[46] The intervening period, as L. F. Orr discusses in her essay (pp. 83–95), saw a remarkable succession of artist-voyagers beginning with the so-called Romanists and Mannerists in the sixteenth century and culminating in the seventeenth with several generations of gifted landscape and genre painters.[47]

At the beginning of the seventeenth century, the Twelve Year Truce led to a peaceful hiatus that encouraged many Dutch painters and draftsmen to set off for Rome, especially artists from Utrecht, which remained an important center of Roman Catholicism in an officially Calvinist Republic. But regardless of religious affiliation, northern landscapists were attracted to Italy because its terrain and climate were so dramatically different from the flat countryside and cool, rainy weather they knew at home. Moreover, the experience of being in Rome surely expanded their conception of time as well as place, for the city presented an unequaled concentration of ruins much older and far more numerous than the medieval sites on Dutch soil. Whether at home or in Italy, artists of this period who depicted ruins were less concerned with archaeological specificity than with creating a convincing illusion of time and place, frequently revising what they saw or inventing monuments that were not actually there. Understandably, they allowed themselves an even greater degree of imaginative freedom when they turned to foreign scenes. Thus, while most Dutch depictions of local landscapes with crumbling or fallen buildings appear to take place in the viewer's present, those set in Italy often show artists attempting to bring to life the vanished world of antiquity, using ruins to attach the scene to the distant past. It is not surprising that such settings came to be employed frequently for biblical, mythological, and historical narratives,

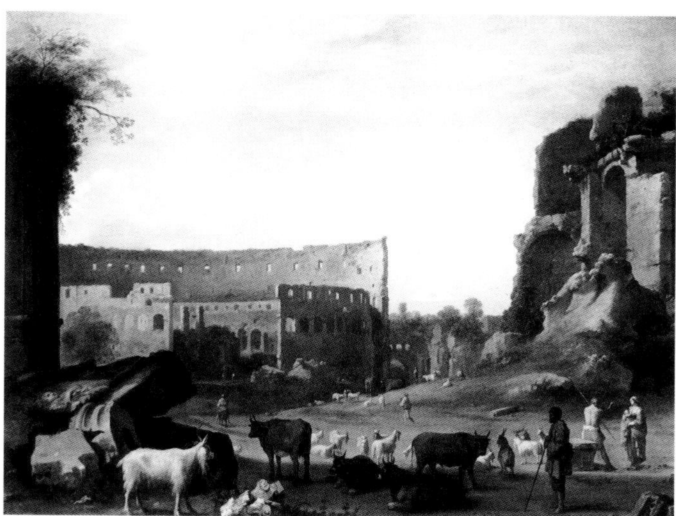

FIGURE 17. Cornelis van Poelenburch, *Roman Landscape*, c. 1620, oil on panel. Toledo Museum of Art, Ohio.

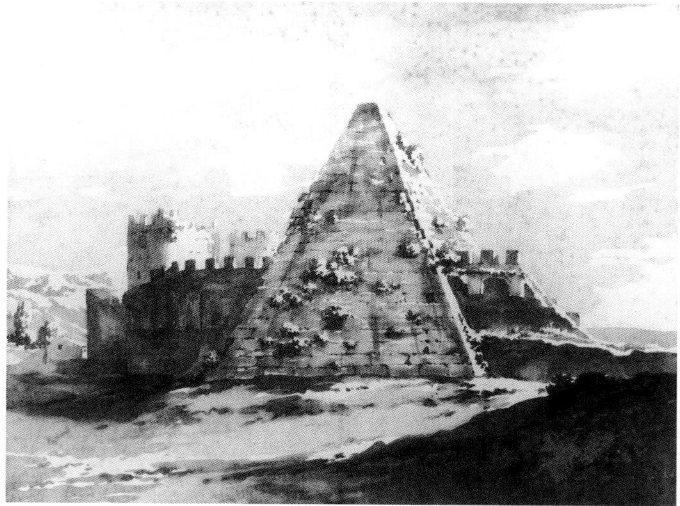

FIGURE 18. Jacob van der Ulft, *The Pyramid of Caius Cestius, Rome*, c. 1665–70(?), pen and brown ink, black chalk on paper. Museum of Art, Rhode Island School of Design, Providence.

even those that took place far from Rome (Cats. 15, 49, 50, 53, 54, 56, and 57).

When Cornelis van Poelenburch (q.v.), the most celebrated of the first generation of Italianate landscapists, painted a Roman landscape with a view of the Colosseum (Fig. 17), he combined the most familiar monument in the city with invented ruins and architectural debris whose scale dwarfs the cows, goats, and herdsmen wandering freely through the site. As in so many of these scenes, time seems to operate fluidly in some liminal realm between past and present, for although the buildings are no longer whole as they would have been in antiquity, their fallen state testifies to the great age of a place whose inhabitants continue to occupy themselves in utterly timeless ways. The shepherd leaning on his staff could be living in the early seventeenth century or hundreds of years earlier. The standing woman holding her baby at the far right might almost be Mary with the Christ child during their flight into Egypt, as Poelenburch repeatedly represented them in other Italianate landscapes with ruins (Cat. 67). Later in the century, Jacob van der Ulft (1621–89), an artist strongly influenced by De Bisschop (Cats. 29 and 62), made a memorable drawing of the Pyramid of Caius Cestius of 12 BC, the impressive structure that is part of the third-century city wall erected by Emperor Aurelianus at the Porta San Paolo on the southern edge of Rome (Fig. 18). Whether he drew the pyramid directly or after another artist's representation of it is not known, but his revisions to the actual site are obvious when his drawing is compared with views by other artists that show a much flatter wall at left.[48] In Van der Ulft's version, the wall becomes a curving, shadowed surface, which helps bring to vibrant life this most stable of all structures, whose ancient blocks sprout foliage and whose triangular face shimmers in the soft afternoon light.

Not all voyages, of course, involve actual journeys to faraway places. A surprising number of Dutch artists who never left their homeland responded to imagery that had been recorded by their predecessors or contemporaries, using it to develop their own imaginative evocations of Roman sites. One of the most surprising examples is a painting, dated 1629, by Pieter Saenredam (1597–1665) representing the Roman Church of Santa Maria della Febbre (Fig. 19). Saenredam never visited Italy, but he did have access to a famous sixteenth-century Roman sketchbook by Maerten van Heemskerck that was then in Haarlem (Fig. 79).[49] As in the earlier drawing, the round mausoleum at left, which came to be known as the Church of Santa Maria della Febbre (and after 1506 became the sacristy of St. Peter's) stands with other outbuildings in front of a huge, seemingly ruined structure with coffered vaults. This is the unfinished crossing of St. Peter's as it looked in the 1530s while still under construction. By Saenredam's time, Michelangelo's dome had been completed and the obelisk in the foreground moved to St. Peter's Square. This scene therefore depicts the invention of what is made to seem an ancient ruin, while isolating the complex of buildings in an imaginary rural setting, adding foliage and modulating wall textures and colors to emphasize weathering and age. Yet in the immediate foreground, the cardinal in his coach and the travelers in seventeenth-century costume also connect the scene to the present. Time here seems to accumulate, becoming denser and more deeply layered as one moves further into the scene. This, in fact, has always been the experience of Roman visitors, who find

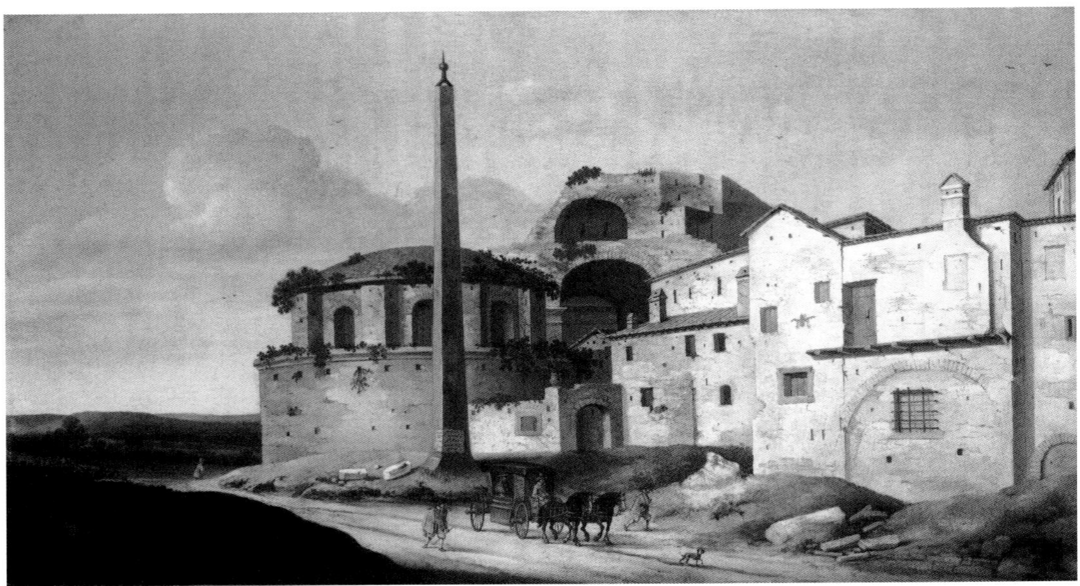

FIGURE 19. Pieter Jansz. Saenredam, *Church of Santa Maria della Febbre, Rome*, 1629, oil on panel. National Gallery of Art, Washington, D.C.

themselves confronted on all sides by the remains of different historical eras. A similar effect is conveyed by an Italianate landscape of about 1650–55 by Jan Baptist Weenix (Cat. 68), which combines ancient and Renaissance motifs from different locations, even transforming a famous (intact) Renaissance sculpture into a fictive ruin. Unlike Saenredam, however, this artist had spent five years in Italy.

Side by side with their enthusiastic appreciation of Italianate landscapes was the Dutch interest in pastoral imagery (i.e., imagery pertaining to shepherds), which began to emerge shortly after 1600 in both literature and art (Cat. 15) and continued to be popular into the later years of the century (Cats. 11, 28, 61, 64, 66, 68, and 69). Such idyllic scenes of herders and animals in pleasant rural surroundings derive ultimately from the bucolic poetry of Roman writers such as Horace and Virgil, who celebrated the beauty and harmony of nature as a timeless realm offering tranquility and safety from the vices, discord, and peril of the civilized world. Their common designation as "arcadian" images refers to Arcadia, a mountainous district in Greece, celebrated by poets as the home of contented shepherd folk. As A. Kettering has discussed, pastoral or arcadian imagery had a particular appeal for noble patrons and prosperous members of the middle class, who recognized its associations with literary and courtly traditions and who appreciated its celebration of leisurely rural existence.[50] The vogue for pastoral themes generated a flood of paintings, prints, and book illustrations such as the etching from J. H. Krul's drama *Pastorel musyck-spel van Juliana en Claudiaen*, published in Amsterdam in 1634 (Fig. 20). Here a young man pipes a serenade to his beloved—neither realizing that they are brother and sister, separated by circumstance and failing to recognize each other in their guises of shepherdess and beggar. Both figures wear elegant theatrical costume, while the youth holds an object that recalls both a beggar's staff and a shepherd's crook. The large ruin at the left background is a motif commonly employed in pastoral landscapes (Cats. 52, 61, 64, 68, and 69) to connect

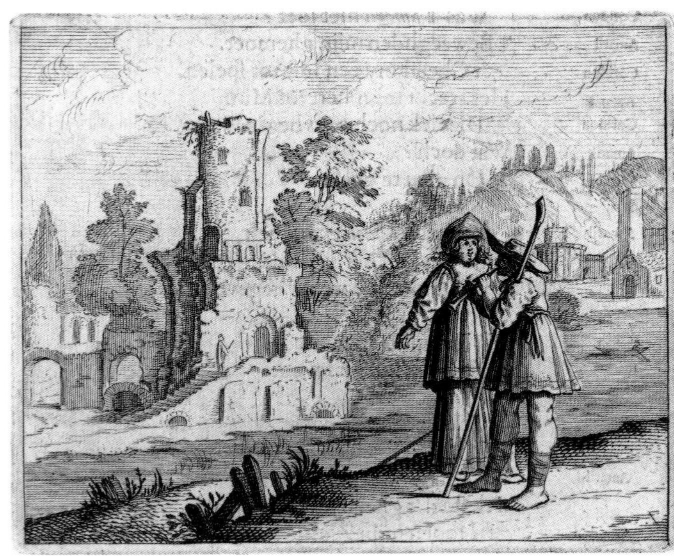

FIGURE 20. Salomon Savery, illustration from J. H. Krul, *Pastorel musyck-spel van Juliana en Claudiaen*, Amsterdam, 1634, page 23. Department of Printing and Graphic Arts, The Houghton Library, Harvard College Library, Cambridge, Massachusetts.

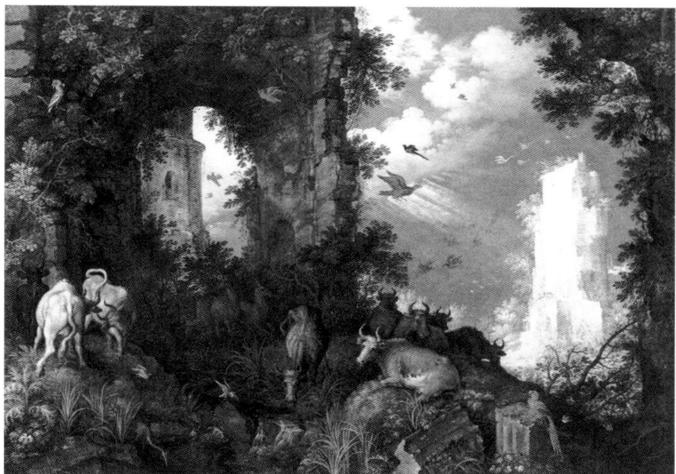

FIGURE 21. Roelandt Savery, *Landscape with Ruins and Animals*, 1624, oil on panel. Norton Simon Foundation, Pasadena, California.

such figures to their ancient origins and to enhance the aura of enduring serenity. In fact, pastoral figures became so popular that artists even incorporated them into local landscapes with recognizable Dutch ruins such as Brederode Castle (Cat. 7) or Rijnsburg Abbey (Cat. 11).

By far the most unexpected and exotic Dutch landscapes of this period were depicted by artists who traveled with the far-flung trading fleet to record the terrain and inhabitants of commercial outposts or colonies far from home. Frans Post's startling views of the New World in the Dutch settlement at Recife in Brazil (Cat. 71) are of particular interest in this context because they illustrate a translation into South American imagery of the type of landscape schema developed slightly earlier in Haarlem. Thus, it is not unusual to find the artist sometimes incorporating ruins, as Buytewech and Jan van de Velde II had done in the early years of the century (Cats. 2a–b and 4), but replacing familiar local monuments with crumbling Brazilian churches or monasteries, perhaps as references to the waning of Roman Catholic influence during the Dutch occupation of the region.[51] To a viewer living in Haarlem, Amsterdam, or Delft, Post's vivid scenes offered armchair travel to a corner of the world much more distant and foreign than the Italian campagna. But in both cases (and in local Dutch scenes as well), fallen and fragmentary structures inject both time and history into the landscape, making it seem more alive by alluding to the constantly evolving processes that mark and transform every part of the physical world, whatever its location on the globe.

Dutch artists who invented fantastic, imaginary landscapes were no less drawn to ruins, whose inherent irregularities and frequently bizarre shapes so enhance the dramatic strangeness of such scenes. Such is the case in the colorful paintings of the Utrecht artist Roelandt Savery (1567–1639), who worked for the court of Rudolf II in Prague. Inspired by Rudolf's *Wunderkammer* and menagerie and by his own travels in the Tyrolian Alps, Savery produced delicately painted vistas such as the mountain scene *Landscape with Ruins and Animals* of 1624 (Fig. 21), in which a large ruin overgrown with foliage becomes a sanctuary and display area for various animals and exotic birds. No less fantastic is a patently invented composite ruin that looms as a huge presence beside a river in an etching of about 1640 by Simon de Vlieger (Cat. 60). A charmingly eccentric gouache of the 1670s by Gerrit Battem (Cat. 65) shows an interpretation of the ruined Temple of the Sibyl at Tivoli perched incongruously beside a roaring, Ruisdael-like waterfall, yielding an effect quite unlike the actual site (Cat. 59).

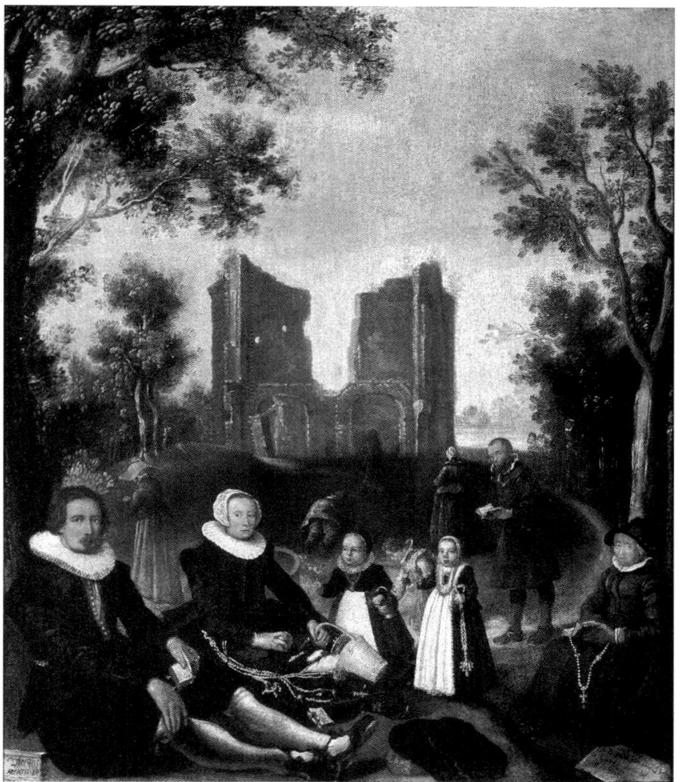

FIGURE 22. Pietersz. de Jongh, *Portrait of a Family at Heiloo*, 1630, oil on canvas. Catherijnconvent, Utrecht.

Yet another evocative (though less frequent) use of ruins occurs in Dutch family portraiture, where such motifs—either actual or imaginary—were sometimes included as allusions to time or travel. In at least one instance, a family portrait was combined with a ruin-portrait in order to commemorate a pilgrimage to a significant religious site. Gerrit Pietersz. de Jongh's (d. 1642) painting of 1630 shows a Dutch family, along with other visitors, in front of the

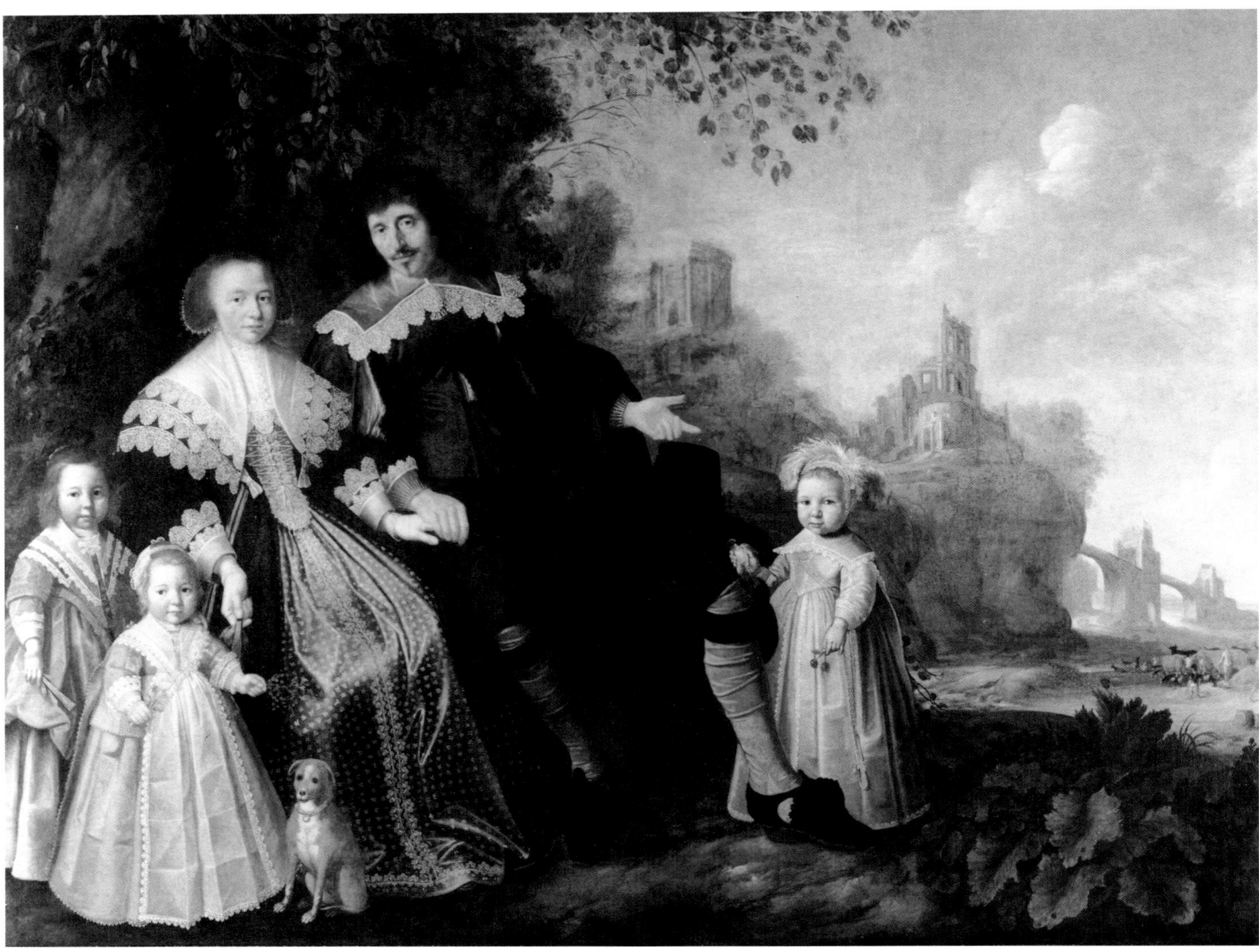

FIGURE 23. Herman Mijndertsz. Doncker, *Family Portrait with Three Children and Ruins*, 1644, oil on canvas. Sarah Campbell Blaffer Foundation, Houston.

ruined Capel van Ons Lieve Vrouw (Chapel of Our Dear Lady) at Heiloo (Fig. 22), not far from Egmond Castle (Fig. 10), a site that began to attract pilgrims after its destruction during the Siege of Alkmaar of 1573. More often, however, portraits of this type show the figures near ruins that may allude to the dynastic longevity of the family within the Dutch Republic (Cat. 82) or suggest connections to Italy through travel or classical learning. Such is the case in a number of single and family portraits with ruins by Herman Mijndertsz. Doncker (c. 1620–after 1656), who was active in Haarlem and Enkhuizen.[52] Doncker's portraits, some huge in scale—including one in Houston that is more than six by eight feet (Fig. 23)—may have been commissioned to demonstrate that their sitters had made the journey to Rome, but it is more likely that they reflect the popular vogue for pastoral imagery, discussed above. In any case, placing contemporary individuals near ancient ruins with their aura of poetic timelessness produces a complex duality of effect. On the one hand, such paintings emphasize how portraiture allows its mortal subjects to live on (if only in paint) beyond their actual span of years, while on the other they remind viewers that all aspects of the material world are subject to time.

Buildings, Bodies, and Mortality

The frequent appearance of ruins in local, foreign, and imaginary landscapes by Dutch artists makes sense when one considers their exceptional range of shapes, sizes, and potential meanings. Fragmentary and timeworn structures also tend to evoke universal human responses, probably because they

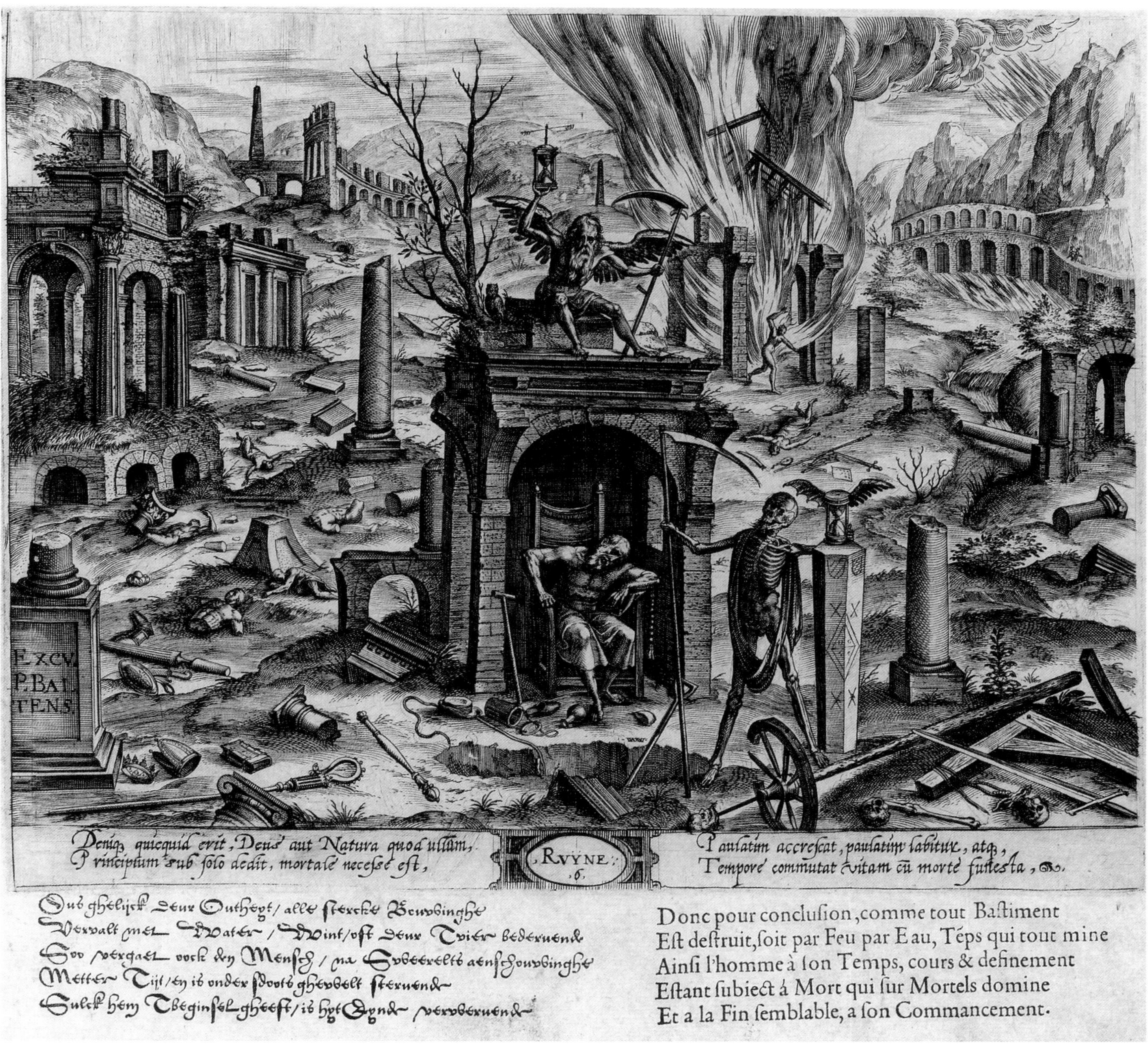

FIGURE 24. Jan Wierix, "Ruyne (Old Age)," engraving from *Theatrum vitae humanae*, 1577. Print Collection, Miriam and Ira D. Wallach Division of Art, Prints and Photographs, The New York Public Library.

remind viewers that they too exist within time. This association is intensified by the realization that there are certain analogies between buildings and bodies: both structures of containment in which life is lived and both subject to metamorphosis. Interestingly, this correlation was explored in various ways by Netherlandish artists in both the sixteenth and seventeenth centuries. Jan Wierix's (1459–c. 1618) *Theatrum vitae humanae* of 1577, for example, takes the viewer through the various stages of human life, ending with a final sheet entitled "Ruyne" (Fig. 24), which depicts a desolate landscape of fallen statuary, broken columns, and other vestiges of Roman architecture.[53] At the center foreground is an old man, framed by a ruined building that surrounds him as if it were his second mortal cage. As Father Time looks down from the rooftop above him, the skeletal figure of Death waits on the ground before him. While the meaning of the image itself is perfectly clear, its inscription reiterates the parallel between buildings that are destroyed by fire or water and man whose condition of mortality rules his life from beginning to end.[54] A similar idea seems to have inspired a witty drawing of about 1650 (Fig. 25) by Herman Saftleven, who was responsible for some of the most evocative Dutch drawings of fallen architecture (Cats. 41 and 48). Here the silhouette of a ruin merges with the contours and foliage of a rocky hillside to form a man's profile; a second figure stands within the arched doorway that reads as an eye.[55]

Both Wierix's and Saftleven's works relate to the category of images, noted earlier, that the Dutch classified as vanitas representations or meditations on the transience of human life (Cats. 74, 77–79 and Fig. 11). In vanitas scenes, which encompass a great range of subjects, the viewer repeatedly encounters juxtapositions of intact and ruined structures to show time's transformation of the physical world. An especially subtle and lovely example is the pen drawing of 1614 by Hendrick Goltzius (1558–1617) (Fig. 26), which shows a bust-length view of a handsome young man wearing an elaborate doublet and a slashed, plumed beret. Framing his happy face is a ruined wall that displays an hourglass and an inscription at the right that reads: "Quis evadet" (Who escapes?) and, in smaller letters, "nemo" (no one). In his left hand, the youth holds a skull and in his right, a long-stemmed tulip that springs upward from the death's head. Because he holds the stem as one might hold a pen or burin, he appears to be drawing the skull as well as holding it.[56] The tulip's curving leaves and stalk lead the eye up to the fragile, cup-shaped flower and the ruined masonry just above it, where Goltzius has placed his monogram and the date, as if commenting on the artist's capacity to simultaneously reveal and transcend the evanescence of the physical world by representing it. The death's head, a motif that makes frequent appearances in Dutch vanitas paintings and prints (Cats. 77–79), is turned toward the right, in the same direction as the young man's head, and it is further linked to the living face by the framing edges of the boy's elaborate tunic. The viewer is thus encouraged to compare the two not only as different states of existence but also as materially different physical entities—one soft and pliant, the other hard and unyielding—one convex, the other concave. As the brain's hollow container, where the major perceptual receptors once resided, the skull (along with the other skeletal bones) is the only part of the body that outlasts the lifespan of the living person. In their sculptural play of solids and voids, and as the shells of organisms that were once more complete, skulls present certain obvious analogies to ruins, which also outlive the buildings they once were.

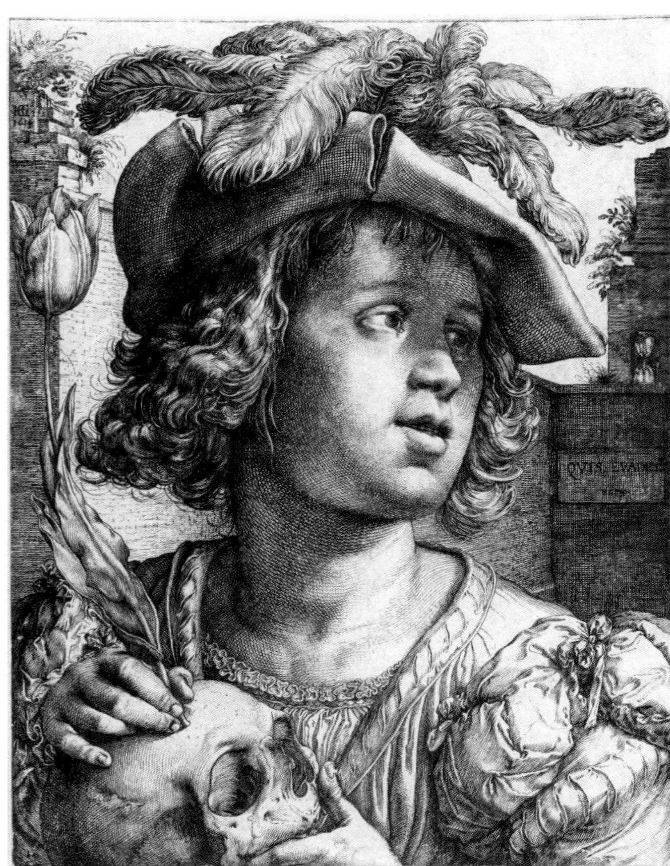

FIGURE 26. Hendrick Goltzius, *Young Man with Skull, Tulip, and Ruin*, 1614, pen and brown ink on paper. The Pierpont Morgan Library, New York.

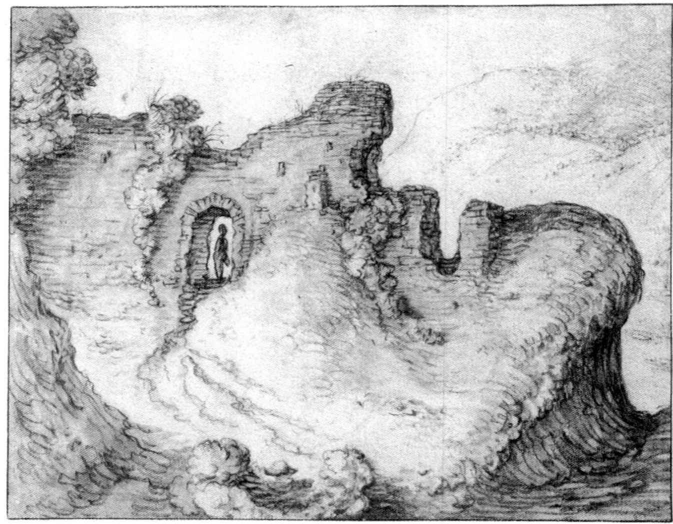

FIGURE 25. Herman Saftleven, *Rocky Landscape with Ruins Forming the Profile of a Man's Face*, before c. 1650, black chalk and brown wash on paper. Centraal Museum, Utrecht.

A painting of about 1627–28 by Hendrick Terbrugghen (1588–1629), which scholars have titled either *Melancholia* or *The Repentant Magdalene* (Fig. 27), illustrates a similar

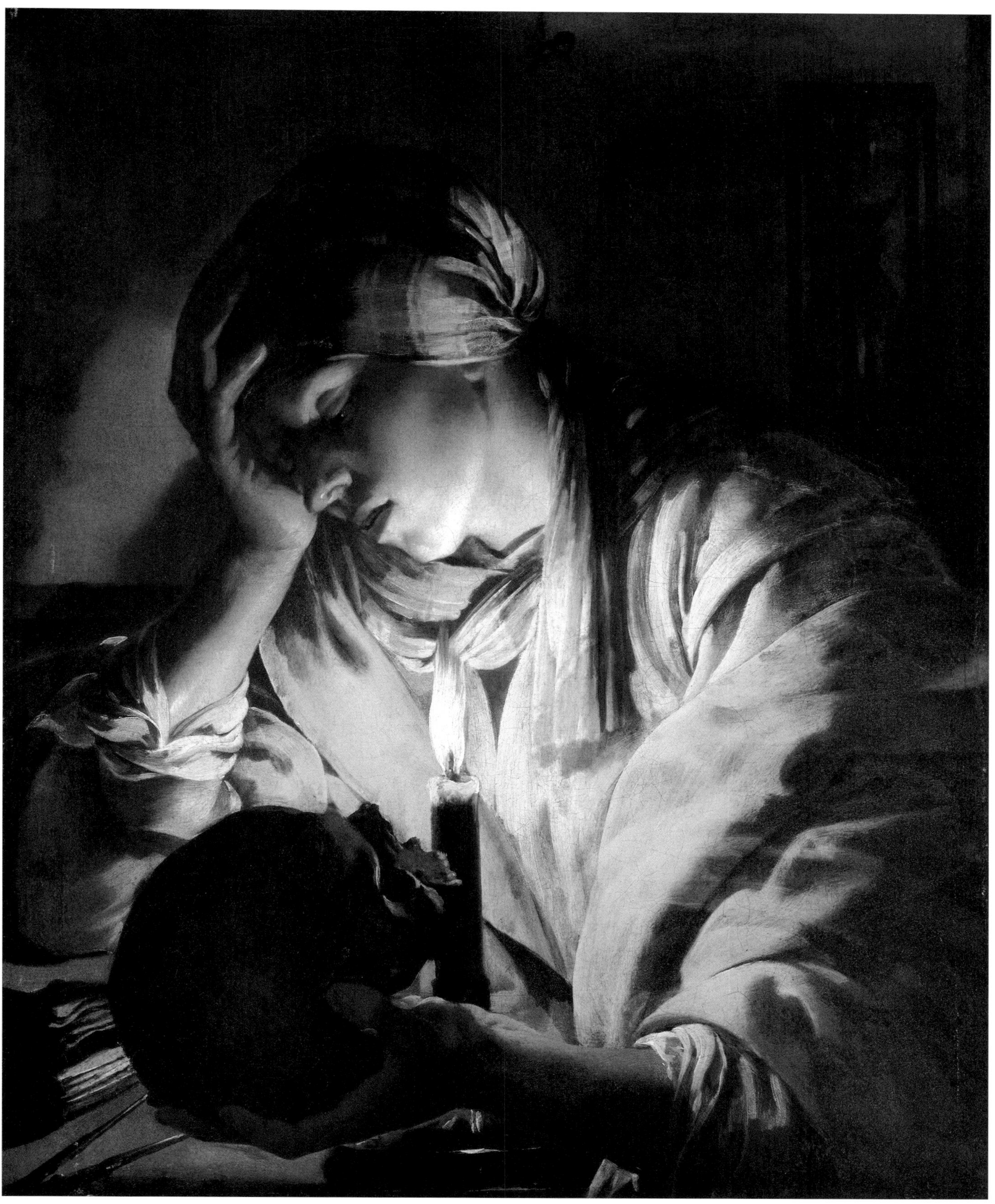

FIGURE 27. Hendrick Terbrugghen, *Melancholia (The Repentant Magdalene?)*, c. 1627–28, oil on canvas. Art Gallery of Ontario, Toronto, on loan from a private collection.

interplay between skull and living face, but now revealed by candlelight.[57] Like other Utrecht followers of Caravaggio, Terbrugghen developed a style in which this ambience is used to evoke moments in the process of passing. The flickering glow of the candle, which consumes itself as it burns and discharges its substance into evanescent smoke, produces a dramatically fluid atmosphere, in which figures and objects appear to shift constantly between tangible visibility and obliteration. In Terbrugghen's painting, the candle's flame emits a soft but intense illumination, which reveals a young woman in half-length, surrounded by shadow and leaning her head on her right hand. With downcast eyes, she contemplates the darkly silhouetted skull in her left hand, as if reflecting on the inevitable end of her earthly time, as measured by the hourglass in shadow at the upper right. Whether or not this painting represents Mary Magdalene, the repentant sinner who became a follower of Christ, the figure recalls depictions of St. Jerome and other devout hermits who commonly appear with vanitas imagery such as candles or lanterns, skulls, dead trees, and ruins (Cats. 72–74).

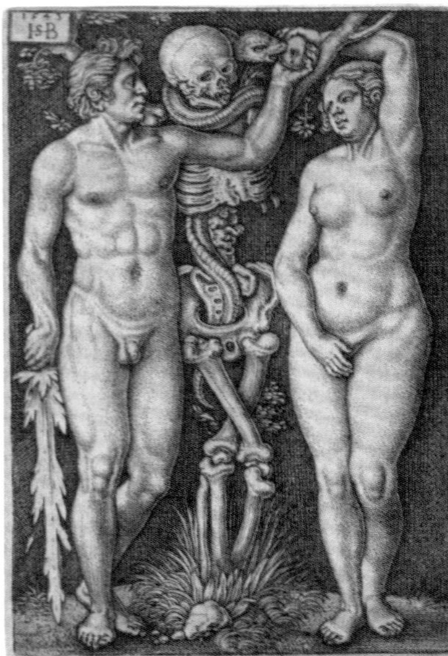

FIGURE 28.
Hans Sebald Beham, *Adam and Eve*, 1543, engraving. Courtesy of the Fogg Art Museum, Harvard University Art Museums, Cambridge, Massachusetts.

Behind all vanitas representations, of course, is the biblical account of the origin of human mortality as described in the second and third chapters of Genesis. This was the so-called fall of Adam and Eve, who disobeyed God's command by eating the forbidden fruit of the Tree of Knowledge and thus lost their primal innocence and immortality. Thereafter, they and all their descendants became subject to physical deterioration and death. Accordingly, the Latin verb *cadere* (to fall) is the root of the word cadaver, or corpse.[58] The ruinous consequences of Adam and Eve's fall are vividly illustrated, for example, in an engraving of 1543 (Fig. 28) by the German artist Hans Sebald Beham (1500–1550). Here the first man and woman stand on either side of the Tree of Knowledge, which the artist has transformed into a full-length human skeleton, its skull leering between their heads as the serpent twined around its neck presents the fatal apple to Adam. Christianity offered recourse from this cycle of sin, bodily corruption, and death by teaching that Christ's sacrificial death on the Cross atoned for the sin of the first parents and gave humanity a second chance for eternal life. Indeed, according to medieval legends about the Cross, the skull marking the site of Golgotha ("place of the skull") was believed to be the skull of Adam, in which seeds from the fatal fruit sprouted and grew into the tree from which the cross was made.[59]

Typological connections between Adam and Christ continued to be widely drawn during the Protestant Reformation in northern Europe, which spawned intense debate about the mortal state of humanity and the conditions needed for salvation. Thus, depictions of the dead Christ, especially in sixteenth-century German art, often elaborate on the corpse in all its decaying materiality in order to emphasize the inevitability of death and humanity's consequent need for salvation.[60] One recalls this theological and art-historical background when confronting another subject that became popular in the Dutch provinces during the seventeenth century: the anatomy lesson, either in the form of group portraits of doctors with their students or as scientific illustrations of dissections in printed manuals. In these depictions of what might be called the ruined body, yet another form of physical transformation is vividly explored.

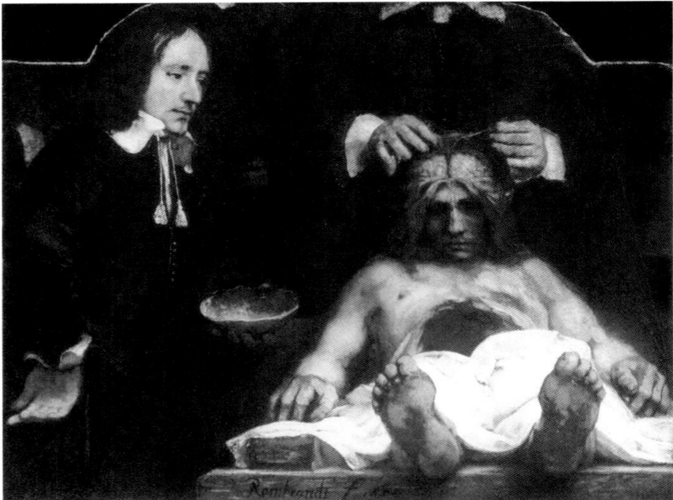

FIGURE 29. Rembrandt van Rijn, *The Anatomy Lesson of Dr. Joan Deyman*, 1656, oil on canvas. Amsterdams Historisch Museum.

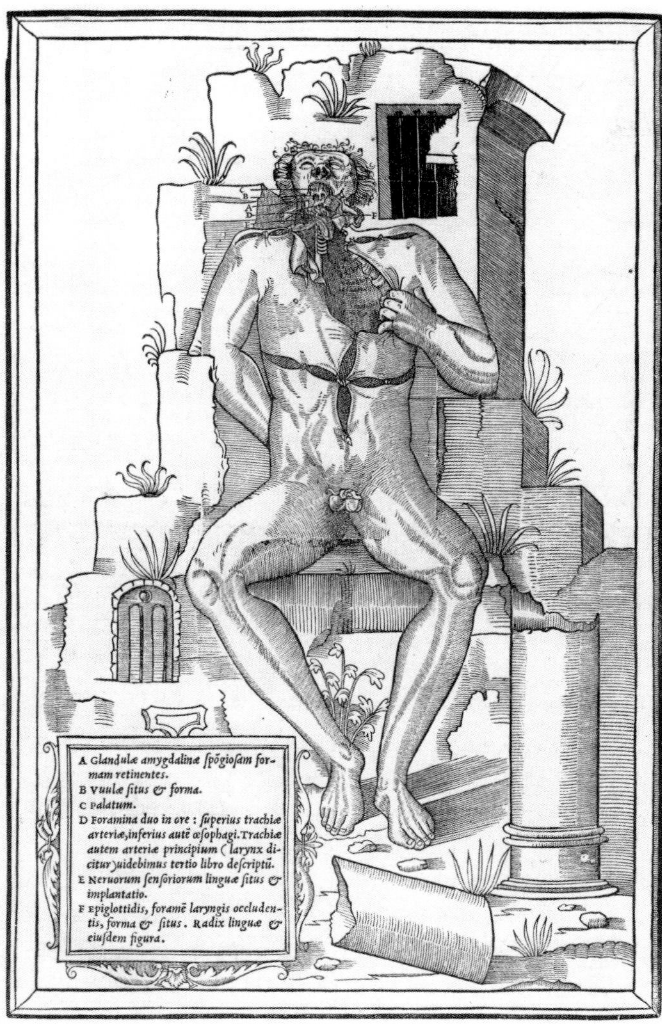

FIGURE 30. Estienne de la Rivière, anatomical insert, "Corpse resting on Ruins," woodcut, from Charles Estienne, *De dissectione partium corporis humani*, Paris 1545. Research Library, The Getty Research Institute, Los Angeles.

The Anatomy Lesson of Dr. Joan Deyman of 1656 (Fig. 29), the second of Rembrandt's two anatomy portraits, is the fragment of an originally larger composition that focuses on a powerfully foreshortened, anatomized corpse.[61] Joris Fonteyn, or "Black Jan," one of the executed criminals used as specimens in public demonstrations of the structure of the human body, appears here as the very shell of man, his gaping abdominal cavity emptied of its organs and his scalp peeled down to frame his face. As the anatomist dissects the brain, his assistant at left holds the bony cap of the skull. To a person of this period who saw an anatomy portrait or witnessed an actual dissection, the progressive evisceration and fragmentation of the physical self conveyed awe-inspiring scientific knowledge, but it must have prompted religious reflection as well. Secular sacrificial figures, these cadavers were also used to demonstrate the miracle of divine creation as revealed in the mysterious internal world of the human body. This idea is clearly expressed in Caspar Barlaeus's (1584–1648) poem on Rembrandt's earlier *Anatomy Lesson of Dr. Tulp* (c. 1633, Mauritshuis, The Hague), which reads in part: "Listeners learn yourself! And while you proceed through the parts, believe that even in the smallest detail God lies hid."[62]

The same sense of wonder is evident in the pages of the scientific materials of this period, such as Govert Bidloo's anatomical treatise of 1685, with illustrations designed by Gerard de Lairesse (Cat. 81 and Fig. 160). This large and beautifully designed book leads the reader through the human body (both male and female) from the skin that sheaths its intact form to its smallest and most hidden internal parts. In the process, the illustrations show how the anatomist must, in effect, gradually destroy the object of his study in order to investigate it fully. Not surprisingly, early scientific illustrators noticed a parallel between anatomized corpses and ruined buildings, as in a woodcut from Charles Estienne's *De dissectione partium corporis humani*, published in Paris in 1545 (Fig. 30).[63] In this poignant image, the condition of fallen-ness applies equally to the remains of the ruined building and to the corpse propped against it, who pulls apart the incision on his chest to reveal its hollow core.

Time

Anatomical research was only one of the many areas of empirical and theoretical inquiry that flourished in the Dutch Republic in the seventeenth century, encouraged by the country's openness to new ideas and relative lack of censorship.[64] The development and improvement of lenses and other scientific tools, which made possible closer analysis of the material world, fostered new understanding of what had seemed utterly unreachable aspects of the universe, from miniscule microscopic organisms to distant planetary spheres. Among the most important advances of the Age of Observation was the increased capacity to compute and measure, as evidenced in major developments in mathematics, physics, cartography, and astronomy. Closely related to the interest in these areas of research was a new impetus to understand and more accurately gauge time. This elusive concept, which had provoked speculation since antiquity, came to be of great practical interest for the commercial society and expanding global empire of the Dutch Republic, whose economy was largely dependent upon seafaring.[65]

Early physicists and philosophers had considered time to be either a fundamental property of the universe or the aspect of human consciousness that involves awareness of its own thought progression and memory. Two important early figures, Aristotle and St. Augustine, should be mentioned here because their extensive commentaries on time continued to influence so much subsequent thinking on the subject. Aristotle (384–322 BC) defined time in a famous phrase as "the measure of motion according to before and after," arguing that it depends upon observable changes in the physical world as manifested in the movements of the celestial bodies.[66] In struggling with the celebrated Paradoxes of Zeno (c. 450 BC), who had questioned how motion is possible if time consists of infinitely divisible "nows," Aristotle responded that time is not merely made up of indivisible points or moments and is not identical with motion, but depends upon it, just as motion reciprocally defines time.

Centuries later in the Early Christian era, St. Augustine (AD 354–430) wrote at length about what he termed "the large and boundless inner hall" of memory, which retains pictures, knowledge, emotions, and past actions but is unable to determine where in human consciousness God resides.[67] For Augustine, time is not a property of the physical world but exists in the impressions retained in memory. As he meditated on the mysteries of where time comes from, how it passes, and where it goes, he asked how time can be measured if past, present, and future exist only in the mind. Observing that resting and moving bodies may occupy equal temporal intervals, and that time may seem to pass slowly or rapidly under different circumstances, he concluded, in contrast to Aristotle, that "time is not the movement of a body."[68] Augustine's lament on the indefinable familiarity of this most mysterious of all concepts is one that still resonates today: "What, then, is time? If no one asks me, I know; if I wish to explain to one who asks me, I know not."[69]

In the seventeenth century, intense interest in time in and beyond the Dutch Republic was stimulated by a variety of factors. For Europeans of this period, the displacements and upheavals of war, as well as devastating episodes of the plague, were potent enough reminders of individual mortality, as they had often been in the past. Scientific research, which since the Renaissance had been circulating through an international network of scholars, was also creating changing perceptions of the universe and the human position within it. In a period that saw increasing acceptance of Nicolaus Copernicus's (1473–1543) revolutionary proposal of a heliocentric universe (1543), two interacting areas of inquiry contributed to an evolving world view: continuing research in astronomy and major discoveries in mathematics. The rational, mechanistic conception of nature that marked this era in Europe emerged from the activities of a succession of extraordinary figures: Galileo Galilei (1564–1642), who invented the pendulum and constructed the first telescope to confirm the Copernican theory; Johannes Kepler (1571–1630), who formulated the laws of planetary motion; René Descartes (1596–1650), who developed algebraic notation and analytic geometry (in addition to his theory of mind/body dualism); Blaise Pascal (1623–62), who laid the foundation for the theory of probability; and Sir Isaac Newton (1642–1727), who discovered the laws of gravitation and motion and invented differential and integral calculus.[70] In the Netherlands, the new science, which often married abstract theory to concrete practical invention, was specifically directed toward the measure of time by Christiaan Huygens (1629–95), the brilliantly gifted second son of the poet and diplomat Constantijn Huygens (1596–1687).

As a young boy tutored privately in the home of his learned father, Christiaan Huygens was introduced to major thinkers of his day, including his father's friend Descartes, who may have encouraged his study of mathematics. He went on to study law and mathematics at the University of Leiden between 1645 and 1647, subsequently becoming interested in optics, lens grinding, and telescope construction, which resulted in his discovery of the first ring of Saturn in 1655.[71] Because research in astronomy required accurate timekeeping, Huygens's attention soon turned to clocks. Here his mathematical training served him well, for his studies of oscillation and cycloidal motion, building upon Galileo's earlier research, led him to invent the first pendulum clock in 1656.

Large clocks driven by weights had existed in Europe since the early fourteenth century, but the invention of mechanical timepieces capable of measuring minutes and seconds only occurred later and is credited to Huygens. His preliminary plan for a pendulum clock is preserved at Leiden University in a letter he sent to his friend, Jean Chapelain, in Paris on 25 December 1656.[72] This initial research on the clock, which he patented and published in 1658, had immediate local application when pendulums were installed in the church clocks at Scheveningen and Utrecht. Indeed, Huygens's chief clockmaker, Samuel Coster of The Hague, was able to guarantee the Utrecht church fathers that their clock would not deviate more than eight minutes a week—an extraordinary degree of accuracy for this period.[73]

The major purpose of Huygens's research, however, was to develop timepieces capable of determining precise longitude at sea—a problem (not to be solved until the late eighteenth century) that was of the most pressing concern for a nation extensively involved in seafaring and global trade.[74] His major work on the pendulum clock was published in Paris in 1673: *Horologium oscillatorium*, which also includes treatises on cycloidal motion, on the evolutes of curves and

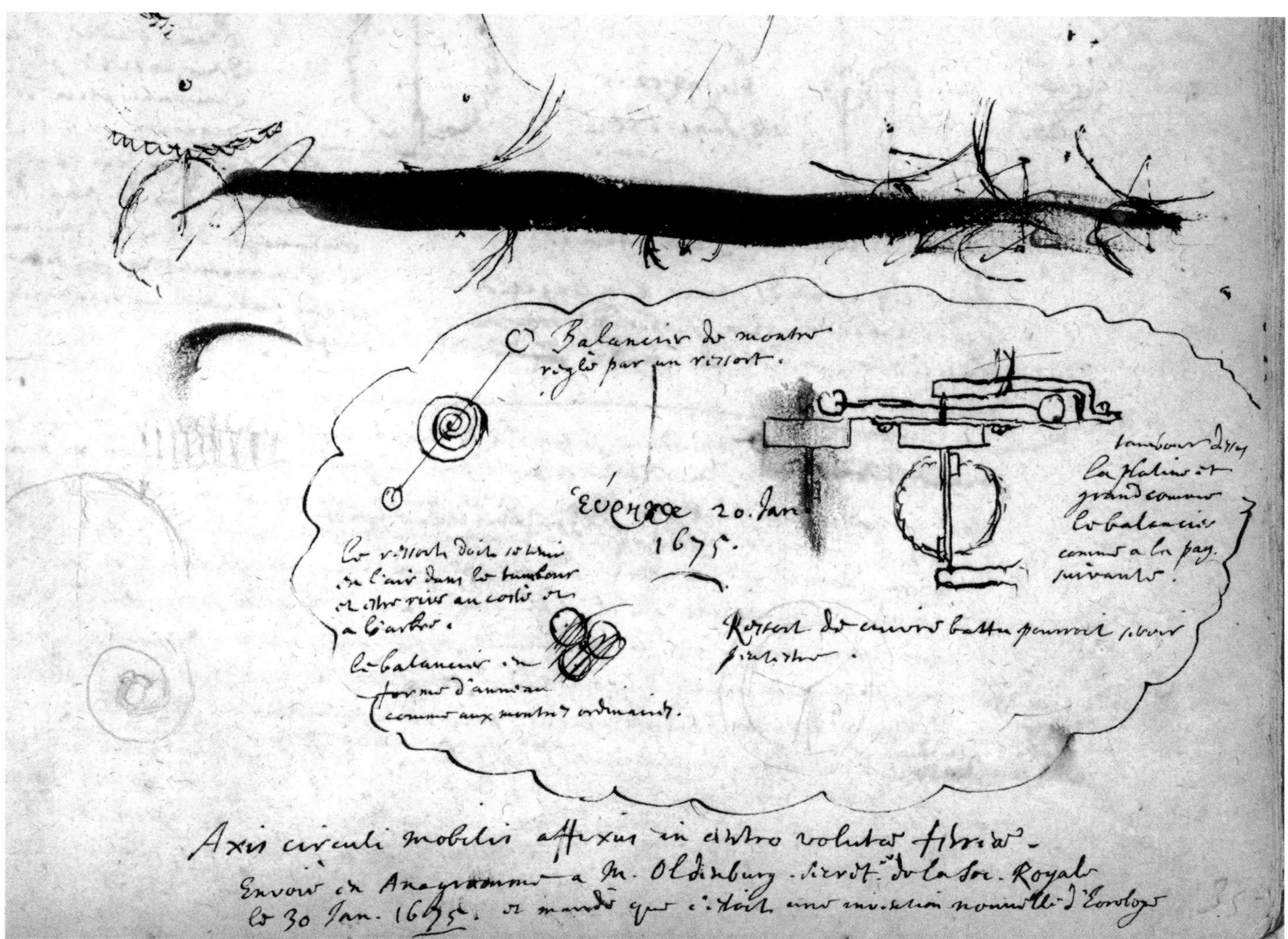

FIGURE 31. Christiaan Huygens, earliest sketch of a balance spring to control motion in a watch, Paris, 20 January 1675. Department of Western Manuscripts, University Library, Leiden.

centers of oscillation, as well as theorems on centrifugal force.[75] In 1675, in an attempt to produce portable timepieces able to function accurately on sea voyages, he developed the balance spring watch, which yielded significantly better results than the spring-driven clocks that had begun to appear in the early fifteenth century.[76] His notebook records his earliest sketch for this mechanism with his annotations in French and—in the center in Greek—the triumphant exclamation: "Eureka [I have found it] 20. Jan[uary] 1675." (Fig. 31).[77]

Huygens's attempt to measure exact temporal intervals, which depends upon the notion that specific moments can be marked, recorded, and compared, parallels his period's broader philosophical interest in time, which also involved conceptualizing the extended aspect of time known as duration: a state of temporal being that is not connected to motion. While early thinkers, including Aristotle and Augustine, had recognized time's persistent, extended continuity, later philosophers would explore this aspect of it in a more pointed way. Interestingly, both Descartes, who spent the twenty most productive years of his career in the Dutch provinces, and the Dutch rationalist philosopher Baruch Spinoza (1632–77) reflected on durational time, though in slightly different ways. In his *Principia philosophiae*, published in 1644, Descartes defined duration as a mode of considering the perseverance of the existence of a thing (by which he meant either a physical entity or an idea).[78] Spinoza's *Ethics* of 1677, whose second book includes extensive discussion of duration, time, and eternity, introduced the term "actuality" to indicate that anything considered durational must exist in the real world: "Duration is the attribute under which we conceive the existence of created things, in so far as they persevere in their own actuality."[79] To put this complex and subtle concept another way: duration offers a way of thinking about the physical world that recognizes it has a cumulative existence, in that the things it contains can endure over extended periods. Philosophers (including more recent thinkers from Bergson to Bachelard) have explored and articulated this concept in more than one way, but in a broad sense, duration implies that the material realm is not only acted upon by time but, in effect, contains and absorbs it in a manner that is neither fleeting nor temporary.

The idea of duration as non-momentary temporality probably reached a rather extensive audience in the Dutch provinces during this period through a contemporary figure much less known today than Descartes or Spinoza: Franco Petri Burgersdijk (1590–1635), who in 1629 was appointed professor of philosophy and ethics at the University of Leiden.[80] Classified by modern historians as a neo-Aristotelian, Burgersdijk has not been judged an especially innovative thinker in his own right, but he wrote a series of introductory handbooks on physics, logic, and ethics that because of their clarity would be reprinted and widely used in Dutch university courses for more than a hundred years. Students at Oxford, Cambridge, and Trinity College, Dublin, also read them in translation until the mid-eighteenth century, as did their American counterparts at Harvard and Yale.[81] In his writings, Burgersdijk repeatedly addressed the question of how to understand time and explain its properties. A believer in the Copernican system, he approached his discussions through physics more than metaphysics, linking time to observable celestial movement and attempting to relate it to ordinary experience. Of particular interest in the present context is his *Institutionum metaphysicarum*, published posthumously in 1640, in which he distinguishes among what he calls momentary temporality (the being-in-time of momentary entities), duration as the non-momentary continuity of existence, and persisting duration as eternity. He concludes that every part of time corresponds to some part of existence.[82] While the finer shadings of these and other seventeenth-century discussions of time must be left for other studies, we may safely conclude for present purposes that this was a period that was enthralled, if not obsessed, with the subject and, further, that contemporary reflections on time addressed both its momentary and durational aspects.

Conclusion

To assume that one-to-one connections can be made between art and the scientific or philosophical concerns of its period would be too easy. Yet it is clear that an intense and highly concentrated interest in time emerged simultaneously in many areas of thought and expression during the seventeenth century. Indeed, the Dutch Republic was an environment that encouraged heightened time-consciousness. On the most individual level, the Calvinist religion placed conspicuous emphasis on recognition of human mortality, as many a vanitas still life testifies. Moralizing poems and sermons of this period likewise reminded people to use their earthly time wisely in full knowledge that its span would be limited. The point is even made in explicitly horological terms in Jan Luyken's poem entitled "The Clockmaker," which was apparently inspired by Huygens's invention:

> O Man, set straight your soul's abode
> While life's clock ticks its measured road;
> For when the pendulum runs down,
> Which marks the span of life's short round,
> There is no upstroke to be found
> For art, or money, or renown.[83]

Within society as a whole, broad economic factors also came into play, for, in addition to the Dutch involvement in global sea trade noted above, an open-market, mercantile society built upon individual initiative had evolved at home. Entrepreneurship and commercial competition created a sharpened awareness of time, since gaps in communication or delayed shipments of goods could have serious financial and legal ramifications. In this milieu, the most basic organizing systems of daily life, from consignment schedules to postal services, called for closer attention to timekeeping.[84] That artists came to be as much engaged with time as the scientists, philosophers, and merchants of the day is therefore hardly surprising. How, then, might they give visual form to this fundamental condition of existence that affects it so profoundly in every aspect, yet is not itself visible?

The paintings, drawings, and prints considered here provide a partial answer. As material objects, they exist perpetually in the present: canvases, panels, or sheets of paper that display the result of someone's creative process. Yet they transcend the stillness—the inherent now-ness—of their media by creating illusions that time is a living presence, visibly transforming the material world they depict. While the evocation of fleeting moments within a larger temporal flow is almost the hallmark of seventeenth-century art, these representations of ruined, fallen, and fragmentary things focus directly and analytically on the actual processes that shape and alter the physical world—sometimes instantaneously, more often through gradual accretion and erosion. Jacob van Ruisdael's drawing of a ruined farmhouse of about 1655 (Cat. 30) captures the intriguing paradox of these scenes, for in the demise of this small rustic dwelling, the observer recognizes the force of time itself, potent and unmistakable in

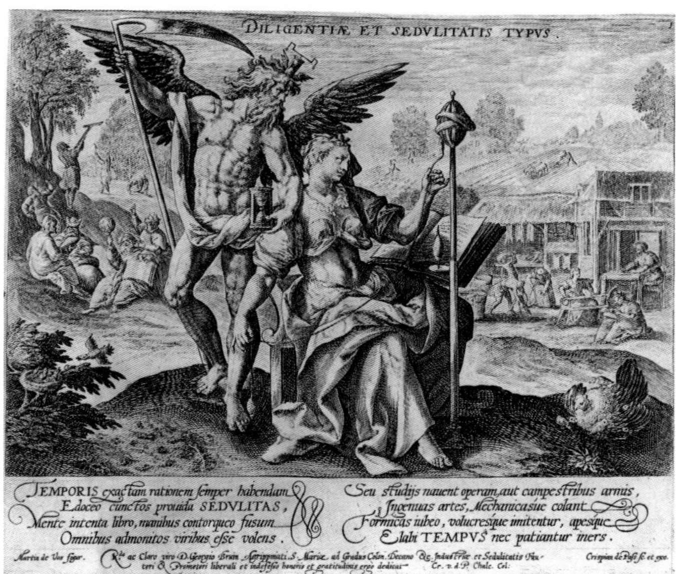

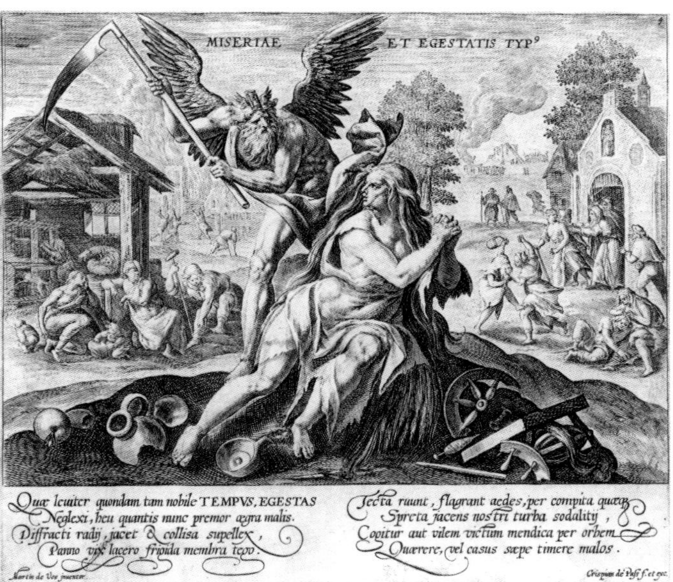

FIGURES 32 and 33. Crispijn van de Passe the Elder after Maerten de Vos, nos. 1 and 4 from the series *The Use and Abuse of Time*, c. 1570, engraving. British Museum, London.

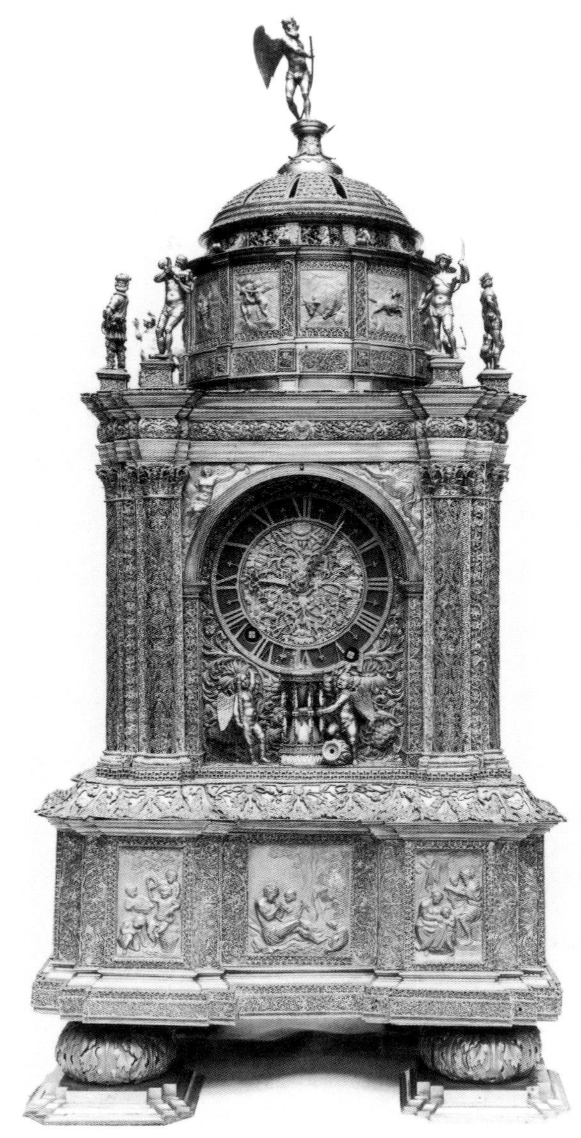

FIGURE 34. Hans Coenraet Breghtel and Adriaen van den Bergh, *Clock*, c. 1660, silver, partly gilt. Victoria and Albert Museum, London.

the strokes of chalk that capture the structure's softening surfaces and its sequence of collapsing walls. Viewed within the process of its dissolution, the farmhouse appears more—not less—alive.

Ruisdael's drawing and images like it reveal a striking departure from traditional attempts to visualize time through allegory and symbolic allusion. A case in point is the late sixteenth-century cycle of engravings by Crispijn van de Passe the Elder (c. 1565–1637) entitled *The Use and Abuse of Time*. Here the familiar personification of Father Time appears as an old man wielding his scythe and balancing an hourglass on his grizzled head.[85] A benevolent partner for those who use their lives well (Fig. 32), Time becomes a ruthless adversary for those who waste them (Fig. 33), engendering misery and poverty in deteriorating farmhouses, ragged garments, and broken wagon wheels—the very motifs that would later appear in the works of Ruisdael and his contemporaries as naturalistic manifestations of temporality.

Yet if Father Time would be superceded by new forms of expression in the seventeenth century, he would not vanish from the scene. He appears again, holding his scythe and balancing at the apex of an elaborate silver clock (Fig. 34) created about 1660 by the Dutch silversmith Hans Coenraet Breghtel (1608–75) to encase a movement made by Adriaen van den Bergh of The Hague.[86] This magnificent object, a production of art and technology combined, displays other conventional indicators of time's passing in the signs of the zodiac encircling the drum of the dome and the reliefs of the Twelve Months on the base of the structure. Within its central zone two putti flank an hourglass beneath a circular dial with twelve numerals and moving hands. They mark the world of explicit temporality that emerged with such startling vibrancy in the art and thought of the seventeenth century: then and ever after.

NOTES

1. The true-to-life appearance of much of Dutch art, which E. Fromentin (writing in the late nineteenth century) called "the portrait of Holland" (Fromentin 1876/1960, 97), has been addressed in various ways by modern scholars such as E. de Jongh, who has shown how its "realism and seeming realism" often involve moralizing symbolism derived from prints and emblems (De Jongh 1997, 21–36); S. Alpers, who has analyzed its descriptive emphasis in relation to the empirical science of the time (Alpers 1983); and M. Westermann, who has explored "the reality effect" of art in the worldly society of the Dutch Republic (Westermann 1996, 7).

2. A vast bibliography exists on the definition of ruins and the use of ruin motifs by writers, artists, and architects (much of which concerns the eighteenth and nineteenth centuries or belongs to recent discourse on contemporary art and architecture and the role of museums). Sources that have been particularly interesting or useful to this author are Macauley 1966, Zucker 1968, Ginsberg 1970, Zimmerman 1989, Hamon 1992 (chap. 1); Benjamin 1999; the volume on ruins in the Netherlands produced by the Rijksdienst voor de Monumentenzorg in Zeist, esp. essays by A. J. Schulte, A. de Vries, J. Michels, and M. J. Kuipers-Verbuijs (Schulte et. al. 1997); the essays by M. S. Roth, C. Lyons, and C. Merewether for an exhibition at the Getty Center entitled *Irresistible Decay: Ruins Reclaimed* (Los Angeles 1997–98); and Maleuvre 1999 (esp. 56–63 and 82–87). My thanks to Marni Kessler for consultations on the ruin literature from the nineteenth century to the present.

3. Panofsky was the first to articulate this symbolic use of ruins in both fifteenth-century Netherlandish panel painting and in the calendars of early manuscript illuminations, in which a building tumbling into rubble indicates the ending of the old year (Old Dispensation under Jewish law) before the beginning of the new. In the *bas-de-page* for the December page of Jean Pucelle's *Belleville Breviary* of c. 1325 (Bibliothèque Nationale, Paris), a prophet pulls the brick from the fabric of the synagogue that causes it to collapse into ruin, handing it to the apostle who will use it for the construction of the new Church. Panofsky 1958, 1:33, 135–36 and 2: pl. 5, fig. 11.

4. For further discussion of *The Adoration of the Magi* in the Cincinnati Art Museum, see Scott 1987, 84–87.

5. Panofsky 1958, 1:133–37.

6. Amsterdam 2001.

7. For discussion of Netherlandish artists' travels to Italy, see Montreal 1990, Brussels/Rome 1995, Amsterdam 2001, and Dulwich 2002.

8. L. B. Harwood in Dulwich 2002, 8.

9. According to T. A. Riggs, Cock's depictions of Roman ruins suggest that he visited Italy before 1550, but there is no evidence that these prints were based on his own designs rather than copied after drawings by other artists such as his brother Matthys. Hieronymus himself etched *Views of Roman Ruins* (most of which are inscribed with variations of "H. Cock fecit"), but he is listed only as the publisher ("H. Cock ex.") of *The Small Book of Roman Ruins*, whose authorship remains problematic. Riggs 1977, 256–66 and 299–305, and T. A. Riggs in Chapel Hill/Chicago 1993, 17.

10. For discussion of Heemskerck's complex print, see Veldman 1977, 80–81. C. M. Armstrong, among others, has noted that the proliferation of sixteenth-century Netherlandish images about pride, ambition, and vanity (the Tower of Babel, the Prodigal Son, etc.) may also be a response to the rapid growth of mercantile activity in northern Europe during this period, making pride in material acquisition and other kinds of worldly ambition the target of moralizing prints. Armstrong 1990, 19, 68–69.

11. For example, Karel van Mander, in his theoretical treatise on painting (*Het schilder-boeck: Den grondt der edel vry schilder-const*) published in 1604, advised young artists to travel to Rome because seeing its "vervallen bouwinghen" would reveal to them the former greatness of the city (Van Mander/Miedema 1973, 1:97, fol. 7v, verse 77). Bartholomeus Breenbergh entitled his print series of Roman ruins of 1639–40 (Cats. 55a–f) "Verscheyden vervallen gebouwē."

12. Roemer Visscher, *Sinnepoppen*, Amsterdam, 1614, no. XLIV.

13. The fall of the tower of Babel, also illustrated in Heemskerck's print series *Clades Judeae gentis* (The disasters of the Jewish people) of 1569, is mentioned not in the Bible but in other sources, such as the *Jewish Antiquities* written by Flavius Josephus in the first century AD (chap. 1, verse 4). Josephus elaborated on the story by having the construction ordered by a ruler named King Nimrod and situating the tower in a place called Babylon.

14. For unknown reasons, the number 11 that follows the word Genesis was rather clumsily altered in all known impressions of this print to a 14, creating a reference to a chapter that bears no relationship at all to the scene depicted. C. M. Armstrong plausibly suggests (assuming the revision was not an error) that this change may refer to chapter 14 of the Apocaplyse, where Babylon's fall is first mentioned (Armstrong 1990, 113).

15. For discussion of the conflation of Babel/Babylon/Rome and their fall as prophesied in the Old Testament books of Jeremiah and Isaiah and in the Apocalypse, see Armstrong 1990, chap. 11, esp. 105–14. Although Armstrong recognizes the more frequent use of the metaphor of Rome as Babylon in Protestant writings, she points out that Catholics, who accused Martin Luther of being a "Babeltürmer," likened the dissension among various Protestant sects to the chaos of Babel (Armstrong 1990, 111). A very different consideration of the tower of Babel, Jacques Derrida's essay on translation, considers the linguistic problems inherent in translating the phrase "Tour de Babel" (Derrida 1991, 243–53).

16. For discussions of iconoclasm in the Netherlands, see Freedberg 1988, Crew 1978, Freedberg 1982, and Amsterdam 1986.

17. Like other art-historical period designations such as Mannerism and Baroque, the usefulness of the term Romanticism has been debated in recent years. For basic discussions of this period, see Brookner 2001 and Brown 2001. I am indebted to Brian Lukacher for these references.

18. Buckley's watercolor belongs to a collection of some 3,700 works on paper, primarily by nineteenth-century British and American artists,

which, along with Hudson River School landscapes, constitute the majority of the founding art collection of Vassar College. This large group of paintings, drawings, and prints was purchased in 1864 by Matthew Vassar from Reverend Elias Magoon of Albany, a member of the new college's board of trustees. The Magoon purchase (which would undoubtedly be judged a conflict of interest today) established a college museum of original works representing the modern art of its time. The taste for ruins is everywhere evident in the Magoon collection, which includes examples such as the Buckley watercolor that Magoon (probably the standing figure in Buckley's painting) apparently commissioned himself. The subject of a recent exhibition, this collection and its period have been thoroughly analyzed by B. Lukacher, F. Consagra, and S. Smiles in Poughkeepsie/Chicago/Pittsburgh/Athens 1999–2002, esp. 87–88.

19. The urban aspect of Dutch landscape in art and literature in the fifteenth through seventeenth century is discussed in Leeflang 1997, while A. J. Adams and C. Levesque have explored the social and political context of Dutch landscape of this period, notably in relation to the new nation's quest for self-definition: Adams 1994, Levesque 1994, and Levesque 1997 (as well as her essay herein).

20. I am greatly indebted to J. M. Montias for sending me the text of his article that subsequently appeared in *Simiolus* (Montias 2003). In this study of how notaries and other scribes recorded works of art in seventeenth-century sales and inventories, he investigates the development of standardized vocabulary to designate specialized subjects in Dutch art. Surveying records kept by notaries and clerks for auction masters over the years 1597–1679 in Amsterdam and 1600–1665 in Antwerp, he has identified seventeen specialized terms for landscape types, excluding citations in which the term *landschap* was used. The sixty-three Amsterdam citations to ruins (which refer to ruins of all types, including Italianate and rustic) indicate that the subject must have been depicted very often, for the term *ruijnen* is exceeded in number only by *gebercht* (mountain scenes) and *strand* or *zeestrand* (beach scenes). In a subsequent communication to the author (October 2004), Montias noted that his data base of records from the Desolate Boedelskamer of Amsterdam (the city organization concerned with inventorying and dispersing the assets of bankrupt citizens) has revealed the interesting fact that paintings or drawings of ruins belonged quite often to the estates of those who suffered financial ruin themselves: further testimony of the great popularity of this subject.

21. On the development of terminology to describe categories of subjects and the use of diminutive suffixes, Montias cites R. Falkenburg in Falkenburg 1997, esp. 135.

22. This painting is probably an eighteenth-century imitation of a lost work by Pieter Janssens Elinga (Haverkamp-Begemann 1978, 155). A painting of a ruin within a domestic interior appears in Jacob Duck's (c. 1600–1667) *Merry Company* of c. 1630, Musées d'Art et Histoire, Nîmes, where it is flanked by Pieter Codde's (1599–1678) *The Dancing Lesson* (Musée du Louvre, Paris) and Leonart Bramer's (1596–1674) *Salome Receiving the Head of John the Baptist* (Thott collection, Gauno). In this context, the ruin seems a comment on the moral situation of the young man being undressed by two women (repr. Washington/Detroit/Amsterdam 1980–81, 255, fig. 4). Princely collections also included *ruijntjes*, as illustrated in Willem van Haecht's (1593–1637) *Interior of the Salon of the Archduchess Isabella of Austria* of c. 1628, Norton Museum of Art, Palm Beach, Florida, in which Isabella's *Kunstkammer* displays a large painting of a ruin in the style of Willem van Nieulandt (q.v.) at the left foreground.

23. The exhibition that this volume accompanies includes three fine works by Ruisdael (Cats. 30–32), but for paintings of ruins by this artist in both American and European collections, viewers are referred to the large upcoming Ruisdael exhibition, organized by S. Slive for the Los Angeles County Museum of Art, the Philadelphia Museum of Art, and the Royal Academy, London.

24. On the history of Egmond Castle, see Burger 1988, Schulte et al. 1997, 232–36, and Slive 2001, 43–46.

25. Slive 2001, 43. Ruisdael's involvement with Egmond Castle is further documented in drawings that show the site from various viewpoints: Rijksprentenkabinet, Rijksmuseum, Amsterdam (nos. A 4560 and A 4561); Kupferstichkabinett, Staatliche Museen, Berlin (no. 14726); formerly Kunsthalle, Bremen (no. 917, dest. World War II); private collection, Germany; Groninger Museum voor Stad en Lande, Groningen (no. 1931-217); Staatsgalerie, Stuttgart (no. C 64/1329). Cf. Slive 2001, nos. D2, D3, D18, D33, D57, D59, and D120.

26. The identity and history of the castle in the Chicago painting are discussed in Slive 2001, 43–44. Slive cites J. G. N. Renaud's research on Egmond Castle as the source for identification of most of Ruisdael's views of the this site. Renaud 1940, 339–40.

27. Art historians have long debated how to date the two versions of *The Jewish Cemetery*. Recent cleaning of the larger and more elaborate painting in Detroit has revealed a range of colors and spatial effects formerly obscured by darkened varnish. G. S. Keyes, chief curator of the Detroit Institute of Arts, argues that the robust and dynamic effect of this painting supports a date of c. 1653–55, while the more meditative Dresden version should be dated a decade later. G. S. Keyes in Keyes, Kuretsky, Rüger, and Wheelock 2004, 198–203.

28. Ruisdael's drawings of the Beth Haim cemetery are preserved in the Teylers Museum, Haarlem (nos. Q*48 and Q*49). Slive 2001, nos. D60 and D61.

29. While the symbolic content of *The Jewish Cemetery* is generally agreed upon, J. Bruyn's advocacy of what he has termed "scriptural reading" of Dutch landscape (in Amsterdam/Boston/Philadelphia 1987–88, 84–103) has been debated—some scholars are more inclined to find religious and moralizing meanings (Walford 1991, 15–28) and others more cautionary (Gibson 2000, 50–65).

30. Becket 1970, 64, as cited in Slive 2001, 183.

31. Johan de Brune, *Emblemata of zinne-werck*, Amsterdam, 1624, 139, no. XVIII.

32. Jan Luyken, *De bykorf des gemoeds*, Amsterdam, 1711, 6. Cited in Schulte et al. 1997, 45–46.

33. On the depictions of the ruined city of Grave by Valentijn Klotz, see D. Farr and W. Bradford in New York/London 1986, 120–21.

34. Tobias van Domselaer, *Het ontroerde Nederlandt: Door de wapenen des konings van Vrankryk dat is een waarachtigh verhaal van den Fransen, Engelsen, Keulsen, en Munstersen oorlogh, tegen de Vereenigde Nederlanden*, 2 vols. (Amsterdam, 1674 and 1676). The signature "I. Sorions" on the printed illustrations has been identified as that of the painter Johan Horions, mentioned in Utrecht documents between c. 1652 and 1662. Thieme-Becker 17 (1924):512.

35. I am greatly indebted to Diane Cearfoss Mankin for sending me the text of her 1996 Ph.D. dissertation for the University of Kansas: *Dutch Seventeenth-Century Images of Classicizing Palaces and Villas inside the Netherlands*. In her first chapter, she examines Van Domselaer's text and illustrations and suggests relating the destruction of villas on the Vecht to the imposition of taxes by the French invaders.

36. Nijenrode appears in its intact state in early seventeenth-century prints such as the etching of Spring (Hollstein 17) by Hessel Gerritsz. (1581–1632) after David Vinckboons (1576–before 1633), from a cycle of the Four Seasons (Hollstein 7 [1949]:107, no. 1, repr.), and, after its

renovation, in paintings by Jan van der Heyden (Wagner 1971, 98–99, nos. 141–46).

37. The symbolic implications of trees have been discussed by L. Stauch in Reallexikon 2 (1948):63–73; and in Davies 1988 and Kuretsky 1994, 166–69, 179–80, 182.

38. On the association between the tree and the cross in images of St. Jerome, see Kuretsky 1974.

39. On the interpretation of this print, see J. Bruyn in Amsterdam/Boston/Philadelphia 1987–88, 86–87; and Walford 1991, 34. Dead and living trees are also juxtaposed to comment on the condition of human life in Roemer Visscher's emblem "Keur baert angst" (Choice causes worry), which illustrates the difficulties of choosing between flourishing and barren alternatives: the dead tree is in the immediate foreground and the living one some distance beyond. Visscher 1614/1949, no. XI. Repr. Amsterdam/Boston/Philadelphia 1987–88, 15, fig. 11.

40. Gibson 2000, esp. chap. 7, 141–77, 225–34. Gibson distinguishes between "rustic ruins" and the grander structures he calls "noble ruins," a term that encompasses both ancient Roman sites and the vestiges of medieval structures on Dutch soil.

41. Van Mander's comments about the two alternative painting techniques appear in his chapter on painting in *Den grondt der edel vry schilder-const*, fol. 48v, verses 26–29ff (Van Mander/Miedema 1973, 1:261). On the distinction between rough and smooth techniques of painting in reference to Rembrandt, see Alpers 1990, chap. 1, esp. 16–20.

42. De Bisschop 1671; translated in Van Gelder and Joost 1985, 1:28; cited and slightly amended in Gibson 2000, 145. As Gibson rightly observes in his essay herein, De Bisschop beautified his drawing of a ruined windmill (Cat. 29) by using golden-toned ink.

43. De Lairesse 1707. Quoted from the English translation, *The Art of Painting*, published in London in 1738. Book VI, chapter xv, is entitled "Of the Word (Painter-Like) against Ruins and Beggars" (330–31). Book VI, chapter xvii, is entitled "Of Things Deformed and Broken Falsely Called Painter-Like" (338–43).

44. The varied meanings of the term *schilderachtig* as used by writers from Van Mander on are discussed in Bakker 1995 and in Gibson 2000, esp. 145–50. As both authors point out, later seventeenth-century writers used the word primarily as a basis for criticizing what they considered to be the mistakes of earlier artists such as Rembrandt who were known for producing roughly painted, down-to-earth subjects. See also Slive 1953, 160–66.

45. De Lairesse 1707 (1738 ed.), from chap. VI ("Of Ruins"), 390. Book VIII of De Lairesse's treatise, which he devoted to architecture, includes a chapter, entitled "Of Ruins" (389–90). How De Lairesse's ideas were translated into painting can be seen in the cycle of four huge illusionistic murals he painted in collaboration with Johannes Glauber (1646–c. 1726) for the house of the Amsterdam merchant Jacob de Flines (now Rijksmuseum, Amsterdam). Looming, life-sized foreground figures, cropped at the waist, are shown against landscapes filled with lush foliage and varied classical architecture; both the intact and the ruined buildings appear imposing and graceful.

46. "Ik kan my naeulijx zonder laechen onthouden, als ik onze landslieden zie geheele bundels papier uit Italie meede brengen, waer in zy de gebroke mueren en uitgegeete steenen van zoo veel Vorstelijke Paleyzen, als 'er te Rome zijn, hebben afgeteykent, zonder datze eens hebben nagespeurt de ordinantie en gedaente der gebouwen, waer uitze iets bezienwaerdigs zouden geleert hebben, aen den dach te brengen" (I can hardly keep from laughing as I see our fellow citizens bringing back with them from Italy whole bundles of paper wherein they have drawn the broken walls and corroded stones of as many princely palaces as there are in Rome, but without having bothered to trace the plan or formation of the buildings out of which they could have brought to light something worth seeing). Hoogstraten 1678, 127. Following these remarks in *Inleyding tot de hooge schoole der schilderkonst* (Introduction to the high school of the art of painting; bk. IV, chap. 2), Hoogstraten goes on to describe for the benefit of art students the size, plan, and decoration of a series of ancient buildings.

47. The development of Dutch Italianate painting, which includes both landscapists and the circle of genre painters known as the Bamboccianti, is discussed in Blankert 1978, 5–47, and in several recent exhibition catalogues: F. J. Duparc in Montreal 1990, 13–44; P. Schatborn in Amsterdam 2001, 11–32; and by L. B. Harwood in Dulwich 2002, 12–33.

48. See, for example, the drawing of the Porta San Paolo (Museum Boijmans Van Beuningen, Rotterdam, inv. no. JA 3) by Jan Asselijn (c. 1615–52), who was active in Rome between about 1639 and 1644. Repr. Cambridge/Montreal 1988, 53. Although Houbraken stated that Van der Ulft had never been to Italy (Houbraken 2 [1719]:197), more recent art historians who have admired his lively and highly specific Italian scenes have found this statement hard to believe. See F. W. Robinson in Washington/Denver/Fort Worth 1977, 66, and F. J. Duparc in Cambridge/Montreal 1988, 206.

49. My description of Saenredam's painting in the National Gallery of Art is greatly indebted to A. K. Wheelock Jr.'s discussion of this work in Wheelock 1995, 350–53.

50. Kettering 1983, 10.

51. H. Honour put forward this suggestion in Washington/Cleveland/Paris 1975–77, no. 80 (unpaginated).

52. Doncker produced both single and family portraits with ruins (an important example of which is in the Rijksmuseum, Amsterdam), as well as families in pastoral garb. See Laarmann 2000, esp. figs. 11, 13, and 17 and nos. 15, 19, 23, and 38. For other family portraits with figures in pastoral dress, see Smith 1982, chap. 7, 145–64, figs. 69–70; Kettering 1983, chap. 5, 63–81, figs. 55–93; and Haarlem 1986, 316–17, no. 79.

53. My thanks to Elizabeth Wyckoff for bringing Wierix's print cycle to my attention.

54. The inscription reads as follows: "Donc pour conclusion, comme tout Bastiment / Est destroit soit par Feu, par Eau, Téps qui tout mine / Ainsi l'homme à son Temps, cours & definement / Estant subiect à Mort qui sur Mortels domine / Et a la Fin semblable, à son Commancement" (Thus in conclusion, as every building is destroyed, be it by fire, by water, or time through which everything finishes, so man in his brief time is subject to death which reigns similarly over mortals in the end as from the beginning).

55. Schulz 1982, 421, no. 1153, and repr. in Schulz's biographical essay on Saftleven in *Dictionary of Art* 1996, 27:518, which suggests a date of "before 1650." This unusual image is somewhat reminiscent of an etching by Jacques de Gheyn III (c. 1596–1641) entitled *Grotesque Heads in Clumps of Earth*, dated 1638. Repr. Boston/St. Louis 1980–81, 140, no. 88.

56. Goltzius made other such visual puns in his works, as in the magnificent pen and chalk drawing of 1606 in the State Hermitage Museum, St. Petersburg, entitled *Sine Cerere et Libero friget Venus* (Without Bacchus and Ceres Venus grows cold). Here the artist projects himself into the scene in a self-portrait at left. He stands beside Cupid's altar but holds engravers' tools (burins) that recall Cupid's arrows of love. Repr. Amsterdam/New York/Toledo 2003–4, 279.

57. L. J. Slatkes has reviewed the debate over the title of Terbrugghen's painting in Baltimore/San Francisco 1997–98, 196–98.

Slatkes argues that the artist adapted for Melancholia a schema traditionally used for Mary Magdalene and notes that the dividers on the table at the lower left (symbolizing geometry or mathematics) were associated with the melancholic temperament but not with Mary Magdalene.

58. This connection was made by J. L. Koerner in his discussion of the hermeneutics of death during the Protestant Reformation of the sixteenth century, specifically Martin Luther's emphasis on the scriptural origins of the corruptible body. Koerner 1993, chap. 14, esp. 294. For further discussion of the imagery of Adam and Eve during this period, see H. D. Russell in Washington 1990, 113–14, and Pagels 1988, esp. 109.

59. For discussion of the symbolism of the tree as an instrument of death and redemption linking Adam's sin and Christ's sacrifice, see O. Erich in Reallexikon 1 (1937):157–67; L. Stauch in Reallexikon 2 (1948): 63–73; and Schiller 1971–72, 2:130–36.

60. The best-known examples of cadaverous Christ figures in sixteenth-century German art are Hans Holbein the Younger's (1497/98–1543) *Dead Christ Entombed* (1521, Kunstmuseum, Basel) and the predella of Matthis Grünewald's (c. 1470/80–1528) Isenheim Altar (1515, Musée d'Unterlinden, Colmar). In the seventeenth century, the English theologian Thomas Burnet (1635?–1715) would concoct an eccentric, pseudoscientific global theory about the ruinous consequences of sin by arguing that the Deluge turned the entire planet into a mighty ruin, as manifested in the rough irregularities of mountains. Burnet/Willey 1691/1965 and Zimmerman 1989, 1–16.

61. Among the extensive writings on seventeenth-century anatomy lessons and their appearance in group portraits, see especially Heckscher 1958, Hodges 1985, Middelkoop 1994, Ottawa 1996, and London 2001.

62. For the full text of the Barleus poem, see Heckscher 1958, 112, and *Rembrandt Corpus* 2 (1986):185.

63. Andreas Vesalius's (1514–64) fundamental anatomical treatise, *De humani corporis fabrica* of 1543, also includes illustrations that juxtapose anatomized figures with ruins or dead trees. Cf. Saunders and O'Malley/Vesalius 1950, pls. 23, 25, and 31.

64. As D. J. Struik has discussed, tolerance to scientific research and other new ideas in the Dutch Republic can be related to both religion and commerce, for Calvinism (which, unlike Roman Catholicism, had no Index of Forbidden Books) taught that the majesty of God is revealed in the majesty of nature. At the same time, a developing mercantile society was putting its citizens in touch with a vastly expanded range of beliefs, moralities, and ways of life. Struik 1981, 64–66.

65. In preparing this section of the essay, I have been greatly assisted by a discussion with Joy Kenseth of the art history department, Dartmouth College, and by consultation with colleagues in the philosophy department (Douglas Winblad and Michael McCarthy) and the mathematics department (John Feroe) at Vassar College. I am no less grateful for research assistance and lively conversation on the philosophical, scientific, and technological aspects of time generously provided by student assistants Margaret Horn, Jason Schreiber, Adam Tessier, and Anna Gutman.

66. Aristotle *Physics* 4.11.219b1–2. As M. McCarthy has pointed out (personal conversation, Vassar College, October 2004), Aristotle's idea of time encompassed not only kinesis but also actuality, or the striving to actualize the potential of an entity or substance.

67. Augustine *Confessions* 10.10.15; quoted in Augustine/Cutler 1955, 7:210.

68. Augustine *Confessions* 11.25.31; quoted in Augustine/Cutler 1955, 7:210.

69. Augustine, *Confessions*, 11.14.17 in Augustine/Cutler 1955, 7:254.

70. To this list should be added the Scottish mathematician John Napier (1550–1617), who invented and named logarithms and introduced the decimal point. By 1620 a form of the slide rule, based on the principles of logarithm, was in use. A large bibliography exists on the scientific revolution of the seventeenth century as it influenced research on time. In addition to citations that appear in other notes herein, the following works have been useful to this author: Burtt 1954, Toulmin and Goodfield 1965, Fraser, Haber, and Müller 1972, Boorstin 1983 (chap. 1), and Cohen 1994.

71. Christiaan Huygens, also the first to propose the wave theory of light, wrote the first printed treatise on probability, produced an unpublished study of the mechanics of impact, wrote studies on centrifugal force and an analysis of percussion, as well as inventing what is now known as the Huygens ocular for telescopes. He lived a reclusive life at Voorburg, near The Hague, keeping up an intense correspondence with other scientists in London and Paris, which he also visited. He moved to Paris in 1666, having been invited to help found the Académie Royale des Sciences. On Huygens's life and scientific achievements, see Bell 1947 and Yoder 1988.

72. Repr. Sobel and Andrewes 1998, 47.

73. H. M. Bos in Huygens/Blackwell 1986, xi.

74. The importance of precise calculation of longitude cannot be overestimated, as even the smallest temporal deviation can send a fleet of ships to disaster. Huygens's pendulum clocks performed well on long sea trials to the North Atlantic, the Cape Verde Islands, and the west coast of Africa, but only in calm weather. In 1714 the British Longitude Act offered bounties of up to £20,000 for methods to determine longitude within half a degree (i.e., a timepiece that would gain or lose no more than three seconds in twenty-four hours). The prize was finally won in 1773 by the clockmaker John "Longitude" Harrison. Sobel and Andrewes 1998, esp. chaps. 6 and 7.

75. Christiaan Huygens, *Horologium oscillatorium sive de motu pendulorum ad horologia aptato demonstrationes geometricae* (The pendulum clock or geometrical demonstrations concerning the motion of pendula as applied to clocks), Paris, 1673. For a modern English translation with commentary, see Huygens/Blackwell 1986.

76. Since the force of a spring diminishes as it unwinds, spring-driven timepieces required the introduction of an intermediary fusee wheel to equalize tension over time. Small, portable timepieces began to appear around 1430, such as the so-called Burgundy Clock owned by Philip the Good. The invention of the watch has been credited to a certain Peter Henlein (or Hele), active in Nuremburg in the early sixteenth century, although similar developments were occurring simultaneously in Italy. In Huygens's time, the balance spring or hairspring regulator that could make a timepiece impervious to motion (as on ships at sea) appears to have been developed at almost exactly the same moment by the British scientist Robert Hooke (1635–1703). Huygens, however, was the first to insert one into an actual watch. The verge movement in balance spring watches (with a contrate wheel that turns once every sixty seconds) made possible the insertion of a second hand, although watches with second hands, known as "doctors' watches," were not made until around 1690. The invention and evolution of mechanical timepieces are thoroughly discussed in Landes 1983, esp. 124–30. It should be noted that the small, beautifully crafted watches with wind-up keys that often appear in Dutch still-life paintings (cf. Pieter Claesz.'s *Breakfast Piece*, 1641, Frances Lehman Loeb Art Center, Vassar College) were probably all equipped with the less accurate, pre-Huygens movements.

77. Sobel and Andrewes 1998, 49, repr.

78. Descartes, *Principia philosophiae* (Meditations on first philosophy), I, 55, 60, and 62. Descartes's *Discours de la méthode* (Discourse on method), which included his influential essay on geometry, had previously been published in Leiden in 1637. Interestingly, in his mechanistic description of the human body in *La description du corps humain*, Descartes used a clock analogy to argue for the distinction between mind and body, stating that there is no reason "... to judge that there is a soul in a clock because it shows the hours." Quoted in Des Chene 2001, 97. Cf. Descartes/AT 1964–76, 2:226.

79. Spinoza, *Ethics* I and *Cogitata metaphysica* I, 4 and II, 1. As M. McCarthy notes (personal conversation, Vassar College, October 2004), by "duration," Spinoza did not simply mean an object's static state, for he argued that every mode of physical being (people, buildings, trees, etc.) strives to endure through an active interior disposition to preserve itself. In his philosophy, only God is eternal—and it is very relevant to this period that Spinoza saw God mathematically, as the geometric essence (*natura naturans*) from which all other properties derive.

80. I am greatly indebted to my student assistant, Jason Schreiber, for unearthing a useful article by S. H. Daniel (Daniel 1981) on scholastic treatments of time in the writings of Burgersdijk and the Spanish Jesuit scholar Juan Suarez (1548–1617), by whom he was influenced. Burgersdijk's biography and his activities at Leiden are thoroughly discussed in essays in Bos and Krop 1993.

81. So standard were the Burgersdijk volumes that they were often passed down in families from one generation to the next. By the mid-eighteenth century, they had begun to elicit violently negative reactions from the best students at Oxford, Cambridge, and Trinity College. An exasperated tirade by the young Edmund Burke (1729–97) is revealing: "Never look Burgy in the face! Divine, the Black<guard> stuff, the hoard of exploded nonsense, the Scrum of Pedantry, the refuse of the Boghouse school-Philosophy..." M. Feingold in Bos and Krop 1993, 160.

82. Burgersdijk, *Institutionum metaphysicarum libri duo*, Lyons, 1640, 1.21.13–4. Cited in Daniel 1981, 604.

83. The original verses of "De Horologiemaaker" read as follows: "ô Mens, beschik uw zielenstaat, / Terwyl des levens uurwerk gaat; / Want als 't gewigt is afgeloopen / Van deezen korten leevenstyd, / Daar is geen ophaal weêr te koopen, / Voor konst, noch geld, noch achtbaarheid." Dutch text and English translation from Segel 1974, 244. In a broader sense, L. Nelson Jr. has argued that the new awareness of time in the Baroque period led poets to begin to use it as a significant structural device by emphasizing time's relativity to subjective experience and by employing devices such as the repeated use of exclamations or the present tense to create an effect of the instantaneous (Nelson 1979).

84. The handling of risk by Dutch merchants and other entrepreneurs in the early modern period is discussed in articles by P. Mathias and L. Kooijmans in Lesger and Noordegraaf 1995, 5–24 and 25–34. My thanks to J. M. Montias for bringing this useful volume to my attention. The Dutch postal service, which comprised municipal messengers, mounted carriers for longer distances, and a separate military communications system, is discussed in Greenwich/Dublin 2003–4, 27–32, by P. C. Sutton, who includes useful citations to additional bibliography (48 n. 15).

85. The iconology of Father Time is analyzed in a classic essay by E. Panofsky (Panofsky 1962). Father Time was also shown in a classical context of Roman ruins, as in a pen and ink drawing by Michael Coxcie (1497/1501–1592) of *The Triumph of Time* (Szépmüvészeti Múzeum, Budapest) which shows an old man with a long beard, a crutch, an hourglass, and spectacles surrounded by Roman ruins (repr. Armstrong 1990, fig. 110). Or artists could picture time by showing the Months or Seasons, either as landscape cycles and/or as personifications of the Ages of Man. An emblem of 1612 by Otto van Veen illustrates the irrevocable flight of time as a procession of four figures of different ages who represent the Seasons, marching away from the viewer beneath an airborne putto holding a sundial. Van Veen/Orgel 1979, 206.

86. This unusually elaborate clock, which could only have been commissioned by a very wealthy patron, displays dials on three sides that have eight-day movements. Each measures a twelve-hour cycle, but only the one at the front of the structure indicates minutes as well as hours. Greenwich 1999, 160.

Haarlem Landscapes and Ruins: Nature Transformed

Catherine Levesque

Time and Transformation in Seventeenth-Century Dutch Art poses a paradox—how works of art by their continued presence transcend the processes of time, mutability, and decay that they depict. Though the printmakers associated with Haarlem considered here do not resolve this contradiction, their shared preoccupation with the interrelationship of history, memory, art, and nature manifests mutual concerns with time and transformation. Hendrick Goltzius (1558–1617) and Hercules Segers (q.v.), the artists whose careers frame this essay, most obviously examine the relationship between art and nature in their work. Prints by the other artists considered here, Claes Jansz. Visscher (1587–1652), Willem Buytewech (q.v.), and Jan van de Velde II (q.v.), seem to treat more directly the connections between time and place. Nonetheless, for all their apparent differences, each of these printmakers exploits technique, style, and subject matter in ways that realize the potential role of ruins in landscape.

This essay does not attempt to address fully the Haarlem artists' complex attitude toward ruins. For example, I consider neither the role of classical ruins nor earlier artistic traditions. The essay does, however, explore something of Haarlem's special sensitivity to its own historical past and artistic tradition.[1] Artists no less than local historians draw attention to the city's antiquity and to its role more recently in history in the revolt against Hapsburg Spain.[2] Certainly, too, the longstanding importance of printmaking and printers in Haarlem heightened the Haarlemmer's sensitivity to the technique and labor of printmaking and its importance in the transmission of history and memory.[3]

Though ruins appear rarely in the work of Hendrick Goltzius, those few instances explore a complex interplay between the processes of nature and artistic style. The most prominent examples appear in the final engraving (Fig. 35) of his *Roman Heroes* series and in a pen and wash drawing of Brederode Castle (Fig. 36). Landscapes showing the depredations of war play a subordinate role in two other instances,

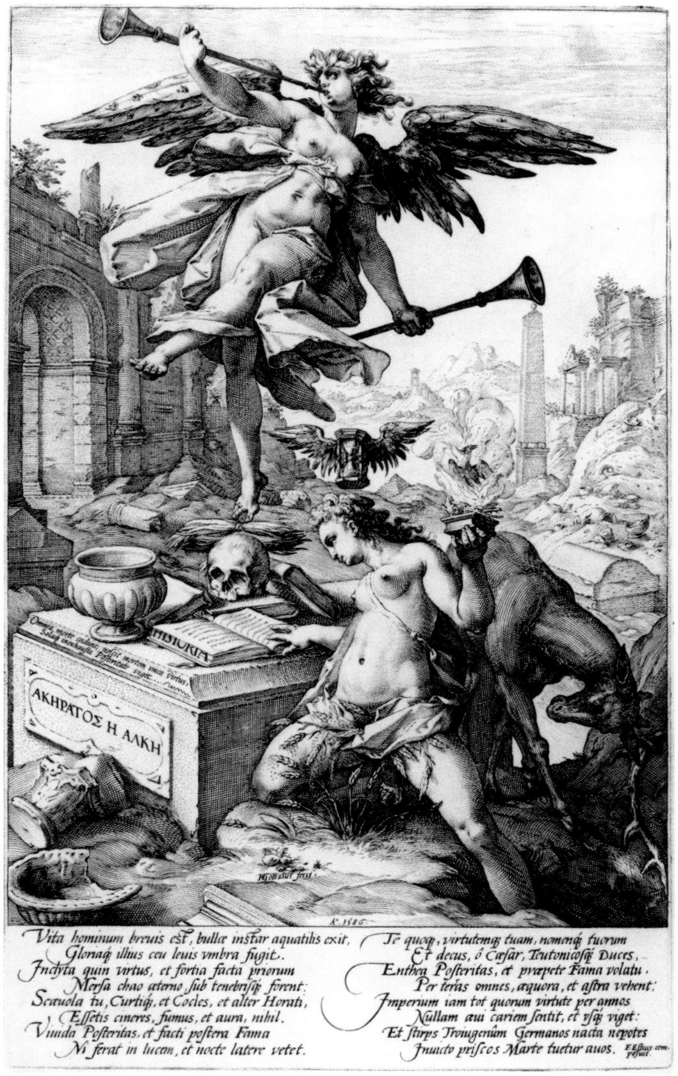

FIGURE 35. Hendrick Goltzius, *Fame and History*, 1586, engraving. British Museum, London.

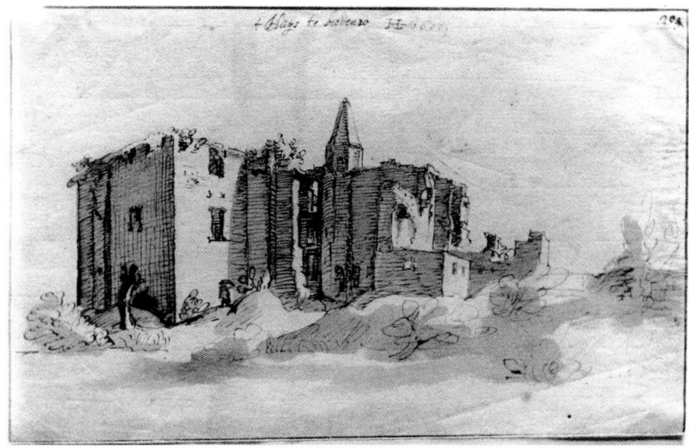

FIGURE 36. Hendrick Goltzius, *Brederode Castle*, c. 1600, black chalk, brown ink, and green watercolor drawing. Rijksprentenkabinet, Rijksmuseum, Amsterdam.

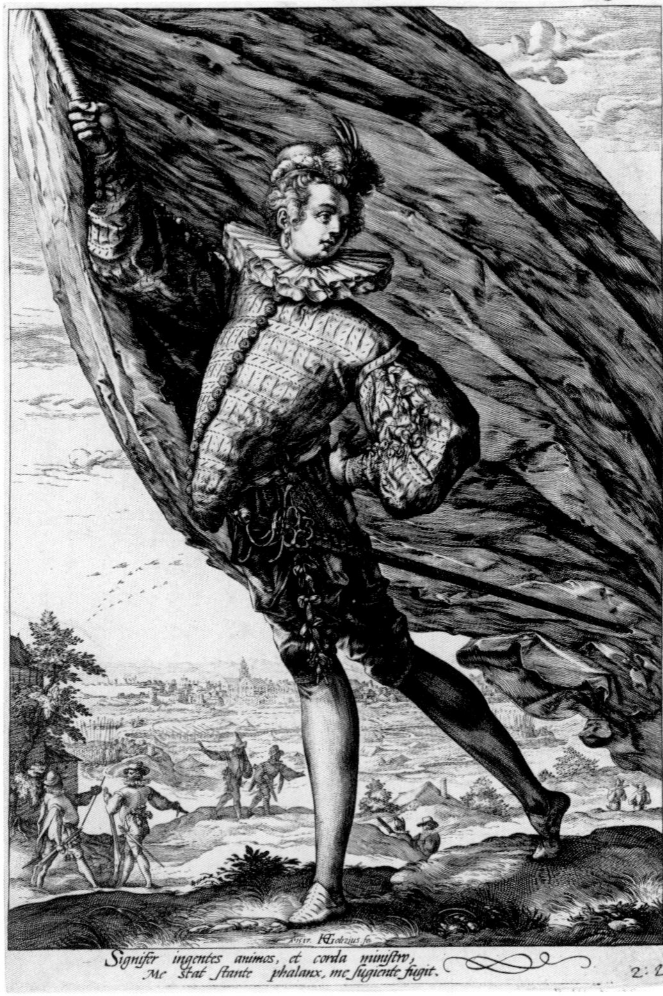

FIGURE 37. Hendrick Goltzius, *The Standard Bearer*, 1587, engraving. British Museum, London.

The Standard Bearer (Fig. 37) and *Fortitude and Patience* (Fig. 38), in which views of Haarlem with reminders of the Spanish siege of 1572–73 appear in the background. In very different ways, all of these works also evoke a more pervasive theme in Goltzius's oeuvre—the transformative power of art.

If the final print of Goltzius's *Roman Heroes* (1586; Fig. 35) emphasizes the dissolution wrought by time, it also presents the possibility of regeneration.[4] The engraving shows two female personifications, History and Fame, in a landscape replete with fragments and ruins. History is reading a chronicle and holding a tablet of ashes from which a phoenix rises. In an even more explicit allusion to generation, ears of grain sprout from her loincloth. Fame, poised above symbols of transience and death, blows her trumpet. In the landscape, too, several elements—notably a triumphal arch and obelisk—stand largely intact. The inscription below the scene alludes to the earlier title page dedication of the series to Emperor Rudolf II. Both the title and final print call for the renewal of ancient virtues. After all, even the well-placed personification of Rome, who dominates the title page, sits on a throne decorated with an image of the burning city of Troy. It is typical of Goltzius to place the final scene depicting history and fame within the context of time and regeneration. Moreover, as W. Melion points out, in *Roman Heroes*, both the heroes and the emperor rely on the engraver, "whose images are proof of art's power over death, of the burin-hand's ability to conquer time and oblivion, enemies the sword cannot master."[5]

The main body of the *Roman Heroes* series portrays a sequence of individual figures from Roman antiquity. Each man is set against a landscape that is the setting for his heroic deed. The labor and sacrifice of these men is at the heart of the series; their heroism is inscribed in the book of history and trumpeted by fame. Implicit, too, is the suggestion that in the emulation of such deeds is the hope of renewal. The formal parallels between the *Roman Heroes* and the *Dutch Warriors* series, created around the same period, was remarked on by O. Hirschman in 1919.[6] More recently, G. Luijten and M. Royalton-Kisch have pointed to the similar framing of *Dutch Warriors* with Goltzius's four drawings of biblical heroes and heroines.[7] In all of these works, figures stand prominently above and before a landscape in which related actions take place. Royalton-Kisch notes that the series' subjects may have been chosen in response to contemporary political events.[8] This allusion to events in Haarlem is explicit in Goltzius's *Standard Bearer* (1587; Fig. 37), in which a distant view of the city (from the north) provides a background for the pairs of men with guns who parade before

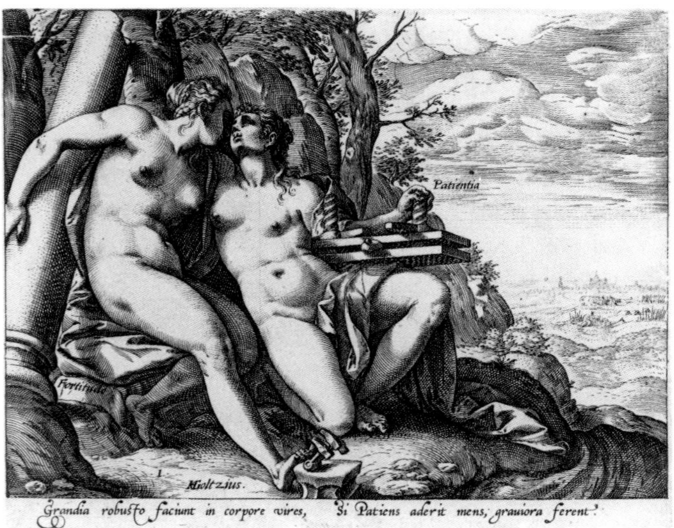

FIGURE 38. Hendrick Goltzius, *Fortitude and Patience*, 1583, engraving. British Museum, London.

well-provisioned redoubts. The declaration of standing firm, asserted in both the print and its inscription, confirms the willingness to die, endure, and discipline oneself for the well-being of the land that is set forth in the inscriptions on previous prints.[9] In this context, the technical audacity of the print's style mirrors the audacious bravery of the heroes.

Goltzius's depiction of Haarlem in the background of *Fortitude and Patience* (1583; Fig. 38), one of a group of four prints personifying pairs of Virtues, specifically associates the city with those virtues.[10] Here, too, though in quite a different vein, the last print portrays the rewards of concord and repose.[11] Notably, both *The Standard Bearer* and *Fortitude and Patience* associate Haarlem and its surroundings with endurance that, ultimately, is rewarded. Both works also suggest a parallel with art in the bravura technique of *The Standard Bearer* and in the small press held by Patience.

For the most part, allusions to politics in Goltzius's prints are couched in allegorical and mythological terms.[12] If *The Standard Bearer* is unusual in its inclusion of Haarlem, then Goltzius's evocative drawing of Brederode Castle (Fig. 36) is even more exceptional in his oeuvre as a precise description of an identifiable landmark.[13] Brederode, the old castle of the Brederode family in the dunes and woods near Santpoort, was destroyed in 1426 and partially rebuilt, then burned again in 1573 by the Spanish.[14] Goltzius's drawing is one of the earliest with a Dutch ruin as its main subject.[15] The rendering of Brederode is topographically accurate, but the artist does not dwell on details of the building or of the surrounding dunes and scrubby bushes. Rather, his use of brown pen lines and pale green wash suggests a play of light that conveys the old walls' dereliction. By using the same tone on the building and its surroundings, Goltzius strengthens the impression of the structure's gradual dissolution. Such sensitivity to the interplay between line and color and ability to portray natural effects through self-consciously artful means reassert themselves in the work of Hercules Segers.

The changes evident in Gerrit Adriaensz. Gouw's later print of Brederode Castle (Cat. 1) based on Goltzius's drawing are significant. The print presents a view that emphasizes the solid, blocky tower rather than the many openings that pierce the fabric in Goltzius's drawing. Moreover, the print adds figures and fills in the landscape. As D. Freedberg points out, the ruin has become "a fit and autonomous image for contemplation, both in image and in reality."[16] Hunters and couples gather near the ruin, one pair of lovers sits at the base of a tree, and a more decorous couple stands to the far right. A man with a pack and staff approaches the doorway. Even the inscription's emphasis on the old family name is counterpoised with the focus on couples and the hope for continuity that they evoke. The text spells out the etymology of the word Brederode and the date of the building's destruction. The transition from a private drawing to more public print reflects a different framework for viewing.[17] The figures in Gouw's print anticipate responses to landscapes and ruins that appear throughout the print series associated with Haarlem.

Haarlem Print Series

Claes Jansz. Visscher (1587–1652) was the first artist to incorporate recognizable Haarlem monuments into a print series.[18] Although the etchings in his *Pleasant Places* (c. 1611) display the evident prosperity and well-being of Haarlem's surroundings, the title page, table of contents, and images of identifiable ruins allude to the depredations of the past. The title page (Fig. 39) dedication to Haarlem presents the city's emblems—the dry tree, ship, and sword—and motto *VICIT VIM VIRTUS* (Virtue has overcome force). The symbols allude to Haarlem's past bravery and endurance.[19] The emblem is flanked by personifications of Time and Diligence (who holds a book open to a full-page spread that depicts St. Bavo's Church). No doubt the personifications also allude to history and to the endurance and labor of the Haarlemmers, who after the Spanish siege had to work to revive their land and prosperity (an important theme in just these years).[20] The titles of the personifications are also juxtaposed with the name of the artist, Visscher (meaning "fisher"), and so relate these qualities to him, an allusion that is reiterated by the inclusion of a fisherman in the background. The emblem of the fisherman appears in Roemer Visscher's *Sinnepoppen* (1614; illustrated by Claes Jansz. Visscher) as representing the diligent man in search of wealth.[21]

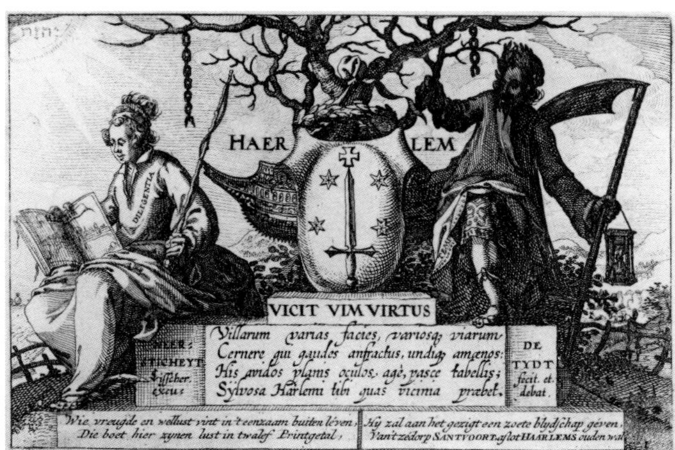

FIGURE 39. Claes Jansz. Visscher, *Title Page: Pleasant Places*, c. 1611–12, etching. Rijksprentenkabinet, Rijksmuseum, Amsterdam.

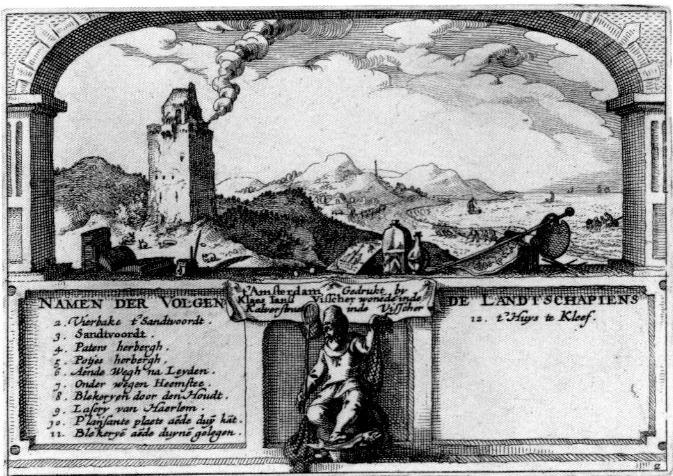

FIGURE 40. Claes Jansz. Visscher, *Contents: Pleasant Places*, c. 1611–12, etching. Rijksprentenkabinet, Rijksmuseum, Amsterdam.

The association of Visscher with time and diligence—a theme repeated in the subsequent page, the table of contents (Fig. 40)—is not merely witty byplay, but sets up parallels between the rebirth and cultivation of the arts and of the land. This theme has precedents in poetry; it is a major theme in the anthology *Nederduytschen Helicon* (Haarlem, 1610).[22] The emphasis, in Visscher's print, on diligence and wealth is also comparable to that in Hendrick Goltzius's print series *The Rewards of Labor, Industry, Practice, and Art* (1582). The first three prints of the series each show a nude couple signifying the conjunction of two qualities that lead to fortune; the last print shows a recumbent female figure who personifies well-earned rest.[23] Visscher, like Goltzius, asserts the role of his own labor and diligence. Moreover, in Visscher's prints, labor and diligence make possible the cultivation of land and art that in turn promote the inevitable transformations of time and history. These parallels are even more explicit in the series' table of contents.

Goltzius's personification of the themes of time and diligence and their resultant wealth, well-being, and justified rest appear as motifs throughout Visscher's print series. In the later series, themes evocative of memory and history intertwine seamlessly within the overall context of the ongoing cultivation of art and nature. Not only do the tools of Visscher's trade frame the view that leads into the series, but a figure of a fisherman stands in for the artist himself—an image reiterated in the first scene, where several spectators watch as the artist draws the old church.

The series of landscapes begins with a landmark—the church at Zandvoort (Fig. 41). This fishing village was an outpost of the Dutch forces during the siege and was subsequently destroyed by the Spanish. The scene is marked by the diligence of the fishermen and of the artist, who is shown sketching the still-damaged church. Ruins appear in only three of the landscapes, but they frame the series. Besides the first view of the church at Zandvoort, several scenes of monuments prominent in the siege of Haarlem appear toward the end. The Lasery (leper asylum; fourth from last) shows no evidence of damage, while the final print shows a ruin: the Huis ter Kleef (Fig. 42). This ruin is, however, set amid a bustling and prosperous landscape. Moreover, the Huis ter Kleef provides a focus for a number of figures who stop to regard the derelict building at their leisure. Thus the evident well-being in *Pleasant Places* is set against reminders of past depredations and endurance, ongoing labor and diligence, and well-earned rest. The themes are strikingly similar to those of Goltzius's series but are a commonplace in the prints and literature of the period.[24] Equally noteworthy

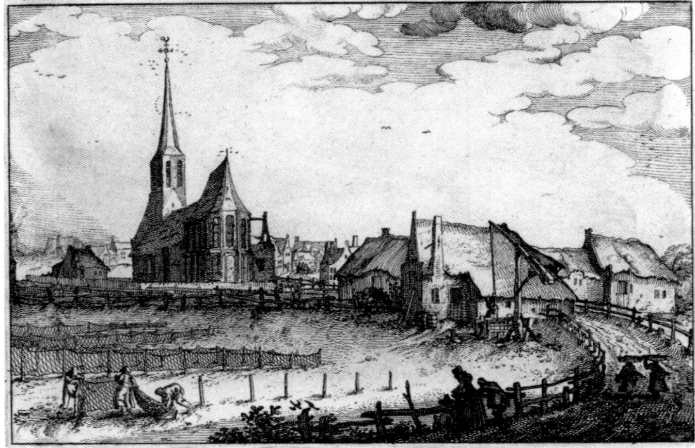

FIGURE 41. Claes Jansz. Visscher, *Zandvoort*, c. 1611–12, etching. Rijksprentenkabinet, Rijksmuseum, Amsterdam.

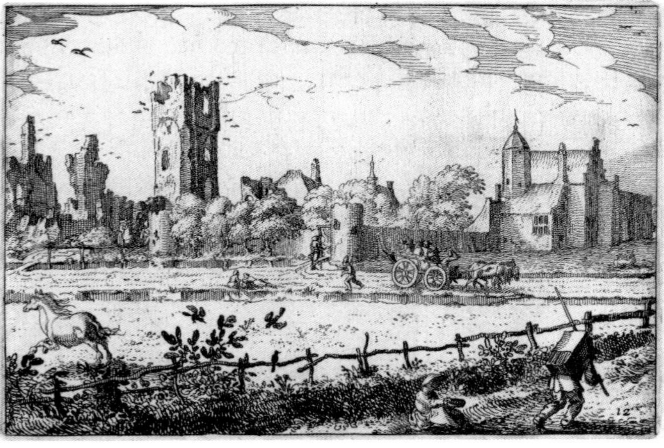

FIGURE 42. Claes Jansz. Visscher, *Huis ter Kleef*, c. 1611–12, etching. Museum of Fine Arts, Boston.

is Visscher's shifting perspective on ruins within the series. The ruin at Zandvoort is presented as the subject of the artist's attention, the Lasery has been reconstructed, while the Huis ter Kleef stands as a monument worthy of contemplation. Here, as in the title and contents pages, the prints appear to refer to art as well as landscape. Visscher as fisherman leads to Zandvoort, where we see the artist drawing the scene before us; the series ends with an image in which various pairs of lovers look at the ruins of the Huis ter Kleef. By implication, Visscher (along with our guides Time and Diligence) leads us through the series and so teaches us how to look at these ruins. In his treatment of the monuments here, he achieves a balance in which the structures act as landmarks but also as the subject for art: a celebration of printing as well as of place.

Ruins play an even more important role in Willem Buytewech's *Ten Small Landscapes*.[25] His series is distinctive in its unity of graphic style and subject matter. The unassuming technique, at once delicate and expressive, is especially appropriate to the treatment of vegetation and of ruins. With Buytewech we are aware of the processes of dissolution and regeneration—in nature and in art. The prominent title-page allusion to the farmers' well-earned abundance introduces the themes of labor and bounty reiterated in the scenes of cultivation framed by ruins: Brederode (Cat. 2a), the Huis ter Kleef (Cat. 2b), the charcoal burner (Fig. 43), and the Chapel at Eyckenduyn (Fig. 44).

The ruins at the beginning and end of the series frame a sequence that, like the title print, evokes nature's abundance. The first prints with ruins portray Brederode and the Huis ter Kleef, two monuments in the vicinity of Haarlem. Both were buildings of historical significance even in the late sixteenth century, when they were destroyed in the siege of Haarlem and its aftermath. The last two prints show quite different ruins. In the second to last print—the charcoal burner—we see only the derelict remains of a building behind a screen of trees. The Chapel at Eyckenduyn (near The Hague), though more intact, also appears in a ruinous state. The emphasis in this, the final print is on the reuse of ruins—the church land is shown as a furrowed plot. In 1581, by order of the States of Holland, the chapel was broken up out of fear that it would be a focus for Roman Catholic worship.[26] The ruin and surrounding cemetery did in fact attract pilgrims. In Buytewech's print, the building's derelict condition is evident and provides a marked contrast with the potential fertility of the surrounding landscape.

Buytewech's evocation of "the continuous cycle of decay and renewal to which also man-made buildings are subject" is marked by a distinctive graphic style as much as by subject matter.[27] The subtle stippling, meticulous parallel lines, and delicately sinuous forms convey the interpenetration of vegetation and buildings—even the cottage and country house are subsumed among trees, bushes, and shrubs. The processes of nature are still more evident in the derelict ruins that merge into the thicket behind the charcoal burner. Here nature and architecture are barely distinguished, and at one point the ruin—a bare trace—almost merges amid Buytewech's carefully differentiated strokes. As Freedberg points out, Buytewech's artistry resides in his ability to convey "how any ordinary scene—and not only those with dramatic or imaginary features—merits the twofold act of distancing and immersion that is an essential element in any kind of aesthetic response."[28] Certainly, such attentive judgment and reflexive distance are compatible with cultivating more

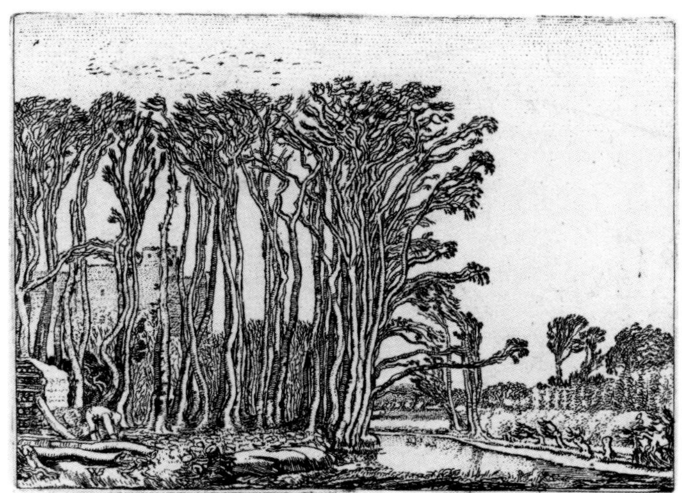

FIGURE 43. Willem Buytewech, *Charcoal Burner*, c. 1616, etching. Rijksprentenkabinet, Rijksmuseum, Amsterdam.

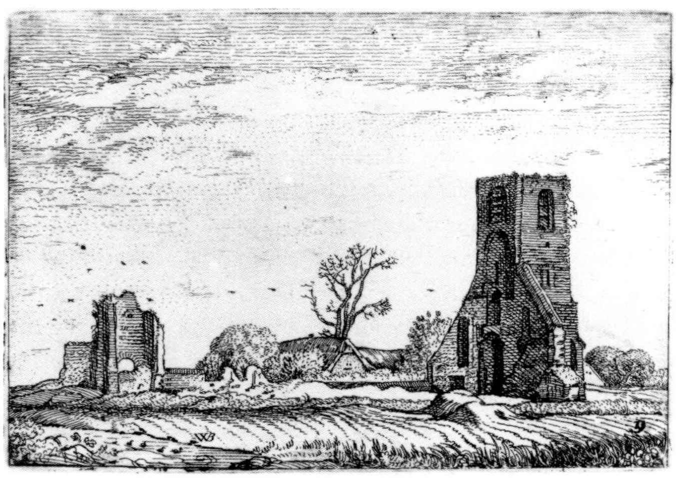

FIGURE 44. Willem Buytewech, *Chapel at Eyckenduyn*, c. 1616, etching. Rijksprentenkabinet, Rijksmuseum, Amsterdam.

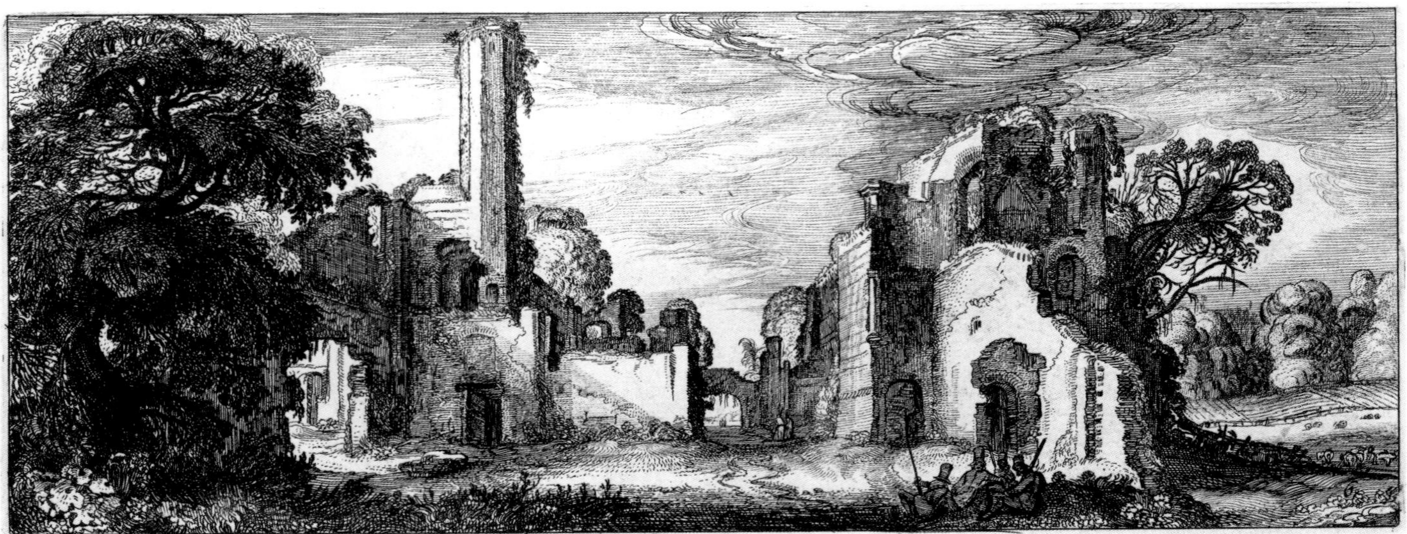

FIGURE 45. Jan van de Velde, *A Ruin with a Six-Sided Tower in a Densely Wooded Landscape*, 1615, etching. Rijksprentenkabinet, Rijksmuseum, Amsterdam.

general discernment of the processes of art no less than those of nature.

The play between the framing ruins and the central landscapes suggests themes of continuity as well as change. The inclusion of recognizable monuments and ruins in the print series by Visscher and Buytewech are not merely reminders of past events or historical associations. Rather, they make the history of the landscape palpable. Such ruins in identifiable local places embody the dense overlay of past, present, and future. They evoke, by their very survival, the perdurance emphasized in the literature and histories of the period. Moreover, set within prosperous landscapes, such scenes are manifest reminders of the rewards of time and diligence that are explicit in Visscher's series.[29]

Monuments and Ruins

While monuments and ruins play a significant role in the series by Visscher and Buytewech, they are even more prevalent in the prints of Jan van de Velde II (q.v.).[30] Among his earliest works are two series that show the range of his approach to this subject: *Eighteen Landscapes and Ruins* of 1615 (Cats. 3a–d and Fig. 45) accentuates artistic invention, whereas *Six Monuments* (Fig. 46) portrays identifiable buildings.[31] The still later prints of old buildings (Cat. 4) that Van de Velde did after Pieter Saenredam for Samuel Ampzing's *Description of Haarlem* (1628) emphasize even more the documentary and topographical depiction of monuments.

Eighteen Landscapes and Ruins is Van de Velde's earliest known dated work. The title page (Cat. 3a) of the prints introduces diverse types of ruins, a theme that is played out in the remainder of the series. Ancient buildings, recognizable Dutch monuments, and more or less derelict ruins appear in different landscape settings. The variety of monuments and ruins is matched by Van de Velde's carefully differentiated manners of etching. Throughout the series, his technical virtuosity is displayed in a nuanced range of graphic marks. The difference between a lighter, soft, sweet, and fluid style made up of delicate parallel lines, cross-hatching, and stipples and another, somewhat harsher and darker style characterized by richly ornamented flourishes evokes two contemporaneous calligraphic styles, the *net* and *klad*.[32] The *net*, or the old, traditional way of writing, is characterized as a neat fair copy, while the *klad*, or rough style, is characterized as a *loopend schrift* (running hand).[33] Though Van de Velde utilizes different approaches with each scene and his works present stylistic distinctions rather than any crude dichotomy, the darker, ornamental style appears most frequently in his depiction of dead or overgrown trees and derelict ruins. More important, his subtle use of various styles and portrayal of diverse subjects encourages the viewer's discrimination.

The distinction among different types of landscapes and ruins is even clearer in the later, longer series *Landscapes and Ruins*. These prints show Van de Velde as self-consciously artful; his command of different styles and techniques, as well as his diverse subject matter, display his ingenuity. Van de Velde's extensive series provides a virtuoso's perspective on the theme. Moreover, with this series, the parallels—between landscapes and ruins, nature and art—suggested in the series by Visscher and Buytewech are explicit. Here, too,

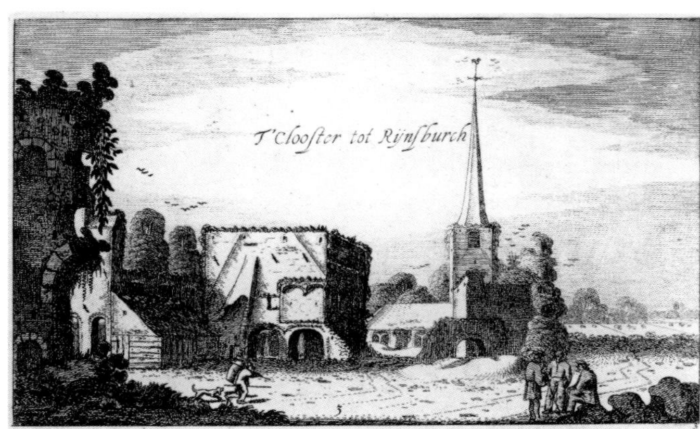

FIGURE 46. Jan van de Velde, *t' Clooster tot Rijnsburch*, 1616, etching. Rijksprentenkabinet, Rijksmuseum, Amsterdam.

invention, fantasy, and technique are foregrounded with elaborate coulisses and framing devices. The artfulness of such effects is remarked on by Franciscus Junius later in the century.

> Great masters use sometimes to blaze and to pourtray in most excellent pictures, not only the dainty lineaments of beauty, but they use also to shadow round about it rude thickets and craggy rocks that by the horridness of such parts there might accrue a more excellent grace to the principall ...[34]

Van de Velde, no less than Visscher and Buytewech, evokes themes of hard-earned prosperity and well-being. In Van de Velde's series *Sixty Landscapes and Ruins*, the title pages especially convey such communal values. Moreover, themes of destruction and regeneration implicit in Visscher's and Buytewech's works are alluded to specifically in Van de Velde's title prints. His subtle references to Ceres, Bacchus, and Venus and the associated values of peace, cultural production, and rest are reminiscent of Goltzius. Like Goltzius, Van de Velde draws attention to technique. The ox head, painter's palette with brushes, and printmaker's tools on the final title pages explicitly point to parallels between the cultivation of the land and the arts.

Van de Velde shows a different attitude to ruins in his etchings of six particular Dutch monuments: *Teijlinghen*, *Egmont op de Hoeff*, *t' Clooster tot Rijnsburch* (Fig. 46), *t' Huijs te Cleef bij Haarlem*, *Weerdenburch*, and *Rossum*.[35] This series represents identifiable places. Several including, the Huis ter Kleef, figured in the Dutch Revolt. With one exception, this series depicts great houses associated with the aristocratic past. Even the exception, Rijnsburg Abbey, was associated with the nobility. Rijnsburg, an old Benedictine abbey (see also Cats. 5 and 11), was a noble foundation for aristocratic women, founded in 1133 and destroyed in 1574 during the siege of Leiden[36] (the last remains were removed in the nineteenth century).[37] The abbey was a burial place for the nobility, and up to the dissolution of the monastery, the nuns were from patrician families. Much was made after the destruction of the abbey that the nuns of Rijnsburg were not called *zusters* (sisters) but *juffers* (young ladies).[38] Overall, the buildings in Van de Velde's series of monuments were treated as accurate topographical descriptions. This depiction of Rijnsburg was used as the source for prints documenting the appearance of the old abbey as late as the nineteenth century.[39]

Van de Velde's portrayal of Rijnsburg Abbey in several different contexts provides an index of the diverse treatments and associations ruins might take on in his work. In *Eighteen Landscapes and Ruins*, one of the most dramatically derelict monuments, *A Ruin with a Six-Sided Tower in a Densely Wooded Landscape* (Fig. 45), incorporates fragments—the rectangular block with the refectory and the church behind—of the actual abbey.[40] In contrast, the overall construction of the building, as well as the heavily worked overgrown tree and vegetation in the foreground and the delicately etched fields in the background, are fantasies.

The Ruin of Rijnsburg Seen from the Southwest (Fig. 47), from Van de Velde's series *Twenty Landscapes and Ruins*, provides a different perspective on the monastery ruins.[41] Here, the elements taken from Rijnsburg are closer to actuality. Though Van de Velde still added dark, overgrown ruins as a framing device, the building itself is accurate and readily identifiable. Nonetheless, the landscape, while seemingly a straightforward Dutch locale, does not accord with what we know about the surroundings of the monument. This print provides a good instance of what Freedberg has described as a "distinctly Dutch way of combining buildings, figures, and motifs—however imaginary or inventive they might be—into

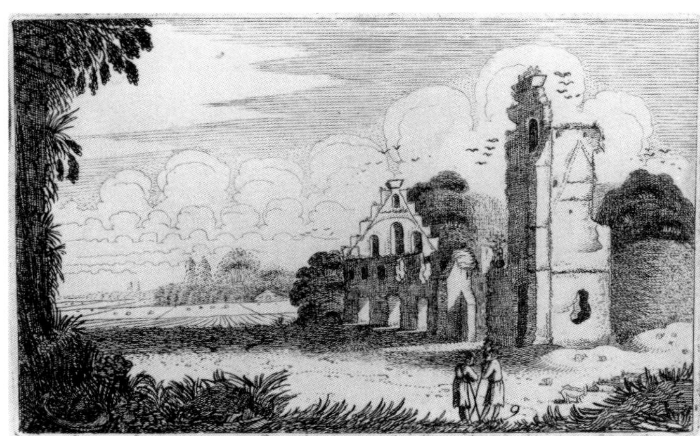

FIGURE 47. Jan van de Velde, *The Ruin of Rijnsburg Seen from the Southwest*, 1616, etching. Collection Frits Lugt, Institut Néerlandais, Paris.

apparently realistic or recognizably local (and specifically Dutch) scenes."[42]

Van de Velde's treatment of Rijnsburg in his etched views is instructive. In each instance, from the more-or-less topographical image to the fantasy view, he treats the monument as something that can be manipulated, a source to be broken up into bits and pieces and used as motifs. Moreover, ruins in these examples seem to have encouraged a self-consciously artful technique. The cloister, drained of functional meaning, has become a subject for art. The more decorative and imaginative treatment of Gothic churches and overgrown chapels in Van de Velde's work is suggestive. It evokes something of Constantijn Huygens's (1596–1687) preference for the classical style, as, for example, when he praises Jacob van Campen, "who admonished idiotic Gothic decoration with stately Roman and drove out old heresy with older truth."[43] Similar sentiments are evident in earlier works such as the *Nederduytschen Helicon* and contemporary histories by writers such as the legal scholar and historian Hugo Grotius (1583–1645).[44] Nonetheless, attitudes toward Gothic art were complicated. Old buildings might convey the status of an ancient family or evoke particular historic associations.[45] Huygens, for example, writes in quite a different vein when he describes the patriotic associations evoked by the old Klooster Kerk in the Voorhout of the Hague.[46] Nor was disdain for Gothic universal. The Utrecht humanist Arnoldus Buchelius, who describes the ruins of Rijnsburg, was one of the few with an eye for the beauties of medieval architecture.[47]

Still, Joachim van Oudaen's (1628–92) poem on Rijnsburg (published in 1724) is fairly typical in its ironic commentary on the "luxurious court of the noble nuns" who went from morning prayers in the cloister to afternoons sitting behind young noblemen on their horses, thereafter dancing and finally feasting.[48] In this poem, as in Van de Velde's etching of Rijnsburg Abbey or Buytewech's of the Chapel at Eyckenduyn, the building's ruinous state places it in time. The abbey's evident loss of its timeless liturgical function is counterpoised with the site's renewed fertility.

The prints of monuments that Van de Velde made after Saenredam's designs for Ampzing's *Description of Haarlem* (Cat. 4) display yet another attitude toward old buildings. These illustrations articulate the same interest in topographical accuracy as Saenredam's *Reconstruction of the Siege of Haarlem*. The monuments here are depicted in a neutral, descriptive style (tight parallel lines and muted stippling) appropriate for documenting particular places. The emphasis on old houses (in the sense of families as well as buildings) suggests that status and continuity were one motivation for an interest in old structures. Notably, the inscriptions for each image not only mark the building's history but also point to new beginnings. To judge by the inscriptions, even Brederode Castle and the Huis ter Kleef, though celebrated as ruins—respectively mementos of vanity and a heroic past or of past oppression—evoke thoughts of rebuilding.[49]

Thankfulness, pride, and the pleasure to be had in present-day independence and well-being are implicit in all the views, but only the inscription for the Huis ter Kleef alludes more specifically to the siege and calls up explicitly patriotic associations. Several scholars who have written on *The Description of Haarlem* have drawn attention to the political situation in Haarlem and the significant collaboration of writers and artists who represented a range of religious views.[50] Whatever the motivations behind the project, Ampzing's description embodies Haarlem's special sensitivity to its own historical past and artistic tradition.

One detail, the inclusion of the artist, alluded to in the inscription for the picture of Brederode ("You see here Brederode drawn from life. As nice as our pen or pencil could make it") is made explicit in the large view of Haarlem shown from an artist's perspective and more subtly in the view of the Huis ter Kleef. The depiction of artists sketching ruins is a consistent motif that appears in the work of Visscher as well as Saenredam. The most prominent example, *Wide Landscape of Haarlem* with the Huis ter Kleef (1621, Fig. 8), by Van de Velde after Pieter Molijn (q.v.), foregrounds the artist's act of sketching the monument. This self-consciousness suggests that by the second decade of the seventeenth century, ruins were taken for granted as subject matter for artists. This effect is further enhanced by the printmakers' evident self-awareness of technique and self-conscious artfulness. The monuments in Haarlem print series are *schilderachtig* in the sense of being worthy to be depicted as well as being portrayed after life.[51] The parallel development of ruins as subject and of style as decorum is even more prominent in the work of Hercules Segers.

The Texture of Reality

Ruins figure significantly among the limited subjects that appear in the prints of Hercules Segers (q.v.). Besides ruins such as those depicted in the *Monument of the Curatii* or an *Unknown Monastery*, he portrayed two identifiable Dutch subjects, Brederode Castle and Rijnsburg Abbey. The two versions of the latter, *The Ruins of the Abbey at Rijnsburg, small version* (Cat. 5) and the *Large Ruin of Rijnsburg* (Figs. 48 and 49), are especially complex.[52] In both, the abbey is viewed from the south. Segers's depiction of the monastery is correct though not topographical. The two versions of the print—small and large—exist in different states: six of the former and seven of the latter.[53] The prints of the small *Rijnsburg* are

FIGURE 48. Hercules Segers, *Large Rijnsburg*, etching. Rijksprentenkabinet, Rijksmuseum, Amsterdam.

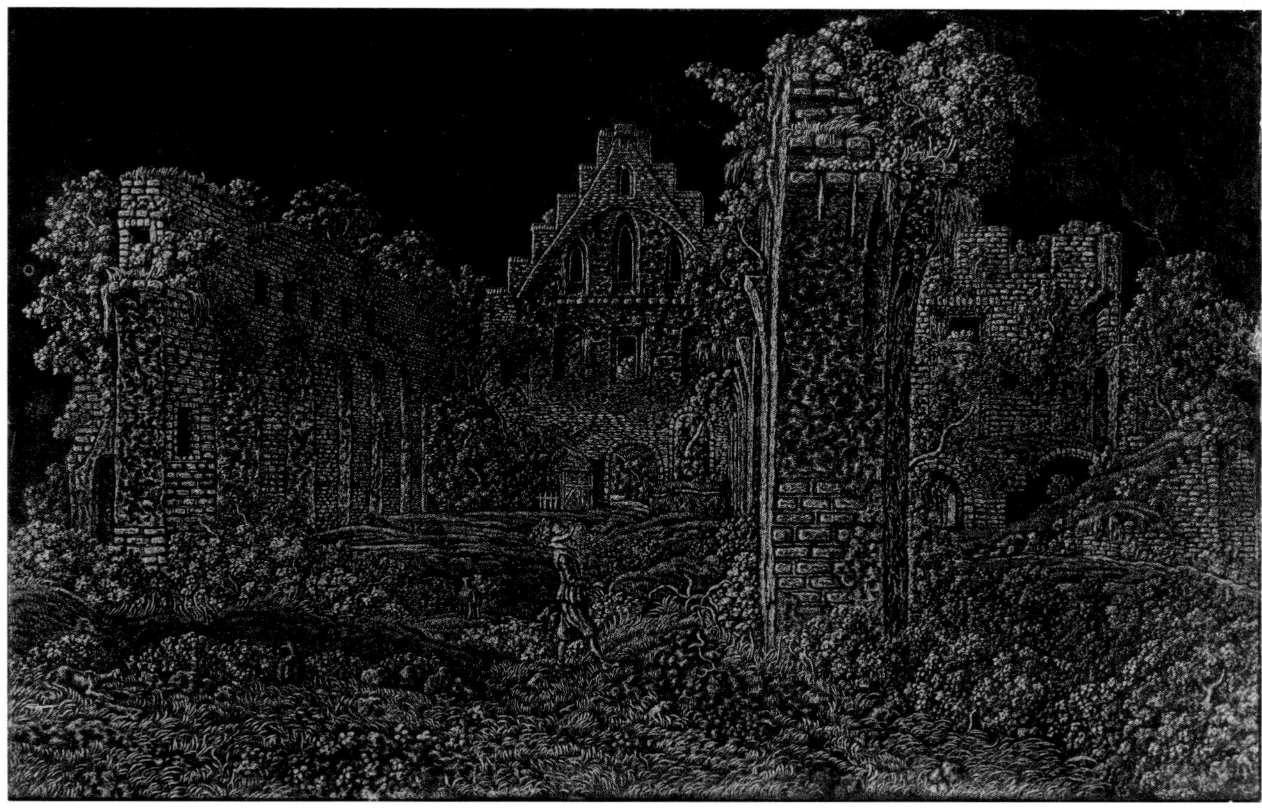

FIGURE 49. Hercules Segers, *Large Rijnsburg*, etching. British Museum, London.

printed in dark ink on light cloth or paper; those of the larger are printed light on dark. In all of the prints, Segers fully exploits the contradictions and idiosyncrasies of his craft, the play between virtuoso control and chance accidents, between ritual technical processes and personal handwriting, and between line and color.

Segers's small *Rijnsburg* is similar in size and subject to prints of monuments by Visscher, Buytewech, and Van de Velde. Indeed, Segers's view of the abbey (Cat. 5) is very much like Van de Velde's etching from the *Series of Twenty Landscapes and Ruins* (Fig. 47). Yet the differences are significant. Segers's concentrated close-up provides almost no background, whereas Van de Velde's view suggests the overgrown site with a coulisse of dense vegetation in the left foreground and large bushes beyond the abbey that contrast with the more lightly etched building and still finer distant fields. These transitions from dark to light contribute to the scene's believable depth and atmosphere. Although the emphasis in the small *Rijnsburg*, as Haverkamp-Begemann points out, is on clarity and linearity, the modulated density of varied textures gives a rich tonal effect.[54] Ruins, here, have an almost geological character; the buildings and their immediate surroundings are covered in overgrowth. The sense of decay is heightened by the meticulously worked texture of the bricks and crumbling walls. Even the sole viewer is hard to distinguish from his surroundings.

In contrast to the small *Rijnsburg*'s more traditional dark-on-light printing, the large *Rijnsburg* is printed light on dark. The large *Rijnsburg* in Amsterdam (Fig. 48) was printed in yellow on paper prepared with black and subsequently overpainted in red (for the masonry) and greenish blue (for the sky) and is varnished, whereas the British Museum's (Fig. 49) print is in yellowish white on paper prepared with dark brown paint.[55] In both examples, the print takes on a luminescent quality. This makes the different effects all the more dramatic. The building in the Amsterdam print looms against the gloomy sky, while ruins in the London print show up as ghostly against the dark background. Although the larger version is much more detailed than the smaller version, the minutely worked surface in the Amsterdam and London prints obscures and subsumes the architecture and the figure.

Segers's labor-intensive approach draws attention to his works' materiality even as his technical skill and practical experience dissolve and reconfigure matter into art. The themes of destruction and regeneration explicit in Segers's ruins already appear in a more muted version in the series by Visscher, Buytewech, and Van de Velde, but with Segers, building and figure are subsumed in nature. In his work, the emphasis on the mutability and transience of the material world, evoked by eroded rocks, broken walls, and overgrown bricks, is equally manifest in the creviced lines and microstructures that convey the material stuff of nature while they record the processes of art. Segers's subject matter embodies interest in materiality, process, and transformation that is only hinted at in other prints considered here.[56]

Segers's preoccupation with processes of transformation is evident in the different impressions of Rijnsburg Abbey. His approach exemplifies the fluidity, for him, among painting, drawing, and printmaking. Samuel van Hoogstraten refers to Segers's work as "printschildery" and "druckte schilderij," which suggests both colors printed with painterly means and printed paintings.[57] Notably, too, Hoogstraten praises these works for both their naturalism and their art.[58] According to this view, Segers's works reconcile qualities—the artful and the natural—usually considered as contradictory. Hoogstraten's comment draws attention to the prints' combination of artifice (art made out of art) and natural order (echoed in the processes of art). Indeed, Segers's "ordering of nature" lays bare the two ingredients Hoogstraten singles out as essential for naturalism—color and handling.[59]

Hoogstraten recommends that a landscape painter who aspires to the highest rung of his art needs to attend to perfecting imagination and fantasy. He notes that Segers was especially gifted in this and especially commends the artist for the way his printed paintings adapted their color scheme to the thing in nature. Hoogstraten's discusses these effects of painting like nature in conjunction with so-called "natural paintings."[60] Franciscus Junius notes the desirablity of such effects:

> Pictures which are judged sweeter than any picture, pictures surpassing the apprehension and Art of man, works that are sayd to be done by an unspeakable way of Art, delicatly [*sic*], divinely, unfeisably [unfeasibly], &c. insinuate nothing els [*sic*] but that there is something in them which doth not proceed from the laborious curiositie prescribed by the rules of Art, and that the free spirit of the Artificer marking how nature sporteth her selfe in such an infinite varietie of things, undertooke to doe the same.[61]

Junius's emphasis on diligence coupled with nimble facility, of "laborious curiositie ... and free spirit," is reminiscent of Segers's combination of meticulously worked line and evocative use of color as well as his combination of highly refined technique and exploitation of accident, trial, and chance. Junius's discussion of the relationship between color and fantasy is equally pertinent to Segers's work:

> Democritus was of [the] opinion, that Colours are nothing in their owne nature, but that the mixtures made of them do then onely stir our phantasies, when upon a meete and

> proportionable application their appeareth in them order, figure, and disposition. It is certaine therefore that colours being laid on after a seasonable and good order, doe sometimes make up whole figures which never shall be able to affect our minde ...[62]

The delight men take in the imitation of nature, Junius points out, can stir up the imagination and can also embolden them to pry into the most profound mysteries of nature. This is true of Segers, whose interest in materiality, process, and transformation is consistent with his repeated treatment of fragments, ruins, and traces. In his prints of ruins, the emphasis on the subject's mutability and transience is echoed in the means of making. In these prints, play between artifice and outward appearances embodies insight through the evident application of experimental techniques that probe the nature of creation—*fantasia* in the deepest sense. *Fantasia*, from this point of view, suggests the Stoic belief that nature might embody both those things bestowed by God and an active principle acting upon matter. Such a view of nature calls for both contemplation and imitation.[63] In his brief account, Hoogstraten conveys just these characteristics of Segers's work.

> He had a keen and steady perception, mastered the design of landscape and background; was entertaining in imaginative mountains and caves and was as it were pregnant of whole Provinces to which he gave birth with wide spaces, and which he showed with wonder in his paintings and prints. He exercised his art with incomparable industry.[64]

Ruins, in the series by Visscher, Buytewech, and Van de Velde, are part of sequences where, for the most part, native landscapes dominate and provide an unfolding context for looking. In contrast, Segers's various versions of Rijnsburg Abbey immerse the viewer in the means by which the very subject alters. His treatment of the ruins conveys time and transformation both in the processes of art that transform the physical structure of the ruin (processes that parallel those of nature) and also in the way that the different versions condition the viewer's optical experience. Though the interrelation of art, nature, time, and memory are shared in all the prints of ruins considered here, Segers's work is extraordinary in its self-consciousness and in its intensity of vision.

The Necessity of Ruins

In her recent fine study of the Utrecht antiquarian Arnoldus Buchelius, J. Pollmann points out that "In a society in which claims of religious and political legitimacy were based almost exclusively on proving continuity with the past, historians and antiquaries were actively involved in shaping national and cultural identities."[65] The printmakers considered here shared in this endeavor. Moreover, though no doubt they reflect broader antiquarian interests of the period, they are the first to emphasize specifically ruinous native monuments in works of art, a type of ruin unique to Dutch art at that time. Such prints provided a nuanced means to mediate a complex attitude toward history. Not only did the ruins depicted make concrete the presence of the human past within nature, the prints also provided different frames for memory. Ruins in prints mark the land for commemoration but also provide reminders of the more general processes of dissolution and renewal. Such contexts, as well as stylistic distinctions among different kinds of ruins, encouraged spectators to look at individual structures with discernment and judgment. To some extent prints instructed the viewer on how to look at the past.

References to local ruins are peripheral to Goltzius's main concerns, but the motifs and associations he touches on are developed by later artists. Moreover, the themes of endurance, patience, and fortitude—sometimes associated with scenes that include views of Haarlem—are reworked by later artists, as is Goltzius's preoccupation with the reciprocal relationship between the cultivation of art and the benefits of peace, well-being, and prosperity. Equally sophisticated in his knowledge of past styles of art and the workings of nature, Goltzius, the "Proteus" of art (as Van Mander referred to him), showed that an original quality of vision is in no way inconsistent with truth to nature. The interdependence of ruins and landscape in the Haarlem prints continued to reflect this complex interplay between nature and style. Moreover, the artists' obvious pride in equating their own labor with the larger cultural endeavor suggests continuity with the artistic past.

The interrelationship of art with themes of time and transformation that is seminal to Goltzius's work remained an ongoing concern for subsequent artists. Though only Segers is so directly engaged in the parallels between the processes of art and those of nature, this relationship is important for all of the prints considered here. The Haarlem print series are noted for their unassuming descriptive naturalism, but they achieve this lifelike rendition with notably different technical effects. Each draws attention to the making of the prints; Visscher literally frames his series with references to print culture, while Buytewech's unassertive but expressive marks and Van de Velde's carefully calculated technique also presuppose an audience highly attuned to nuances of graphic style. It might even be argued that the more understated Haarlem series normalize the relationship between natural images and graphic convention. Segers, in contrast, makes the dialogue between the two his subject. In any case, all these artists assume an audience whose literacy in graphic form ought not to be underrated.

The printmakers considered here played a significant role in opening up a new vision of landscape. They exemplify the French sociologist Maurice Halbwachs's (1877–1945) view that "the society of yesterday could indeed be diverted from the contemplation of its own image—reflected in the mirror of the past—only if little by little there appeared in the same mirror other images, perhaps less clear and less familiar, but that opened up to that society vaster perspectives."[66] Indeed, a number of the prints that portray artists drawing or spectators regarding the ruins depicted show Halbwachs's process in action. Gouw's translation of Goltzius's evocative drawing of Brederode (Cat. 1) illustrates the move from a personal response to a historically allusive monument to a more public presentation. This explicit involvement of the viewer emphasizes the shared experience of looking. Even the many figures who pass by the monuments as they go about their everyday business convey that these buildings are part of the quotidian world. The presence of such figures—artists, spectators, and passers-by—within prints assert, no less than does the awareness of style, a community of viewers. Ruins in such a context form a necessary backdrop to the Golden Age; they embody the power of art to assert continuity while putting the past in its place. That these developments take place in prints affirms the traditional association of printmaking with the values of humanism and truth—and with the history of Haarlem.

NOTES

1. De Bièvre 1988, 303, 312–27, considers artistic developments and self-awareness in the context of Haarlem's particular history and politics. Leeflang 1997, 54–69, 80–84, provides a more general overview.

2. For accounts of the siege, see Temminck 1972, and Wijn, 1982. Levesque 1994, 45–54, 59–71, considers the historical associations of particular sites that appear in Haarlem print series.

3. Petrus Scriverius's *Laure-cranz voor Laurens Coster van Haerlem, eerste vinder vande boek-druckery* was published with Samuel Ampzing's *Beschryvinge ende lof der stad Haerlem in Holland* (both Haarlem, 1628). This panegyric to Haarlem printmaking not only "brings to light" the true account of the invention of printing in the Haarlem woods but also, by its very construction, embodies the centrality of prints and printmaking to Haarlem's self-image. Indeed, the collaborative nature of the project exemplifies how Haarlem's print culture mediated a dynamic cultural milieu within and beyond the city. Scriverius (78) suggests something of this interaction in his "Dialogue between an Artist and a Poet." Notably, Hugo Grotius (1801–3, book 3:39) repeats Scriverius's account, reiterating the role of printing in "enlightening" the world. Grotius considers printmaking in conjuction with his discussion of calligraphy and painting—all of which he lists as *handwerken*. Veldman 1974, 37–38, and Melion 1992 consider different instances of this fruitful mingling within this group of printers, artists, and humanists. See also Lacuelle-van der Kerk 1951.

4. Amsterdam/New York/Toledo 2003–4, 89–92; Strauss 1977, 402–3; and Hirschmann 1976, 119, no. 255. Los Angeles 1992, 29, notes associations with the political situation. See also Melion 1995, 1096–1105, and Melion 1989.

5. Melion 1995, 1105. Of course, metamorphosis and transformation were longstanding interests of Goltzius. His chiaroscuro woodcut *Demogorgon in the Cave of Eternity* (c. 1588) reveals his preoccupation with themes that symbolize processes of art and nature as well as utilizing a technique that draws attention to its own artfulness. Indeed the theme—creation out of chaos and the entry of eternity into time—suggests the process enacted in the making of the print itself. Notably, Demogorgon holds a tablet and writing instrument as well as a wand. By implication, nature, here, is imitable by art. For a discussion of this print and the *Deities* series, see Amsterdam/Cleveland 1992, 115–37. Mazur-Contamine 1994 provides a thorough consideration of the series's relationship to natural philosophy. Reznicek 1989, 62, notes the importance of Goltzius's chiaroscuro woodcuts *Arcadian Landscape* and *Landscape with a Peasant Dwelling* for later developments in landscape, especially the work of Hercules Segers.

6. Strauss 1977, 272, refers to Hirschmann's comment (Hirschmann 1919, 98) in discussing *The Standard Bearer* (434–35). The comparison is suggestive, since the *Dutch Warriors* is a group of prints that Goltzius worked on sporadically over a number of years. The first print is from 1582, four years before he began work on the *Roman Heroes*. The last print by Goltzius (his student Jacques de Gheyn II [q.v.] continued work on the subject) was only completed in 1597, one year after the *Roman Heroes* series was completed.

7. Amsterdam 1993–94a, 348–49. See also Amsterdam/New York/Toledo 2003–4, 78–79, on the seventeenth- and eighteenth-century tendency to associate the figures with specific individuals.

8. Amsterdam 1993–94a, 348–49.

9. The inscriptions under the prints read:

> *Mortales fugitis mortem? Patriamq[ue] tueri*
> *Horretis pauidi? mors sua quenq[ue] manet*
> *Vita Nimis nulli placeat quem mors terit vsq[ue]*
> *Qui si HODIE est aliquid, CRAS NIHIL esse potest.*
> (Are you mortals fleeing death? And trembling do you dread to watch over your fatherland? Your death awaits each of you. Let life please nobody too much whom death wears out continuously. If anybody is anything today, he can be nothing tomorrow.)
>
> *Voyant vostre angelycque face,*
> *Je puis dire pour le myeulx*
> *En pardonnant mon audace*
> *Que sans vous AULTRE NE VEULX*
> (Seeing your angelic face, / I can say very well, / if you will pardon my boldness, / that, without you, I want no other.)
>
> *Des lants welvaert / moet zijn bewaert / byden getrouwen,*
> *Die aen elcken cant / voor tvaderslant / haer trouw bewysen*
> *Daermen int begin / sonder gewin / op mochten bouwen,*
> *Sulck een men plach / DIE NOCH TOE SACH, lofflick te prysen.*
> (The lands well-being must be protected by the faithful,
> Who on every side prove their loyalty to the fatherland
> Because men without victory in the beginning may build up
> Such a one still has faith in action on the field, laudable to praise.)

Praeuius infractos redo Dux Martis alumnus,
Spernere dum doceo cuncta perida meo.
(Taking the vanguard, as leader, I make the students of Mars unbroken,
By teaching them from example to scorn all danger.)

Signifer ingentes animos, et corda ministro,
Me stat stante phalanx, me sugiente fugit.
(I, the standard-bearer, bestow great courage and daring:
The line holds while I stand firm, but were I to flee it would break and run.)

My thanks go to John Oakley and James Baron for help with the Latin in the first stanza and to Don Monson for the French in the second. The translations of the last two Latin stanzas are from Amsterdam 1993, 348.

10. Levesque 1997, 230–33. The subject, fortitude and patience, echoes a theme, the complaint of peace, found in a number of didactic prints and title pages, in which Belgica's rape is set in front of scenery depicting the land's depredation. In Leicester's entry into Haarlem, such complaints, made by a female personification of the city, are presented as part of a reenactment of the siege.

11. Goltzius's four prints include *Fortitude and Patience*, *Hope and Confidence*, *Justice and Prudence*, and *Concordia and Peace.*

12. Holman 1991–92, 397–412, gives a good account of this tendency. See also Levesque 1997, 223–30, 247–54.

13. Reznicek 1961, 423; Freedberg 1980, 27; and Amsterdam/New York/Toledo 2003–4, 198–99.

14. See Schulte et al. 1997, 239–45, for a thorough history of the building, description of the ruins, and discussions of archaeological research and restoration.

15. Reznicek 1961, 423, notes that Goltzius may also have drawn the Huis ter Kleef.

16. Freedberg 1980, 27.

17. Freedberg 1980, 27. See, Amsterdam 1993–94a, 650, for a discussion of the relationship between Visscher's drawings and prints; for example, those of the Zandvoort lighthouse.

18. Simon 1958, 48–50; Freedberg 1980, 28, 30–32; Amsterdam 1993–94a, 653–55; and Levesque 1994, 35–54.

19. De Bièvre 1988, 305–8, 325–27, and Levesque 1994, 36–37; 50.

20. De Bièvre 1988, 307–9, 312–18.

21. Amsterdam 1993–94a, 653.

22. Nederduytschen Helicon 1610, 78, 81–84, 264.

23. Strauss 1977, 252–59; and Amsterdam/New York/Toledo 2003–4, 44–46.

24. Nederduytschen Helicon 1610, 78, 228–30; Van Borsselen 1613, 8, 27–28; and Huygens/Worp 1892, 214–19. For discussion of the literature, see Levesque 1994, 82–88; De Bièvre 1988, 305–12; Leeflang 1997, 60–64; and Levesque 1997, 239–52.

25. Hollstein [1949]–, nos. 35–44; Haverkamp-Begemann 1959, 18, 21–30; Rotterdam/Paris 1974–75, 105–11; Boston/St. Louis 1980–81, 64–66; De Groot 1979, nos. 12–21; Freedberg 1980, 31–32; Amsterdam 1993–94a, 671–72; and Levesque 1994, 73–88.

26. Schulte et al. 1997, 278–79.

27. Haverkamp-Begemann 1959, 35–45.

28. Freedberg 1980, 32.

29. Hermanus Follinus (1613, fols. 6–7) recommends specific and well-known images to evoke memories and even strong emotions that could eventually lead to general abstract concepts such as time and morality.

30. Franken and Van der Kellen 1883 (rev. 1968); Van Gelder 1933; Boston/St. Louis 1980–81, 70–72; De Groot 1979, nos. 69–80; and Freedberg 1980, 37–38.

31. Franken and Van der Kellen 1883 (rev. 1968), 101–2, nos. 217 and 222 and 93, no. 198.

32. De Keyser 1943–44, 232 and 250–51, discusses the elder Jan van de Velde's (1569–1623) *Spieghel der schrijfkonst*, of 1605; the title page was designed by Karel van Mander (1548–1606) and engraved by Jacob Matham (250). Among the inscriptions is a panegyric to Goltzius (251, no. 20). See also De la Fontaine Verway 1976, 73–78, which comments on Van de Velde I's command of every hand and goes on to describe the audience of wealthy amateurs and semi-professionals who collected expensive writing books such as those he produced. Croiset van Uchelen 1976, 319–46 discusses the calligrapher's need to codify his hands and to obtain the service of expert engravers. Melion 1993, 62–64, points out that Van de Velde I's praise of Goltzius in the *Spieghel* draws attention to the parallels between the artist's "superior penmanship" and his own. Melion further notes the shared assumptions behind Van Mander's use of the Proteus metaphor for Goltzius and Van de Velde I display of his command of the canonical scripts. For Van de Velde I's technique and ingenuity, see also Levesque 1994, 89–93.

33. De Keyser 1943–44, 232.

34. Junius 1638, 317.

35. Franken and Van der Kellen 1883 (rev. 1968), 93, no. 198.

36. Bolten 1994, 3–6, 9–12; and Glasbergen and Leenheer 1974, 24–37.

37. Glasbergen and Leenheer 1974, 42.

38. Bolten 1994, 5.

39. Bolten 1994, 22–23.

40. Franken and Van der Kellen 1883 (rev. 1968), 102, no. 222. Bolten 1994, 20–21, describes the print as "Een Ruïne met een seshoekige toren in een boomrijk landschap" (A ruin with a six-sided tower in a densely wooded landscape) and identifies the parts of the actual building.

41. Franken and Van der Kellen 1883 (rev. 1968), 105, no. 243, and Bolten 1994, 22–23 (as *De ruïne van Rijnsburg, gezien vanuit het zuidwesten* [The ruin of Rijnsburg seen from the southwest]).

42. Freedberg, Burnstock, and Phenix 1984, 157.

43. De Jongh 1973, 85–88, 102–104.

44. Nederduytschen Helicon 1610, 40, 98, 104, 124–35, 233–38. See, Grotius 1714, 104, 151 and Grotius, 1801–3, 26. For an overview of the question in seventeenth-century histories see Kampinga 1980, 21–23, 42–45. Haitsma Muller 1993 discusses the treatment of reminders of Roman Catholicism in the city descriptions. Of particular interest is city historian J. J. Orlers's downplaying the origin of Leiden's old churches and his emphasis that at the moment of his writing they were restored and made ready for the practice of religion.

45. De Jongh 1973, 96–99, 101.

46. Huygens/Worp 1892, 214–36. De Jongh 1973, 111, notes that Huygens owned Saenredam's painting of the interior of the Mariakerk (a Gothic church with a Romanesque choir). Schwartz 1966–67 draws attention to the rich historical and theological allusions that, in this instance, can be documented.

47. Kampinga 1980, 194. See also Pollmann 1999. In her nuanced analysis of Buchelius' gradual movement away from the Roman Catholicism of his youth to his prominent activity as a Counter Remonstrant later in life, J. Pollmann provides an exemplary case study that highlights the complex motives and beliefs that characterize confessional choice in this period. Her account also sets forth the web of aesthetic,

historic, and political motives that helped to shape individual attitudes toward medieval architecture and history.

48. Bolten 1994, 10–11.

49. Utrecht 1961, 247–51, illustrates all the prints and also provides the original inscriptions and their English translations. Several prints combine old and new buildings (Bredero and Assumberg) or allude to the dynastic line (Bredero and Berkenrode). The translated inscription for Brederode reads:

> You see here Bredero drawn from life.
> As nice as our pen or pencil could make it,
> As it at present still lies destroyed
> What is all peoples' doing more than vanity
>
> You see from the massiveness of the walls and stone,
> that this castle must formerly have been something wonderful
> Founded by our Count on the bank of the Rhine.
> Than it were again as it was, that it were again erected!
>
> You see at the same time an avenue with trees
> Before you could arrive here at the house of Bredero,
> Which leads towards the House of Burgomater Loo,
> Just against the dune and near Bredero.

50. Schwartz and Bok 1990, 35–50.

51. Bakker 1995, 149–154. See also the essay herein by W. S. Gibson, pages 63–72.

52. Haverkamp-Begemann 1973, 90–91.

53. Haverkamp-Begemann 1973, 90–91.

54. Haverkamp-Begemann 1973, 91, further notes that these etchings, without drypoint or lift-ground, are with one exception printed on cotton (in most cases a form of it called casos) of the same fine weave. Some prints of this group are of cotton dyed the same light gray color; others were subsequently prepared with the same light gray watercolor.

55. Haverkamp-Begemann 1973, 90. Freedberg 1980, 46–50, notes Segers's use of the lift-ground technique in the London print of the large *Rijnsburg*.

56. Morath 1996, 62–69.

57. Hoogstraten 1678, 196, 240 and 312, refers to his work as "printschildery" and "druckte schilderij," which suggests both colors printed with painterly means and printed paintings. Haverkamp-Begemann 1973, 50 n. 117, states that the term "printschildery" could refer to both chiaroscuro prints and Segers's colored etchings.

58. Hoogstraten 1678, 312. In Amsterdam 1988, 35–157, J. van der Waals provides a perceptive account of how Segers's prints fit within the context of the Amsterdam regent Michiel Hinlopen's (1619–1708) print collection with its interest in history and the classics, but also in connection with collectors' more general interests in wonders and "natural paintings." Van der Waals (141) points out that in Hinlopen's collection, Segers's prints were filed with Van de Velde's *The Four Times of Day* and *The Twelve Months*, which explored cycles and changes in nature.

59. Brusati 1995, 249.

60. Hoogstraten 1678, 232; and Amsterdam 1988, 148–56.

61. Junius 1638, 331.

62. Junius 1638, 306.

63. Junius 1638, 4, quotes Cicero ("Man born to contemplate and imitate the world"). Morath 1996, 169–74, discusses the importance of neo-Stoicism in seventeenth-century Netherlands and points out the pertinence of Stoic ideas on *techné* to Segers's work.

64. Hoogstraten 1678, 312.

65. Pollmann 1999, 119.

66. Halbwachs 1992, 166.

Bloemaert's Privy: The Rustic Ruin in Dutch Art

Walter S. Gibson

Abraham Bloemaert, we are told by Karel van Mander, produced a number of "very subtle landscapes ... with some well-observed and burlesque ['drollig'] peasant houses, peasant implements, trees and pieces of ground—things which are to be seen in great variety about Utrecht and which are drawn by him; for he does a great deal after life and he has a very clever manner of drawing and penmanship to which he adds some water colors so that it looks particularly good."[1] Bloemaert began producing these drawings perhaps as early as 1585, when he returned to the Northern Netherlands from France, but certainly not much later than 1593, when he settled in Utrecht for the rest of his life.[2] A prime example is a sheet now in Berlin (Fig. 50)[3] depicting the type of scenery that the artist must have encountered in his rambles through the Utrecht countryside, including the ubiquitous thatched-roofed cottage hugging the very earth out of which it seems to grow. On the slope above is another kind of structure Bloemaert would also have frequently seen, a flimsy structure leaning against a crumbling wall. There can be no doubt that it is a privy, more specifically what our ancestors might have called a "one-seater," for its door has swung open to expose its single occupant to view. This privy is clearly the protagonist of the drawing, eclipsing even the cottage: Bloemaert has carefully recorded its slapdash construction, the crudely nailed door, and the ruinous interior into which daylight streams through gaps in the wall. All else seems an afterthought: the man reclining at lower right amid some rustic implements; two children playing on the ground nearby; and perhaps even the young lady ensconced within the privy who, we may suppose, enjoys the bucolic prospect afforded from her seat.

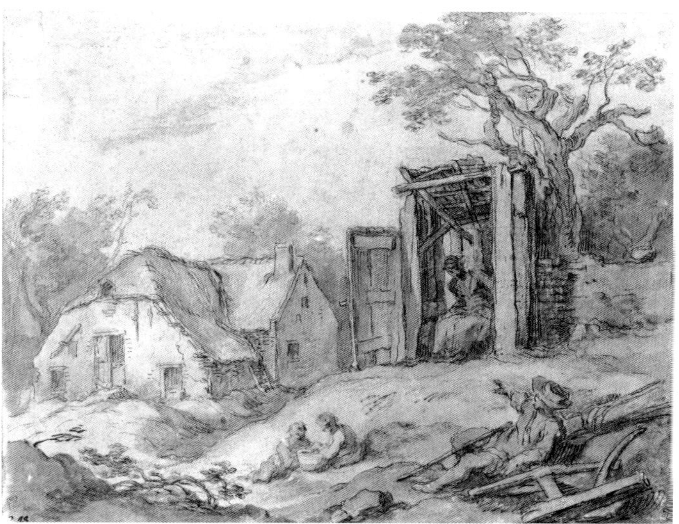

FIGURE 50. Abraham Bloemaert, *Landscape with Cottage and Privy*, c. 1605/6, pen, black chalk, and brown wash drawing. Kupferstichkabinett, Staatliche Museen, Berlin.

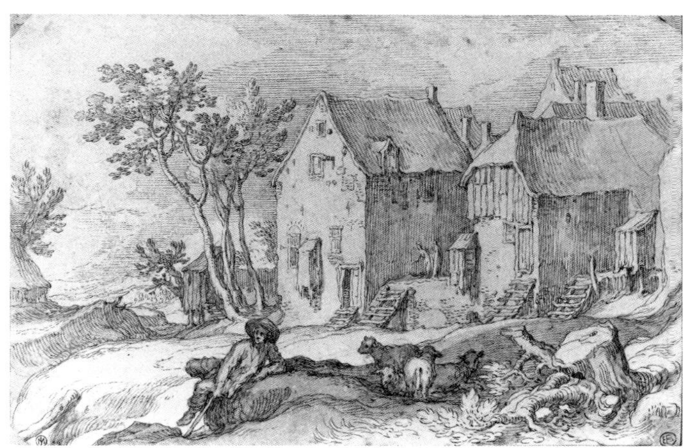

FIGURE 51. Abraham Bloemaert, *Landscape with a Group of Houses*, pen, ink, and wash drawing. École Supérieure des Beaux-Arts, Paris.

This outdoor privy, or "house of Speciall Office," as an English writer of the period called it,[4] is the modest counterpart of the *secreten* or *gemakskofferjes* (literally "secret [places]" and "closets of ease," the latter a portable privy), the indoor facilities found in the more prosperous houses of the period.[5] Bloemaert may have recorded several of these interior conveniences in another drawing (Fig. 51): attached to the walls of two houses, some feet off the ground, are small wooden structures with shed roofs.[6] Their shape suggests that they are *secreten*, and although rather slovenly built, they afford better protection from the elements than the privy in the Berlin drawing. But the latter has even less in common with the public latrines that presumably were erected in the market places and other public areas of Dutch towns, if we may accept the evidence of an etching from the late seventeenth century (Fig. 52).[7] The two conveniences depicted here are more solidly constructed, and although their open doors, as in Bloemaert's Berlin drawing, reveal their occupants, they are clearly designated as to gender use by the placards attached near their doors. Showing a man and a woman respectively, in bust format, these two images

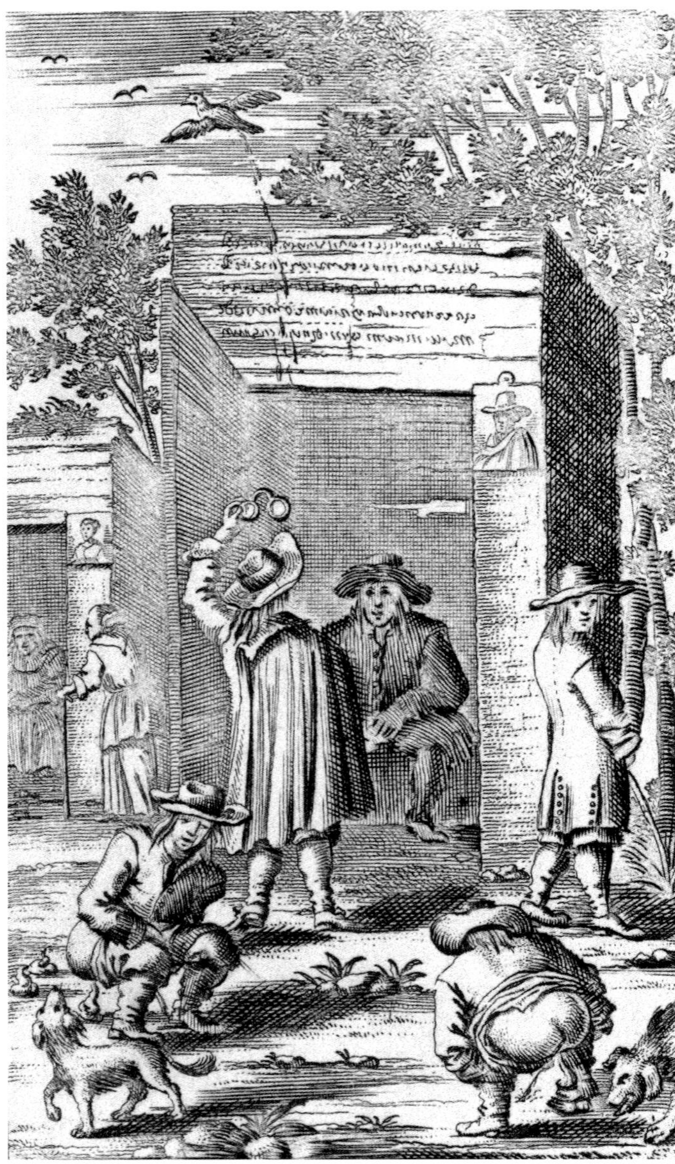

FIGURE 52. *Two Public Latrines*, etching from Hieronymus Sweerts, *Koddige en ernstige opschriften*, 3rd ed., Amsterdam, 1698–1700, p. 9. Koninklijke Bibliotheek, The Hague.

are among the distant predecessors of the "His" and "Hers" signs upon which their makers have exercised so much ingenuity in our own time, including a pair I recently encountered, displaying photographs of Humphrey Bogart and Ingrid Bergman.

Outdoor privies, of course, have long been the subject of bawdy humor. In the last century or so, they have inspired comic postcards, a wall calendar celebrating the outhouses of Alaska, and several tongue-in-cheek histories.[8] Matters, it would seem, were not much different in the Dutch Golden Age.[9] Indeed, the etching of two public latrines shown in Figure 52 illustrates a book by Hieronymus Sweerts, *Koddige en ernstige opschriften* (Serious and comical inscriptions), of which the first volume was published in 1682. Undertaken while the author was traveling on a rest cure through the Netherlands, it is a compilation of amusing graffiti assiduously copied from walls, signboards, and the like, including privies, in order, as Sweerts assured his readers, to amuse them with these buffooneries.[10] His labors must have been well received, for this work, ultimately grown to four volumes, was frequently reprinted in the next two centuries (the latest printing was in 1846).[11] In the etching, the foreground shows three would-be users of the privy apparently unable to await their turn, while a fourth man, presumably the author himself, raises his spectacles to scan the inscription above the door of the "Gents," unaware of a bird passing overhead and about to baptize him with its droppings.

If Bloemaert pondered the risible potential offered by his drawing, we have no way of knowing, but the privy in the Berlin drawing (or perhaps a close cousin), this time viewed from the side, reappears on a sheet now in Paris (Fig. 53). Again, the artist has painstakingly described this rickety structure, which is seemingly kept upright chiefly by the vines twined around several of its boards.[12] What is unmistakably the same privy in reverse appears in *Landscape with Argus and Mercury*, a print etched about 1612—probably sometime later than the Berlin drawing—by Boëthius Adam Bolswert (1580–1633) after Bloemaert's design (Fig. 54). Bloemaert recorded at least one other privy in a drawing now in Windsor Castle, which his son Frederick Bloemaert included in his *Large Landscape Series* etched after his father's designs about 1635 (Fig. 55).[13] Nevertheless, the elder Bloemaert's fascination

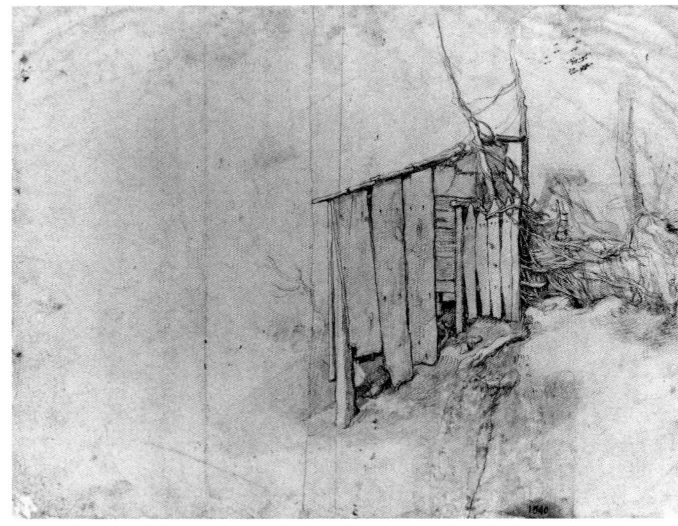

FIGURE 53. Abraham Bloemaert, *Landscape with Privy*, drawing, verso. École Supérieure des Beaux-Arts, Paris.

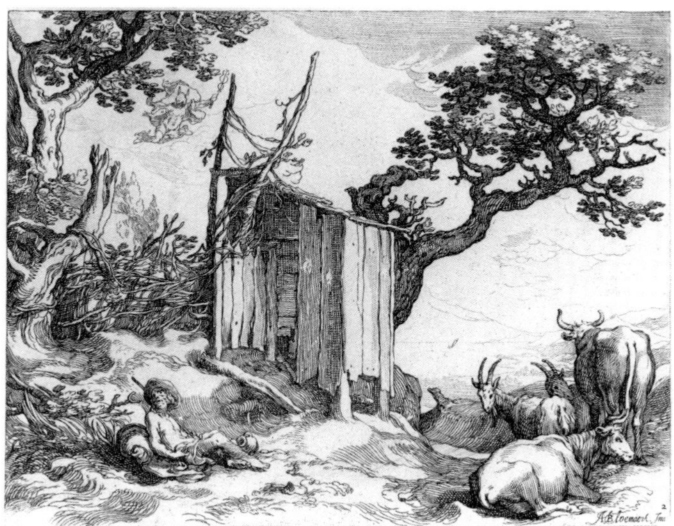

FIGURE 54. Boëthius Adam Bolswert after Abraham Bloemaert, *Landscape with Argus and Mercury*, c. 1612, etching. Museum Boijmans Van Beuningen, Rotterdam.

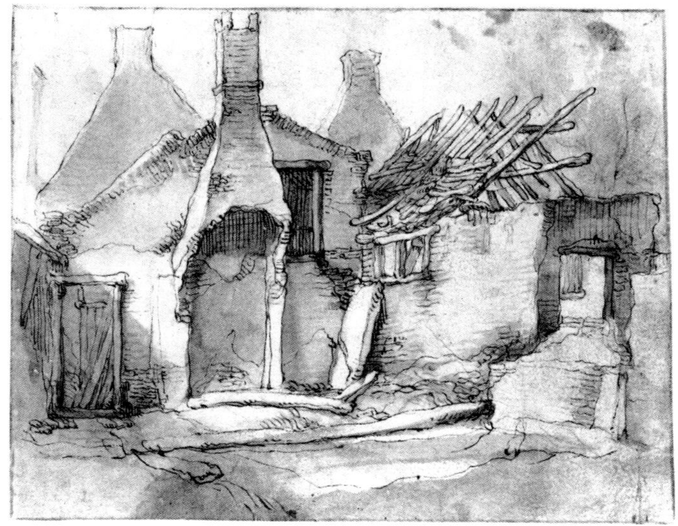

FIGURE 56. Abraham Bloemaert, *Ruined Peasant Cottage*, drawing. Kupferstichkabinett, Staatliche Museen, Berlin.

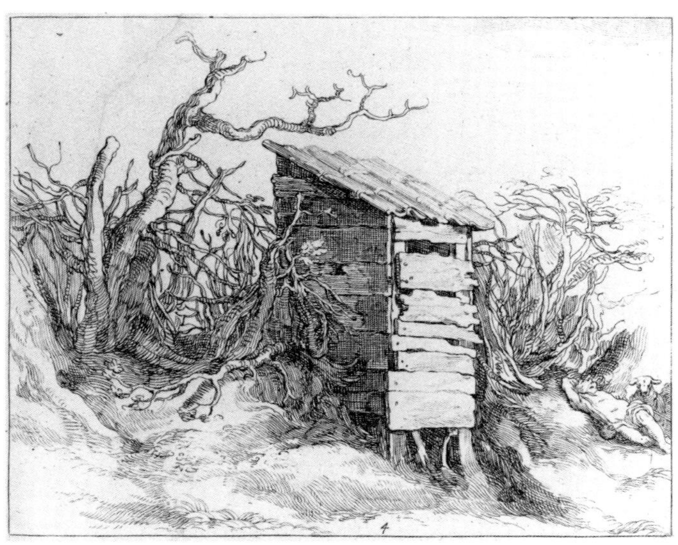

FIGURE 55. Frederick Bloemaert after Abraham Bloemaert, *Landscape with Shed and Sleeping Shepherd*, c. 1635, etching. Museum Boijmans Van Beuningen, Rotterdam.

with ramshackle structures was not confined to outhouses. He sketched many views of dilapidated farm buildings, ruinous cottages (Fig. 56 and Cat. 18), and dovecotes, scrupulously recording their weathered boards, peeling plaster, crumbling brick walls, rotting doors, and thatched roofs falling away in places (Cat. 17).[14] And such tumbledown and decaying structures must have found favor with the public, for not only were his drawings collected by the *Const-beminders*, or art lovers, as Van Mander tells us,[15] but they formed an inexhaustible source from which he drew motifs for his landscape paintings and for the many prints after his designs produced by other artists, including his sons Cornelis and Frederick, as well as Bolswert.[16]

Bloemaert was not unique in his abiding fascination with dilapidation and decay. It was shared by many landscapists active in Holland in the first half of the seventeenth century. They include Roelant Savery (1576–1639), a Fleming of Bloemaert's age who worked for Emperor Rudolph II before settling in Utrecht in 1619,[17] as well as such younger contemporaries as Esaias van de Velde (q.v.), Pieter Molijn (q.v.), Jan van Goyen (q.v.), and Rembrandt (q.v.). They all favored weather-beaten cottages and farm buildings. Indeed, a dune landscape painted by Van Goyen features little else than a stretch of derelict fencing that supports a rotting door (Fig. 57). Nor were these artists averse to depicting privies. In a landscape drawing later etched by Jan van de Velde II (q.v.), Molijn introduced a hut probably modeled on Bloemaert's privy in the Paris drawing (Fig. 58), but this time provided with a ragged piece of cloth to shield any occupant from view,[18] while Jacob van Ruisdael (q.v.) included privies in at least two of his early paintings.[19] These artists also depicted natural decay in the form of dead and fallen trees and tree stumps; a spectacular example is Ruisdael's *View of Egmond on the Sea* (Fig. 59), dominated by a dead tree, its skeletal form looming dramatically against the sky.[20]

For the sake of convenience, these forms of ruin and decay, both man-made and natural, can be designated as "rustic ruins." Ranging from simple weathering and neglect to downright dereliction, rustic ruins should be distinguished from ruins of the "noble" variety. Noble ruins, of course, had

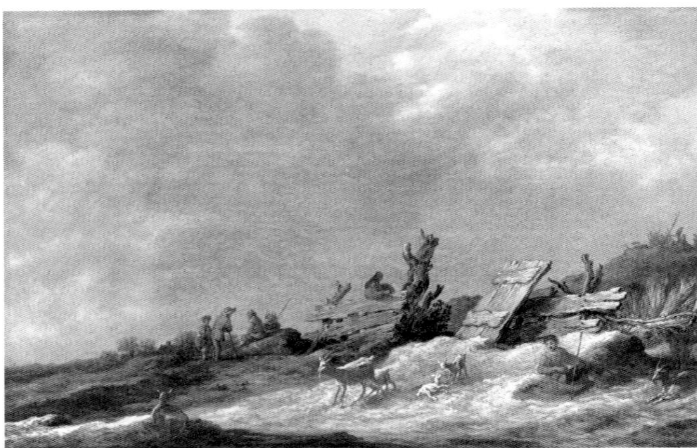

FIGURE 57. Jan van Goyen, *Landscape with Old Fence*, 1631, oil on panel. Herzog Anton Ulrich-Museum, Braunschweig.

long enthralled the European imagination. This was especially true of the remains of ancient Rome, which eloquently testified to the "[b]arbaric insanity and the terrible maelstrom of the years," as we read on the title plate of a series of etchings depicting Roman ruins and published by Hieronymus Cock in the mid-sixteenth century.[21] And noble ruins of the domestic variety, such as Rijnsburg Abbey and Brederode Castle,[22] reminded the Dutch of their own turbulent past. "I do love these ancient ruins," someone aptly remarks in a play of the period, "We never tread on them but we set / Our foot upon some reverend history."[23]

Rustic ruins, however, at least the man-made variety, are the remains of a people without history, evoking not momentous deeds and events, but a hardscrabble existence eked out of the land, crop failures, and abandoned farms. To my knowledge, such humble ruins are never encountered in

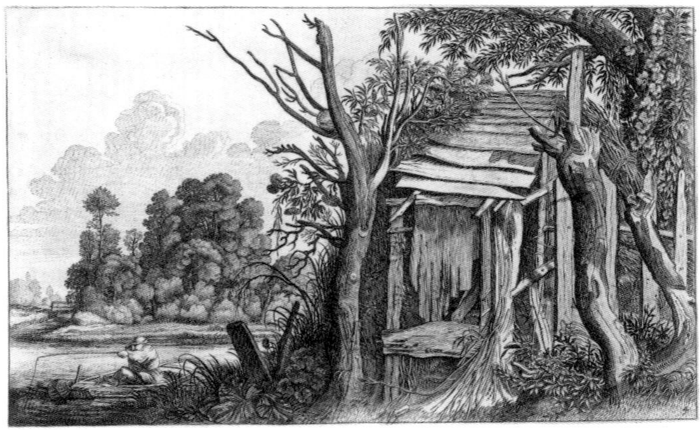

FIGURE 58. Jan van de Velde II after Pieter de Molijn, *Landscape with Shed*, etching. Rijksprentenkabinet, Rijksmuseum, Amsterdam.

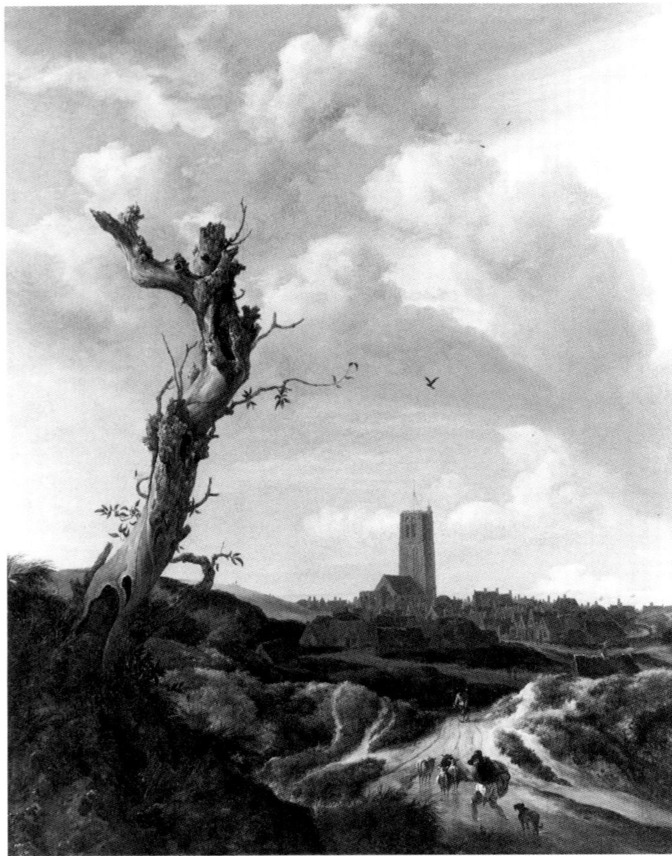

FIGURE 59. Jacob van Ruisdael, *View of Egmond on the Sea*, 1648, oil on panel. The Currier Gallery of Art, Manchester, New Hampshire.

seventeenth-century literary descriptions of the Dutch landscape. Neither the *hofdichten* (country house poems) nor other nature poems celebrate neglected farmsteads, collapsing walls, and dead trees.[24] So this brings us to the question: just why do these forms of physical decay appear so frequently in depictions of the Dutch countryside?

Formerly, when it was assumed that the Dutch artists were engaged in making "a sort of photography" of their country, as a nineteenth-century critic put it,[25] this question would have been easily answered: Bloemaert and his colleagues simply recorded what they saw. This is possible, if only because ruined cottages and deserted farmsteads must have existed, especially during the war with Spain, when parts of the Dutch countryside were ravaged by the enemy. In the last half-century or so, however, we have come to understand that Dutch artists were far from being merely visual journalists, but that their "realism" was actually a "selective naturalism" (*keurlijke natuurlijkheid*), as the Dutch painter and writer Samuel van Hoogstraten (1627–28) later characterized the seascapes of Jan Porcellis (1584–1632).[26] We now realize, in fact, that Dutch artists selected only a limited range of themes from the diverse and visually complex world around them. So why did they so often choose the kind of scenery that people most likely would have sought to avoid if they encountered it in real life?

In recent years, some scholars have sought to answer this question by equating material decay with moral decay; they claim that when Dutch artists introduced dilapidated farm buildings, rotting fences, and dead trees into their landscapes, they intended these forms to symbolize the transience of human life, sin, and death.[27] There is no doubt, of course, that ruinous buildings had traditionally been employed to express moral failings. "By slothfulness a building shall be brought down, and through the weakness of hands, the house shall drop through," according to Ecclesiastes 10:18 (Douay-Rheims version). A good example occurs in a print of about 1603 after Jacques de Gheyn II (Cat. 20). It shows a neglected cottage, its door hanging by one hinge, in the middle of a farmyard littered with a broken wheel, fragments of fencing, and tree stumps. H. Mielke has plausibly interpreted these details as symbols of sloth and lust, reflecting the spiritual condition of the young couple dallying at lower left.[28] But did rustic ruins, whatever their context, invariably symbolize moral or spiritual decay? The emblem books so popular during this period offer surprisingly little help on this point. In Jacob Cats's emblem book *Sinne en minnebeelden*, first published sometime before 1627, for instance, the penultimate image shows a corpse laid out on a pallet before a collapsing house. The Dutch verse begins "When the house falls, then leave all the mice, / When the body dies, then flee all the lice" and goes on to say that in like manner, when death approaches, the desire to engage in amorous dalliance also departs, and frivolous cupid flees elsewhere with his torch.[29] Similarly, in his *Sinnenpoppen* of 1614, Roemer Visscher includes an emblem that pairs a healthy tree with a desiccated one almost devoid of leaves, yet the issue here is hardly one of life and death. Prefaced by the motto "Keur baert angst" (Choice engenders anxiety), the accompanying text explains that faced with two or more choices, a person may choose the worst.[30] We would be hard put to apply either lesson to the rustic ruins so prevalent in the Dutch landscapes of the period, and there is evidence, in fact, that these images of rural decay and neglect could evoke ideas of a quite different kind.

This is strongly suggested by the two unlikely contexts in which Bloemaert inserted his privies. One of these is *Elijah in a Landscape* (Fig. 60), painted most likely between 1605 and 1615, for which he turned to the Paris sketch; the other is a drawing now in Amsterdam of the hermit Paul of Phermae, done probably in the 1620s, inspired by the drawing in Windsor Castle.[31] In both cases, these structures presumably provide shelter, however meager, for the holy men. Concerning *Elijah in a Landscape*, M. Roethlisberger has suggested that the privy "may stand for earthly trivia,"[32] but a clue to Bloemaert's real motive in using this structure can be found in his *Landscape with Praying Hermit and Twisted Trees* (Cat. 72), a print that Frederick etched after his father's design. Like Elijah and Paul of Phermae, the hermit is shown in prayer, and nearby, behind the great gnarled tree trunks and roots that Bloemaert employed so often, can be glimpsed his shelter, not a privy this time, but an even more primitive refuge hastily thrown together from twigs and grasses. The inscription proclaims: "Oh truly happy [he] who loves to spend life in the solitary woods, fleeing the pleasures of the world! Thus hiding and ready to serve only God, he seeks with continuous prayer the supreme kingdom."[33]

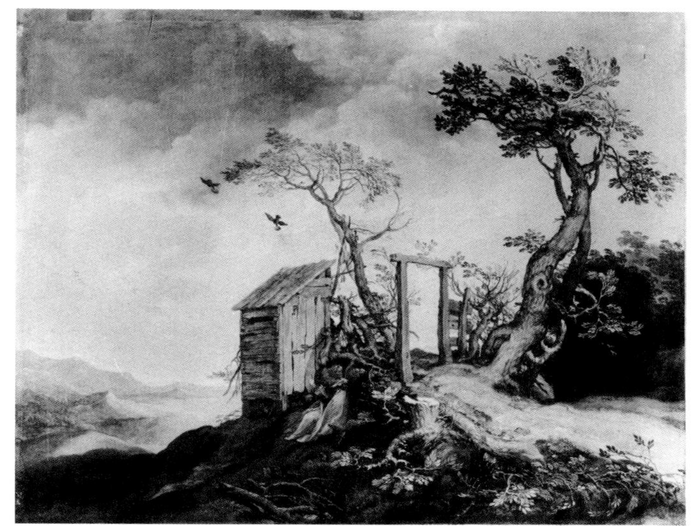

FIGURE 60. Abraham Bloemaert, *Elijah in a Landscape*, c. 1605–15, drawing. The State Hermitage Museum, St. Petersburg.

Artists had long associated biblical prophets and the hermit saints with rude shelters (Cats. 73 and 74). Many examples occur in the two series of saintly and eremitic personages designed by Bloemaert, one etched by Bolswert in 1612, the other by Frederick Bloemaert sometime after 1630. The holy anchorites huddle in caves, within dilapidated huts and sheds, or beneath simple pieces of thatch supported by tree branches.[34] Similarly, scenes of the Nativity and Infancy of Christ are often placed in impoverished surroundings: the simple manger to which Joseph perhaps has made a few repairs in order to shelter Mary and the Christ child. A quite decrepit manger appears in Robert Campin's (1378/79–1444) *Nativity*, now in the Musée des Beaux-Arts, Dijon, full of gaping holes; its daub-and-wattle walls afford little protection for the mother and newborn child.[35] Bloemaert reverted to this tradition in a painting of 1632 (Fig. 61), in which the Holy Family huddles in a dilapidated cottage kitchen with sagging walls, window frames askew, and the roof open in places to the sky. This latter picture, incidentally, gives us some notion of what the artist must have encountered inside the tumble-down cottages he so often sketched.

It is not unlikely, thus, that Bloemaert was attracted to the rickety outhouse in the Paris sketch not for its scatological associations, but because it could serve as an apt shelter for the eremitic life and for virtuous poverty in general. A related concept of rustic dilapidation informs the *Cottage Series*, a suite of etchings produced by Bolswert after Bloemaert around 1612; it presents a whole repertoire of farm buildings (Figs. 62 and 63), many exhibiting sagging rooflines and walls with missing boards, as well as farmyards littered with broken wheels and other agricultural detritus.[36] The verses inscribed on the title plate, however, do not condemn lazy farmers, as we might expect, but rather praise the fortunate man "who may spend his years free from civic burdens, living safely under the roof of his own cottage; ...with a serene spirit he gathers the large flocks to his pastures." And if he has a good wife to share his work, "oh, ever so happy and blessed with a supreme fate is he!"[37] Bloemaert's weather-beaten, run-down cottages and outbuildings thus constitute the physical setting for this rustic felicity, and they were not without precedent. The cottage of that impoverished but outstandingly virtuous peasant couple of antiquity, Baucis and Philemon (who entertained the disguised Jupiter and Mercury), is described by Ovid as "indeed a humble dwelling roofed with thatch and reeds from the marsh," and it was often shown by Renaissance artists in a state of disrepair.[38] Dilapidated sheds and shelters also occur frequently in paintings of the Labors of the Months produced in Venice by Jacopo Bassano and his workshop, compositions reproduced in prints that circulated throughout Europe.[39]

The humble but peaceful life of the country had long been contrasted with the pomp and intrigues of court and city. Horace's Epode 2, "Beatus ille," for example, begins, "Happy the man who, far from business cares ... works his ancestral acres with his steers, from all money-lending free."[40] And in his *Georgics*, Virgil tells us that far from the "stately mansions" with their "proud portals inlaid with lovely tortoise-shell," their inhabitants in "raiment tricked with gold," the farmer enjoys a "repose without care, and a life that knows no fraud," plucking "the fruits which his boughs, which his ready fields, of their own free will, have borne."[41] In later centuries, such exalted sentiments inspired countless descriptions of the rustic life, including, in Bloemaert's time, the *Bauw-heers wel-leven* (The farmer's good life), a poem attributed to Pieter Janssoon Schaghen.[42] Basically an elaboration of "Beatus ille,"[43] it celebrates the peaceful life of the farmer in his simple, unpretentious cottage ("slecht recht lant-huys"). In an anonymous Dutch song of the period, the peasants sing of their hard but simple life: they are free from care and sorrow, even if they live in houses without walls or chimneys. Each verse of this song ends with the proverbial phrase: "Lord, daily bread and clothes, heaven, and then nothing more."[44] These descriptions of rustic habitations—a *slecht recht lant-huys* and houses without walls and chimneys—thus suggest that for seventeenth-century viewers, the cottages and farmyards of Bloemaert and his colleagues, with their signs of neglect and decay, would have evoked the supposedly carefree but virtuous simplicity of country life, far from the "stately mansions" of court and town. This is, of course, a wholly idealized view that conveniently ignores the vicissitudes of country life, but however ill founded, it is a dream of untrammeled freedom and peace of mind that has appealed to townspeople of every age.

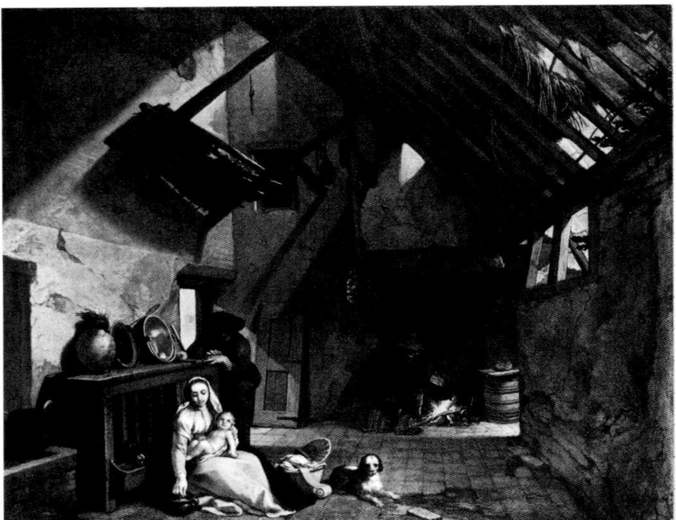

FIGURE 61. Abraham Bloemaert, *Holy Family in a Peasant Cottage*, 1632, oil on canvas. Rijksmuseum, Amsterdam.

Equally important, however, rustic ruins in their various manifestations, man-made and natural, also reflect a premeditated striving for certain pictorial effects. This, in fact, was precisely what was recommended by two writers on art active in Bloemaert's lifetime. In the chapter on landscape in his *Leergedicht* (1604), a versified manual on painting, Van Mander explains how to depict shepherds' huts and peasant hamlets: do not paint the roofs in bright, strong colors like vermilion or red-lead, but show everything as seen in reality. Roofs and walls are not to be shown with bright red bricks, but rather with turf, reeds, or straw, holed and patched; they can also be plastered in a fantastic manner ['vreemd'lijck'], with the moss growing on them.[45] Van Mander further advo-

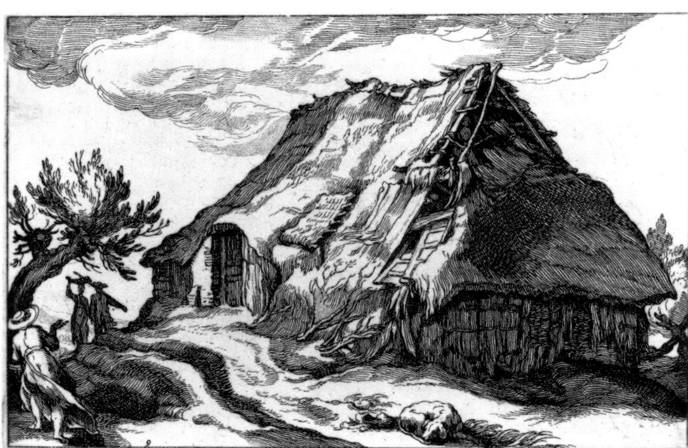

FIGURE 62. Boëthius Adam Bolswert after Abraham Bloemaert, *Farm Cottage*, c. 1612, etching. Rijksprentenkabinet, Rijksmuseum, Amsterdam.

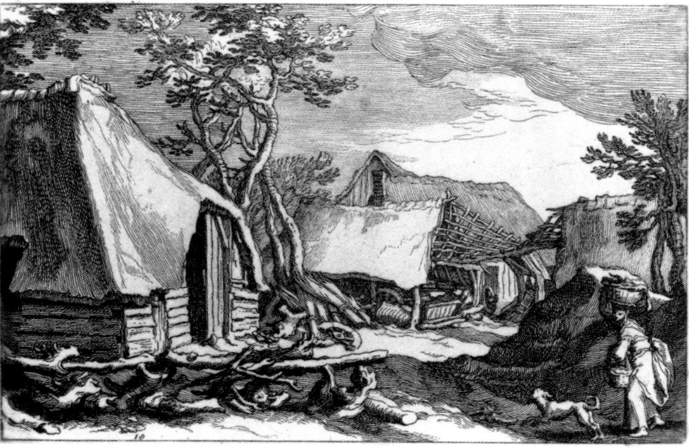

FIGURE 63. Boëthius Adam Bolswert after Abraham Bloemaert, *Farm Cottage*, c. 1612, etching. Rijksprentenkabinet, Rijksmuseum, Amsterdam.

cates depicting peasant cottages as "vreemde" and as "seldtsamer cluchten," that is, "strange" and "bizarre or grotesque whimsicalities"—in a word, what we might term "quaint."[46] This is not so much a moral judgment as an aesthetic one.

About a generation after Van Mander, the same aesthetic sensibility was evinced by Cornelis Pietersz. Biens, poet and amateur draftsman. His publications include a manual on drawing, *De teecken-const*, published in 1636, in which, among other things, he discusses the proper choice of landscape subjects. "For the cottages," he advises, "choose the old, curious broken and half-fallen peasant houses covered with reeds or straw, overgrown with vegetation, with old walls, broken doors and windows, accompanied by curious ['drollig'] hay stacks, dovecotes ['vogelhuysen'], ploughs, wagons, animals or fowls, and ... such like."[47] Although Biens was an author of moralizing tracts, including one dedicated to improving Christian youth, he ignores the symbolic possibilities of decrepit houses in favor of their visual qualities. In fact, while he undoubtedly had cribbed from Van Mander's *Schilder-boeck*, he exceeded his predecessor by far in his enthusiasm for picturesque decay. Supplementing Van Mander's prescriptions with a passage on the depiction of trees, Biens counsels that the artist should mix tall, well-grown trees with those that are old and crooked.[48]

Although Biens names no individuals, he may well have had in mind such artists as Bloemaert and Savery, as well as some of their younger colleagues, all of whom exploited rustic ruins to display their artistic virtuosity in depicting the complex play of light and shadow over rough-textured and disintegrating surfaces.[49] Rustic dilapidation appears even when not justified by the subject matter, as in the *Expulsion of Hagar*, a print of 1603, engraved by Jacob Matham after Bloemaert (Cat. 16). The great farmhouse that rises behind the figures is in a precarious state of preservation, with a broken window, brick and lath work exposed by crumbling plaster, a collapsing wall in the upper story. Nevertheless, nothing in the biblical account (Genesis 21:14) indicates that Abraham was anything but prosperous. But most often, of course, such ruins were associated with ordinary country life. In a series of four etchings of rustic scenes dated 1626, Pieter Molijn depicted crumbling buildings and fences, most sensationally in *Landscape with Peasants Conversing beside a Ruined Hut* (Cat. 22a), where the hut totters on the brink of collapse. And among Jacob van Ruisdael's weather-beaten cottages and water mills, we encounter a drawing of a ruined cottage subsiding totally into a pile of rubble (Cat. 30). It was one of his most popular motifs, reproduced in a number of paintings by other artists, including Emanuel Murant (1622–1700), a landscape painter of whom little is known but who seems to have specialized in subjects of this type.[50] Van Goyen's sketchbooks reveal how the artist searched out such motifs on his tours through Holland and elsewhere. During a trip to Brabant around 1648, he largely ignored the imposing Renaissance and Baroque structures he would have seen in Antwerp and Brussels in favor of the medieval city gates and the villages in the surrounding countryside.[51] And at least once he even invented a ruin: in sketching the tower of the church at Warmond, near Leiden, he substituted a crumbling upper stage for the well-preserved spire. He must have been pleased with the results, for he later introduced it into several paintings.[52] Thus transformed, the Warmond church qualifies more as a noble ruin than one of the rustic variety; nevertheless, we may assume that it appealed to Van Goyen for its visual qualities. The same is probably true in the case of Kostverloren (meaning, roughly, "money down the drain"), a medieval manor house near Amsterdam, which artists continued to represent in its former ruinous state even after its restoration in 1658.[53]

The taste for rustic ruins spanned approximately three generations of landscapists, from Bloemaert through Van Goyen and Jan van de Velde II to Ruisdael and Murant. But long before Ruisdael's death in 1682 and Murant's in 1700, this taste began to receive vigorous condemnation from the Dutch critics. The earliest objections known to me were raised in the *Paradigmata graphices variorum artificum* of Jan de Bisschop (q.v.), a talented amateur artist and writer on art.[54] Published shortly after his death in 1671, the *Paradigmata* was a collection of images inspired chiefly by classical and Italian art, intended for both practicing artists and art lovers. In the dedication, De Bisschop insists that

> [It is] an obvious perversity of our judgment to be persuaded that whatever is unsightly in nature is pleasing and praiseworthy in art, and that consequently a deformed, wrinkled and tottering old man is more suitable for painting ["meer schilderachtig"] than a handsome and youthful one; a dilapidated and irregular building than a well-built one in good repair ... Yet only recently ... this error had taken such hold of many of even the greatest of our artists, that everywhere it had the strength of an accepted opinion; and to such a degree that almost everything unpleasing was especially chosen as an excellent thing to paint and draw.[55]

De Bisschop fails to name these "greatest of our artists" who so tastelessly dedicated themselves to the depiction of ugliness, nor is it clear what he means by the term *schilderachtig*. This word may be translated, literally, as "painter-like" or "painterly" or "suitable for a painting," but he never defines it precisely. In any case, when De Bisschop came to record a rustic ruin on his own, in this case an old windmill missing its sails (Cat. 29), he rendered the structure in the generalizing tones of a golden-brown wash that deals gracefully with its weathered surfaces.

De Bisschop reflects the growing classicism that characterized Dutch culture from the late seventeenth century on, inspired in part by the growing influence of the French court and manifested visually in the taste for graceful, idealized forms and smooth surfaces.[56] De Bisschop's objections were developed at great length early in the next century by the painter Gerard de Lairesse (q.v.), who, incidentally, had engraved the title page to a later edition of De Bisschop's *Paradigmata*. In his *Groot schilderboeck* of 1707, De Lairesse clearly comes down on the side of the classicists.[57] Deploring artists who represent ugly subject matter of any type, he devotes three chapters to landscape, where he vehemently condemns scenes that show "deformed trees, widely branched and leafed, and disorderly ... full of knots and hollowness, also rugged grounds without roads or ways, sharp hills, and monstrous mountains filling the distance, rough or ruined buildings with their parts lying up and down in confusion; likewise muddy brooks, a gloomy sky abounding with heavy clouds ..."[58] He ends this tirade by asking: "Can anyone without reason assert him to be a *schilderachtig* subject, who appears as a lame and dirty beggar, clothed in rags, and splayfooted ... Would you not rather conclude such things to be the jest of the painter?"[59] He then lists some artists who were considered *schilderachtig*, among them the landscapists Bloemaert and Savery.[60] In the same chapter, De Lairesse also criticizes the misuse of the word *tekenachtige*, which might be translated as "design-like," or "suitable for a drawing," a word, he tells us, that has been as much perverted as *schilderachtig*: "for instance, crooked trees abounding with knots and hollowness, rugged clods of earth, broken and sharp rocks," and the like, that have been extolled as *tekenachtig*, "though as absurdly and improperly, as it is to fetch light out of darkness and virtue from vice."[61] Although he does not name them, De Lairesse probably regarded with similar distaste the later landscapists, especially Van Goyen, Rembrandt, and Ruisdael, for he complains at one point about good artists who leave the beautiful green color out of their palettes, using instead black, yellow, and more such faded colors.[62] Indeed, De Lairesse's strictures on gloomy skies, heavy clouds, and subdued colors recall the pictures of Van Goyen, Molijn, and their colleagues working during the so-called tonal period of Dutch painting.[63]

De Lairesse appropriated the word *schilderachtig* for what he considered as the "correct" kind of natural scenery, which he explained at length in the two final chapters of the section on landscape. In the penultimate chapter, titled "Of the *schilderachtig* beauty in the open air," he strolls through a park-like *locus amoenus*, or "pleasant place," pointing out to us the marble fountains, temples, and neatly kept peasant houses with classical architectural details, as well as strategically placed ancient ruins and antique tombs; the weather is fair and the roads are "so neat and level, that in walking you hardly seemed to touch the ground."[64] Such scenery may call to mind the landscapes of Poussin or, closer to home, to De Lairesse's own theater designs and landscape backgrounds.[65] The final chapter offers a landscape of quite the opposite sort, as indicated by its title, "Of things ugly ['onschone,' literally 'unbeautiful'] and broken, unjustly called *schilderachtig*."[66] The author now struggles through a rugged, desolate terrain, without paths or roads, strewn with dead trees and tree stumps, and plagued by quakes and storms. Even the ruins differ from those encountered in the previous landscape: they lie on the ground at awkward angles, affording no comfortable seats for the weary traveler; a corpse spills out of a shattered tomb. In this inhospitable region, nevertheless, our author meets various artists busily sketching the motifs that it offers, because, as one draftsman tells him, "Oh! You cannot imagine how extraordinary, and full of variety these objects are. This is the finest place on earth to a curious artist; all is *schilderachtig*; everything lies so loose, pretty, and wild." De Lairesse confesses that he is almost persuaded by such enthusiasm, but he soon recovers and elsewhere draws the moral of his two parables: "It is therefore indisputable that the painter-like [*schilderachtig*], or most beautiful choice, implies nothing else than what is worthy to be painted; and that the most mean, or what is not beautiful, least deserves that honour ..."[67]

It seems that De Bisschop and De Lairesse were correct when they insisted that the Dutch painters of the earlier seventeenth century had deliberately cultivated the ugly in nature because they considered it *schilderachtig*, that is, "worthy of being painted." But when these two critics employed *schilderachtig* in its pejorative sense, they also remarkably anticipate the later meaning of the word "picturesque" as employed by English writers of the later eighteenth and nineteenth centuries.[68] There is probably no direct connection between these two words, but there is equally no doubt that the landscapes of Van Goyen, Jacob van Ruisdael, and their colleagues, exerted a profound influence on the English picturesque.[69] And when William Marshall Craig published his English edition of De Lairesse's *Groot schilderboek* in 1817, he heartily endorsed the author's animadversions on the depiction of the ugly in art, with one exception. In a section titled "On the Picturesque in Rural Landscapes," he described the subjects appropriate for a picturesque landscape, among them "[a] cottage nearly falling to pieces, ... a piece of shattered railing; a thatched roof covered with moss and ivy; the ill-marked pathway through a green lane: or, a carriage road cut into deep furrows," because, as he concluded," it has been most happily remarked ... that things generally become more picturesque in proportion as they become unfit for the purpose to which they were destined."[70] This is an opinion with which Bloemaert and the other Dutch landscapists of his time would have most heartily concurred.[71]

NOTES

1. Van Mander/Miedema 1994–99, 1: fol. 298r (p. 450).
2. For Bloemaert's life, see Amsterdam 1993–94a, 300–301; and Roethlisberger 1993, 551–87; and for his earliest drawings, Bolten 1998.
3. See Bock and Rosenberg 1930, 11, no. 288.
4. *The Parliament of Women*, 1640, a royalist pamphlet quoted in Brown 2003, 99.
5. Muizelaar and Phillips 2003, 26, 31.
6. Muizelaar and Phillips 2003, 35, refers to an Amsterdam house of the period with a *secreet* attached to its back wall. In Bloemaert's drawing, it is unclear whether the somewhat larger but similarly constructed shed at the extreme right is another indoor convenience.
7. See also Westermann 1997, 108, fig. 45.
8. See, for example, the amusing but very informative history in Barlow 2000.
9. For this subject in early modern Europe, see Persels and Ganim 2004.
10. See Sweerts 1698–1700, 5, for the quote and 9–10 for several graffiti he recorded from various *secreten*.
11. For Sweerts and the publication history of his *Koddige en ernstige opschriften*, see *Nieuwe Nederl. biog. woordenboek* 1911–27, 3:1223–25.
12. It is possible, as Roethlisberger assumes, the same privy is depicted in both the Berlin and Paris drawings; see Roethlisberger 1993, 1:306, no. 466.
13. For Bloemaert's original drawing, see Puyvelde 1944, 22–23, no. 93. It is dated to the 1610s in Roethlisberger 1993, 1:306, no. 466.
14. There is as yet no comprehensive catalogue of Bloemaert's drawings, but for examples of his landscape drawings, including rustic ruins, see Boon 1978, nos. 69–70; Benesch 1928, nos. 431–43; and Gerzi 1971, nos. 10–11.
15. Van Mander/Miedema 1994–99, fol. 292r (p. 450).
16. See the many examples illustrated in Roethlisberger 1993 and, more recently, Roethlisberger 2000, 163–64, figs. 14–15.
17. For Savery, see Gibson 2000, 151–53.
18. It is the last sheet in a set of four landscape prints after Molijn; see Hollstein 33–34 (1989): nos. 324–27.
19. For several examples, see Slive 2001, 404, no. 564, and 406–7, no. 569; Haarlem 2002, 68–71, nos. 10–11, which identifies the structures in question as privies. A privy appears in a third early painting attributed to Ruisdael, but Slive places it among the dubious works; see Slive 2001, 659, no. dub136; Haarlem 2002, 68–69, no. 10.
20. For other examples of rustic ruins, see Cats. 15–33 herein.
21. Hieronymus Cock, *Praecipua aliquot Romanae antiquitatis ruinarum monimenta* ... (Suite of Roman ruins ...), 1550–51. See Hollstein 4 (1949): 283, no. 22; Riggs 1972, 256–57, no. 1a; dedication page, with verses by Cornelis Graphaeus that begin: "Barbaric insanity and the terrible maelstrom of the years have her, Rome, the queen of the world, so sadly destroyed." The Dutch translation of these lines is from Bakker 1996, 53.
22. For other "historical" ruins, see Cats. 5 and 11 (Rijnsburg) and 1, 2a, 7, and 8 (Brederode) herein.
23. John Webster, *The Duchess of Malfi*, act 5, scene 3; quoted from Webster and Ford 1933, 176.
24. For the country house poems, see Van Veen 1985; and for the treatment of nature in Dutch literature in general, Beening 1963.
25. Thoré-Bürger (W. Bürger), *Les Musées de la Hollande* (Paris, 1858), quoted in Hecht 1986, 175.
26. Hoogstraeten 1678, 238; quoted in Stechow 1966, 11.
27. For the equation of rustic ruins with sin, see Gibson 2000, chap. 3. For other scholars, rustic ruins evoke the idea of human transience in contrast, or subordinated, to eternal nature; see Haverkamp-Begemann 1959, 42.
28. Mielke 1980, 46; see also Bruyn 1987–88, 86.
29. Cats/Luijten 1996, 1:336–37.
30. Visscher 1614/1949, 11 (Het eerste schock, XI).
31. For the *Elijah*, see Roethlisberger 1993, 1:203, no. 262. For the Amsterdam drawing, see Boon 1978, 1:19, no. 40. Boon does not comment on the shed, but its source was already noted in Puyvelde 1944,

22–23, no. 93. The Amsterdam drawing was used in reverse for a print in the so-called *Second Series of Hermits*, etched after 1630 by Frederick Bloemaert, who, however, omitted the latrine. See Roethlisberger 1993, 1:364, no. 637.

32. Roethlisberger 1993, 1:203, no. 262.

33. Quoted from Roethlisberger 1993, 1: no. 89, 138.

34. See Roethlisberger 1993, 1:171–83, nos. 163–214 (etched by Bolswert), and 355–67, nos. 577–657 (*Thebais Sacra*, etched by Frederick Bloemaert), a series that apparently was never published.

35. Friedländer 1967–76, 2: pl. 76, no. 53. For the tradition of the humble life of Christ, particularly as manifested in Protestant thought, see Baldwin 1985.

36. Roethlisberger 1993, 1:195–99, nos. 230–29; Gibson 2000, 155–57.

37. Quoted from Roethlisberger 1993, 1:196–97, no. 230.

38. Ovid, *Metamorphoses*, book 8; quoted from Ovid/Innes 1955, 212. For the visual tradition, see Stechow 1940–41.

39. For the paintings, see Aikema 1996, 131–45, and for the prints, Bassano 1992, 30–34, nos. 9–12; 48–51, nos. 28–35; 55–56, nos. 39–40.

40. Horace/Bennett 1914/67, 365.

41. Virgil, *Georgics*, 2: lines 461–63; 500–501; see Virgil/Fairclough 1974, 1:149, 151.

42. In *Den Nederduytschen Helicon*, Haarlem: Passchier van Westbusch, 1610, 233–38. For the author, see Strengholt 1977.

43. See Knuttel 1927.

44. Meertens 1942, 48–50.

45. Van Mander/Miedema 1973, 1:212–15 (fols. 36v–37, bk. 8, vv. 31–32).

46. Van Mander/Miedema 1973, 1:212–13 (fol. 36v, bk. 8, v. 31). In a marginal note, Van Mander refers to "*vreemde* peasant houses and shepherds' huts." Miedema translates *vreemde* and *seldtsamer cluchten* into modern Dutch as *bizarre* and *bizarre grilligheden*, respectively.

47. De Klerk 1982, 51.

48. De Klerk 1982, 51.

49. Cf. Zucker 1961, 120, in which some seventeenth-century Italian painters of ruins are characterized in rather similar terms.

50. For Murant, see H. Gerson in Thieme-Becker, 25:281; his works bear dates between 1658 and 1696.

51. Buijsen 1993, 25.

52. Buijsen 1993, 51 and fol. 26; Leiden 1996, no. 32, 118.

53. It was so depicted by Meindert Hobbema and Jan van Kessel; see Slive 1988, esp. 137. For other views of the site by Ruisdael, see Slive 2001, 97–102.

54. See Van Gelder and Joost 1985.

55. See Van Gelder and Joost 1985, 1:228, with some emendations to reflect the original Dutch text more faithfully.

56. See Slive 1995, 295–327.

57. For an excellent account of De Lairesse's life and his aesthetic theories, see De Vries 1998.

58. De Lairesse 1817, 1:286 (bk. 6, chap. 15).

59. De Lairesse 1817, 1:286.

60. De Lairesse 1817, 1:286; the passage on the Netherlandish cited from De Lairesse 1740, 1:419.

61. De Lairesse 1817, 1:286 (bk. 6, chap. 15).

62. De Lairesse 1817, 1:241 (bk. 6, chap. 5).

63. For the *schilderachtige* skies of Van Goyen and other landscapists, see Falkenburg 1996; Falkenburg 1997. For the tonal phase of Dutch landscape painting, see Slive 1995, 186–94.

64. De Lairesse 1817, 1:287–92 (bk. 6, chap. 16).

65. See De Vries 1998, 158–63, figs. 43–46. De Vries 2003, 316, observes that Dutch artists did not follow De Lairesse's formulas for genre paintings; to what extent his prescriptions might have influenced the landscape painters is a topic yet to be pursued.

66. De Lairesse, 1817, 1:292–96 (bk. 6, chap. 17).

67. De Lairesse 1817, 1:285 (bk. 6, chap. 15).

68. For the English picturesque, see Gibson 2000, 149–51, with further references.

69. Gibson 2000, 151–52.

70. De Lairesse 1817, 2:284.

71. Various issues raised in this essay are treated at greater length in Gibson 2000, 141–7.

Accidents and Disasters

Arthur K. Wheelock Jr.

Accidents and disasters happen. And, as a rule, they tend to occur at inconvenient times, disrupting well-laid plans and orderly existence. At best, accidents are a temporary inconvenience, like spilling a cup of coffee, and can be overcome with a modicum of patience and good will. At worst, they devastate communities and take lives, sometimes in untold numbers, and their effects may last for generations. Disasters such as hurricanes and earthquakes tend to be cataclysmic events, ones that have far-reaching implications for a community or a nation, but they can also be more personal, as when one experiences acute embarrassment or disgrace.[1]

Humans respond to accidents in various ways. They can elicit a range of emotions from sympathy to scorn that reflect the relative culpability of the individual or individuals affected. The sight of someone slipping while walking on a freshly polished floor or while running beside a swimming pool, for example, creates very different responses in the observer. Accidents to innocent bystanders almost always evoke sympathy, stemming from the awareness that, but for the grace of God, it could have been me—as in me standing on the bridge that collapsed or driving the car when the truck swerved into it.

Unlike accidents, disasters create a sense of awe and horror that seamlessly blends with empathy for those affected. The magnitude of many natural disasters poignantly reminds humankind of its helplessness in the face of nature's destructive forces, whether fire, wind, or water, whereas those suffering from personal disaster become acutely aware of their vulnerability in the face of society. In either instance, one experiences helplessness in controlling events, which often leads to a search for spiritual help or to the placing of responsibility in a strong political or social leader. Perhaps for this reason, even more than their inherent dramas, disasters resonate on a universal level that has made them the focus of art and literature throughout the centuries.

The seventeenth-century Dutch, like everyone else, presumably had their share of accidents and disasters, but few of them were allowed to enter the realm of art. The overall impression one receives from prints, drawings, and paintings is that this land was a veritable Arcadia and that its people, blessed by God's munificence, lived a life of peace and prosperity. Peace, of course, had come to the nation only after years of war and strife, hunger and hardship during the revolt against Spain. But it had come, in large part because of the perseverance and vision of its wise leaders and the sacrifices of its brave citizens, who likened their struggle to reach their "promised land" to that of the ancient Israelites. Through the building of dikes and windmills, the hard-working and industrious Dutch had successfully reclaimed an inhospitable terrain, filled with bogs and areas unfit for crops or pastures, transforming it into fertile and productive lands. They constructed a complex network of waterways to allow goods to pass easily from city to city. Finally, wealth had come from successful trading practices, as Dutch ships had brought back untold riches, not only spices, but also exotic flowers and rare shells, from distant lands.

Dutch artists emphasized these positives in their work, for clearly they, like the rest of that society, were fully committed to the idea that they had entered into a "Golden Age."[2] Indeed, a certain element of propaganda exists in their prints, drawings, and paintings, in which the land, the people, and their society in general are celebrated for their overridingly positive qualities. In viewing these works, one can only be amazed at how well maintained are the fields and barns, how contented are the cattle and sheep, how filled with ferries and pleasure boats are the waterways, how prosperous are the cities and towns, how filled-to-the-brim are the overflowing tabletops, whether with exotic flowers in Wan Li vases or arrays of cheeses, fruits, and wines. Portraits similarly depict a well-dressed people proud of themselves and

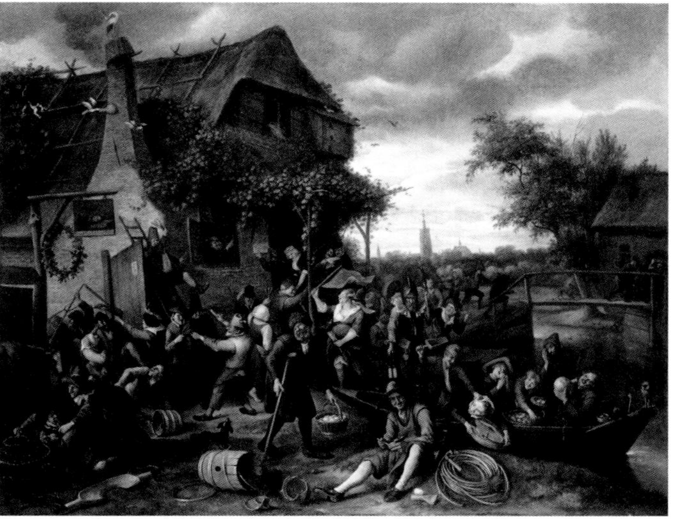

FIGURE 64. Jan Steen, *A Village Revel*, 1673, oil on canvas. The Royal Collection, Her Majesty Queen Elizabeth II.

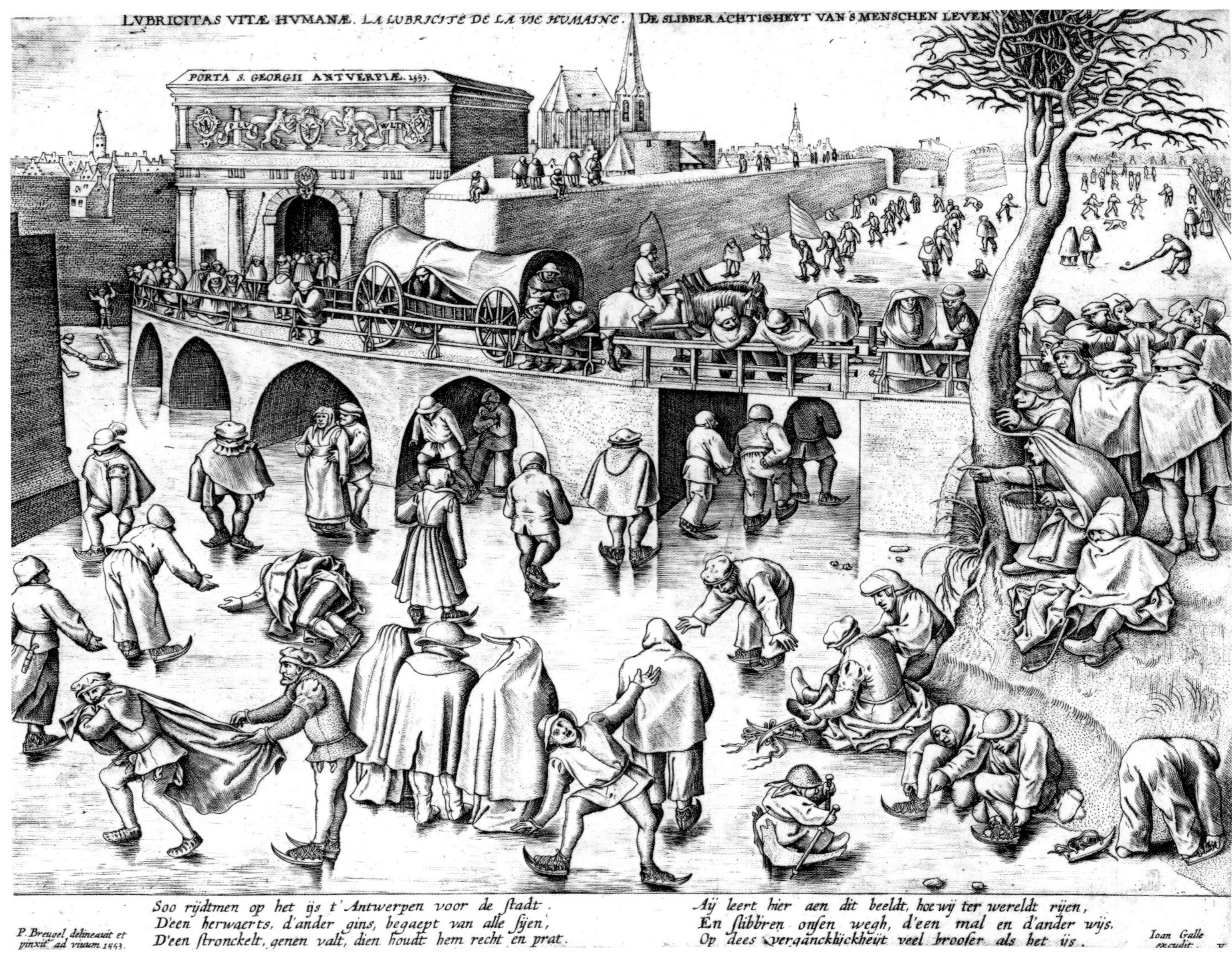

FIGURE 65. Frans Huys after Pieter Bruegel the Elder, *Skaters before St. George's Gate in Antwerp*, late sixteenth century, engraving, state ii. Biblioteque royale de Belgique, Brussels.

their heritage, while genre scenes generally portray individuals positively engaged in domestic life, with only an occasional ruffian or village quarrel to add color to the image of peace and harmony (Fig. 64).

The Dutch only allowed certain types of accidents to impinge on the perception that they were a self-sufficient and industrious people: those to which certain moral beliefs or maxims of life could be attached. Except for an occasional fire, specific accidents were virtually never depicted, only generic ones that could provide moral lessons about proper behavior, as, for example, a figure falling on the ice. The most prevalent moralizing meaning attached to this all-too-common incident was that it represented "the slipperiness of human life," the caption added to the second state of a late-sixteenth-century engraving of an ice scene by Pieter Bruegel the Elder (c. 1525–69; Fig. 65). A poem accompanying the print further provides the explicit moral lesson to be learned from the skaters who traverse a frozen waterway near Antwerp:

> See how they skate on the ice in Antwerp, outside the city,
> One this way, the other that, watched from every side.
> One stumbles, another falls, that one stands proud and tall.
> Oh learn from this scene how we pass through the world,
> Slithering as we go, one foolish, the other wise
> On this impermanence, far brittler than ice.[3]

A figure falling on or through the ice, however, provided the Dutch with multiple emblematic warnings, ranging from the dangers inherent in reckless behavior to the uncertainties of love.[4] On the other hand, as evident in an emblem by Roemer Visscher, one who had mastered the art of skating was held up as an exemplar of proper behavior: just as skaters only achieve their proficiency through diligent practice and learning, so one should prepare oneself for life's vagaries.[5] For Visscher, even a fallen skater provided an opportunity for a positive emblematic message: the best of skaters will occasionally fall, but they will get up and proceed as though nothing had happened (Fig. 66). In like manner, one should deal with small setbacks in one's financial fortunes, personal accounts, chivalrous deeds, or love affairs.[6]

If accidents to individuals rarely surface in Dutch art, disasters, both real and imagined, excited the Dutch imagination to a far greater degree. Natural disturbances of all types, from beached whales to high winds, provided excellent opportunities for moralizing about human behavior.[7] For example, the image of trees bent by raging winds was one that suggested the enormous power of nature's forces when unleashed on the seemingly strong and sturdy (Fig. 67). Jacob Cats observed that large trees are most likely to be affected by such adversities, while low-lying areas often remained unaffected by the winds, interpreting such a natural phenomenon as a warning that individuals who have received honors and power need to expect criticisms and jealousy from others.[8]

The mother of all Dutch disasters was, without question, the dramatic explosion of the powder magazine in Delft on 12 October 1654, the aftermath of which is recorded in Daniel Vosmaer's (q.v.) and Herman Saftleven's (q.v.) compelling views of the devastated city (see Cats. 41, 42). This horrific event, described at length by Dirck van Bleyswijck in his *Beschryvinge der Stadt Delft* (Delft, 1667), occurred when between eighty and ninety thousand pounds of gunpowder ignited in a tremendous explosion that was even heard on the island of Texel, over eighty miles away. The destruction in Delft was extensive. The whole northeastern section of the city, where the powder magazine was located, was leveled, with great loss of life. Van Bleyswijck vividly recounts how roofs had been blown off houses in nearby neighborhoods, how old trees had been blown over, and how gardens had been destroyed, a poignant account further brought to life by Vosmaer's and Saftleven's depictions of this devastated area. Precious stained-glass windows were blown out of the Oude Kerk and Nieuwe Kerk. Throughout Delft, valuable objects, such as porcelain and glass, had fallen from shelves and smashed on floors.

The "howling and crying" of the injured, according to a heart-wrenching missive that Van Bleyswijck published alongside his own account, "was so very pitiful and deplorable, that a heart of stones and diamonds would be moved to bemoan

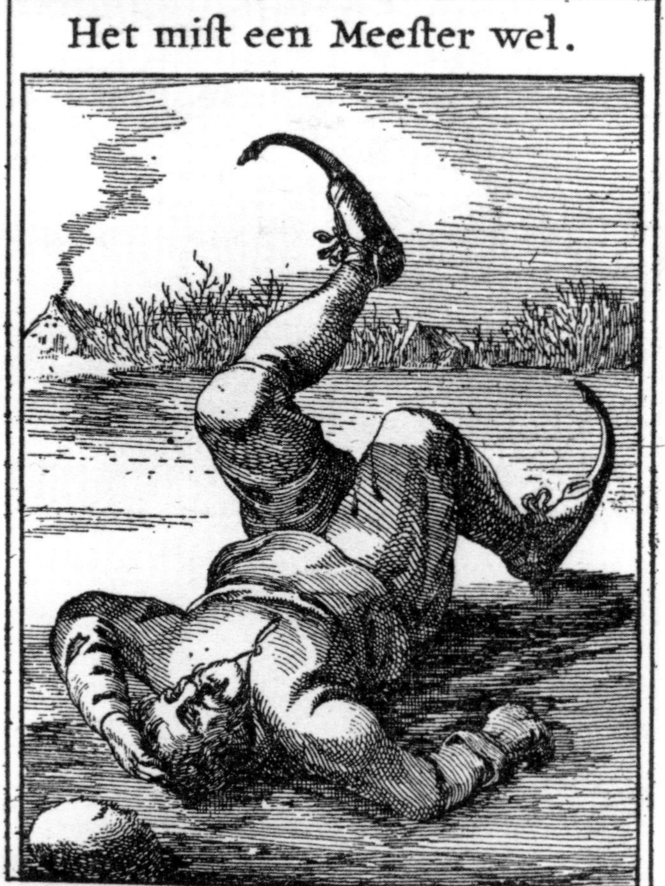

FIGURE 66. Claesz Jansz. Visscher, "Het mist een meester wel," 1614, engraving, from Roemer Visscher, *Sinnepoppen*, Amsterdam, 1614, pt. 3, emblem 24. National Gallery of Art Library, Collection of Rare Books, Washington, D.C.

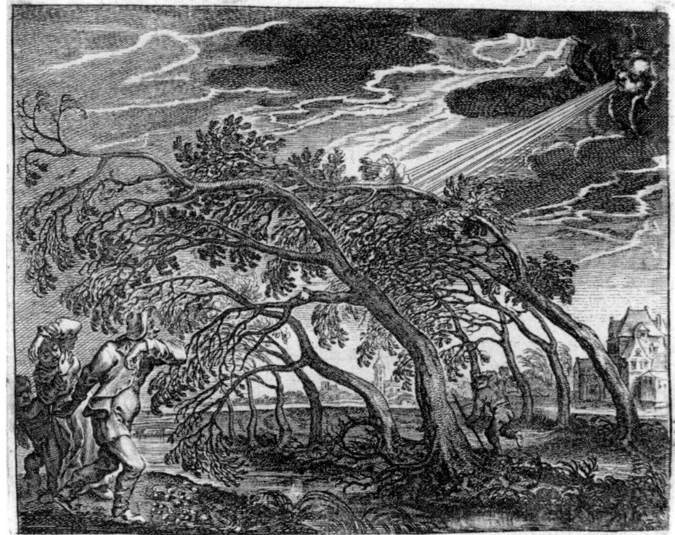

FIGURE 67. Adriaen van de Venne, *Trees Threatened by High Winds*, 1655, engraving, from Jacob Cats, *Hof-Gedachten*, Amsterdam, 1655. National Gallery of Art Library, Collection of Rare Books, Washington, D.C.

and bewail by these sad lamentations."[9] Vosmaer (Cat. 42) tugged at these same heartstrings by depicting in the immediate foreground of his painting a wounded woman being attended by her loved ones. Other figures wander through the wreckage, surveying the damage and searching for survivors. On the other hand, Saftleven (Cat. 41), in his large, panoramic drawing, represented the scene of devastation in a remarkably dispassionate manner, with not a victim in sight. His drawing, and the extended commentaries he included beneath the image, describe both the damage inflicted on the buildings and the treasures that were spared, as, for example, the "coats of arms and sepulchre on his majesty's grave" in the Nieuwe Kerk. Whether he meant his drawing to serve as a basis for a printed broadsheet is not known but seems likely.[10]

The literary and artistic responses to the explosion in Delft were remarkable, not just because of Van Bleyswijck's extensive description of the damage to life and property, but also because of the large number of images of the explosion and resulting devastation that were executed in succeeding years. For example, Daniel Vosmaer (q.v.) and his Delft contemporary Egbert van der Poel (q.v.) executed more than twenty paintings of this subject (see Fig. 133 under Cat. 42). They are quite similar in character, which indicates that a ready market for commemorative images of this disaster existed. On many of these works Van der Poel inscribed the date, 12 October 1654, which, not unlike 9/11, had become immediately seared into the collective memory.

The site, in fact, became a sort of tourist destination (see Cat. 43). Viewers, among them Saftleven, who had traveled from Utrecht, and the Winter Queen, Elizabeth Stuart, who came from The Hague, felt the need to see the devastation for themselves. The area was left in ruins for some time, so visitors could wander along paths adjacent to scattered bricks and low-lying walls that were once parts of houses, and they could reminisce about events that had occurred on that fateful day.[11] Among the stories circulating about the effects of the explosion were a few positive accounts, including that of an eighty-year-old man who had been rescued after having been trapped for thirty-six hours under a pile of debris.[12] Another celebrated the miraculous rescue of a fifteen-month-old girl, who was found in the rubble twenty-four hours after the explosion. When discovered, she was still in her high chair, virtually unharmed, and still clutching an apple.

The Dutch, however, were not about to allow such a disaster to occur without finding in it an important lesson to be learned. Van Bleyswijck reported that many who were experienced in this awful tragedy felt that the thunder of the explosion signaled the end of the earth and that they would soon be brought before God for his judgment on how they had conducted their lives. For Van Bleyswijck, this disaster was a poignant reminder that one can never know when death will arrive, and he quotes the Second Epistle of St. Peter the Apostle (3:10): "But the day of the Lord shall come as a thief, in which the heavens shall pass away with great violence, and the elements shall be melted with heat, and the earth and the works which are in it, shall be burnt up."[13]

The unpredictability of life is a theme that runs through much of Dutch art, but nowhere more consistently than in marine painting. Artists as diverse as Jan Brueghel the Elder (1568–1625), Bonaventura Peeters (1614–52), Paulus Bril (1554–1626), Simon de Vlieger (q.v.), and Jacob Adriaensz. Bellevois (1620/22–76) found a ready market for tempest scenes, not only because of the inherent drama of their subjects, but also because these scenes spoke to a deep-seated fear in all those whose lives depended on the sea.[14] Rocky shores, in particular, had ominous overtones. On a practical level, they were to be feared in the midst of a storm, but they also symbolized inhospitable, distant foreign lands, the Dutch coast being predominantly lined by dunes.

One of the most dramatic of such scenes is Bellevois's *Sea Storm on a Rocky Coast* (Fig. 68), where a number of ships are being tossed about in turbulent seas. Some survivors of a wreck, having made it safely to a large rock near the shore, pray to thank God for their safe deliverance. In the allegorical mindset of the Dutch, however, such an image alluded to far more than the dangers faced by sailors at sea. In a broader sense, the tumultuous storm represented the turbulence of life, from which the fortunate sailors have been saved through God's intervention.[15] Ludolf Backhuysen's dramatic *Ships in Distress off a Rocky Coast* (Cat. 34) is less anecdotal than Bellevois's painting, but the fervid prayers of the sailors in the central ship similarly appeal to God's intervention to save them from being cast upon the threatening rocks that line the stormy coast. In this instance as well, it seems that the sailors' prayers will be answered, for the clearing skies in the upper left indicate that the storm is relenting and that they will not suffer the same fate as those in the ships whose masts are seen floating in the waves. In depicting this scene, Backhuysen pushed the limits of his pictorial techniques to express fully the impact of the disaster. By flicking a brush loaded with lead-white paint against the canvas, he indicated the spray from the waves crashing against the rocks and ships, thereby suggesting the terrifying effects of the storm in ways that could be vividly felt by the viewer.

Steadfastness in the face of disaster was, in fact, a virtue that the Dutch saw as a fundamental component of their national character. It was one that had been sorely tested during the revolt against Spain, a struggle that would surely have been lost without the sacrifices of so many over such a

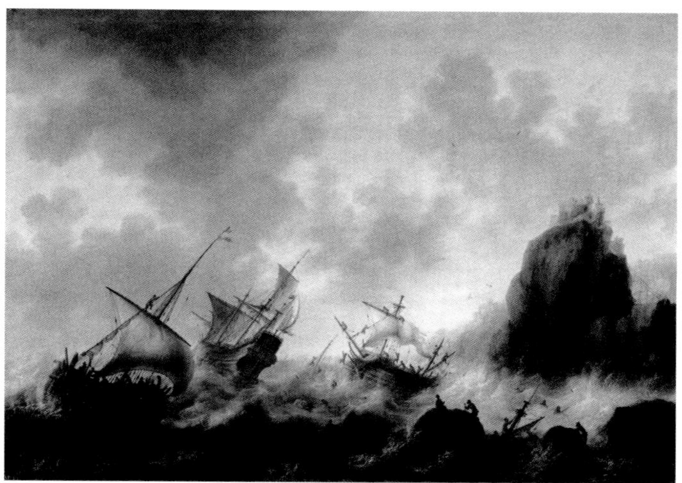

FIGURE 68. Jacob Adriaensz. Bellevois, *Sea Storm on a Rocky Coast*, 1664, oil on canvas. Herzog Anton Ulrich-Museum, Braunschweig.

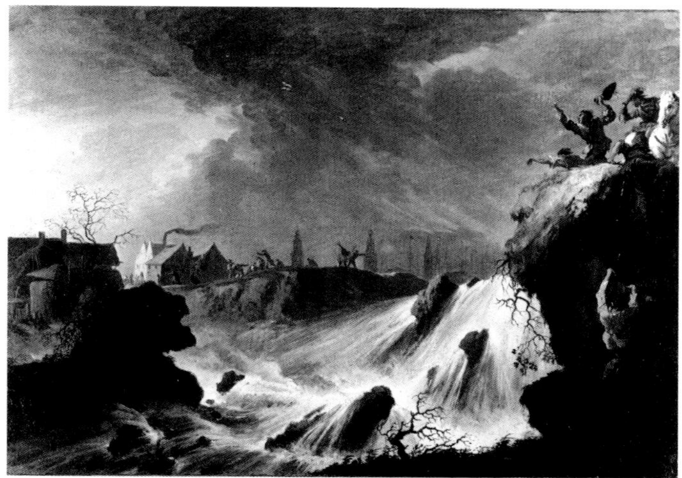

FIGURE 69. Willem Schellinks, *The Breach in the St. Anthonis Dike near Houtewael*, 1651, oil on canvas. Amsterdams Historisch Museum.

long period of time. As one Calvinist author wrote about the revolt: "Truly was the violence of these calamities so great that men could only weigh the suffering as a *test* sent from heaven ... [to try] the virtue and steadfastness of this people in burdensome affairs."[16] Steadfastness, however, was a necessary virtue even in times of peace, for the Dutch had to be continually wary of another foe that was constantly threatening to overrun the countryside—the tidal waters that so often flooded low-lying lands after heavy rains, high winds, or, most dramatically of all, burst through breaches in the dikes (Cats. 36–38).

Building these dikes had been a great engineering feat, carefully conceived and carried out to allow the Dutch to reclaim rich and fertile lands suitable for crops and the grazing of cattle. These reclamation projects also helped create a network of canals and roads that facilitated transportation from town to town and from city to city. Dikes also served a defensive function, for, as was demonstrated in the Dutch Revolt, they could be purposely breached to flood low-lying lands to hinder the enemy. Nevertheless, when floods and breached dikes happened unexpectedly, they wreaked havoc on the countryside. One of the most severe of these occurred on 5 March 1651, when water burst through the St. Anthonis dike at Houtewael, just east of Amsterdam. According to a contemporary report, a strong northwest storm battered the area "at full moon and springflood" and inundated the low-lying land behind the dike with sixteen feet of roiling sea water.[17] Joost van den Vondel, writing in an allegorical mode about the breaching of the dike, painted a graphic description of the toll it took on the Diemermeer polder:

> Neptune ... spares neither dike nor piles
> Nor planks of oak, and comes just above Outewael
> Bursting into the pastures and roaring on his oars
> Proceeds and sinks and rises and falls in Diemen's lake.
> Puts farms and crops and cattle below the water that
> Aforetimes had been forced to leave that great expanse ...
> The haystack keeps the cattle, farmers with families
> Put through the roofs their heads, to stave off threatening death.[18]

Like the explosion in Delft, breached dikes drew visitors, including artists such as Willem Schellinks, who traveled to witness and record the devastation caused by the torrents of water that had spilled out into the surrounding countryside (Fig. 69). Some Calvinists assuredly saw in these floods indications of God's displeasure with contemporary society's desire for financial gain, but surprisingly little indication of such concerns is evident in images of such tragedies.[19] Quite remarkably, as in Esaias van de Velde's depiction of the repairing of the broken dike on the river Lek of 1624 (Cat. 35), most of the prints depicting the St. Anthonis dike focus on its reconstruction rather than on the actual disaster and its dire consequences. These are, in essence, images that celebrate the steadfastness and ingenuity of the Dutch in coping with the destructive forces of nature. In these prints, there is no shortage of pride in the magnitude of the achievement: dikes, which had been so essential for creating a flourishing agricultural environment, had helped the Dutch transform their small country into that arcadian world they so frequently celebrated in song and verse.

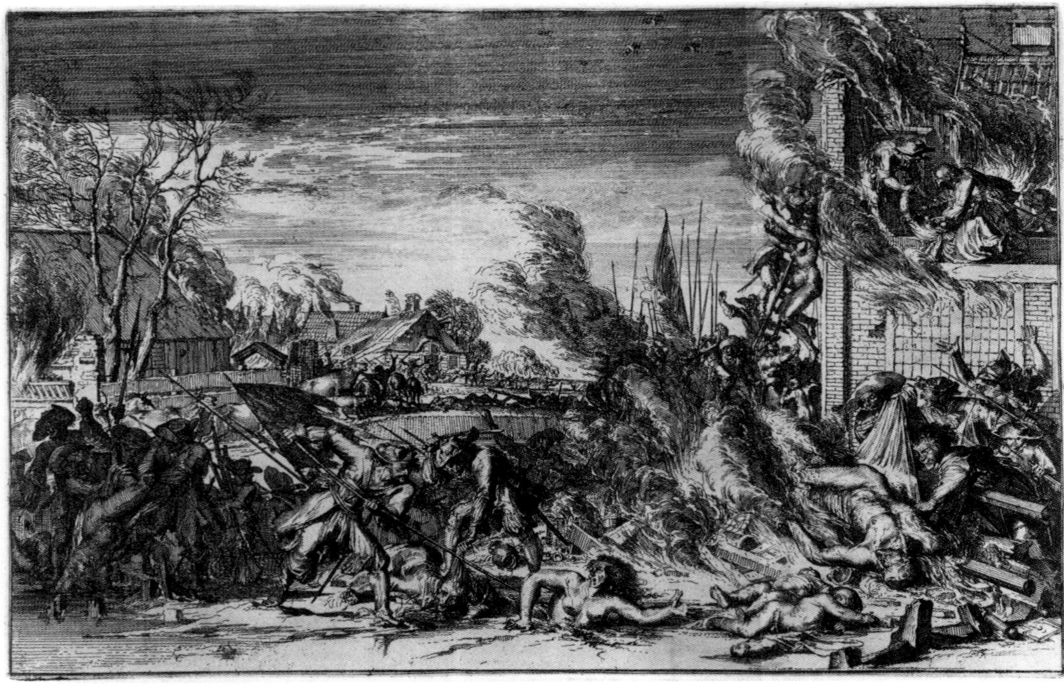

FIGURE 70. Romeyn de Hooghe, *A Scene of French Tyranny*, 1673, engraving, from Abraham de Wicquefort, *Advis fidelle aux véritables hollandois*, Amsterdam, 1673. National Gallery of Art Library, Collection of Rare Books, Washington, D.C.

The attitude toward the breaching in 1673 of the lengthy dike across the river Vecht was entirely different. This dike, one of the longest and most expensive in the Netherlands, was also one of the most despised construction projects of the period, and its demise was seen in biblical terms. This notorious dike had been constructed not by the Dutch for peaceful, agrarian purposes, but by an invader, the bishop of Münster, who intended to use it to hold back the waters of the river Vecht to drown the nearby garrison town of Coevorden. Thus, when the dike broke on 1 October 1673 and hundreds of soldiers in the bishop's army were swept to their death, the disaster was seen as God's retribution for the bishop's evil designs against the Dutch. H. Selijns's poem about the event, which was printed at the upper right of Romeyn de Hooghe's dramatic rendering of the cataclysmic disaster (Cat. 38), recalls in its allusions the miracle of the parting of the Red Sea: "At Coevorden: Miraculous deliverance from the Bishop who dug with his mitre in the mud / to let the waters rise in order to win Coevoerden. He broke his solemn vow / so God broke his dike / that godlessly was begun."

Prints such as these serve as reminders that disaster scenes, despite the infrequency with which they figure in Dutch art, had great pictorial appeal, and in depicting them, artists often rose to heights not generally associated with their work. No artist responded to disasters with greater enthusiasm and visual power than De Hooghe, particularly when the disasters had political implications. The image of the bishop of Münster's drowning soldiers being cast into the turbulent waters of the river Vecht provided De Hooghe an opportunity to exercise the full range of his expressive techniques. He emphasized the overwhelming nature of the event occurring on the broken dike by the large scale of the print, by his panoramic viewpoint, and by the powerful diagonals and chiaroscuro effects that heighten the drama of the scene. He used similar effects in his unrelentingly gruesome illustrations for *Advis fidelle*, Abraham de Wicquefort's anti-war treatise chronicling the brutal atrocities that French troops committed against Dutch citizens in small towns near Utrecht during the "Rampjaar" (Disaster Year) in 1672 (Cat. 39). With his vigorous, slashing strokes and vivid pictorial imagination, De Hooghe brought home the brutality of the killings, rapes, and general debasement of men, women, and children who had been dragged out of their burning homes by these bloodthirsty troops (Fig. 70).

Fire, even when it was not a backdrop to the horrors of war or the result of a powder-house explosion, was a type of disaster that was all too common in seventeenth-century city life. Wooden houses with thatched roofs, most of which had been erected in close proximity, caught fire all too easily. Conflagrations spread rapidly and without warning, generally overwhelming the rudimentary fire-protection methods—primarily bucket brigades—then available. The spectacle of a raging fire was particularly dramatic at night, and onlookers would stand in awe at the searing light of raging flames and shower of red-hot sparks soaring into the darkness above.

A long pictorial tradition of biblical and mythological scenes depicting night fires served seventeenth-century Dutch artists well when they sought to convey the drama of conflagrations in their homeland. Jan Brueghel the Elder, in particular, had painted numerous biblical and mythological scenes with fires raging in the distance, such as *Lot and his Daughters*, where Sodom and Gomorrah are seen being consumed in flames, or the *Sack of Troy*, where similar background effects create a comparable nocturnal spectacle (Fig. 71).[20] The primary Dutch specialist in night scenes, Aert van der Neer (1603/4–77), must have drawn inspiration from such works, although he removed all suggestion of a narrative from his conflagration scenes (Fig. 72). Van der Neer's paintings of fires in villages and cities are more atmospheric than terrifying—not far removed, in fact, from his depictions of peaceful evening sunsets. Images of death and destruction were of no interest to him. Instead, he focused on the gentle orange glow of the distant fire in the night sky, an effect that the onlookers lining the bridge seemingly gaze upon with fascination. Van der Poel, on the other hand, delighted in bringing the viewer close to the fervid activities of those trying to control fires bursting through the thatched roofs of country cottages and farmhouses (Fig. 73). The artist, who focused much of his career on depicting disasters, including the explosion in Delft, invariably painted these fires as night scenes, with flickering chiaroscuro effects adding to the drama (see Cat. 45).

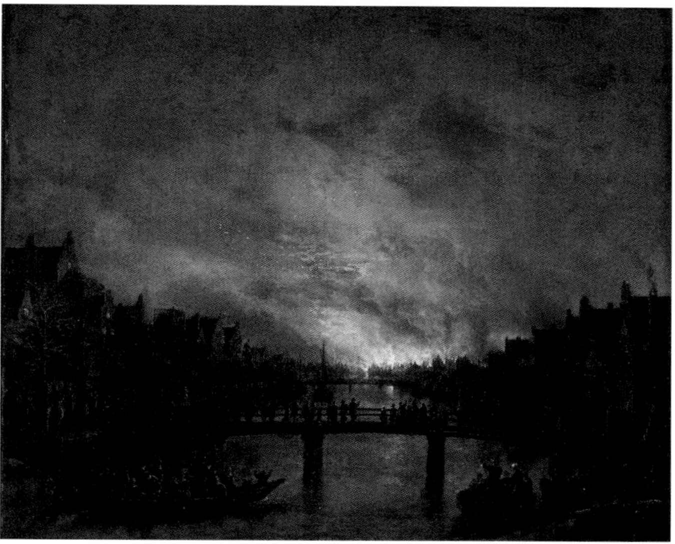

FIGURE 72. Aert van der Neer, *A Burning Fire in an Amsterdam Canal*, c. 1645, oil on canvas. Statens Museum for Kunst, Copenhagen.

A night conflagration of an entirely different nature occurred when the Old Town Hall in Amsterdam caught fire at two o'clock in the morning on 7 July 1652. Although this municipal structure was already outmoded, and a new town hall designed by Jacob van Campen (1595–1657) was in the process of being built, it was still the seat of government for the largest and most important city in the Dutch Republic. A youthful artist by the name of Jan de Baen (q.v.) recognized the importance of the event and, acting almost as a contemporary news photographer recording a local disaster, created an expressive print of the disaster for widespread

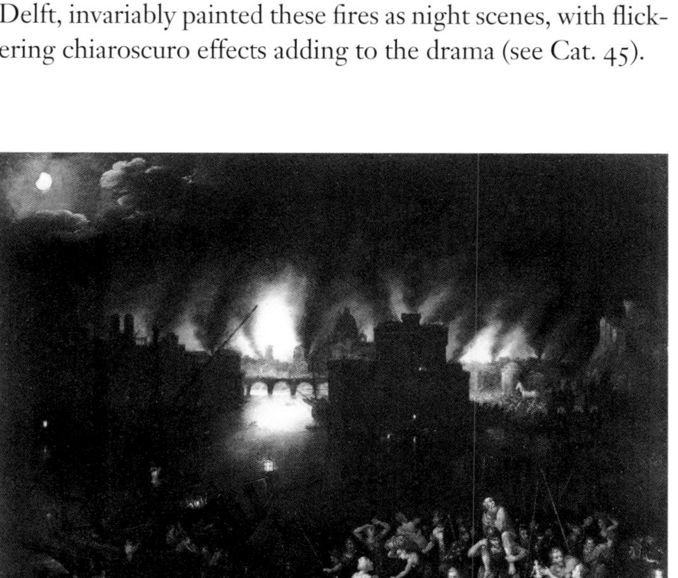

FIGURE 71. Jan Brueghel the Elder, *The Sack of Troy*, c. 1595, oil on copper. Bayerische Staatsgemäldesammlungen, Munich.

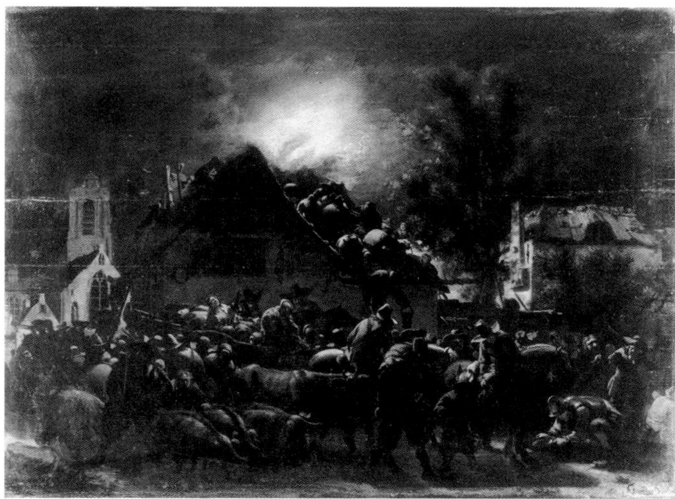

FIGURE 73. Egbert van der Poel, *The Burning City*, c. 1655, oil on panel. Seattle Art Museum, Eugene Fuller Memorial Collection, 47.160.

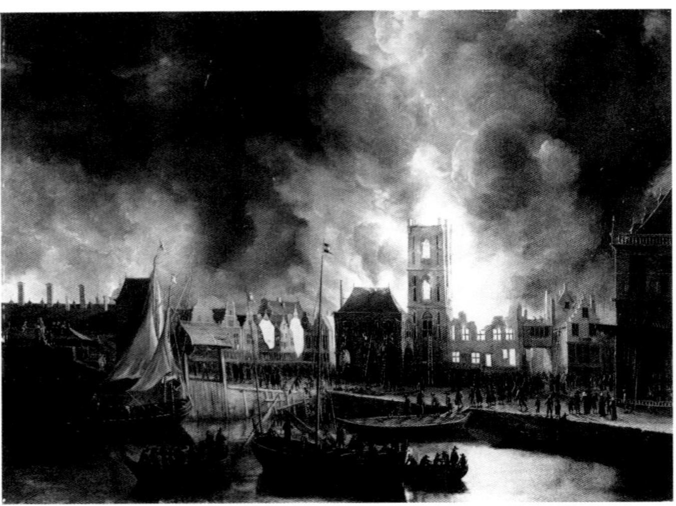

FIGURE 74. Jan Abrahamsz. Beerstraaten, *The Burning of the Old Town Hall in Amsterdam*, c. 1652, oil on panel. Amsterdams Historisch Museum.

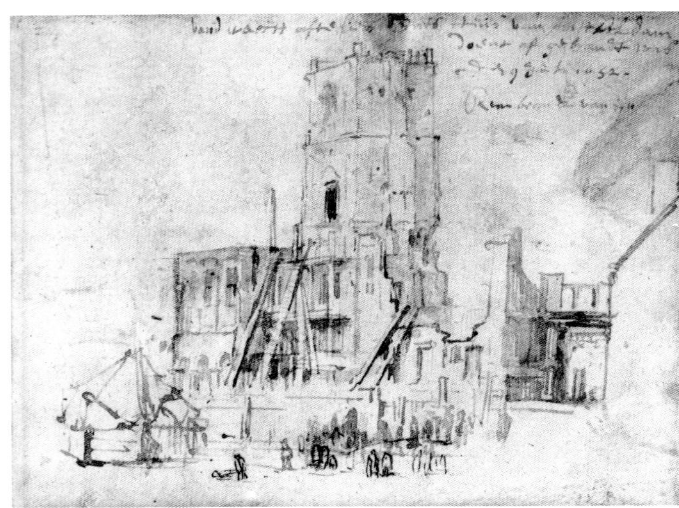

FIGURE 75. Rembrandt van Rijn, *The Ruins of the Old Town Hall of Amsterdam*, 1652, pen, brush, reed pen, and touches of red chalk. Museum Het Rembrandthuis, Amsterdam.

dissemination (Cat. 40). As flames reach into the night sky from all areas of the building, one can almost feel the heat of the fire and sense the panic of the onlookers as they flee from the falling debris. De Baen makes it quite evident that, despite the best efforts of those carrying buckets of water to men climbing ladders propped against the burning edifice, the building would be a total loss.

Much like the explosion in Delft, the destruction of the Old Town Hall became the subject of a number of commemorative paintings and drawings that recorded both the event and its aftermath. One artist that specialized in such scenes was Jan Abrahamsz. Beerstraaten (1622–66), whose panoramic painting of the Town Hall at the height of the fire effectively captures the raging inferno within the building's interior (Fig. 74) and whose subsequent depiction of the building as a stark ruin standing in a barren wasteland is equally haunting.[21] Rembrandt, who never recorded the appearance of the old Town Hall before the fire, was also fascinated by the devastation and recorded the burned-out structure in one of his most haunting images (Fig. 75).

Joost van den Vondel, in the allegorical poem he wrote for the dedication of the New Town Hall in 1655, took a different approach to the disaster than had De Baen and Beerstraten in their expressive, yet descriptive renderings of the scene. Vondel blamed the fire on Vulcan, who, according to the poet, wanted to destroy the building himself rather than having it taken down by humankind. Vondel wrote that when the fire and its soaring flames woke the town, proud citizens rushed to the site to save letters, books, and treasures contained within the burning edifice, thereby preserving the city's soul. Thus, while the God of Fire left behind only walls, rubble, and stone, he did not succeed in destroying the building's spirit. Like the mythological phoenix, a new town hall was rising out of the ashes and rubble, one that would become a crown of the land and would last for centuries.[22]

Just as they rebuilt broken dikes, the Dutch did not let such disasters dampen their sense of destiny. Vondel addressed this issue head-on when he wrote that it was not true that the city's good fortunes were bound to the Old Town Hall. For him, the building of the New Town Hall promised an even grander future for Amsterdam.[23] However accurately Vondel's celebratory poem captured the sense of optimism in the city, the threat of fire had to be faced in order to prevent even worse tragedies from occurring in the future. Dealing with this situation would require invention and ingenuity, both of which the artist Jan van der Heyden (q.v.) possessed in good measure. Van der Heyden, who lived on the Dam Square, had witnessed the devastating fire of the Old Town Hall. Although he was only fifteen years old at the time, his vivid memory of the event is evident in the way he described the fire and depicted it in his remarkable illustrated book on the fire hose, *Beschryving der nieuwlyks uitgevonden en geoctrojeerde slang-brand-spuiten en haare wyze van brandblussen, tegenwoordig binnen Amsterdam in gebruik zynde*, which he published in Amsterdam in 1690 (Figs. 76, 135, and 136 and Cat. 46).

Although this engraving dates some thirty-eight years after the fire, Van der Heyden's print has a remarkable sense of immediacy. A far better artist than the youthful De Baen was when he made his etching of the fire (see Cat. 40), and one who had had the opportunity to study De Hooghe's expressive depictions of conflagrations, Van der Heyden captured the urgency of the moment as workers in the long lines of the bucket brigades feverishly tried to fill the pumps at the base of the burning structure. As opposed to De Baen's earlier print, Van der Heyden's engraving is a panoramic view of the Dam Square, where one sees not only boats bringing empty buckets to the figures climbing on ladders to reach the water, but also wet sails being held aloft on distant buildings to try to keep them from catching fire as well. No one flees here, for so intent are they in fighting the fire, they do not notice that a huge section of the tower is about to crash down upon them.

Van der Heyden's purpose, however, was not primarily to report on the fire but to indicate how it could have been better fought if only his new invention of the water hose had been available at the time. In his extensive text, he enumerates all of the limitations of the earlier fire-prevention methods. For example, they did not provide adequate amounts of water to reach the flames, and none of the water reached the inner portions of the building where the fire was at its worst. Moreover, firefighters had to get too close to the fire, where they were endangered by extreme heat and falling debris. His report is quite contrary to the impression given by Vondel: according to Van der Heyden, the fire spread too quickly to save letters, and money in the exchange bank smelted together in large clumps.[24] To demonstrate how these problems could have been overcome had the water hose and pump been available in 1652, Van der Heyden anachronistically included his inventions in this scene, which he carefully captioned to be sure that the point was not lost (see Cat. 46, letter C).

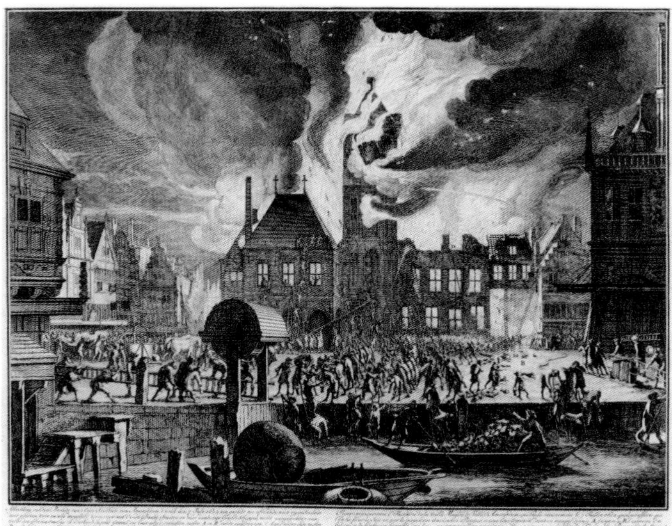

FIGURE 76. Jan van der Heyden, *The Burning of the Old Town Hall in Amsterdam*, 1690, engraving, from *Beschrijving der nieuwlijks uitgevonden en geoctrojeerde slang-brand-spuiten*, Amsterdam, 1690. National Gallery of Art, Washington, D.C., Ailsa Mellon Bruce Fund.

While Van der Heyden's book is a marvelous promotional piece, both compelling in its images and carefully descriptive in its accounts of the fires, it is also a powerful summation of the various ways the Dutch responded to disasters. To begin with, disasters elicited enormous empathy for those affected, particularly disasters caused by water and fire, the most volatile of the four elements. Dutch artists, who so effectively depicted the movements and vagaries of nature in their landscape paintings and prints, were also able to capture the extremes, when strong winds blew spray from the waves as they crashed upon floundering ships or fed angry flames searing through windows and roofs. The paintings and prints of disasters always involve a human element, with which the viewer can immediately identify. Disasters were also seen allegorically, often as an indication of Divine retribution for one's transgressions or those of one's enemies. Although most warnings, and their contingent moralizing message, were biblically inspired—as in warnings to conduct each day of one's life as though it were the last—they could also have a more practical character, such as emphasizing the necessity of having proper fire-fighting equipment handy.

Finally, in the Dutch mind, disasters belonged to the broader spectrum of life. While often frightening and even devastating at the moment of their happening, they could be overcome. Fires could be contained, dikes could be rebuilt and strengthened, new town halls could arise that would promise even greater glory and good fortune. Building upon their strong sense of self, which was formed during their successful revolt against Spanish control, and with a thoroughly ingrained belief that they, like the ancient Israelites, were a chosen people living in a promised land, the Dutch continually accepted the challenges that disasters afforded and moved on, always hoping to create a better world.

NOTES

1. I would like to thank Anneke Wertheim and Adriaan Waiboer for their thoughtful comments about this essay.

2. For this issue, see A. K. Wheelock Jr., "Aelbert Cuyp and the Depiction of the Dutch Arcadia," in Washington/London/Amsterdam 2002, 17–23.

3. Translation taken from Amsterdam 1997, 51. This state was published by Johannes Galle (1600–1676).

4. Jacob Cats's, *Spiegel van den ouden en nieuwen tijdt* (The Hague, 1632; reprint Amsterdam, 1968), pt. 2, p. 8, emblem 2 depicts a donkey having fallen on the ice, the moral being that he should not have gone where he was unprepared; and Cats's *S'Weerelt begin, midden, eijnde, besloten in den Trou-ringh* (Amsterdam, 1657; reprinted in Jacob Cats, *Alle de wercken* [Amsterdam, 1700], 2:71) includes an engraving of a woman being rescued by her lover after falling through the ice in a story entitled "Liefde, gekocht met gevaer des Levens" (Love, bought with danger to life).

5. Roemer Visscher, *Sinnepoppen* (Amsterdam, 1614), pt. 3, emblem 7: "Gheoeffent derf." "Die ghy in eenige dingen wilt seecker ende vast doen gaen / die moet ghy daer in oeffenen eer't in't werck komt" (Dare to be skillful. He who seeks to be sure and constant in some things must practice before he will succeed).

6. Roemer Visscher, *Sinnepoppen* (Amsterdam, 1614), pt. 3, emblem 24: "Het mist een meester wel." "Het is niet nieuws inde plaetsen daet men ghewoon is Schaetsen te ghebruycken, dat een Man valt, soo hy de moet heeft dat hy weder op staet, en gaet zijn gangh oft niet gheschiedt en waer: daer men mede te verstaen wil gheven, dat niemand haeft om een kleyn ongheval den moet verliesen sal, het zy in zijn Rijckdom, in zijn Reeckeninghe, in zijn Ridderlijcke daden, in zijn Amoreusheden ..." (Even a master fails: It is not news in places where men generally use skates that when a man falls he has the courage to stand up again and proceed as though nothing happened: from that one should understand that a small mishap need not create loss, whether in one's financial fortunes, personal accounts, [or] love affairs).

7. For the various portents associated with beached whales, see Schama 1987, 130–44.

8. Jacob Cats, *Hof-Gedachten* (Amsterdam 1655), 25–26, provides the moral with this French proverb: "Qui se veut gardet de foudre, qu'il s'abaisse" (He who wishes to avoid lightning must bend low).

9. Van Bleyswijck 1667–80, 2:623: "Het gehuyl dat hier is ... is soo seer erbarmelick en betreurlick, dat een hart van steenen en Diamanten sigh soude bewegen, om dese treur- en klaegh-redenen te beschreyen ende te beweenen ..."

10. For further information about Saftleven's drawing, see the entry by M. Plomp in New York/London 2001, 486–87, no. 124. One possible reason that a broadsheet based on Saftleven's drawing was not made is that Jan Philipsz. Schabaelje immediately published a pamphlet about the explosion (*Historisch verhael van het wonderlick en schrickelick opspringen van 't Magasyn-huys, voor-gevallen op den 12 october 1654 binnen Delft*). For a discussion of the pamphlet, see M. Plomp in New York/London 2001, 470–71, no. 114.

11. In 1659 the site of the former powder magazine was leveled and left as an open space for a horse market.

12. Van Bleyswijck 1667–80, 2:630. These stories had previously been published in a pamphlet published shortly after the explosion (see note 10). They were illustrated in the pamphlet by a dramatic etching depicting both the discovery of the eighty-year-old man under a pile of rubble and the infant in her high chair. The print was based on a drawing by Gerbrand van den Eeckhout (q.v.). For illustrations of the etching and the drawing, see M. Plomp in New York/London 2001, 470–71, no. 114.

13. Van Bleyswijck 1667–80, 2:631.

14. Schama (1987, 28–30) describes a number of disaster epics written in the mid-seventeenth century about voyages of exploration, where ships are described being battered by a tropical storm or trapped in Arctic ice, where fire on board causes dramatic explosions of powder kegs, and where the threat of starvation and, consequently, the temptation to cannibalism is ever present. As so often occurs in the paintings, the protagonists of these stories generally survive, not only because they manage to overcome huge obstacles through skill and perseverance but also because of God's grace.

15. See Braunschweig 1991, 28–31.

16. As translated in Schama 1987, 26. The Dutch text by the Calvinist writer J. Lydius appeared in an anthology of poems entitled *'t Verheerlikt Nederland* (1668, 28): "Doch die Godt tot groote heerlijkheydt verheffen wil, besoeckt hy eerst met ghevaren ende uytterste onheylen. En waarlyck was 't gewelt van dese rampen soo groct, dat men licht afmeten kost dat het ons hemel tot en beproeving opgheleydt was, willende dien onsterslicken Godt eens onderstaen of de deught to lijden en uyt te voeren onkreuckbaer blijven soude."

17. This report is quoted from the *Hollandsche Mercurius*, 1651, by M. Carasso-Kok in Bussum 1975, 82.

18. Vondel's text is taken from *Inwydinge van't Stadhuis t'Amsterdam*, a poem written for the dedication of the Amsterdam Town Hall in 1655. See Vondel 1930, 460: "Neptuin ... ontziet noch dijck, noch pael, / Noch eicke planck, en komt u, boven Outewael, / Geborsten in de weide, en, bruizende op zijn riemen, / Vaert voort, en zackt, en ryst, en valt in 't meer van Diemen. / Zet hofsteên, vee, en vrucht in 't water, dat wel eer, / Zijns ondancks, ruimen moest den boezem van zyn meer ... / De hoybergh berghde 't vee. De droeve huisman stack, / Met vrouwe en kindren, 't hooft gedootverft uit het dack ..." The English translation is taken from M. A. Schenkeveld-van der Dussen, "Nature and Landscape in Dutch Literature of the Golden Age," in London 1986, 77.

19. See Schama 1987, 42–46, for discussion of the allegorical importance of water to the Dutch.

20. For Brueghel's night scenes, see Ertz 1979, 129–36.

21. For this latter work, *The Old Town Hall of Amsterdam in Ruins*, 1652, Rijksmuseum, Amsterdam, see Amsterdam/Toronto 1977, 202–3, no. 99.

22. Vondel 1930, 462: "De gansche stadt waeckt op. De vlam ging op, en stack / Het torenbuskruit aen. Nu rusten geene bedden. / De trousten schieten toe, en reppen zich, en redden / De brieven, boecken, gelt, trezoor, en banck en schat; / En bergen in dien brant de ziel der gansche stadt; / Terwijl de vlam in top blijft weiden, als een wonder, / Uit gunst, die 't vier ons droegh, dat tijt gaf, om van onder / Te redden have, en goet, ten oirbaer van 't Gemeen. / Dus liet Vulkaen hier niets dan muurwerck, puin, en steen, / Waerna de bouwkunst breet haer vleugels ging ontvouwen, / De nieuwe fenixpluim en kroon van 's lants gebouwen, / Als ryzende uit den grave en d' assche en 't lijck van 't out, / En een geduurzaemheit van eeuwen toebetrouwt." This text, roughly translated, reads: "The entire city awoke. The flame rose up and lit the tower's gunpowder. Now no beds rested. The proud rushed there and took letters, books, money, and treasure to save them, thereby hiding from this fire the soul of the entire city. Although the flame continued to enlarge, as a marvel good fortune gave us time to pull from under the fire, and to save, the city's stork. Thus Vulcan left here nothing other than walls, rubble, and stone, after which architecture unfurled her wings wide to build the new phoenix-plume and crown of the land, rising from the grave and the ashes as of old and entrusted to the enduringness of centuries."

23. See Vondel 1930, 462: " ... Hoe onvast staen dees gronden: / 't Geluck der steden is aen 't out stehuis gebonden: / Men vraege Schelt en Eems; zy hebben 't ons geleert / Moe met den raethuisbouw 't geluck der steden keert;" (How unstable are these arguments [that] the luck of a city is bound with its old town hall: One [need only] ask Scheldt [Antwerp] and Eems [Emden]; they have taught us [that] the luck of a city turns with the building of a town hall). See also Vondel 1930, 475–76, in which the author expands on the concept that the New Town Hall was as a phoenix being born from the flames of the Old Town Hall, a phoenix that signaled a rich future for Amsterdam.

24. Van der Heyden 1690, 9: "Men had nauwlyks tyd om de papieren, en 't geen daar 't meest aangeleegen was, te bergen, de rest verbrandde; de gelden van de Wisselbank smolten veel aan groote klompen" (One barely had time to hide [save] the papers, which was most necessary; the rest burned; much of the gold from the exchange bank smelted into large clumps).

Embracing Antiquity: The Dutch Response to Rome

Lynn Federle Orr

Roma quanta fuit, ipsa ruina docet
(The ruin itself teaches the grandeur that was Rome)

Hildebert de Lavardin, twelfth century[1]

[Rome] This spectacle of the world, how fallen it is! How changed! How defaced! The path of victory is obliterated by vines, and the benches of the senators are concealed by a dunghill.

Poggio Bracciolini, 1430[2]

Captivated by the decaying remains of ancient Roman architecture, seventeenth-century Dutch artists—perhaps more than artists of any other country—exploited the artistic potential of these remnants of classical antiquity. Literally thousands of "Dutch Italianate"[3] paintings, drawings, and prints record the response of successive generations of Dutch artists to Italian history, culture, and topography. Within this genre, an extensive sub-set focuses specifically on the ruins of ancient Rome as subject or setting. Seventeenth-century Dutch painters and draftsmen combined an understanding of the evocative and paradoxical nature of ruins with the Dutch propensity for realism. This formula led to the creation of some of the most sensuous images of architecture (Fig. 77) in the Western tradition. Particularly in the drawings of Dutch masters working directly before the ancient monuments in Rome, the material remains of distant history are artfully described through revealing luminosity and tactile immediacy.

From the mid-sixteenth through the early eighteenth century, the Northern visual interpretation of Roman ruins fluctuated among accurate renderings, fantastic reconstructions, warm evocations, and the blond city views and capriccios of the *veduta*, or view, painters. Over the course of the seventeenth century, the formal role of ruins within Dutch works also evolved. Each generation sought different effects and utilized the architectural motifs accordingly. As narrative components, ancient ruins helped to establish a foreign setting, distant in both time and place. As iconographic elements, Roman ruins presented a paradox, functioning concurrently as symbols of the grandiose achievements of the past and elegiac reminders of the destructive power of time. As compositional elements, ruins could be manipulated in many ways: isolated or clustered together for picturesque effect; shown in situ or transported to a new location; shown as a distant element in a landscape or placed in the foreground to encourage close study. While drawing on an established repertoire of identifiable buildings, individual artists also followed personal preferences, favoring specific monuments or generic structures, as well as restricting or expanding the prominence of the ruin motif within their works. In fact, seventeenth-century Dutch artists exercised great freedom in their interpretation of Roman ruins and rarely depicted identifiable structures with much precision. This approach changed only late in the century, as the Dutch specialization of cityscape painting was transported to the Roman milieu. Prior to this, factual observations were usually confined to graphic works. Indeed, there is a striking variance in topographical accuracy between images sketched out of doors and those painted in the studio. As we shall see, these differences in approach reveal much about seventeenth-century art theory, practice, and markets.

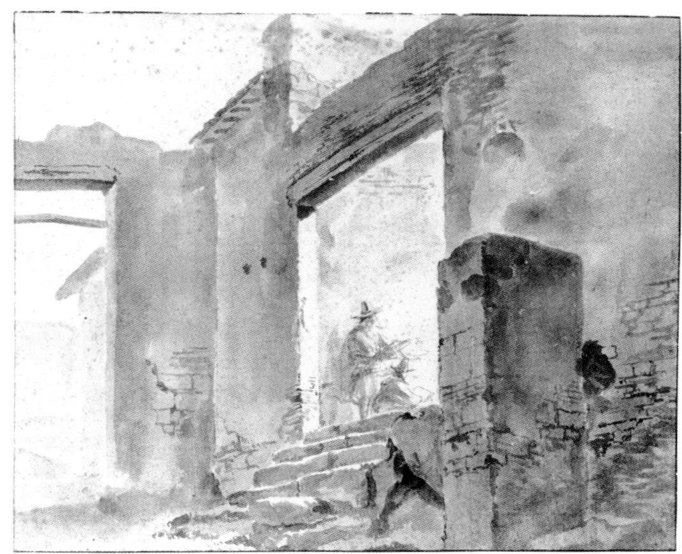

FIGURE 77. Jan Baptist Weenix, *Two Artists Drawing in a Ruin*, c. 1645, gray wash on paper. Museum Boijmans Van Beuningen, Rotterdam.

Historical Background

In the seventeenth century, Rome occupied a privileged position among European cities, recognized simultaneously as the seat of the Catholic popes, the repository of Europe's ancient classical heritage, and the center of artistic innovation. Rome was the premier destination of artistic pilgrims, as much as it was for Catholic pilgrims. Encouraged by the success of their compatriots, Northern artists visited Rome in increasing numbers, seeking to hone their skill in the "capital" of the schools of painting.[4] From the distant vantage point of our era of "how to" travel films and videos, electronic booking, and comfortable transportation, it is difficult to imagine the hardships of a seventeenth-century journey taking weeks on foot, horseback, coach, and/or ship to reach Italy from Northern Europe. But the obligatory trip to Italy was a common topos in art commentary of the period.[5] For artists, the value of such an experience lay in the unparalleled wealth of visual sensations that awaited: the celebrated artistic achievements of Renaissance masters, including Raphael and Michelangelo; the novel works of Caravaggio and the Carracci, who had revolutionized contemporary Italian painting; to say nothing of the impact of the beauty, color, and warmth of the Italian countryside. The promise of patronage also provided a practical reason for Northern artists to seek their fortunes in Rome, as the city experienced a surge of expansion and construction under the aegis of the Counter-Reformation popes. Having reached their destination, seventeenth-century travelers were confronted by two realities: the spectacle of modern Christian Rome and the vast, decaying fabric of ancient imperial Rome. Then, as today, Early Christian, Renaissance, and Baroque churches, palaces, and civic buildings competed with pagan structures for the visitor's attention.

Over a thousand-year span, Rome had declined steadily and precipitously, the victim of barbarian invasion and occupation. Its population, once numbering almost a million, constricted to a few tens of thousands, and about 80 percent of land within the ancient city walls was uninhabited, reclaimed by swamplands or used for vineyards or grazing.[6] With time, the abandoned imperial structures deteriorated, their crumbling walls offering shelter to the poor and/or providing ready building materials for the ruling classes. But slowly, during the Middle Ages, a European-wide appreciation for the intellectual and physical legacy of antiquity emerged, and it sharpened during the Renaissance and Baroque centuries. Growing interest in ancient Greek and Roman literature and culture spurred efforts to save the remaining classical structures. Several Renaissance popes advocated for the preservation of Rome's ancient monuments, realizing both their intrinsic value and the symbolic value of building a new, Christian Rome amid, if not actually from, the pagan ruins.[7] Nonetheless, the destruction of the ancient structures continued; structures such as the Colosseum were assaulted by builders carrying papal permits granting salvage privileges. Blocks of travertine and other worked stones were carried off to be reused "as is." More destructive was the burning of incalculable quantities of marble, including even statuary, in the limekilns to make powdered lime for use as aggregate for mortar. Decrying the process, Raphael said: "I would be so bold to say that all of this new Rome, however great it may be, however beautiful, however embellished with palaces, churches and other buildings, all of this is built with mortar made from ancient marbles."[8] But the laments of artists and antiquarians, as well as the edicts of sympathetic popes and the city's governing council, proved ineffectual.[9] In fact, the destruction of Rome's architectural remains continued well into the eighteenth century.

A number of important monuments were despoiled during the seventeenth century; for example, during the reign of Urban VIII Barberini, Gianlorenzo Bernini (1598–1680) supervised the removal of the bronze cladding from the porch of the Pantheon. Melted down, it was recast into his Baldacchino for St. Peter's high altar. Contemporary critics charged, "What the barbarians didn't do, the Barberini did!"

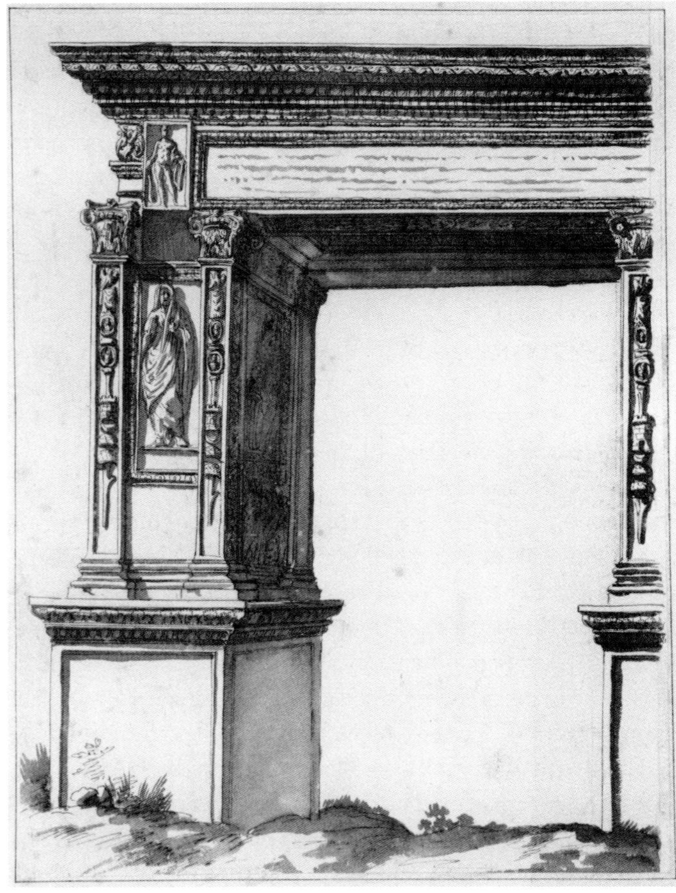

FIGURE 78. Unidentified artist, *Arch of the Argentarii, Forum Boarium, Rome*, c. 1625–35, pen and ink on paper. The Royal Collection, Her Majesty Queen Elizabeth II, Royal Library, Windsor.

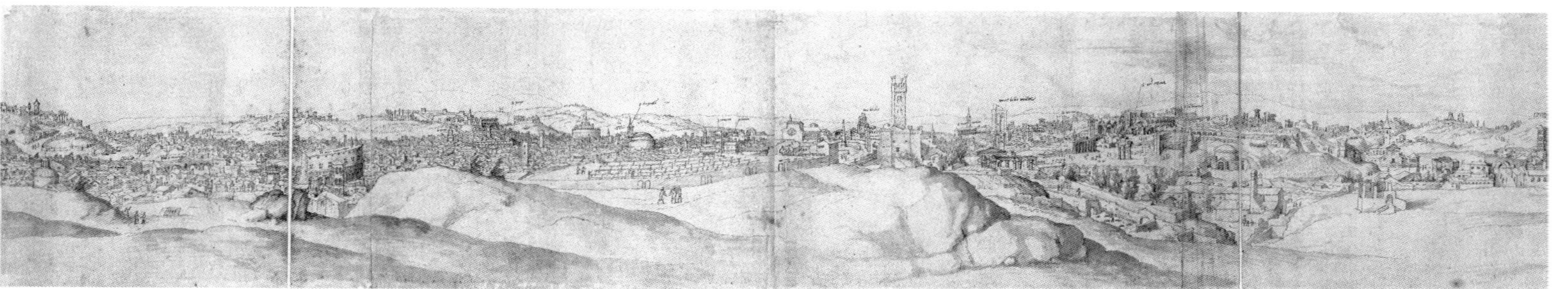

FIGURE 79. Maerten van Heemskerck, *Panoramic View of Rome*, c. 1535, pen and ink on paper. Kupferstichkabinett, Staatliche Museen, Berlin.

Fortunately, thousands of careful drawings (Fig. 78), such as those ordered by the antiquarian Cassiano dal Pozzo, catalogue various types of antiquities and aid in our understanding of what has been lost.[10]

Sixteenth-Century Precedents

In the seventeenth century, unlike our own image-flooded era, prospective travelers had to rely on the verbal or written recollections of returning travelers or on the Italian imagery of the few Northern artists who had ventured south in the late fifteenth and early sixteenth centuries.[11] The remarkable sketchbooks of Maerten van Heemskerck (1498–1574) now provide some of the most complete visual records of sixteenth-century Rome.[12] Among the many images of the city and its architectural and sculptural monuments is a panoramic view of Rome (c. 1535; Fig. 79). The city spreads before us, a combination of pockets of population, scattered vineyards, and deserted expanse. Ancient monuments appear, some in ruins, others well preserved; some in isolation, others in the midst of the sixteenth-century town. Mirroring reality, Heemskerck contrasts ancient and modern, pagan and Christian, derelict and functioning elements of the cityscape.[13]

Heemskerck's own assessment of the value of his exposure to the culture of antiquity is suggested by his self-portrait of 1553 (Fig. 80). As if to document his travels, the artist juxtaposes his visage with the Colosseum, the grandest of Rome's ruins. Here Heemskerck plays with concepts of time and illusion, depicting himself twice—the larger image represents him in his mid-fifties (his age when the self-portrait was actually painted) and a reduced image represents his younger self in the fictive painting within this painting. The smaller self-portrait recaptures Heemskerck's appearance during his Italian sojourn in the mid-1530s, when seated out of doors he drew the ancient monuments around him. The motif of the artist working not in his studio but out in the field is of great significance to our understanding of the evolution of European artistic procedures and reveals direct observation as the key to Dutch realism.[14] Here, in addition to suggesting the importance of personal retrospection, which the ruins encourage, Heemskerck declares his firsthand Italian experience as an important aspect of his artistic credentials.[15]

A wider Northern audience was introduced to the marvels of the ancient city by Flemish artist and publisher Hieronymus Cock (c. 1510–70). In Antwerp in 1551, Cock published the first of several print series featuring views of Roman ruins.[16] These widely popular engravings convey the complex layering of monuments from different eras—ancient, Early Christian, medieval, and Renaissance—that gives the city of Rome its essential personality even today. To a Northern public with no direct experience, the Cock prints, such as *Forum Roman a Colosseo* (Fig. 81), conveyed much information about the vast number, configuration, scale, and condition of Rome's ancient monuments. However, except for later prints after Sebastian van Noyen's (1493–1557) reconstruction of the baths of Diocletian,[17] Cock's renderings are

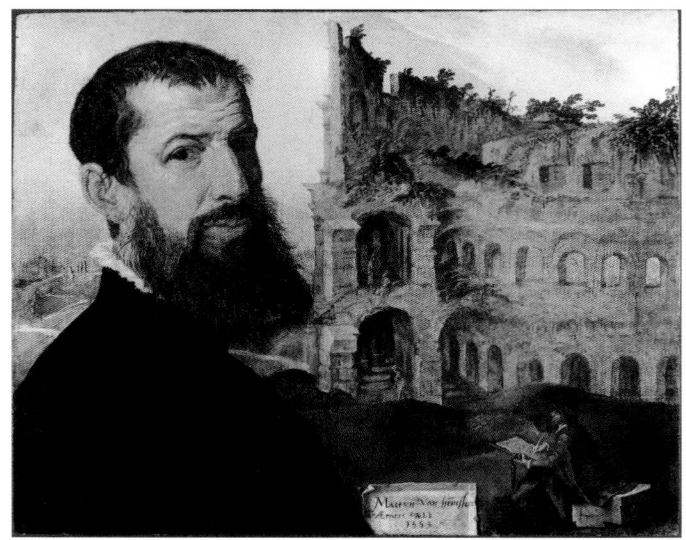

FIGURE 80. Maerten van Heemskerck, *Portrait of the Painter, with the Colosseum*, 1553, oil on panel. Fitzwilliam Musuem, Cambridge.

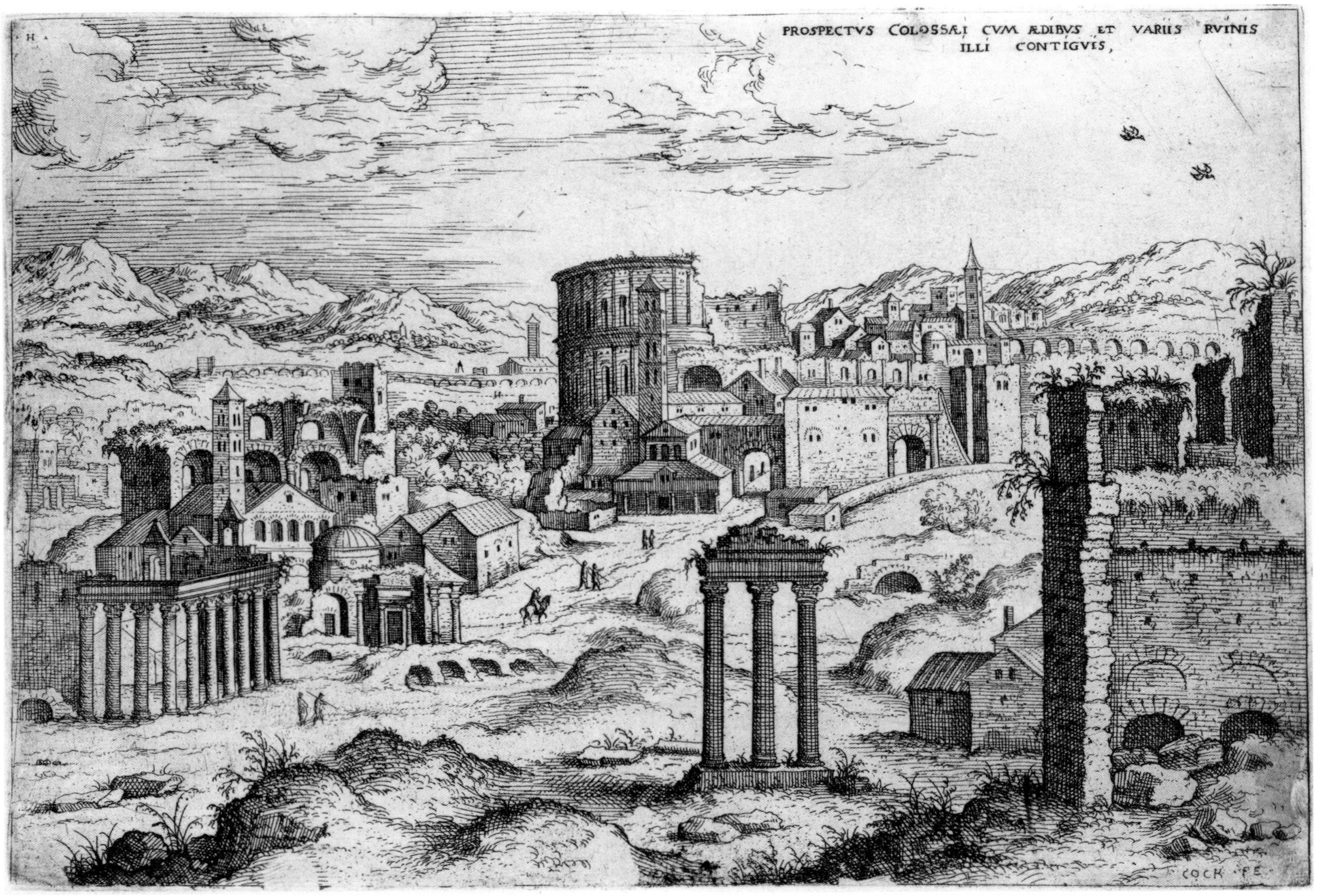

FIGURE 81. Hieronymus Cock, *Roman Forum and Colosseum*, 1551, engraving. Rijksprentenkabinet, Rijksmuseum, Amsterdam.

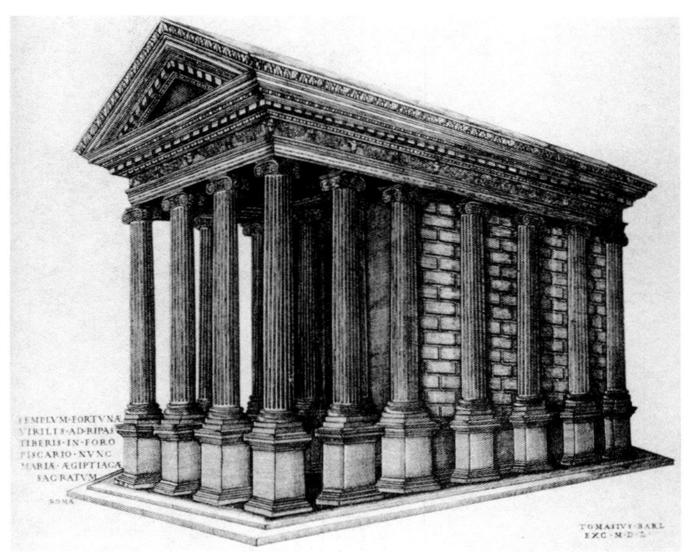

FIGURE 82. Nicolas Beatrizot, *Temple of Fortune*, 1550, engraving. British Museum, London.

informative but not scientific. Comparison with Italian prints of the same period reveals the picturesque nature of Cock's images. For example, the *Temple of Fortune* (Fig. 82) by Nicolas Beatrizot (1507/15–c. 1565) is isolated from any setting, the building rendered like a specimen, drawn with a precise, analytical line. In contrast, Cock delighted in the patterns created by the fragmentary arches of tunnels and vaults of the Colosseum, for example (see Fig. 3), and the lacy designs of invasive foliage. Overall, the approach casts the ancient ruins as an extensive backdrop of picturesque, if decaying, grandeur that dwarfs and trivializes contemporary life. Cock's original images established for Northern artists both the standard for print series of Roman ruins and a favored repertoire of monuments and viewpoints.[18] With subject matter so different from the typical Netherlandish fare of portraiture and scenes of everyday life, these novel prints found a wide market.

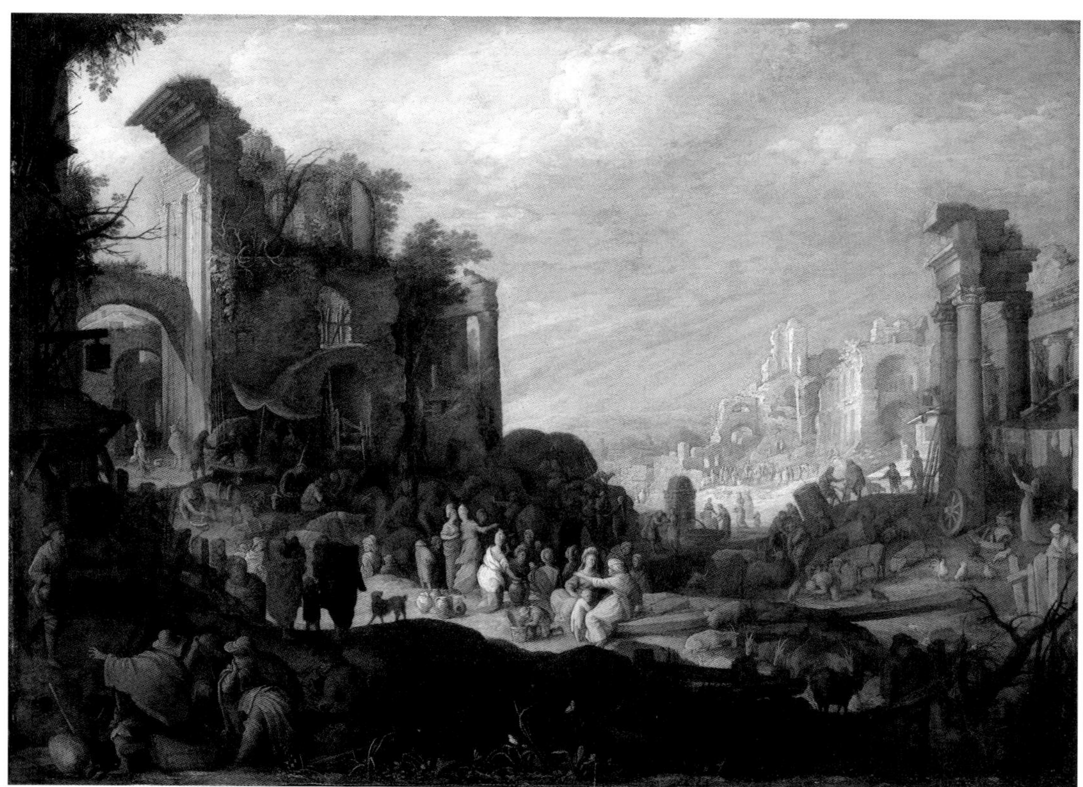

FIGURE 83. Paulus Bril, *Landscape with Roman Ruins*, c. 1610–15, oil on copper. Rijksmuseum, Amsterdam.

A Repertoire of Ruins

Although the identity and function of many of Rome's imperial ruins were known, such historical associations seem to have mattered little to Dutch artists as they selected pictorial motifs for their paintings. From the onset, the primacy of the Colosseum as historical artifact and pictorial subject was acknowledged by Cock, who devoted the first six prints of his Roman series to it.[19] Some famous monuments, such as the well-preserved Pantheon and Castel Sant'Angelo, appear relatively infrequently, while other structures, such as the Septizonium with its multistoried façade, continued to be depicted even after demolished.[20] Among recognizable buildings, it is often the most damaged that are depicted. Artists seemed to have taken special pleasure in the irregular outlines and repetitive light/dark patterns of such complex structures as the badly disfigured Palatine, the Temple of Minerva Medica (see Cat. 56), and the substructure of the Palace of Septimius Severus.[21] Generic structural types, again particularly those with complex systems of arched forms—the technology that allowed the Romans to span vast spaces—as well as isolated columns or fragmentary porticoes, predominate in their paintings. More compact monuments, such as the triumphal arches and the pyramid of Caius Cestius (Fig. 18), provided classical quotations where desired. In addition, favored sights beyond the city such as hill-top structures at Tivoli (Cats. 3b, 59, and 65) or the Claudian aqueduct in the Roman campagna provided appealing visual drama. Netherlandish artists certainly warmed to this foreign vocabulary of grand architectural forms, so different in scale from most Northern buildings.

Transitional Generation

For landscape painters, as for figure painters, Rome was a major center of Baroque innovation. Imported by specialists, including Adam Elsheimer (1578–1610) and Jan Brueghel the Elder (1568–1625), the Northern landscape tradition mixed with the artistic preoccupations of the Italian painters who experimented with this newly acceptable subject matter, including Annibale Carraci (1560–1609), Domenichino (1581–1641), and less-known artists such as Agostino Tassi (c. 1580–1644) and Filippo Angeli, called Napoletano (c. 1587–1638). During this period, intense focus on landscape painting led to major advancements in the genre. Among the community of foreign landscape artists working in Rome in the late sixteenth and early seventeenth centuries, the Flemish artist Paulus Bril (1554–1626) became a pivotal figure. Reaching Rome by 1582,[22] Bril capitalized on contacts with influential individuals that had already been established by his brother Matthijs (1550–83).[23] These initial contacts served Paulus well throughout his own career. Unlike the majority of traveling artists, particularly landscape specialists, he enjoyed the steady patronage of popes, members of the curia and Roman aristocracy, as well as wealthy Northern merchants.[24] Financial security allowed Bril to establish a large workshop, which became the focal point of contact and potential employment for other Northern artists in Rome. There, artistic ideas, elements of style, and attitudes toward subject matter would naturally have been shared and expropriated.

Bril frequently used Italian buildings, whether imaginary structures or identifiable ruins, in the background of his paintings, as in *Landscape with Roman Ruins* (Fig. 83). Here is laid out the essential formula used in many early seventeenth-century images of Roman ruins: a dark repoussoir element introduces the viewer into the pictorial space; the figural action is carried out in the middle distance by relatively tiny players; and the architectural elements, functioning as stage flats, partially screen the view into the distance. The ruins operate on two levels within the image; first as a compositional device to order the pictorial space. Second, although based on actual ruins (here including the Temple of Minerva in the Forum of Nerva), the fantastic and towering fragmentary ruins remove the action from the mundane world. It is instructive to compare Bril's painted depiction with a drawing of the Forum of Nerva (Fig. 84) by his brother. Obviously, they sought different effects, one descriptive and topographical, the other theatrical.

Bril gradually discarded the typical mannerist stylizations of the late sixteenth century for the more realistic and balanced compositions of the emergent Baroque. This may be due in part to his greater interaction with nature itself; his drawings suggest that he had begun to take more seriously Karel van Mander's (1548–1606) advice to go out into nature every day to observe and draw.[25] The drawings of younger artists in Bril's orbit, such as Willem van Nieulandt the Younger (q.v.) and Gerard ter Borch the Elder (1582/83–1662),[26] reflect this practice. Compared with the imaginative paintings by these artists, such drawings reveal a much more realistic approach and are particularly instructive for the student of Rome's antiquities.

Bril's less well-known student Willem van Nieulandt adopted many of Bril's characteristics, including the taste for ruins.[27] He recorded his impressions of Rome during a brief sojourn there around 1602–4.[28] Typical of his generation, Van Nieulandt's draftsmanship is characterized by a quiet, descriptive idiom, as seen in these appealing pen drawings (Fig. 85). Artists usually kept such sketches, as they provided a portfolio of motifs.[29] After his return north, some of Van Nieulandt's Roman drawings were engraved and included in his series of views of Rome. Even some of his later drawings, such as the *View of the Colosseum from the Caelian Hill* of 1620 in Leiden,[30] are most likely re-workings of sketches drawn in Rome. From the early seventeenth century onward, this pattern of creative progression is repeated: informal sketches done out of doors become the source material for more for-

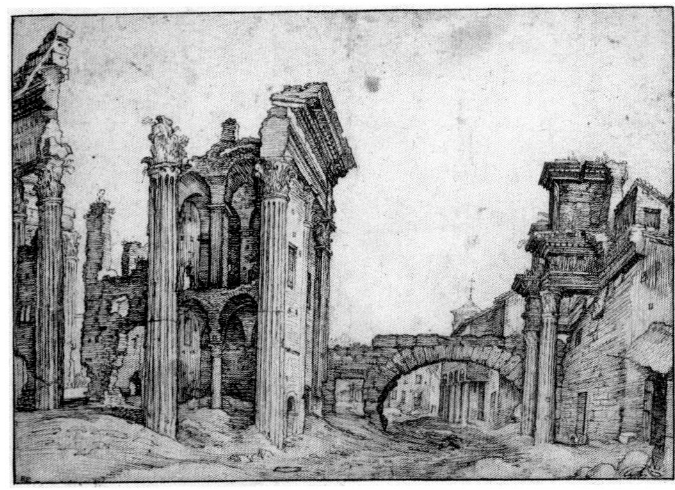

FIGURE 84. Matthijs Bril, *View of the Forum of Nerva*, c. 1580, pen and brown ink on paper. Cabinet des Arts Graphiques, Musée du Louvre, Paris.

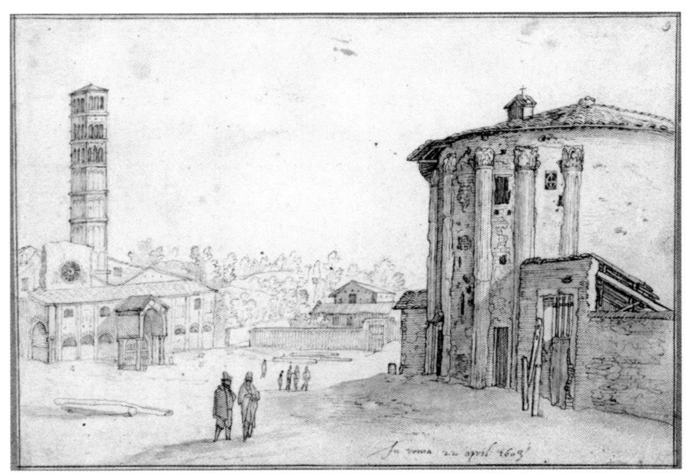

FIGURE 85. Willem van Nieulandt the Younger, *The Temple of Vesta and Santa Maria in Cosmedin in the Background*, 1603, pen and ink and brown wash on paper. Curtis O. Baer Collection, on deposit in the National Gallery of Art, Washington, D.C.

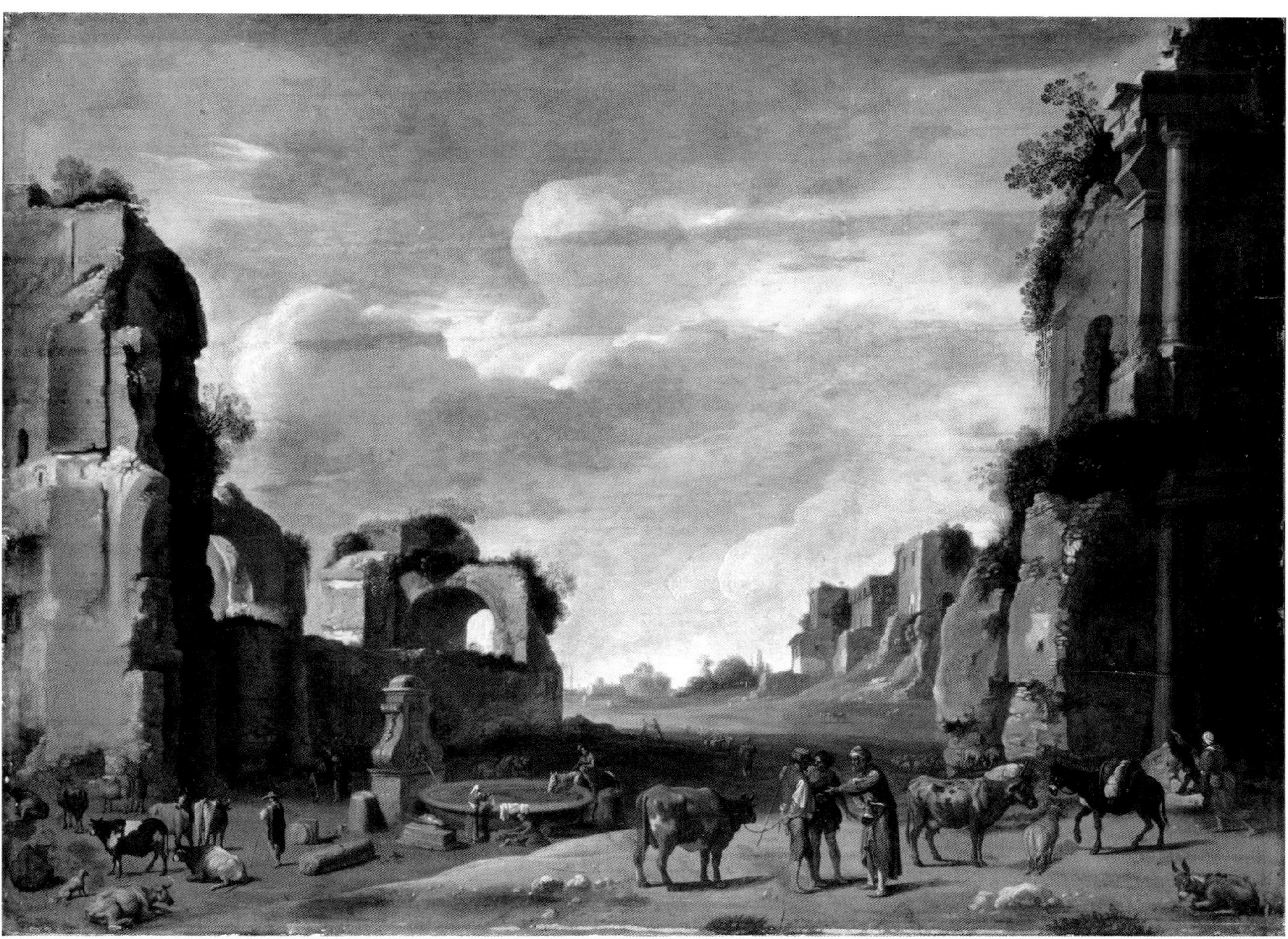

FIGURE 86. Cornelis van Poelenburch, *Fantasy View of the Campo Vaccino with Two Donkeys*, 1620, oil on panel. Musée du Louvre, Paris.

mal painted compositions. This follows artistic conventions of the time: the formality of "art" interjects itself between first impression and finished work. For the Dutch Italianate artists, their drawings made in Italy continued to supply popular foreign motifs for new compositions, whether paintings or prints, long after they returned home.[31]

First Generation of Dutch Italianate Landscape Artists

This relationship between drawn and painted images is also seen in the work of the next generation of Dutch landscapists active in Rome, whose contribution to the Dutch genre of ruins painting is a matter of both interpretation and technique. Cornelis van Poelenburch (q.v.) and Bartholomeus Breenbergh (q.v.), who both trained in the studio of Abraham Bloemaert (q.v.) in their native Utrecht, reached Rome separately late in the second decade of the century.[32] By 1619 they were both recorded living in the neighborhood of the Piazza del Popolo. This colorful area was favored by foreigners living in Rome, in part because papal tax incentives encouraged settlement of this previously underpopulated district. Northern artists congregated there, their movements from house to house recorded in the yearly Easter census. Together Poelenburch and Breenbergh were founding members of the eccentric confraternity of Northern artists resident in Rome, called the Schildersbent (artists' clique).[33]

Poelenburch's early style reflects the influence of Bril. But dispensing with Bril's artificialities, he achieved a more realistic formula of his own, which he repeated throughout his career (Fig. 86). Poelenburch increased the believability of the spatial construction by lowering the ground plane and changing its relationship, now almost perpendicular, to the pictorial surface. As had become conventional (Cats. 15, 50, 51, 53, 54, 56, and 57), Poelenburch included classical archi-

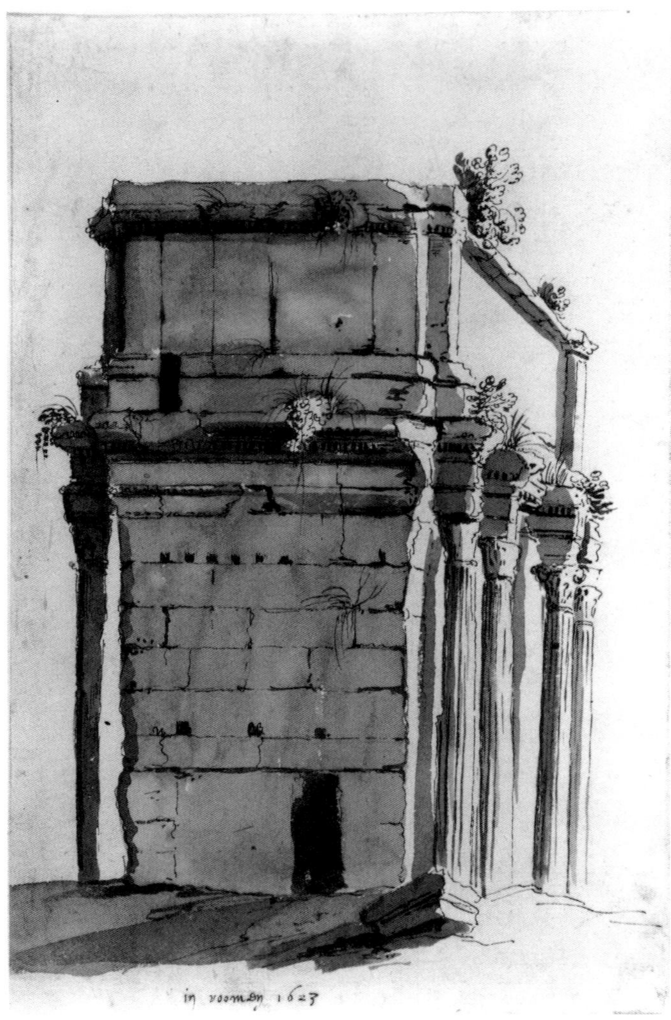

FIGURE 87. Cornelis van Poelenburch, *Arch of Septimius Severus, Rome*, 1623, pen and brown ink and wash over black chalk. The J. Paul Getty Museum, Los Angeles.

tectural elements in his landscapes to set his narratives of biblical, historical, or mythological origin in a distant past (Cat. 67). While his scenery is recognizable as Roman, or at least Italian, he displayed a selective interest in the realities of Roman topography. The Musée du Louvre's *Fantasy View of the Campo Vaccino* of 1620 (Fig. 86), one of a set of four early views of the Roman Forum, is a case in point (see also Fig. 17). Poelenburch plays with the actual placement of the various buildings, rearranging them to suit his sense of composition. The weighty ancient buildings serve to anchor the ground plane and figures, heightening the stability of the image and establishing a mood of calm, enhanced by the subtle color scheme. The result is a quiet, measured, and seemingly factual presentation of an imaginary landscape that is not really topographically accurate.

In contrast to his paintings, Poelenburch's drawings are dramatic, suggesting the artist's immediate response to the motif before him. His luminous technique augments the pen strokes with a fluid wash; the paper itself is given a greater role to play, simulating brilliant sunlight. When it is turned on the classical ruins, the result is dazzling (Fig. 87). In comparison, the tight, analytical penmanship of earlier artists seems very clinical. Poelenburch's lush technique captures the effect and intensity of strong contrasts of sun and shade typical of southern locales. While inherent in the subject itself, the achieved theatricality is also in keeping with the Baroque taste for the dramatic.

While Breenbergh employed a more expansive format in his paintings than Poelenburch, the broad spatial recession is still marked off by outcroppings of ruins, whether generic or identifiable (see, for example, Cats. 52–55). The human drama of his chosen subjects, often episodes from the Bible, is diffused, the comparatively small figures swallowed up by the spacious setting. Often it is the ruins themselves that create

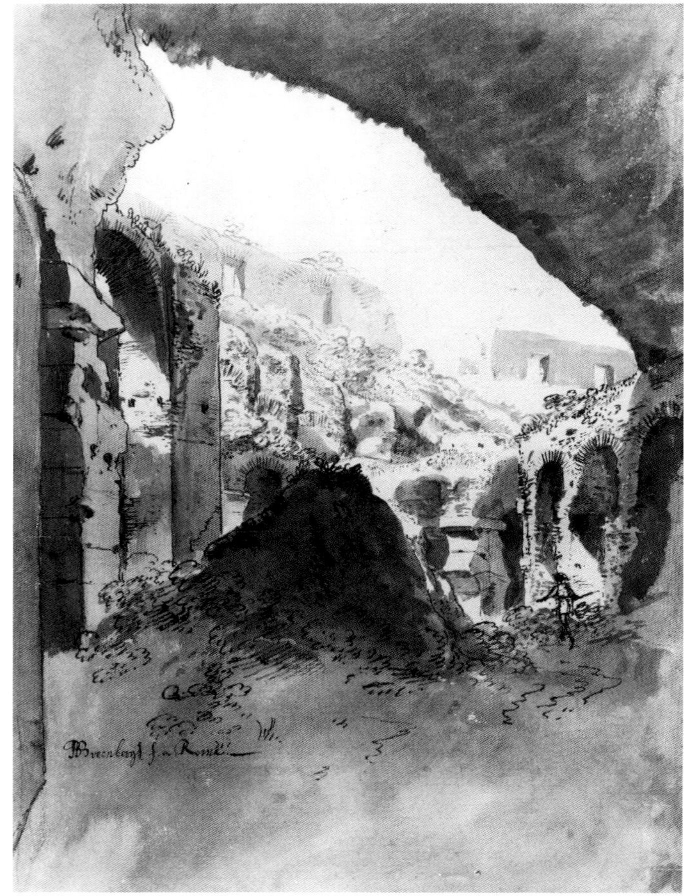

FIGURE 88. Bartholomeus Breenbergh, *View of the Colosseum*, c. 1620–25, pen and brown ink and wash over black chalk. Graphische Sammlung, Staatliche Museen, Kassel.

the compositional crescendo within Breenbergh's paintings. But a similar duality between painted and sketched works appears in the output of Breenbergh.

Together Breenbergh and Poelenburch produced some of the most brilliant drawings of the Italian scene. Their technique is particularly well suited to rendering awe-inspiring monuments, lush gardens, and picturesque hill-top towns, such as the perennial favorite, Tivoli, seen under an intense Mediterranean sunlight. Again we sense the presence of Paulus Bril at the foundations of this style.[34] But in the hands of the younger artists, the full dramatic potential of the medium is realized. Note, for example, Breenbergh's drawing of the Colosseum (Fig. 88) now in the Staatliche Museen, Kassel.[35] The artist's vantage point is low: he has positioned himself deep within the tunnel-like archways of the structure, looking toward the arena's sunlit center. This sightline creates a typically Baroque theatricality as the building rises up around, above, and in front of the viewer. The dramatic angle is further accentuated by the light/dark contrasts of wash and paper, evoking the strong lighting effects; in such works, the subject and medium are perfectly aligned.

Patronage

Recognized as leaders in the landscape genre, a number of foreign artists found patronage among European aristocratic collectors. For example, Herman van Swanevelt (q.v.), Claude Lorrain (1600–1682), Nicolas Poussin (1593/94–1665), and Jan Both (q.v.), among others, were commissioned by Don Manuel de Moura, marqués de Castel Rodrigo, for paintings to decorate Buen Retiro Palace, a country retreat planned for Philip IV in Madrid. Such royal patronage was rather unusual for Northern landscape artists, especially since throughout this period, "history painting"—concerning itself with stories of biblical, historical, or mythological origin—commanded the preeminent position among art theorists and critics. Nonetheless several of the artists that we have discussed did attract the attention of leading collectors in Rome and beyond.[36] For example, arriving in Rome about 1575, Matthijs Bril worked on decorative projects in the Vatican palace for Gregory XIII.[37] Poelenburch found patronage in Rome, as well as in Florence with Cosimo II de' Medici and in London with Charles I.[38] Jan Baptist Weenix (q.v.) had a number of wealthy patrons, both in Rome, where he worked for Innocent X and Prince Camillo Pamphili, and in his native Utrecht, where on his return from Italy, he collaborated with the collector Baron van Wyttenhorst.[39] Dutch Italianate paintings, with their Mediterranean warmth and pastoral imagery, found favor with markets in Northern Europe; especially in England, they were highly prized well

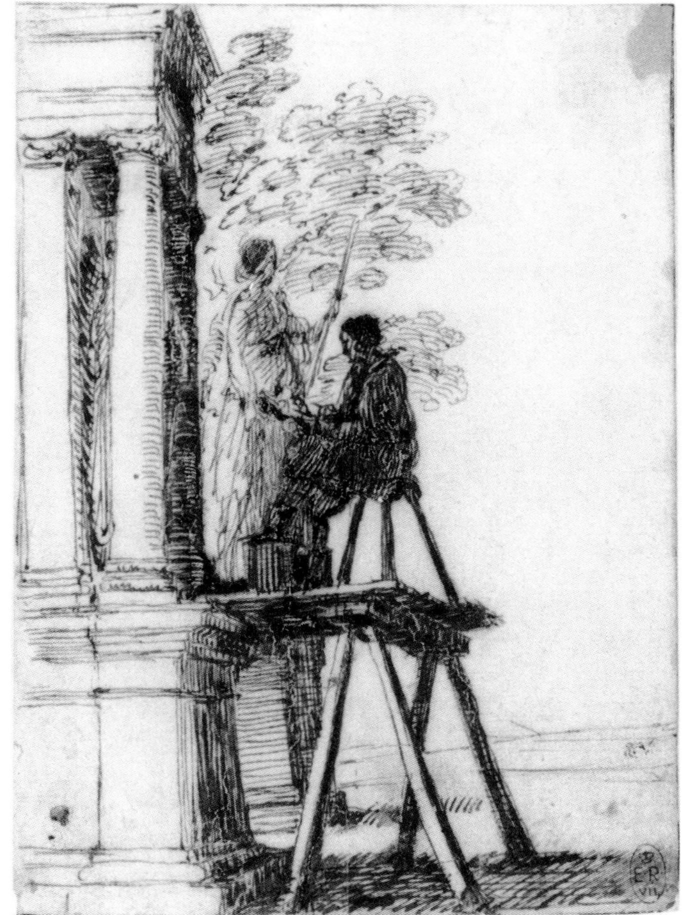

FIGURE 89. Claude Lorrain, *Draughtsman in Front of a Statue*, c. 1630, pen and brown ink on paper. The Royal Collection, Her Majesty Queen Elizabeth II, Royal Library, Windsor.

into the nineteenth century. Typically, the many painters specializing in small landscapes painted for a popular market.

Direct Study of Nature

What distinguishes the paintings of the leading foreign landscape artists working in Rome is their ability to evoke a mood through their depictions of nature. As others had done, they relied on standard motifs—temples or ruins—to place their narrative beyond the contemporary world. But through their direct experience of nature, studied from life, these artists imbued their images with greater realism and, at the same time, made them more powerfully evocative of the arcadian landscape of antiquity, known through literature. In an often-cited passage, Joachim van Sandrart (1606–88) references going into the Roman countryside on sketching trips with Claude, Poussin, and the Dutchman Pieter van Laer (1599–1642).[40] Earlier generations of artists had sketched out of doors; see, for example, Heemskerck's self-portrait (Fig. 80). But the seventeenth-century confrontation with nature was intense and sustained. The same concentration was directed toward observation of ancient monuments (Fig. 89). While perfecting their renderings of specific places and monuments, these artists became increasingly perceptive of actual atmospheric conditions. Illusionistic effects began to pervade their landscape paintings. The warm sunlight and hazy atmospherics of Swanevelt's depictions of the Roman countryside were to influence subsequent Dutch Italianates, including Jan Both (q.v.) and his contemporaries.

Second Generation of Dutch Italianate Painters

A new wave of Dutch artists congregated in Rome in the 1630s and 1640s, and they dealt with the ruin motif very differently. Artistically, this generation coalesced around Pieter van Laer, and they were collectively known as the *Bamboccianti*, after his nickname, "Bamboccio" (Clumsy Doll).[41] Following his example, these artists, including Andries (1612/13–42) and Jan Both and Johannes Lingelbach (1622–74) specialized in low-life scenes based on their observations in the slums of Rome. There, the daily life of the poor and working classes intersected with the classical ruins. The relationship between architectural setting and figures has shifted: the field of vision constricted, the figures increased in size, and the architectural backdrop gained in importance. The spectator experiences the colorful ambience of Roman street life through proximity with street types and architecture. Images of generic ruins add regional flavor to their paintings. In the occasional painting where identifiable monuments appear, as for example Jan Both's *Roman Street Scene* (Fig. 90), signature monuments, such as a reconstructed Colosseum, are grouped together in an imaginative configuration. It has been argued that in such works, the artists consciously constructed a paradox, the Roman ruins exemplifying both "Rome's eternal greatness and ... its transience."[42] Whether or not this is the case, the reality of seventeenth-century Rome was that the ruined remains of imperial Rome formed the backdrop to the trivial, but universal, activities of everyday life; the juxtaposition is inherently ironic.

The Dutch appreciation for Roman ruins reached its evocative high point in the works of Jan Asselijn (after 1610–52) and Nicolaes Berchem (q.v.), whose flushed color schemes invest their depictions of ruins with a truly romantic character. Asselijn often depicted large-scale ruins viewed at close range, as in a series of drawings (Fig. 91) later engraved by Gabriel Perelle (c. 1603–77).[43] Asselijn emphasized the disparity of scale between the vast, yet fragmentary, architectural forms and the tiny figures of travelers and herdsmen. Internal contradictions between light and shade, spatial projections and recessions, and figural movement animate the otherwise quiet compositions. Yet the timeless rhythms of human activity prove insignificant when juxtaposed with the increments of time relevant to ancient ruins. Asselijn creates a palpable sense of time and place through careful observation and transcription of effects of light and atmosphere. Bathed in a warm afternoon glow, his painted Italian landscapes (Fig. 92) establish a slow rhythm. Time lengthens as one contemplates the ruins, and such contemplation provokes a conscious sense of the passage of time.

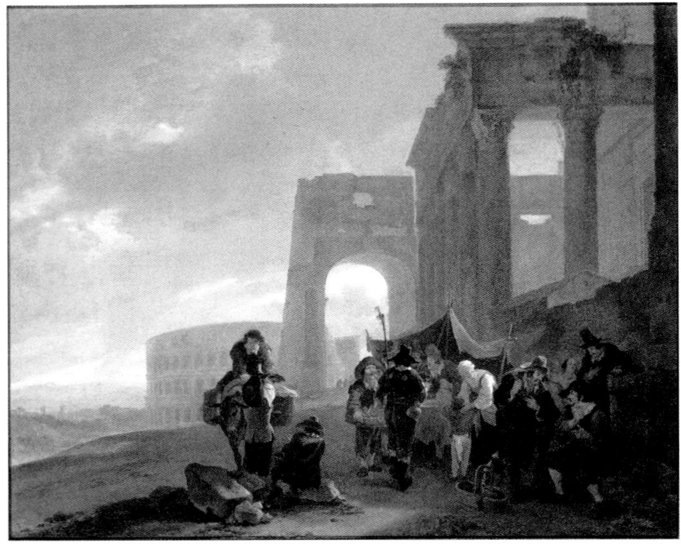

FIGURE 90. Jan Both, *Roman Street Scene*, c. 1641, oil on canvas. Rijksmuseum, Amsterdam.

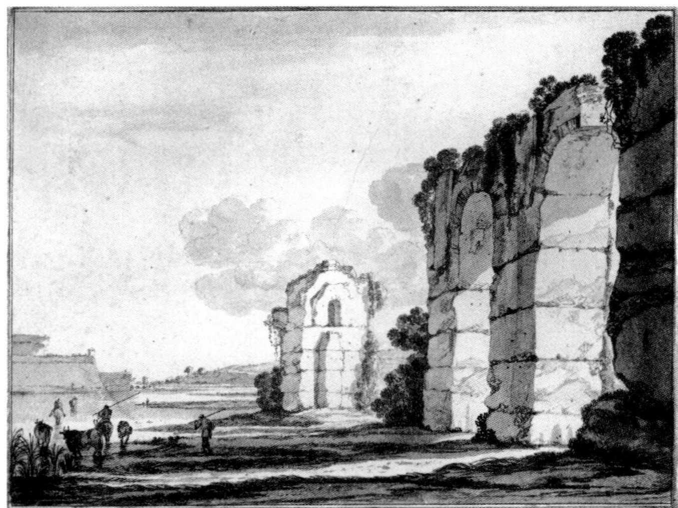

FIGURE 91. Jan Asselijn, *Aqueduct at Frascati*, c. 1640–45, pen and ink and wash on paper. The Pierpont Morgan Library, New York.

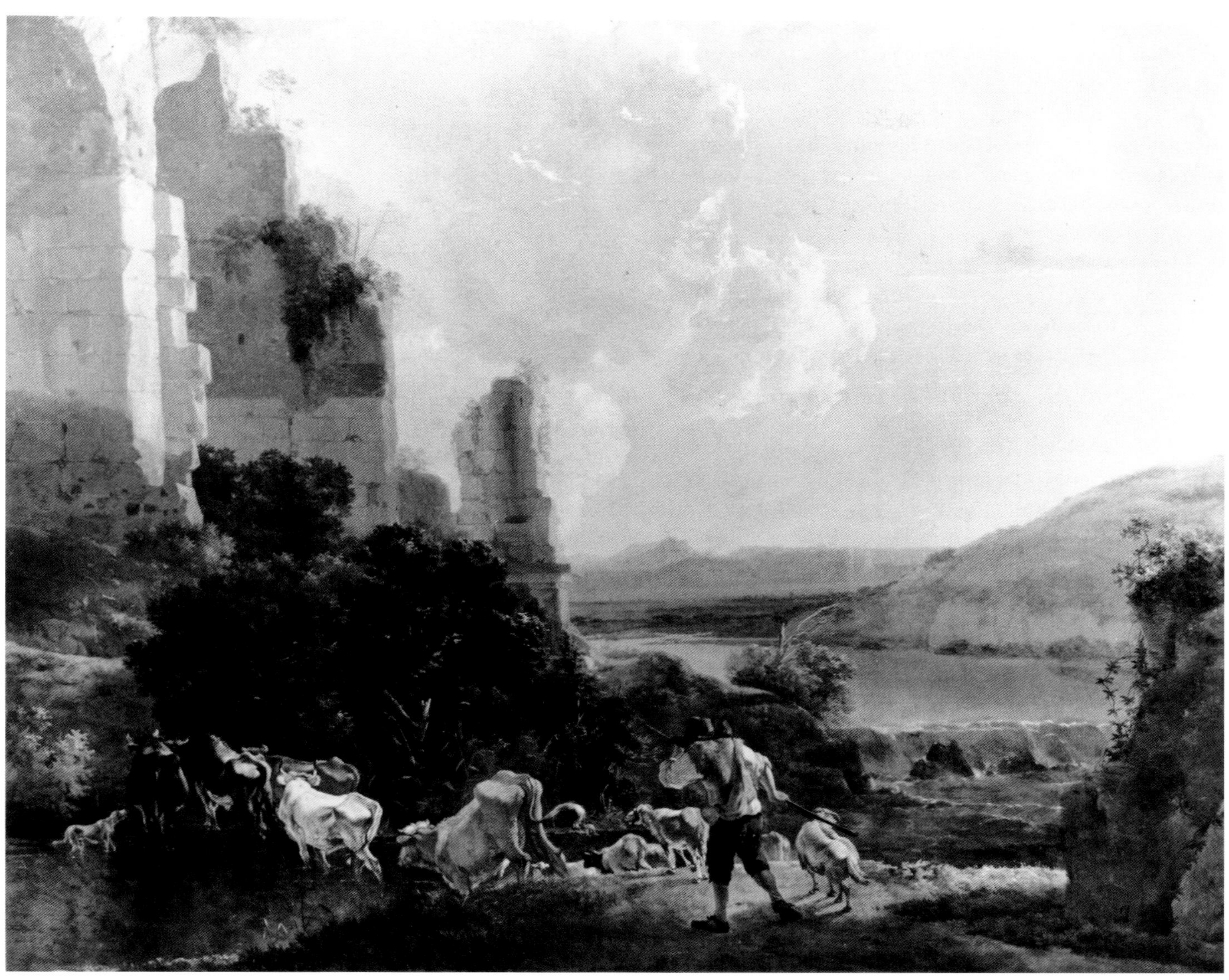

FIGURE 92. Jan Asselijn, *The Ford*, c. 1649, oil on canvas. Gemäldegalerie der Akademie der bildenden Künste, Vienna.

Coda

The achievements of the last generation of seventeenth-century Dutch artists working in Italy serve as a coda to the those of their counterparts earlier in the century. Less vigorously individualistic artists such as Hendrik Frans van Lint (1684–1763) and Jacob de Heusch (1656–1701) adapted to shifts in fashion and/or adopted the idiom of others more talented than they. Preference was shown for the styles of the leading French landscapists, particularly the classical mode established by Poussin and Gaspard Dughet (1615–75). In these late seventeenth-century Dutch classicizing landscapes, the ancient monuments are once again relegated to establishing an arcadian setting for their historical narratives or used to punctuate their geometrically ordered compositions. Reflecting the transfer of artistic authority from Rome to Paris, the influence of French art overpowered many Dutch artists. However, through the work of Gaspard van Wittel, called Vanvitelli (1653–1736), the Dutch school made one more major contribution to Italian art. His artistic approach shared much with the early topographical efforts of the first Northern artists working in Rome. It was the modern city of Rome that preoccupied Vanvitelli. However, while the ancient ruins that had dominated the art of his countrymen figure relatively infrequently in his output, Vanvitelli was not completely immune to their pictorial potential. The Colosseum, in particular, figures in a number of his paintings, many of almost postcard size. See, for example, *The View of the Colosseum and the Arch of Constantine* in the collection of Viscount Coke.[44] Vanvitelli's pictures, his gouache medium often giving them a delicate pastel coloring, function as pleasant souvenirs of Italy. Turning his trained Dutch eye on Rome's urban vistas, Vanvitelli laid the groundwork for the great *veduta*, or view, painters of the eighteenth century, including Giovanni Paolo Panini (c. 1692–1765/68), Giovanni Battista Piranesi (1720–78), and Giovanni Antonio Canaletto (1697–1768). While not as highly keyed coloristically as the works of the previous generation, the blond tonalities of Vanvitelli's Italian city views became treasured as souvenir postcards of the Grand Tour.

With Vanvitelli, the Dutch representation of ancient ruins comes full circle, returning to a topographical approach, similar to that of Hieronymus Cock (Fig. 81), yet newly updated and fashionable—an approach that sought to describe the picturesque Roman cityscape with its wealth of monuments of divergent age and style. Generations of Dutch Italianate artists responded enthusiastically to the visual stimuli of seventeenth-century Rome, producing a wide range of interpretations of the city, its inhabitants and monuments. The vacillation between topographical accuracy and fanciful imagination evident in their works was the expression of both personal and generational preferences and mirrored general developments in seventeenth-century art. But through their painting, prints, and drawings, these masters share with the viewer something of the wonder they experienced in front of the architectural legacy of classical antiquity.

NOTES

1. For an extended passage from Hildebert de Lavardin's poem "De Roma" with its "interweaving of ... love of ancient Rome, of her divinely preordained destruction and the victory of Christ," see Krautheimer 1980, 200–201.

2. As translated in Woodward 2001, 10.

3. The term "Dutch Italianate" refers to Dutch artists who worked in Italy and brought a distinctive Italian vocabulary to their landscapes, cityscapes, harbor views, and genre scenes. Sometimes realistic, but more frequently imaginary, their topography evokes the realities of Italian scenery or the arcadian landscape described in classical, Renaissance, and Baroque literature. The term is also applied to those artists who adopted this idiom, even though they themselves never visited Italy, such as Aelbert Cuyp (q.v.). Several recent exhibitions and their beautiful and fully illustrated catalogues have focused on this aspect of seventeenth-century Dutch art. See Amsterdam 2001 and London 2002.

4. For a translation of Karel van Mander's poem *Den grondt der edel vry schilder-const* (Foundations of the noble free art of painting; bk. 1, fols. 6–7)—in which he both recommends and cautions against a trip to Rome—see Montreal 1990, 20–21.

5. Baltimore/San Francisco 1997–98, 100–102.

6. Krautheimer 1980, 231–332.

7. Woodward 2001, 7–8; on the general topic of the Renaissance appreciation for classical ruins, see Weiss 1969, 59–72; for an overview of the destruction of ancient ruins in the sixteenth through eighteenth century, see Lanciani 1903.

8. Woodward 2001, 8; for a discussion of the many Dutch Italianate depictions of limekilns and their meaning, see Levine 1988.

9. Lanciani 1903, 190–92, 251–52.

10. Vermeule 1956, 32 n. 3.

11. Among the earliest Northern artists to travel to Italy was Rogier van der Weyden (c. 1399–1464), who reached Rome c. 1450. For a short list of early artist-travelers, see Montreal 1990, 19.

12. Heemskerck was in Rome 1532–36/37.

13. Early maps of Rome traditionally took one of two approaches: mapping (1) the location of principal Christian churches and shrines, such as A. Lafréy's *Seven Churches* map of 1575 (Krautheimer 1980, 249, fig. 194); or (2) the location of major ancient buildings, as J. Blaeu's map of ancient Rome in *Theatrum Civitatum ... Italiae ...* (D'Onofrio 1968, frontispiece).

14. In *Den grondt*, Karel van Mander (Van Mander 1604, chap. 8, paragraph 2, fol. 34v; see Van Mander/Miedema 1973, 202–5) encouraged landscape artists to go out into the country to observe nature; however, drawing out of doors was not common practice until the seventeenth century.

15. On the benefits that accrued to artists who traveled to Italy, see Baltimore/San Francisco 1997–98, 112–13.

16. Riggs 1977, nos. 1–25, figs. 4–24.

17. Riggs 1977, no. 174, figs. 78–81.

18. For Cock and subsequent print series of Roman views, see Grelle 1987.

19. Until the building of the Crystal Palace in London in 1851, the Colosseum encompassed more space than any other man-made structure in the world. A recent and beautifully illustrated history of the building is Gabucci 2001.

20. The towering remains of the Septizonium (the south-facing façade of the Palace of Severus) were pulled down in 1588–89 by papal architect Domenico Fontana on the orders of Sixtus V; Lanciani 1897, 181–83.

21. P. Schatborn reproduces dozens of Dutch Italianate prints and drawings representing Roman ruins, as well as ruins of Italian domestic architecture (Amsterdam 2001).

22. Ruby 1999, 2.

23. Arriving in Rome about 1575, Matthijs Bril had successfully established himself, working on decorative projects in the Vatican palace for Pope Gregory XIII.

24. Ruby 1999, 35–38.

25. Ruby 1999, 29.

26. In addition to his beautiful images of Rome and its environs, a drawing by Ter Borch represents the Palace of Galienus and the Temple of Tutela at Bordeaux (Kettering 1988, 12, Gsr3, repr.). This reminds us that Ter Borch, as would any modern tourist, encountered Roman ruins on his way across France to or from Italy. Such drawings are important historical documents, as well as works of art. The Temple of Tutela was destroyed in 1677. But the ruins of the third-century amphitheater of Galienus, the so-called Palais Gallien, still stand. Greatly diminished in size, it is located in the heart of central Bordeaux, where nineteenth-century residential buildings encroach up to the ruin's edge.

27. Compare, for example, Van Nieulandt's *Fantastic Landscape with Roman Monuments and Buildings*, Rijksdienst Beeldende Kunst, The

Hague ('s-Hertogenbosch/Heino/Haarlem 1984, 92, fig. 17) and the painting by Bril just discussed.

28. In his suite of topographical drawings, a number are inscribed with precise dates; the earliest is 22 April 1603, the latest 18 December 1603.

29. Valuable assets, drawings were important tools of the painter's trade, used as teaching aides as well as records of various motifs. They frequently were itemized in an artist's will. After his death, Matthijs Bril's studio drawings were inherited by Paulus and copied by other artists in his circle (Ruby 1999, 44–45). Schatborn also reproduces several examples, such as a drawing of a hill-top town by Breenbergh after Bril (Amsterdam 2001, 66, figs. A and B).

30. Willem van Nieulandt the Younger, *View of the Colosseum from the Caelian Hill*, Prentenkabinet van de Universiteit Leiden (Amsterdam 2001, 41, fig. F).

31. Print series were published by Ter Borch the Elder, Breenbergh, Swanevelt, Jan Both, and Asselijn, among others.

32. On the artistic relationship between Poelenburch and Breenbergh, see Roethlisberger 1981, 13–15.

33. For an introduction to the members, professional purpose, and antics of the "Bent," as it was called, as well as a bibliography, see C. Brown in London 2002, 34–41.

34. On Bril's experimentation with wash, see Ruby 1999, 105–6, no. 66, pl. 74.

35. Roethlisberger 1969, 22, no. 12, pl. 12.

36. Haskell 1980 remains the principal survey of Italian patronage in the seventeenth and eighteenth centuries.

37. Ruby 1999, 139 n. 106.

38. On Poelenburch's patrons, see M. J. Bok in Baltimore/San Francisco 1997–98, 387–88.

39. On Weenix's patrons, see M. J. Bok in Baltimore/San Francisco 1997–98, 390–91.

40. Sandrart 1675, 183–84. The practice of painting outdoors did not become common until the nineteenth century. However, while in Rome in 1649, the English traveler Richard Symonds made a diagram of a painting box designed to be used out of doors. See Varriano 2004.

41. The literature on the *Bamboccianti* has continued to grow; the best surveys in English are Levine 1984 and the English edition of Briganti, Trezzani, and Laureati 1983.

42. Levine 1984, 94.

43. Steland 1989, 15ff.

44. 's-Hertogenbosch/Heino/Haarlem 1984, 150.

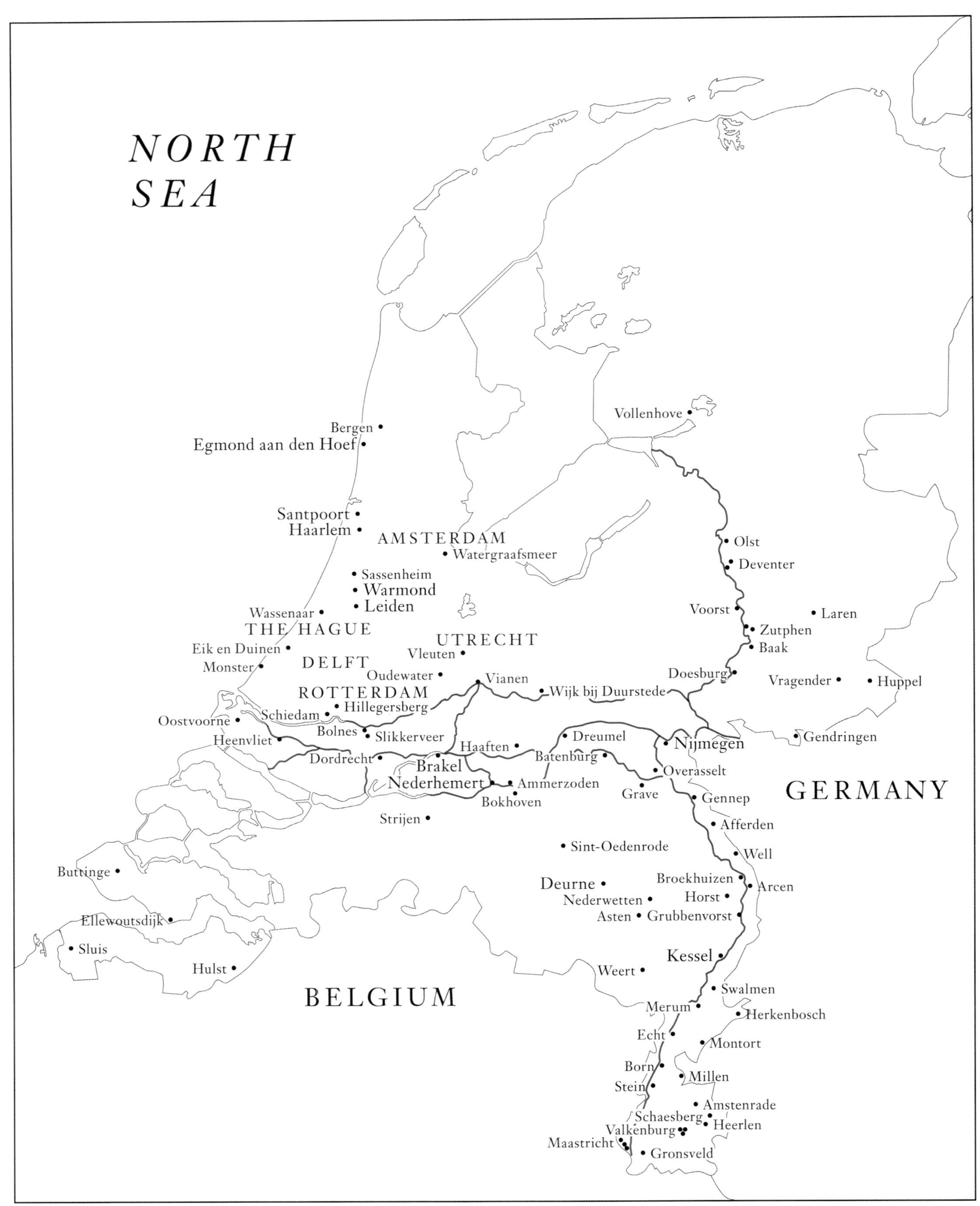

FIGURE 93. Map of existing ruin sites in the Netherlands. Adapted from a map by A. Reinstra, Rijksdienst voor de Monumentenzorg, Zeist.

Ruins in the Netherlands: The Present Situation

Erik P. Löffler

Today, some eighty important ruins of buildings dating before 1800 exist in the Netherlands (Fig. 93). The largest categories include ruined churches, chapels, and castles such as the well-known site of Brederode, near Haarlem (see Fig. 104). For the sake of comparison: the number of existing castles of medieval origin in the Northern Netherlands amounts to about three hundred, while the total number of castles that ever existed, including those of which no traces are left, can be estimated at approximately 2,300—one of the highest densities in Europe. The ruinous state of the buildings discussed here may date equally from the Middle Ages or from after World War II. Ruins of buildings dating from after 1700 are rare, however, as their protection has been considered less important from a historical point of view.[1]

The history of the care of ancient ruins in twenty-first-century Europe is full of paradoxes. Maintenance of the status quo by regular restoration means replacing more and more original bricks and stones with new material. If this is done, in the end, nothing old will be left. But if the ruin is left untouched, or if only small repairs are made to retard decay, ultimately none of the original building will remain either. The general public tends to favor total reconstruction, even when there is not enough historical evidence to prevent creation of a work of complete fantasy. For a nonspecialist, authenticity is less important, and a complete medieval castle, even if essentially new, may seem more impressive than its ruins. Different ideas about how ruins should be cared for are also influenced by how specialists think a ruin should look: well restored or crumbling and overgrown.[2]

How Dutch Ruins Came into Being

From the Middle Ages on, ruins must have been a common feature in both the urban and rural landscapes of the Netherlands. Devastation caused by wars, storms, or fires was often more than one generation could repair. For example, the debris of the nave of the St. Maartensdom (St. Maartens Cathedral) in Utrecht (begun in 1254), destroyed by a hurri-

---

ALPHABETICAL LIST OF RUINS IN THE NETHERLANDS ACCORDING TO TOWN (*adapted from a map by A. Reinstra in Schulte et al. 1997, 131*).

Afferden (Bergen): Kasteel Blijenbeek (kasteel = castle)
Ammerzoden: ruins of a reformed church
Amstenrade (Schinnen): folly grotto
Arcen: Schanstoren (toren = tower)
Asten: Kasteel Asten
Baak (Steenderen): Baakse kapel (kapel = chapel)
Batenburg (Wijchen): Kasteel Batenburg
Bergen: church ruins
Bokhoven: ('s-Hertogenbosch): Kasteel Bokhoven
Bolnes: folly at Huis ten Donck
Born: Kasteel Born
Brakel: Slot te Brakel (slot = castle)
Broekhuizen: Kasteel Broekhuizen
Buttinge (Veere): St. Michaëlskerk (kerk = church)
Deurne: Groot Kasteel Deurne
Deventer: Ceceliaconvent en Heer Florenshuis
Deventer: Mariakerk
Doesburg: remains of the St. Catharine Cloister
Dordrecht: Huis te Merwede (huis = house)
Dreumel (West Maas and Waal): nave of a reformed church
Echt: Kasteel Annendael
Egmond aan den Hoef (Egmond): Kasteel Egmond
Eik en Duinen (The Hague): church ruins
Ellewoutsdijk (Borssele): folly at Zorgvliet
Gendringen: Kasteel Swanenburg
Gennep: Genneperhuis
Grave: St. Elisabethskerk
Gronsveld (Eijsden): Kasteel Gronsveld
Grubbenvorst: Het Gebroken Slot
Haaften (Neerijnen): Kasteel Goudenstein
Haarlem: Huis ter Kleef
Heenvliet (Bernisse): Kasteel Ravesteyn
Heerlen: Kasteel Eyckholt
Herkenbosch (Melick and Herkenbosch): Kasteel Daelenbroeck
Hillegersberg (Rotterdam): Huis ten Berghe
Horst: Huis te Horst
Hulst: Bollewerkspoort (poort = gate)
Huppel (Winterswijk): Huis t'Waliën
Kessel:l Kasteel De Keverborg
Laren (Lochen): Kasteel Nettelhorst
Leiden:Vrouwenkerk
Maastricht: cloister chapel De Beyart
Maastricht: Kasteel Lichtenberg
Maastricht: king's chapel at St.-Servaaskerk
Merum (Roermond): Kasteel Oude Borg
Millen (Susteren): Kasteel Millen
Monster: folly 'Oud Polanen'
Montfoort (Posterholt): Kasteel Montfort
Nederhemert (Kerkwijk): Kasteel Nederhemert
Nederwetten (Neunen): Kerktoren
Nijmegen: Barbarossa's ruins of the Valkhof
Olst: tower folly at De Haere
Oostvoorne: Kasteel Oostvoorne
Oudewater: Kasteel Te Vliet
Overasselt (Heumen): St. Walrickskapel
Santpoort (Velsen): Kasteel Brederode
Sassenheim (Voorhout): Kasteel Teylingen
Schaesberg: Kasteel Schaesberg
Schiedam: Mathenesse / Huis te Riviere
Sint-Oedenrode: St. Maastenskerk
Slikkersveer (Ridderskerk): Huis te Woude
Sluis: Stene Beer of Westpoort
Stein: Kasteel Stein
Strijen (Oosterhout): Kasteel Strijen
Swalmen: Kasteel De Ouborgh
Valkenburg: Berkelpoort
Valkenburg: Grendelpoort
Valkenburg: Kasteel Valkenburg
Vianen: Kasteel Batestein
Vleuten (Veldhuizen): Kasteel Nyeveld
Vollenhove (Brederwiede): Kasteel Toutenburg
Voorst: Kasteel Nijenbeck
Vragender (Lichtenvoorde): St.-Jacobskapel
Warmond: St.-Matthiaskerk
Wassenaar: village church
Watergraafsmeer (Amsterdam): Hermitage at Frankendael
Weert: Kasteel De Nijenborgh
Well (Bergen): mill tower near Well Castle
Wijk bij Duurstede: Kasteel Duurstede
Zutphen: Berkelpoort
Zutphen: Oude Nieuwstadspoort

cane in 1674 (Fig. 138), was only cleared away in 1826. A new nave was often planned but never built.

Many buildings were ruined during times of war, occasionally even by local authorities to prevent appropriation by the enemy. Most castles were destroyed and reconstructed several times. Holland's longest-standing ruin "created" by military action is Huis te Woude Castle in Ridderkerk, south of Rotterdam. It was destroyed in 1418, during the war of succession between the competing political factions known as the *Hoeken* (Fishhooks) and the *Kabeljauwen* (Codfish). The castle was easy to conquer, for although its construction had been initiated much earlier, in 1371, it was still unfinished in the early fifteenth century.[3] Later conflicts that created numerous ruins were the invasion by France, Münster, and Cologne in 1672–74; France in 1794–95; and Germany during the Second World War in 1940–45. The Eighty Years' War (1568–1648) was not a war in the modern sense, but rather a long period of small, local military actions. Castles and towns were besieged more than once, and the continuous unrest in this period also hampered reconstruction work. The violent early phase of the war in the 1570s led to the destruction of a large number of castles and cloisters (monasteries and convents), the former because of their military function, the latter because many of them were outside the town walls, which made them easy to plunder (Cats. 2a and 2b, 4, 5, 7, 8, 11, and 14). It is probably no coincidence that from the end of the sixteenth century, realistic depictions of ruins started to play a role in Dutch art, as their number increased so rapidly. The historical actuality of these ruins is sometimes accentuated in artists' representations by the presence of visitors who seem to be discussing the historical events that created them.

Many other ruins were created by nature. The flood that caused the most casualties and destruction was the St. Elisabethsvloed, which occurred on (or shortly before) St. Elizabeth's day, 19 November 1421. One of its casualties was Huis te Merwede, a fourteenth-century castle west of Dordrecht that would become one of the most commonly depicted ruins in Dutch art (Cat. 13). Hurricanes are rare in Europe, but on 1 August 1674, a severe storm destroyed a large number of church towers and domestic buildings (Cat. 48) in the town of Utrecht, among them the aforementioned St. Maartensdom. Many of the church buildings were never completely reconstructed. Fires, caused by lightning or accidents, also frequently wrecked single buildings or large areas in densely populated towns (Cats. 40, 41 and 42).

Yet another cause of decay was abandonment. For example, after the childless death of Stadtholder William III in 1702, the palaces Huis ter Nieuwburch in Rijswijk (built 1630; Fig. 94) and Honselaarsdijk in the homonymous village near The Hague (1629) were inherited by his nephew, King Frederick I of Prussia. This was the beginning of a period of neglect and decay that ended with the demolition of the houses in 1790 and 1815, respectively, as restoration was considered too expensive. Abandoned castles were often sold in lots to building contractors, who reused timber, brick-, and stone-work in new projects. When demolition was only partial, these castles became ruins, but by this same process, other ruins disappeared completely.

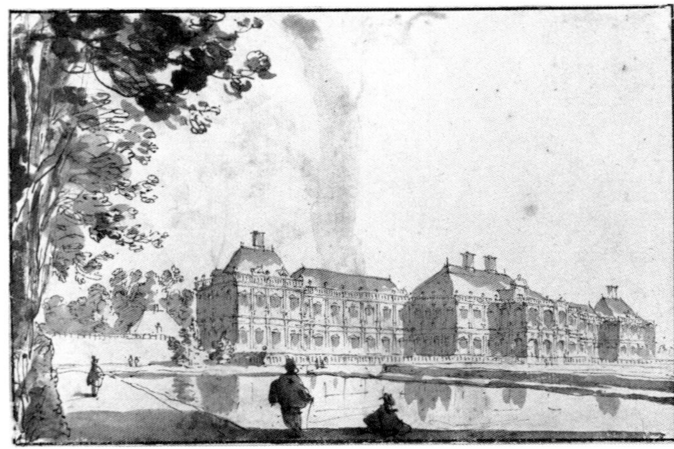

FIGURE 94. Jan de Bisschop, *Huis ter Nieuwburch in Rijswijk*, drawing, c. 1665–70. Private collection, Amsterdam.

Demolitions were often caused by demographic developments: since the Middle Ages, the Netherlands has developed into one of the most densely populated areas in the world. In 1500 it had approximately 1 million inhabitants; in 1650, 1.9 million; in 1800, 2.1 million; and in 1900, 5.1 million. Today the Netherlands has a population of about 16 million, which amounts to about 435 people per square kilometer (the density in the United States is currently about 27 per square kilometer).[4] This expansion has created a larger demand for building materials and growing pressure on available space, which explains the demolition of many ancient city walls, ruins, and other obsolete structures during the first half of the nineteenth century. Examples of this process are the ruins of the abbey of Rijnsburg near Leiden (founded in 1133; Cats. 5 and 11), Egmond Castle at Egmond aan den Hoef (originally built in the middle of the twelfth century; Figs. 10 and 96), and Huis ter Kleef in Haarlem (founded at the beginning of the fourteenth century; Cats. 2b and 4), whose decay can be followed in paintings, drawings, and prints over the course of two centuries until their (almost) complete demolition at the beginning of the nineteenth century (Fig. 95).[5]

Some ruins were even constructed deliberately. At the end of the eighteenth century, during the Romantic period, a new kind of landscaping became fashionable in Europe and

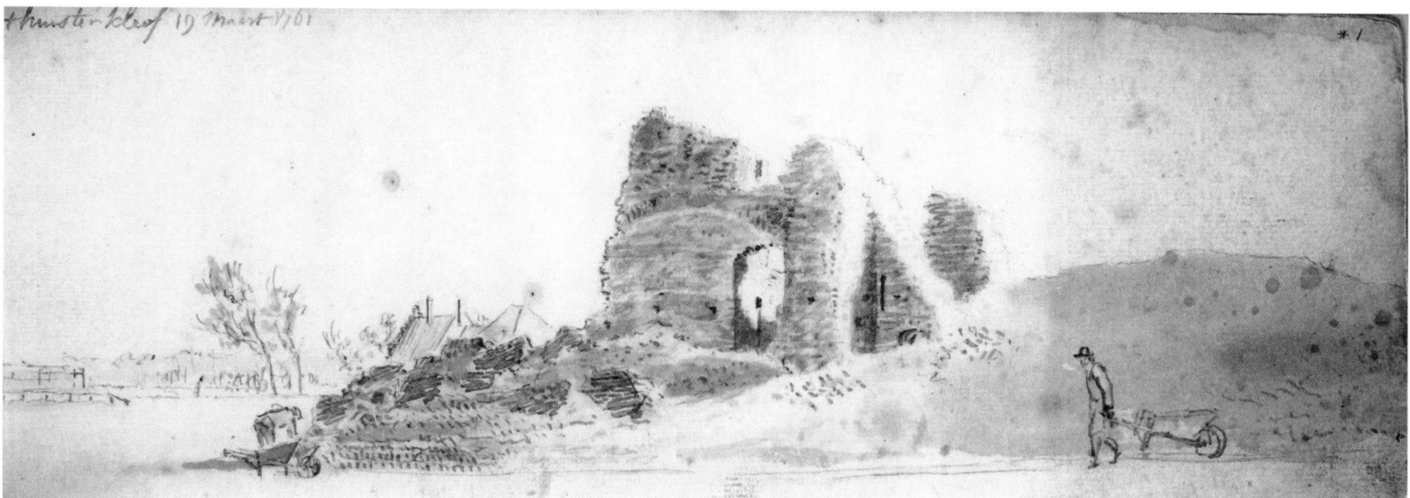

FIGURE 95. Cornelis van Noorde, *Demolition of Huis ter Kleef*, 1761, drawing. Archiefdienst voor Kennemerland, Haarlem.

England. Romantic gardens often included authentic ruins, and if a real ruin was not available, a folly could be created; the later decay of such a structure produced the subcategory of "ruined ruin." The earliest Dutch example can be found in the garden of Huis ten Donck in Bolnes, east of Rotterdam, which dates from the 1770s.[6] The Romantic park of Huis te Brakel in the province of Gelderland, begun in 1811, incorporated an authentic medieval ruin: the remnants of Brakel Castle, founded in the thirteenth century and destroyed by French troops in 1672. In the second half of the nineteenth century, it was even remodeled to make the ruinous state appear more ancient and imposing (Fig. 97).[7]

Importance of Ruins

Until the end of the eighteenth century, the Dutch interest in ruins was historical rather than architectural or archaeological. They were considered reminders of important historical periods, events, and individuals. Probably the first example of the deliberate protection of a ruin concerns Huis te Merwede (Cat. 13). As mentioned above, the castle was ruined by the flood on St. Elizabeth's day in 1421, but it had in fact already been damaged in 1418 by the inhabitants of nearby Dordrecht as revenge for the siege of their town. As early as 1449, the council of Dordrecht forbade exploitation of the ruin as a quarry. It was considered an historic monu-

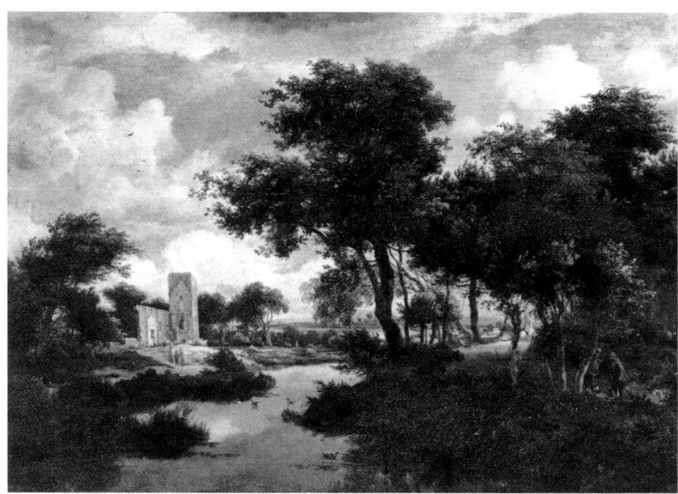

FIGURE 96. Meindert Hobbema, *Egmond Castle*, c. 1671, oil on panel. Clark Collection, Corcoran Gallery of Art, Washington, D.C.

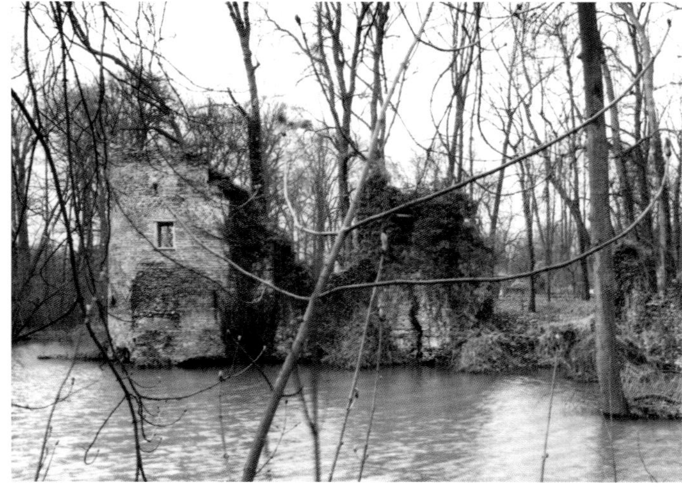

FIGURE 97. Remodeled authentic ruin in the park of Huis te Brakel, 1995. Rijksdienst voor de Monumentenzorg, Zeist.

ment, as it was said to have housed Jacoba of Bavaria, an important figure in fifteenth-century Dutch history.[8] Another example is the ruin of Strijen Castle in Oosterhout (originating about 1290), which was consolidated in 1753. A large part of the ruin had already been demolished for reemployment of the materials, but it was decided that a last fragment had to be preserved, again for historical reasons: it had belonged to the house of Orange. This was one of the earliest cases of restoration of a ruin without the intention to reconstruct it.[9]

From the sixteenth century onward, modernization of warfare diminished the strategic importance of castles, but their function as status symbols increased, and many castles were (re)built in the medieval style.[10] Ruins also served to enhance their owners' prestige. In the eighteenth century, the Van Egmond family bought back the ruin of Egmond Castle (Fig. 10) and had two towers restored to accentuate the importance and ancient lineage of the family.[11] Many ruins depicted in the backgrounds of portraits should also probably be interpreted as dynastic markers rather than as symbols of vanity and transience (Cat. 82).[12]

In the province of Utrecht, in the sixteenth and seventeenth centuries, one had to own an officially recognized *ridderhofstad* (manor farm) to be eligible to serve on the influential political council, the *staten*. The actual state of the building appears to have been less important for such recognition: in 1641 Zuileveld Castle (mentioned in early documents of 1443) was declared a *ridderhofstad*, even though nothing was left of the building itself by then. Possession of such a *ridderhofstad* could also play a role in the acquisition of an aristocratic title.[13] In the province of Overijssel, a similar political role was played by the *havezathes* ("court seat," the vernacular name for manor farm in that province), but in this case, only houses acquired by marriage or inheritance could give the owner access to the local council.[14]

Sometimes ruins had a religious function. After the Calvinist Reformation, Roman Catholicism was still widespread and more or less tolerated in the Northern Netherlands. The ruins of churches or chapels sometimes became pilgrim sites: a good example is Eik en Duinen chapel near The Hague, founded in 1247, which was destroyed in 1581 and still exists as a pilgrim site. The ruin's deterioration can be followed in the many paintings, drawings, and prints representing it, one of the earliest examples being an etching by Willem Buytewech (Fig. 44) from the print series that also includes images of the ruins of Brederode and the Huis ter Kleef (Cats. 2a and 2b). Since the beginning of the eighteenth century, the condition of the ruin has hardly changed, which suggests that renovations have been made regularly since that time. The fifteenth-century Onze Lieve Vrouw ter Nood chapel in Heiloo also became a site of pilgrimage only after its destruction, during the siege of Alkmaar in 1573 (Fig. 22). Its popularity with Catholics led to its complete demolition by the Calvinist authorities in 1637, but pilgrimages continued, even after a large number of trees were planted on the site in 1768. Only now with the secularization that has taken place since World War II has this kind of pilgrimage activity almost died out.[15]

The Development of Restoration Ethics

With the advent of Romanticism at the end of the eighteenth century and the beginning of the nineteenth, ruins also began to be appreciated for purely aesthetic reasons rather than for their individual histories.[16] As discussed above, old and new ruins were even incorporated into Romantic gardens. But in general, until about 1850, it was difficult to conceive of restoration of ruined buildings with any end in view other than the reconstruction of the original structure (as was the case, for example, with the Nieuwe Kerk in Amsterdam after a fire in 1645). Restoring a ruin as a ruin would have meant spending money on building activities without an economically practical purpose.[17] The first ruins ever to undergo large-scale, state-funded restorations were Brederode Castle (first restoration, 1862–82; discussed below; Fig. 104 and Cats. 1, 2a, 7, and 8) and the twelfth-century castle of Valkenburg in the southeast Netherlands (in the 1860s). Particularly remarkable is the early "restoration" of St. Matthew's church in Warmond near Leiden. This church was founded in the eleventh century, but the oldest part of the building as we know it today dates from the fourteenth century. The church was heavily damaged in 1573, at the beginning of the Eighty Years' War, and in 1591 only the choir was rebuilt. In 1874, having fallen into disuse, it was demolished to recreate the ruinous state of 1573, which is still visible today (Fig. 98).[18]

In 1873 Victor de Stuers (1843–1916) published the fundamental article "Holland op zijn smalst" (Holland at its narrowest) in the periodical *De gids*, which is still considered a turning point in Dutch politics concerning monuments, national museums, and art education.[19] De Stuers, who had studied law at Leiden University, published his first articles in the 1860s, denouncing the demolition of medieval fortifications in his native town of Maastricht. In the article in *De gids*, he laments what he considered to be the total lack of interest in the monumental symbols of Dutch history, which were being destroyed on a large scale, and in national art treasures, which were badly stored in depots or sold off at auction. Occasionally, the state or the king himself intervened, but only in a very haphazard way and almost exclusively to protect items that had played an important role in

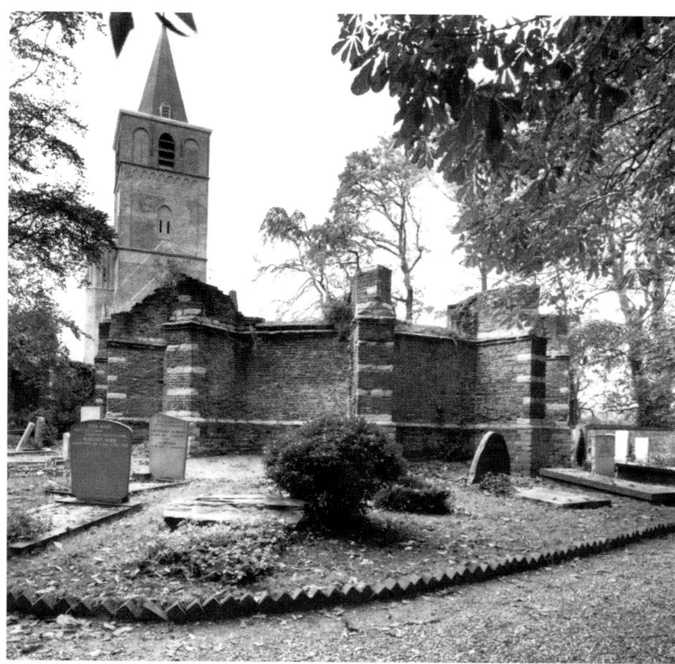

FIGURE 98. Warmond, ruined choir of St. Matthew's church, 1993. Rijksdienst voor de Monumentenzorg, Zeist.

the country's history.[20] Indeed, De Stuers's immediate reason for publishing the article was his discovery that the Renaissance rood screen had been removed from the Gothic cathedral of St. John in 's-Hertogenbosch (dating from about 1380). This very important example of Netherlandish Renaissance sculpture was sold to the Victoria and Albert Museum in London, where it remains today. The bishop and his advisers argued that the screen did not match the church's Gothic style, but in fact they wanted it to be removed for practical reasons: the rood obstructed the view to the altar. In a similar way, many medieval fortifications, churches, castles, and private houses were demolished because space was needed for roads, buildings, or a nice view.[21]

De Stuers compares the Dutch situation with that in some other European countries. These had already had their industrial revolutions: England at the end of the eighteenth century, Belgium and France in the 1830s, and Germany in the 1860s. In such countries, a new middle class had developed, for whom interest in, and knowledge of, the arts were new pastimes; moreover, they were a sign of social distinction and hence a way of achieving upward social mobility. Industrialization also created the financial surpluses necessary to support the arts. Remarkably enough, the Netherlands had experienced a similar situation long before. In the Dutch Golden Age of the seventeenth century, it was also mainly the new middle class that had stimulated the arts on an unprecedented scale. The stadtholders did have a court, and especially under the "stadtholdership" of Prince William III (1650–1702), its members built country houses in order to emulate the style of the French nobility, albeit on a very limited scale in comparison with other European countries. After a decline in the eighteenth century, what was left of the Dutch patriciate was startled by a sudden growth of a new industrial middle class in the 1870s. With the development of democracy, the interest of this new class in the arts and architecture had to be taken into account. De Stuers's involvement was, in fact, symptomatic of this development.[22]

One year after the publication of "Holland op zijn smalst," the young De Stuers was nominated head of the Department of Arts and Sciences at the Ministry of the Interior. In the following decades, he was able to realize many of his plans and wishes. Important monuments were restored to an intact state, and a new national museum was built: the now world-famous Rijksmuseum in Amsterdam. De Stuers's ideas about restoration were typical for his time. In his article he states, when discussing the church of St. John in 's-Hertogenbosch, that every building has its own history and that in some cases it is good to keep the later improvements and additions. But when discussing a recent restoration to the Hooglandse Kerk in Leiden, he expresses sorrow that a Renaissance addition to this medieval church has not been replaced by something in the Gothic style.[23] In restorations done under his supervision, it is clear that his appreciation for later additions was limited and that he did not shy away from reconstructing a building based on a historical ideal, even when documentation was lacking. The merlons (battlements) on the walls of Muiderslot, a castle east of Amsterdam dating from the end of the thirteenth century, were added during restoration. While the original founders of the castle might have appreciated them, it is a fact that merlons had never been there before.[24]

In 1874, a year after the publication of his famous article, De Stuers met Pierre J. H. Cuypers (1827–1921), who had studied architecture in Antwerp and was influenced by the Neogothic schools in France, England, and Germany. During his long career, he restored several medieval buildings and designed a large number of churches in the Neogothic style.[25] Today he is best known as the designer of the Rijksmuseum (1885) and, in a very similar style despite its entirely different function, the Amsterdam Centraal Station (1882–89).[26] Both Cuypers and De Stuers were Roman Catholics who loved medieval arts and crafts. The great irony of their lifelong collaboration and friendship is that the demolition of the rood screen in 's-Hertogenbosch, discussed above, was approved by and carried out under the supervision of Cuypers. Several of the other dubious restoration activities denounced in *Holland op zijn smalst* were completed in accordance with

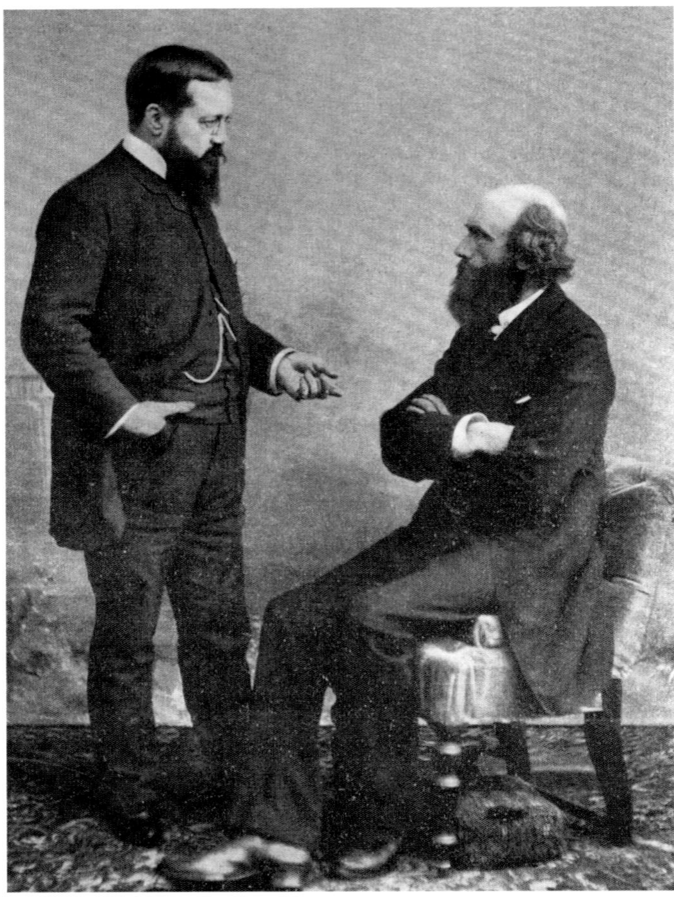

FIGURE 99. Victor de Stuers (left) and Pierre Cuypers (right), c. 1880. Rijksdienst voor de Monumentenzorg, Zeist.

his plans before, but also after, the two men had met for the first time (Fig. 99).[27]

Cuypers's influence on Dutch monuments was not limited to the restorations he designed and supervised himself. From 1875, thanks to his friendship with De Stuers, he consulted on an almost endless number of restoration projects all over the country. In these activities, he showed himself to be a follower of the French architect Eugène Emmanuel Viollet-le-Duc (1814–79), for whom restoring meant completing a building according to an ideal plan.[28] The best example of this mentality is the reconstruction of De Haar Castle near Utrecht, dating from the end of the thirteenth century (discussed below). Nevertheless, in some cases Cuypers's approach could be totally different. For example, his restoration of the early fifteenth-century Berkelpoort (one of the gates in the fortifications of the town of Zutphen), dating from 1888–89, was mainly a consolidation, for hardly any new material was added, and the ruinous state was even enhanced by the addition of new vegetation.[29] Much depended on the tastes of owners or local authorities, but a detailed study of Cuypers's oeuvre also demonstrates that in several cases, it was his own choice to respect the patina or other picturesque aspects of an ancient building.[30]

In 1915 the Nederlandsche Oudheidkundige Bond (Netherlands Antiquarian Society) discussed their new *Grondbeginselen en voorschriften voor het behoud, de herstelling en de uitbreiding van oude bouwwerken* (Principles and regulations for the conservation, restoration, and development of old buildings). Ideas had changed—far-reaching reconstructions in the original style were now rejected.[31] In their respect for the architectural history of monuments, the new ideas and regulations that constituted the *Grondbeginselen* sound very modern, but they also permitted the completion of ancient structures in a modern style. In 1925–27, for example, the spire of the sixteenth-century church in IJsselstein was completed in Dutch Art Deco style after a design by Michiel de Klerck (1884–1923).[32] Even though this approach was already heavily criticized in the 1930s, now and then it is still applied; for example, in the recent plans for the ruins of Deurne Castle, near Eindhoven in the province of Brabant, dating from the end of the fourteenth century. As this building was destroyed relatively recently, in 1944, proposals for reconstruction were easier to accept: unlike Brederode Castle, it had not had time to become a famous national icon in its ruined form. Nevertheless, the plan, launched in 1994, to complete the ruin of Deurne in functional style, was abandoned. For political, technical, and financial reasons, only a limited restoration of the ruin took place (Fig. 100).[33] On the other hand, developments in archaeology in the 1960s made extensive reconstruction work in historical styles tempting. Detailed research on foundations, building traces, and other evidence stimulated restoration of castles to their earliest appearance, even if hardly anything original was left and even if this was against the principles propagated by the *Grondbeginselen*.[34]

Several historical buildings that had been (almost) totally destroyed during World War II were later rebuilt, although shortly after the war, proposals were made to leave two churches unrestored: the Laurenskerk in Rotterdam (built in 1445–1525) and the Eusebiuskerk in Arnhem (begun in 1450). Here, too, however, reconstruction was preferred; the Laurenskerk was rebuilt in its original form; the same was done with Eusebiuskerk, but its tower was rebuilt in a modern form, according to the principles of the *Grondbeginselen*.[35] As a consequence, Holland does not have war monuments like Coventry Cathedral and the Gedächtniskirche (Church of Remembrance) in Berlin. Only a few war ruins were left untouched, but these relatively unimportant buildings are not located in densely inhabited areas, which means that they did not acquire symbolic meaning.[36] Although vanitas sym-

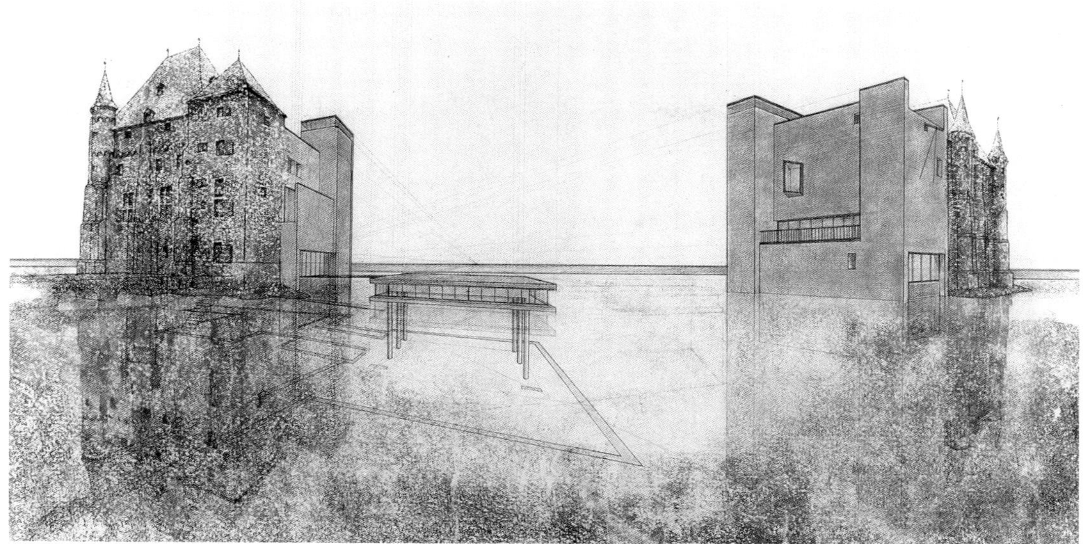

FIGURE 100. Quist Wintermans Architects, proposal for reconstruction of Groot Kasteel in Deurne, 1994.

bols have always been popular in Dutch art, after the war, public opinion favored a new start to mourning the past. A Calvinist mentality may have played a role in this policy, for Calvinism discourages feelings of defeat, teaching that Christians should rely on God and look forward in optimism. Retaining war ruins as reminders of mortality did not fit into that world view. In any case, several Dutch castles were destroyed by the Allied Forces because of the presence of German troops; this made their ruins less suitable for such a symbolic function. For most of these castles, reconstruction plans were made, and if they were not executed, it was for financial reasons.[37] One of the most remarkable post-war restorations was that of Keverberg Castle in Kessel, in the province of Limburg. Here, too, a reconstruction of the castle's pre-war state was planned, but archaeological research proved that the building had originally been a so-called ring fortress, an oval fortified house on a hilltop, dating from the twelfth century. For this reason, it was left as a ruin, later additions were demolished, and only some older remnants were restored in order to reconstruct the castle's original structure as faithfully as possible (Figs. 101a and b).[38]

Opinions about how a ruin should be treated still differ. In *Ruïnes in Nederland* (Ruins in the Netherlands), the first extensive study of Dutch ruins, published in 1997, several

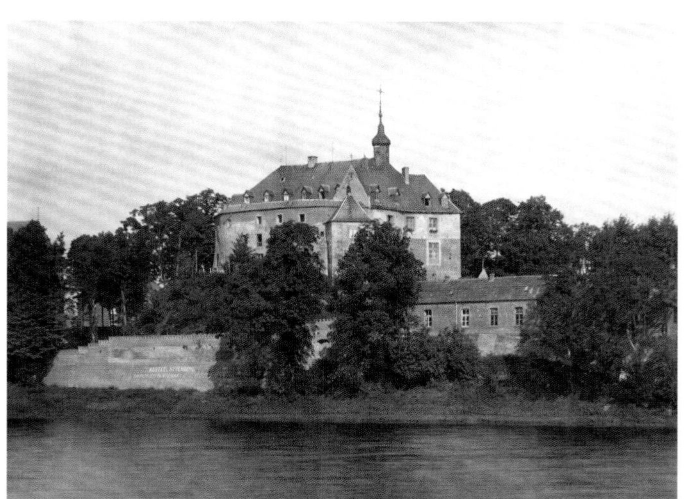

FIGURE 101a. Keverberg Castle in Kessel before war damage and restoration, 1929. Rijksdienst voor de Monumentenzorg, Zeist.

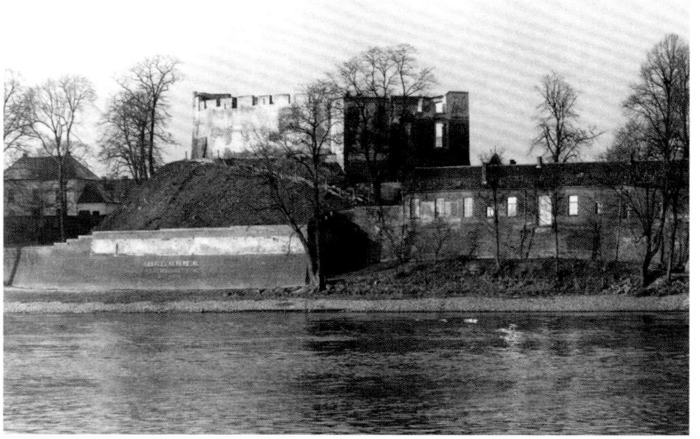

FIGURE 101b. Keverberg Castle in Kessel, after restoration, 1963. Rijksdienst voor de Monumentenzorg, Zeist.

restorations are judged both positively and negatively by different authors.[39] Another paradox is that although nowadays scholars are unanimous in condemning reconstructive restorations such as those of Brederode and De Haar castles (discussed below), stripping the nineteenth- and twentieth-century additions from these (former) ruins would be unthinkable. These are now considered important examples of older restoration principles, and the later additions are essential to their popularity. Even today, when an ancient ruin is restored, there is a tendency to do more than merely consolidate it. For a more lasting effect, much original material is often replaced, and to ease financing, part of the original building is sometimes reconstructed for commercial exploitation. Recent examples are the reconstructed cellar of twelfth-century Heusden Castle in Heusden on the Maas River or the donjon of Wijk bij Duurstede Castle (started about 1270) in the homonymous town southeast of Utrecht, where conflicts about the status of protected monuments and their modern use still remain unresolved.[40]

The development of restoration principles in other European countries is somewhat comparable to the situation in the Northern Netherlands. England has always had the strongest tendency to respect ruins as ruins, while in France, the preference has been to reconstruct. In Belgium (i.e., the former Southern Netherlands) and Germany, as in Holland, the two options have alternated.[41]

Ruins in the Twenty-First Century

Today ruins are no longer endangered by the practice of recycling their materials for new buildings. Most problems are now caused by claims on their surrounding areas. Whereas in France, the protection of the immediate surroundings of monuments was regulated as early as 1913, in the Netherlands, consciousness of the importance of their context dates only from the 1930s, and the protection of monuments is still problematic.[42] Often the immediate surroundings do not belong to the owner of the ruin itself, and in this densely populated country, every free lot of ground is at risk of being claimed for housing, industry, or infrastructure. Building activities not only threaten open vistas and archaeological remains, but can also cause a decline in the underground water level, which can cause ruins to sink. When, instead of visible structures, only subterranean traces remain, total destruction is an especially real danger, as most archaeological sites are still unprotected by law. Fortunately, in October 2003 a new law was proposed that would make archaeological research a required step in preparation for large building projects.[43]

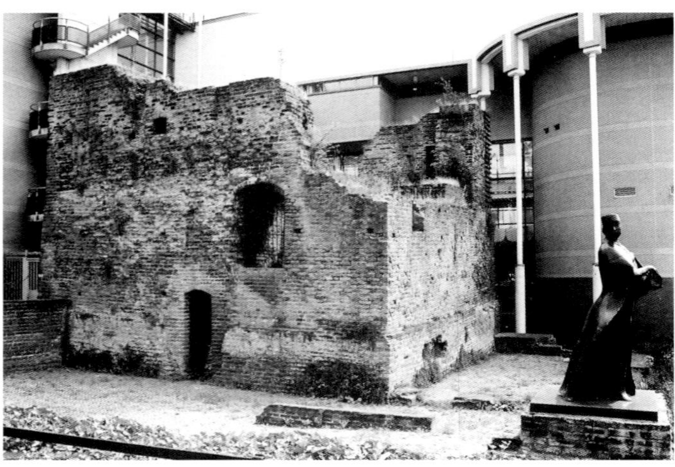

FIGURE 102. Huis te Riviere, Schiedam. Photo by the author, 2004.

The organizations that administer ruins generally do not, like museums, have directors, managers, or curators with contacts in the cultural and political sector who could lobby for their interests. They are mostly managed by nonspecialized civil servants and volunteers at a very local level, which makes them more vulnerable to arbitrary decisions by local or national authorities. A further political problem in the protection of the environments of monuments is that not only the Ministry of Education, Culture, and Science but often also the Ministry of Agriculture, Nature, and Food Quality and the Ministry of Housing, Spatial Planning, and the Environment are involved. Their points of view vary, and their interest in the protection of ancient monuments is often limited. One of the strongest examples of the spoiling of the surroundings of a ruin is Huis te Riviere in Schiedam, west of Rotterdam. This ruin of a castle, founded in 1258 and destroyed in the sixteenth century, is considered a symbol of the ancient history of Schiedam, but, paradoxically, awareness of its importance became the motive for constructing a new town hall in its immediate vicinity in 1997. The new building almost touches the ruin, which in turn was so heavily restored that it looks rather like a construction site (Fig. 102).[44] To facilitate better protection of historical environments, since 1994 the so-called *Culture-Historical Effects Report* (Cultuur Historische Effecten Rapportage, or CHER) was conceived by the archaeological department of the town of Utrecht. It was intended to serve as an example, to be applied throughout the country, for locations where large developments are planned. In such a report, the cultural value of a local historic environment would be inventoried in an effort to protect it. The idea was based on the *Environmental Effects Report* (Milieu Effecten Rapportage, or MER), which is a requirement in the planning of large developments. The problem is that as yet preparation of a CHER is not mandatory.[45]

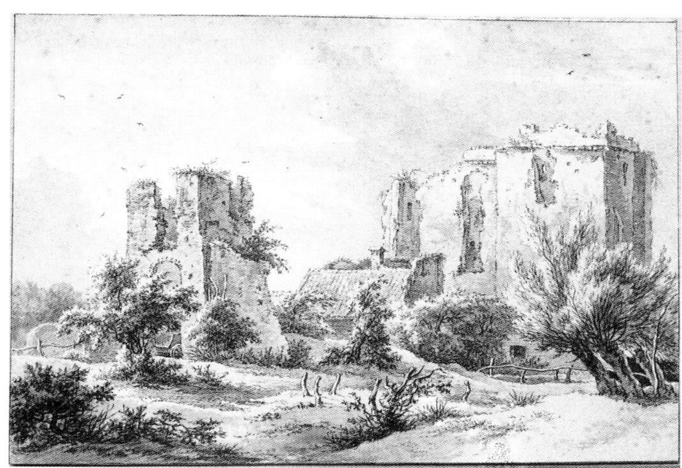

FIGURE 103. Egbert van Drielst, *Brederode*, c. 1800, drawing. Coll. C. P. van Eeghen, The Hague.

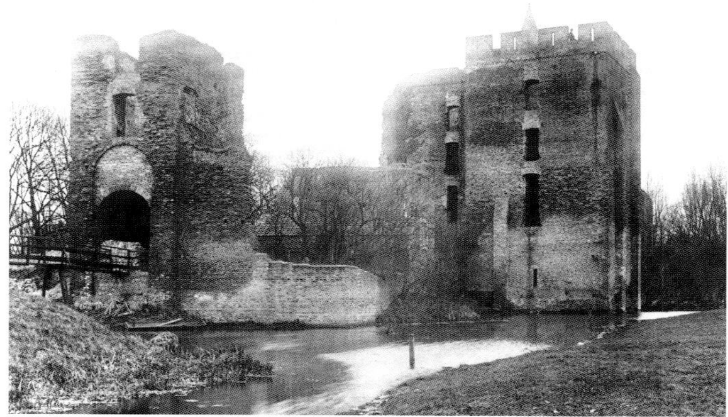

FIGURE 104. Brederode Castle after restoration, c. 1883. Rijksdienst voor de Monumentenzorg, Zeist.

Public support is important for the survival of ruins. This support can be enhanced by the development of activities in and around the site, but, as contradictory as this may sound, a ruin is easily damaged, and overexploitation can also threaten its ecological value. The aesthetic appreciation of vegetation on ruins reached its peak during the Romantic period, but nowadays, awareness of the ecological importance of ruins is developing. Their often isolated location in combination with their many sheltered, humid corners are favorable for the growth of species that are in danger of extinction, such as certain rare ferns. Many ruins also provide shelter for bats and other kinds of small mammals. Some recent restorations try to spare vegetation, and when species are protected by the Dutch Nature Protection Law (*Natuurbeschermingswet*), their removal is only allowed with special permission.[46]

Some Ruins and Their Restoration History

BREDERODE CASTLE

Brederode Castle (Fig. 104) is situated near the village of Santpoort (municipality of Bloemendaal), north of Haarlem. A first castle was built at the end of the thirteenth century. After being destroyed, it was rebuilt between 1354 and 1426, but in the latter year, it was ruined again. In 1573, the partially reconstructed castle was destroyed by fire during the siege of Haarlem by the Spanish troops. What was left was inhabited until about 1600; after that date it again fell into decay. Only a dwelling adjacent to the ruin of the gate seems to have been regularly inhabited or used as a barn through the centuries, probably always by farmers, as agricultural activities around the remnants of the castle can be seen in paintings, drawings, and prints dating from after 1600 (Cats. 1, 2a, 7 and 8).

Plans for restoration were developed in the 1860s, and from 1873 on, Victor de Stuers was involved in the project. He invited Pierre Cuypers to participate, and it was after his designs that the first large-scale restoration of the ruin was completed in 1880–82. The work was already being criticized, however, in an 1886 article in *De Nederlandsche spectator*, in which the restorers were accused of reconstructing too much and with too much fantasy.[47] This discussion went on throughout the entire restoration period, which indicates that even in the nineteenth century, reconstructions were not acceptable to everyone. Of the present-day ruin, only some 40 percent of the brickwork dates from before about 1850, as indicated by a drawing by Egbert van Drielst (1745–1818) of about 1800 (Fig. 103). As all the upper parts of the walls, merlons, and other outstanding details were (re)constructed, the appearance of the complex totally changed (Fig. 104). This is also true of many other buildings that were heavily restored during the same period, such as the Ridderzaal (Knights' Hall) in The Hague and Muiderslot Castle, west of Amsterdam.[48]

Brederode Castle is no longer threatened by enthusiastic restorers, but now the problem of claims on the surrounding grounds has become more pressing. A CHER (as discussed above) was drawn up for the area south of the ruin belonging to the village of Bloemendaal. The importance of this area derives from the presence of several ancient country houses, or remains of their parks, and of a hospital dating from the first half of the nineteenth century. Several of these buildings are listed by the Dutch state as national monu-

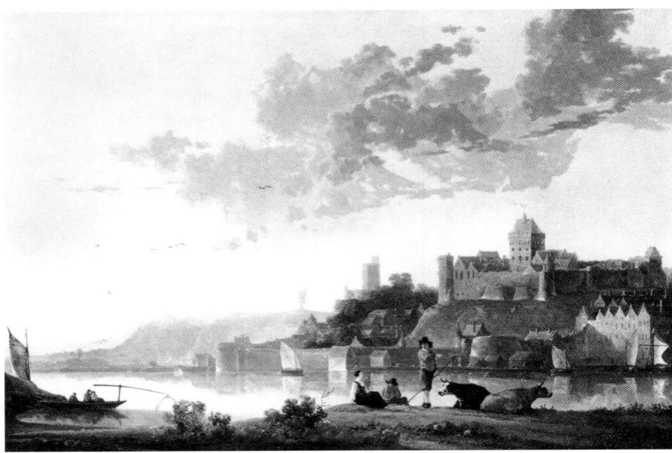

FIGURE 105. Aelbert Cuyp, *The Valkhof at Nijmegen*, mid-1650s, oil on panel. Indianapolis Museum of Art.

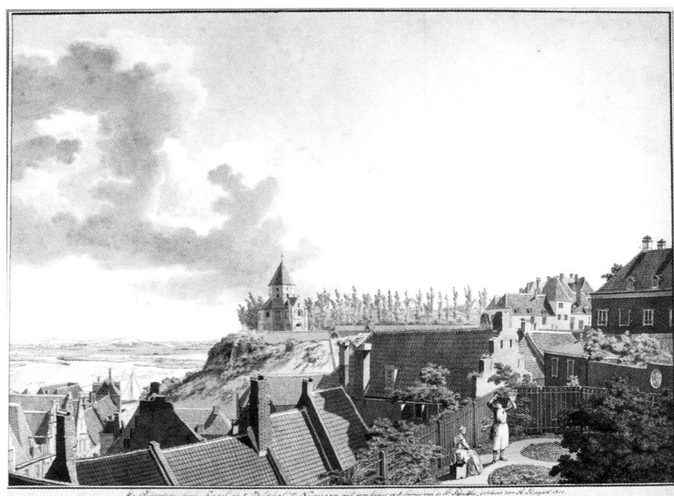

FIGURE 106. Hendrik Hoogers, *Valkhof*, St. Nicholas chapel (left) and apse of St. Martin chapel (behind the trees), 1810, drawing. Centrum voor Stads-en Streekhistorie, Nijmegen.

ments. But the ruin of Brederode is situated on the boundary between Bloemendaal and the municipality of Velsen, and construction plans in Velsen do not respect the view of the castle in neighboring Bloemendaal. Protection of the surroundings of this ruin is all the more important because of the area's ecological value. Many species of birds breed in and around the ruin. Building activities in the surrounding area may also cause a decline of the underground water level, which could damage the ruin itself as well as the many ancient trees nearby.[49]

VALKHOF CASTLE

Valkhof (falcon's court) Castle, a major strategic fortress, is situated in the historic town of Nijmegen on the Waal River in the province of Gelderland, where it was frequently depicted by seventeenth-century artists such as Aelbert Cuyp (q.v.; Fig. 105). As early as the ninth century, Charlemagne had built a palace on this site, and a new castle was constructed by Holy Roman Emperor Frederick I Barbarossa beginning in 1155. Throughout the following centuries, it was enlarged, plundered, and reconstructed until it was heavily damaged by French troops in 1794, and demolition of the remains was proposed: the profits from sale of the Valkhof's tufa (a light stone of volcanic origin), bricks, and wood were needed to cover the costs of more urgent reconstruction work in the town of Nijmegen. Furthermore, the castle was considered a symbol of the old regime, especially since the stadtholder, Prince William V of Orange, had resided there in 1786–87.

Johannes In de Betouw (1732–1820), an antiquarian who published on local history, fiercely opposed demolition. The political situation was unfavorable to his opinion, however, and demolition was started in 1795, but he managed to save some structures, which still stand today: a chapel and a ruined apse. A tower and part of the ring wall also survived, as their demolition would have endangered some private houses and the chapel and apse, which were then thought to be remnants from Roman times. This was an important argument in favor of their protection, as interest in the earliest history of the Netherlands was developing in that period.[50] Yet although building materials from a Roman settlement (first–fourth centuries AD) had been found on this site, today we know that the ruined apse belonged to a twelfth-century chapel dedicated to St. Martin, once part of the castle built by Frederick Barbarossa, and that the polygonal chapel, dedicated to St. Nicholas, dates from the eleventh century (Fig. 106). If this had been known at the time, it is unlikely that anyone would have bothered to save any part of the castle, as interest in medieval buildings was still very limited.

In 1797 it was decided that some necessary restorations to the structures that had escaped demolition would be carried out "in the same stones and in the same style." This is in fact one of the earliest statements about how a ruin should be restored.[51] In a document of 1798, mention was made of theft of stones from the ruins; nevertheless, the four structures mentioned still survive.[52] As early as 1797, a park was established, and in the 1880s it was enlarged. The ruins became tourist attractions for historical reasons but probably also because of the romantic atmosphere they evoked: the site gave rise to meditations about the vanity and transitoriness of human endeavor, an effect enhanced by weeping willows planted for that purpose.[53]

In 1978 the Valkhofvereniging was founded, an association with the stated aim of reconstructing the castle. A 1988 plan could not be financed, but in 1995 a second plan was presented. The Nijmegen town council was in favor of reconstruction; it had probably been influenced by lobbying building contractors who hoped to create shops, pubs, restaurants, and a luxury hotel in the new castle. They argued that restoration of the "toothless mouth," as they called it on this occasion, would provide significant economic stimulus for the town. Of the local population, 44 percent was in favor of reconstruction, 47 percent against. An association of opponents was also created, and the Dutch government as well as specialized institutions in the field of monuments and archaeology were among those opposed to the plans. Reconstruction, they argued, would destroy an important archaeological site and a park that is now a protected monument itself. The result was that the second plan has not been realized either, although discussion still continues.[54]

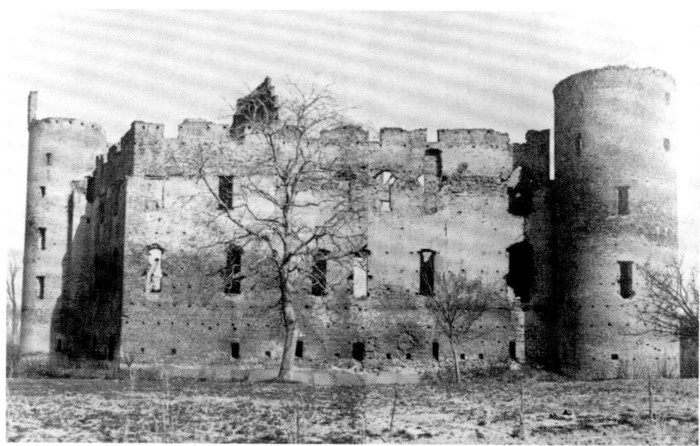

FIGURE 107a. De Haar Castle before reconstruction, 1887. Rijksdienst voor de Monumentenzorg, Zeist.

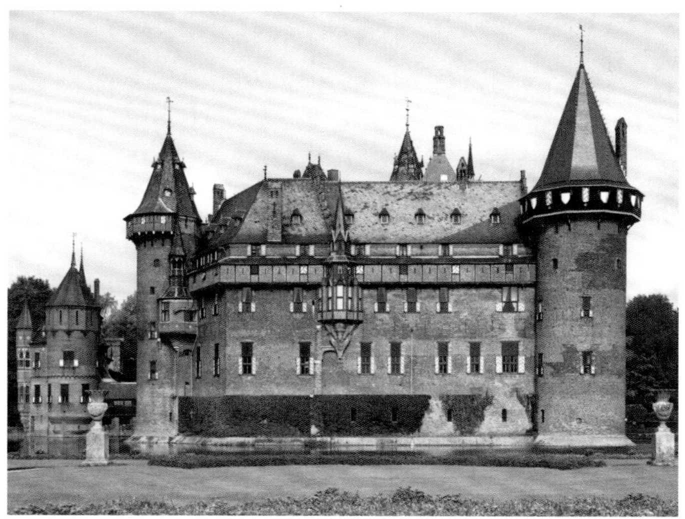

FIGURE 107b. De Haar Castle after reconstruction, 1974. Rijksdienst voor de Monumentenzorg, Zeist.

DE HAAR CASTLE

De Haar Castle, west of Utrecht, already existed in 1391 and probably dates back even earlier, to the thirteenth century. After destruction in 1482, it was rebuilt in the sixteenth century. From 1641, when the owners' male line died out, it was inhabited irregularly, and its gradual decay began. At the end of the nineteenth century, the castle, now a ruin (Fig. 107a), was inherited by Etienne Gustave Frédéric Baron van Zuylen van Nyevelt. In 1887 this French-Dutch nobleman married Hélène Caroline Betsy Baroness Rothschild, a member of the extremely wealthy banking family. It was Etienne's dream to reconstruct the castle, and not only his: Victor de Stuers's wedding present to the couple was a first reconstruction sketch. The castle was to become the family's holiday home—as it still is—but also a symbol of the age and nobility of the family. It was through De Stuers that Pierre Cuypers became the project's lead architect, along with his son Jos. The ruin of what had been one of Holland's largest castles was reconstructed with help of seventeenth- and eighteenth-century topographical drawings by, among others, Jan de Beijer (1703–80). The (still very important) ruin was not demolished but completely incorporated into the reconstructed castle. New additions and interiors were rebuilt according to the taste of the architect and the family who commissioned the work. The owners had grown up in France, and in that period Cuypers himself preferred the French Gothic style, so this was used for the reception areas. The technical installations (elevator, kitchen, central heating, electricity) were extremely modern. The reconstruction, started in 1892, was originally planned on a modest scale but eventually grew into one of the largest projects of its kind ever carried out. It was not completed until 1913 (Fig. 107b).

At the end of the twentieth century, the building began to sink, for the reconstruction had produced a castle that was higher, larger, and heavier than the original, with the consequence that its foundations could no longer support it. Although specialists consider this castle an eccentric, ahistorical folly, and although they still regret the "loss" of one of the most impressive of Dutch ruins, it was nevertheless decided that this unique example of a nineteenth-century pseudo-historical reconstruction should be saved: as a monument to Dutch history, as an icon of nineteenth-century architecture, and as a tourist attraction. The owners helped by initiating the fund-raising and converted their property into a foundation, while the Dutch state allocated forty million euros to the project. Specialists in the fields of architecture, architectural history, and interior decoration are now

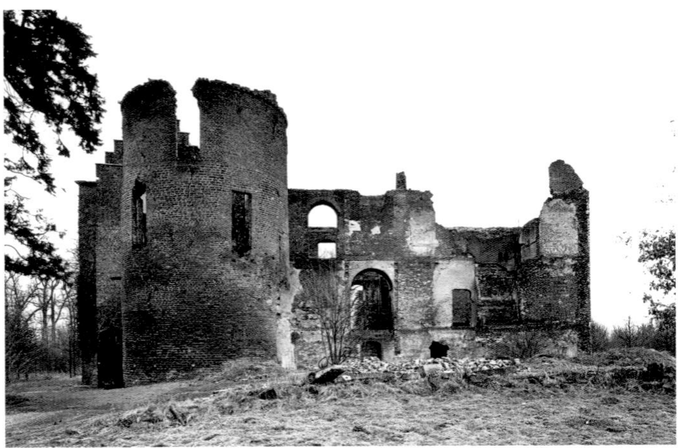

FIGURE 108a. Nederhemert Castle before reconstruction, 1962. Guelders Trust, Arnhem.

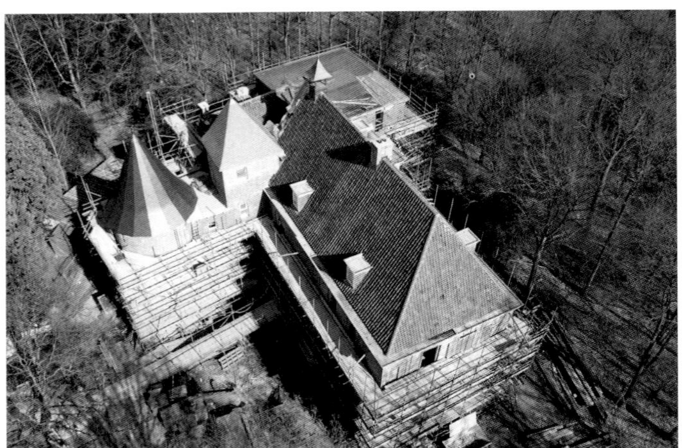

FIGURE 108b. Nederhemert Castle under reconstruction, 2003. Rijksdienst voor de Monumentenzorg, Zeist.

collaborating on a restoration project of unprecedented scale. After a long period of preparatory research, major work is scheduled to begin in 2005.[55]

NEDERHEMERT

The ruin of Nederhemert Castle was situated east of Dordrecht, in the province of Gelderland (Fig. 108a). The castle was founded probably at the beginning of the fourteenth century, and since then it was successively enlarged, partly demolished, reconstructed, and refurbished. It was destroyed by fire in the winter of 1944–45, when it was in the front line of the Allied advance. The last owners, the aristocratic Van Wassenaer family, had been forced to leave the castle in November 1944. In 1957 they sold the ruin to the state, which handed it over to the Vrienden van de Geldersche Kasteelen (Guelders Trust) in 1961.

Due to lack of funding, early restoration plans were cancelled. The ruin continued to deteriorate even though, after the collapse of the main staircase in 1966, small-scale repairs were made regularly to stop the decay. This situation remained unchanged until the end of the 1990s, when the Dutch state finally decided to finance reconstruction. The newer part of the castle, of which nothing was left, was not reconstructed, and in the interior, only one central room was returned completely to its original state according to pre–World War II photographs.[56] One of the cellars, which had become the winter shelter of several protected bat species, was deliberately left untouched.[57] Part of the building will be lent to a computer enterprise, the older part is to be accessible to the public and the cellar with the bats will be left untouched (Fig. 108b).[58]

The restoration of Nederhemert Castle raised many of the major questions that are often asked about the treatment of old monuments. Hadn't the destruction taken place too long ago? What is the use of reconstructing a castle in such an isolated area? Finding a tenant was also difficult, partly because a listed monument cannot be as multifunctional and well equipped as a modern office building. The debate about this reconstruction was sharpened by fund-raising problems, which caused much publicity, and by the fact that the proposal was initiated by a castle society, originally even by the Dutch state. In comparison, the reconstruction of Heemstede Castle, south of Utrecht, drew very little public attention. The restoration of this castle, burned down in 1987, was financed by a real estate developer who needed a new office building. As far as the exterior is concerned, this latter reconstruction was executed relatively well and with approval of the Rijksdienst voor de Monumentenzorg (Netherlands Department for Conservation). The interior, on the other hand, was adapted to suit its new function.[59]

The Future of Dutch Ruins

In the Netherlands, opinions still differ about how ruins should be treated. Every ruin is unique in its location, state of preservation, and historical importance, which makes it difficult to formulate strict, consistent rules for their restoration and use. Nevertheless, some general remarks can be made. As Holland's population is still growing, town and country planning is starting to seriously endanger the surroundings of castles and ruins. It is hoped that the CHER can form a new basis for the integration of the often conflicting interests involved in new building development projects. Nowadays, thoughtful planning is becoming more and more important, as financial support by the Dutch state is diminishing. In the early twenty-first century, national funding is seldom granted for a ruin without a development plan that not only articulates its cultural function, but in the future will generate part of the money necessary to its maintenance.

In our own time, the public's appreciation of national history may be diminishing, but in its place a more general interest in history and culture is developing, as the number of visitors to Dutch museums and sites of historical interest increases. In the Netherlands, we now face the challenge of finding a new role for the monuments of the past in order to keep them alive for future generations.

NOTES

1. I wish to express my gratitude to the following specialists who corrected this article: Annemieke Kylstra-Wielinga (director of the NKS/Dutch Castle Society), Johan Carel Bierens de Haan (director of the Geldersche Kasteelen/Guelderlands Trust), Maria Sherwood-Smith, and R. van 't Zelfde.

2. For a recent discussion of this subject, see R. J. Wielinga, "Ruïnes herstellen of de tand des tijds vrij spel geven?" in Schulte et al. 1997, 87–94; and Denslagen 1997.

3. Schulte et al. 1997, 297.

4. Ekamper 2003, 8, 13.

5. Examples of castles that were reduced to small ruins through selling of their materials are Strijen near Oosterhout and the Valkhof at Nijmegen, both discussed herein. The bricks of the ruined abbey in Egmond (which was situated not far from the castle) were sold in 1652 for 12,500 guilders; material from Medemblik Castle (north of Amsterdam) was sold in 1890 and used for the reinforcement of dikes. It is probable that the bricks of almost all demolished castles were reused elsewhere, and that the value of the materials was in many cases reason enough to demolish castles. On this subject, see Kuipers-Verbuijs 1993, 5–7, and Bierens de Haan and Jas 2000, 60–61.

6. Schulte et al. 1997, 69, 273.

7. Schulte et al. 1997, 67, 138–39; Bierens de Haan and Jas 2000, 63–65.

8. Schulte et al. 1997, 16.

9. Schulte et al. 1997, 31, 228.

10. Janssen, Kylstra-Wielinga, and Olde Meierink 1996, 145–66.

11. Schulte et al. 1997, 233.

12. Schulte et al. 1997, 46.

13. Bok 1996, 221.

14. Olde Meierink et al. (ed.) 1995, 45–47; Janssen, Kylstra-Wielinga, and Olde Meierink 1996, 165; Aalbers 1987, 58–59.

15. For Eik en Duinen, see Dumas 1991, 213–18; a print of the ruin by Willem Buytewech (1621) belongs to the same series as his depictions of Brederode and Huis ter Kleef included in this catalogue (Cats. 2a and 2b). For Heiloo, see Utrecht 1997, 22–24.

16. Kuipers-Verbuijs 1993, 9–10.

17. Beek et al. 1975, 31–33.

18. Schulte et al. 1997, 301–2.

19. De Stuers 1873. *De gids*, founded in 1837, still exists as a cultural and literary periodical.

20. An important example is the late thirteenth-century Muiderslot Castle in Muiden, west of Amsterdam. King William I prevented its demolition in 1825 because of the important role it had played in Dutch history, an action that is often considered to be a starting point in the protection of monuments by the Dutch state.

21. De Stuers 1873, 367. The argument was that the rood screen was a later addition in a different style. This subject is discussed below; see also Tillema 1973, 122.

22. Beek et al. 1975, 132.

23. For the St. Janskerk in 's-Hertogenbosch, see De Stuers 1873, 370, and De Stuers 1875, 77. In the latter, he is positive about later additions. For the Hooglandse Kerk, see De Stuers 1873, 375.

24. Janssen, Kylstra-Wielinga, and Olde Meierink 1996, 215–16.

25. In the period 1853–1914, Cuypers built many churches. Some important examples are the church of St. Willibrordus in Amsterdam (started in 1864; never completed; demolished in 1969), the Vondelkerk, also in Amsterdam (1870), and the church of St. Vitus in Hilversum (1891–92).

26. Van Leeuwen 1995, 253.

27. Beek et al. 1975, 163–64 n. 377. It is probable that De Stuers never discovered Cuypers's role in the removal of the rood screen; for further details, see Tillema 1973, 128 n. *m*.

28. Beek et al. 1975, 143.

29. Van Leeuwen 1995, 146–48; Schulte 1997, 35, 162.

30. On Cuypers as a restoration architect, see Van Leeuwen 1994.

31. Kalf 1917; Beek et al. 1975, 145; Janssen, Kylstra-Wielinga, and Olde Meierink 1996, 234–36.

32. Denslagen 2004, 85–86, 102.

33. This plan was in fact the winner in a competition in which three architects participated; Provoost and Wilkins 1995, 106–13; Schulte et al. 1997, 43, 90, 222–23.

34. An early example is Keverberg Castle in Kessel, discussed herein.

35. Denslagen 2004, 102.

36. Some examples are Nijenbeek Castle in Voorst (destroyed in 1945), Broekhuizen Castle in Broehuizen, and Asten Castle in Asten (destroyed in 1944); Schulte et al. 1997, 158–61, 175–76, 219–21; Bierens de Haan and Jas 2000, 66–69.

37. Van Nispen tot Sevenaer 1995. For a general overview of reconstruction practice in the Netherlands in an international context, see Temminck Groll 1988.

38. Schulte et al. 1997, 90, 189–91.

39. Schulte et al. 1997; for example, the restoration of Batenburg Castle is assessed negatively by J. Michels (41–42) and positively by R. J. Wielinga (94). The restoration of the Berkelpoort in Zutphen is criticized by Michels (41), but H. Klomp (162–64) is rather approving. In both cases, the difference in opinion concerns the question of how far a restorer is allowed to go to prevent further decay. Especially with Batenburg, a lot of new bricks had to be added to prevent collapse of large parts of the remaining walls.

40. For Heusden, see Netherlands Castle Society (Nederlandse Kastelenstichting, NKS), dossier *Heusden*. For Wijk bij Duurstede, see Schulte et al. 1997, 41, 261–65; NKS, dossier *Wijk bij Duurstede*. For discussion about the creation of functional rooms in general, see Schulte et al. 1997, 42–43.

41. Schulte et al. 1987, 23. For the history of restoration principles in England, France, and Germany, see Denslagen 1987, 22–150. This latter book and Denslagen 2004 contain a good overview of the development of restoration ethics in the Netherlands (153–213).

42. Beek et al. 1975, 122; Schulte et al. 1997, 37.

43. Press release from the Dutch Ministry of Education, Culture, and Science, 22 October 2003.

44. Schulte et al. 1997, 295–97; NKS, dossier *Huis te Riviere*.

45. Van den Brand 2003, 6. An example is *Cultuurhistorische effectenrapportage Meerenberg*, Bloemendaal (Bloemendaal District Council), 2001.

46. N. C. M. Maes, "Flora en fauna in en om ruïnes," in Schulte et al. 1997, 95–111.

47. Gosschalk 1866.

48. Schulte et al. 1997, 33–34, 239–45.

49. Schulte et al. 1997, 37.

50. Lemmens 1984, 97–106; Altena 2000.

51. In 1797 the town council at Nijmegen formed a commission—consisting of, among others, the antiquarian Johannes In de Betouw and the artist Hendrik Hoogers (1747–1824), who was also secretary to the council—to investigate the situation of the protected ruins. The quotation comes from their report, dated 10 July 1797, now in Nijmegen Town Archive (OAN 45, Raadssignaat 1797-II). Hoogers made many drawings of Valkhof Castle before and after demolition (for example, Fig. 106). See also Lemmens 1984, 98, 105, 122.

52. Lemmens 1984, 105; Schulte et al. 1997, 36, 154–55.

53. Lemmens 1984, 113.

54. NRC Handelsblad 1996; Schulte et al. 1997, 155; Cobouw 1997; Van Leeuwen and Pantus 1997.

55. Olde Meierink et al. (ed.) 1995, 218–24; Kok 1996; Janssen, Kylstra-Wielinga, and Olde Meierink 1996, 219–25; Schulte et al. 1997, 34–35.

56. Schulte et al. 1997, 149–52; Hielkema 2000.

57. Schulte et al. 1997, 102, 151.

58. Bollebakker 1998; Bierens de Haan and Jas 2000, 68–69.

59. De Jong 2000.

MONUMENTAL RUINS IN THE DUTCH LANDSCAPE

GERRIT ADRIAENSZ. GOUW, AFTER HENDRICK GOLTZIUS

active c. 1604–38

Little is known about the life of the printmaker Gerrit Gouw (who sometimes signed his works Gauw), except that he was active by 1604 and by 1622 was recorded in Haarlem as a member of the St. Luke's guild.[1] He made his own printed portraits but also produced engravings after designs by such major printmakers as Jacob Matham (q.v.) and Hendrick Goltzius (1558–1617). An important aspect of his career involved engraving the lettering for manuals on calligraphy, such as Jan van de Velde I's (1568–1623) *Deliciae variarum insigniumque sculpturarum* (Haarlem, 1604), G. de Carpentier's *Schriftuirlik zedevormisch alphabetum* (Haarlem, 1620), and H. Friesenborch's *Lusthoff der schriftkonst* (Embden, 1628), as well as the text for the title page of G. Thibault's *Académie de l'espée* (Brussels, 1628). Gouw's burial in Haarlem was recorded on 16 January 1638.

NOTE

1. Material on Gerrit Gouw is drawn from Thieme-Becker 11 (1920):295.

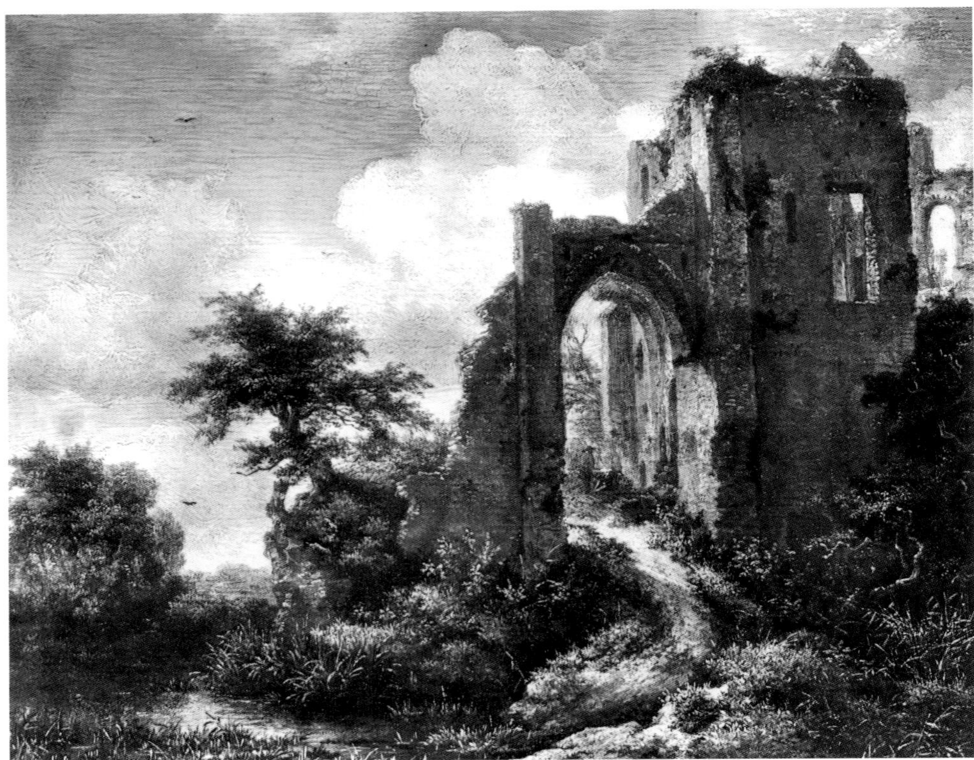

Fig. 109. Jacob van Ruisdael, *A Ruined Entrance Gate of Castle Brederode*, c. 1655, oil on panel, John G. Johnson Collection, Philadelphia Museum of Art

[1]

Landscape with the Ruins of Brederode, c. 1600–1610

Inscriptions: bottom center, 2; far right, *Cum. privileg. IM (ineen) escudit*; in Latin and in Dutch below the scene,

ARNVLPHVS. Comes Hollandiae III.C qui in Winckel ao. 993-caesus est Ziphrido natu minori Filio / latifundia ac dominia amphoribus Iusto decempedis dimensa donavit: inde arci, quam pater eidem quoque, / dederat Brederodiae et postentati agnomen mansit. Arx ao 1426. deformata, non procul Harlemo, ut hic videre licet.

ARNVLPHVS. De derde Grave van Hollandt C (dien i Winckel .ao 993. verslagen is) heeft syn ionckste soon / Ziphrido toe gemeten landen ende domÿnen met breede roeden, Waer deur het Casteel, welck de Vader hem oeck / gegeuven hadde, ende den naecomelingen de naeme Brederode gebleven is. Ao. 1426 is dit casteel geschent leyt niet verre van Haerlem alsmen hier siet.

(Arnulphus, the third count of Holland, defeated in [the village of] Winkel in the year 993, vested his youngest son Ziphrido with lands and domains broad in measure ["breed roeden"], which his father had given him and from which to him and his descendents the name Brederode derives. In the year 1426 this castle was destroyed, and it is not far from Haarlem, as one sees here.)

Etching and engraving, 239 × 328 mm (9⅜ × 12⅞ in); state ii/iii

Courtesy of the Fogg Art Museum, Harvard University Art Museums, Cambridge, Massachusetts, Light-Outerbridge Collection, Richard Norton Memorial Fund, M24558

References: Hollstein 8 (1949):133 (as after H. Goltzius); Hollstein 11 (1955):234, no. B304 (as Jacob Matham, engraved by G. A. Gouw); Reznicek 1961, 1:423, under no. 391; Boon 1978, 1:99, under no. 280; Berlin 1979, 46–47, no. 50; Freedberg 1980, 27 and fig. 17; Van der Wyck and Kloek 1990, 2:57–58, fig. 81; Amsterdam 1993–94, 46, no. 4, with transcription of caption; Kloek 1993, 57–58; Widerkehr 1993, 258, no. M14-2; Leeflang 1997, 61–63; Amsterdam/New York/Toledo 2003–4, 199, fig. 73a.

This etching of Brederode Castle near Haarlem (see also Cat. 2a) is one of the earliest depictions of what would soon become a popular subject for Dutch draftsmen, printmakers, and painters throughout the seventeenth century: the ruins of local medieval structures, many of which had been destroyed during the long Dutch conflict with the Spanish that led to national independence from Hapsburg rule.[1] It belongs to a series of four landscape prints designed by Hendrick Goltzius (1558–1617) and issued by his stepson Jacob Matham (q.v.), as indicated by an inscription on the first print in the series that displays Matham's address with the royal print privilege and the inscription: *IGoltzius Iuen(tor); G. Gouw incidit.*[2] Goltzius's even earlier signed and dated drawing of 1600 in the Rijksprentenkabinet, Amsterdam, shows another view of this site, probably made on the spot, that captures the shattered shapes of the building, isolated on the page and modeled by sunlight and soft shadow (Fig. 36), while an informal sketch by Matham, dated 1603 (Kupferstichkabinett, Berlin) shows the courtyard of the farm at Brederode with the castle at the left background.[3]

Gouw's print, rendered with the control and finish of an engraving, appears to have been made with a different intention in mind, for the ruin is now placed within a fully articulated environment. Below the scene is a short inscription in Latin and Dutch about the history of

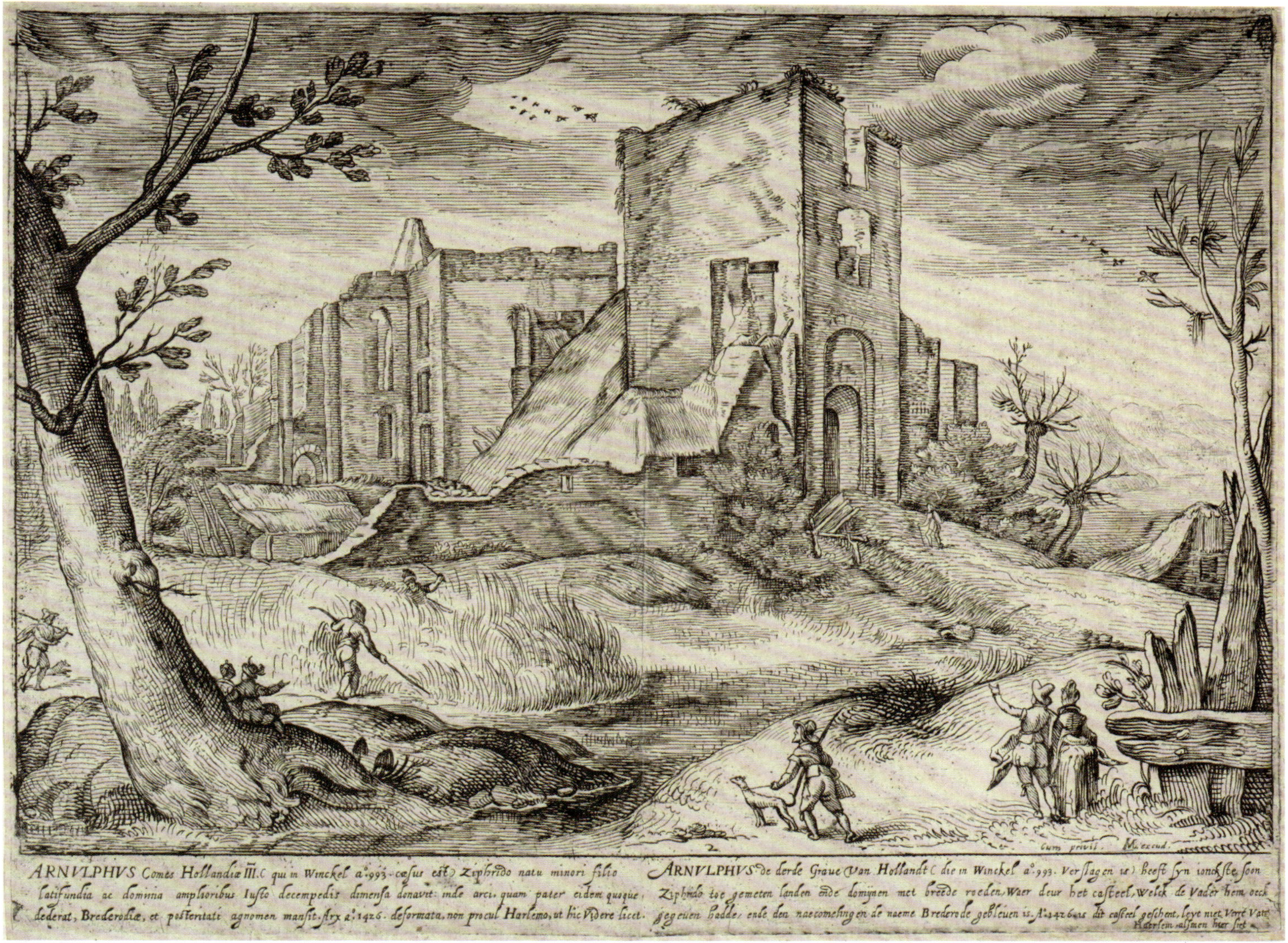

the Brederode family and the building. Here are recounted the legendary origins of the family in the tenth century with Arnulphus, third count of Holland, and his son, Ziphrido.[4] To a seventeenth-century Dutch viewer of this time, however, any image of Brederode must have immediately recalled more recent events still in the memory of many living citizens: the traumatic Siege of Haarlem of 1572–73, after which the castle was blown up by the Spanish. Yet Gouw's inscription cites only the much earlier destruction of the castle that had occurred in 1426 (it would be partially restored in 1478) during the long conflict known as the quarrel between the Hoeks and the Kabeljauws.[5] As this print appears to have been issued close to the time of the Twelve Year Truce with the Spanish (1609–21), a direct comment on recent history might have seemed more inflammatory than invoking a parallel from the distant past as a reminder of Brederode's historic importance.

Most depictions of Brederode, such as Willem Buytewech's well-known etching of 1616 (Cat. 2a), show it from the side in order to expose the distinctive faceted tower, whose conical top is just visible at the upper left in Gouw's print. Gouw, however, has elevated Brederode to the upper half of the sheet, making the entrance gate the dominant section of the larger complex of structures. This heavy, crenellated block, which was called "de Poortboog" (the arch gate), attracted the attention of several major artists, who explored it from various vantage points and with very different interpretations. In Hercules Segers's eerie etching (Fig. 111), ancient, corroded bricks convey an almost tomblike effect, while Jacob van Ruisdael's lively little oil sketch in the Philadelphia Museum of Art (Fig. 109) emphasizes the ruin's interaction with the luxuriant natural growth all around it.

In Gouw's print, the scene is enlivened by figures engaged in pleasantly peaceful occupations: men cutting the tall grass, hunters with their dogs, couples at left and right who gesture toward the castle as if discussing its appearance or history, and a small traveler with a staff and a pack on his back who climbs the path to the gate. By using figures and trees in the foreground and clouds in the background to create a frame for the ruin, Gouw intensifies focus on Brederode, whose mass is silhouetted against the light behind it. As a result, what seems at first no more than a matter-of-fact depiction of a local landmark takes on something of the aura of a pilgrimage site.

NOTES

1. For further discussion of Brederode Castle and its history in relation to Buytewech's print, see Cat. 2a.

2. Amsterdam 1993–94, 46.

3. Repr. Widerkehr 1993, 240, fig. 151.

4. Modern historians date the earliest construction of the castle to around 1282 after Willem van Brederode had acquired the land through exchange with Floris V, count of Holland. The history of the building is discussed in Van Reyen 1965, 71–73, and Schulte et al. 1997, 240–42. See also Allan 1983 and Slive 2001, 41.

5. The conflict between the competing factions of the Hoeks (Fishhooks) and the Kabeljauws (Codfish) began after the death of Willem IV in 1345: through dynastic marriage, the Bavarian house of Wittelsbach acquired possession of Holland, which then included parts of Zeeland and Friesland. Brederode, destroyed in 1351 by the Kabeljauws under the command of Gijsbrecht van Nijenrode, was rebuilt between 1354 and 1426, when it again faced destruction. In 1433 Philip the Good, duke of Burgundy, seized the territory of Holland from Jacqueline (Jacoba), countess of Holland, Zeeland, and Friesland. The Hoeks were the party of nobles who supported Jacqueline and were against the House of Burgundy, while the Kabeljauws, representing the cities, took the opposite position and allied themselves with Burgundy. The clash continued until the end of the fifteenth century, with the defeat of the Hoeks (1490) following the death of Mary of Burgundy in 1482, when control of the Netherlands passed to Archduke Maximilian of Austria. In 1491 Brederode withstood yet another assault when it was plundered by German troops.

WILLEM PIETERSZ. BUYTEWECH
1591/92–1624

Painter, draftsman, and etcher, Buytewech (known in his time as "Geestige Willem," or Witty Willem) was an influential figure in the development of Dutch landscape and genre subjects, even though his career was short.[1] In addition, he produced historical scenes, costume studies, allegories, designs for book illustrations, and even two etchings of stranded sperm whales. Born in Rotterdam, he entered the Haarlem guild of St. Luke in 1612 along with Esaias van de Velde (q.v.) and Hercules Segers (q.v.). Both were also innovative printmakers, as was Jan van de Velde II (q.v.), who joined the guild in 1614. Of the thirty-two known prints by Buytewech, his series of ten etchings entitled *Verscheyden landschapjes* (Various little landscapes) of about 1616 can be considered particularly original in their technique and interpretation of landscape, blending linear pattern with acute observation of nature. Two of the three scenes that represent local medieval ruins are exhibited here (Cats. 2a and 2b). Buytewech returned to Rotterdam in 1617, and on 16 September 1624 he drew up his will. He was buried a week later in the Grote Kerk, Rotterdam, at the age of thirty-three.

NOTE

1. For information on Buytewech's life and art, see Haverkamp-Begemann 1959, 3–5; Rotterdam/Paris 1974–75, x–xxi; and M. van Berge-Gerbaud's extensive essay in *Dictionary of Art* 1996, 5:323–26.

[2]
Two etchings from *Verscheyden landschapjes* (Various small landscapes), c. 1616

[2a] *Ruins of Brederode Castle near Haarlem* (no. 2), c. 1616

Inscriptions: lower left, *WB*; lower right, 2.

Etching, 89 × 127 mm (3½ × 5 in.) (platemark), 97 × 134 mm (3 3/16 × 5¼ in.) (sheet); state ii/iii

Museum of Fine Arts, Boston, Helen and Alice Colburn Fund, 34.19

References: Van der Kellen 1867–73, no. 29; Hollstein 4 (1949):72, repr., and 75; Haverkamp-Begemann 1959, 42, 174, no. vG 22; Rotterdam/Paris 1974–75, 108, no. 133, pl. 137; De Groot 1979, no. 13; London 1986, 136; Levesque 1994, 74, 80, fig. 73.

Buytewech's *Verscheyden landschapjes* (Various small landscapes), a series of nine small landscape prints plus an illustrated title page, conveys an intimate yet curiously elegant view of the early seventeenth-century Dutch countryside. Tall trees with slender, anemone-like trunks and neatly patterned foliage are the main emphasis in six of these small sheets, but the remaining prints focus on medieval ruins in the vicinity of Haarlem or The Hague. As C. Levesque has argued, this juxtaposition of imagery, which displays the abundance of the cultivated Dutch landscape in the present next to scenes of architectural remains from the past, seems calculated to encourage meditation on connections between then and now, especially as Brederode Castle and the Huis ter Kleef were both destroyed by the Spanish in 1573 during the long struggle that preceded Dutch independence.[1]

Brederode Castle, which Buytewech placed immediately after the title page, is probably the most frequently represented of all the Dutch historic ruin sites (Cats. 1, 7, and 8). Built by Willem van Brederode and subsequent members of his family in the woods at Santpoort, five kilometers (three miles) northwest of Haarlem, it is a large complex dating from the thirteenth and fourteenth centuries that includes a fortified entrance gate, or barbican, a moat, an exterior courtyard, and a square castle with three rectangular towers and one round one.[2] The faceted, cone-shaped cap of the round tower helps identify Brederode in many representations such as Buytewech's, where it rises behind the bulk of the ruin at the upper right. Even before the Spanish troops set fire to the castle, it had sustained earlier destruction, beginning in 1351 with the assault of the Kabeljauws under the leadership of Gijsbrecht van Nijenrode. After a period of rebuilding, further destruction followed in 1426 and again in 1491, when plundering German troops reduced sections of the castle to ruin. The extensive devastation of the site, following the Spanish siege of Haarlem, is evident in the many seventeenth-century depictions of its remains. Because of its historic importance, efforts to preserve Brederode, begun in 1862, have continued, and the complex, although heavily restored, remains an important tourist site that demonstrates the layout of a medieval castle as well as the sense of temporality that old ruins can evoke.[3]

Like Breenbergh's diminutive series of Roman ruins (Cat. 55), Buytewech's etchings have a compressed intensity that is partly the consequence of reducing monumental structures to intimate scale. A small figure seated at the center foreground suggests the actual size of Brederode, whose solid, irregular forms rise at the right, with the smaller ruin of the entrance gate in the distance at the left. Fused with the landscape, the castle has attracted vines and grasses that soften its shattered top, smoothing transitions between the broken walls. Buytewech's disciplined, confident technique is displayed in the range of small etched touches and parallel hatchings that capture surface textures and the shapes of the building, whose remains include a windowed section at the left and the flat surface of an exposed interior wall at the right. Despite pervasive damage that has rendered the castle uninhabitable, Buytewech's interpretation of Brederode stresses tenacity and survival in the structure's transformation into a new sequence of powerful sculptural shapes. A strong, vertical spine joins the two sections of the ruin, while stable horizontal accents throughout the scene extend even to the stippled touches that evoke transparent layers of cloud.

NOTES

1. Levesque 1994, 74. The third ruin print in this cycle represents Eyckenduyn chapel (no. 10 in the sequence and Fig. 44) between The Hague and Loosduynen, a Roman Catholic chapel, sold by the States of Holland in 1580, when Calvinism became the state religion, and largely demolished the next year. See Hollstein 4 (1949):75 and De Groot 1979: no. 21.

2. For a discussion of the building and its history, see Van Reyen 1965, 71–73; Allan 1983; and Schulte et al. 1997, 240–42, which includes floor plans and diagrams of the various stages of construction and renovation. E. P. Löffler has analyzed drawings that represent Brederode's entrance gate or were made from this vantage point (Löffler 2002, 10–14 and 16). Brederode's history is also discussed in Slive 2001, 41.

3. Discussion of archeological surveys and repeated restoration campaigns at Brederode can be found in Schulte et al. 1997, 242–43.

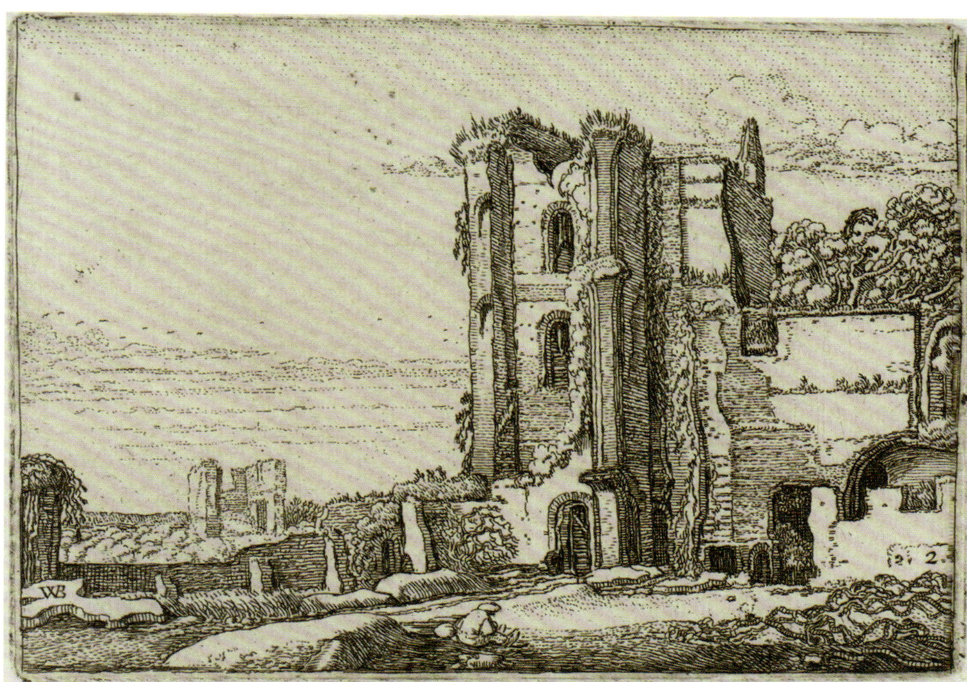

[2a]

[2b] *Ruins of the Huis ter Kleef near Haarlem* (no. 3), c. 1616

Inscriptions: lower left, *WB;* lower right, *3*.

Etching, 89 × 124 mm (3 7/16 × 4 7/8 in.) (platemark), 96 × 131 mm (3 3/4 × 5 3/16 in.) (sheet); state ii/iii

Museum of Fine Arts, Boston, Helen and Alice Colburn Fund, 34.18

References: Van der Kellen 1867–73, no. 30; Hollstein 4 (1949):75, no. 37; Haverkamp-Begemann 1959, 42, 174, no. vG 23 and fig. 85; Rotterdam/Paris 1974–75, 108–9, no. 134, pl. 138; De Groot 1979, no. 14; Boston/St. Louis 1980–81, 64–65, no. 37; Levesque 1994, 74, 80–81, fig. 74.

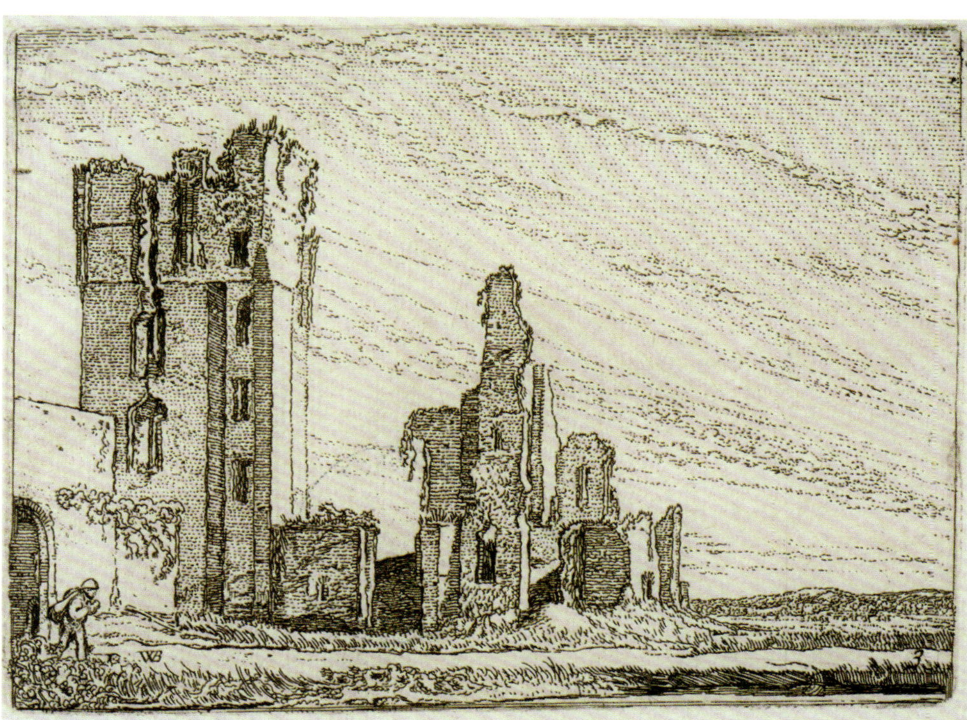

[2b]

Today only a few large chunks of rubble mark the ancient foundations and walls of the Huis ter Kleef, located in the middle of the municipal garden (*stadtskweektuin*) just north of the old center of Haarlem. This castle, whose foundations date partly from the thirteenth century, was originally called Huis te Schoten after the nearby hamlet of Schoten.[1] Listed in the feudal register of the counts of Holland of 1329, it was transferred in 1403 to Margaretha van Kleef, countess of Holland, from whom its name apparently derives. Around 1500 it came into the possession of the noble Van Brederode family. The Huis ter Kleef acquired a conspicuous historic role during the brutal siege of Haarlem (1572–73), when it was taken over as headquarters for the Spanish commander Don Frederick de Toledo, son of the duke of Alva. With the surrender of the city in 1573, the Spanish blew up the castle to prevent its being used by Protestant rebels. Although some restoration was done to the building in 1634, it remained—like Brederode—in a state of ruin that would have reminded early seventeenth-century visitors of the Dutch Republic's long struggle for independence from foreign rule.

Buytewech's memorable interpretation of the Huis ter Kleef, which follows the image of Brederode in his print series, stresses the fragmentation and irregularity of the remains of the castle, split into separate sections by the explosion that destroyed it. Beside the square tower at left, the fragmented walls at right seem fragile and vulnerable to further erosion and collapse, though they still stand firmly upright. In contrast to the stable, timeless effect of Brederode, the Huis ter Kleef has been captured within an ongoing temporal process. At the lower left, a small figure with a pack on his back walks into the picture space. Suggestions of clouds are evoked by diagonal streams of dots that seem to move across the sky as if magnetically pulled toward the horizon at the right, where low dunes rise in the distance. As C. S. Ackley has observed, Buytewech's highly original graphic vocabulary, which employs short hatches, dots, and stipples to avoid defining continuous contours, gives silhouettes and sky an unusual eloquence.[2] A falling light suggestive of sunset intensifies the scene's expression of the impermanence of human works. How radically Buytewech has reduced and concentrated his subject is obvious when it is compared to an etching of the same site from Claes Jansz. Visscher's *Pleasant Places around Haarlem* of 1611–12, in which the Huis ter Kleef is relegated to the background of a delightfully anecdotal scene of people and animals enjoying the outdoors (Fig. 42).

NOTES

1. On the Huis ter Kleef and its history, see Temminck 1995 and Schulte et al. 1997, 236–39.
2. Ackley in Boston/St. Louis 1980–81, 64–65.

JAN VAN DE VELDE II
c. 1593–1641

Son of the famous calligrapher Jan van de Velde I (1569–1623) and student of the engraver Jacob Matham (q.v.), Jan van de Velde II entered the Haarlem painters' guild in 1614, a year or two after several major printmakers had joined it: his uncle Esaias van de Velde (q.v.), Willem Buytewech (q.v.), and Hercules Segers (q.v.).[1] Major suites of etchings by Jan appear from 1615 on, beginning with his cycle of eighteen etched landscapes with ruins (Hollstein 178–95), published by Claes Jansz. Visscher of Amsterdam, four of which are included in this catalogue (Cats 3a–d). Indeed, no Dutch artist was more intensely engaged in representing ruin motifs, as further illustrated in Van de Velde's series *The Twelve Months*, published by Visscher in 1616 (Hollstein 46–57) and in *Sixteen Landscapes and Ruins* (Hollstein 196–215), published by Robert de Baudous in the same year. His prolific output in 1616 continued with the five-part series known as *Sixty Landscapes with Ruins* (Hollstein 232–91), also published by De Baudous. Various kinds of ruins also appear frequently in genre and historical scenes by Van de Velde, who contributed prints of major local ruin sites (after drawings by Pieter Saenredam) to Samuel Ampzing's historical description and praise of Haarlem (*Beschrijvinge ende lof der stad Haerlem in Holland*), published in 1628 (Cat. 4). In these and other prints, Van de Velde developed a fluid, elegantly patterned, highly clarified approach to etching that greatly influenced contemporary Dutch printmakers, including Rembrandt (q.v.).

Following his marriage to Stintje Fredericksdr. Non in Enkhuizen in 1618, Van de Velde settled in Haarlem, where he would produce almost five hundred prints—primarily landscapes but also portraits, genre scenes, and book illustrations, as well as a few landscape paintings. From 1618 on, most of his prints were based not on his own drawings but on those of other artists, such as Buytewech, Esaias van de Velde, Pieter Molijn (q.v.), and Moses van Uyttenbroek (c. 1600–after 1646). In 1636 he and his wife moved to Enkhuizen, where the artist died in 1641.

NOTE

1. Information on Jan van de Velde II is based on C. S. Ackley's biography in Boston/St. Louis 1980–81, 70, and on G. Luijten's essay in *Dictionary of Art* 32 (1996):140. The earliest research on the artist's prints was done in the late nineteenth century: Franken and Van der Kellen 1883 (rev. 1968); while a monograph on the paintings and drawings was published by J. G. van Gelder in 1933.

[3]

Four etchings from *Amoenissimae aliquot Regiunculae et antiquorum monumentorum ruinae* (Some very pleasant places and ruins of antique monuments, or *Eighteen Landscapes with Ruins*), 1615

[3a] *Frontispiece* (no. 1), 118 × 309 mm (4⅝ × 12³⁄₁₆ in.) (trimmed within platemark); state ii/iv; 58.461

[3b] *Wooded Landscape with Circular Temple (the Temple of the Sibyl at Tivoli)* (no. 3), 120 × 315 mm (4¾ × 12⅜ in.) (platemark), 122 × 317 mm (4³⁄₁₆ × 12½ in.) (sheet); state ii/ii; 58.463

[3c] *Ruins with a Dead Tree* (no. 10), 119 × 317 mm (4¹¹⁄₁₆ × 12½ in.) (platemark), 120 × 318 mm (4¾ × 12½ in.) (sheet); state ii/ii; 58.470

[3d] *Ruins of a Hexagonal Tower, Bridge, River and Town Buildings* (no. 14), 120 × 317 mm (4¾ × 12½ in.) (platemark), 122 × 318 mm (sheet) (4¹³⁄₁₆ × 12½ in.); state ii/ii; 58.474

Inscriptions: on title page, *Amoenissimae aliquot Regiunculae, et / antiquorum monumentorum ruinae: / a Ioanne Veldio Iuniore delineate / et perchalcographiam in lucem edi: / te a Nicolao Ioannis Vischerio / anaglÿptario / Anno. CIII CXV. / Amstelodami*

(Some very pleasant places and ruins of antique monuments drawn by Jan van de Velde, Junior, and brought to life [i.e., published] by the engraver Nicolaes Johannes Visscher in the year 1615. Amsterdam)

Museum of Fine Arts, Boston, George Peabody Gardner Fund, nos. 58.461, 58.463, 58.470, 58.474

References: Franken and Van der Kellen 1883 (rev. 1968), 217, 219, 226, and 230; Van Gelder 1933, 48, pl. XI, fig. 22; Hollstein 33 (1989):60–65, nos. 178, 180, 187, and 191 and 34 (1989):96, 99, and 100; Boston/St. Louis 1980–81, 72; New Brunswick 1983, 134, no. 122; Levesque 1994, 89–113, figs. 102, 104, 111, and 115.

The earliest dated prints by Jan van de Velde II belong to his magnificent cycle of 1615, *Eighteen Landscapes with Ruins*, whose refinement of technique and originality of interpretation place this series among the finest of all seventeenth-century Dutch print productions. Unusually long and narrow in format, they offer a stunning variety of local and foreign scenery, mixing observation and imagination and alternating between peaceful and dramatic moods. Despite the title, only ten of these wide panoramic images actually focus on ruined buildings, although all prints in the cycle suggest the passing of time, individually and as a group.

A temporal context is established immediately in the triptych-like title page (Cat. 3a), where the viewer encounters a group of young men playing dice or another game of chance—a common vanitas motif (see Cat. 78)—in front of a weathered, hexagonal Roman structure at the center foreground. The building displays a billboard of inscriptions in cursive script and Roman lettering announcing that the scenes to follow will consist of "pleasant landscapes" and the ruins of antique monuments. In this sheet, old buildings on both sides rise out of dense, variously patterned masses of foliage within the countryside beyond: an elaborate medieval church at the left and farmhouses with a tall, ruined tower at the right beside a low field with

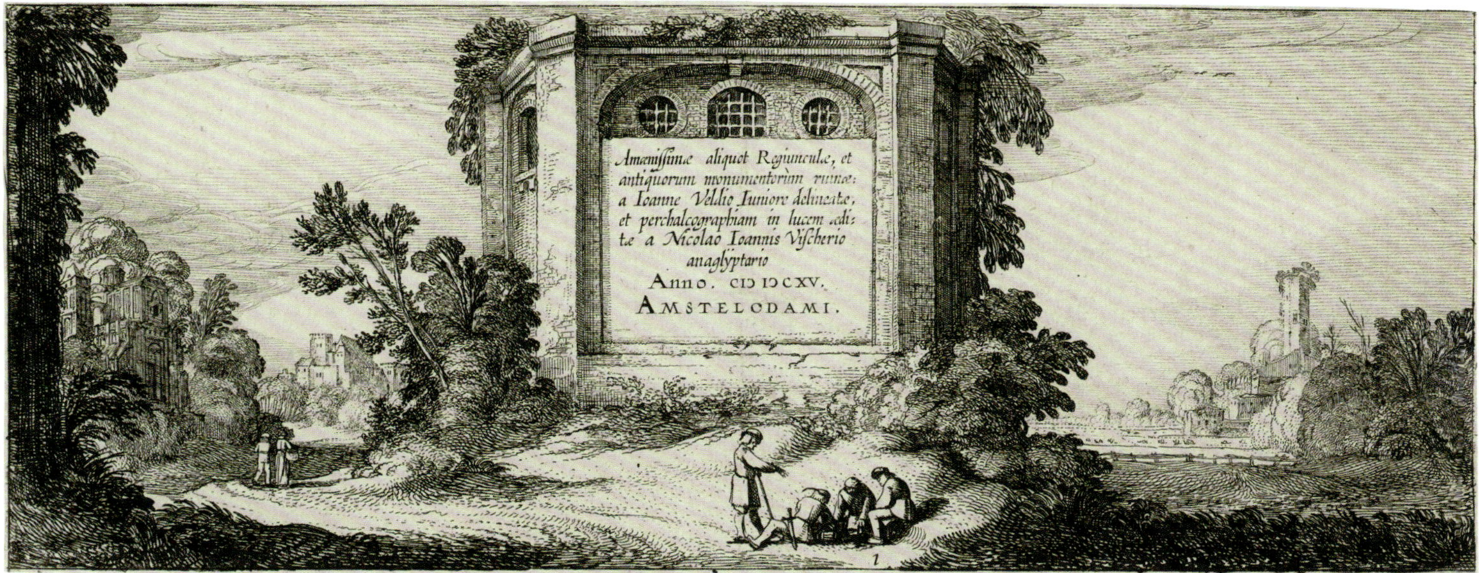

[3a]

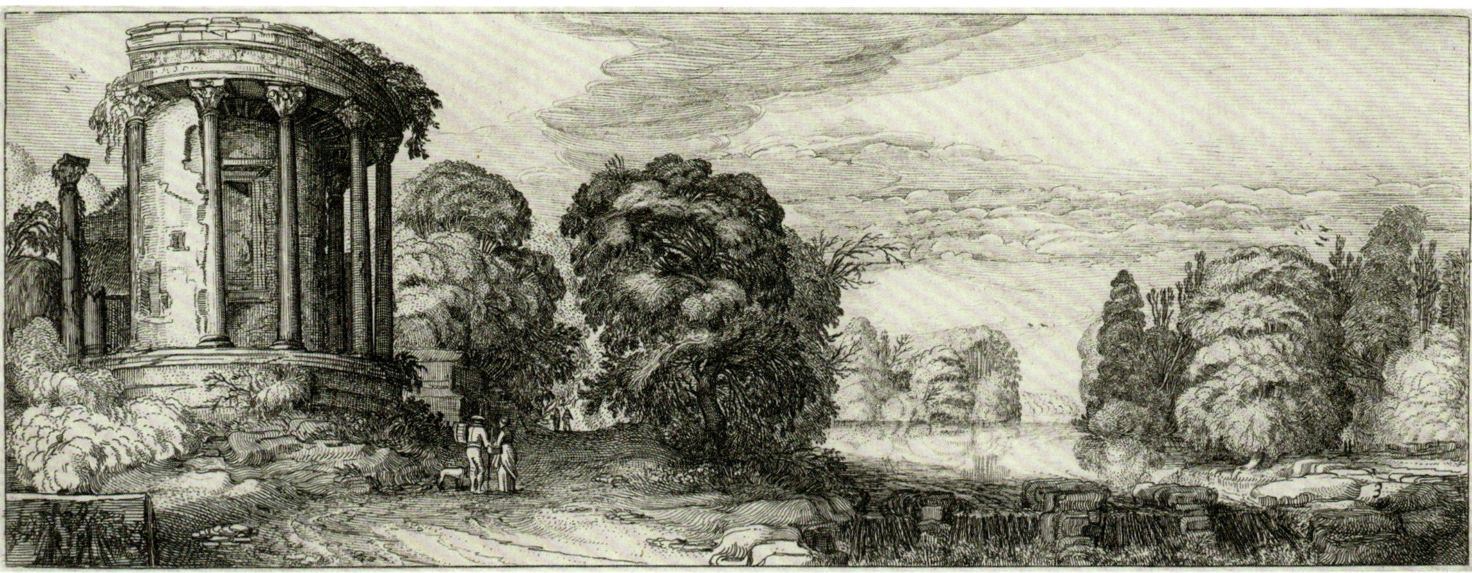

[3b]

grazing sheep. The couple walking into the landscape at the left encourages the observer to do the same.

While none of the buildings in the title sheet (or in most prints in the cycle) can be connected to specific structures, Van de Velde chose the famous ruined Temple of the Sibyl at Tivoli for the third landscape in his series (Cat. 3b), probably basing his depiction on an earlier image, as there is no evidence that he ever visited Italy himself. Most representations of this site emphasize the dramatically elevated position of the round temple on its precipice over the Aniene Falls (Cats. 59 and 65), but Van de Velde gives the structure a homier, more accessible effect by choosing a ground-level vantage point and representing couples walking peacefully along the path beside it.[1] In this remarkably original interpretation, he devotes the entire right half of the immediate foreground to the waterfall but shows only its uppermost rim before the water's plunge down the mountain below. The very process of time seems to come alive here in the transition from the calm water of the river with its reflections of surrounding trees to the accelerating line of eddies crossing the edge of the drop just where the picture space ends and the viewer's world begins.

In contrast to the peaceful effect of these prints, *Ruins with a Dead Tree* (Cat. 3c), number 10 in the series, is dramatic and foreboding both in its imagery and in its bolder, more agitated line. In the center is an enormous dead tree whose twisting trunk and bare branches writhe in an almost human way, an effect intensified by how it seems to push against the upper edge of the narrow sheet as if confined by the picture space. While all other prints in the sequence include extensive vistas, this

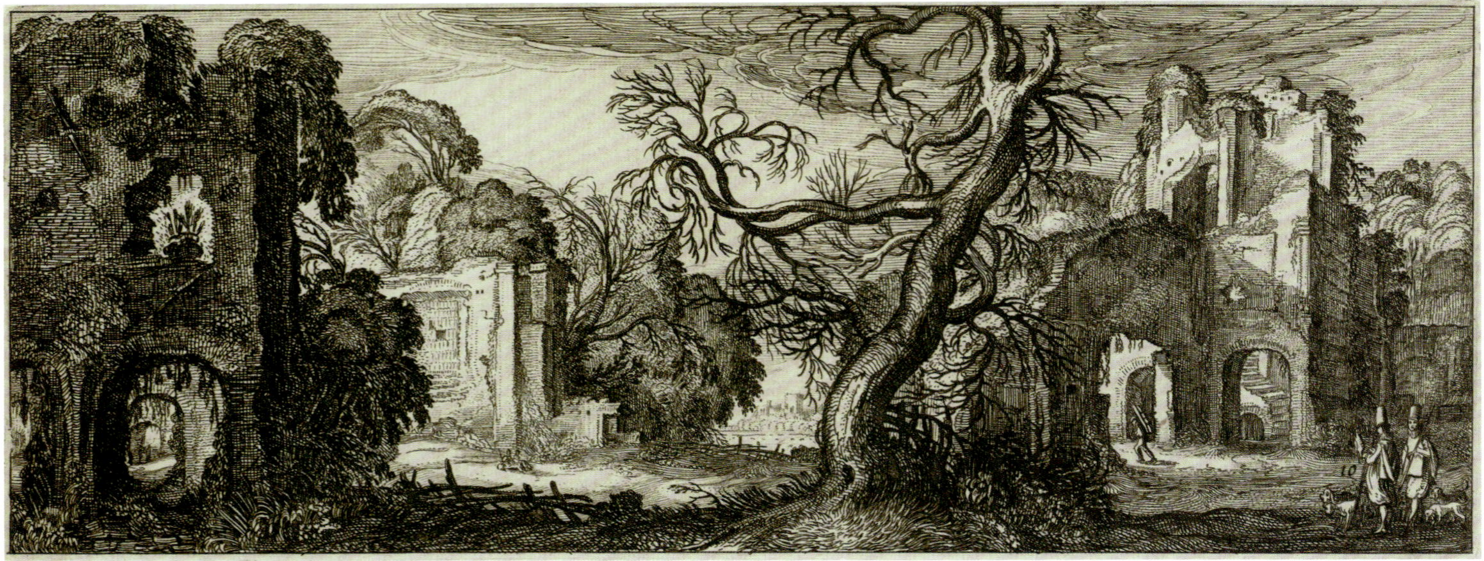

[3c]

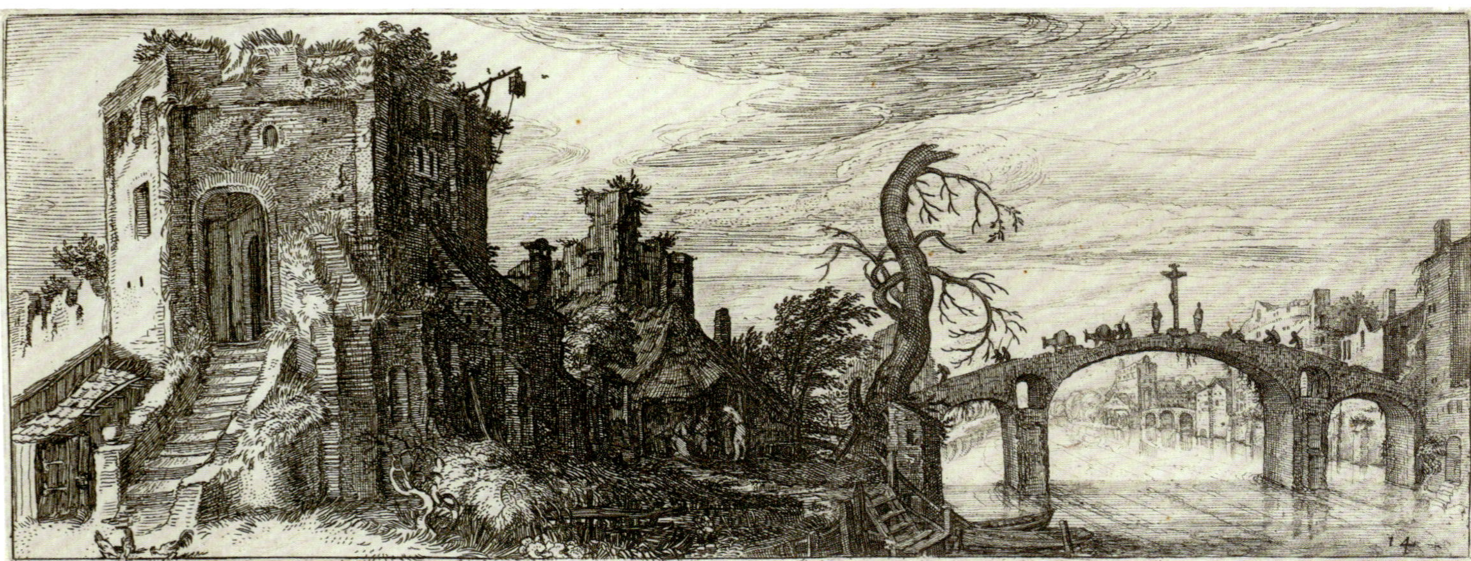

[3d]

scene, filled with the densely overlapped shapes of trees and ruins, restricts spatial penetration to small "views-through" (for which the Dutch coined the terms *doorsien* or *doorkijkje*): at left, a passageway of arches within arches penetrates the mass of the dark ruin, framing two tiny figures in the distance; in the center, dead and living trees frame a small illuminated view of a faraway castle. The large ruin at the right displays additional views-through, exposing the interior stairway of the building. Beside it, two elegant, top-hatted falconers stand with their pack of hunting dogs.[2]

The intention and meaning of such print series (addressed herein by C. Levesque; see pages 49–62) are especially thought provoking, especially in the case of these images, which combine observation with imagination and use both local and foreign scenery, as was also the practice in Dutch poetic sequences of this period.[3] *Ruins of a Hexagonal Tower, Bridge, River and Town Buildings*, number 14 in the cycle (Cat. 3d), combines motifs found elsewhere in the series, such as a weathered hexagonal Roman building, a dead tree, and a view-through, here framed by a curving Italianate bridge. While the figures in the deep shadows of the dilapidated tavern in the center recall traditional Netherlandish genre scenes (Cat. 27), the imagery of this landscape remains predominantly Italian. The Roman Catholic crucifixion shrine on the bridge at the right (the kind of icon for public worship that was banned in the officially Calvinist Dutch provinces after independence from Spain had been won) raises the question of whether ruined structures in this context were meant to suggest darker associations with the past, suggesting the fall of the old order. Levesque has argued that, by contrast, ruins on Dutch soil that had been destroyed during the Spanish conflict—such as the medieval castles of Brederode and Huis ter Kleef (nos. 8 and 12 in this series)—tended to be presented in more peaceful landscapes, rendered in a simpler, more clarified style to illustrate the harmony of the native countryside as a product of peace and labor.[4]

In any case, ruins clearly attracted Van de Velde because their uniquely irregular forms offer such unexpected visual effects. His stunningly refined technique, which often recalls engraving, captures the shapes and surfaces of all aspects of his varied landscapes, even their changing skies, where his controlled, supple line renders cloud movement with his distinctively elastic flexibility. Such a range of effects is particularly evident in *Ruins of a Hexagonal Tower, Bridge, River and Town Buildings*, whose rather somber imagery is enlivened with a touch of pictorial wit: three chickens at the lower left, pecking *through* the lower border of the print.

NOTES

1. The Flemish artist Paulus Bril (1554–1626), who had settled in Rome by around 1575, made two dramatic drawings of the site (Musée du Louvre, Paris) that emphasize its high vantage point over the waterfall (Fig. 143; Amsterdam 2001, 34–35, figs. B and C).

2. In 1616 Van de Velde made a series of four prints of falconers, published by De Baudous. Hollstein 33 (1989):54, nos. 155–58 and 34 (1989):84–85, repr.

3. See Levesque 1994, 93–101, in which the author draws parallels between Van de Velde's print cycle and Dutch poetic sequences, based on the Georgic tradition, such as the *Nederduytschen Helicon* (1610), Philibert van Borsselen's *Den Binckhorst* (1613), and Hendrick Laurensz. Spiegel's *Hertspiegel* (1614), which employ the framework of a journey through nature to evoke the harmony and fertility of native landscapes in contrast to more turbulent and barren foreign scenery.

4. Levesque 1994, 106–10, and her essay herein. For additional depictions, see Cats. 1, 2a, 7, and 8 (Brederode) and Cats. 2b and 4 (Huis ter Kleef).

[4]

Landscape with the Huis ter Kleef (after Pieter Saenredam), from Samuel Ampzing, *Beschrijvinge ende lof der stad Haerlem in Holland* (Description and praise of the city of Haarlem in Holland), Adriaen Rooman, Haarlem, 1628

Inscriptions: upper left, *P. Zaenredam inv. J.V. Velde Sculp.* below the image,

Dit is het Huys te Kleef so 't huyden word gevonden
In ons Beleg vernield, in ons Beleg geschonden:
Daer Frederico lag als hy de stad besloot.
Daer Frederico lag als hy de Stad beschoot.

Wie dattet heeft gesticht, kan niemand seker weten,
Maert hoe het is verwoest, en is noch niet vergeten.
Foey Spanjaerd die ons land soo deerlyk heb geprangd!
En foey hem die ook noch na syne konst verlagd!

Wat dit nu voor een huys mag syn geweest voor desen
Begrypt eeynder licht die op syn huydig wesen,
En hoog en wyd begryp syn wacker oge slaet.
Waert soo weer opbeboud, het waer ons lants zieraed.

(This is Kleef manor as it looks today,
Damaged and destroyed during our siege,
Here Frederico camped when he surrounded the city.
Here Frederico camped when he bombarded the town.

Who founded it, nobody knows for certain,
But how it was destroyed has not yet been forgotten.
Fie on the Spaniards who oppressed our country so sorely!
And fie on him who still longs for their return!

How this house looked before, can be understood easily
By anyone who sees it with open eyes at its present state,
And casts an attentive eye on its high and wide extension.
Were it to be rebuilt that way, it would be the jewel of our land.)[1]

Etching, 159 × 235 mm (6¼ × 9¼ in.) (image), 330.2 × 203.2 mm (13 × 8 in.) (overall)

Department of Rare Books, The Houghton Library, Harvard College Library, Cambridge, Massachusetts, Neth 3407.1* (Poughkeepsie); The National Gallery of Art Library, Washington, D.C., David K. E. Bruce Fund (Sarasota and Louisville)

References: Boston/St. Louis 1980–81, 104–5; Schwartz and Bok 1990, 35–46; Leeflang 1997, 78–79, 109 nn. 88 and 89.

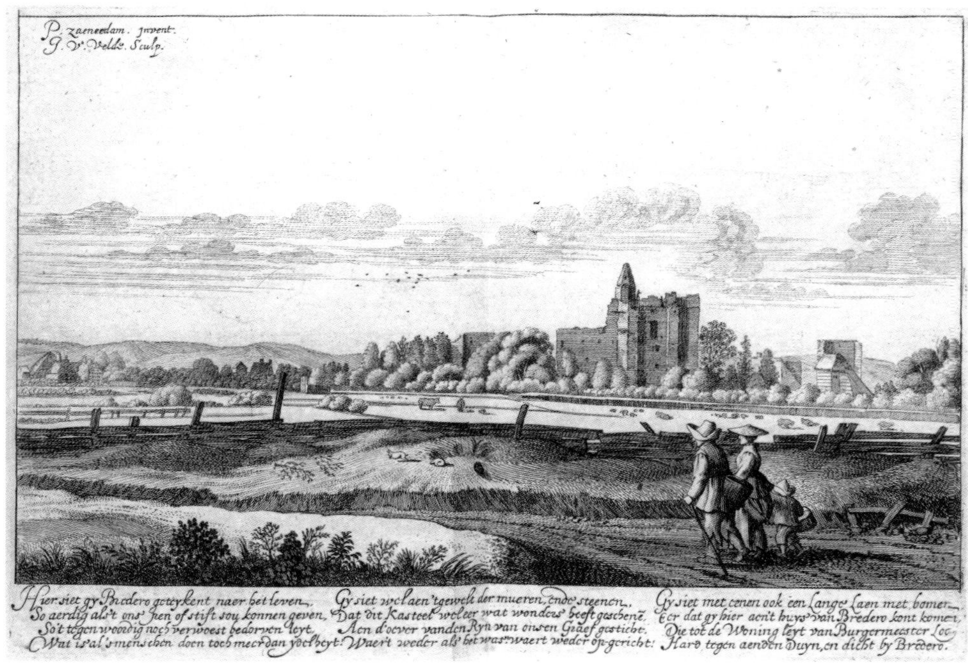

Fig. 110. Jan van de Velde II, after Pieter Saenredam, *Landscape with Brederode Castle*, from Samuel Ampzing, *Beschrijvinge ende lof der stad Haerlem in Holland*, Haarlem, 1628, Department of Rare Books, The Houghton Library, Harvard College Library, Cambridge, Massachusetts

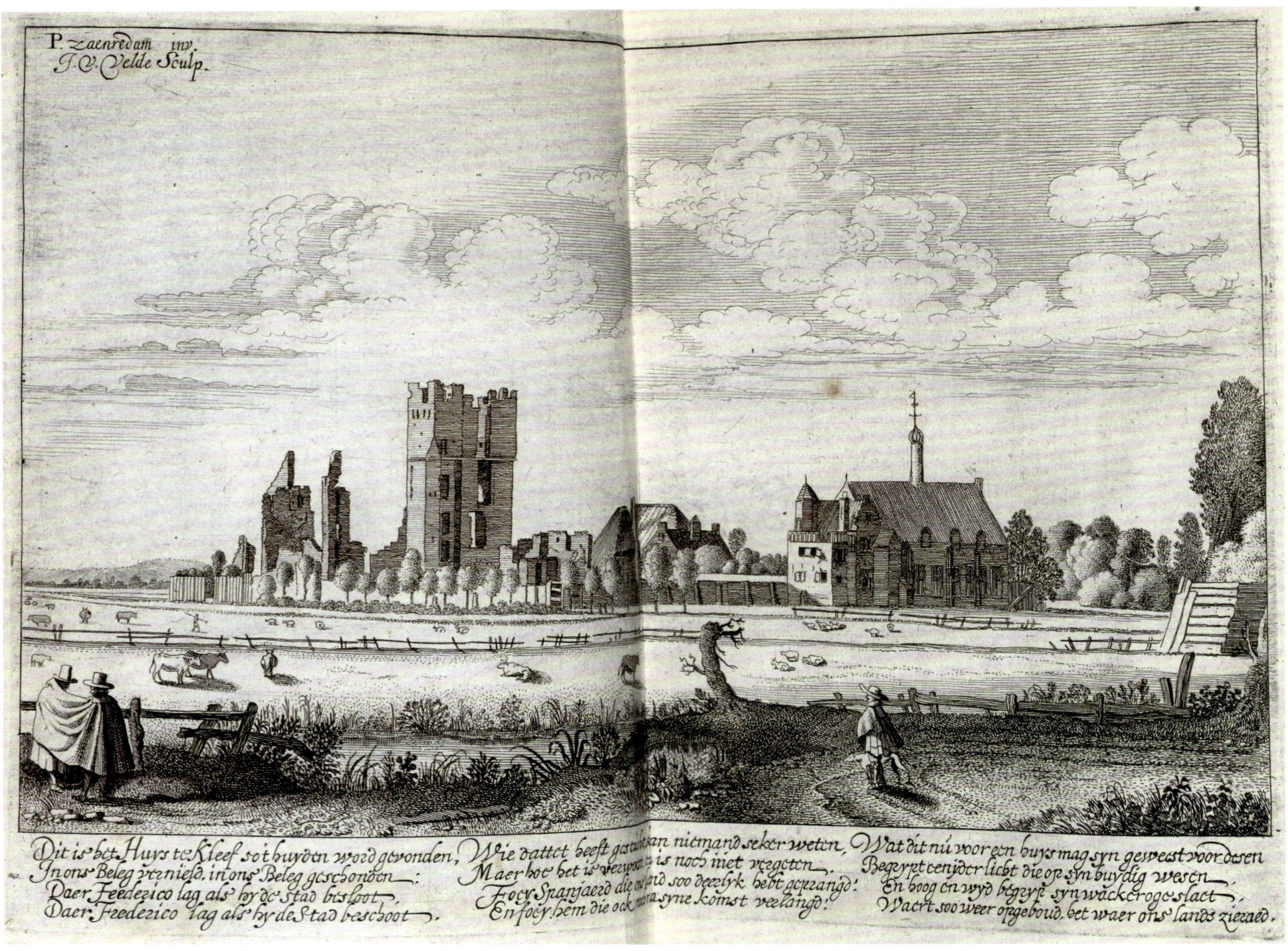

Samuel Ampzing (1590–1632), an orthodox Calvinist preacher at the Church of St. Bavo in Haarlem, published his description and praise of his native city in 1628. The text, composed in rhymed couplets, describes the history of Haarlem, its most celebrated citizens, and its major buildings. The illustrations, contributed by several artists, were primarily the work of Jan van de Velde II, who based his prints on drawings by the architectural painter and draftsman Pieter Saenredam (1597–1665). Ampzing's book makes a point of emphasizing the traumatic period in Haarlem's history, when it suffered under the Spanish Siege between December 1572 and July 1573. Accordingly, two of Van de Velde's prints represent major medieval castles in the vicinity that were destroyed by the Spanish in 1573: Brederode Castle (Fig. 110) and the Huis ter Kleef (Cat. 4), which had been appropriated as headquarters for the Spanish commander Don Frederick de Toledo. Both are accompanied by Ampzing's verses, in which the author laments the loss of handsome local monuments, comments on the vanity of human deeds, and vows not to forget the Spanish oppressors and their destructive acts.[2]

In contrast to the prints Van de Velde designed and executed himself (Cats. 3a–d), these images made after another artist's designs have a more stringent selectivity and directness. In both, the ruined monuments appear as irregular silhouettes against the sky at some distance so that the viewer visually traverses an expanse of the low landscape in order to reach them. The idea of visiting such sites in order to witness them (which the prints, in a sense, also make possible) is also suggested in both scenes by the attitudes of the figures in the foreground. A man and woman walk with their child into the picture space toward Brederode, as a man and dog pause on the path at the right foreground of the Huis ter Kleef. The latter scene also includes a draftsman sketching the site at the left, whose companion thoughtfully opens his cape to protect him from the wind.[3] With their depictions of calm skies and wide horizontal terrain occupied by cows and sheep, these landscapes emphasize the civilized peace, order, and prosperity of the Dutch countryside at the time Ampzing's book was published, while reminding the reader, as his text does, that the past still lives in memory behind the present.

NOTES

1. Translation from Schwartz and Bok 1990, 290.

2. The verses under the image of Brederode read as follows (original text and translation in Schwartz and Bok 1990, 289–90).

Here one sees Brederode drawn from life,
As nicely as pen or pencil could render it for us,
The way it still lies in ruins today;
Are human deeds anything more than vanity?

You can see the massiveness of the walls and stones
That this castle used to be a wonder to behold,
Founded by our count on the banks of the Rhine.
That it were again as it was! That it were once
more rebuilt!

At the same time you can see a long avenue with
trees
Before you arrive at Brederode Manor,
Which leads towards the house of Burgomaster Loo,
Just against the dunes and near Brederode.

3. The same motif appears at the left foreground in a print of a beached whale (repr. Hollstein 23 [1980]:94, no. 121) by Pieter Saenredam's father, Jan Saenredam (q.v.), as noted in Schwartz and Bok 1990, 44.

HERCULES SEGERS
c. 1589/90–c. 1638

Segers stands alone among Dutch printmakers, his special character as an artist recognized by Samuel van Hoogstraten as early as 1678.[1] His intensely evocative etchings—of remote rocky landscapes, trees, waterfalls, or ruins—were made by using experimental techniques that produced texture, tone, and color analogous to the effects of painting. The fact that Segers tended to treat each impression as a unique work of art makes his prints all the more rare and precious. Fifty-four etchings by him are known, and while their authorship is immediately obvious, their chronology remains unclear, because there seems to be no discernable development in his choice of themes or way of rendering them.[2] Only eleven of his paintings survive, which suggests that much of what he created during his short, ten-year career has been lost. Although Segers apparently had no pupils, his influence, on Rembrandt among many others, was great.

The son of Pieter Segers, a Mennonite textile merchant, Hercules Segers fled the southern Netherlands with his family to escape religious persecution, settling in Amsterdam around 1595.[3] Hercules (who signed himself in documents before 1620 as Hercules Pietersz.) apparently studied with the Amsterdam landscape painter Gillis van Conninxloo (1544–1607), purchasing a number of works from his teacher's estate in 1607. By 1612 he had moved to Haarlem, as attested by his registration in the guild of St. Luke, along with Willem Buytewech (q.v.) and Esaias van de Velde. (q.v.), who joined it in the same year. Amsterdam documents of 1614 mention not only his betrothal to Anneken van der Brugghen (a woman sixteen years his elder), but also his agreement to support an illegitimate child he had had by another woman whom the couple would bring up as their daughter. Segers and his wife purchased a large house on the Lindengracht in 1619 but would later be forced to sell it in 1631, probably because of mounting debts. Segers then settled in Utrecht, where he was active as a picture dealer. Archival evidence suggests that he spent the final years of his life in The Hague, where a picture seller named "Hercules de Haerlem" is cited. The fact that a woman named Cornelia de Witte (presumably the artist's second wife) is mentioned in a document of 1638 as the "widow" of Hercules Pietersz. suggests that he died in or before that year.

NOTES

1. Hoogstraten 1678, 312.

2. On the difficulty of establishing a chronology for Segers, see Haverkamp-Begemann 1973, 53–55.

3. Biographical material on Segers is drawn from Haverkamp-Begemann 1973, 17–22 and C. S. Ackley in Boston/St. Louis 1980–81, 53; and from the essay by B. P. J. Broos in *Dictionary of Art* 1996, 28:357–60.

[5]
The Ruins of the Abbey at Rijnsburg, small version, c. 1620

Inscriptions: none

Etching printed in black ink on plain weave cloth prepared opaque gray with added double brown wash borderline, 95 × 173 mm (3¾ × 6 13/16 in.) (sheet); state i/ii

Cincinnati Art Museum, Bequest of Herbert Greer French, inv. no. 1943-345

References: Springer 1910–12, no. 53; Cincinnati 1941, 32, no. 160; Collins 1953, 40, pl. 28, fig. 41 (Cincinnati); Haverkamp-Begemann 1973, 38, 54, 90–91, no. 47 Ic (Cincinnati); Rowlands 1979, 31, pl. 39 (Amsterdam); Hollstein 26 (1982):217, no. 47 Ic (Cincinnati); New Brunswick 1983, no. 113, repr. 126 (Cincinnati); Cincinnati 1993, no. 75.

Segers's etchings frequently depict landscapes, trees, and buildings that are ancient, fragmented, or timeworn. The artist's exceptional originality of interpretation is evident not only in his way of drawing, but also in his choice and handling of materials, for the actual printed sheets often convey weathered or eroded effects highly appropriate to their subjects. A porous ground and long immersion in acid allowed lines to be deeply bitten, yielding a ragged effect, while drypoint was frequently added over etched crosshatching to produce extensive surface tone.[1] Segers also liked to make unique impressions by tinting his thick paper or linen supports with additional tone or color, by printing in differently colored inks, and by partially and individually wiping each plate. The Cincinnati Art Museum's fine impression of the first state of this etching is printed in black on linen prepared with a light gray wash and with a borderline of brown wash.[2]

Segers's eight etchings of ruins (both Dutch and Roman) include two almost identical compositions of different sizes representing the old Benedictine convent of Rijnsburg Abbey that once stood northwest of Leiden.[3] The smaller version, shown here, places more focus on the factual details of the monument, emphasizing the textures of its weathered brick walls and the shapes of its remaining windows. Impressions of the larger, more elaborated version (Figs. 48 and 49) have a more atmospheric and moody effect, with detail obscured by deeper tones suggesting corrosion and decay.[4]

Founded in the early twelfth century as a convent for noblewomen, Rijnsburg Abbey acquired additional historical significance as the mausoleum of the counts of Holland (for further discussion of Rijnsburg, see Cat. 11). Like Brederode Castle near Haarlem, which Segers represented in two distinct views, Rijnsburg was reduced to a ruin in 1573 during the Dutch conflict with the Spanish that preceded national independence.[5] Both sites attracted artists and other visitors throughout the seventeenth century, as indicated by the figure who appears at the center of this scene looking up at the building. While Brederode's ruins still stand outside Haarlem, the last vestiges of Rijnsburg disappeared in the early nineteenth century.

Comparison of this print with Aelbert's Cuyp's painting of the same site (Cat. 11) reveals very different ways of seeing and interpreting the abbey. Instead of presenting the ruin within a larger landscape, Segers has tightly framed it, allowing its irregular broken walls to occupy most of the picture space, as did Willem Buytewech in his similarly small-scale prints of ruins (Cats. 2a and 2b). In Segers's etching, nature has encroached everywhere upon the building, as vines climb its broken walls and shrubs and grasses carpet the ground inside and outside the ruin. Perhaps the most unusual aspect of Segers's print is that he shows Rijnsburg from the inside, allowing the

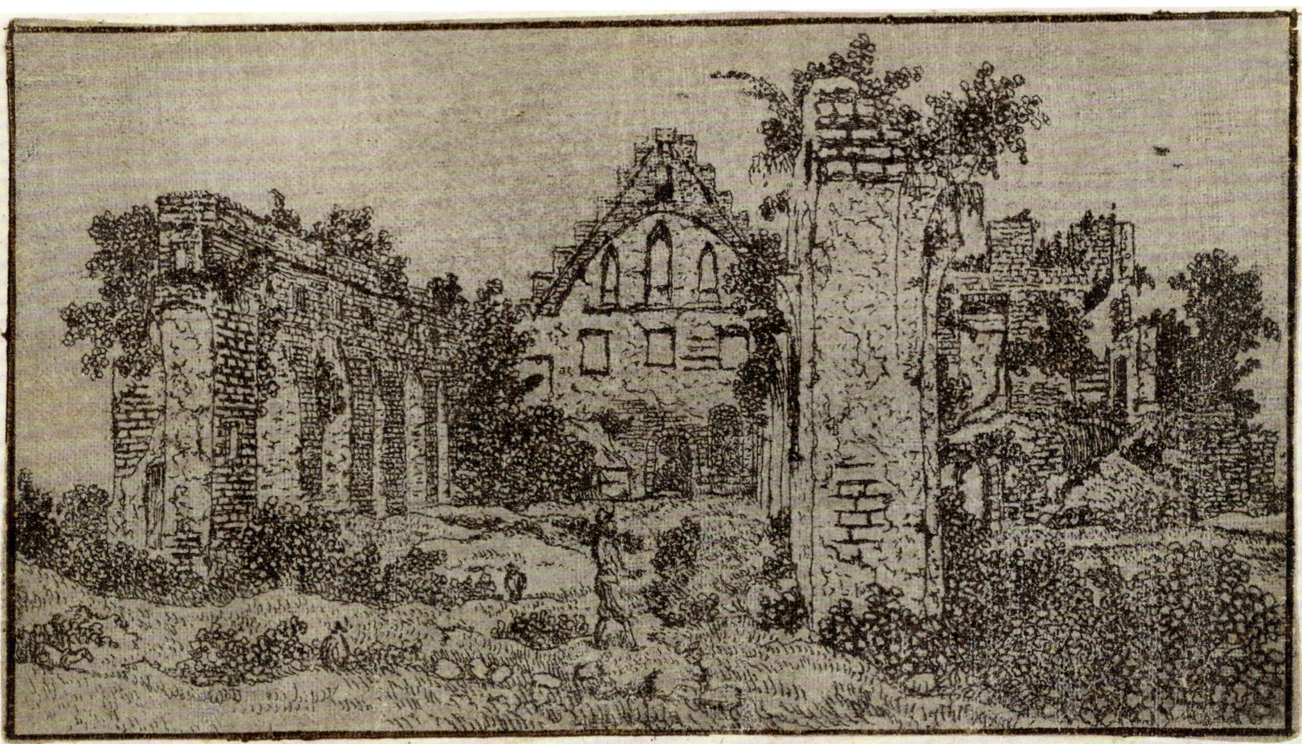

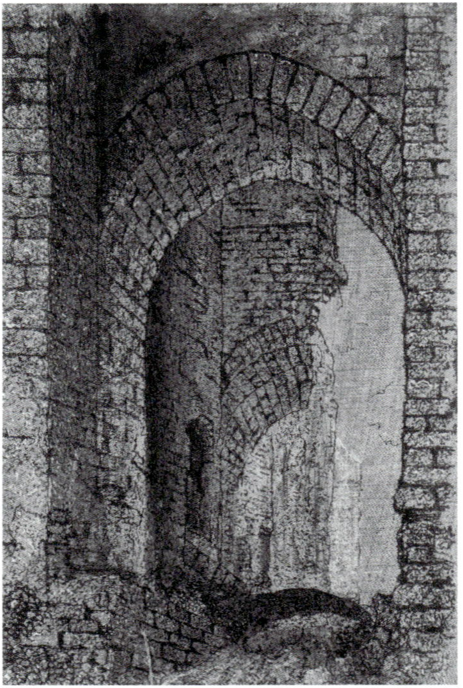

Fig. 111. Hercules Segers, *The Entrance Gate of Brederode Castle*, c. 1625–35, etching, Rijksprentenkabinet, Rijksmuseum, Amsterdam

viewer to enter the main hall of this roofless, three-sided shell of a structure as an actual visitor might. One of the abbey's heavy walls, rendered in extreme foreshortening at the right, is juxtaposed with the building's distinctive step-gable façade, seen from behind, as it would have appeared from within the empty interior of the abbey. Segers's interest in showing ruined structures from the inside also produced his haunting depiction of the entrance gate of Brederode Castle (Fig. 111), in which the viewer feels enclosed within the heavy, roughly textured stone walls and arches of the castle. Its intact Gothic entranceway frames a sheared-off archway just beyond that draws attention to a single, narrow slice of open space.

NOTES

1. For discussion of Segers's materials and techniques, including his innovative use of a lift-ground technique that did not come into wider use until the eighteenth century, see Van Leusden 1961 and Haverkamp-Begemann 1973, 42–48.

2. The impression of this print in the Rosenwald Collection, National Gallery of Art, Washington, D.C., is also printed in black on gray prepared linen but has additional blue-gray coloring. The impression in the Staatliche Kunstsammlungen, Dresden, is printed in green on paper prepared with a pink ground and subsequently colored with green, while the impression in the Bibliothèque Nationale, Paris, was printed in dark green on light green prepared paper. Hollstein 26 (1982):217–18, nos. 47 Id, 47 IIe, and 47 IIf. Hollstein lists a total of seven impressions of this print (Hollstein 26 [1982]:217–18), the last of which is known only through a citation in Springer 1910–12, no. 53f.

3. Segers's eight ruin prints include his large and small versions of Rijnsburg Abbey (Hollstein 46 and 47), two very different views of Brederode Castle (Hollstein 39 and 40), the ruins of an unidentified monastery (Hollstein 44), and two etchings of Roman ruins (Hollstein 42 and 43). For a third depiction of Roman ruins with the tomb of the Horatii and Curiatii (Hollstein 45), he apparently borrowed the motif from an etching, *Landscape with the Dismissal of Hagar*, attributed to Adam Elsheimer (1578–1610) (Haverkamp-Begemann 1973, 37 and fig. 18).

4. Hollstein lists six impressions of the larger version of the ruins of Rijnsburg whose scale (depending on how the prints were trimmed) is approximately 100 × 300 mm and whose grounds are dark brown or grayish brown with printing in yellowish white or yellowish blue. Hollstein 26 (1982):216–17, nos. 46a–f.

5. For other depictions of Brederode, see Cats. 1, 2a, 7, and 8.

HENDRICK HONDIUS THE ELDER
1573–1650

Hendrick Hondius, unrelated to the famous Amsterdam cartographer and printer Jodocus Hondius (1563–1612), was born in Flemish Brabant in 1573 and trained first with a goldsmith in Brussels and subsequently with the printmaker Jan Wierix (c. 1549–after 1615) in Antwerp.[1] After a period of travel to Cologne, London, and Paris, he moved to The Hague, where he registered in the artists' guild in 1597 and in the same year received his first print privilege (a form of copyright) for a portrait of Prince Maurits. After short periods of residence in Amsterdam in 1603 and Leiden in 1604–5, he settled permanently in The Hague, where he became a printmaker and print publisher. Hondius published some three hundred prints after designs by other Netherlandish artists, with an equal number reissued from the plates of earlier publishers.[2]

Between 1614 and 1640, Hondius owned a house on the Buitenhof, where he published drawings, prints, and books, including perspective and architectural treatises. During the 1630s he restricted himself primarily to publishing maps and official portraits, but he returned to etching in the 1640s. His works, influenced by Jacques de Gheyn II (q.v.) and Paulus Bril (1554–1626), also include pen and brown ink drawings with watercolor washes. Hondius produced an exceptionally wide variety of subjects, after his own designs and those of other artists, including portraits, biblical scenes and allegories, animals, anatomical studies, maps, perspective drawings, and even Roman ruins. In his last years, he turned primarily to reproductive engravings after sixteenth-century artists.

NOTES

1. Biographical material is based upon Orenstein 1996, 38, and the essay by N. Orenstein and C. Schuckman in *Dictionary of Art* 1996, 14:708–9.

2. On Hondius's activities as a print publisher, see Orenstein 1995 and Orenstein 1996, 86–137.

[6]

Ruins of Castle Spangen, c. 1640–50

Inscriptions: none

Pen and brush in brown ink over black chalk; laid down; traces of black chalk framing lines, 224 × 340 mm (8¾ × 13⅜ in.)

Private collection

References: Chapel Hill/Ithaca/Worcester 1999, 64–65, no. 16.

Many of the medieval ruins on Dutch soil came into being in the late sixteenth century during the series of conflicts with the Spanish. At this time, castles and other fortified structures were destroyed by one side or the other, so that the buildings could no longer be appropriated by the invaders or used for defense by the local population. Castle Spangen in the vicinity of Rotterdam, named for the family of that name, was built in 1310 between Overschie and

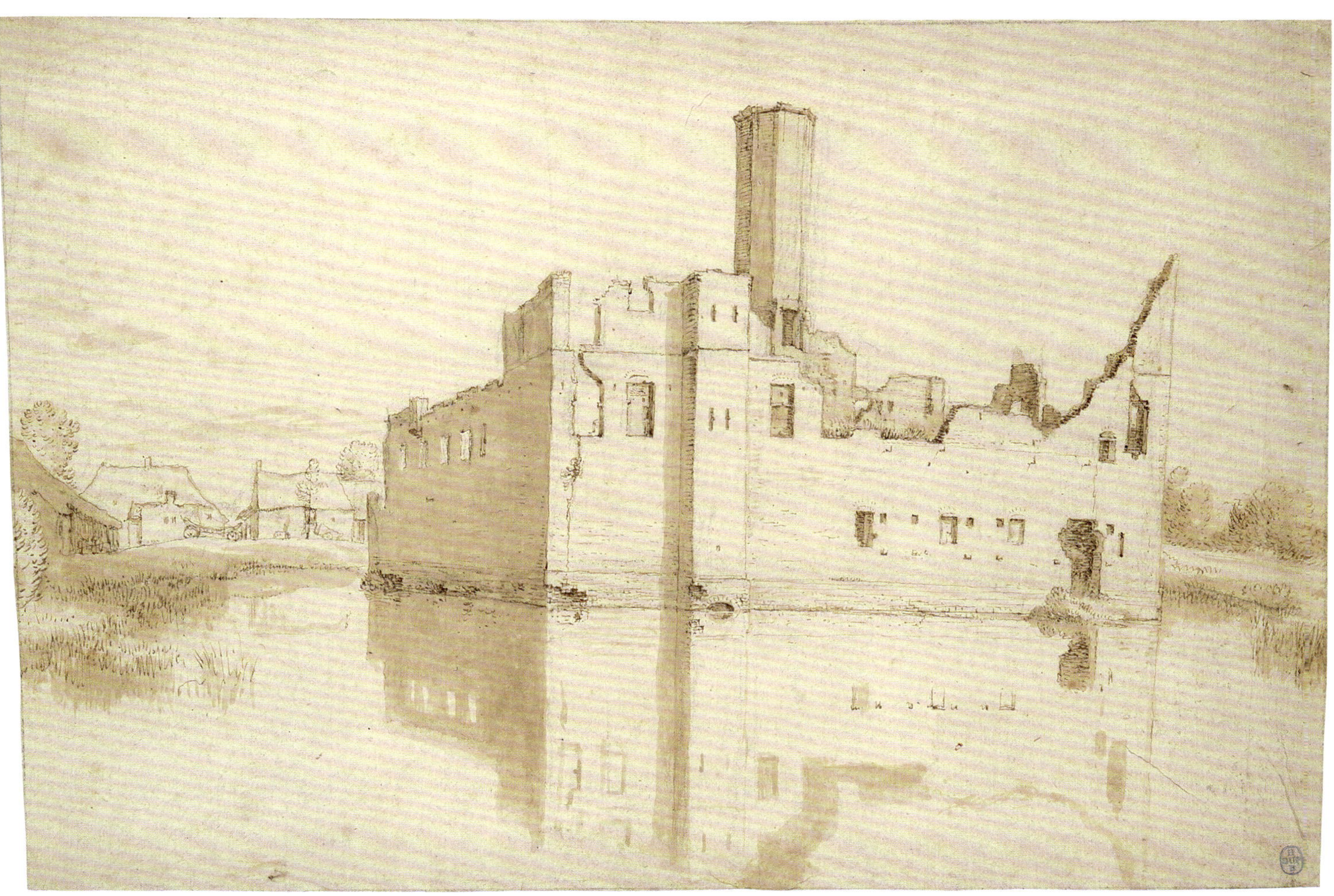

Delfshaven by Philip Spangen, whose great grandfather Jacob had been a knight, burgrave of Leiden, and lord of Rhineland.[1] Burned by the Spanish in 1572, Castle Spangen became the subject of numerous topographical prints and drawings during the seventeenth and eighteenth centuries. Abraham Rademaker (1675–1735) devoted six illustrations to Spangen in his extensive compendium that compares the original, intact state of Dutch castles and other historic buildings with their subsequent appearance as ruins (Figs. 112 and 113).[2] Although none of Rademaker's prints exactly replicates the castle in Hondius's drawing, his early eighteenth-century depictions of the ruins of Spangen as they appeared in 1573 allow the building in Hondius's drawing to be identified by the distinctive polygonal staircase tower that is clearly exposed as it rises from the central courtyard. (Fig. 113).[3] Remains of Spangen were still visible in the nineteenth century, but it was apparently demolished long before the excavations that unearthed its ground plan in 1942, two years after German bombs had leveled much of Rotterdam and its surroundings.[4]

Hondius's drawing of Castle Spangen shows the monument surrounded by water and isolated in the center of the sheet, with the irregular silhouette of its gaping, broken roofline silhouetted against the sky. Unlike most depictions of ruins, this shattered structure is neither overgrown with foliage nor surrounded by trees, so that its condition is starkly revealed, further emphasized by its contrast with the intact farm buildings at the left background. Thus, the ruin seems to float on the quiet water that catches its reflection in reverse. Implications of both permanence and transience are evoked, as the mirroring of the structure captures its shape while dissolving its mass, as if the water were simultaneously holding onto the building and letting it go.[5]

NOTES

1. Van der Aa 1852–78, 6:276 n. 1, cited by E. Haverkamp-Begemann in New York/Paris 1977–78, 38 n. 4, and by C. van Hasselt in New York/Paris 1977–78, 37.

2. Rademaker 1725, 1: nos. 139–44. See also Willem Buytewech's (q.v.) early seventeenth-century drawing of Spangen, in which the ruin is closely merged with surrounding trees (Institut Néerlandais, Paris; repr. Rotterdam/Paris 1974–75, pl. 111); and Roelant Roghman's (q.v.) drawing of Spangen screened by trees, from his well-known series of topographical views (Teylers Museum, Harlem, no. O**47; repr. Van der Wyck and Kloek 1990, 1:196, no. 177).

3. Identification of the castle in Hondius's drawing was made by F. W. Robinson, who compared the drawing to Rademaker's prints of the building. Chapel Hill/Ithaca/Worcester 1999, 64.

4. Renaud 1942, as cited by E. Haverkamp-Begemann in Rotterdam/Paris 1974–75, 75–76, no. 102.

5. A similar depiction of a ruined castle that appears to rise from surrounding water appears in Albert Cuyp's (q.v.) depiction of Ubbergen Castle (c. 1655, National Gallery, London, inv. no. 824), a structure that once stood near the eastern Dutch city of Nijmegen (Fig. 118).

Fig. 112. Castle Spangen seen from the front in the year 1550, and in ruins, from Abraham Rademaker, *Kabinet van Nederlandsche outheden en gezichten*, Amsterdam, 1725, part 1, nos. 139–40, Department of Rare Books, The Houghton Library, Harvard College Library, Cambridge, Massachusetts

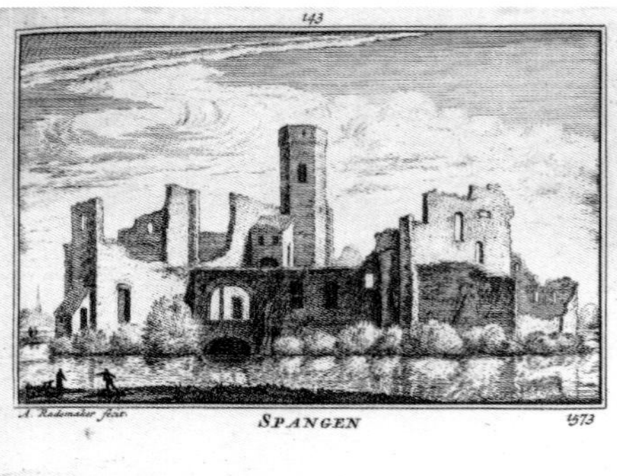

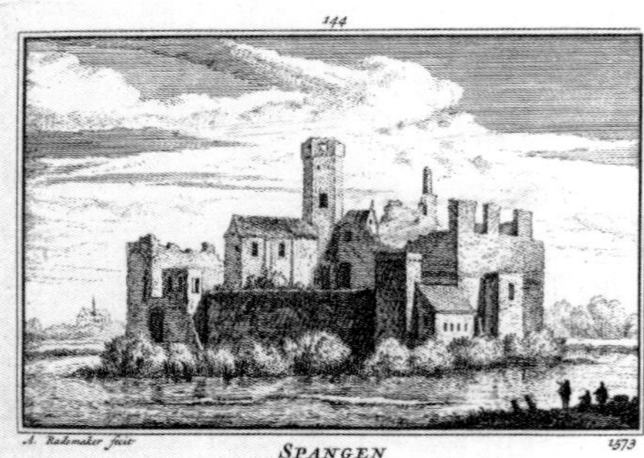

Fig. 113. Castle Spangen seen from the rear in the year 1573, from Abraham Rademaker, *Kabinet van Nederlandsche outheden en gezichten*, Amsterdam, 1725, part 1, nos. 143–44, Department of Rare Books, The Houghton Library, Harvard College Library, Cambridge, Massachusetts

VINCENT LAURENSZ. VAN DER VINNE (attr.)

The large Van der Vinne family of draftsmen, printmakers, and painters originated in Friesland but settled in Haarlem, where they remained active from the seventeenth through the nineteenth century. Vincent Laurensz. van der Vinne began as an apprentice in a Haarlem weaving mill before becoming a student of Frans Hals (who painted his portrait, now in the Art Gallery of Ontario, Toronto, around 1655–60). He went on to join the Haarlem guild of St. Luke in 1649.[1] His only known paintings are a few vanitas still lifes (1649, Musée du Louvre, Paris), although he also painted landscapes and received commissions for portraits, ceiling paintings, and signboards. Known best as a draftsman, Van der Vinne produced numerous drawings in black and red chalk of views in and around Haarlem, including the medieval ruins in the neighboring countryside. Between 1652 and 1655 he traveled through Germany, Switzerland, and France in the company of Guillam Dubois (c. 1610–80) and Cornelis Bega (1631/32–64). The illustrated diaries he made during and after this journey are preserved in the Gemeentearchief, Haarlem, along with a sketchbook of his Rhineland landscapes.[2] He married Anneke Jansdr. de Gaver in 1656 and, after her death in 1668, Catalijntje Boekaert. A journey through the Netherlands in 1680 yielded additional townscape drawings in pen and gray wash. Laurens Vincentsz. van der Vinne (1658–1729) was his student and follower, as was Jan Vincentsz. van der Vinne (1663–1721), who was active as a painter and draftsman in both England and Haarlem.

NOTES

1. Biographical material on Vincent van der Vinne is based on the essay by B. C. Sliggers in *Dictionary of Art* 32 (1996): 592–93.

2. On the travel journal of 1652–55, see Sliggers 1979.

[7]

Landscape with the Ruined Castle of Brederode, c. 1675

(Poughkeepsie and Louisville only)

Inscriptions: at lower left margin, partially trimmed, *Berghem*. On verso, upper-left corner with Röver code in black chalk, *23/45*. Below this in black chalk, *Breederoode*; in another hand in black chalk at lower center, *Ruins of the Castle of Brederode*; at lower right, *Berghem / Mr Peels is by Hobema*.

Black and red chalk with accents in oily black chalk on paper; traces of framing line in black ink along lower edge, 307 × 511 mm (12 1/16 × 20 1/8 in.)

The Pierpont Morgan Library, New York, Gift of J. P. Morgan, Jr., Acc. no. I, 140

References: Fairfax Murray 1905–12, I (1905): no. 140, repr. (as Berchem); Von Sick 1930, no. 23 (as Berchem); Ann Arbor 1964, no. 10 (as Berchem); Berlin 1974, under no. 16 (as Berchem); Paris/London/Antwerp/New York 1979–80, no. 103 (as formerly attributed to Berchem, perhaps by Laurens van der Vinne); New York/London 1986, under no. 31 n. 7 (as perhaps by Laurens van der Vinne).

Probably the most frequently depicted of all the medieval ruin sites in the Dutch provinces was Brederode Castle (see also Cats. 1 and 8 and discussion under Cat. 2a). Erected in the thirteenth century at Santpoort just north of Haarlem, the castle had been the seat of the counts of Brederode, and its ruins retained powerful patriotic associations because it had been destroyed—as were many other ancient fortified buildings—during the Dutch war of independence from Hapsburg dominion. Following the traumatic Siege of Haarlem by the Spanish in 1572–73, the large, red-brick grouping of structures was left in ruins that would attract the interest of Dutch draftsmen and painters throughout the seventeenth century. In this extensive view of the site, the artist has taken a vantage point from the back and side that allows the full length of the castle complex to be visible, including its gateway, framed by trees and rising behind a low hill at the center background. Selective use of red chalk (only for the architecture) vividly captures both the color and the texture of Brederode's weathered brick walls, which emerge from behind a stand of tall trees rendered in black chalk. Within the broad stage-like space of the foreground is a pool where lively ducks frolic in the water. The four cows with their male and female herders recall the pastoral staffage commonly found in Dutch Italianate landscapes (Cats. 52, 64, and 66).

This drawing has an impressive provenance that can be traced back to Valerius Röver (1686–1739), the distinguished Delft collector who wrote the earliest oeuvre catalogue of Rembrandt's etchings.[1] Its long attribution to Nicolaes Berchem (q.v.), who also depicted Brederode and made similar large-scale chalk drawings, has, however, been doubted by recent scholars based on discrepancies such as the oversize scale of the ducks and the regularity of the foliage, which is uncharacteristic of Berchem.[2] Two drawings of the central section of Brederode

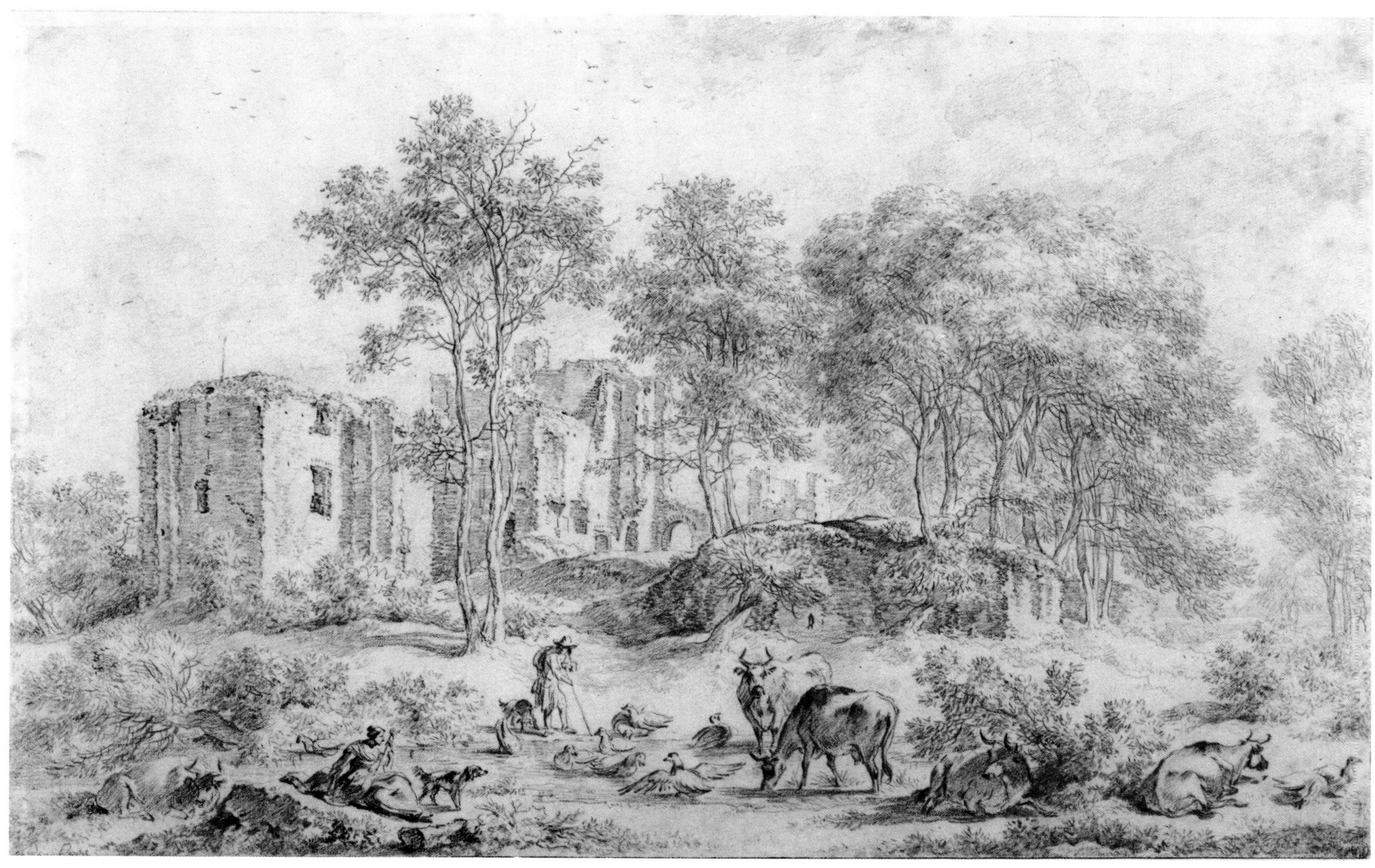

attributed to Laurens van der Vinne (1658–1729) and now in the Rijksprentenkabinet, Amsterdam, have been related to the style of the present sheet, but it is a drawing assigned to Laurens's father, Vincent, of a dune landscape near Brederode (Prentenkabinet der Universiteit, Leiden) that appears closest to the example at the Morgan Library.[3] That the Leiden drawing is dated 1676 on the verso provides an approximate date for this work.

NOTES

1. On Valerius Röver as a collector, see Van Gelder 1938 and Slive 1953, 174–76.

2. The history of opinions relating to the attribution of this drawing is recounted both in F. Stampfle's exhibition catalogue of Netherlandish drawings from the Morgan Library (Paris/London/Antwerp/New York 1979–80, 129–30) and in the entry on Laurens van der Vinne in J. S. Turner's forthcoming catalogue of the Dutch drawings in the Morgan Library collections catalogue of this material, which I am grateful to have been able to consult.

3. The drawings in the Rijksprentenkabinet are inv. nos. A1806 and A127, both of which depict the central portion of the Brederode ruins left of the archway. Interestingly, a variant of A1807 in the collection of the Ecole des Beaux-Arts, Paris, was also originally attributed to Berchem until F. Lugt reassigned it to Laurens van der Vinne (Lugt 1950, 87, no. 710, pl. xci, as noted in Paris/London/Antwerp/New York 1979–80, 129).

JAN LIEVENS
1607–74

The son of a Leiden embroiderer and hatmaker who had emigrated from the Flemish provinces, Lievens was sent at the age of eight to study with Joris van Schooten (c. 1587–c. 1653) but then became a pupil of Pieter Lastman (1583–1633) in Amsterdam around 1617–19, a few years before Rembrandt did (q.v.).[1] Between 1625 and 1631, he worked closely with Rembrandt in Leiden (very likely sharing his studio), painting historical themes and portraits in a very similar style. Constantijn Huygens, the secretary of the Stadholder Frederick Henry, penned the earliest praise of the two young artists in his autobiography, written between 1629 and 1631. Late in 1631 Lievens moved to Amsterdam, but he soon relocated to England, where he painted portraits for the court of Charles I and met Sir Anthony van Dyck (1599–1641), by whom he would be profoundly influenced. In 1635 he was listed as a member of the St. Luke's guild in Antwerp. Lievens married Susanna de Nole in 1638 in Antwerp, but financial difficulties arose (his property was seized in 1642), and he moved to Amsterdam in 1644. In 1642, following the death of his first wife, he married Cornelia de Bray, daughter of the Haarlem painter Jan de Bray (c. 1627–97). During the 1650s Lievens worked for the elector of Brandenburg in Berlin. He also won major portrait commissions (both paintings and drawings) from various leading citizens of Amsterdam and was asked to paint two large historical scenes for the new Amsterdam State House in 1656 and in 1661. He died in 1674 in Amsterdam.

An important aspect of Lievens's oeuvre is his involvement in landscape, which seems to have become a significant aspect of his work during the early 1640s while he was in Antwerp and was exposed to the landscapes of both Adriaen Brouwer (1605/6–38) and Peter Paul Rubens (1577–1640). Boldly calligraphic woodcuts of trees date from this period, but Lievens also produced delicate pen and wash drawings of recognizably Dutch landscapes during the 1650s and 1660s after his move to Amsterdam.[2]

NOTES

1. Biographical material on Lievens is based upon the account of his life in Schneider 1932/1973, 1–10; on C. S. Ackley's analysis of his career in Boston/St. Louis 1980–81, 113–14; and on E. Domela Nieuwenhuis's essay in *Dictionary of Art* 1996, 19:347–50.

2. Lievens's development as a landscape painter has been discussed by S. Jacob in Braunschweig 1979, 21–26, and his work as a draftsman by R. E. O. Ekkart in Braunschweig 1979, 27–32.

[8]

Ruins of the Castle of Brederode, c. 1655–65

Inscriptions: verso at center right, *slot te brederoo 3 guilden*

Pen in brown ink, brown ink framing lines, 292 × 383 mm (11½ × 20⅛ in.)

Private collection

References: Schneider 1932/1973, 218, 366, no. Z. 185; Amsterdam 1956, no. 67; Amsterdam 1964, no. 52, fig. 20; Sumowski 1979–92, 7:3872, no. 1741; Van der Wyck and Kloek 1990, 2:86, fig. 134; Chapel Hill/Ithaca/Worcester 1999, 68–69, no. 18.

Brederode, the frequently depicted medieval castle at Santpoort, three miles northwest of Haarlem, was destroyed by the Spanish in 1573 during the Dutch war of independence (see discussion under Cat. 2a). Dutch artists represented this major historic site throughout the seventeenth century in prints, book illustrations, drawings, and paintings, nearly always in views from the side that allow the building's distinctive conical turret to be visible (Cats. 1, 2a, and 7). Lievens, on the other hand, has taken an unusually low and oblique vantage point, bringing the viewer very close to Brederode but below it, so that its shattered walls rise above eye level and are elevated in sunlight beyond the shadowed foreground. This effect of ascending, which implies amplification or importance of meaning, is accentuated by the sharp rise of the hill with its uneven sequence of flat stones that climb like steps through dense vegetation to become lost in the underbrush. The same rising contour is reiterated in the darkly hatched and overgrown segment of ruin in the immediate foreground, which may represent part of the entrance gate of Brederode.[1] Interestingly, the actual site of Brederode as it appears today shows no evidence of such hilly terrain.

Working with pen and warm brown ink, Lievens was able to develop a free yet controlled graphic touch, partly under the influence of Rubens, in which repeated diagonal hatchings are overlaid with smaller loops of line to create a shimmering effect.[2] Thus, this scene not only pictures the effects of time, but also seems to exist within a visible temporal process, as further suggested by shifts in tone from one spatial zone to another. Toward the lower, more level background the artist gradually dilutes his ink to paler tones and loosens his stroke to sketch in a stand of young trees, whose foliage seems

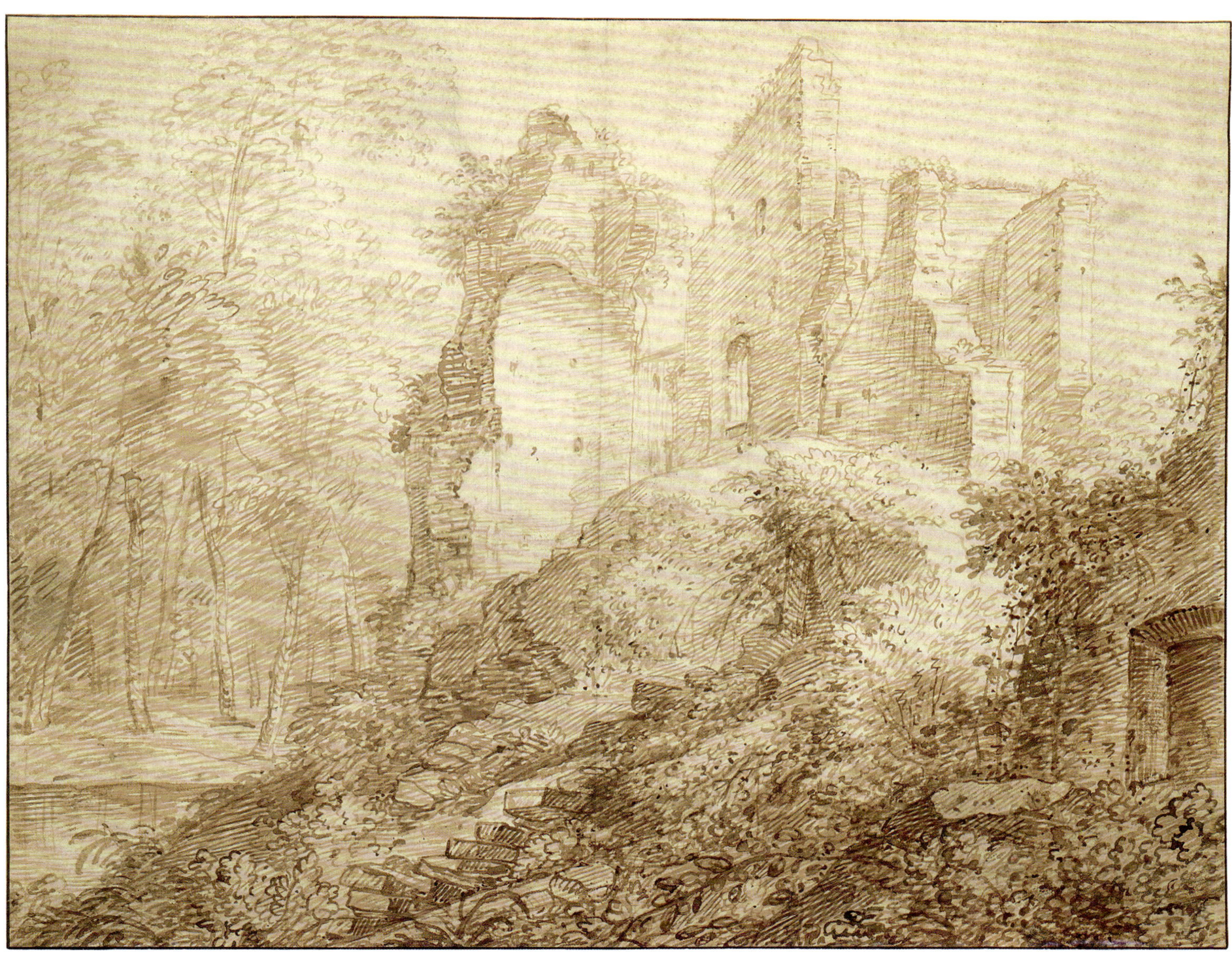

to tremble in the breeze and whose slender trunks are reflected at the edge of a pool of water. That Lievens has included no visitors or sightseers within this scene also sets his drawing apart from most other depictions of the site. Here the viewer is allowed a private encounter with Brederode, whose elevation in the middle ground places it just out of reach.

Establishing a chronology for Lievens's drawings is difficult, because, with the exception of a few portraits, he rarely dated his graphic works and always worked in pen and brown ink. This drawing, which presumably postdates his return to the Dutch provinces in 1644, seems similar to a group of drawings R. E. O. Ekkart has dated to the period between the mid-1650s and the early 1660s, which he considers to be the highpoint of Lievens's development as a landscape draftsman.[3] All of these works display a similarly delicate touch in scenes that fully occupy the picture space without views into the distance.

NOTES

1. Lievens made another, broadly sketched pen drawing of this outer fortified structure (pen and brown ink), whose present location is unknown. Sumowski 1979–82, 7:3874–75, repr., no. 1742. Another drawing by Lievens of castle ruins, incorrectly labeled in eighteenth-century script on the verso *Ruine van 't huis te Brederode* was formerly in the collection of the late J. Q. van Regteren Altena, Amsterdam. Sumowski 1979–82, 7:3808–9, repr., no. 1711.

2. See, for example, Rubens's pen and brown ink drawing over black chalk *Landscape with a Fallen Tree* of c. 1618 in the Musée du Louvre, Paris. Repr. White 1987, 127, fig. 144. Adriaen Brouwer's loosely painted landscapes with diagonal strokes forming foliage may also have had an effect on Lievens, as in his *Twilight Landscape*, also in the Louvre. Repr. Knuttel 1962, 162, fig. 109.

3. R. E. O. Ekkart in Schneider 1932/1973, 31 and 166–71, nos. 72–75.

ALLART VAN EVERDINGEN
1621–75

Younger brother of the classicizing history painter Cesar van Everdingen (1616–78), Allart was also from Alkmaar but went on to follow an entirely different path as an artist.[1] According to Houbraken, he studied with two of the major landscape specialists of the period: Roelandt Savery (1576–1639) in Utrecht and Pieter Molijn (q.v.) in Haarlem.[2] In 1644 Everdingen traveled to Scandinavia, where he made annotated sketches of the southeast coast of Norway and the Göteborg district of western Sweden. By February 1645 he was back in Haarlem, where his marriage to Janneke Cornelisdr. Brouwers was recorded, and in the same year joined the Dutch Reformed Church. In 1646 he became a member of the Haarlem guild of St. Luke and in 1648 enlisted with his brother Cesar in the Civic Guard of St. George.

By 1652 he had moved to Amsterdam, where four of his eight children were born, and during the 1660s he was hired to help decorate the Amsterdam townhouse of the Trip family of munitions makers, whose business was centered in Sweden.[3] His Nordic landscapes with log cabins, fir trees, and waterfalls deeply influenced a number of his contemporaries including Jacob van Ruisdael (q.v.), Roelant Roghman (q.v.), and Jan van Kessel (1641–80). Aside from paintings, which include a number of topographical landscapes, at least five hundred landscape drawings of Dutch and Scandinavian views by Everdingen are known, as well as numerous small, etched landscapes and early experiments with the technique of mezzotint.[4]

NOTES

1. On Allart van Everdingen's biography, see A. I. Davies in *Dictionary of Art* 1996, 10:660–61, and Davies 2001, 15–39.

2. Houbraken 1718–21, 2:95–96.

3. According to A. I. Davies (written communication, October 2004), there is no reason to believe that Everdingen returned to Scandinavia during the 1660s. He was the artist hired to produce this kind of scenery for the Trippenhuis, however, because he had been the first to introduce Scandinavian landscapes to his countrymen. In making these later works, he apparently relied on a boundary map and on his own earlier sketches.

4. A. I. Davies, who is now completing a catalogue of Everdingen's drawings, has identified approximately 650 works in this category, which include watercolors and oils on paper (written communication).

[9]

Landscape with Cottage and Ruined Castle, c. 1655

Inscriptions: lower left in pen and brown ink, *AVE*

Point of brush in brown ink with brown wash over graphite on cream antique laid paper, 177 × 279 mm (6⅞ × 10¹⁵⁄₁₆ in.)

Courtesy of the Fogg Art Museum, Harvard University Art Museums, Cambridge, Massachusetts, Loan from the Maida and George Abrams Collection, 25.1998.115

References: London/Birmingham/Leeds 1962, 20, no. 99; Washington/Denver/Fort Worth 1977, 65–66, no. 62, fig. 62; Cambridge/Montreal 1988, 99, no. 28; Beck 1990, 376; London/Paris/Cambridge 2002–3, 168–69, no. 71.

The topographical drawings Everdingen made to record his travels in Sweden and Norway are so accurate that the places he visited can sometimes be recognized, while the small, anonymous ports in many of his sketches are often identified in his careful annotations. Yet the majority of his works—as was the custom among Dutch landscapists—are composite scenes that he assembled in his studio. This predilection for creating a convincing but fictive world out of experiences the artist had in different places, and even at different times, is particularly evident in this horizontal drawing, which brings together Dutch and Scandinavian scenery. The compositional structure, based on a popular Netherlandish type traceable to the late sixteenth century, consists of a triangular foreground wedge of land, buildings, and trees, beyond which is a more distant vista. In his fundamental survey of Dutch landscape painting, W. Stechow aptly used the terms "one-wing" or "two-wing" panorama to describe the kinds of landscapes in which such inwardly projecting lateral wedges of ground or trees allow the artist to focus on individual foreground motifs that counterpoint the spatial recession beyond.[1]

Everdingen's one-wing landscape, defined in tones of warm brown ink and wash, belongs to a group of similarly composed scenes with shadowed foregrounds that A. I. Davies has dated to the late 1650s.[2] All include cottages, travelers, and fishermen in front of a diagonally receding river whose opposite shore is visible. In this example, the enormous round tower that rises from the distant riverbank at the far right is a variation on the donjon, or castle keep, of Kasteel Rosendael near Velp in Gelderland,

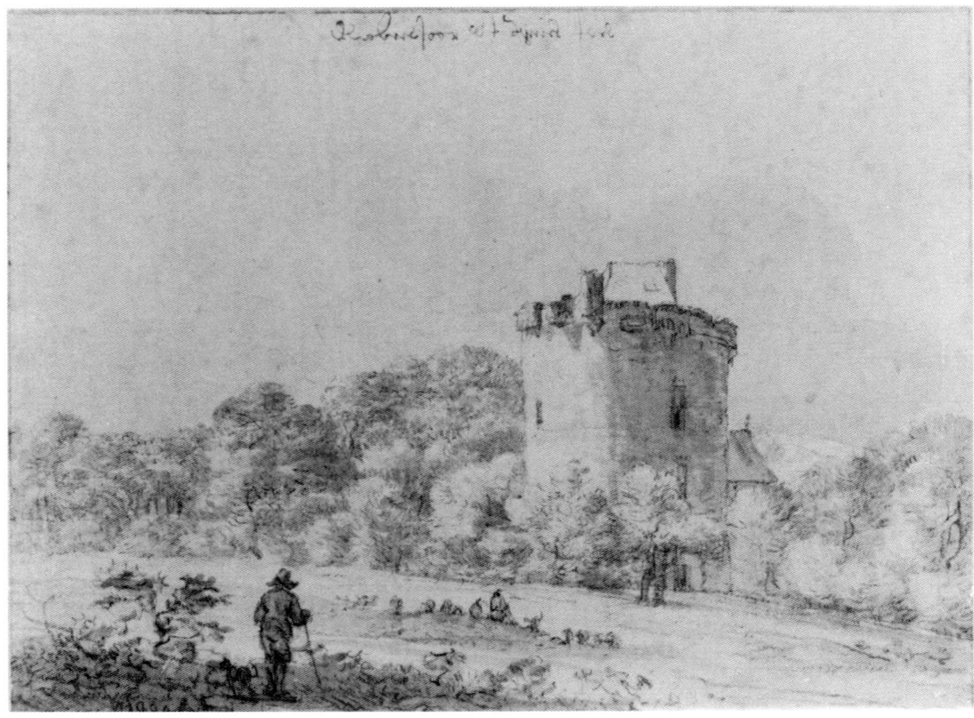

Fig. 114. Karel Dujardin, *Kasteel Rosendael in Gelderland*, c. 1650–55, chalk drawing, Collection Frits Lugt, Institut Néerlandais, Paris

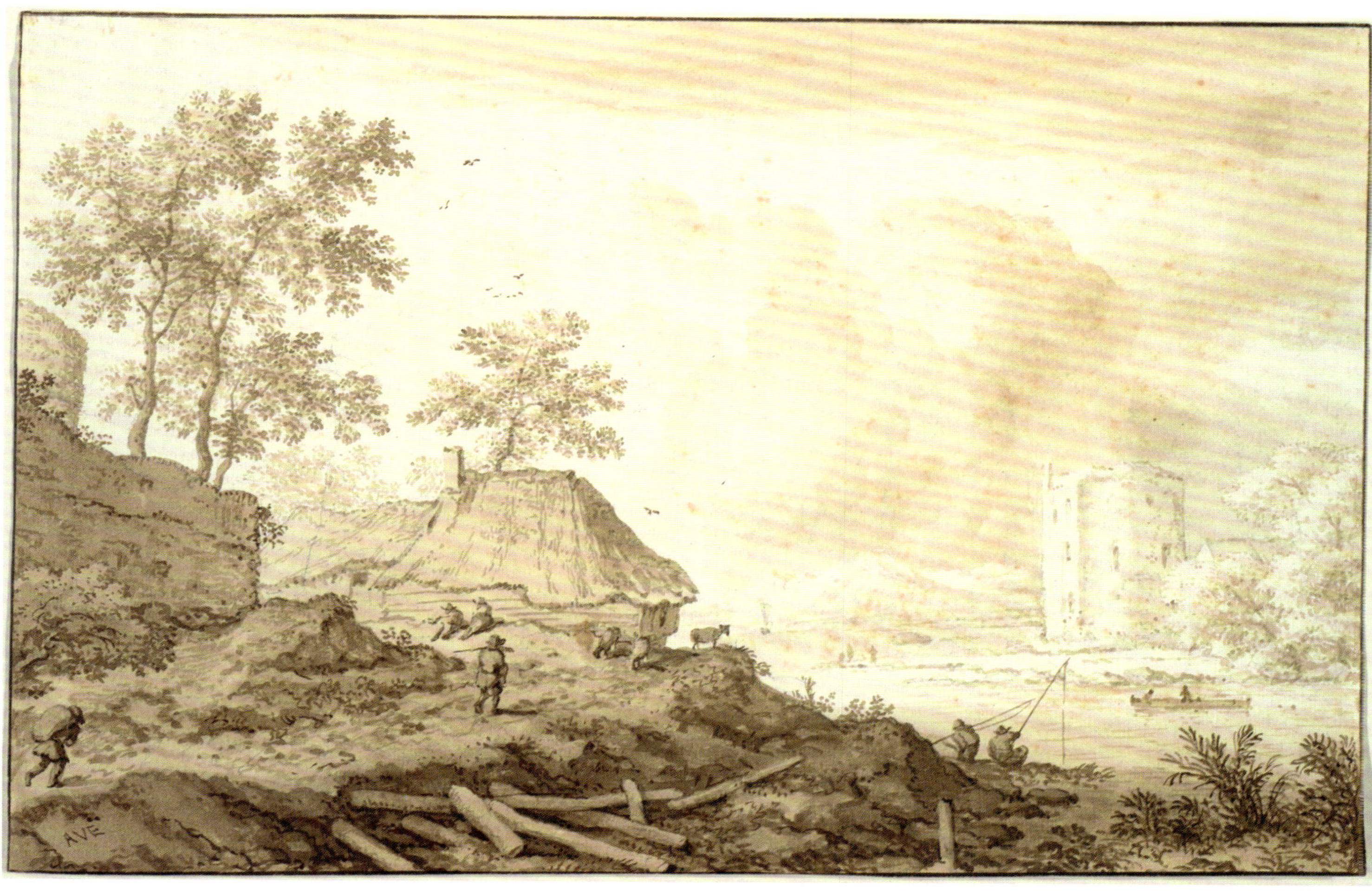

originally the residence of the counts of Gelre (Gelderland). Begun as early as 1314, this medieval tower, which is the largest in the Netherlands, still stands today, although both the upper part of the tower and its adjoining buildings have been reconstructed and renovated over the centuries, most recently in 1986–89.[3] In 1615 a house was built beside the tower whose roof can also be seen in Everdingen's drawing. A closer view of the castle and house appear in a drawing of similar date by Karel Dujardin (q.v.) in the Institut Néerlandais, Paris (Fig. 114).[4] As C. van Hasselt has observed, however, it is possible that neither Everdingen nor Dujardin based his drawing of this monument on direct observation of it, because by 1628 Rosendael and its gardens had been extensively redesigned and reconstructed in Renaissance style.[5]

In Everdingen's drawing, the castle, the quiet waterway, and the clouds—motifs often found in Dutch landscapes—are evoked in pale washes of ink, as are the distant mountains that appear to be imported from some Nordic locale. The more deeply toned foreground features other Scandinavian elements such as scattered logs and a thatch-roofed log cabin along with figures walking, conversing, or fishing. The immediacy of this vivid part of the scene is created by lively calligraphy whose varied touches capture leaves, grasses, and other natural forms. The great contrast in tone and brushwork between foreground and background encourages comparison between the rustic hut and the imposing castle: buildings of different type and age that seem to coexist within different layers of time.

NOTES

1. Stechow 1966, 35–41.

2. Cited by W. W. Robinson, who notes that A. I. Davies (in conversation) has compared these drawings to a group of similarly designed paintings by Everdingen (Davies 2001, 112, 117–18, and 121–23 and nos. 89, 90, 111, 117, and 119). W. W. Robinson in London/Paris/Cambridge 2002–3, 168.

3. The history of Rosendael has been discussed by C. van Hasselt in Brussels/Rotterdam/Paris/Berne 1968–69, 48–49, and in Bierens de Haan and Jas 2000, 167.

4. W. W. Robinson, citing J. Bosch van Rosenthal (personal conversation), has identified the castle in Everdingen's drawing as Rosendael, also illustrating Karel Dujardin's (q.v.) drawing in the Institut Néerlandais, Paris. London/Paris/Cambridge 2002–3, 168, fig. 2. See Fig. 114.

5. C. van Hasselt in Brussels/Rotterdam/Paris/Berne 1968–69, 49.

JAN VAN GOYEN
1596–1656

J. J. Orlers, the historian of the city of Leiden, reported that Van Goyen, the son of a shoemaker, had apprenticeships with several local artists beginning at age ten, then worked for two years with Willem Gerritsz. (fl. 1657) in Hoorn.[1] Van Goyen's most important and influential teacher was the landscape painter Esaias van de Velde (q.v.), with whom he studied for one year in Haarlem, following a period of travel in France in 1615–16. Back in Leiden, Van Goyen married Annetje Willemsdr. van Raelst in 1618. One of the couple's three daughters would marry the genre and history painter Jan Steen (1626–79), and another the still-life painter Jacques de Claeuw (fl. 1642–76). Van Goyen's continuing residence in Leiden is documented between 1627 and 1632, but in 1632 he moved to The Hague, where he became head of the guild of St. Luke in 1638 and 1640. One of the greatest Dutch landscapists, Van Goyen produced more than twelve hundred paintings and eight hundred drawings; among his pupils were Nicolaes Berchem (q.v.) and his son-in-law Steen. Nonetheless, he developed severe financial problems despite his activities as an art dealer, appraiser, and auctioneer. A speculator in real estate and tulip bulbs, he sustained heavy losses after the crash of the tulip market in 1637. In 1652 and 1654, he was forced to sell his possessions at public auctions; at the time of his death two years later, his widow auctioned his remaining possessions, including their house.

Van Goyen's detailed early works show the influence of Esaias van de Velde, but during the late 1620s, he and several Haarlem contemporaries, including Pieter Molijn (q.v.) and Salomon van Ruysdael, developed a new "tonal" approach to landscape, using looser brushwork and a more monochromatic brown-gray coloring to unify all aspects of the landscape. This effect remains in the more structured paintings Van Goyen produced after 1645. Usually horizontal in format, his landscapes tend to focus on rivers and waterways, as well as panoramas with views of distant towns. Recognizable churches, gateways, and castles frequently appear in his paintings and drawings, although they may be imaginatively modified in construction or setting. The ruins of Merwede Castle near Dordrecht (see also Cat. 13) are visible in many scenes, but, more often, the ruins in Van Goyen's landscapes cannot be identified.[2]

NOTES

1. Orlers 1641, pt. 1, 373–74. For discussion of Van Goyen's biography, see H.-U. Beck's essay in *Dictionary of Art* 1996, 13:255–57.

2. For Van Goyen's paintings of Merwede Castle, see Beck 1972–73, 2: nos. 63, 66, and 67, 80, 812, 826, 847a, 862, 878, 880, and 910. For landscapes with unidentified ruins, see Beck 1972–73, 2:169, 176, 190, 203, 205, 631, 659, 666, 677, 686, 688, 694, 699, 702, 745, 771, 753, 782, and 1210a. Although certain details seem different, A. J. Adams has suggested that no. 659 may be a version of the Pellecussen Gate as a ruin (A. J. Adams in New York 1988, 70).

[10]

River Landscape with the Pellecussen Gate near Utrecht, 1648

Inscriptions: on the boat at left, *VGOYEN 1648*

Oil on panel, 64.1 × 94 cm (25¼ × 37 in.)

The Minneapolis Institute of Arts, Gift of Bruce B. Dayton, 83.84

References: Dieren 1937, 9, no. 24; Stechow 1938, 207; Beck 1972–73, 2:316–17, no. 693 and repr.; Amsterdam 1981, 126–27; Keyes 1984, 67 and 396, fig. 40; Keyes 1986, 59, 61, and 66; Sutton 1986, 157 and fig. 224; Beck 1987, 226, no. 693; Lipschitz 1988, 96; Bordeaux 1990, 120–21, repr. 121; The Hague/San Francisco 1990–91, 249–52, no. 24.

Van Goyen's landscapes seem saturated with time. His monochromatic coloring and loose but controlled brushwork capture the damp atmosphere and moisture-laden clouds of the Dutch lowlands in a way that evokes temporal flux not only by representing it, but by appearing to absorb it into the medium itself.[1] In his paintings, life unfolds in small, simultaneous incidents that all belong to everyday existence but whose individual pace is not the same: fishing boats moored or under sail, birds in flight, people walking or waiting. All are subordinated to what C. O. Baer has aptly described as "... a gradual coming and departing, in which the present moment is a slight crescendo. The pace is leisurely but persistent ..."[2] The fluid ambience of Van Goyen's landscapes is greatly enhanced by the presence of waterways as well as old castles, towers, gates, and churches—either intact or in ruins—whose presence further implies the workings of time. In the Minneapolis painting, a quiet river catches the reflections of boats and of the buildings at the right: their varied shapes form a rough wedge pointing into the distance, where the water's surface brightens in the light. The dominant structure in this scene, a tall tower silhouetted against the cloudy sky, is the fourteenth-century Pellecussen Gate, or Pellkus-Poort, outside Utrecht, which Van Goyen painted at least a dozen times.[3]

This building, which once stood just north of Utrecht on the river Vecht, was erected in 1371 not as a town gate but as a privately owned

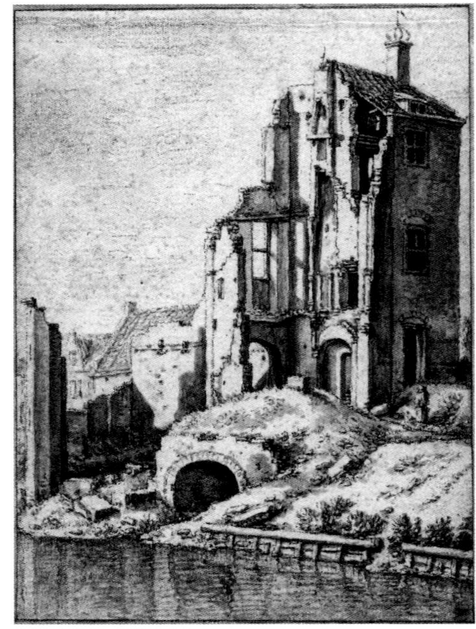

Fig. 115. Herman Saftleven, *The Ruins of the Pellecussen Gate*, 1674, drawing, Teylers Museum, Haarlem

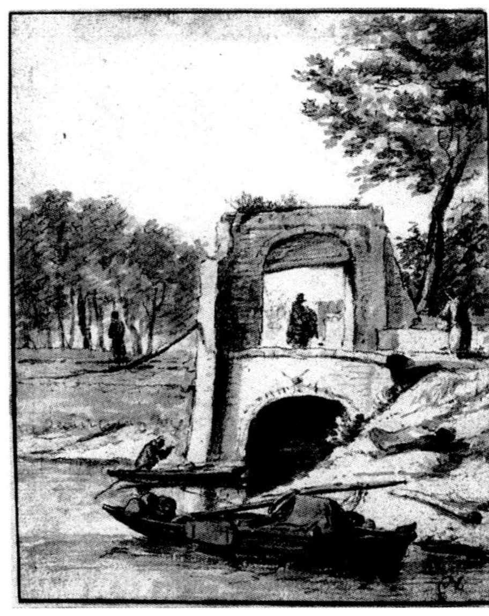

Fig. 116. Herman Saftleven, *The Remains of the Pellecussen Gate*, c. 1675–76, chalk and wash drawing, Gemeentearchief, Utrecht

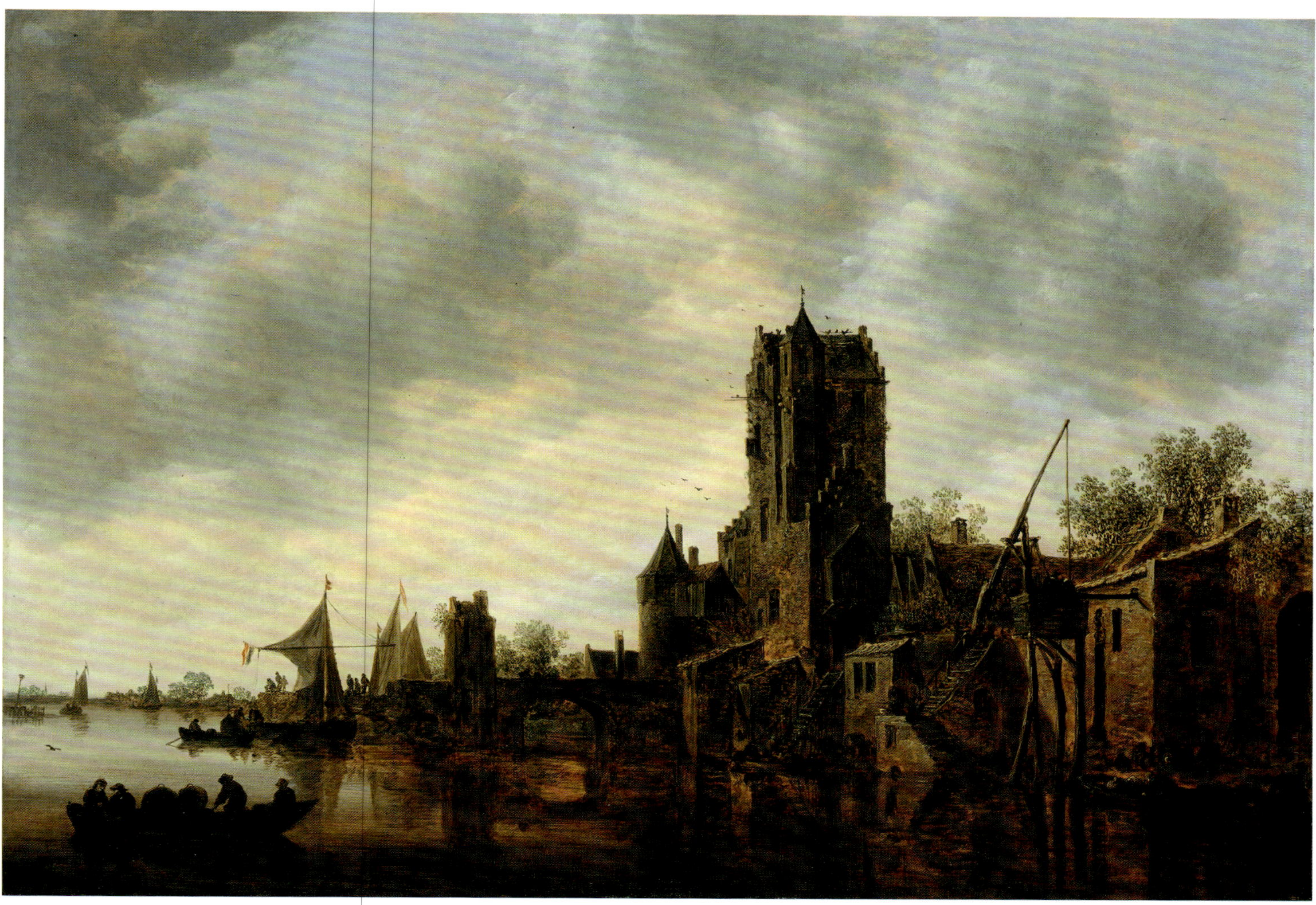

castle immediately outside the city walls.[4] Its name derives from the Pellecussen family, whose lineage is traceable to the medieval period and who owned the nearby Lauwerecht estate. Later the gate became the residence of the lords of Lauwerecht. One of the most picturesque structures in the Dutch countryside, the Pellkus-Poort attracted the attention of both Van Goyen and Salomon van Ruysdael (?1600/1603–1670), who repeatedly painted and drew it after 1640.[5] Sited at an attractive spot where a small brook flowed into the larger river, the gate marked the place where a traveler, coming out of Utrecht, would turn toward Amsterdam. In Van Goyen's time, the tall structure with its distinctive step gable, hexagonal stair tower, and bricked-in cannon balls was still intact. But in accordance with his frequent practice of modifying what he saw, he has made additions in this version of it: stairways leading down to the water, bridges, and even a well installation at the right.[6]

Renovations beginning about 1660 led to the demolition of the Pellecussen Gate's wooden bay window and the addition of a new wing facing the Vecht. During the trials of the so-called Rampjaar (Year of Disaster) of 1672, the French invasion would inflict extensive destruction upon the area around Utrecht (see also Cats. 38 and 39). The Pellecussen Gate would not be spared, as B. P. J. Broos has shown in his discussion of drawings by Herman Saftleven (q.v.) that show it as a ruin in 1674 (Teylers Museum, Haarlem, Fig. 115) and then, a year or so later, as no more than a vaulted foundation with remains of the lower walls (Gemeentearchief, Utrecht, Fig. 116).[7] Although he could not have known it, Van Goyen's depictions of this landmark are all views of a ruin-to-be.

NOTES

1. As R. L. Falkenburg has discussed, however, the strong emphasis on damp weather and dense cloud cover in Van Goyen's landscapes after 1640 appears to have been influenced by a wish to create more picturesque, or "schilderachtig," scenes. Falkenburg in Leiden 1996, 60–69; on the term *schilderachtig*, see also the essay by W. S. Gibson herein. On the taste and market for Van Goyen's scenes with inclement weather, see Falkenburg 1997, 117–61.

2. For a perceptive discussion of the *Stimmung* (tone or pitch) of Van Goyen's landscapes and how it differs from that of Rembrandt's landscapes, see Baer 1973, 20–23.

3. For Van Goyen's paintings with views of the Pellecussen Gate, see Beck 1972–73, 2: nos. 74, 639, 640, 690, 693, 711, 721, 760, 762, 765, 788, and 1210a. Broos has found only one drawing of the site that he believes may be by Van Goyen (Rijksprentenkabinet, Amsterdam, inv. no. A 2947), although it has been attributed to Antoni Waterloo (1609–90). Broos in The Hague/San Francisco 1990–91, 249, fig. 1.

4. Broos has compiled a thorough account of the history, site, and structure of the Pellecussen gate in an excellent catalogue entry on the Minneapolis painting, to which my discussion is greatly indebted. Broos in The Hague/San Francisco 1990–91, 249–52, no. 24. On the representation of this and other sites in the vicinity of Utrecht, see Wilmer 1980, esp. 32.

5. W. Stechow was the first to investigate Van Goyen's and Ruysdael's depictions of the Pellecussen gate in Stechow 1938.

6. Broos reproduces an anonymous drawing of c. 1600 (Gemeentearchief, Utrecht, no inv. no.) that shows the original appearance of the building, allowing modern scholars to recognize Van Goyen's additions. Broos in The Hague/San Francisco 1990–91, 251, fig. 3, and 252. As A. J. Adams has noted, a dramatic alteration to the gate is visible in Van Goyen's dated painting of 1643 (private collection), in which it appears with an attached Gothic choir. Adams in New York 1988, 70.

7. Broos in The Hague/San Francisco 1990–91, 252 n. 16 (Schulz 1982, 280, no. 571) and n. 17 (not catalogued in Schulz), fig. 6.

AELBERT CUYP
1620–81

Aelbert Cuyp, the most widely known member of the Dordrecht family of painters, made important contributions to seventeenth-century landscape, although his works seem not to have been known outside his native city during his lifetime.[1] His teacher was probably his father, the portraitist Jacob Cuyp (1594–?1652), but the major influence on his early works was clearly the tonal landscapes of Jan van Goyen (q.v.) and Salomon van Ruysdael.[2] Family connections with Utrecht on his mother's side seem to have encouraged the artist to make an extensive sketching tour, around 1642, of both Holland and Utrecht. Only two or three years later, he came under the influence of such Utrecht Italianate landscapists as Herman Saftleven (q.v.) and Jan Both (q.v.). In 1651–52 he made a second sketching trip along the Rhine, during which he studied the area around Nijmegen and Cleves. Cuyp never went to Italy, but his river scenes and landscapes with cows often convey the clear, sunny radiance of early morning or late afternoon, giving even the most Dutch vistas a flavor of the south, especially those that feature ruins drenched in a golden light. Cuyp also painted seascapes, elegant family and equestrian portraits in landscape settings, and a small number of biblical narratives.

In 1658 Cuyp married Cornelia Boschman, a wealthy widow whose social position helped him become prominent in Dordrecht as deacon, then elder, in the Dutch Reformed Church, as regent of the local hospital, and as a member of the High Court of South Holland. Cuyp apparently stopped painting after about 1660. Records indicate that at the time of his death in November 1691, he had become one of the wealthiest citizens of Dordrecht.

NOTES

1. On the artists of the Cuyp family, see the exhibition catalogue Dordrecht 1977–78.

2. Biographical material on Aelbert Cuyp is based on A. Chong's essays in Amsterdam/Boston/Philadelphia 1987–88, 290, and in *Dictionary of Art* 1996, 8:293–98.

[11]

Landscape with the Ruins of Rijnsburg Abbey, c. 1645

Inscription: bottom center: *A. cuyp*

Oil on canvas, 101.6 × 142.2 cm (40 × 55 15/16 in.)

The Detroit Institute of Arts, Gift of Mrs. Lillian Henkel Haass and Mrs. Trent McMath in memory of Julius H. Haass, 33.7

References: Smith 1829–42, 5 (1834):358–59, no. 258, and 9 (1842):662, no. 42; Hofstede de Groot 2 (1907):95, no. 319 (as Brederode Castle); Holmes 1930, 169, repr.; Glasbergen and Van Regteren Altena 1965, 146, repr.; The Hague 1980, 21–23, under inv. 822 n. 5; Chong 1991, 610; Chong 1992, 196–97, 312, no. 65; Bolten 1994, 45, under no. 35; Keyes, Kuretsky, Rüger, and Wheelock 2004, 60–61.

Rijnsburg Abbey, five miles northwest of Leiden, was one of the great medieval structures on Dutch soil that became ruins in the late sixteenth century during the war with Spain that preceded national independence. The last vestiges of its remains were dismantled by about 1815, but the site had been thoroughly recorded in numerous paintings, prints, and drawings throughout the seventeenth and eighteenth centuries.[1] Founded in 1133 by Petronilla van Lotharingen, widow of Count Floris II, as a Benedictine convent for women of noble birth, Rijnsburg acquired additional historic significance as the burial place of the counts of Holland who were interred in its church.[2] The exact date of its destruction is not known, but Rijnsburg had sustained damage by iconoclasts even before it was overrun and burned by Spanish soldiers in 1573–74 during the siege of Leiden. Like the other medieval monuments destroyed during this period, such as Brederode Castle (Cats. 1, 2a, 7, and 8) and the Huis ter Kleef (Cats. 2b and 4), the ruins of Rijnsburg remained a prominent local landmark that continued to attract artists and sightseers because of its associations with Dutch history as well as its picturesque appearance. The grounds apparently continued to have religious significance until at least 1620, when the last abbess of Rijnsburg was buried there.[3]

Cuyp made at least four paintings and one drawing of Rijnsburg that depict the site from various vantage points and under different lighting conditions.[4] In the Detroit painting, the abbey is seen from the southwest, much as it appears in a print in Abraham Rademaker's *Kabinet van Nederlandsche outheden en gezichten*, an early eighteenth-century compilation of views of Dutch towns, castles, and ruin sites that shows the building as it looked in 1630 (Fig. 117).[5] While certain distinctive aspects of the structure, such as the remains of its stepped gable (see Cat. 5) are not apparent, Cuyp has emphasized the deep, ground-level arches and windows of the two-story elevation as well as the extreme irregularity of its damaged roofline. Ruins occupy various spatial zones throughout this hilly landscape, for the segment of a tall, overgrown wall forms a repoussoir at the left foreground, while in the distance a ruined castle rises into the light on the other side of a river.

More than his other depictions of Rijnsburg, Cuyp's painting in Detroit conveys an intensely brooding atmosphere, with stormy clouds gathering overhead and the entire foreground cast into deep shadow. As a result, irregular shapes of the shattered architecture are powerfully projected against the light in a manner that emphasizes their silhouettes more than any details of surface texture. Within the darkened foreground, small touches of light pick out a herd of sheep, two cows, and a standing and a seated man. Like the spectators in many landscapes with ruins, this pair appears to be discussing the condition or history of the building. While the standing figure is dressed as a con-

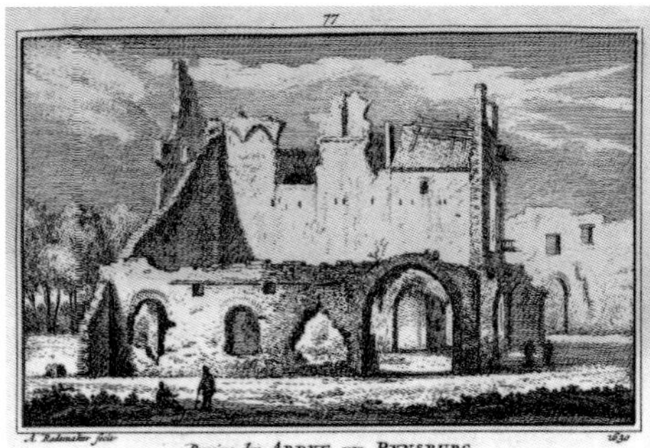

Fig. 117. The ruins of Rijnsburg Abbey from the southwest in 1630, from Abraham Rademaker, *Kabinet van Nederlandsche outheden en gezichten*, Amsterdam, 1725, part 1, no. 77, Department of Rare Books, The Houghton Library, Harvard College Library, Cambridge, Massachusetts

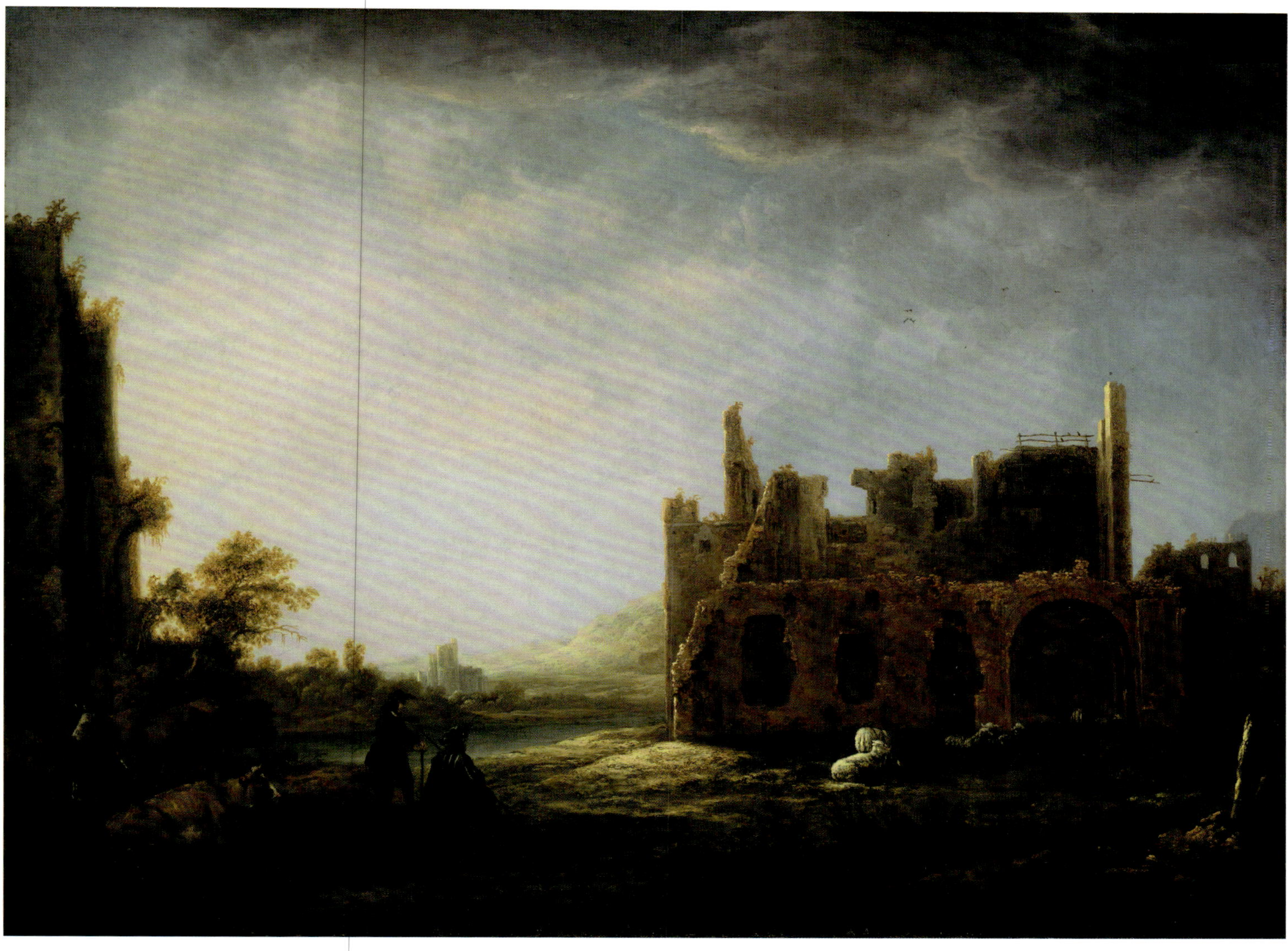

temporary gentleman with a broad-brimmed hat and walking stick, his seated companion, holding a long staff, wears theatrical garb, his slashed jacket and feathered beret giving him the look of a costumed shepherd. Pastoral imagery, which became popular with the Dutch public in paintings, poems, and plays, was meant to transport its audience into an idyllic realm outside time and therefore impervious to death or decay. Scenes of this type often feature ruins in order to evoke connections with ancient bucolic poetry (Cats. 13 and 66), but the darker, more foreboding effect of Cuyp's painting suggests that these onlookers may be conversing about more serious matters involving the evanescence of human builders and their works.

NOTES

1. The latest representation included in J. Bolten's extensive study of the prints and drawings of Rijnsburg is a drawing in the Gemeentearchief, Leiden, dated 1814, by Hermanus Numan (1744–1820); repr. Bolten 1994, 117, no. 158. For further discussion of Rijnsburg's ruins, see Glasbergen and Van Regteren-Altena 1965 and Löffler 2000, which concentrates on examples with imaginary settings.

2. On the history of Rijnsburg Abbey see Van Leeuwen 1685, 1317–21; Glasbergen and Leenheer 1974, 20–32; New York/London 1986, 156; and A. A. W. van Gestel in Bolten 1994, 3–6.

3. Schotel 1851, 207, as cited in New York/London 1986, 156, n. 4.

4. Cuyp's depictions of Rijnsburg include a dated painting of 1645 in a Dutch private collection (panel, 40.5 × 53 cm; repr. Chong 1991, 611, fig. 51); an undated painting from the same period in the Mauritshuis, The Hague (inv. 822, panel, 49.7 × 74 cm; The Hague 1980, 21–23, 160, repr., no. 822); and a signed painting at Bridgewater House, London (panel, 45 × 75 cm; photo RKD, The Hague, no. L69399). There is also a drawing of Rijnsburg by Cuyp in the Dordrechts Museum (repr. Bolten 1994, 33, no. 19).

5. Rademaker 1725, pt. 1, no. 77. The building in the Detroit painting, previously thought to be Brederode Castle, was first matched with Rademaker's view of Rijnsburg Abbey in Glasbergen and Van Regteren Altena 1965, 146.

[12]

Horsemen before Ubbergen Castle, c. 1650–55

Inscriptions: signed lower left: *A. Cuÿp*

Oil on panel, 58.4 × 73.7 cm (23 × 29 in.)

Sarah Campbell Blaffer Foundation, Houston, 1977.8

References: Von Bode 1913, no. 155; Capetown 1952, 9, no. 11; Wright 1981, 144–45.

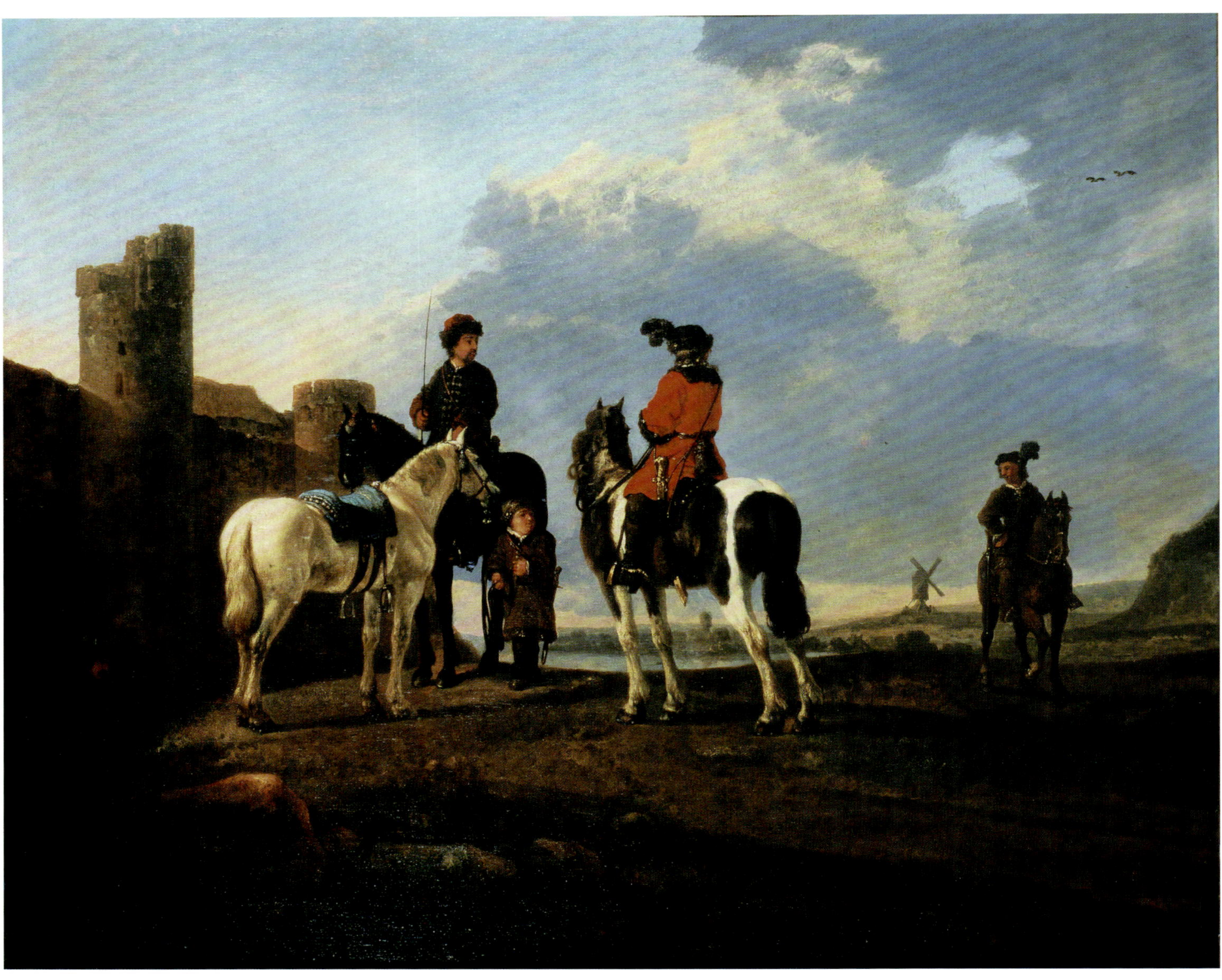

Ubbergen Castle, no longer extant, once stood four kilometers southeast of Nijmegen near the eastern border of the Dutch provinces.[1] Cuyp would have seen its ruins during his travels around the area in 1651–52. This exceptionally scenic setting of the lower Rhine included a large mountain (the Ubberger Berg), rising behind the castle, as well as a lake known as the Ubberger Meer, also since vanished from the landscape. Cuyp used the site for a major landscape painting in the mid-1650s (National Gallery, London; Fig. 118), in which the shell of the castle was based upon the artist's direct examination of the structure, as recorded in his preparatory drawing with identifying inscription in the Albertina, Vienna.[2]

Built in the late fourteenth century for Johann van Ubbergen, count of Nijmegen, Ubbergen had a square plan with towers at the corners like those of Brederode Castle (Cats. 1, 2a, 7, and 8) and Huis te Merwede (Cat. 13). According to documentary evidence, on the evening of 23 August 1582, during the period of Dutch rebellion against the Spanish, the castle was set on fire by the local citizens, probably to prevent its falling into Spanish hands.[3] Like other Dutch ruins that came into being in similar circumstances, Ubbergen retained potent associations with the national struggle for independence. Its remains were demolished in 1742.

In the Houston painting, only a portion of the ruin with round towers appears at the far left beyond the foreground figures, but its presence is crucial to the scene's mood and meaning. Within the soft light and long, end-of-day shadows, elegant horsemen and their young page gather informally in a setting that might almost be Italian, were it not for the level waterway and the obviously Dutch windmill at the right background. The men wear exotic costumes with elaborate gold-trimmed velvet jackets and soft hats or berets, as seen in other paintings of aristocratic equestrians by Cuyp, such as his *Portrait of Michiel and Cornelis Pompe van Meerdervoort and Their Tutor* (Metropolitan Museum of Art, New York), in which a background ruin also appears.[4] Lowering the viewpoint to enhance the projection of figures and

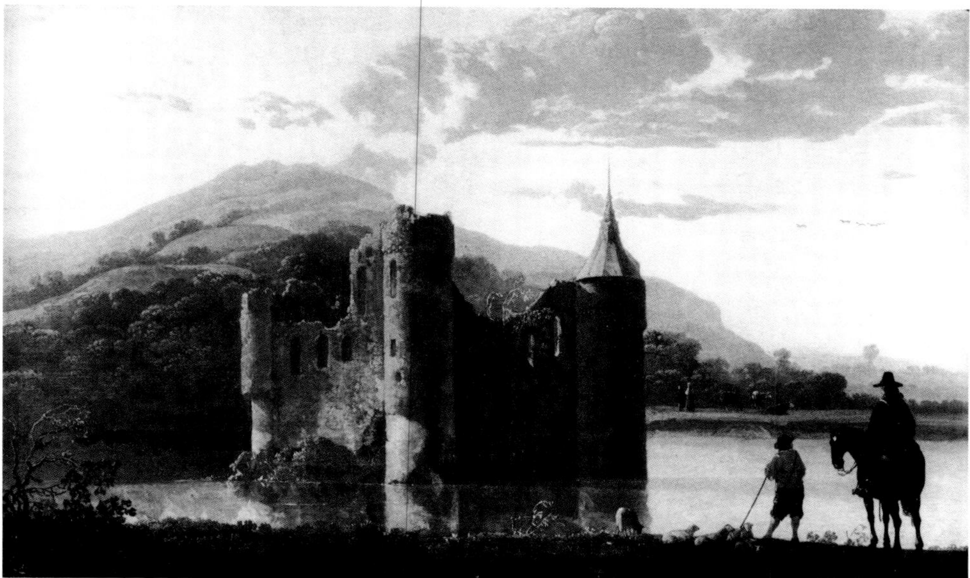

Fig. 118. Aelbert Cuyp, *Ubbergen Castle*, mid-1650s, oil on panel, The National Gallery, London

castle against the lighted sky has the effect of elevating and connecting both, reminding the viewer that horsemanship (and related activities such as hunting) were ancient privileges of the nobility. Thus, like many of Cuyp's landscapes, this scene seems to take place in a temporal realm somewhere between past and present.

NOTES

1. Discussion of Ubbergen Castle and its history is based primarily on the account by A. Rüger (Washington/London/Amsterdam 2002, 154), who notes the major source of his material as Gorissen 1959.

2. Repr. Washington/London/Amsterdam 2002, 256, no. 88.

3. The document is quoted in Gorissen 1959, 159: "Heft die burgerie het huis Ubbergen den avot (23 august 1582) in brant gesteken"; and cited by A. Rüger in Washington/London/Amsterdam 2002, 201 n. 3.

4. Similar attire appears in *Horsemen Resting in a Landscape*, Dordrechts Museum, and *Horsemen and Herdsmen with Cattle*, National Gallery of Art, Washington, D.C. A. Chong suggests that the elaborate costumes in these scenes were probably part of Cuyp's stock of studio gear (Washington/London/Amsterdam 2002, 166).

[13]

Herdsmen Tending Cattle, c. 1655–60

Inscriptions: lower left, *A. cuijp*

Oil on canvas, 66 × 87.6 cm (26 × 34½ in.)

Andrew W. Mellon Collection, National Gallery of Art, Washington, D.C., 1937.1.59

References: Smith 1829–42, 5 (1834):305, no. 76; Cundall 1891, 161; Hofstede de Groot 2 (1907):68, no. 203; Graves 1913–15, 1:245, 247, and 250; Reiss 1975, 129, no. 92, repr.; Spicer 1983, 251, fig. 2; Sutton 1986, fig. 456; Wheelock 1995, 44–46.

This peaceful, light-saturated scene shows a man and a woman with long herders' staffs guarding cattle by a quiet river and two travelers in conversation at the far right. It offers the rather idealized interpretation of rural life found in paintings, drawings, and prints by Dutch artists who had spent time in Italy. Cuyp, who had not, was strongly influenced by landscapes of this type by Jan Both (q.v.), Jan Asselijn (after 1610–52), and others (Cat. 61 and Figs. 91 and 92), in which shepherds or herdsmen appear within similarly clear, sunny illumination that suggests a timeless, perfect world free of earthly cares and concerns. This kind of arcadian idyll, whose origins can be traced to ancient poets such as Virgil, was also being revived in seventeenth-century Dutch *hofdichten* (country house poems) and pastoral plays.[1] Although Cuyp's figures do not wear theatrical garb, their elegant red and blue costumes and the relaxed demeanor of both people and animals enhance the bucolic character of a scene that does not, however, exist outside time. Delicately waning light and the long shadows falling across the foreground suggest that this is the end of day. A sense of departure is also implied, as the male figure turns back to his seated female companion, gesturing to the right, toward which the herd is beginning to move.

One of Cuyp's most evocative and poetic landscapes, this painting employs a low viewpoint so that figures and cows are framed by a towering mass of cumulus cloud that has absorbed the golden light and seems suspended in the clear atmosphere beyond them. The cows, somewhat glorified within this ambiance, exhibit a diversity of colors and are shown from multiple viewpoints. Thus the artist displays the excellence of a domestic beast that, along with its pastoral associations, became something of a symbol of Dutch prosperity during the seventeenth century, as new breeding produced dairy herds acclaimed throughout Europe for the quantity and quality of their milk, butter, and cheese.[2] While the herd occupies the right side of this scene, a long vista opens at the left into a distant view of tall cliffs

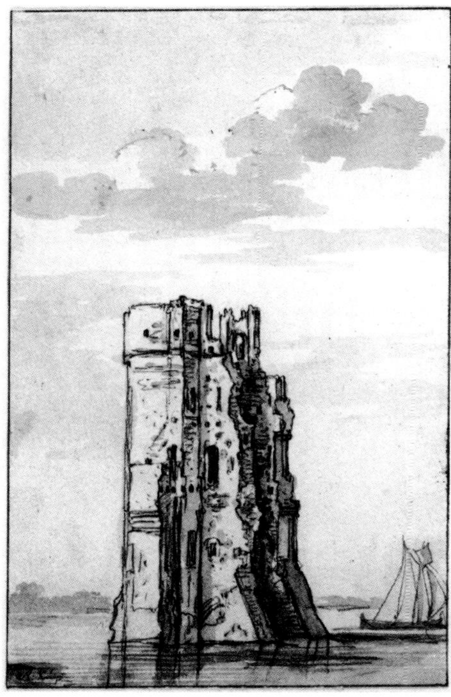

Fig. 119. Aelbert Cuyp, *Ruins of the Huis te Merwede*, chalk drawing, British Museum, London

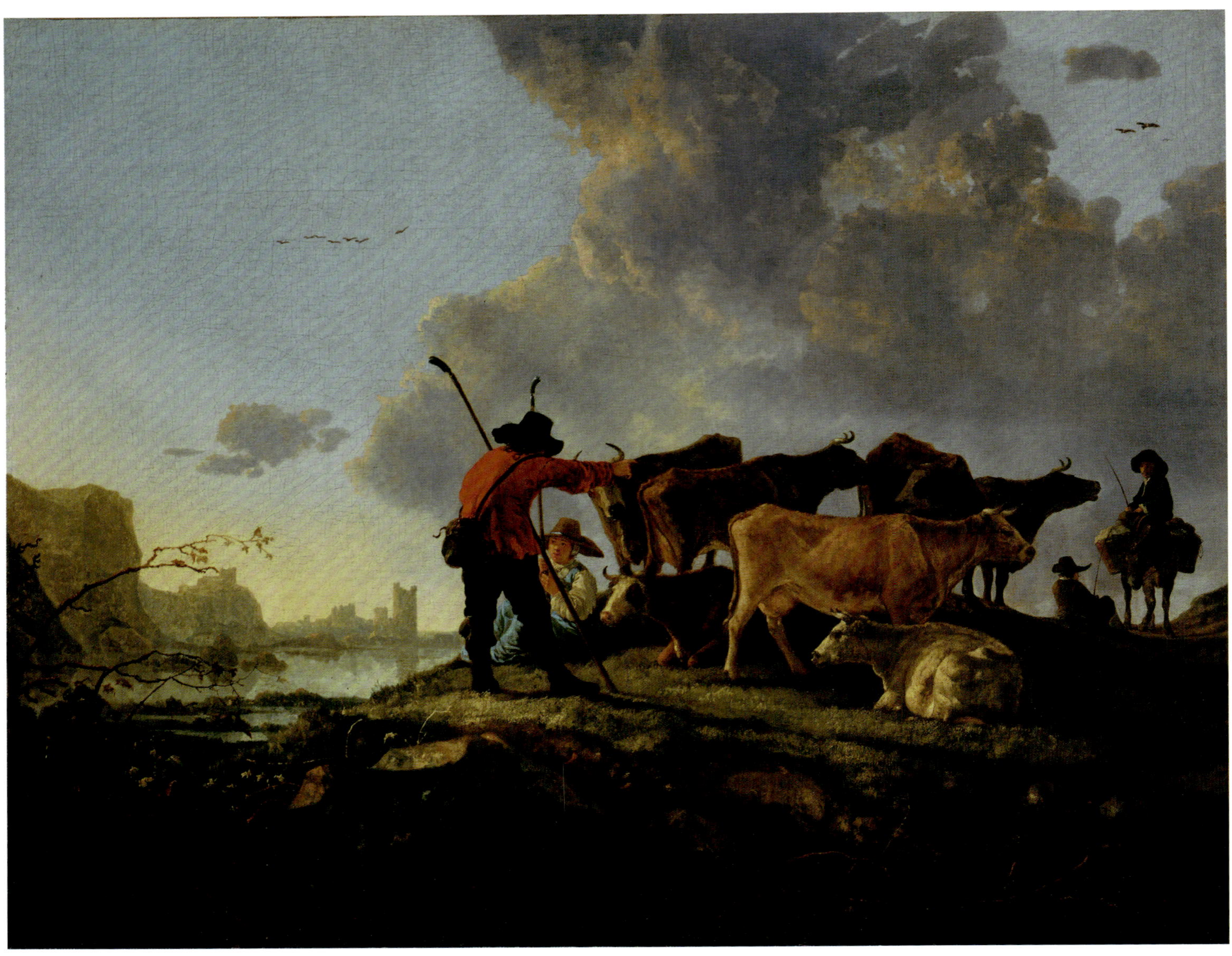

and ancient castles reflected in the water.[3] The ruined structure at the end, which has been identified as a free adaptation of the tower of Huis te Merwede outside Dordrecht, acts as a small pictorial foil for the standing herdsman, connecting him to both past and present.[4]

Unlike many of the other ruined castles in the Dutch landscape, Merwede was destroyed long before the late sixteenth-century conflict with the Spanish.[5] Built on land leased from the count of Holland for Daniël van der Merwede (whose daughter Margaretha would marry Willem van Brederode), this early fourteenth-century structure suffered two distinct episodes of damage. The first occurred during the Siege of Dordrecht of 1418, when the duke of Brabant (Jan IV van Beijeren) appropriated the building as his personal residence, and a vengeful local population tried to destroy it. Only a few years later, in 1421, the historic St. Elizabeth's Flood, one of the most devastating natural disasters in Dutch history, submerged the land around Merwede, inflicting further damage on the castle. By the mid-seventeenth century, Merwede had been reduced to a large irregular tower of masonry at the northwest corner—still surrounded by water, as seen in other depictions of it by Cuyp (Fig. 119).[6] The tower's remains, consolidated by modern restorers, are still standing.

NOTES

1. Dutch pastoral imagery and its development have been thoroughly explored in Kettering 1983. On the taste for *hofdichten*, see Van Veen 1985.

2. A. Chong has discussed the depiction of cows as symbols of the Dutch nation and as emblems of national wealth in Amsterdam/Boston/Philadelphia 1987–88, 294–95, and in his essay in the exhibition catalogue *Meesterlijk vee* in Dordrecht/Leeuwarden 1988, 56–86. On the origins and development of the Dutch cattle piece, see Spicer 1983.

3. As A. K. Wheelock Jr. has noted, however, a copy of the painting in the collection of Baron Ash of Wingfield Castle, Diss, Norfolk, England, shows the cattle somewhat more centered in the picture space, which suggests that the Washington canvas has been slightly trimmed. Wheelock 1995, 46 and fig. 1.

4. Wheelock 1995, 44.

5. The history of Merwede has been discussed in Dordrecht 1976; Chong 1992, 197, 171–72 and n. 7; Schulte et al. 1997, 274–77; and A. Rüger in Washington/London/Amsterdam 2002, 156, 203 nn. 2 and 3.

6. Depictions of the site (repr. Reiss 1975, nos. 40,

70, and 111) include paintings attributed to Cuyp in the Musée Fabre, Montpellier (panel, 53 × 83 cm) and in the Musée des Beaux-Arts, Strasbourg (panel, 49 × 66 cm), as well as Cuyp's winter landscape with Merwede tower in the collection of the earl of Yarborough, Brocklesby Hall (panel, 64 × 89 cm). Cuyp also made drawings of the ruined tower, two of which (seen from the west) are in the British Museum, London, and one (from the northeast) in the Institut Néerlandais, Paris.

COENRAET DECKER
1651–85

A student of Romeyn de Hooghe (q.v.), Decker was an Amsterdam engraver and book illustrator whose marriage to Agatha Jans Leygue was recorded in Sloterdijk in 1673.[1] The marriage was apparently an unhappy one, for in 1682, Decker left his wife and two children and went to live with a woman named Margriet Both, with whom he had had a liaison as early as 1679. Among Decker's most significant prints are the thirty-two illustrations he contributed to Dirck Evertsz. van Bleyswijck's *Beschryvinge der stadt Delft* (History of the city of Delft), whose first volume was issued in 1667 (the second would appear in 1680). In 1675, when van Bleyswijck was commissioned by the municipality of Delft to produce a large pictorial record of the city, he again selected Decker as one of two engravers for this important and complex project. The *Kaart figuratief* (illustrated map), published in 1678 by Pieter Smith under van Bleyswijck's supervision, consisted of two elaborately framed combinations of prints, including a bird's-eye-view map of the city, two large skyline vistas, and depictions of significant buildings and surrounding villages. Like *Beschryvinge der stadt Delft*, it was intended to promote the beauty, importance, and fame of the city, both locally and throughout Europe.[2]

Decker's printmaking activities were wide-ranging, for like his teacher Romeyn de Hooghe, he produced topographical views, political allegories, and depictions of contemporary figures and events, including representations of battles on land and sea during the French invasion of the Dutch provinces in 1672–73 (see also Cat. 39). Other book illustrations by Decker include engravings for Jansonius van Waesberghe and Johannes van Someren's *Asiographica* of 1672; for W. Schouten's *Oost-Indische voyagie* of 1676; and for J. Nieuhof's *Brasiliaense … reyse* of 1682.

NOTES

1. For biographical information on Decker, see the essay by R. Feurer in Saur/Künstler-Lexikon 1992, 25 (2000):124–25.

2. As M. C. Plomp has discussed, the *Kaart figuratief* was intended as a presentation piece to visiting Dutch magistrates, ambassadors, and foreign princes. For discussion of this project, see Weve 1997 and M. C. Plomp in New York/London 2001, 189–90, 506–8, nos. 134 and 135.

[14]

The Ruins of the Carthusian Monastery, Delft, in Three Views, from Dirck van Bleyswijck, *Beschryvinge der stadt Delft*, Arnold Bon, Delft, 1667

Inscriptions: lower right, *verae, genuinae, indubitataeque demonstrationes / vestigiorum Monasterii Carthusianorum pro: / pe Delphos Batavorum, ad vivum de: / lineatae ano M.D.LXXV.—*

(A true, genuine, and unquestionable demonstration / of the remains of the Carthusian monastery of the Batavians [i.e., the Dutch] near / Delft drawn from life the year 1575.)

Waere, en onfeÿlbaere afgebeeldingen, van / 't Carthuÿsers Klooster buÿten Delft soo / als het selve geruineert Lagh in 't / jaer 1575. Sÿnde een, vande drie / Kloosters die van dese ordre in ge: / heel Hollant geweest sÿn.

(True and direct representations of / the Carthusian cloister outside Delft / as it lay in ruins / in the year 1575. This is one of three / cloisters of this religious order / to exist in all of Holland.)

Engraving, 180 × 271 mm (7 1/16 × 10 10/16 in.) (image), 355.6 × 215.9 mm (14 × 8 1/2 in.) (overall)

Department of Rare Books, The Houghton Library, Harvard College Library, Cambridge, Massachusetts, Neth 3310.7* (Poughkeepsie); National Gallery of Art Library, Washington, D.C., David K. E. Bruce Fund (Sarasota and Louisville)

References: Van Bleyswijck 1667–80, 1:354; Schulte et al. 1997, 19–21; Weve 1997, 10–15; New York/London 2001, 200, 886 n. 28.

Like Samuel Ampzing's history of the city of Haarlem, published in 1628 (Cat. 4), Dirck Evertsz. van Bleyswijck's (1639–81) history of Delft was written to celebrate the author's native city and to record its important citizens and architectural monuments and the significant

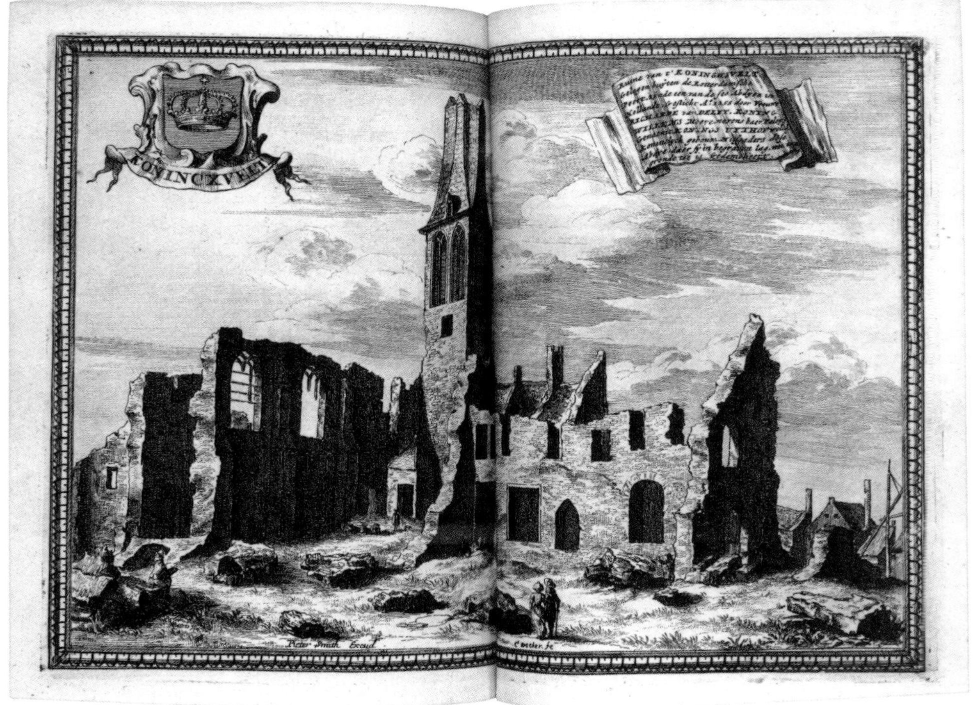

Fig. 120. Coenraet Decker, *The Ruins of Koningsveld*, from Dirck van Bleyswijck, *Beschryvinge der stadt Delft*, Delft, 1667, Department of Rare Books, The Houghton Library, Harvard College Library, Cambridge, Massachusetts

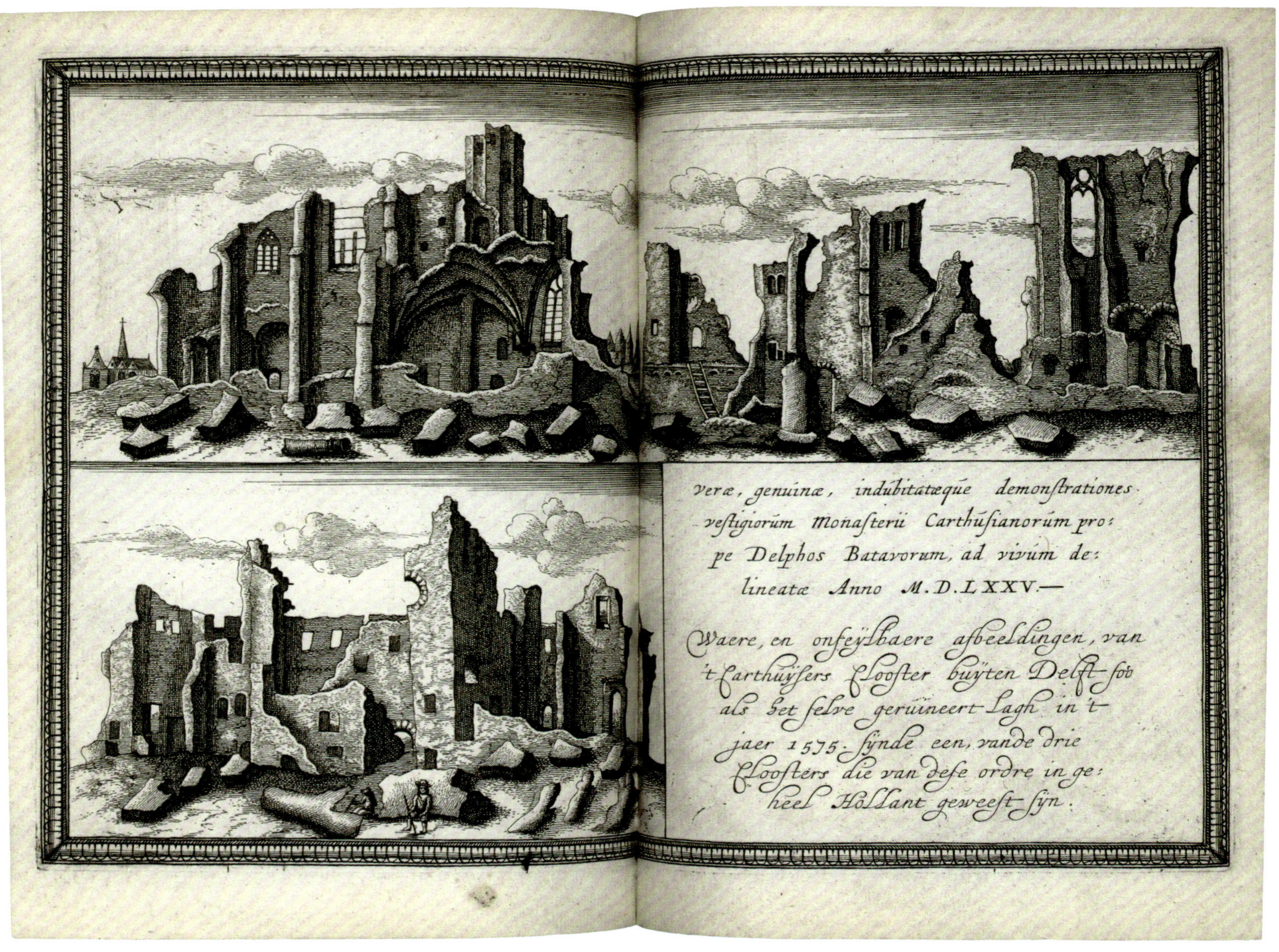

events of its past. But while Ampzing's book was written when the war with Spain was still fresh in the memory of at least some local citizens, Van Bleyswijck was addressing himself to a later generation. As M. J. Bok has noted, the preface of Van Bleyswijck's book indicates that the author had become concerned that increasing affluence and the global expansion of the Dutch Republic was causing its citizens to become less interested in their own heritage and more concerned with faraway lands.[1] There was good reason for Van Bleyswijck to celebrate Delft, because, in addition to its beauty and prosperity, the city had great historic importance as the residence and headquarters of William of Orange (William the Silent), leader of the rebellion against the Spanish, who was assassinated in the Prinsenhof in 1584 and whose remains are interred in Delft's Nieuwe Kerk.

The son of a wealthy Delft brewer and burgomaster, Van Bleyswijck studied at Leiden University, traveled, collected art, and went on to serve a term as burgomaster of the city and to become a member of the Admiralty of Zeeland. As he states in the introduction to his book, he had planned a grand tour of the Netherlands, France, and Italy as a young man, but after illness confined him to his bed, he decided to write the history of his native city. The first volume of *Beschryvinge der stadt Delft*, published by Arnold Bon, appeared in 1667, the second in 1680. A new edition was issued by Renier Boitet in 1729.

Coenraet Decker's illustrations for Van Bleyswijck's history include views of two important local ruins, both built as convents for young women and both destroyed during the struggle with the Spanish. Neither stands today. The Carthusian convent, established in 1430 and located on the west side of the city, was destroyed in 1573 by the citizens of Delft to prevent its being appropriated by Spanish troops. Its importance as one of only three Carthusian cloisters in Holland is emphasized by inscriptions in Latin and Dutch and by the fact that the building is presented in an unusually prominent way from three vantage points.[2] This repetition of views, which reveals the extent of the destruction on all sides, magnifies the utter devastation of the site, as does the complete lack of grass or other plant life. Silhouetted against floating clouds in the sky beyond, these shattered walls retain almost nothing of the building's original shape. Their extreme fragmentation as well as the many chunks of masonry scattered across the ground make the building's remains appear to be falling, even as large shards of the structure continue to stand.

Another important ruin illustrated in Van Bleyswijck's book is Koningsveld (also spelled Koningxvelt or Coningsvelt), an abbey outside the Rotterdam Gate that had been founded in 1255 by Richardis, daughter of Willem I and sister of Floris III, count of Holland and Zeeland (Fig. 120). This print, according to its inscription, was made ("fe.") by Decker, but published ("excud.") by Pieter Smith. Unlike in the depiction of the Carthusian convent, however, an intact tower with narrow gothic lancets still rises above the broken shell of the structure, whose truncated walls are punctuated by empty windows of varied sizes and shapes. Among the visitors who have come to examine and discuss the ruin is a seated draftsman sketching the site at the left foreground.[3]

NOTES

1. M. J. Bok in New York/London 2001, 200.

2. The same three views of the Carthusian cloister were reproduced in Abraham Rademaker's compendium of city views, buildings, and monuments, published in 1725. Rademaker 1725, nos. 132, 133, and 135.

3. Some of the copies of Van Bleyswijck's book (such as the ones in the New York Public Library and the National Gallery of Art Library, Washington, D.C.) include additional views of the ruins of Koningsveld in images made entirely in line, without any shading, so that the abbey appears almost as the ghost of itself. As A. Blankert has pointed out, the often-quoted poem by Arnold Bon about the death of Carel Fabritius in Van Bleyswijck's book is also worded differently in different copies of the book, even though there was only one edition. Blankert 1978, 61.

RUSTIC RUINS

JOACHIM WTEWAEL
1566–1638

One of the leading Dutch practitioners of the elegantly artful, classically influenced style that has come to be known as mannerism, Wtewael (also spelled Uytewael) began as a student in his father's glassworks in Utrecht and then apprenticed with Joost de Beer (fl. 1575–91), according to Karel van Mander's (1548–1606) account of his life.[1] Between about 1588 and 1592 he traveled in Italy and France with his patron, Charles de Bourgneuf de Cucé, bishop of St. Malo. During this period, he absorbed the styles of Italian mannerists such as Parmigianino and French artists of the School of Fontainebleau. By 1592 he returned to Utrecht, where he joined the saddlers' guild (to which artists also belonged) and began to respond to developments initiated by Haarlem artists such as Hendrick Goltzius (1558–1617) and Van Mander. In 1594 or 1595 Wtewael was commissioned to design a stained glass window for the recently reconstructed St. Janskerk in Gouda. Since Utrecht (a bishopric) had remained predominantly Roman Catholic, Wtewael was probably baptized in that faith, but in 1595 he married Christina van Halen in the Reformed Church and in subsequent years appears to have become a Calvinist sympathizer and supporter of Prince Maurice of Orange and the Counter-Remonstrant faction.

Until about 1600 Wtewael's polished and colorful biblical and mythological scenes, many painted on copper, display the crowded, convoluted designs, exaggerated muscular poses, and jewel-like finishes of the more extreme form of mannerism initiated by the influential Flemish painter Bartholomaus Spranger (1546–1611). After 1600, however, Wtewael and his contemporaries in Utrecht and Haarlem moved toward more spatially clarified, more naturalistic images, while still retaining a graceful refinement of color and contour. A flax merchant and politician as well as a painter, Wtewael was repeatedly elected to the Utrecht town council and became one of the founders, in 1611, of the town's new St. Luke's guild for artists. His works have sometimes been confused with those of his son Pieter Wtewael (1596–1660), who closely followed his style.

NOTE

1. Van Mander 1604, fols. 296v2–297r10. For a translation of Van Mander's account see Lowenthal 1986, 25–26 and Van Mander/Miedema 1994–99, 1 (1994):445–46. Further biographical material on Wtewael has been drawn from A. Lowenthal's monograph (Lowenthal 1986, 25–37) and from her biographical essay on the artist in *Dictionary of Art* 1996, 33:417–19.

[15]

Adoration of the Shepherds, 1598–99

Inscriptions: signed on a rock, left foreground, *IOACHIM WTEN WAEL FECIT*

Oil on canvas, 86.7 × 112.1 cm (34⅛ × 44⅛ in.)

Fine Arts Museums of San Francisco, Museum purchase, European Art Trust Fund, The Roscoe and Margaret Oakes Income Fund, and by exchange from the Mildred Anna Williams Collection, André J. Kahn-Wolf, Julia Wise, Donald McLeod Lewis in Memory of Mabelle McLeod Lewis, Dr. T. Edward and Tullah Hanley, Bradford, Pennsylvania, Herbert Fleishhacker, Sydney Menzie Wynn and the Ernest M. P. Wayne Estate, Forrest Engelhart and Julia May Babcock, 1999.130

References: Amsterdam 1955, no. 126, pl. 27; Manchester 1965, no. 243; London 1974, no. 1, repr.; Kettering 1983, 40, 49, 168–69 n. 86, and fig. 26 (Utrecht version); Lowenthal 1986, 71, 85–86, no. A-7, pl. 9; New York 1988, 141, no. 61; Orr 2000.

One of the most frequently depicted incidents in the New Testament, this scene features the first earthly witnesses to the birth of Christ: shepherds who had been sleeping beside their flocks in the nearby countryside and were startled awake by a glory of heavenly light and an angel telling them that a savior had been born in Bethlehem (Luke 2:15–18). That this divine manifestation allowed the simplest rustic folk to be the first arrivals at the Nativity underlines the democratic character of Christianity, which teaches that even people from the most humble stations in life can achieve salvation. Significantly, Christ would later refer to himself as the Good Shepherd who watches over the flock of humanity (John 10:11).

In Wtewael's brilliantly colorful painting, a complex grouping of figures and animals have come together in a setting of Roman ruins with brick archways and broken barrel vaults. The foreground, strewn with rubble, displays a fallen Corinthian capital, two broken logs or trees, and, at the far right, crumbling brickwork that discloses part of an underground basement or grotto. Such ancient ruined settings for scenes of the Adoration of the Shepherds or the Magi were first elaborated in fifteenth-century Netherlandish painting to indicate the falling away of the Old Dispensation of Mosaic law when the New Dispensation of the Christian era began. This traditional distinction is further expressed here in the contrast between the ass at the far left (representing the era before Christ) who turns his back on the scene to nibble hay, while the ox (a sacrificial beast symbolizing the Christian era) noses his huge head devoutly toward the tiny newborn child.[1]

As in this painting, uneven holes in the ground (sometimes grated) occasionally appear in depictions of the Nativity, beginning in early Netherlandish art of the fifteenth century, to indicate that the ruins of the old Jewish synagogue became the foundation for the new Christian church.[2] Such crevices may also allude to early reports that the birth of Christ took place in an underground grotto or cave beneath the stable of the Nativity, as vividly illustrated in an early sixteen-century miniature of the *Adoration of the Magi* from Sebastian Brandt's *Hortulus animae* in the Österreichische Nationalbibliothek, Vienna (Fig. 121).[3] Framing Adoration scenes within ruined architecture of the past, whose irregular and incomplete shapes embody temporal transformation, emphasizes the fact that those who have come to pay tribute to Christ also experience transformation through spiritual conversion.

As a mannerist painter, Wtewael renders almost every aspect of his scene with polished elegance, from the trio of silky, long-horned goats at the right to the shepherds whose bodies twist gracefully in their garments of blue-green, violet, and gold. Their broad-brimmed hats and the red filets woven into their hair are

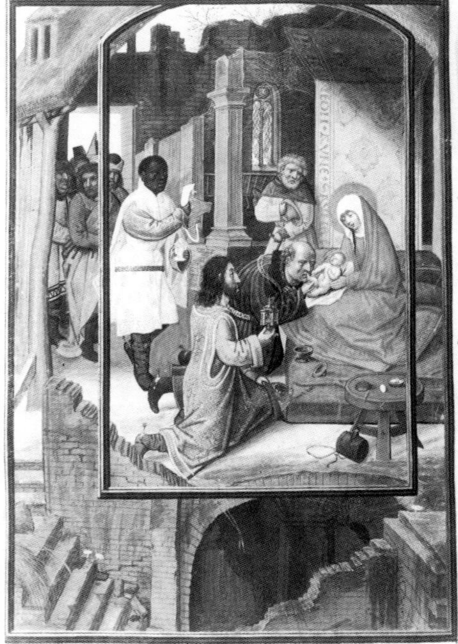

Fig. 121. *Adoration of the Magi*, from Sebastian Brandt, *Hortulus animae*, c. 1510, Bildarchiv, Österreichische Nationalbibliothek, Vienna

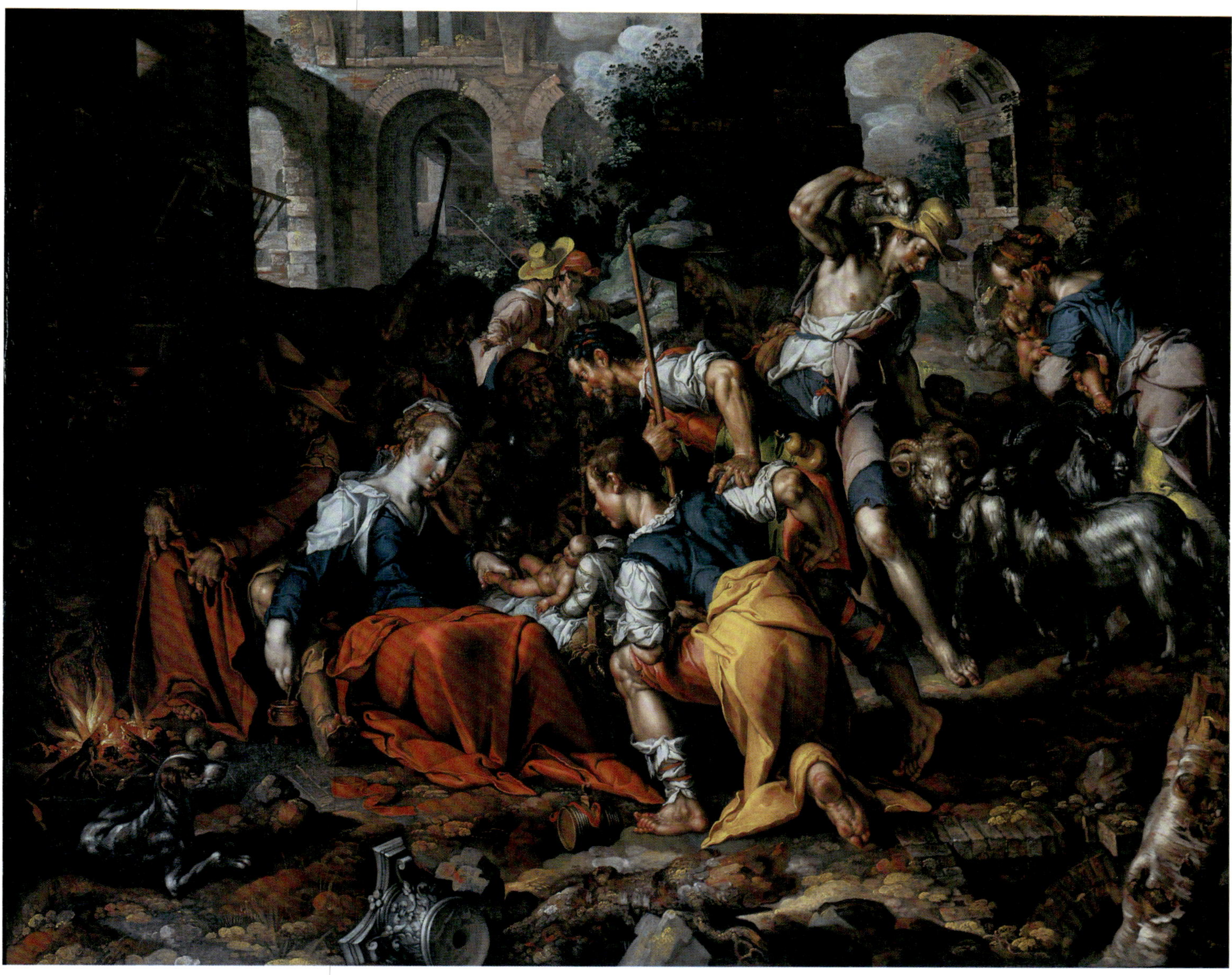

not everyday rustic dress, nor is the off-the-shoulder *all'antica* costume of the standing figure at the right. As A. Kettering has discussed, these motifs are important early examples of the kinds of pastoral imagery that would become popular in Dutch art, poetry, and theater from about 1620 on.[4] Originating in the bucolic literature of antiquity, pastoral imagery was revived, beginning in the Renaissance, primarily for an educated audience who appreciated both its idealizing interpretation of nature (including refined rustic figures like Wtewael's) and its learned connections with antiquity.

No less evident in Wtewael's painting is the mannerist predilection to quote from earlier artists, thus drawing attention to the borrower's knowledge and virtuosity.[5] At the same time, daringly arbitrary lighting juxtaposes illuminated and shadowed figures in a way that emphasizes each one, while setting up sinuous visual pathways throughout the complex design. With all his artful blending of quotation and invention, however, Wtewael has also incorporated passages of surprisingly direct observation such as the firelight flickering on the shadowed Joseph at left, or the way Mary proudly displays the infant's tiny foot to a kneeling shepherd while stirring food in the small ceramic pot at her side. It is not surprising that this composition was so successful that the artist produced more than one version of it. According to A.W. Lowenthal, a somewhat smaller painting (86.5 × 106.5 cm, dated 1598) in the Centraal Museum, Utrecht, predates the San Francisco variant, which is somewhat bolder in color and more vigorous in technique.[6]

NOTES

1. E. Panofsky was the first to articulate the ways in which time has been symbolized in Netherlandish Nativity scenes, drawing attention to ruined wooden sheds such as the setting of Robert Campin's *Nativity* of c. 1625, Musée de la Ville, Dijon, and to the more commonly used Romanesque stone ruins found in later paintings such as Rogier van der Weyden's *Bladelin Altarpiece*, c. 1452, Staatliche Museen, Berlin, and his *Columba Altarpiece*, c. 1459, Alte Pinakothek, Munich. Panofsky 1958, 1:158–59, 276–78, and 286–88, 2: figs. 201, 337, and 353.

2. Although Panofsky did not elaborate on this detail of nativity–ruins, holes (grated and ungrated) are featured in the foreground of both altarpieces by Van der Weyden's *Bladelin Altarpiece* and *Columba Altarpiece*.

3. As G. Schiller has discussed in relation to depictions of the Nativity in a Cave, rocky caves and grottoes commonly exist under houses in Bethlehem, out of which cellars and stables were and are still frequently hewn. Pilgrims' accounts as late as the eighth century mention that the church in Bethlehem had an opening through which visitors could look down into the grotto of the Nativity, while the early church fathers connected the cave of the Nativity to the cave of Hades, in which the dead of the Old Covenant await salvation. Schiller 1971–72, 1:62, 78, and 83. G. Bandmann's analysis of this motif points out that the dungeon-like *Geburtshöhle* along with the column may also allude to Christ's later imprisonment and flagellation (Bandmann 1970, 136–37). My thanks to Walter Gibson for discussing this iconographical detail with me and for drawing my attention to additional bibliography on holes in the ground in Nativity scenes: Von der Oosten 1964 and Bandmann 1970.

4. Kettering 1983, 40–41, and Orr 2000, 8.

5. According to A. W. Lowenthal (1986, 85), Wtewael borrowed his setting, the Corinthian capital on the ground and the ass nibbling hay, from an engraving of 1579 of the same subject by Jan Sadelaer (1550–1600) after Jacopo Bassano (c. 1510/18–92), while the shepherds' hats and some of their gestures were taken from a print by Cornelis Cort (1533–before 1578) after Taddeo Zuccaro's (1529–66) *Adoration of the Shepherds* of 1567. The seated dog, lower left, is a quotation from Albrecht Dürer's *St. Eustace* engraving.

6. Lowenthal 1986, 85–86. This catalogue raisonné lists multiple depictions of *The Adoration of the Shepherds* that have been attributed to Wtewael, not all of which are accepted as autograph works (letter B is used to indicate "problematic" and letter C, "rejected"). Aside from the Utrecht and San Francisco paintings (nos. A-6 and A-7), see nos. A-8, A-17, A-42, A-78, A-82, A-83, A-91, B-8, C1–11 (copies), and C57–59 (rejected).

JACOB MATHAM
1571–1631

Matham became an apprentice of Hendrick Goltzius (1558–1617), the celebrated Haarlem engraver, in 1579, when Goltzius married Matham's mother.[1] Thereafter, he became Goltzius's closest associate, concentrating his activities primarily on producing engravings after Goltzius's paintings and drawings in a style that closely reflected his master's.[2] Between 1593 and 1597, Matham was in Rome and Venice, where he made prints after Italian painters such as Jacopo Tintoretto (1518–94) and Taddeo Zuccaro (1529–66), which he continued to produce later in his life, along with engravings after Abraham Bloemaert (q.v.) and such eminent northern Renaissance painters and printmakers as Albrecht Dürer (1471–1528) and Pieter Aertsen (1508/9–75). A signature on one of his engravings indicates that he was court engraver in The Hague the year before his death. An exceptionally prolific printmaker, Matham has yet to be studied thoroughly enough that all of the works attributed to him can be definitively accepted. Nor have his drawings been fully catalogued. The engraving techniques he learned in Goltzius's workshop were handed down to his three sons, Adriaen (1599–1660), Jan (1600–1648), and Theodor (1605/6–76).

NOTES

1. Biographical material on Matham is based upon D. Limouze's essay in *Dictionary of Art* 1996, 20:812.

2. On the relationship between Matham and Goltzius, see Widerkehr 1993, 219–60.

[16]

JACOB MATHAM,
AFTER ABRAHAM BLOEMAERT

Abraham Casting out Hagar, 1603

Inscriptions: signed at the bottom, *Cum privil. Sa. Cae. M. / Abrahamus Bloemaert Inven. I. Martham sculp. / et excud Ao. 1603*; in the margin, *Gen. XXI Dum petulans Dominae non insultare veretur, / Cum nato Iussa est vertere serva solum. / Rupert. In Gen. Sic, Christo, Christique gregi dum illudere certant, / Judaeos meritò par quoque poena permit SSH* [Simon Sovius Harlemsis]

(Genesis 21: Unable to refrain from petulantly insulting her mistress, the servant is ordered to leave along with the son. Rupert [of Deutz] Genesis commentary: As long as the Jews strive to maltreat Christ and the Christian community, they will be rightly harassed with the same punishment)

Engraving, 479 × 370 mm (18⅞ × 14⁹⁄₁₆ in.); state i/ii

Courtesy of the Fogg Art Museum, Harvard University Art Museums, Cambridge, Massachusetts, Bequest of Arnold H. Knapp, M13304

References: Müller 1927, 193–95, repr.; Hamann 1936, 478–80; Hollstein 2 (n.d.):67, no. 475; Hollstein 11 (1955):216; Bartsch (Illustrated) 4 (1980):53; Berlin 1979, no. 57; Cologne 1981, no. 24; E. McGrath in Vekeman and Muller Hofstede 1984, 78, 88, fig. 6; Basel 1987, 88; Roethlisberger 1993, 1:114–15, no. 69, 2: fig. 118; Amsterdam 1993–94a, 552–53, no. 223; Kuretsky 1997, 73 n. 9.

Of the sixteen prints Matham made after Abraham Bloemaert (q.v.), this is one of the largest and most brilliantly rendered, comparable in scale and complexity to Jan Saenredam's engraving, *Farmyard with the Prodigal Son* after Bloemaert of about 1600 (Cat. 17), in which a large, dilapidated farmhouse also plays a major role. The story (Genesis 16–21), which became popular with Netherlandish painters and printmakers from the sixteenth century on, involves the banishment of the Egyptian servant girl Hagar, who had had an illegitimate son (Ishmael) by Abraham at the request of Abraham's barren wife Sarah. When the elderly Sarah miraculously bore her own son, Isaac, she asked Abraham to send Hagar and Ishmael away. As the book of Genesis recounts (Genesis 16:4–5, 21:9), their expulsion from the household was precipitated by Sarah's anger at Hagar's arrogance ("She looked on me with contempt"), as well as her concern that Ishmael would be a threat to Isaac's inheritance. In Matham's print, an inscription at the lower left summarizes the biblical passage, adding a brief comment at the right, from the twelfth-century theologian Rupert of Deutz. This passage has been related to St. Paul's typological interpretation of the narrative as an allegory of the two covenants, with Hagar's dismissal illustrating how the ancient law of Judaism was expelled by the New Dispensation of Christianity, as personified by Sarah and her son Isaac (Galacians 4:22–31).[1]

In this intensely detailed vertical composition, the large house—a weathered edifice of extraordinary character that has been assembled of brick, wood, and thatch—rises high above the small figures, as if to emphasize the homey sanctuary that Hagar and Ishmael must now abandon. Hagar bends weeping in distress with her son behind her, as Abraham gestures insistently to the right (Isaac leaning out the window behind him). Under his pointing hand

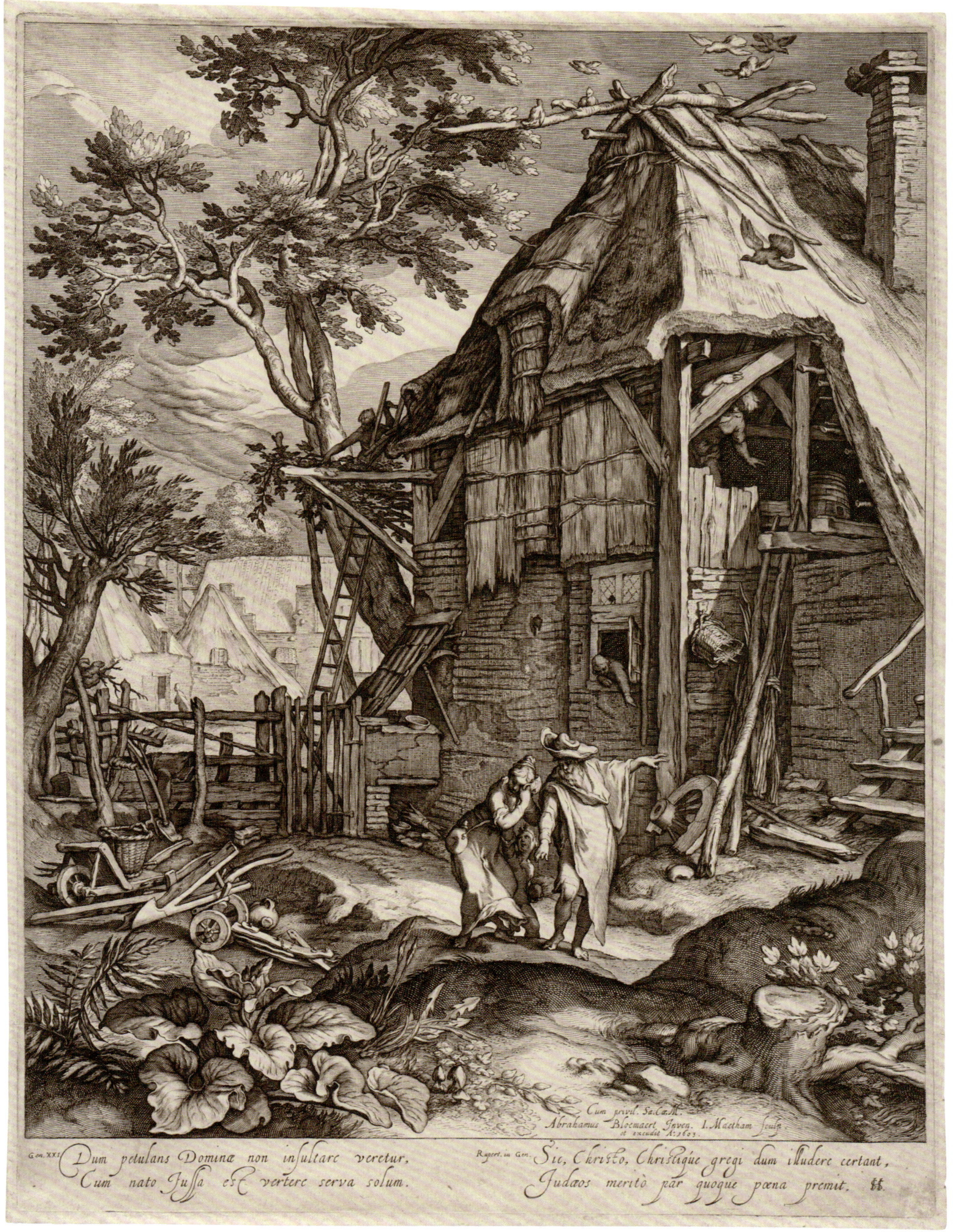

Cum privil. Sa. Cæ. M.
Abrahamus Bloemaert Inven. I. Maetham sculp. et excudit A: 1603.
Gen. XXI Dum petulans Dominæ non insultare veretur,
Cum nato Jussa est vertere serva solum.
Rupert. in Gen. Sic, Christo, Christique gregi dum illudere certant,
Judæos meritò par quoque pœna premit.

is a broken wagon wheel, a motif also found in Saenredam's engraving after Bloemaert, where, as here, it may symbolize lost fortune.[2] At the left, lush vegetation and a heap of wheelbarrows and farming tools display the comfortable assets of this household. Pictorial structure serves the narrative too, for the precariously pitched diagonals throughout Matham's print seem to evoke the perilous uncertainty that Hagar and Ishmael face as they leave the protection of Abraham's house.

Abraham Bloemaert, the designer of this print, was deeply interested in the story of Hagar's expulsion, for he made at least three paintings of the incident in about 1615, 1635, and again in 1638—all of which feature elaborate farmyard settings.[3] Aside from drawings of tumbledown farmhouses by Bloemaert himself (Cat. 18), similar rustic motifs appear in print series that were made after his designs in 1613/14 by Boëthius Adam Bolswert (c. 1580–1633); after 1635 by his son Frederick (q.v.); and after 1638 by his son Cornelis (1603–c. 1684).[4]

NOTES

1. The translation of the inscriptions, reproduced above, is taken from Roethlisberger 1993, 1:114. For exegesis of the inscription by Rupert von Deutz, see L. Widerkehr in Amsterdam 1993–94a, 553. For further discussion of the typological interpretation of the Hagar and Ishmael story, see Roethlisberger 1993, 1:115, and Kuretsky 1997, 62–63.

2. Roethlisberger has identified a potential source for this motif in an emblem by G. Montanea (Georgette de Montenay, 1540–81), which appears in various editions of her collections of Christian emblems (cf. *Emblemes ou devises chréstiennes*, Lyon, 1571). Emblem no. 31, "Frangor patientia" or "Frangor Fortuna" (I am broken by hardship), shows a wheel, broken by the hand of God as a symbol of lost fortune, illustrating how the faithful Christian must patiently accept all of God's actions. Roethlisberger 1993, 1:119. A similar wagon wheel appears in an engraving of the Prodigal Son by Jan Saenredam after Abraham Bloemaert (Cat. 17) and in a landscape with a ruined farmhouse after Jacques de Gheyn II (Cat. 20). As E. J. Sluijter has pointed out (conversation, December 2004), broken wagon wheels need not have symbolic meaning, however, for such fragments of ruined farm equipment were commonly put to new use as gates.

3. Listed in Roethlisberger 1993, 1:193–94, no. 225, 2: fig. 344, American private collection, c. 1615 (canvas, 86.5 × 137 cm); 1:325–26, no. 522, 2: fig. 694, private collection, 1635 (canvas, 199 × 148.5 cm); 1:341, no. 547, 2: fig. 733, The J. Paul Getty Museum, Los Angeles, 16(3?)8 (canvas, 146.5 × 180 cm).

4. For illustrations, see Roethlisberger 1993, 2: figs. 345–82, 576–77, 647–54, and 573–75.

JAN PIETERSZ. SAENREDAM
c. 1564–1607

An orphan who was raised by his uncle, a bailiff, in Assendelft, Jan Saenredam began his career as a draftsman and mapmaker. In 1589 he worked briefly with Hendrick Goltzius (1558–1617) in Haarlem and in Amsterdam, according to Karel van Mander, as a student of Jacques de Gheyn II (q.v.).[1] Between 1595 and 1597, while Goltzius's assistant and stepson Jacob Matham (q.v.) was away in Italy, Saenredam was hired as a reproductive engraver of Goltzius's designs. By 1595 he was back in Assendelft, where he married. His son Pieter (1597–1665), born two years later, would become a well-known architectural painter. Although he made a few drawings, Saenredam is known primarily for his virtuosity as a printmaker; his fine burin lines capture the most subtle lighting effects, spatial relationships, and strikingly naturalistic details. After 1600 he engraved a number of his own compositions, but the great majority of his prints (at least 115 are known) were made after the designs of other artists.

NOTE

1. On Jan Saenredam's biography, see D. Limouze in *Dictionary of Art* 1996, 27:507, and C. S. Ackley in Boston/St. Louis 1980–81, 44.

[17]

JAN SAENREDAM,
AFTER ABRAHAM BLOEMAERT

Farmyard with the Prodigal Son, c. 1603–5

Inscriptions: signed at the bottom right, *J. Saenredam sculp. Et excudebat / A. Bloemaert. Inve*

In the margin, *Qui modò delitys Gratus Bacchoq-maderet / Prodogus, et lentos luxu irretaret amores / Nudus opum, et lacera male tectus membra lacerna / Languida degeneri traxit vestigial gressu / Suasit enim importuna fames ad tecta coloni: / Illum, supplicitor plorantem acmulta precantem / Villicus excipiens, dignito indice pascere stantes / Imperat, immundum pecus, ad praesepia porcos, / Ille inhians rabidi solvit ieiunia ventris / Immersasq- sero siliquans avidae ingerit alvo / Tshrevelius*

(The Prodigal Son, who was recently in love with pleasure, soaked with wine and stirring up lusts made sluggish by debauchery, stripped of possessions, his limbs barely covered by a torn cloak, dragged along his weak feet with a feeble step. For nagging hunger urged him to the farmer's house. The bailiff, receiving him as he wept in supplication and begged profusely, orders him with his forefinger to feed the filthy flock of pigs standing at their troughs. Gaping wide, he relieved the hunger of his raging stom-

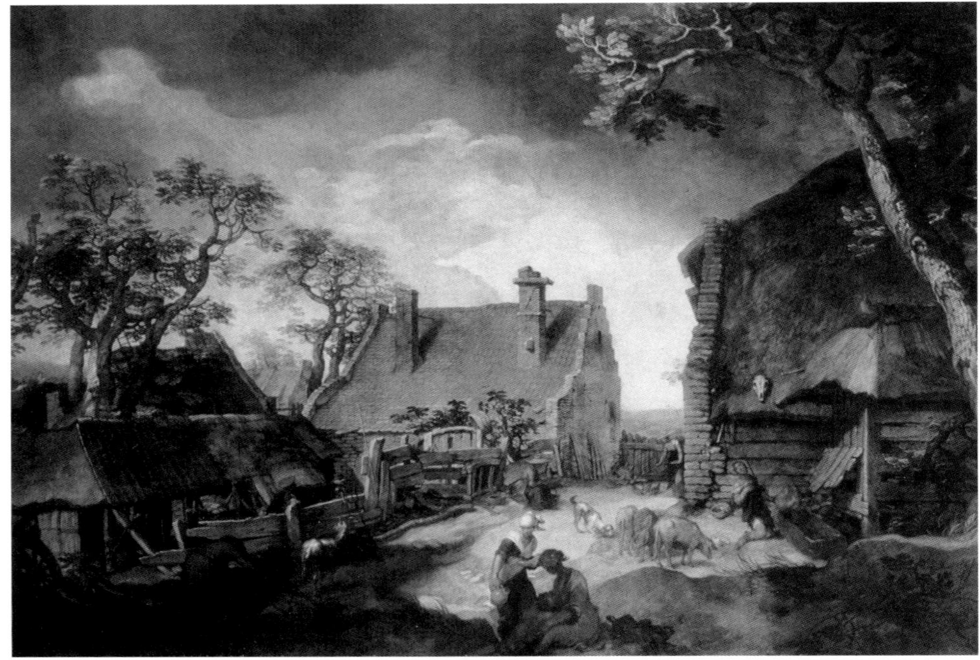

Fig. 122. Abraham Bloemaert, *Farmyard with the Prodigal Son*, c. 1615, oil on canvas, Warwick District Council Art Gallery and Museum, Leamington Spa

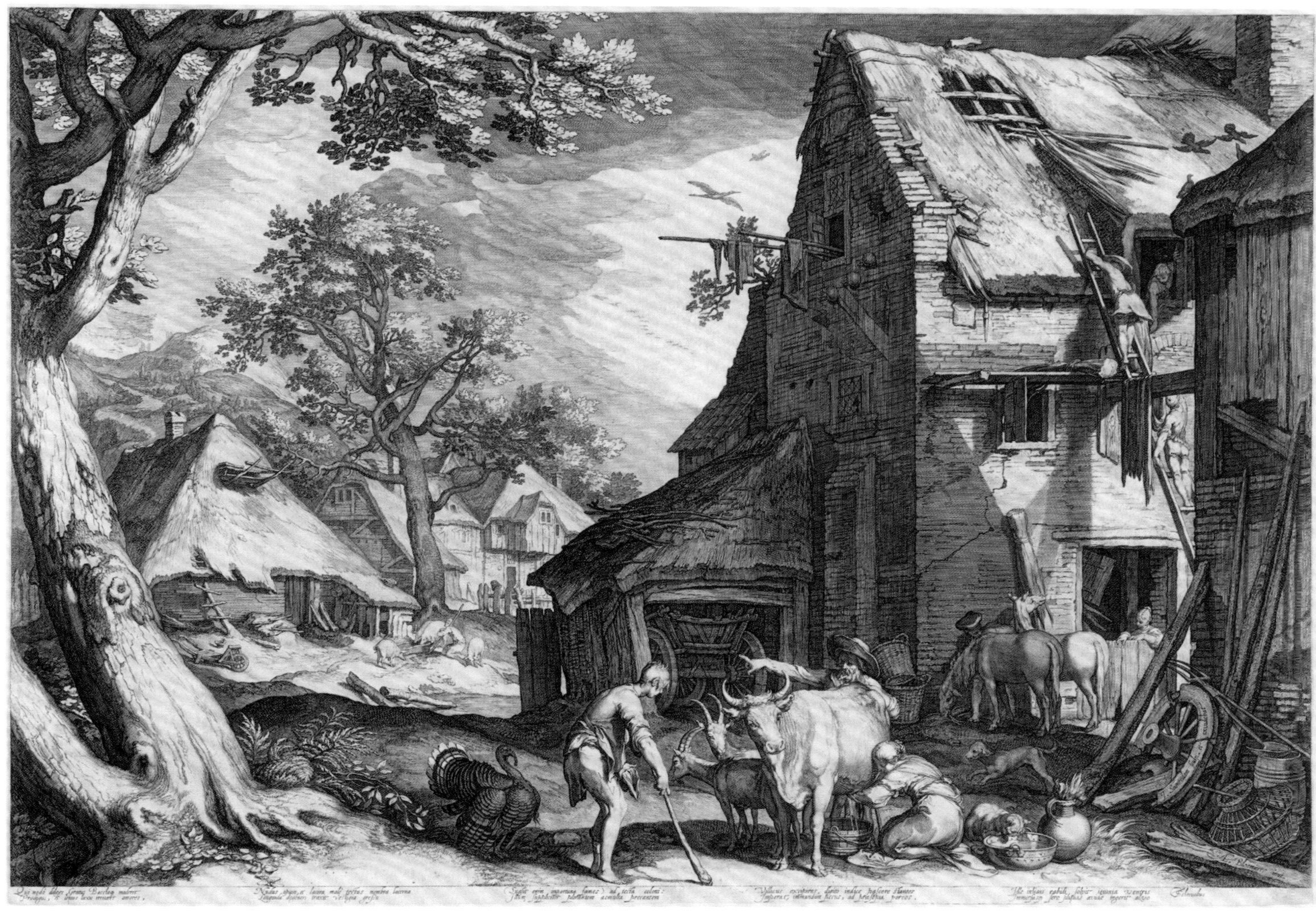

ach and pours the beanpods soaked in whey into his greedy belly.)[1]

Engraving, 436 × 636 mm ($17\frac{1}{8} \times 25\frac{1}{16}$ in.); state ii/v

The Frances Lehman Loeb Art Center, Vassar College, Poughkeepsie, New York, Gift of Matthew Vassar, 1984.20

References: Delbanco 1928, 30, repr.; Judson 1959, 6, fig. 33 (state iv); Hollstein 23 (1980):27, no. 27; Bartsch (Illustrated) 4 (1980):334 (wrong size listed); Dordrecht/Leeuwarden 1988, fig. 26; Roethlisberger 1993, 1:118–19, no. 71, 2: fig. 126; St. Petersburg, Florida 2001, 20 and fig. 4.

The story of the prodigal son, one of Christ's parables on repentance (Luke 15:11–24), is the tale of a foolish young man who, after receiving his inheritance, ran away from home to waste his money and his virtue, finding salvation only after repenting his sins and returning home to seek his father's forgiveness. Sixteenth-century prints, plays, and sermons used the story to demonstrate how the earthly journey of all human beings can lead to salvation through Christ. In northern Europe, where the prodigal son became a prime exemplum in Reformation debates about the conditions required for salvation, Roman Catholics used the story to demonstrate the necessity of repentance through the sacrament of Penance, while Protestants took the parable to mean that God has infinite mercy toward sinners and used it to support the doctrine of Justification by Faith, rather than the quest for salvation through ritual.[2]

During the seventeenth century, Dutch painters and printmakers most often selected scenes from the prodigal's life that show him either as an elaborately dressed celebrant among bad companions (Cat. 49) or as a destitute and ruined vagrant being reunited with his father.[3] That this story involves both spiritual and physical transformation is illustrated vividly in Saenredam's print, which depicts a less common, intermediate moment in the journey. Here, as noted in the engraving's inscription, the destitute and starving young man is compelled to beg for food from a farmer's bailiff, who unsympathetically sends him to the swine's trough.[4] As the biblical text further clarifies, this terrible moment, which reminds the prodigal of all he has lost, is the turning point that finally sends him home with the intention of declaring: "Father, I have sinned against heaven and before thee" (Luke 15:18).

In Saenredam's large, brilliantly executed engraving the prodigal son appears twice, first leaning on his beggar's staff in the center foreground and beseeching the bailiff; the latter points to the left background where the young man is seen again at a slightly later moment, kneeling among the swine. The large tree that rises above him draws attention to his small figure, which appears in a brightly illuminated area beyond the shadowed layer of space nearest the viewer. Here a number of witty motifs comment on the narrative, such as the plump cat crouched at the right that gazes, Narcissus-like, into a metal container full of milk or the turkey, puffing out its feathers behind the prodigal son, as if to imply that pride as well as greed has led to his downfall. The broken wagon wheel at the right, upon which the printmaker's name is inscribed, may refer to lost fortune.[5] Throughout the scene, Saenredam's supple, sinuous line and skillful deployment of light and shadow offer repeated visual surprises: for example, the arc of sharp cow and goat horns that separates the bailiff from the unwelcome visitor or the round rumps of the two horses standing companionably at the far right, one in shadow, one in light. By reducing the scale of the figures, Saenredam gives the setting, which represents the world of everyday life, greatest prominence, particularly the imposing but ramshackle three-story farmhouse whose thatched roof is in the process of renovation. Its cracked wall and crumbling brickwork recall drawings of derelict farmhouses by Abraham Bloemaert (Cat. 18), the designer of this composition.

Bloemaert, whose name is written on the broken board at the immediate right foreground, was intensely interested in this particular incident in the prodigal son's story, perhaps because it allowed him to represent rustic farmyards with all their picturesque details. At least five of his paintings depict the subject, including the impressive *Farmyard with the Prodigal Son* at the Warwick District Council Art Gallery and Museum, Leamington Spa (Fig. 122), which Roethlisberger has dated to about 1615.[6] A similar setting appears in Jacob Matham's large engraving after Bloemaert of 1603, *Abraham Casting out Hagar* (Cat. 16).

NOTES

1. Latin inscription translated by Professor Robert Brown of the Department of Classical Studies, Vassar College.

2. Parente 1987, 71–75 and 80–81.

3. The Utrecht followers of Caravaggio, in particular, produced such scenes of the prodigal's revelry, such as Dirck van Baburen's painting of 1622 in the Museum of Fine Arts, Boston. Rembrandt's so-called *Prodigal Son Self-Portrait with Saskia* of 1636 in the Staatliche Kunstsammlungen, Dresden, takes up the same theme, but the artist also depicted the prodigal's return to his father in an etching of the same year and again in a major late painting of c. 1668 in the State Hermitage Museum, St. Petersburg.

4. On Maerten van Heemskerck's (1498–1574) depictions of the prodigal son among the swine, see Haeger 1988, figs. 3 and 9.

5. The same motif of a shattered wagon wheel appears in Jacob Matham's print after Bloemaert, which represents Abraham casting out Hagar and her son Ishmael (Cat. 16) and in a print after Jacques de Gheyn II, *Landscape with a Man Milking a Cow* (Cat. 20). For an emblematic reference to the broken wagon wheel as a symbol of lost fortune (and the importance of trusting God in times of adversity), see note 2 under Cat. 16.

6. The other paintings of this subject by Bloemaert listed by Roethlisberger are no. 7, fig. 168 (Staatliche Museen, Berlin); no. 100, fig. 175 (collection Richard Feigen, New York); no. 261, fig. 385 (Kunsthaus, Zurich); and no. 546, fig. 732 (Ranger's House, Blackheath, London).

ABRAHAM BLOEMAERT
1564–1651

A prolific painter and draftsman of exceptional distinction, Bloemaert taught numerous pupils throughout his long working life.[1] His fame and influence were also spread by the numerous prints (more than six hundred) made after his designs, all but one of which, an etching of Juno, are the work of gifted reproductive engravers, etchers, and woodcutters, including two of his own sons, Cornelis (1603–c. 1684) and Frederick (q.v.), as well as Jan Saenredam (q.v.), Jan Muller (1571–1628), and Jacob Matham (q.v.).

Van Mander reported that Bloemaert received his first lessons in Utrecht, copying drawings by Frans Floris (c. 1516–1570) under the supervision of his father, Cornelis (c. 1540–93), who was a sculptor and architect.[2] Abraham was then sent to various local painters before traveling in about 1582 to Paris, where he studied with Hieronymus Francken I (c. 1540–1610), among others. He would later complain about his fragmented training under six masters. After encountering mannerist works of the School of Fontainebleau in Paris, Bloemaert returned to Utrecht by 1585, probably to work with his father, and in 1591, when Cornelis was appointed city engineer of Amsterdam, accompanied him there and became a citizen. The following year he married a wealthy spinster twenty years his senior and moved back to Utrecht, where he would spend the remainder of his long life. Following his wife's death of the plague in 1599, he remarried in 1600. He had at least eight children from his second marriage, four of whom became artists.

Among Bloemaert's many students in Utrecht were the major Caravaggesque painters Gerrit van Honthorst (1592–1656) and Hendrik Terbrugghen (1588–1629) and the Dutch Italianate landscapists Cornelis van Poelenburch (q.v.) and Jan Baptist Weenix (q.v.). His *Konstryck tekenboek* (Artistic drawing book), a pattern book for art students, was engraved by his son Frederick and continued to be used in art schools until the nineteenth century. Bloemaert's early works display all the refinement and extravagance of late mannerism. But as his own students returned from Italy, bringing Caravaggio's more naturalistic approach to religious subjects, he moved in this new direction, although his colors would always remain rich and intense, and the contours of his forms would retain a distinctive linear grace. Along with his enduring commitment to pictorial elegance, Bloemaert, who owned a farm in Oostveen north of Utrecht, remained fascinated throughout his long career by the irregularities and visual surprises of dilapidated rural buildings and ancient twisted trees, as illustrated in two drawings by him in this catalogue (Cats. 18 and 19) and four prints by other artists after his designs (Cats. 16, 17, 72, and 77).

NOTES

1. On Bloemaert's biography, see the essay by M. J. Bok in Roethlisberger 1993, 1:551–87; Baltimore/San Francisco 1997–98, 375–76; and C. J. A. Wansink's essay in *Dictionary of Art* 1996, 4:149–53.

2. Van Mander 1604, fol. 297; Van Mander/Miedema 1994–99, 4:87.

[18]

A Dilapidated Farmhouse (recto) *Walls of a Farmhouse* (verso) c. 1600–1603

Inscriptions: lower left corner by a late hand, *ab. Bloemaert*

Brown ink, brown and gray wash, pink and green watercolor and white gouache over black chalk, with framing line in brown ink, on cream antique laid paper, 162 × 215 mm (6⅜ × 8⁷⁄₁₆ in.)

Courtesy of the Fogg Art Museum, Harvard University Art Museums, Cambridge, Massachusetts, The Maida and George Abrams Collection, 1999.130

References: Amsterdam 1971, no. 7; Hanover/Hartford/Boston 1973–74, no. 9; Poughkeepsie 1976, 25, no. 3, fig. 3; Amsterdam/Vienna/New York/Cambridge 1991–92, 60–61, no. 21.

More than 1,500 drawings by Abraham Bloemaert are known, including numerous studies of landscape motifs and picturesque farmhouses that he sketched in the vicinity of Utrecht. Karel van Mander, writing in 1604, praised the charm and variety of these rural scenes, which he said were very popular with collectors of the time, noting that they were drawn from life in pen "… to which he then adds some succulent touches of color …"[1] With its delicate brown and gray washes and touches of pink and green watercolor, this example, both recto and verso, displays Bloemaert's great sensitivity to relationships of tone and line.

This ruined farmhouse is cropped in the views on both sides of this sheet, making partial what time has already rendered fragmentary. The fact that the viewer cannot see the entire structure draws closer attention to the irregular edges of the broken walls, rendered in deli-

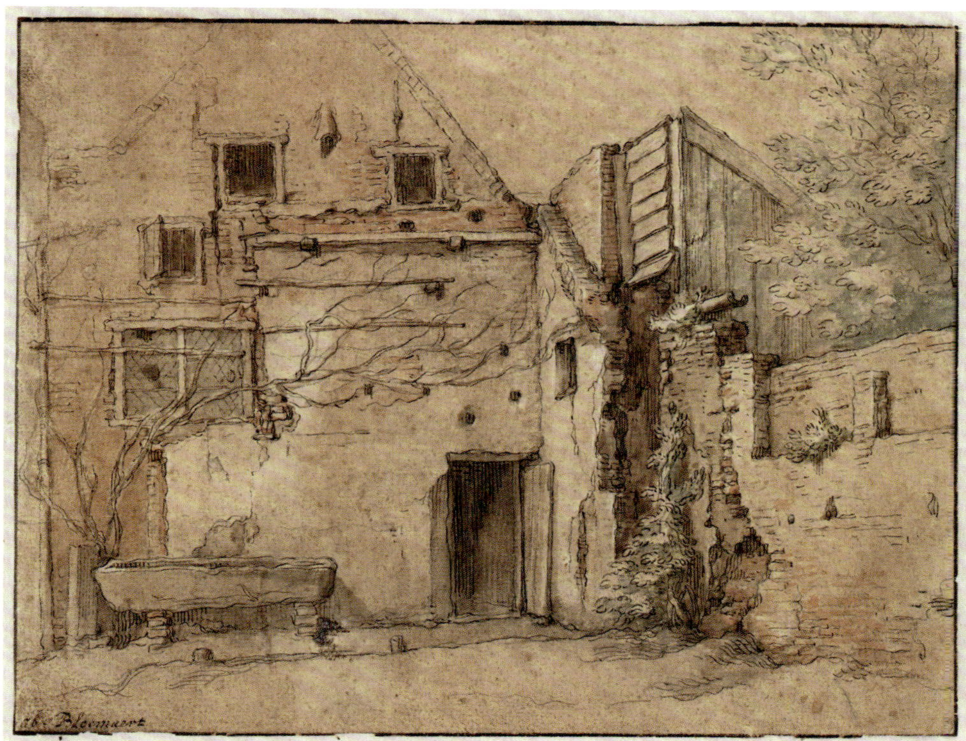

[18] recto

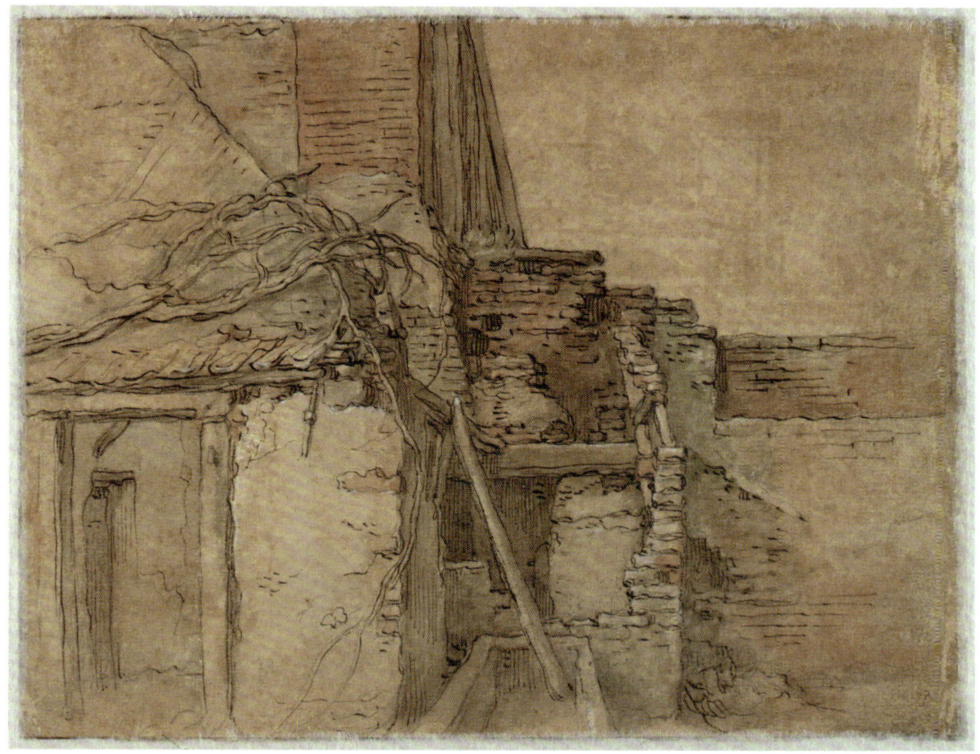

[18] verso

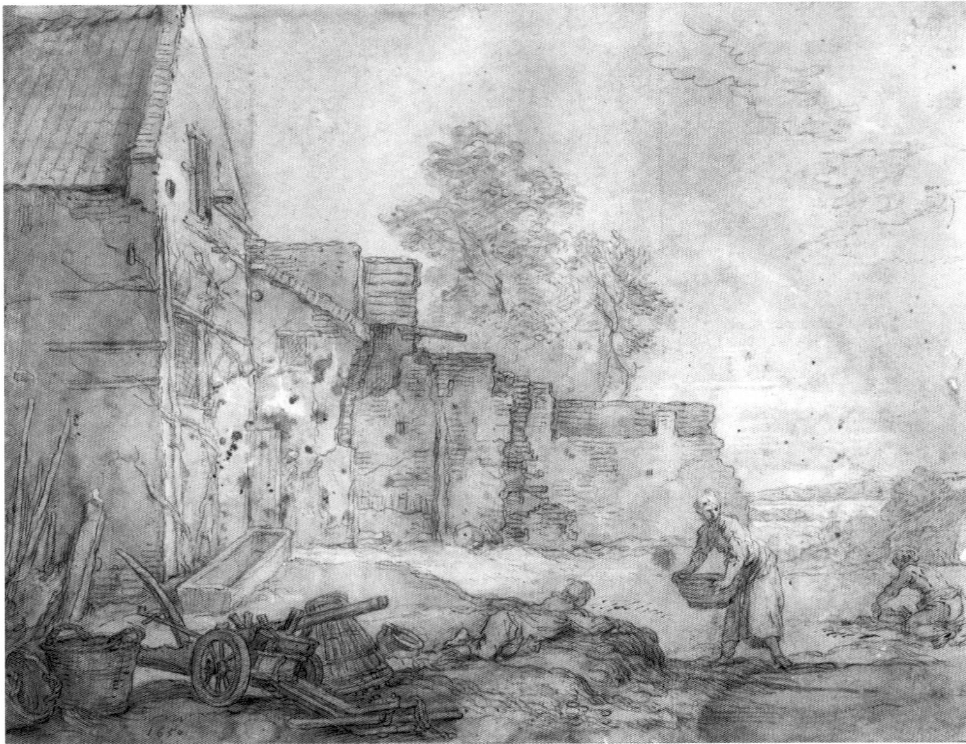

Fig. 123. Abraham Bloemaert, *Ruined Farmhouse with Figures and Farm Implements*, 1650, ink and chalk drawing, Statens Museum for Kunst, Copenhagen

cately quivering pen lines that fade toward the top of the page in the drawing on the recto, as if the farmhouse were being captured within the very process of its transformation. A sarcophagus-sized tub, propped up on stacks of bricks at the lower left, anchors the broad plane of the wall that faces the viewer and is punctuated by a gaping doorway and the rectangles of irregularly spaced windows—one large double casement still retaining most of its glass. Sinuous fingers of vine cross the wall surface toward the right, where sharper segments of masonry that frame an encroaching shrub rise sharply toward the gable. Here overlapping layers of broken bricks reveal the texture and thickness of the wall, as seen also in the sketch on the verso, in which the motif has been so daringly cropped on all sides that it becomes an abstract play of lively contours and unexpected crevices. Emptied of human presence and deprived of its original function, this dilapidated rural dwelling shows how the most ordinary aspects of the visible world can be transformed, through art, into images of arrestingly elegant complexity.

The date of c. 1600–1603 for this sheet, first suggested by J. Bolten, is confirmed by W. W. Robinson's observation of its similarity to a drawing of a landscape with farmhouse dated 1600 in the Rijksprentenkabinet, Amsterdam, which bears the same inscription in the same hand.[2] Almost fifty years later, Bloemaert depicted the identical site again in a larger, more finished drawing, dated 1650 (Fig. 123), apparently basing this work upon another early sketch that has since been lost. Shifting the viewpoint to the left, the later scene adds farm implements and three figures (two working, one reclining), so that the ruined building becomes a setting for human action or repose more than an evocative focus in its own right.

NOTES

1. Van Mander 1604, fol. 298. The full text of Van Mander's biography on Bloemaert is reproduced in English translation in Roethlisberger 1993, 1:41–43. Other depictions of worn farmhouses by Bloemaert in U.S. collections are *Landscape with Worn Farm Buildings* (pen and brown ink, 147 × 228 mm) in the Pierpont Morgan Library, New York, acc. no. I. 229a, and *Worn Farm Buildings* (pen and brush ink with brown, blue, and yellow watercolor over black and red chalk, 172 × 272 mm) in the Cleveland Museum of Art, 1940.737a.

2. In letters to C. O. Baer of 4 September and 2 December 1975, Bolten proposed this date, also pointing out that Bloemaert depicted the same courtyard from a different angle in his drawing in the Statens Museum for Kunst, Copenhagen, no. Tu42, 3b (cited in Poughkeepsie 1976, 25). W. W. Robinson has noted that the same inscription appears not only in the Rijksprentenkabinet drawing, inv. no. A 178, but also in a drawing in the Kunstmuseum, Düsseldorf, inv. no. FP 24-254 Amsterdam/Vienna/New York/Cambridge 1991–92, 60 and n. 3.

[19]

Studies of Two Pollard Willows, c. 1606

Inscriptions: lower right corner, *Bloemaert*

Pen and brown ink, watercolor, traces of black chalk, framing line in pen and brown ink, 210 × 310 mm (8¼ × $12\frac{3}{16}$ in.)[1]

Lent by the Metropolitan Museum of Art, New York, Rogers Fund, 1970, 1970.242.3

References: New York 1973, no. 29; Poughkeepsie 1976, 26, no. 4, fig. 4; Mules 1985, 28–29.

Bloemaert's interest in the irregularities of ancient trees is evident both in his own drawings and paintings and in numerous prints made after his designs by his son Frederick (Cat.72). Willows attracted his notice most strongly because these common deciduous trees and shrubs were often pollarded—cleaved or cut back to their trunks in order to promote the growth of dense foliage that produces the flexible twigs used for basket weaving. Rembrandt, too, featured a pollard willow in his 1648 etching of St. Jerome (Cat.73). A later pen and wash drawing by Bloemaert in the collection of the Fogg Art Museum, Cambridge, Massachusetts (Fig. 124), depicts a single willow split at the top so that its two large sections seem to reach energetically outward and upward at left and right, sprouting a multitude of small branches that fill most of the picture space.[2]

In the New York drawing, two older, more twisted willow stumps have been separated on the page in an effective corner-to-corner arrangement whose impact is intensified by the fact that they lean in parallel diagonals toward the right. Although both are defined by small, energetic pen strokes over soft washes of tone, Bloemaert creates something of a visual dialogue between the two, so similar in size yet so distinct in shape and color. The split stump at the upper left, washed in pale brown, is surrounded by lacy webs of pen and brush strokes that suggest movement, while the one at the lower right, washed in pale green, has heavier

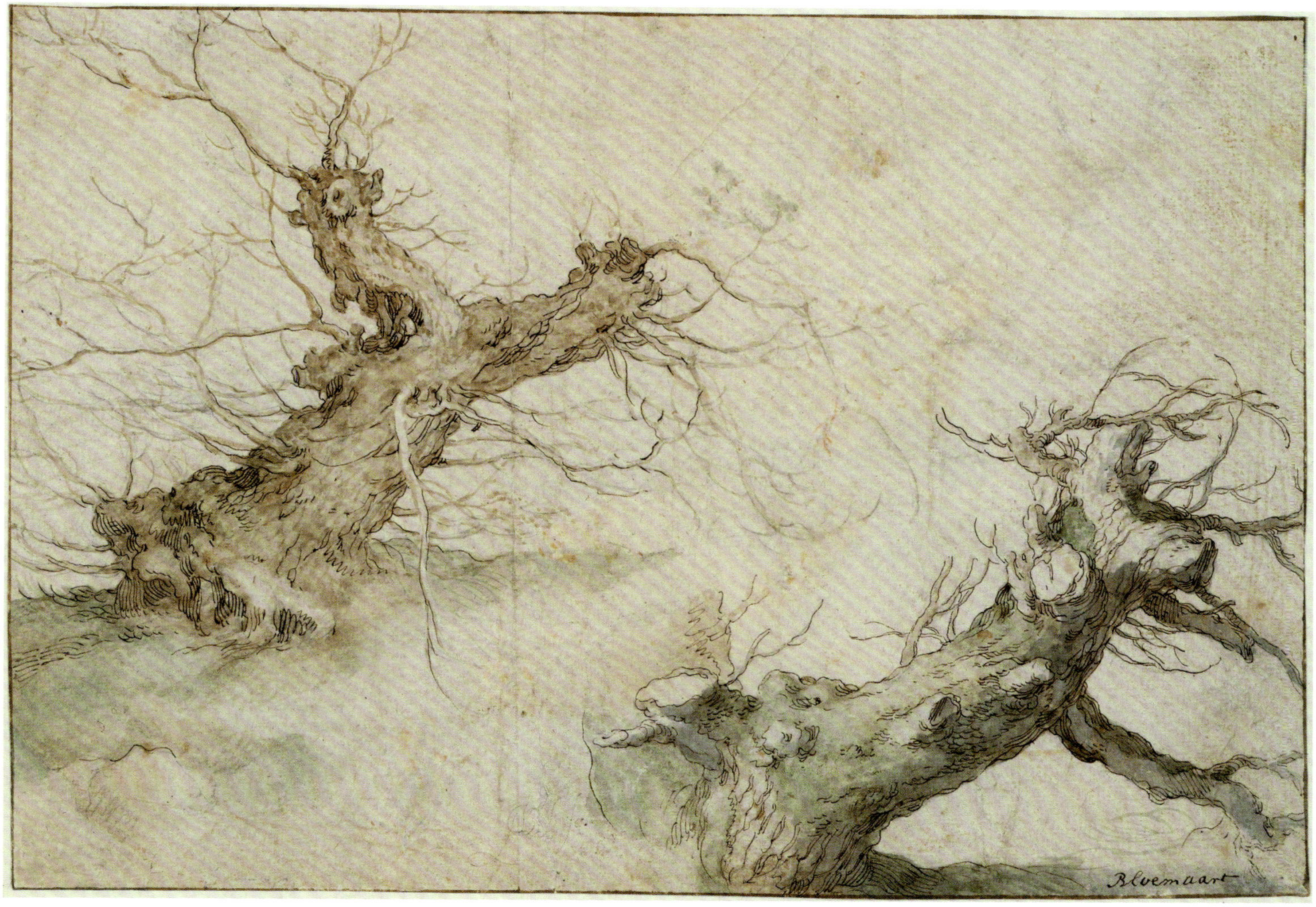

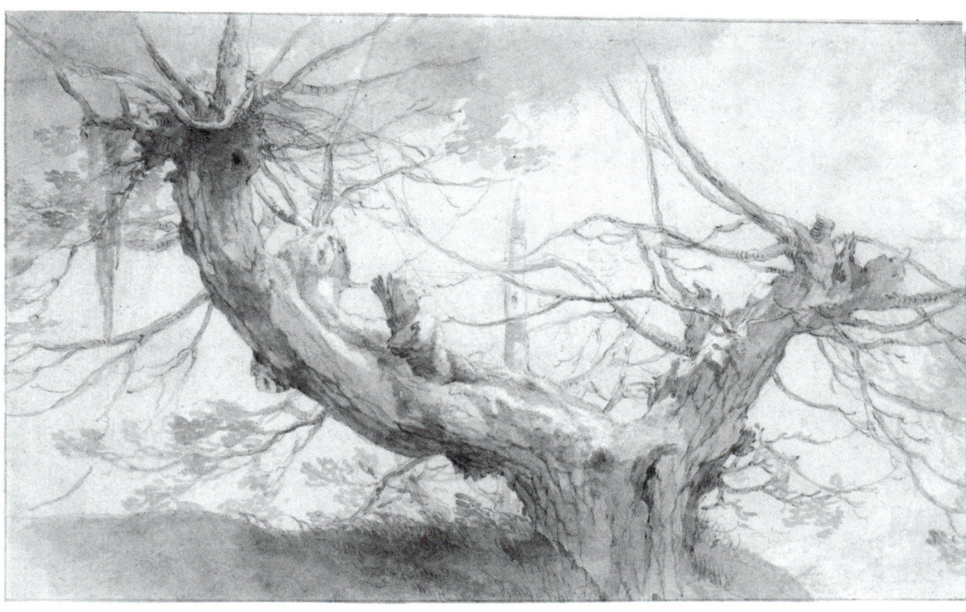

Fig. 124. Abraham Bloemaert, *A Pollard Willow*, c. 1630 (?), pen and ink and brown wash drawing, Courtesy of the Fogg Art Museum, Harvard University Art Museums, Cambridge, Massachusetts

branches, is more solidly modeled, and seems anchored to the bottom of the sheet. That the trees are presented out of their natural context and that neither is seen to be rooted in the ground allows the viewer to concentrate closely on their complex forms, which demonstrate how all natural organisms, even those of the same age and species, respond in their own unique ways to time.

On the verso of this drawing is the delicate sketch of a mountainous landscape, which, according to J. Bolten, was used in a print by Frederick Bloemaert.[3]

NOTES

1. Image on verso: *Wide Landscape Prospect*, black chalk and watercolor.

2. A similar willow with a forked trunk appears in Bloemaert's *Landscape with Mercury and Argus*, dated 1645, in the Prince of Liechtenstein's collection, Vaduz, which Roethlisberger has related to a print by Frederick Bloemaert, suggesting that "an unknown late drawing by Abraham, matching the print, must have been the model for both." Roethlisberger 1993, 1:347, 2: pl. 33 and figs. 744 and 757.

3. Bolten made this suggestion in a letter to C. O. Baer (cited in Poughkeepsie 1976, 26), in which he suggested a date of c. 1606 for the drawing. A similar print by Frederick Bloemaert is *View with Trees*, repr. in Roethlisberger 1993, 2: fig. 379.

JACQUES DE GHEYN II
1565–1629

The De Gheyns were a three-generation family of artists, beginning with the glass painter Jacob de Gheyn I (1537/38–?1581) who was probably the first teacher of his better-known son, Jacques II.[1] Around 1585 De Gheyn II began to work with the celebrated Haarlem engraver Hendrick Goltzius (1558–1617). By 1590/91 he was active as a printmaker in Amsterdam, and in 1595 married Eva Stalpaert van der Wiele, a woman from a wealthy patrician family. The couple settled first in Leiden between 1596 and 1601/2, where De Gheyn collaborated with the distinguished legal scholar Hugo de Groot (Grotius), who composed inscriptions for the artist's engravings. By 1605 he was a member of the St. Luke's guild in The Hague, where he remained for the rest of his life, closely connected to the House of Orange. His design for Prince Maurice's garden in the Buitenhof incorporated the earliest grottoes in the Netherlands.

An artist of brilliant technical facility and exceptional inventiveness and diversity, De Gheyn illustrates the transitional period between the elegantly idealized and polished approach to art known as mannerism and the more naturalistic style and imagery that Dutch artists developed after 1610. Until about 1596 he made prints after the designs of other artists, such as one discussed here (Cat. 49), in which the strongest influence is clearly that of Goltzius. His own prolific production of prints and drawings (I. Q. van Regteren-Altena catalogued more than 1,500) encompasses allegorical scenes, images reflecting close empirical observation of the natural world, as well as strange flights of fantasy including depictions of witchcraft. After 1600 he began to produce etchings and (like Goltzius) paintings, including the vanitas still lifes and flower pieces that would influence the subsequent development of Dutch still-life painting. It is, however, De Gheyn's magnificent graphic works that remain his major legacy, an aspect of his art that was continued in the works of his son and close follower, Jacques de Gheyn III (?1596–1641).

NOTE

1. Material on De Gheyn II's biography and development is based on E. K. J. Reznicek's essay in *Dictionary of Art* 1996, 12:529–32.

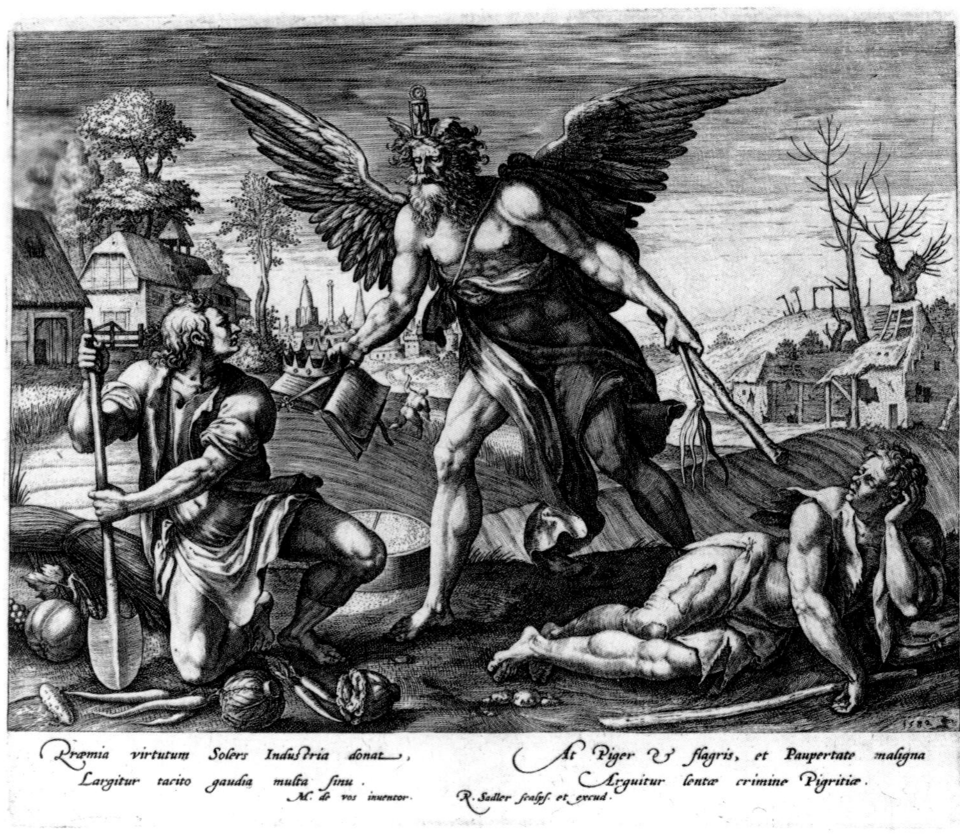

Fig. 125. Raphael Sadelaer I, after Marten de Vos, *Time and Labor*, late sixteenth century, engraving, Rijksprentenkabinet, Rijksmuseum, Amsterdam

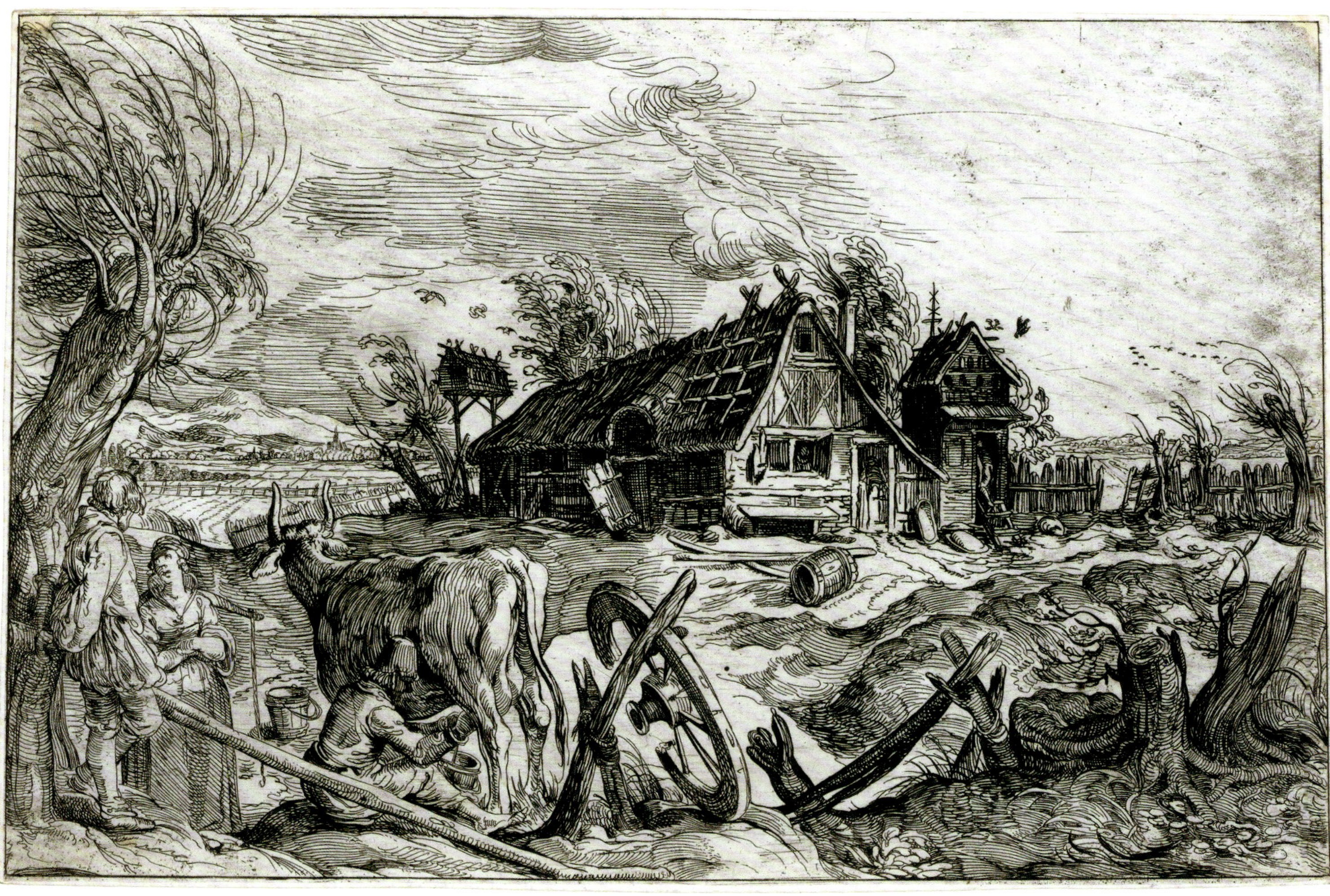

[20]

AFTER JACQUES DE GHEYN II

Landscape with Man Milking Cow, c. 1603

Inscriptions: none

Etching, 216 × 318 mm (8½ × 12½ in.) (sheet, cut to platemark); only state

Lent by the Metropolitan Museum of Art, New York, Gift of Giorgiana W. Sargent, in Memory of John Osborne Sargent, 1924, 24.63.903

References: Burchard 1917, 30; Van Regteren-Altena 1935, 49; Bock 1930, 277; Boon 1978, no. 233; Judson 1973, 21, 25, and 42 and pl. 36; Hollstein 7 (n.d.):144, no. 293; Berlin 1979, 48–49, no. 56; Van Regteren-Altena 1983, 1:93–94, 145–46; Paris 1985, 84–85, no. 47, pl. 66; Rotterdam/Washington 1986, 86; Filedt Kok 1990, 380, no. 293; Walford 1991, 36–37; Gibson 2000, 143–45; *The New Hollstein* 2000, 2:232, no.7 (as rejected).

Dilapidated farmhouses appear frequently in Dutch prints and drawings from Bloemaert (Cat. 18) to Rembrandt (Cat. 23) and beyond. Yet as W. S. Gibson has discussed (see also his essay herein, pp. 63–72), such scenes were quite rare before the early seventeenth century, when a taste developed for picturesquely weathered or ruined domestic structures that carried associations, depending on their context, of either physical neglect caused by sloth or of virtuous poverty and the pleasure of simple rural existence.[1] In any case, as the long conflict with Spain drew toward a close in the period around 1600, abandoned farms and collapsing rustic dwellings would hardly have been an uncommon sight in the Dutch countryside.

The farmyard represented here is not abandoned, but it does show great evidence of human neglect. Beside the man milking a cow, a milkmaid ignores her duties (the yoke on her shoulders holds nothing) to converse with a dandy who lounges against a willow tree at the far left. H. Mielke has interpreted the willow in this scene as the kind of shallowly rooted tree whose easy and rapid growth prevents it from bearing ripe fruit: a parallel to the pleasure-seeking couple beneath it.[2] In the foreground appear dead tree stumps, a shattered fence, and a large, broken wagon wheel, a motif that may have been included to signify lost fortune or the way in which time (often allegorically represented as a rolling wagon) destroys human works.[3]

In the background, smoke rises from the chimney of the farmhouse and figures appear at its open door and window, yet the building stands in a perilous state of decay within a littered farmyard. One door hangs precariously from its hinges, the shutters have deteriorated, and the roof has lost its thatch. The dovecotes at both sides of the farmhouse may be a further allusion to getting by with little effort, since this manner of keeping birds for the cooking pot was considered easier than hunting them.[4] The contrast of this ill-cared-for property to the neatly tilled field in the background makes the moralizing message of the image quite clear. A likely precedent for this scene, pointed out by W. S. Gibson, is a late sixteenth-century engraving by Raphael Sadelaer I (after Marten de Vos) entitled *Time and Labor* (Fig. 125), in which a winged personification of Father Time stands between an industrious and a lazy peasant.[5] The dilapidated farm buildings and dead trees behind the slothful reclining figure form a telling contrast to the well-maintained barns and healthy trees behind the diligent farmer with his shovel.

Frequently reproduced, this etching faithfully records, in reverse, the composition of a signed and dated drawing by Jacques de Gheyn II of 1603 in the Rijksprentenkabinet, Amsterdam.[6] J. Burchard considered the print to be a major work by De Gheyn himself, but a number of more recent scholars have expressed the opinion that it may be by another Dutch printmaker such as Simon Frisius (1580–1629) or may even postdate the seventeenth century, because all known impressions are printed on paper that was unusually heavy for the time.[7]

NOTES

1. Gibson 2000, 143–45.
2. Mielke 1980, 46. Cited and quoted by J. Bruyn in Amsterdam/Boston/Philadelphia 1987–88, 86.
3. Such wheels also appear in prints after Abraham Bloemaert that have farmyard settings, such as *Abraham Casting out Hagar* by Jacob Matham (Cat. 16) and *Farmyard with the Prodigal Son* by Jan Saenredam (Cat. 17). Roethlisberger connects this motif to an emblem by G. Montanea (Georgette de Montenay), discussed in Cat. 16, note 2, in which a broken wheel, symbolizing lost fortune, is used to suggest that Christians must be prepared to accept even God's destructive acts. Roethlisberger 1993, 1:119. E. J. Walford cites *The Triumph of Time*, an anonymous print after Pieter Bruegel the Elder, published in 1574, that depicts a broken wheel among other human artifacts strewn in the path of Time's wagon. Walford 1991, 36, fig. 11 and 215 n. 21. E. J. Sluijter (conversation, December 2004) also notes that such wheel fragments were sometimes used as farmyard gates.
4. J. Spicer offers this reading of the large dovecote in Abraham Bloemaert's *Parable of the Wheat and the Tares* of 1624 in the Walters Art Museum, Baltimore, and cites Giezen-Nieuwenhuys 1987 on the representation of Netherlandish dovecotes and pigeon houses. J. Spicer in Baltimore/San Francisco 1997–98, 184 and 414 nn. 11 and 12.
5. Gibson 2000, 142, repr., and 143.
6. The drawing, however, includes one detail that is not found in the etching: a man trying to hide under the bench at the side of the farmhouse as an old woman attacks him with a stick.
7. I. Q. van Regteren-Altena, who summarized debates about the dating and attribution of this print and cited later copies of it, proposed a late eighteenth-century date for the print because of its paper; he further noted that no other exact reproductions of De Gheyn's drawings are known and that the earliest known reference to this etching is a sale catalogue of 1803 (Van Regteren-Altena 1983, 1:146). According to K. G. Boon, none of the known impressions of this print (all of which have Italian watermarks) are on paper that was used in Holland in De Gheyn's time (Boon 1978, 1:81–82, no. 233) while J. P. Filedt Kok and M. Leesberg reject the print, listing it as "anonymous possibly late 18th century" (*The New Hollstein* 2000, 2:232, no. 7). C. van Hasselt, however, cited another print by De Gheyn (*Portrait of Tycho Brahe*, dated 1586, Hollstein 304), in which he found similar paper with the same seventeenth-century watermark (C. van Hasselt in Paris 1985, 85 n. 6).

LAMBERT HARMENSZ. DOOMER
1624–1700

Lambert Doomer was the son of Harmen Doomer, the well-known Amsterdam frame maker who supplied frames to Rembrandt (q.v.) and whose portrait Rembrandt painted in 1640 (Metropolitan Museum of Art, New York). Baptized in Amsterdam on 11 February 1624, Lambert became a student in Rembrandt's studio in 1644.[1] Two years later he traveled to Nantes, where his two brothers were living, and between July and September 1646, he accompanied Willem Schellinks (q.v.) along the Loire to northern France, where the two artists made topographical drawings of various towns and chateaux.[2] Further topographical views were made on trips throughout the Netherlands and on a journey in 1663 up the Rhine via Cleve and Cologne. In 1668 Doomer married Metje Harmens, after which he moved to Alkmaar. From 1673 to 1681 he was a resident of the old men's home (*mannengasthuis*) in Alkmaar. He remarried in 1679 and moved back to Amsterdam in 1695.

Doomer produced at least twenty-five paintings that include landscapes, still lifes, portraits, and biblical scenes, but his most admired works have always been his drawings, some three hundred of which have been identified.[3] Many, including copies after works by other artists, are topographical landscapes featuring Dutch, French, or German buildings or vistas. In 1665 he made eleven drawings for inclusion in the large volume known as the *Atlas van der Hem* (Österreichische Nationalbibliothek, Vienna), a major collection of topographical landscapes assembled by Laurens van der Hem, an Amsterdam lawyer. Doomer's drawings, regardless of subject, convey a distinctively appealing effect, as his sensitive touch and delicate watercolor washes allow the objects of his observation to express engagingly individual effects.

NOTES

1. On Doomer's biography, see W. Schulz's essay in *Dictionary of Art* 1996, 9:149–50.
2. The journey through France taken by Doomer and Schellinks has been discussed in Van den Berg 1942.
3. Doomer's drawings were catalogued in 1974 by W. Schulz (Schulz 1974). See also Schatborn 1974.

[21]
Hollow Tree, after Roelandt Savery, c. 1665

Inscriptions: none

Pen and black and brown ink, and brush and green, brown, and orange wash, 317 × 473 mm (12 7/16 × 18 9/16 in.)

Cleveland Museum of Art, Delia E. Holden Fund, 1958.315

References: Francis 1959, 40–41, repr. (as R. Savery); Brussels/Rotterdam/Paris/Berne 1968–69, 46 and n. 7 (as Doomer after Savery and thereafter); Schulz 1971, 256, 259, and pl. 38; Schulz 1972, 66, 428, no. 363; Schulz 1974,

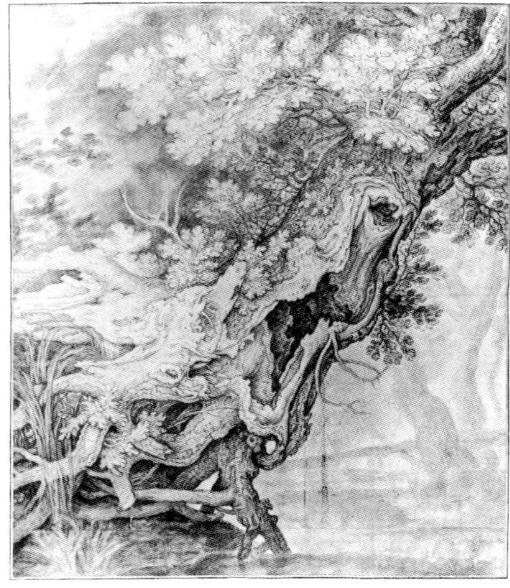

Fig. 126. Roelandt Savery, *Tree Study*, c. 1607, chalk and wash drawing, *Atlas van der Hem* (*Atlas Blaeu*), vol. 46, folio 5, Österreichische Nationalbibliothek, Vienna

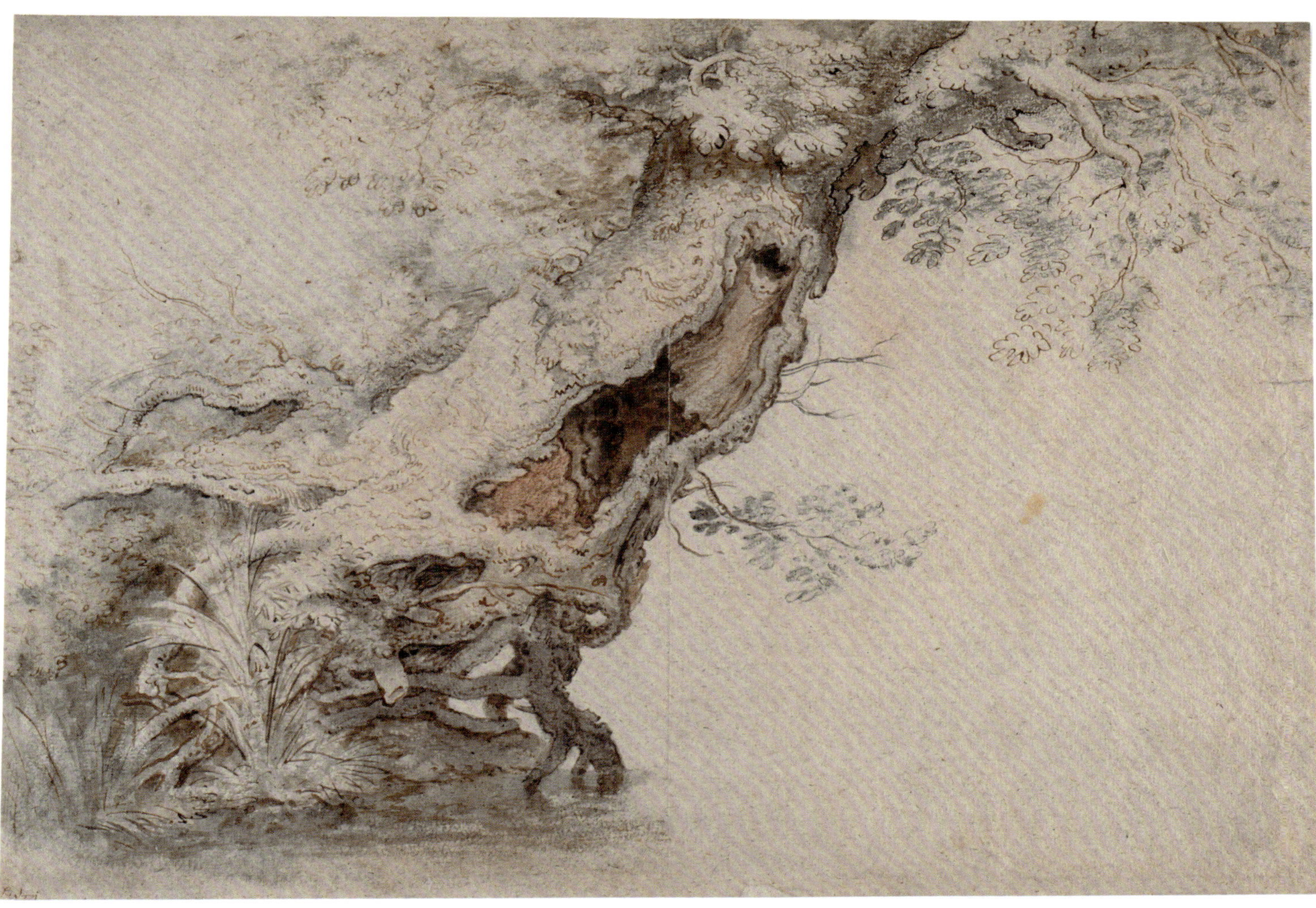

32, 102, no. 253, and repr. 139; Schulz in Berlin 1975, 67, under no. 98; Sumowski 1979–92, 2:1064–65, no. 499; Hamilton 1980, 37, no. 11.

Dutch draftsmen frequently made studies of ancient trees, whose metamorphoses through age, wind, and weather often produce a kind of natural sculpture—each tree twisted and textured in its own unique way (see also Cat. 19). Lambert Doomer, an artist greatly admired for his ability to evoke the individual character of landscape motifs, placed this hollow tree off-center to the left on a rectangular page.[1] Cropped by the upper edge of the sheet, it leans toward the right, its lobed leaves spreading gracefully into the void. Tubular roots reach like fingers into the water at the lower left, where delicate fans of grass rise from the damp ground. Doomer's adroit handling of pen lines and translucent brown washes gives this drawing an extraordinary fluidity: the forms of the tree seem simultaneously solid and soft, recalling water or smoke.

Once attributed to the influential Utrecht landscapist Roelandt Savery (1576–1639), the Cleveland drawing was identified by C. van Hasselt as a copy after Savery by Lambert Doomer.[2] In 1658 Doomer came into possession of an album of Savery's drawings (among many other objects) through one of the auctions of Rembrandt's possessions that followed his bankruptcy of 1656. In 1665, when Doomer was hired by the Amsterdam lawyer Laurens van der Hem to provide drawings for his large atlas of topographical landscapes, he apparently sold to the collector not only his own sketches, but also some of his Savery drawings.[3] In the *Atlas van der Hem*, now in the Österreichische Nationalbibliothek, Vienna, is the Savery *Tree Study* of about 1607 (Fig. 126) that inspired the Cleveland drawing.[4] Comparison of the two works is instructive, for although Doomer borrowed many details from Savery, including the tree's diagonal, hollowed-out trunk and its roots, he created a more spacious effect by changing the shape of the page from vertical to horizontal. Sketching the foliage less densely in pen and wash (rather than Savery's black chalk with colored washes) and omitting indications of a background also give the later drawing a less convoluted, more graceful effect in which forms seem to float lightly on the page.

NOTES

1. According to C. Donnelly Richardson of the Arnold Arboretum at Harvard University, Cambridge, Massachusetts, Savery's tree cannot be identified with a particular species, which would suggest that the artist either invented it or elaborated on what he saw to create a more intricate linear effect.

2. C. van Hasselt in Brussels/Rotterdam/Paris/Berne 1968–69, 46 and n. 7.

3. For discussion of the relationship between the works of Savery and Doomer, see Schultz 1971, 256, 259, and pl. 38. Doomer made at least eight copies after Savery drawings, including landscapes in the Kupferstichkabinett, Berlin, the Institut Néerlandais, Paris, and the Österreichische Nationalbibliothek, Vienna (repr. Schulz 1971, pls. 32–38).

4. Savery's drawing is folio 5 in vol. 46 of the *Atlas van der Hem*, also known as the *Atlas Blaeu* (pencil and black chalk with watercolor, 520 × 455 mm). Repr. Spicer 1970, pl. 1, and Schulz 1971, pl. 39.

PIETER MOLIJN
1595–1661

The son of Flemish-born parents, Molijn was baptized in London on 6 April 1595; he would become an important figure in the early, "tonal" phase of Dutch landscape painting. That he is referred to in later Dutch documents as "The Londoner" may indicate his pride in his place of birth.[1] Molijn's teacher has never been discovered, but his entry into the guild of St. Luke in Haarlem was recorded in 1616, and he remained in that city for the rest of his life. In 1624 he married Mayken Gerards and became a member of the Dutch Reformed Church of Haarlem. He was a member of the Haarlem Civic Guards in 1624, 1627, and 1630 and also served as dean and commissioner of the St. Luke's guild during the 1630s and 1640s. Samuel Ampzing's praise of the city of Haarlem published in 1628 (Cat. 4) places Molijn among important local artists.[2]

Molijn's earliest dated landscape painting was created in 1625; in the following year, he produced an innovative series of four prints that show peasants and soldiers in landscapes with tumbledown inns and huts (Cats. 22a and 22b). Far more numerous are his drawings, most of which were executed in black chalk and signed and dated in the 1650s. As a painter, Molijn produced a variety of rural subjects, but he remains best known for his distinctive landscapes with diagonal compositions. Aside from his activities as an independent artist, he contributed landscape backgrounds to the works of major genre painters such as Frans Hals (1581/85–1666) and Gerard ter Borch (1617–81), who had been his student.

NOTES

1. Biographical material on Pieter Molijn is based on the essay in *Dictionary of Art* 1996, 21:825–27, by E. J. Allen, whose dissertation on the artist was written in 1987 for the University of Maryland, College Park (Allen 1987).

2. Ampzing 1628, 372. Molijn was also cited in Theodor Schrevelius's praise of the city of 1647. Schrevelius 1647, 294.

[22]

Two prints from *Four Landscapes with Figures*, 1626

(The four prints were numbered 1 through 4 in the second state.)

[22a] *Peasants Conversing beside a Ruined Shed* (no. 3)

Inscription: lower right, *3*

Etching and drypoint, 150 × 185 mm (5⅞ × 7¼ in.); state ii/iii

[22b] *Soldiers before a Dilapidated Inn* (no. 4)

Inscriptions: none

Etching and drypoint, 150 × 187 mm (5⅞ × 7⅜ in.); state i/iii

Print Collection, The Miriam and Ira D. Wallach Division of Art, Prints and Photographs, The New York Public Library, Astor, Lenox and Tilden Foundations

References: Hollstein 14 (1956):70, nos. 1–4; London 1986, 154, nos. 53a–d; Bartsch (Illustrated) 5 (1979):10–13.

Only four prints designed and executed by Pieter Molijn are known: landscapes with peasants and travelers or soldiers that he issued in 1626, displaying on the first page the date and his name as artist and publisher (*Pieter de molyn fecit et excudit 1626*) and numbering the sheets in the second state to make a series.[1] The setting for these scenes, whose technique combines etching and drypoint, is the dunes near Haarlem, a sandy, rolling coastal terrain with shifting levels crossed by numerous paths and country roads. All four landscapes, in which figures are given as much emphasis as scenery, focus on moments of encounter: pairs or small groups of people meet and pause for conversation. The prints project a curious blend of stasis and mutability, as if the figures had been fixed in place, but within an ongoing stream of time implied by subsidiary travelers moving through space or by the slope of nearby pathways.

In two of the scenes in the cycle (Cats. 22a and 22b), decrepit structures add further implications of temporality. *Peasants Conversing beside a Ruined Shed* shows an old woman with a market basket and a man with a walking stick (clearly not a couple) standing together on a path and beyond them a seated peasant woman with a toddler. The decaying boards of a wooden shack—some fallen, others haphazardly nailed together—loosely frame the figures, connecting them to their setting and to each other. A large knobby bough above, reiterated in a smaller dead tree to the right, points toward a road that descends to the low landscape beyond. In *Soldiers before a Dilapidated Inn*, this arrangement is reversed, with building and figures massed to the right and distant horsemen moving along a road to the left. Here the spidery shape of a dead tree looms above the inn, which leans toward the right as if commenting on the unstable condition of some of the drinkers. In the foreground, a standing soldier who holds a jug of beer at his side addresses a drunken colleague, perhaps recalling him to duty. The peasant, slumped at the left between an overturned pail and table, is clearly in no better condition.

C. Brown has suggested that this scene illustrates the oppression of the rural population by soldiers during the early years of the seventeenth century and that the cycle as a whole is about the poverty and deprivation of country life.[2] Yet Molijn's prints do not, in fact, display adversarial or problematic relationships between people or between people and nature. Their startling originality lies in the artist's unwillingness to idealize rustic subject matter by connecting it to pastoral traditions, as so many of his contemporaries were doing (Cats. 61, 63, 64, and 66). Molijn's immediate precedents for *Four Landscapes with Figures*, as C. S. Ackley has observed, are the picturesque print series of peasants and tumbledown farmhouses made after designs by Abraham Bloemaert (q.v.), who also produced his own drawings of such subjects (Cat. 18).[3] Molijn's powerfully down-to-earth representations depart from the emphasis on graceful, serpentine contours found in these mannerist-influenced scenes. Yet he, too, emphasizes rhythmic juxtapositions of shapes by maintaining continuous, unbroken contours with his etched line, using drypoint without burr to introduce areas of transparent shadow.

NOTES

1. Molijn did, however, design a second, similar set of four landscapes that were etched by another (unknown) artist. Hollstein 14 (1956):871, nos. 5–8. According to C. S. Ackley, they are probably close in date to the series discussed here. Boston/St. Louis 1980–81, 106, n. 1.

2. C. Brown notes the popularity of this theme in the early years of the century, citing David Vinckboons's (1576–before 1633) pendants in the Rijksmuseum, Amsterdam (inv. nos. A1351, 2), entitled *Boerenverdriet*

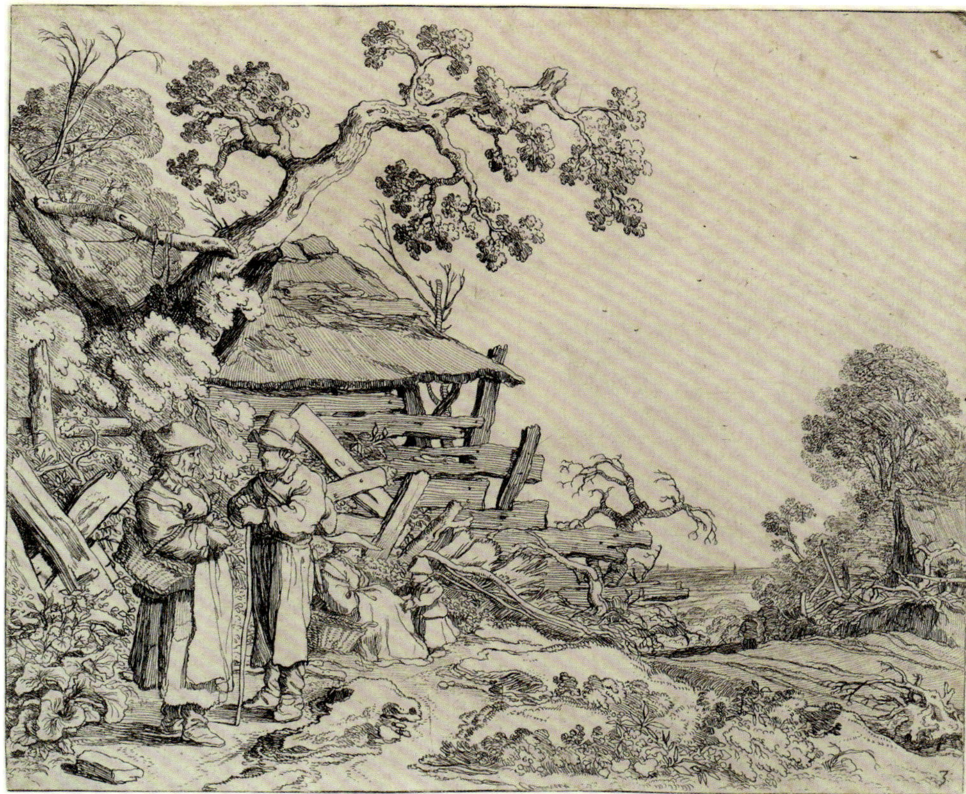

[22a]

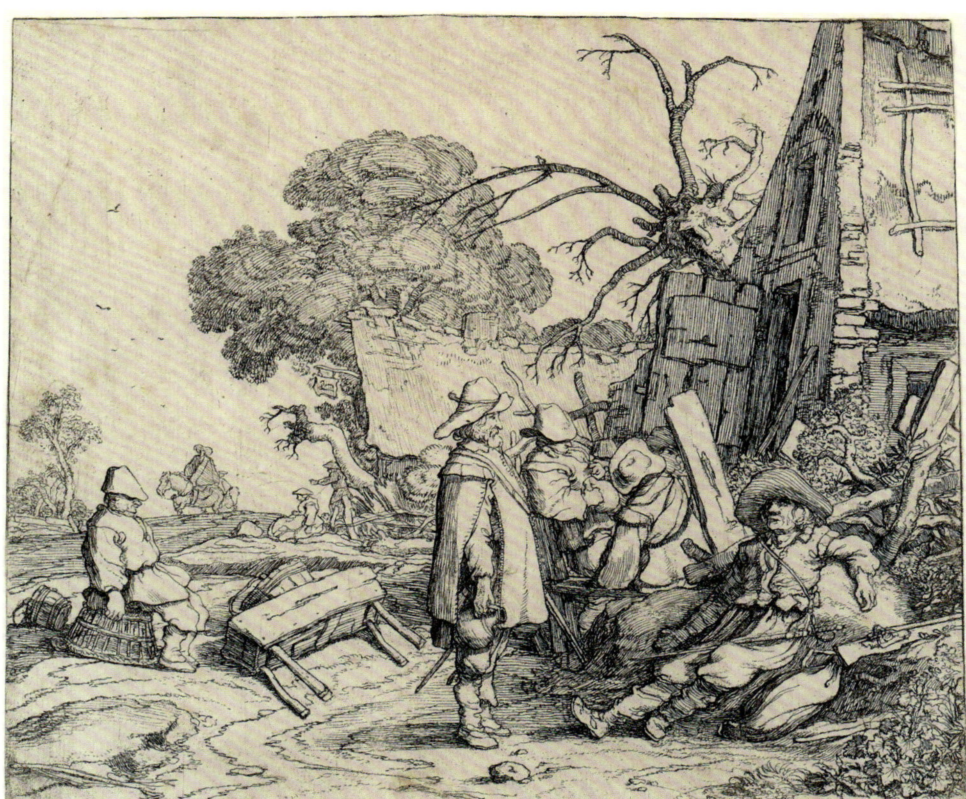

[22b]

(Peasant suffering) and *Boerenvreugd* (Peasant revenge). London 1986, 154.

3. Boston/St. Louis 1980–81, 106. See, for example, the print series by Boëthius Adam Bolswert (1580–1633): *Four Large Rural Views* and *The Farmhouse and Landscape Series*. Roethlisberger 1993, 1:194–95, nos. 226–29, and 195–200, nos. 230–49, 2: figs. 345–48 and 645–59.

REMBRANDT HARMENSZ. VAN RIJN
1606–69

The most profoundly innovative of all Dutch artists, Rembrandt produced a huge oeuvre (some 400 paintings, 290 prints, and more than 1,000 drawings) that encompasses virtually all thematic categories.[1] What remains constant throughout his long career, however, is his acute interest in how people, places, and things exist and evolve within time. While Dutch artists commonly explored the transience of earthly existence, Rembrandt had little interest in vanitas themes. Even the works he made as a young artist suggest that he found time and circumstance to be creative forces that enrich more than they damage or destroy.

Rembrandt made only a few images of ruined buildings, two of which are drawings that record local sites.[2] More often he preferred to examine weathered domestic structures, exploring how they are affected and in a sense recreated by nature and human use. The same interest is evident in Rembrandt's observation of human beings. His portraits, *tronies* (studies of anonymous faces), and narrative scenes all reveal people marked, changed, and enriched by their accumulation of years and experience.

Born in 1606, Rembrandt was the youngest of at least ten children born to the Leiden miller Harmen Gerritsz. van Rijn, a convert to the Dutch Reformed Church.[3] After attending the Latin School in Leiden, he studied briefly at Leiden University but soon left to study painting for three years with the Leiden artist Jacob Isaac van Swanenburgh (1571–1638). In 1624 he went to Amsterdam, where he worked for six months with Pieter Lastman (1583–1633), the most celebrated Dutch history painter of the period. According to Houbraken, he also studied with Jacob Pynas (1592/93–after 1650) before returning to Leiden to set up his own workshop.[4]

By 1632 Rembrandt had settled in Amsterdam, the artistic and commercial center of the Dutch provinces. Major commissions followed, including *The Anatomy Lesson of Dr.*

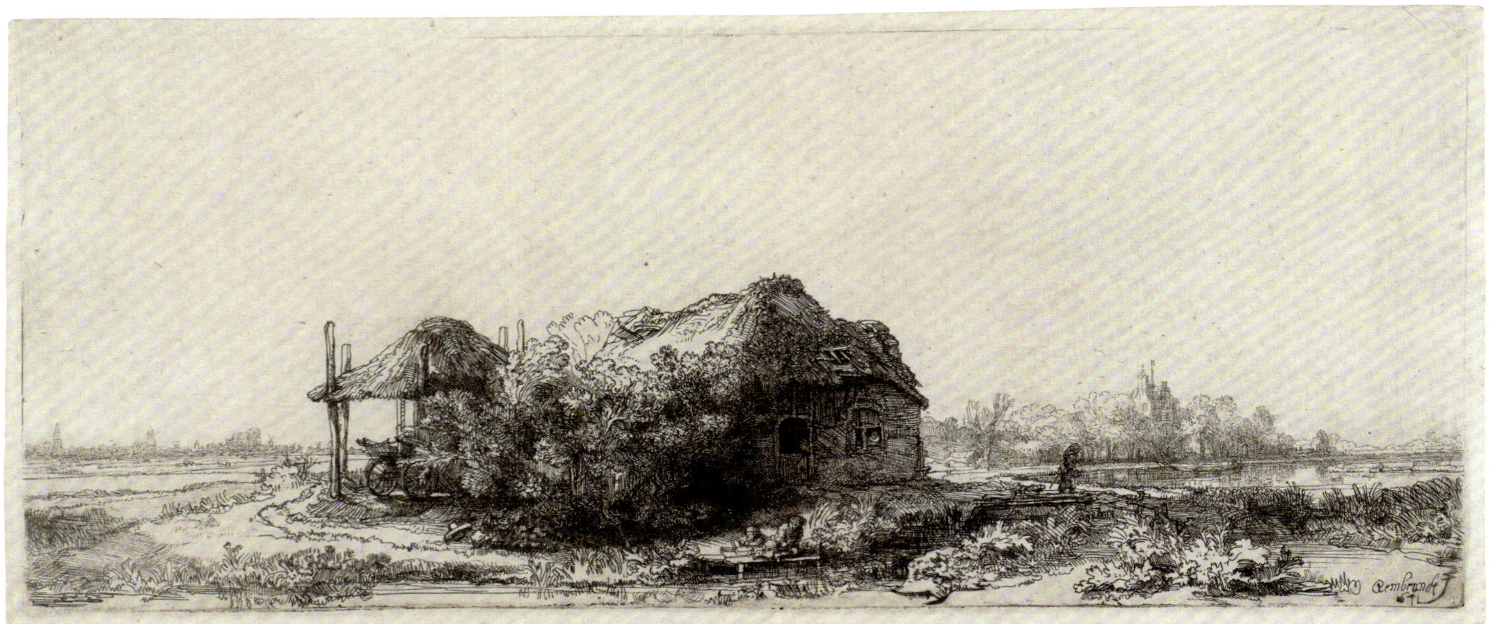

Tulp of 1632 (Mauritshuis, The Hague) and *The Night Watch* of 1642 (Rijksmuseum, Amsterdam), which allowed him to purchase a large house on the Jodenbreestraat, now the museum Het Rembrandthuis, which houses a major collection of the artist's prints.

In 1634 Rembrandt married Saskia van Uylenburgh, with whom he had four children, only one of whom (Titus, b. 1641) survived infancy. Saskia herself died in 1642. During the late 1640s, Hendrickje Stoffels (1626–63) joined Rembrandt's household as a nurse for Titus. Rembrandt's close companion (never his wife because of the terms of Saskia's will), Hendrickje became the model for many of his later works. A daughter, Cornelia, was born to the couple in 1654.

Financial pressures caused by his purchase of his house ultimately led to Rembrandt's bankruptcy in 1656 and the financial difficulties of his late years. Nonetheless, he continued to receive important civic commissions such as *The Anatomy Lesson of Dr. Joan Deyman* of 1656 (Amsterdams Historisch Museum) and *The Syndics of the Cloth Guild* of 1662 (Rijksmuseum, Amsterdam) and to produce major history paintings such as *The Return of the Prodigal Son* (State Hermitage Museum, St. Petersburg, c. 1668–69). In 1663 Hendrickje died during an epidemic of the plague in Amsterdam, while Titus succumbed during another epidemic in 1668. Rembrandt died the following year and was buried in the Westerkerk in Amsterdam in 1669.

NOTES

1. Rembrandt's oeuvre has been progressively contracted, most recently, and sometimes debatably, in the *Corpus of Rembrandt's Paintings*, a multivolume chronological study, begun by a group of Dutch scholars in 1982 and not yet completed (*Rembrandt Corpus*).

2. Although a number of Rembrandt's late landscapes have ancient-looking settings, only one emphasizes a ruin: *River Landscape with Ruins* (Gemäldegalerie, Kassel, no. GK 242), which scholars believe was begun by Rembrandt about 1640, then extensively overpainted in the early 1650s, possibly by his student Ferdinand Bol (1616–80); cf. *Rembrandt Corpus* 2 (1986):514. Two of his drawings record local buildings as ruins: *Ruins after the Fire in the Amsterdam Town Hall* (dated 1652, Het Rembrandthuis, Amsterdam; Fig. 75) and *The Ruins of Kostverloren* (c. 1650, The Art Institute of Chicago; Fig. 128).

3. Rembrandt's father was the only one of his brothers and sisters who converted to Calvinism; his mother, Neeltje Zuytbrouck, seems to have remained Catholic. Rembrandt's own religious affiliation has been debated, but his marriage and the baptisms of his four children took place in the Calvinist (Reformed) church. For discussion of the religious connections of Rembrandt and his family, see Schwartz 1985, 18–19 and 300.

4. Houbraken 1718–21, 1 (1718):254–55.

[23]

Landscape with a Cottage and Hay Barn: oblong, 1641

Inscriptions: lower right, *Rembrandt f. 1641*

Etching, 129 × 323 mm (5 1/16 × 12 3/4 in.) (platemark); 136 × 332 mm (5 3/8 × 13 1/16 in.) (sheet); only state

The Frances Lehman Loeb Art Center, Vassar College, Poughkeepsie, New York, Gift of Mrs. Felix M. Warburg and her Children, 1941.1.73

References: Hollstein 19 (1969):167, no. 225; White 1969, 1:197–98, 2: fig. 294; Slive 1988, 134–35, figs. 3-3 and 6-4; Washington 1990, 83–84, no. 6; Limouze 1995, 121–22, no. 39; Amsterdam/Paris 1998–99, 284–85; London/Amsterdam 2000, 185–86, fig. a.

Rembrandt made prints and drawings of rustic farmhouses and cottages throughout the entire period of his involvement with landscape, from the early 1630s to the late 1650s.

In these works, he was able to explore how manmade structures are acted upon by time and weather, both of which encourage the eventual fusion of a building with its natural surroundings. In many of these scenes, the artist sets up a subtle polarity between country and city, adding the distant skyline of a miniaturized town so that even the most modest rustic cottage, as here, claims the picture space

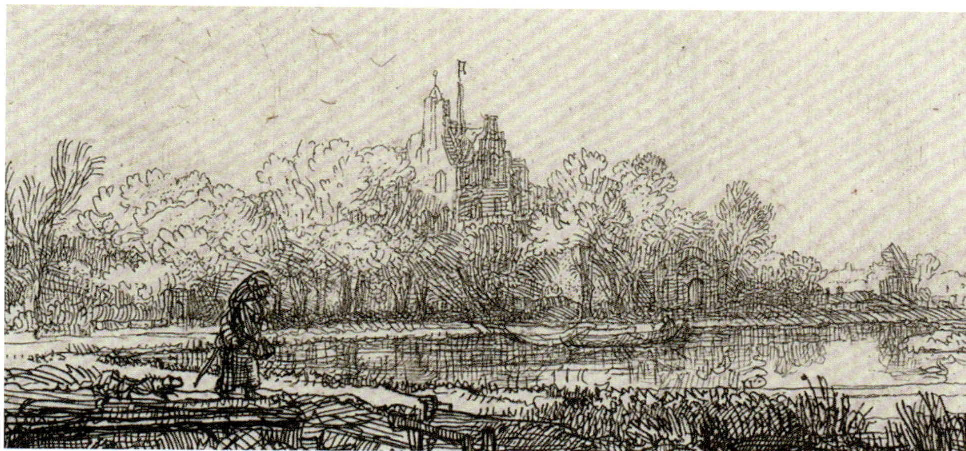

Fig. 127. Detail of Kostverloren, right background of Rembrandt's *Landscape with a Cottage and Hay Barn* (Cat. 23)

fully. In *Landscape with Cottage and Hay Barn*, the towers of a city (possibly Amsterdam) appear at the far left, with the center of this wide scene occupied by the kind of longitudinal farmhouse found in the vicinity of Amsterdam but already becoming somewhat rare and old-fashioned in Rembrandt's time.[1] The typical *langhuis* (long house) was a wooden building developed for dairy farming and cattle breeding that had an attached stable and a thatch and sod roof.

Seen here from the front, the structure, which reiterates the print's oblong shape, is partly masked by dense foliage that bonds its two sections. Against the low horizon, its appealingly humped shape contrasts with the towers of an imposing country villa (Fig. 127) that rises from the riverbank at the right background—probably the early sixteenth-century house on the Amstel popularly known as Kostverloren (Lost Cost) because its damp foundations necessitated perpetual expensive renovation. A popular site for a country excursion, Kostverloren was the subject of numerous paintings, drawings, and prints by seventeenth-century artists, including Jacob van Ruisdael (q.v.), as S. Slive has discussed.[2] Its picturesque interest was only enhanced by its near destruction in a fire of 1650, which Rembrandt recorded in a magnificent pen and wash drawing now in the Art Institute of Chicago (Fig. 128). In it, the shell of the structure, burned bare of vegetation, appears behind a fallen tree. The firm, yet slightly discontinuous strokes of Rembrandt's quill pen capture the shape of the building with its distinctive step-gable tower, while giving it an aura of ghostly fragility.

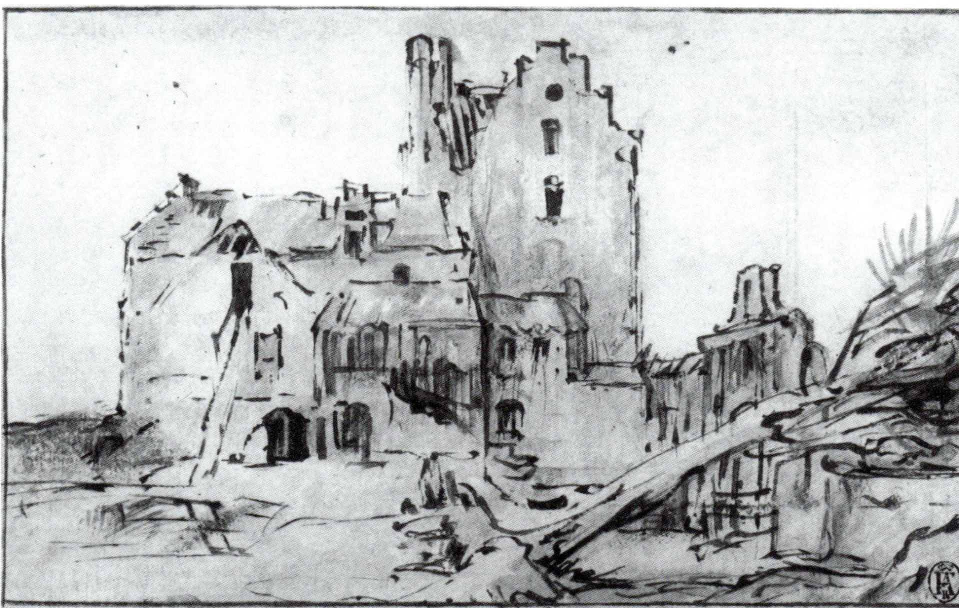

Fig. 128. Rembrandt, *The Ruins of Kostverloren*, c. 1650, pen, brown ink, brown wash, and white watercolor drawing, The Art Institute of Chicago, Clarence Buckingham Collection

In Rembrandt's etching, Kostverloren in its intact state is surrounded by lush foliage and helps to frame the shabby cottage between country estate and city skyline. This farmhouse, whose roof could use re-thatching, takes on an almost human character, especially because it is so thoroughly occupied. People look out of its open door and window, two boys fish from the dock in the center foreground, and a man and dog walk away from the building toward the right. These varied human presences all tie the cottage to the landscape, as does the curving patch of ground that encircles it, emphasizing that it is almost completely surrounded by water. Rembrandt's division of the scene into three kinds of views has a somewhat triptych-like effect, but soft touches of drypoint in this fine early impression create rich passages of light and shade that merge the cottage with the abundant vegetation around it.[3]

NOTES

1. B. Bakker has investigated Rembrandt's depictions of Dutch farmhouse types in his essay in Washington 1990, 33–59, esp. 40 and fig. 5.

2. Slive 1988. Slive discusses the appearance of Kostverloren both before and after the fire, including the views of it made after the ruined estate was purchased in 1658 and largely demolished and rebuilt on a lower foundation.

3. For discussion of Vassar's impression of the print, see Limouze 1995, 121–22.

ISACK VAN OSTADE
1621–49

The short career of Isack van Ostade, whose paintings span only the decade between 1639 and 1649, was an impressive one.[1] Baptized in 1621 in Haarlem, he began painting lively peasant interiors in the style of his brother Adriaen van Ostade (1610–85), who may have been his teacher. After 1642, however, he virtually abandoned Adriaen's specialty in favor of landscapes that show the influence of Salomon van Ruysdael (1600/1603–1670), along with outdoor genre scenes that often focus on the activities outside a modest, often rather ramshackle cottage or roadside inn.[2] He shared this subject with his Haarlem contemporary Philips Wouwerman (1619–68), although it is unclear who developed it first. After 1643, when he joined the Haarlem painters' guild, Isack's manner of painting also shifted strongly. Under the influence of Pieter van Laer (1599–?1642), who had returned to Haarlem from Italy in 1638, he abandoned dark coloring and loose brushwork and began using a more delicate, detailed, and precise technique with lighter tonality. In both his small panels and larger, more ambitious canvasses (many of which are signed and dated), Isack was able to capture the mood of the season through the sky: silvery or golden light for summer scenes and a subtle gray for winter. His many depictions of travelers with peasants often center around a white horse, which almost becomes his signature.

A prolific draftsman, Isack has been credited with 226 of the 500 drawings attributed to the Ostade brothers.[3] Yet Isack van Ostade's profession never made him rich. That his prices were uncommonly low is revealed by a document of 1641 in which he contracts to supply a Rotterdam dealer with thirteen paintings for only twenty-seven guilders for the entire lot.[4] Perhaps for this reason, he supplemented his income by contributing staffage to paintings by other artists.

NOTES

1. Bibliographic material is drawn from Schnackenburg 1981, 1:16–21; Amsterdam/Boston/Philadelphia 1987–88, 390–93; and B. Schnackenburg's essay in *Dictionary of Art* 1996, 23:613–14.

2. While Houbraken stated that Isack van Ostade studied with his brother, a lawsuit brought against Adriaen van Ostade by Ruysdael "for sums due for board and tuition" suggests that Ruysdael was also Isack's teacher. B. Schnackenburg in *Dictionary of Art* 2000, 241.

3. On the drawings of Adriaen and Isack van Ostade, see Schnackenburg 1981.

4. Cited in Schnackenburg 1981, 1:16, and in *Dictionary of Art* 1996, 23:613.

[24]

A Woman Selling Fruit by a Cottage, c. 1645

Oil on panel, 61 × 45.6 cm (24 × 18 in.)

Private collection, New York

References: Smith 1829–42, 1:188, no. 36; Blanc 1869, 123 (with engraving by Bracquemont); Davis 1884, 1: no. 25; Hofstede de Groot 3 (1910):475, no. 129; Eckerling 1977, 100, fig. 36; New York 1988, 102, no. 37; Eckerling Kaufman 1995, 1:302, no. 41 and 2:530–31, fig. 41.

This engaging scene, illustrating the kind of shabbily domestic setting for which Isack van Ostade became known, shows a thatch-roofed cottage built at the top of a dilapidated brick stairway, which is abutted by a crumbling brick archway at the left. At the far left, a large, cracked chamberpot lies on its side next to a small shed or outhouse with a broken door. Seated at a table in the center is an old woman selling fruits and vegetables. She is engaged in conversation with a plainly dressed buyer who has her market basket at one side and her child at the other. This homey incident from everyday life is less realistic than it appears, however, because people in the Dutch provinces were allowed to sell their produce only at marketplaces, not in front of their homes.[1] As L. Eckerling Kaufman has suggested, a number of aspects of this scene (such as the combination of archway and staircase and placement of figures against a large wall) appear to have been derived from works by the Dutch Italianate painter Thomas Wijck (c. 1616–77), like Isack, a student of Adriaen van Ostade, who returned to Haarlem in the early 1640s.[2] Isack's delicate lighting and warm color, as well as his emphasis on a proliferation of finely painted detail, suggest that this painting should be dated to the mid-1640s.[3]

In Dutch paintings and prints, dilapidated architecture may, in certain contexts, express a moralizing message about dereliction of domestic duty, as in an etching of an ill-cared-for farmyard based on a design by Jacques de Gheyn II (Cat. 20). Yet in this scene, all the figures, even the children, are diligently engaged in activity. Furthermore, as W. S. Gibson discusses (see his essay herein, pp. 63–72), Dutch viewers enjoyed rough and irregular pictorial effects, especially as applied to images of ordinary people and rustic places whose worn condition suggests that they been well and thoroughly used. Such effects were equally appealing to a nineteenth-century audience, as indicated by Charles Blanc's response to the painting in 1869: "Quel attrayant désordre, et dans ce désordre, quelle harmonie! Tout est pauvre ici, ruiné, rapiécé, miserable …"[4] (What engaging disorder and in this muddle what harmony! Everything here is poor, ruined, fragmentary, miserable …").

In developing his unusual, double-decker setting, Ostade was able to stage different incidents or motifs throughout the picture space: the woman spinning beside the cottage at the upper left, the clean laundry hung out to dry at the upper right (an orange cat dozes in the doorway beside it), the man descending the stairs with a large basket, and finally the ground-level scene, in which the sunlit archway frames a curious white horse, a motif that became virtually a trademark for Isack van Ostade.[5]

NOTES

1. Eckerling Kaufman 1995, 1:151.On the marketing of goods (which took place in cities, not in rural settings), see Honig 1996.

2. Eckerling Kaufman 1995, 1:150. Wijck's paintings of everyday life are discussed L. Trezzani's article on the artist in Briganti, Trezzani, and Laureati 1983, 223–37, figs. 7.1–7.16, and in Vienna/Salzburg 1986, 212–22.

3. This date has been suggested in an oral communication by B. Schnackenburg to A. J. Adams, as cited in New York 1988, 102, and by L. Eckerling Kaufman in her doctoral dissertation on Isack van Ostade: Eckerling Kaufman 1995, 1:302, no. 41.

4. Blanc 1869, 123.

5. A similar setting with a figure on an exterior stairway linking two levels has been identified by A. J. Adams: Isack van Ostade's *Peasants Listening to a Blind Fiddler*, dated 1646, in the collection of Her Majesty Queen Elizabeth II, London (New York 1988, 102 and n. 3).

WILLEM KALF
1619–93

Baptized on 3 November 1619 in Rotterdam, Willem Kalf was the son of Jan Jansz. Kalf, a successful cloth draper whose activity in the town government included service in the Admiralty of the Maas.[1] According to Houbraken, Kalf was the pupil of Hendrik Gerritsz. Pot (c. 1585–1657),[2] although there is no evidence of this connection in his early paintings. At any rate, by 1639 or 1640 Kalf had gone to Paris, where in January 1642 he was documented in St. Germain-des-Près as a resident of "La Chasse," a pension for Netherlandish artists. Here he made small, freely painted kitchen pieces, whose dilapidated interiors recall the work of such Rotterdam painters as Herman (q.v.) and

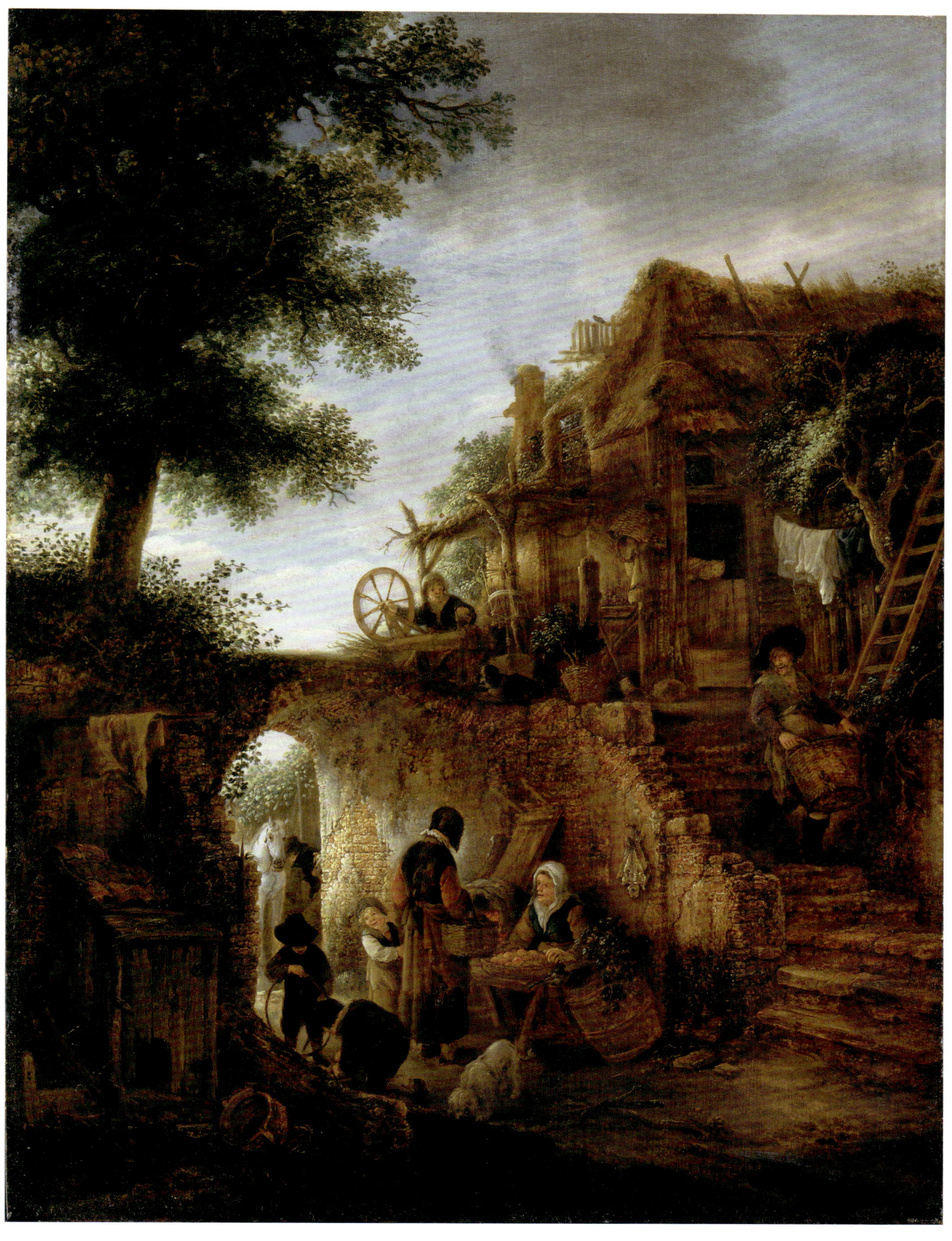

Cornelis (1607–81) Saftleven. I. Bergström has also drawn attention to François Rijckhals of Middelburg and Dordrecht (c. 1600–1647), who he believes may have been Kalf's teacher.[3]

Documents place Kalf back in Rotterdam by 1646 and, in 1651, in the city of Hoorn in West Friesland. There he married Cornelia Pluvier van Vollenhoven, a talented, highly educated woman mentioned in contemporary poems who was a master of calligraphy, a glass engraver, a poet, and a composer of music. Kalf moved to Amsterdam by 1663, spending the rest of his life in this major commercial and cultural center. Unlike many of his Dutch contemporaries, Kalf lived a financially comfortable and stable life as both painter and art dealer. After about 1663 his production of paintings sharply diminished, and by 1680 he was apparently devoting his time exclusively to art dealing. The works for which Kalf became best known are his later *pronkstilleven* (luxurious or sumptuous still lifes), in which he depicted expensive carpets, metalware, and glassware that may in some cases have been objects he owned.

NOTES

1. Archival and biographical material on Kalf is presented in Grisebach 1974, 12–33.
2. Houbraken 1718–21 (1753), 2:218–19.
3. Bergström 1956, 273–78.

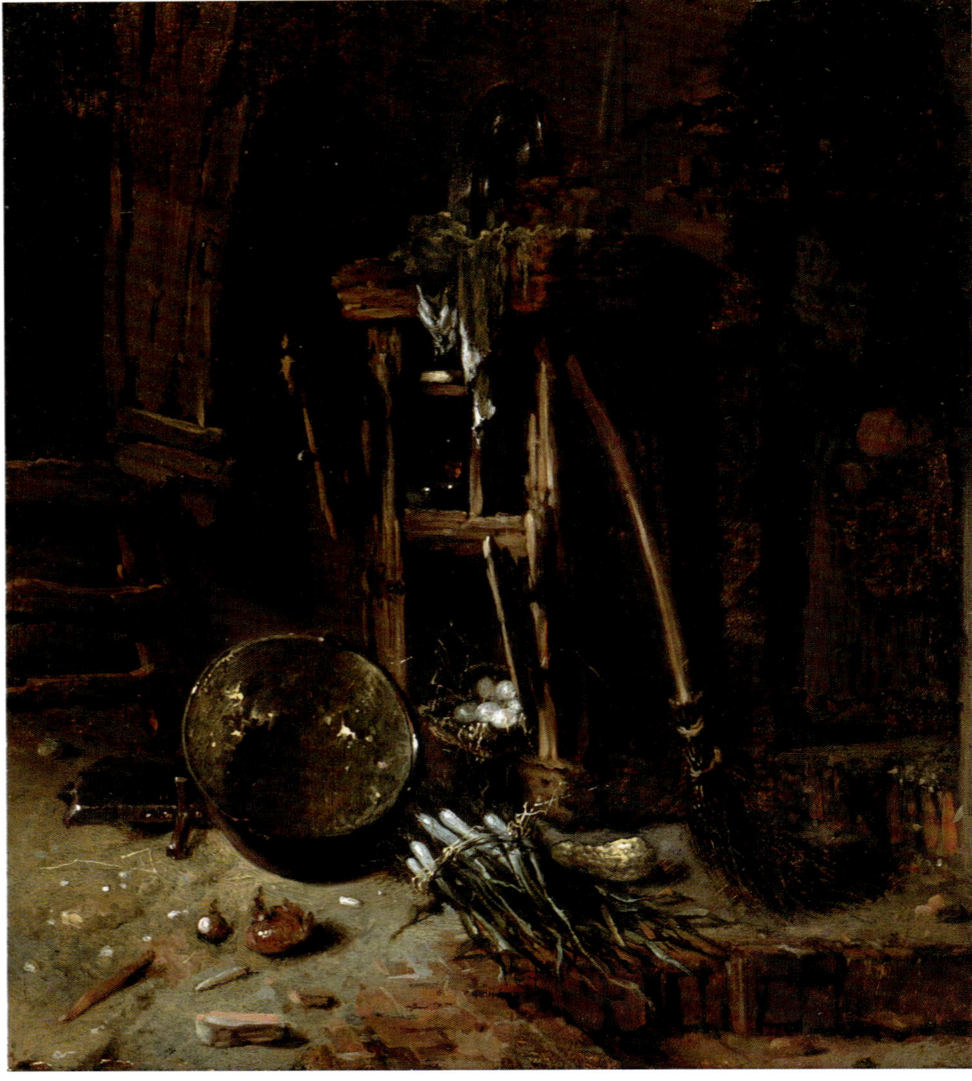

[25]

A Kitchen Corner, c. 1642

Inscriptions: none

Oil on panel, 21.4 × 19.5 cm (8⅜ × 7⅝ in.)

The Detroit Institute of Arts, Gift of Mr. and Mrs. Bernard F. Walker in memory of Robert H. Tannahill, 69.358

References: Detroit 1970, 82; Grisebach 1974, 222–23, no. 29, pl. 31; Amsterdam/Cleveland 1999–2000, no. 47; The Hague/San Francisco 1990–91, 312, fig. 1, under no. 37; Keyes, Kuretsky, Rüger, and Wheelock 2004, 126–27, no. 50.

In this dilapidated, dimly lit larder, a woman with a basket of gourds at the right background becomes an unobtrusive human counterpoint to the artist's primary focus: inanimate objects. Onions, carrots, cucumbers, and leeks are displayed in and around the central motif of a rough wooden cupboard with broken doors, framed by an open doorway at the left and a brick archway at the right. Within the cupboard is a nest of eggs and, surprisingly, the bright accent of a glass of red wine. The round mouth of a shiny brass kettle and the diagonal broom center this grouping of unstably poised objects. Further visual interest is created by the angled fall of light into the left foreground and by the artist's animated brushwork, in which brown, green, and ocher touches of paint are combined with thick, slightly detached white highlights. Characteristic of Kalf's kitchen scenes, this interior conveys not only age and hard use, but also the unexpected harmony that groupings of simple domestic objects can express. Approximately fifty-eight of these scenes are known, four of which are dated between 1639 and 1644, when Kalf was living in Paris.[1]

Domestic interiors featuring kitchen motifs and other housewares became a popular subject in Kalf's native city of Rotterdam. Their earliest precedents in Netherlandish art are the large-scale, late sixteenth-century paintings of Peter Aertsen (c. 1508–75), who was active in Amsterdam and Antwerp. He combined elaborate displays of foodstuffs and kitchenwares with figures, often including a religious narrative in the background, such as Christ in the House of Mary and Martha, to allude to the hazards of gluttony versus the need for spiritual sustenance through Christ.[2] In general, however, Dutch painters of the seventeenth century preferred to use such scenes to demonstrate the virtues of domestic duty and careful household maintenance.[3]

Kalf's small painting clearly has a different intention. The setting, far from being a spotless domestic interior, is the shadowed corner of a cellar or barn which remains functional but has weathered into a kind of ruin with its crumbling brick floor, shattered cupboard, and precariously hanging door. The taste for such rustic, derelict motifs, which encouraged a rough, painterly touch, is also evident in Dutch landscapes of the same period, which often feature tumble-down farm buildings, broken fences or dead trees (Cats. 24 and 31). Some writers have interpreted these scenes as moralizing comments on the transience and inevitable decay of earthly life. W. S. Gibson, on the other hand, has argued persuasively that interest in the roughness and irregularities of crumbling things demonstrates a distinctively Dutch taste for motifs that are *schilderachtig*, or "suitable for painters," as expressed in unidealized images that appear true to life.[4] This more positive reading can be aptly applied to Kalf, for the powerful presence of this deceptively simple little painting is generated by its balance of rather crude motifs, roughly rendered with an assurance that emphasizes both their complexity of surface and the richness of the paint itself.

NOTES

1. Grisebach 1974, 60.
2. Cf. Pieter Aertsen's *Christ in the House of Mary and Martha*, dated 1559, Museum voor Oude Kunst, Brussels, no. 708. This story became popular in northern Europe during the late sixteenth century because it relates to a major debate of the Protestant Reformation: the importance of faith versus works (attending directly to Christ versus relying upon the performance of good deeds and rituals to achieve salvation). In the biblical text, Christ reminds Martha, displeased that her sister Mary has been listening to him instead of helping to serve the meal: "Mary has chose the better part" (Luke 10:42).
3. Franits 1993, 86–90, figs. 67–68.
4. The diverse arguments about the interpretation of Dutch "rustic ruins" are addressed in Gibson 2000, 141–77, and in his essay herein (pp. 63–72).

GERBRAND VAN DEN EECKHOUT
1621–74

The son of a goldsmith, Eeckhout studied with Rembrandt in Amsterdam during the period between around 1635 and 1640, beginning his career as a painter of biblical scenes similar in style to those of his teacher and "great friend," in Houbraken's words.[1] Dated paintings by this prolific artist are known from virtually every year between 1641 and 1674. While biblical scenes and other historical subjects dominate Eeckhout's oeuvre, he also produced a few portraits and mountainous landscapes and, during the 1650s, domestic genre scenes in the style of Gerard ter Borch (1582/83–1662) and Pieter de Hooch (1629–84). An extremely talented draftsman who often depicted landscapes, Eeckhout began under the strong influence of Rembrandt but in the period between 1650 and 1655 responded more to the style of Roelant Roghman's (q.v.) chalk and wash topographical drawings. A trip along the Rhine in 1663 with Jacob Esselens (c. 1627–87) and Jan Lievens (1607–74) yielded panoramic landscape drawings during the early 1660s. In many of Eeckhout's landscape drawings, however, it is unclear whether or not a specific site has been represented. The artist apparently lived his entire life in Amsterdam, where he died a bachelor in 1674.

NOTE

1. Houbraken 1718–21, 1 (1718):174, 2 (1721):100. Biographical material on Eeckhout is based on P. C. Sutton's essay in Amsterdam/Boston/Philadelphia 1987–88, 304–5, and on B. P. J. Broos's essay in *Dictionary of Art* 1996, 9:741–44.

[26]
Landscape with Ruins, 1650

Inscriptions: dated by the artist at lower left, *1650*; inscribed by a later hand in pen and brown ink, *Buyten Brussels*

Pen and brown ink, brown and gray wash, over black chalk, 198 × 229 mm ($7\frac{13}{16}$ × 9 in.)

Lent by the Metropolitan Museum of Art, New York, Rogers Fund, 1965, 65.104

References: Hannema 1955, 2:124, no. 214; Brussels/Rotterdam/Paris/Berne 1968–69, 51–52, under no. 47, nn. 1 and 5; New York/Paris 1977–78, 52, under no. 34; Sumowski 1979–92, 3:1464, no. 677; Mules 1985, 41; Van Berge-Gerbaud 1997, 124 and 126; Plomp 1997, 43, under no. 128.

Despite the inscription (added in a later hand), there is no reason to believe that this mountainous landscape represents the countryside outside Brussels. Its technique, which relates closely to that of Roelant Roghman (q.v.), has led scholars to place it among a group of studies that seem to have been made between 1650 and 1654 in the vicinity of Brabant and Cleves, even though the terrain represented in this drawing is not characteristic of those regions either.[1] In its combination of mountains and ruins with the effects of bright sunlight, Eeckhout's scene might almost have been made in Italy, as further suggested by the donkey and travelers in the

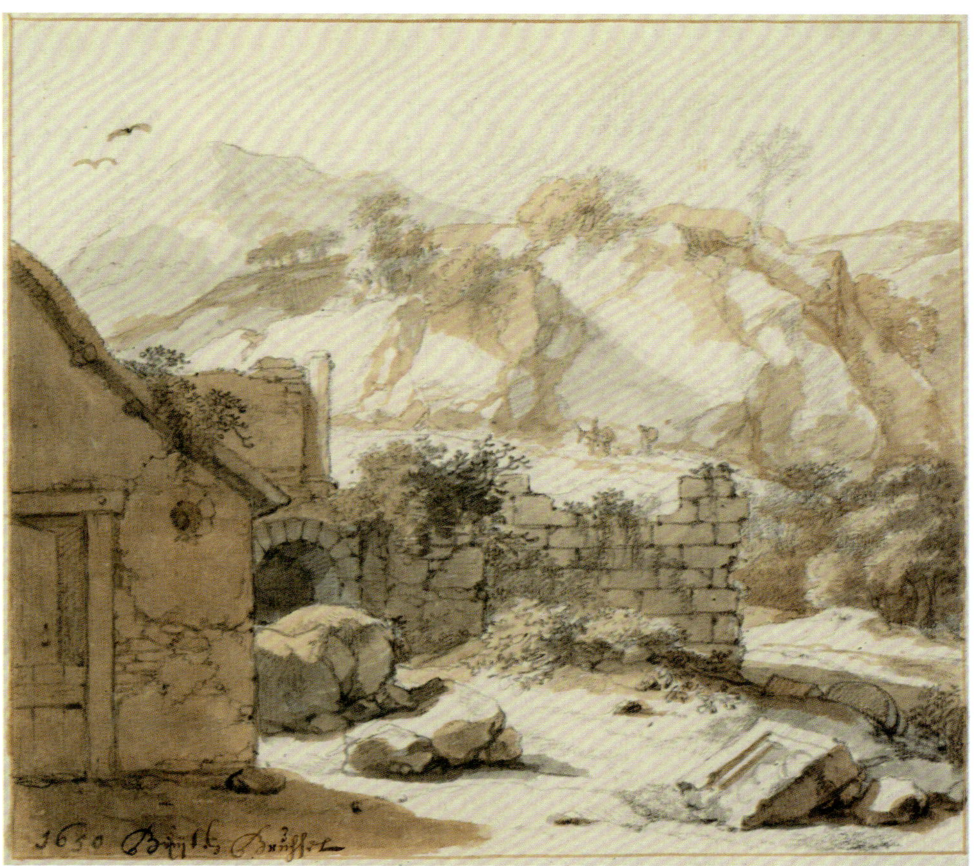

background and by the fallen fragment of a cornice or panel of relief sculpture at the right foreground. Yet Eeckhout is not known to have visited Italy, and the low-lying architectural remains in this landscape seem more medieval than ancient in any case.

The intense vivacity of this quiet scene derives from the fact that its ruined structures illustrate the end of a long temporal process, yet the landscape as a whole seems to exist within a fleeting moment in the present. Brilliant sunlight, falling from the left, casts long diagonal shadows whose intensity diminishes from the deep yellowish-brown washes applied in the foreground to paler, almost transparent shadings of gray on the distant mountains at the far left. Although the scene has a high horizon and little of the sky is visible, its presence is implied by shadows that seem projected onto the landscape by unseen clouds. Within this complex alternation of lighter and darker patterns of tone, the two birds in flight at the upper left and the travelers in the center enliven an otherwise unoccupied scene. Eeckhout emphasizes the emptiness of the ruined structures not only by defining their weathered or fragmented walls, overgrown by foliage, but also by facing the two entranceways at the left directly toward the viewer. The half-door of the stone house in the immediate foreground gapes partly open, while the stone arch beyond it frames a dark void.

NOTE

1. Mules 1985, 41. A very similar ruined structure with an archway appears in Eeckhout's black chalk and gray wash drawing *Sunken Road with Trees*, also dated 1650, in the Institut Néerlandais, Paris (Lugt collection, no. 8725, 206 × 318 mm). Repr. Sumowski 1979–92, 3:1467.

GERRIT ADRIAENSZ. DE HEER
1606–after 1652

Gerrit Adriaensz. de Heer, a draftsman and printmaker who worked in an extremely unusual style, is thought to have been born in the northern Dutch provinces of Friesland or Leeuwarden. His teacher and family history remain unknown, but he produced two portrait drawings, now in the Groninger Museum, and a number of signed etchings and delicate pen drawings on parchment that depict landscapes, inn scenes, and gypsy encampments with ruined buildings. Archival evidence indicates that Gerrit de Heer worked in Amsterdam not only as an artist but also as a *bierbeschoyer*, or retailer in the beer trade. On 3 March 1650 a painter and draftsman by that name was levied with a beer revenue tax of 450 guilders, which had to be paid within fifteen months, although he was allowed to remit paintings and drawings of equal value.[1] Gerrit's son Willem or Guilliam (c. 1638–before 1681), who was probably his student, produced similar genre drawings on parchment. Because he apparently signed many of his works with his father's name, his work has posed problems of attribution for scholars.[2] The rare still lifes of Margarethe de Heer (c. 1600–1665, active in Friesland), who was probably Gerrit's daughter or daughter-in-law, are delicate watercolors and miniatures of the kinds of plants and small creatures that appear in the works of both Gerrit and Willem de Heer.[3]

NOTES

1. According to this document, the bondman, whose name was Jacob Wilthout, retained an option on the art if he paid back the money owed to the creditor. A. Bredius as cited in Thieme-Becker 16 (1923):231. See also F.W. Robinson in Hanover/Wellesley/Providence/Storrs 1969, unpaginated, no. 23, and Karstkarel 1978.

2. F. W. Robinson has argued that Gerrit had a somewhat finer touch and employed more delicate pen work than did his son, whose drawings display greater contrast between light and dark, heavier, more substantial figures, and more clearly defined pictorial space. Hanover/Wellesley/Providence/Storrs 1969, unpaginated, no. 23. For further discussion of attribution problems relating to the De Heers, see M. Kersten in Leiden 1986, 113–14, no. 42, and W. W. Robinson in Amsterdam/Vienna/New York/Cambridge 1991–92, 56, no. 19.

3. On Margareta de Heer's *stukjes* (little pieces), see Karstkarel 1978.

[27]

The Returning Gypsy Family in Front of a Ruined Inn, c. 1660

Inscriptions: lower right, on trunk, *G. de Heer*

Etching on white laid paper, 353 × 432 mm (13⅞ × 17 in.) (platemark), 340 × 430 mm (13⅜ × 16⅞ in.) (sheet); only state

The Art Institute of Chicago, Albrecht H. Wolf Fund Income, 1970, 598

References: Hollstein 9 (1949):3; Lawrence/New Haven/Austin 1983–84, 147–49, no. 38.

Gerrit de Heer's vivid depiction of a congregation of figures around a ruined inn displays a composition very similar to that of his pen drawing of a shepherd and flock (Cat. 28), although the design the artist etched on the plate has been reversed by the printmaking process. The occasion for the gathering is a May Day festival, as indicated by the tall, decorated maypole around which figures drink and dance to the music of a bagpipe played by the young man at the far right. Like the pipe-playing shepherd in De Heer's drawing, he wears a slashed beret and sits beneath a ruined tree with a flowering branch, while the man beside him, also silhouetted against the light, appears to be holding a flute.[1]

Such village festivals, celebrated by local inhabitants in the most uninhibited ways possible, attracted a host of itinerant peddlers, quack medical practitioners, fortunetellers, and beggars who came to amuse (and usually to bilk) the crowds. Gypsies, identifiable by the kinds of ragged capes, floppy hats, and turbans seen within this gathering, attracted intense interest for claiming to be able to predict the future, but they were also frequently jailed or expelled for thievery and deception, which included pretending to be cripples or penniless beggars.[2] The ragged man sleeping in the foreground holds a long beggar's staff. In front of the inn behind him are other figures in morally dubious situations: a well-dressed young lady being encouraged by a sinister group to have her palm read, an old crone performing back surgery on a bare-breasted girl, and a group of drinkers, one of whom lies unconscious on the ground. Within this context, the decaying inn with its partly shattered windows, crumbling brickwork, and loosening shingles has a disturbingly disreputable air. Yet De Heer's scene is not an overall condemnation of human behavior, for the gypsy couple who have set up their temporary camp at the right foreground are shown tenderly feeding their child.

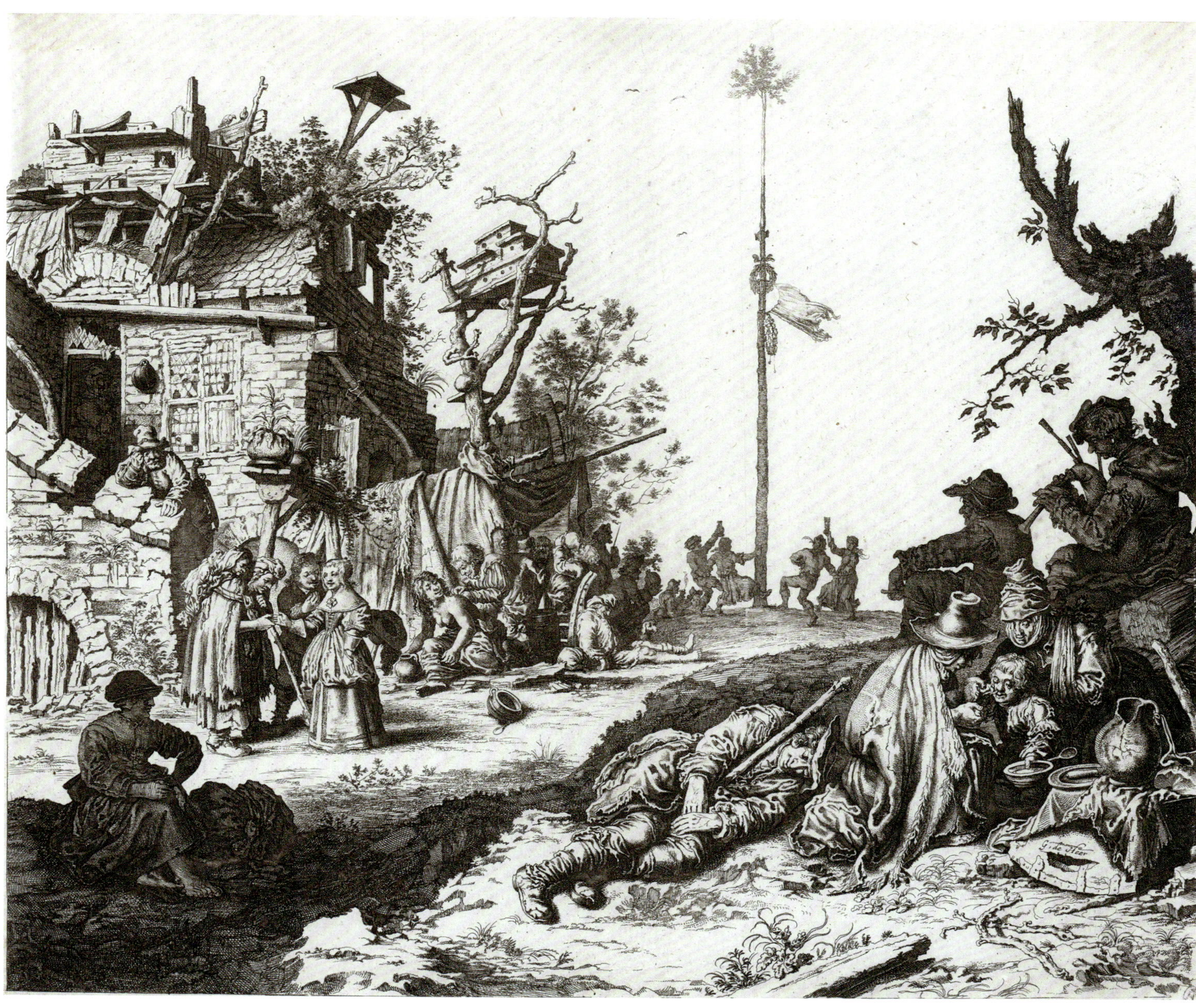

[27]

NOTES

1. L. Stone-Ferrier suggests that in this context the tree may refer to Roemer Visscher's emblem of 1614 that juxtaposes a living and a dead tree under the motto "Keur baert angst" (Choice causes anxiety) to illustrate the quandary of choosing between good and evil or between potentially fertile or barren alternatives. Lawrence/New Haven/Austin 1983–84, 147.

2. Gypsy dress is discussed in De Marly 1970, 388, and Joachim 1959, 22. Both sources are cited in Lawrence/New Haven/Austin 1983–84, 148, along with C. J. Ribton-Turner's study on the history of vagrants and beggars (Ribton-Turner 1972). Gypsies also attracted the interest of the popular Dutch poet Jacob Cats (1577–1660), whose *Het Spaens Heydinnetje* (The Spanish gypsy girl) was published in 1637 (modern reprint: Cats/Vieu-Kuik 1980).

[28]

A Shepherd and His Flock Amidst Ruins, c. 1630–49

Inscriptions: right center on the board in front of the standing man, in pen and brown ink, *G. de Heer*

Brown ink and brown wash (?), with a framing line in black ink on parchment, 267 × 245 mm (10⅞ × 9⅞ in.)

Courtesy of the Fogg Art Museum, Harvard University Art Museums, Cambridge, Massachusetts, The Maida and George Abrams Collection, 1999.149

References: Hanover/Wellesley/Providence/Storrs 1969, unpaginated, no. 23; Amsterdam/Vienna/New York/Cambridge 1991–92, 56, no. 19.

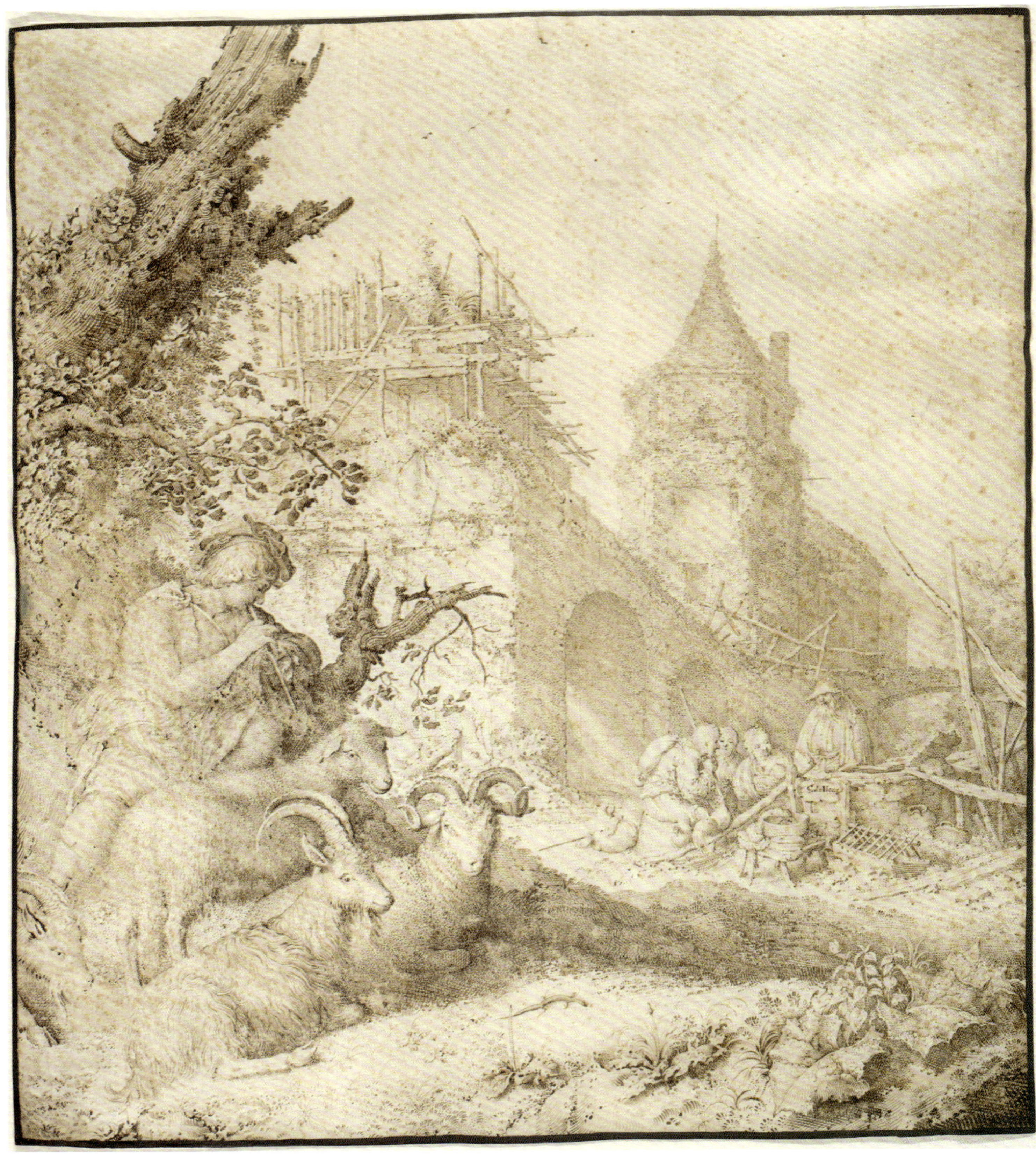

De Heer's remarkably delicate pen drawing consists of two very different pictorial incidents (a pastoral scene in the foreground and a peasant gathering in the background), linked by a large foreshortened ruin whose foundation is an ancient stone arcade or bridge. At its far end rises a hexagonal tower, perhaps part of a church. In front of the tower, at the upper left, is a dilapidated wooden structure with a ladder. At the immediate left foreground, a large tree stump drawn in darker ink towers diagonally over the scene, reiterating the irregular contours of the wooden shack. Under the old tree's last leaves, a young herdsman plays his pipe to three goats and a sheep.

Pastoral imagery in art and literature celebrates an ideal, timeless world in which people, always young, are seen to live in a state of perfect harmony with nature and with each other. Artists often included ruins to evoke the classical origins of this ancient thematic type, which was also adapted for popular seventeenth-century Dutch plays such as P. C. Hooft's *Granida* of 1615.[1] While De Heer has included no narrative, the slashed beret worn by his shepherd is reminiscent of the theater, as is the stagelike foreground space, to which the artist has added a display of varied plants at the lower right. Their finely drawn leaves and the small lizard above them demonstrate the acute responsiveness to nature evident in drawings by all members of the De Heer family.

Contrasts to the arcadian shepherds are the four crude vagabonds in the background, who have set up an informal encampment with their packs and cooking utensils around an old well near the stone arcade. Both Gerrit de Heer and his son Willem often depicted such peasant or gypsy gatherings in the vicinity of ramshackle or ruined buildings, which act as expressive parallels to the rough appearance of the figures (Cat.27).[2] In this drawing, however, the partly classical style of the ruin and the pastoral imagery in the foreground produce a more idealizing effect, further emphasized by the artist's exceptionally refined and finished draftsmanship.

De Heer's minutely hatched and stippled technique, somewhat reminiscent of engraving, allowed him to painstakingly render the different textures of leaves, wood, hair, or fleece by building up tones, using a vocabulary of different pen marks. Also unusual is the artist's use of parchment for his drawing, rather than paper, which had come into widespread use in Europe by the late fourteenth century. The ancestor of paper, parchment or vellum (cured sheepskin or calfskin) allowed medieval scribes and manuscript illuminators to render texts and images of unparalleled durability, clarity, and detail. But although it offers a smoother surface than the finest paper, parchment is more costly to produce, and by the seventeenth century artists rarely used it.[3] De Heer's choice of this manifestly archaic support gives his drawing a charming, oddly eccentric effect, making it seem, in itself, a precious relic of the past.

NOTES

1. As A. M. Kettering discusses in her study of Dutch pastoral art, the fashion for plays and poems of this genre was probably generated by Dutch writers' wish to develop and purify their national language by adapting classical and Renaissance literary traditions. Kettering 1983, 20–21.

2. F. W. Robinson cites three signed De Heer drawings of this type in the British Museum, London, only two of which appear to be by the elder De Heer, who also made two portrait drawings, dated 1634, now in the Groninger Museum voor Stad en Lande (Robinson in Hanover/Wellesley/Providence/Storrs 1969, unpaginated, no. 23).

3. Drawings on parchment were also made by Jacques de Gheyn II (q.v.) and by the Amsterdam peasant painter Pieter Quast (1605/6–47), who, however, preferred graphite or chalk to pen. Rembrandt occasionally printed on vellum impressions of the first state of drypoints, such as *Three Crosses* of 1653 (The National Gallery of Art, Washington, D.C.) and *St. Francis beneath a Tree, Praying* of 1657 (The Pierpont Morgan Library, New York).

JAN DE BISSCHOP
1628–71

A gifted amateur draftsman and etcher, Jan de Bisschop (also know by the Latinized form of his name as Johannes Episcopius) was a lawyer in Amsterdam and The Hague who had close connections with Dutch intellectuals and writers such as Jan Six and Constantijn Huygens the Younger, another amateur draftsman.[1] Having taken his law degree at the University of Leiden, in 1653 De Bisschop married Anna van Baerle, daughter of the celebrated professor and theologian Caspar van Baerle, or Baerleus (1584–1648). As an artist, De Bisschop was most strongly influenced by the Italianate landscapist Bartholomeus Breenbergh (q.v.), two of whose paintings he copied in large etchings. He also designed title pages for books by classical authors and produced figure studies, drawings after famous sculptures and paintings, and views of Rome, although there is no evidence that he ever visited Italy. His deep interest in classical sculpture and Italian painting is evident in his publication of volumes of prints that would strongly influence the training of artists later in the century. *Signorum veterum icones* (Images of ancient sculptures, 1668–69) consists of one hundred prints after classical sculptures, while *Paradigmata graphices variorum artificum* (Examples of the drawings of various artists, 1671) concentrates on prints after sixteenth- and seventeenth-century drawings, most by celebrated Italian artists.[2] In many of his own drawings, however, De Bisschop turned to the most unassuming, unclassical Dutch subjects, presenting them with a dignity and serenity recalling Dutch Italianate landscapes.

NOTES

1. On De Bisschop's life and art, see Van Gelder 1971 and G. Luijten's essay in *Dictionary of Art* 1996, 4:95–96. De Bisschop was the subject of a 1992 exhibition organized by R. E. Jellema and M. Plomp at the Rembrandthuis, Amsterdam (Amsterdam 1992).

2. For a modern reprint and discussion of the *Icones* and the *Paradigmata*, see Van Gelder and Joost 1985.

[29]

Ruined Windmill, c. 1660

Inscriptions: verso, in pencil, *103*; *320*; *J. Ruisdael*

Pen and brown ink, with brown "Bisschop ink," 136 × 84 mm (5⅜ × 3⅞ in.)

Collection George Abrams, Boston, Massachusetts

References: Hanover/Wellesley/Providence/Storrs 1969, unpaginated, no. 60.

Landmarks of the Dutch countryside, windmills were in use in the Netherlands from around 1200 on and were an important factor in the Dutch nation's phenomenal growth and prosperity in the seventeenth century. The wind-driven sails on their crossed blades provided energy to drain the low land for habitation and cultivation and to perform industrial tasks such as grinding grain, sawing wood, and milling paper. Different types were developed for different functions, each with its own distinctive shape and machinery. De Bisschop's small drawing represents a tower mill (*stellingmolen*) used for grinding corn. These tapering cylindrical structures made of stone or brick and topped by a rotatable wooden cap, had large double doors at the base for delivery of the grain and multiple floors marked by windows for various stages of the milling process. Often the miller and his family lived on one or more of the lower floors. Turning the cap to make the blades face the wind was accomplished with a large capstan wheel that was set either at the base of the tower or on an encircling wooden

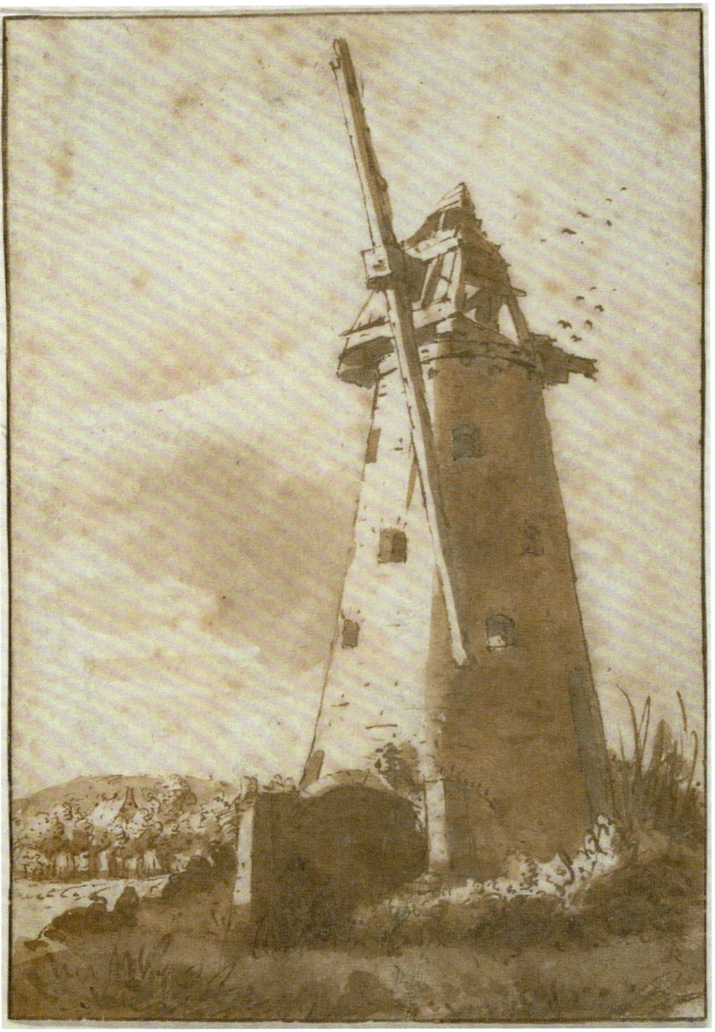

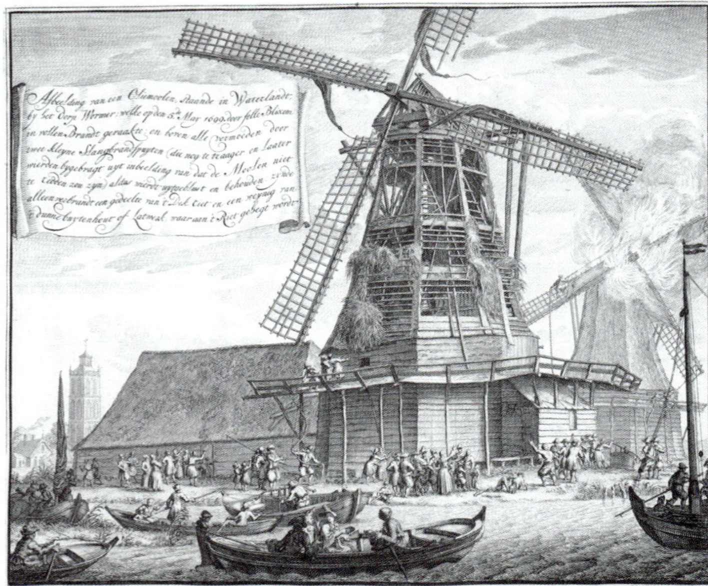

Fig. 129. Laurens Scherm, after Jan van der Heyden, *Windmill in Waterlandt, Burned on 5 May, 1699*, engraving, pl. 21 from Jan van der Heyden, *Beschryving der nieuwlyks uitgevonden en geoctrojeerde slang-brand-spuiten ...*, 2nd ed., Amsterdam, 1735, Smithsonian Institution, Washington, D.C.

stage built halfway up; from there the miller could also rig the sails.[1]

De Bisschop's ruined mill expresses a poignant sense of loss and survival because it stands empty, motionless, and deprived of its intended purpose. Yet its shape remains intact, and the broken fittings remind the viewer of how it once looked and worked. The delivery entrance at the base gaps vacantly, the wooden cap is shattered, and only one broken blade remains, leaning at a slight diagonal. At the opposite side of the tower are the remains of the hoist that once lifted and lowered sacks of grain. A flock of birds rising beyond it suggests that this shell of a structure has become a bird sanctuary. Seen from a low viewpoint, the mill is strongly silhouetted against the sky, rising high above the distant trees and houses across the water at the lower left. De Bisschop's uncanny ability to render the shapes of things in soft but intense light was greatly facilitated by his development of the warm, golden brown ink that came to be known as "bisschopsinkt."[2]

Depictions of windmills fallen into ruin are rare, probably because their functions were so important that they had to be kept in good repair. A very different example dating from later in the century is the engraving of a burned mill (Fig. 129) by Laurens Scherm (fl. 1689–c.1732) after Jan van der Heyden (q.v.) that was made for the second (1735) edition of Jan van der Heyden's treatise on firefighting (see Cat. 46).[3] This oil mill in Waterland near the village of Wormer was struck by lightning on the night of 5 May 1699. Although it was saved by the intervention of fire engines, the illustration shows damage to its blades, thatched roof, and external latticework. At the right background, an intact windmill in flames creates a before-and-after demonstration of the accident.[4]

NOTES

1. For an analysis of various Dutch windmill types with diagrams of their shapes, machinery, and functions, see Stokhuyzen 1962, which also includes material on the history and meaning of windmills. Additional observations on the symbolism of intact windmills may be found in A. K. Wheelock Jr.'s catalogue entry on Rembrandt's *The Mill* in the National Gallery of Art, Washington, D.C. (Wheelock 1995, 237–38 and 240 nn. 35 and 36).

2. According to Willem Goeree, whose treatise on drawing (*Inleiding tot de algemeene teken-konst*) was published in 1697, this unusual ink was made by mixing Indian ink with a small amount of copper red. Goeree 1668, 91. Cited in *Dictionary of Art* 1996, 4:96.

3. The first edition of Jan van der Heyden's *Beschryving der nieuwlyks uitgevonden en geoctrojeerde slang-brand-spuiten en haare wyze van brand-blussen, tegenwoording binnen Amsterdam in gebruik zijnde* (Description of the newly invented and patented hose fire engine and her ways of fighting fires, now in use in Amsterdam) was issued in Amsterdam in 1690. The second edition, published in Amsterdam in 1735, included six additional plates, including plate 21, illustrated here.

4. On Scherm's print see Freedberg 1980, 66–67, fig. 140, and Van der Heyden/Multhauf 1996, 98.

JACOB VAN RUISDAEL
1628/29–82

Ruisdael's vast oeuvre (almost 700 paintings, more than 130 drawings, and 13 etchings) has recently been catalogued by S. Slive, whose monumental corpus underlines the exceptional variety of motifs developed by the artist: Ruisdael specialized in northern landscapes with Dutch, Westphalian, or Scandinavian scenery. The latter (especially the dramatic waterfalls) was borrowed from Allart van Everdingen (q.v.), who had traveled to Norway and Sweden and settled in Haarlem in 1645. Ruisdael's subjects include forests, grain fields, waterfalls, windmills and watermills, townscapes, panoramas, winter scenes, seascapes, views of castles, and—of particular importance here—the ruins of both buildings and trees.[1] In developing his new solid, structural approach to landscape in the late 1640s, Ruisdael departed from the more monochromatic "tonal" approach of artists of the previous generation. Nature seems less tame in his works, which often present a dramatic dialogue between earth and sky or between different aspects of nature such as rocks and moving water. These juxtapositions, along with masterful handling of light and shadow, reveal Ruisdael's ability to capture landscapes that appear to be alive within a temporal process. It is not surprising that he was so often drawn to ruined castles and monasteries, although he never painted Italianate scenery with Roman ruins. Scholars have debated the interpretation of his works, which some have tended to see as visual sermons on the notion of transience.[2]

Ruisdael's teachers are not documented.[3] He may have studied first with his father Isaack (1599–1677), a Haarlem frame maker and picture dealer, and possibly with his uncle, Salomon van Ruysdael (1600/1603–1670), or with Cornelis Vroom (1591–1661).

In 1648 he joined the St. Luke's guild of Haarlem. In about 1650 he traveled around the region of the Dutch-German border, probably with Nicolaes Berchem (q.v.), where he studied Castle Bentheim as well as the local half-timbered houses and watermills. During the 1650s he settled in Amsterdam. His adult baptism in the Dutch Reformed Church was recorded there in 1657, and he purchased citizenship in 1659. A document of 8 July 1660 declares that Meindert Hobbema (1638–1709) had been Ruisdael's student for some years. Among his other students and close followers was Jan van Kessel (1641/42–80). According to Houbraken, Ruisdael never married because he cared for his ailing father for much of his adult life.[4]

NOTES

1. Slive 2001.
2. Symbolic, moralizing interpretations of Ruisdael's work have been put forward in Wiegand 1971; in J. Bruyn's essay "Toward a Scriptural Reading of Dutch Landscape" in Amsterdam/Boston/Philadelphia 1987–88, esp. 98–100; and in Walford 1991, 15–36. S. Slive, who takes a more moderate approach, believes that motifs such as waterfalls should be given vanitas readings only in works with an obviously symbolic program, such as *The Jewish Cemetery* (versions in the Detroit Institute of Arts, no. 26.3, and the Staatliche Kunstsammlungen, Dresden, no. 1502). Slive 2001, 154.
3. For a chronology of Ruisdael's life and dated works, see Slive 2001, 1–6, and Walford 1991, 4–14.
4. Houbraken 1718–21, 3 (1721):65.

[30]
The Ruined Cottage, c. 1655

Inscriptions: monogrammed lower right corner, *JvR* (in ligature)

Black chalk and gray wash on white paper, 200 × 275 mm (7⅞ × 10¹³⁄₁₆ in.)

Thaw Collection, The Pierpont Morgan Library, New York

References: Feitama II, Notatie der Teekeningen, 45; Feitama II, NdT 1297; Josi 1821, 2: unpaginated, under "Jacob van Ruisdael"; De Vries 1915, 39, no. 126; Huffel 1921, 63, no. 144; Cambridge 1958, no. 33; Poughkeepsie 1976, no. 41; Washington/Denver/Fort Worth 1977, 72–74, no. 71; Giltay 1980, 156, 160, 190, no. 15, fig. 24; The Hague/Cambridge 1981–82, no. 71; Washington and elsewhere 1985–87, 82–83, no. 42; Broos 1987, 210; Davies 1992, 75–76; Slive 2001, 563, no. D95; New York 2002, 21–22, no. 9.

Ruisdael's frequent depictions of ruins usually involve much larger and more imposing medieval or Renaissance structures such as Egmond Castle at Egmond aan den Hoef (Fig. 10) or the early sixteenth-century manor house near Amsterdam that was known as Kostverloren (Lost Cost) because of its perpetually collapsing foundations.[1] By contrast, this anonymous little structure, a rustic cottage fallen into ruin, is modest in size and type, but it inspired the artist to produce one of the most memorable of all his works. Indeed, the subject is artfully interpreted in ways that transcend literal recording of a particular place.

Centered in the picture space, the cottage and grassy surrounding are captured in soft touches of chalk and delicate washes that imply weathering and age, making the viewer aware of how natural processes have acted on the

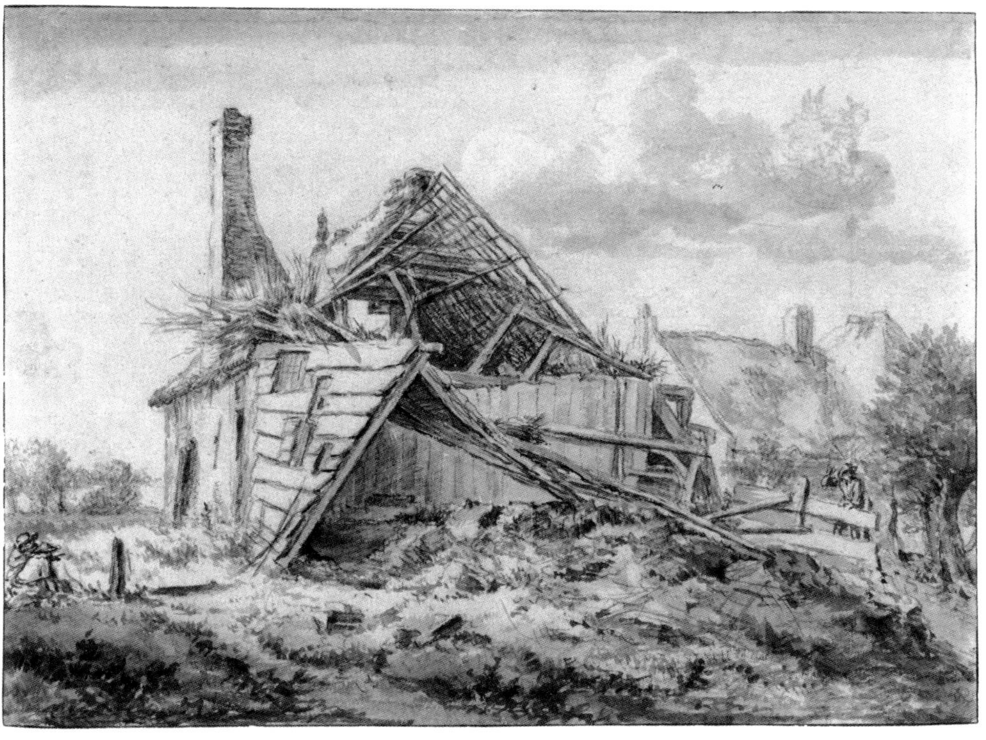

building, gradually but inexorably transforming it into another version of its original self. Ruisdael's drawing might be seen, in a sense, as the biography of a ruin, since his presentation charts the unfolding of the process itself. Contrast of the stable vertical accent of the brick chimney, still solidly intact, with the falling diagonals of the skeletal roof with exposed scaffolding is taken to yet another stage in the repeating tilt of a collapsing wall. From the top, one's attention slides toward the ground following the pull of gravity on the slowly deteriorating structure. As a result, the viewer is encouraged to consider what the building once was but equally to imagine what it will eventually become. Another point of reference is offered by the undamaged houses at the right background. The two seated figures at the left and the man leaning on the fence at the far right appear to contemplate the cottage, encouraging the observer to do likewise.[2]

There is a possibility that Ruisdael intended this highly finished drawing as the preparatory study for a painting. At least four painted copies of his composition by different artists have been identified, each showing different figures. S. Slive suggests that they may have been based either upon a lost painting by Ruisdael or upon a print by Cornelis Brouwer (1733?–1803) after a drawing by Cornelis Ploos van Amstel (1726–98) that carefully records Ruisdael's drawing, including the same figures.[3]

NOTES

1. Egmond Castle inspired two of Ruisdael's finest paintings of ruins: *The Jewish Cemetery* (versions in the Staatliche Kunstsammlungen, Dresden, and the Detroit Institute of Arts, Fig. 11) and *Landscape with the Ruins of Egmond Castle at Egmond aan den Hoef* in the Art Institute of Chicago (Fig. 10). On Ruisdael's many depictions of Kostverloren, see Slive 1988.

2. The possibility that the figures may have been added by a later artist has been raised by J. S. Turner, who points out that that an early owner of the drawing, Sybrand II Feitama (1694–1748), kept notations on drawings in his family collection indicating that he and his father Isaac (and possibly his grandfather Sybrand I) commissioned artists to "embellish" drawings by Ruisdael and others with staffage and additional finishing details. J. S. Turner in New York 2002, 22.

3. On later copies after Ruisdael's *Ruined Cottage*, see Slive 2001, 563 and 654 and J. S. Turner in New York 2002, 21.

[31]

Landscape with a Half-Timbered House and a Blasted Tree, 1653

Inscriptions: lower right, partially legible signature and date of 1653

Oil on canvas, 67.4 × 82 cm (26⁹⁄₁₆ × 32¼ in.)

Collection of the Speed Art Museum, Louisville, Kentucky, no. 1998.3

References: Smith 1829–42, 292; Parthey 1863–64, 2:460, no. 96; Hofstede de Groot 4 (1916):250, no. 793; Berlin 1921, no. 893; Rosenberg 1928, 490; Slive 2001, 410–11, no. 577.

This landscape records Ruisdael's experience of the scenic area along the border of the eastern part of the Dutch provinces and western Germany, which he visited with Nicolaes Berchem (q.v.) during the early 1650s. Unlike the flatter, more cultivated and populated countryside around Haarlem and Amsterdam, the upper Rhine district of Westphalia features much rougher and more uneven terrain, with dense forests, waterfalls, and picturesque half-timbered houses that display a distinctive framework of anchor beams with vertical plank gables and thatched or tiled roofs.[1] As W. Stechow observed, this is territory that would have appeared quite foreign to Dutch eyes, even though its mountains are less than Alpine in scale.[2]

The extreme irregularity of Ruisdael's design intensifies the viewer's impression that everything present in this scene belongs to an ongoing transformative temporal process. Even the house at the right, the most stable form in the landscape, has a well-worn roof and walls; dead branches rise behind it from the midst of a living tree. Smoke puffs from its chimney, while at the top of its stone stairway, a woman leans out of a half-door to observe a man playing with a lively dog. Ruisdael often sets up expressive contrasts in his landscapes between manmade structures and those formed by nature. Here a huge twisted willow stump rises at a sharp angle over the rushing stream at the left foreground, as if pointing toward the house beyond.[3] Large sawn logs from another dead tree lie beside the small cascade of water.

Landscapes with waterfalls and rushing streams constitute the largest category of Ruisdael's paintings, with more than 150 examples of this type attributed to him (see also Cat. 32). Houbraken, whose comments indicate how popular these paintings must have been, suggested that the waterfall be understood as a play on the artist's name ("Ruis-dael" means "noisy valley").[4] Certain more recent scholars have interpreted the motif as a pointed comment on human life, which, like rushing water, never stops and is often turbulent: a metaphor for the fleeting quality of earthy existence and the vanity of human effort.[5] On yet another level, Jan Luyken (1649–1712) described the deafening tumult of the waterfall as a symbol of the earthly hubbub that contrasts to the silence of God.[6]

While it seems unlikely that the Louisville painting incorporates any overtly symbolic or moralizing program, there is no question that the juxtaposition of the dead tree with moving water is an effective way of embodying time's passing. Ruisdael's assured brushwork vividly captures the polished hardness of the weathered stump, stripped of its bark, and the foaming eddies of water rushing below it: materially opposite motifs that express different velocities of change within the same temporal process.

NOTES

1. See Slive 2001, 23 and 27 n. 10, in which the author cites Schepers 1976 for the analysis of Westphalian houses and castles.

2. Stechow 1966, 167. Dutch artists' depictions of Rhine landscape have been explored in several exhibitions cited by Stechow: Krefeld 1938, Düsseldorf 1953, and Bonn 1960–61.

3. In the foreground of Ruisdael's *View of Egmond on the Sea* (dated 1648, The Currier Gallery of Art, Manchester, New Hampshire, no. 1950.4), a similarly twisted tree looms over and seems almost to gesture toward a more distant structure, in this case a church. See Fig. 59.

4. Houbraken 1718–21, 3 (1721):65–66. Cited in Slive 2001, 154.

5. On the vanitas implications of the waterfall, see J. Bruyn who cites, among other references, the following emblem by Jan Luyken from *De bykorf des gemoeds*, Amsterdam, 1711: "Weg water aller idelheid, / Dat stadig na beneden glyd" (Away water all of vanity, / that steadily glides downward). Amsterdam/Boston/Philadelphia 1987–88, 99. J. Walford, who has related biblical texts to many of Ruisdael's paintings, compares rushing torrents to the tumult of earthly life, finding implications of mortality in the association between flowing water and time. Walford 1991, 143.

6. Jan Luyken's emblem "Tot verdooving" (Until deafening) from his *Beschouwing der Wereld* of 1708, which also points out the pun on Ruisdael's name, includes the following verses: "Wel aan de Leven werd bedaard, / Dat nu zo lange en veelde daagen, / Bewoonder van het Ruis-dal waard, / Een Plaas die 't Leven moest mishaagen. / Ô Ruis-dal, aller ydelheid, / Van 't woelend en krioelend leven, / Der wereld geeft in't ryk der tyd. / Men moet u vlieden en begreeven" (Indeed, tranquility came to this life, / which for so long now and for so many days, / inhabited this valley

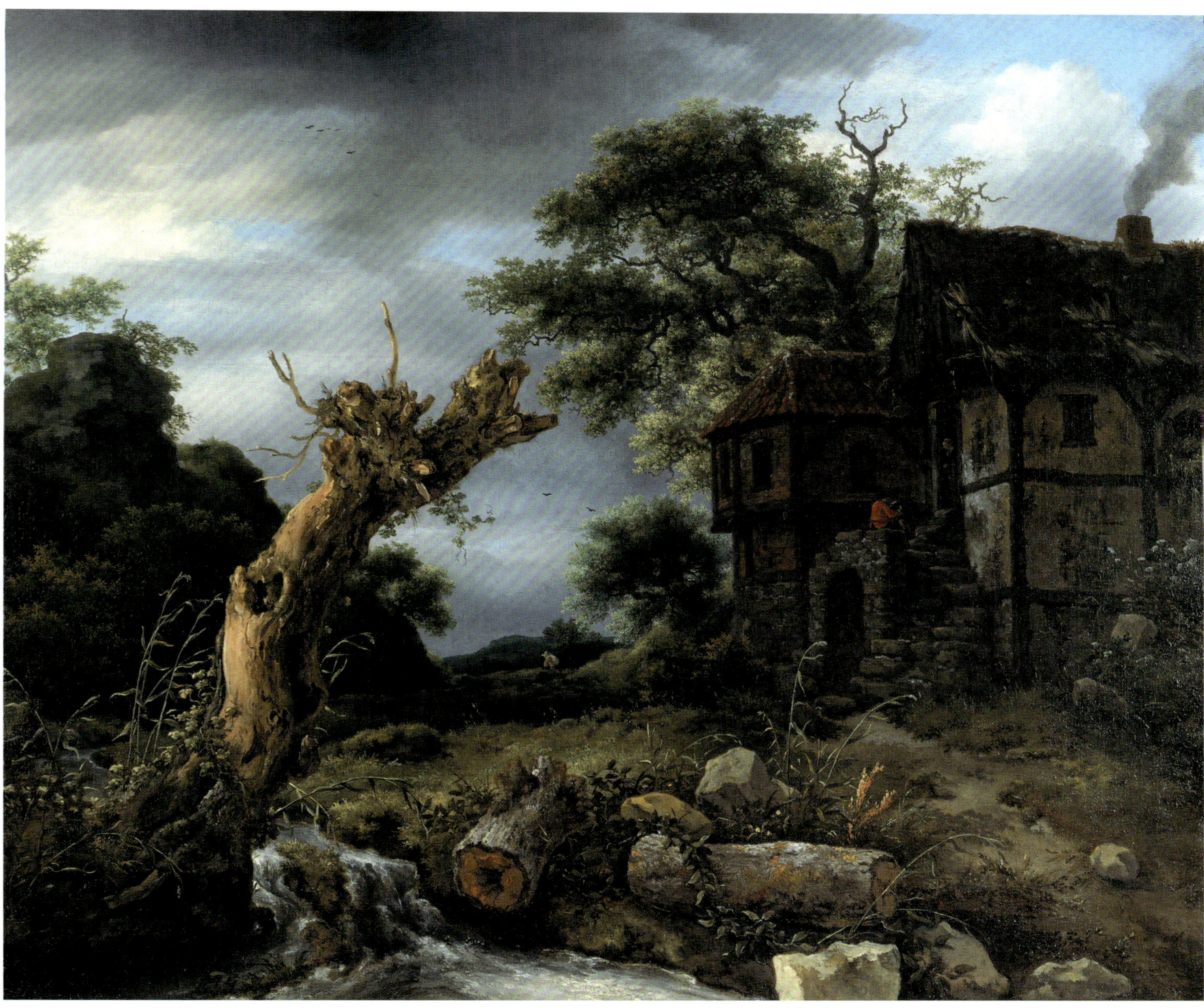

[31]

of noise [*Ruis-dal*], / a place that must displease this life. / Oh valley of noise [*Ruis-dal*], all vanity, / from the turbulent and teeming life, / that the world gives in the realm of time, / one must flee and forsake you). This passage was translated and interpreted by J. Giltay in Amsterdam/Boston/Philadelphia 1987–88, 451 and n. 9. See also Wiegand 1971, 87–98, 265 n. 491, and Brom 1957, 212.

[32]

Landscape with a Dead Tree, c. 1660–70

Inscriptions: signed, lower left, *JRuisdael* (first two letters in ligature)

Oil on canvas, 99.2 × 131 cm (39 1/16 × 51 5/8 in.)

The Cleveland Museum of Art, Mr. and Mrs. H. Marlatt Fund, 1967.63

References: Hofstede de Groot 4 (1912):74–75, no. 220; Rosenberg 1928, 140; Simon 1930, 74; Tokyo/Kyoto 1976, no. 34; Cleveland 1982, 269, no. 118. Walford 1991, 117 (as late 1650s); Slive 2001, 172–74, no. 169 and color repr. (as mid- to late 1660s).

Dead trees, waterfalls, and ruined buildings play major roles in Ruisdael's paintings, alone or in combination, where they give visible form to the process of time. This handsome horizontal landscape includes all three within a setting whose sandy ground is similar to the terrain of the hilly dunes around Haarlem. The medieval ruin largely screened by trees at the right background cannot be identified, but its square, crenellated tower recalls aspects of Brederode Castle at

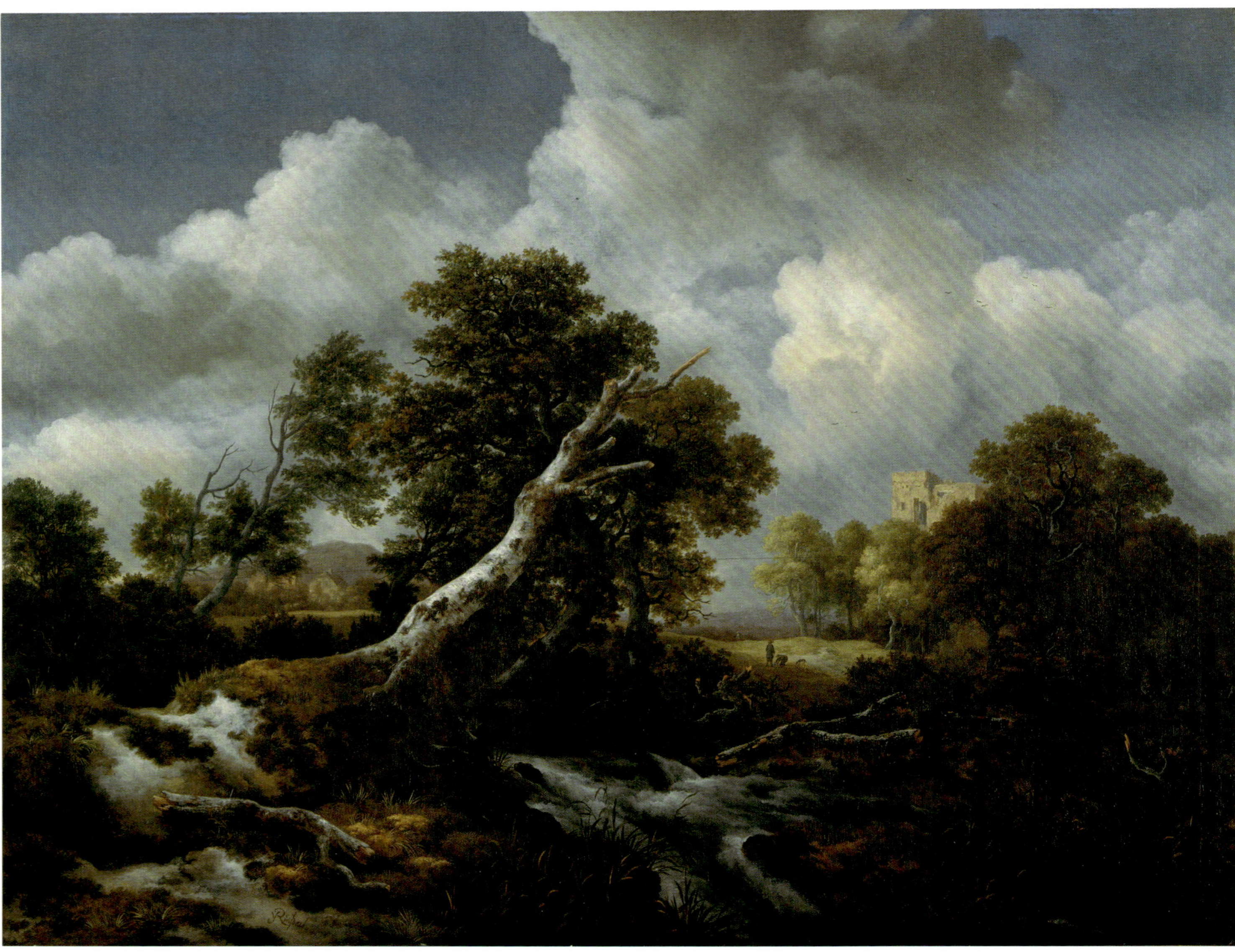

[32]

Santpoort near Haarlem—a frequently depicted site that was the subject of an early painting by Ruisdael now in the Philadelphia Museum of Art (see Fig. 109) as well as numerous paintings and works on paper by other Dutch artists (Cats. 1, 2a, 7, and 8).[1] Like other Dutch landscapists, Ruisdael did not make literal records of what he saw but was in the habit of producing composite scenes, bringing together motifs of diverse origin. Accordingly, the little waterfall that foams over a rocky bed at the center foreground could not have been studied in the Haarlem dunes. This kind of imagery, which appears in Ruisdael's landscapes of the early 1650s (Cat. 31), can be traced to his experiences in the upper Rhine district of Westphalia, where he traveled with Nicolaes Berchem (q.v.) around 1650.[2]

In the Cleveland painting, a large, dead beech, with smooth, hoop-marked bark palely silhouetted against the dark foliage of the oak behind it, leans toward the right over the waterfall. Its broken branches are scattered on the ground at left and right.[3] Ruisdael often juxtaposed such trees with rushing water (Cat. 31), using the diagonal tilt of a dead or fallen trunk to link different spatial zones. Here the beech's smooth body and truncated arms draw attention to the sunlit landscape beyond the shadowed foreground where two men appear with a dog. The tower of the distant ruin that rises from the illuminated stand of trees beyond is further masked by deep foreground foliage at the right, while smaller houses emerge in sunlight at the far left. As in many of Ruisdael's paintings, especially his later works, contrasts of sun and shadow on the ground seem projected from masses of cloud whose puffy cumulus shapes here reiterate the irregular forms of darker foliage below them. No artist was more adept than Ruisdael at the demanding representation of clouds—natural presences that have shape without density, simultaneously absorb and block light, and can take on a multitude of forms that reveal the unseen movements of the wind. That the depiction of clouds was considered a particular test of artistic knowledge and virtuosity is indicated in Gerard de Lairesse's (q.v.) comment in his 1707 treatise on painting: "Een schoone lucht is een proefstuk van een deftig Meester" (A beautiful sky is a test piece for a true master).[4]

NOTES

1. Aside from the painting in the John G. Johnson Collection of the Philadelphia Museum of Art (panel, 30.2 × 27.8 cm), Ruisdael also made a drawing, *Farmstead with the Ruins of Brederode Castle*, c. 1646, Staatliche Kunstsammlungen, Kupferstichkabinett, Dresden, no. C 1277. Repr. Slive 2001, 527, no. D47.

2. On Ruisdael's depictions of waterfalls and the symbolic interpretations that have been attributed to this motif, see the discussion under Cat. 31.

3. Ruisdael, who has been called "the father of tree illustration," was so exacting in his depictions of various tree species that oaks, beeches, willows, elms, hawthorns, and others can be identified not only by their leaves and bark, but also by their patterns of growth. The European beech (*Fagus sylvatica*) sprouts lateral shoots (an arboreal phenomenon known as reiteration) less frequently than many other trees, and its dead branches fall off early and easily, which accounts for the smooth extension of the dead beech trunk in the Cleveland painting. For an art-historical and arboreal analysis of the trees in Ruisdael's paintings, see Ashton, Slive, and Davies 1982, esp. 14 and 15.

4. Gerard de Lairesse, *Het Groot Schilderboek*, Amsterdam, 1707, 371; quoted in Esmeijer 1977, 127. On the depiction of skies in Dutch landscape, see also Walsh 1991.

ADAM PYNACKER
1620–73

Son of a prominent and wealthy wine merchant and shipper from Delft, Adam Pynacker was born in the Dutch port town of Schiedam in 1620.[1] Documents imply that he started out in his father's business, since he did not register in the St. Luke's guild there. A three-year stay in Italy, mentioned by Houbraken, probably occurred between 1645 and 1648, for there are no records of his presence in Holland during this period.[2] That he was not listed among the Netherlandish confraternity of painters in Italy (Schildersbent) suggests that he was there for commercial rather than artistic reasons.

Pynacker's career shift to painting seems to have been influenced by his close association at the end of the 1640s with Adam Pick (c. 1622–before 1666), a Delft wine merchant and innkeeper who was also a painter and art dealer. His earliest paintings (small landscapes with Italianate lighting) date from this period. In 1658 Pynacker married Eva de Geest, daughter of the well-known Leeuwarden portraitist Wybrand de Geest (1592–c. 1661) and a member of the aristocratic Uylenburgh family to which Rembrandt's (q.v.) wife Saskia also belonged. Pynacker's marriage documents indicate that he converted to Roman Catholicism at this time, as further indicated in subsequent baptismal records of the couple's two children.

By 1661 the artist had moved to Amsterdam, where he spent the remainder of his life. His large-scale landscapes of this period, often in an upright format, display powerful light/dark contrasts and frequently feature hunters or travelers in mountainous Italianate settings with prominent foreground trees. Many of these imposing works were probably commissioned as decorations for the large Amsterdam townhouses being built by wealthy middle-class merchants in this commercial center of the Dutch Republic. Pynacker was buried in 1673 in the Roman Catholic cemetery of Amsterdam's Nieuwe Kerk. The fact that he was then living on the Rozengracht, an impoverished district of the city, suggests that he may have faced professional and financial hardship at the end of his life, as did many of his contemporaries—including Rembrandt, who died in the same area in 1669.

NOTES

1. Biographical material on Pynacker is based on L. B. Harwood's monograph on the artist, which includes discussion and full transcriptions of the documents (Harwood 1988, 13–26 and 179–210) and on her biographical essay in *Dictionary of Art* 1996, 25:754–56.

2. Houbraken 1718–21, 2 (1719):96.

[33]

Landscape with Hunters, c. 1665

Inscription: signed lower right, *APynacker* (the A and P in ligature)

Oil on canvas, 82 × 70.5 cm (32¼ × 27¾ in.)

John and Mable Ringling Museum of Art, The State Art Museum of Florida, Sarasota, Florida, SN896

References: Redford 1888, 2:315; Hofstede de Groot 9 (1926):526, no. 14; Robinson and Wilson 1980, 85–86, no. 113; Sutton 1986, 281; Harwood 1988, 34, 96–97, no. 81 and color pl. XVII; Montreal 1990, 158–59, no. 49; The Hague/San Francisco 1990–91, 360–63, no. 48; Williamstown/Sarasota 1994–95, 60–61, no. 12.

The vertical format of this spectacularly fine landscape gives striking prominence to the rising forms of ancient birches and oaks, whose gnarled stumps and broken or mossy trunks loom within the shadowed foreground, dwarfing the two hunters just beyond. Within this densely wooded area, which frames a softly illuminated mountain vista, touches of sunlight delineate the irregular twists of leaves and grasses, igniting with color a stalk of crimson hollyhocks and other wildflowers while defining the skin of peeling birch bark on the shattered stump at the left. Descriptions of this well-known painting have frequently drawn attention to Pynacker's distinctive use of "razor-thin" white lines that model forms yet seem superimposed on the surface of the painting, intensifying the sparkling effects of sunlight.[1] Indeed, Pynacker's unusual and highly effective handling of light has long been recognized, as indicated by Houbraken's praise written in the early eighteenth century: "Artful, natural and amusingly painted: here a copse of trees in the blue shadow: there a sunlight coming down, which paints the green foliage with glowing sparkles."[2]

Landscapes featuring ruined trees or buildings that show nature's cyclical processes are sometimes interpreted as expressions of the inevitable decay and death of all earthly things, a point often made in vanitas prints and emblems of the seventeenth century (Cats. 77–79). In Pynacker's painting, however, the trees in the foreground remain the most tangible and the most visually lively presences in the scene. Touched with vibrant highlights and leaning inwardly at diagonals, their irregular, broken shapes frame the pair of motionless hunters in the middle ground. Beyond these quiet figures, herdsmen and cows make their way slowly up a sunlit hill at the left, while overlapping mountains in the distance seem to gradually dissolve in the radiant light. As a result, the most evanescent things in this scene appear the most solid and immediately accessible within the present moment.

Because Pynacker seldom dated his paintings, his chronology has been difficult to establish. The Sarasota landscape, whose upright format and compositional layout appear in a number of other later works, has been dated to the middle or late 1660s—a time when the artist was filling commissions for wealthy Amsterdam merchants seeking decorations for their elegant townhouses.[3] How such scenes were appreciated by Pynacker's contemporaries is suggested in a poem of 1665, written by the artist's friend Pieter Verhoek (1633–1702) to praise his recently completed paintings for the house of Cornelis Backer, director of the Dutch East India Company. In lively couplets, Verhoek evokes the boldness of Pynacker's brush, densely laden foregrounds, and weathered or mossy trees, concluding that even at times of care, or in the winter when snow covers the ground and the trees are bare, Herr Backer can "... contemplate these leafy crowns. / The green of the foliage, a Summer for the eye. / Here worn out by cares of state, he can unstring / his bow, reveling in their contemplation."[4]

NOTES

1. Robinson and Wilson 1980, 85; Harwood 1988, 96 and 97, n. 4; B. P. J. Broos in The Hague/San Francisco 1990–91, 362; L. Harwood in Williamstown/Sarasota 1994–95, 60.

2. "Ik heb 'er van gezien waar in zig een bosch met dicht geboomte liet zien, Konstig, natuurlyck en vermakelyk geschildert; hier een troep boomen in de blaauwe lommer; daar een invallend zonnelicht, welke de groene meijen met gloeijende tintelingen schildert ..." Harwood 1988, 199. Translation by B. P. J. Broos in The Hague/San Francisco 1990–91, 360.

3. A close comparison is Pynacker's undated *Mountainous Landscape with Waterfall* in the Mauritsthuis, The Hague, of 1665–70 (Harwood 1988, no. 82, fig. 82). Harwood states that the Sarasota painting "belongs compositionally with the finest of Pynacker's output of the mid-1660s" but also notes that its emphasis on elegantly curved lines may support the later date of 1670 suggested by F. W. Robinson and W. Wilson (Harwood 1988, 34 and Robinson and Wilson 1980, 85–86).

4. "... dees bladerryke kruinen, / Beschouwen, groen van loof, een Somer voor het oog. / Hier kan hy afgesloot door staatszorg, weer den boog / Ontspannen; zig in dees bespiegeling verlusten." Verhoek's poem, quoted in Houbraken's account of Pynacker (Houbraken 1718–21, 2 [1719]:97–99), is fully reproduced in its original text and translated into English in Harwood 1988, 32.

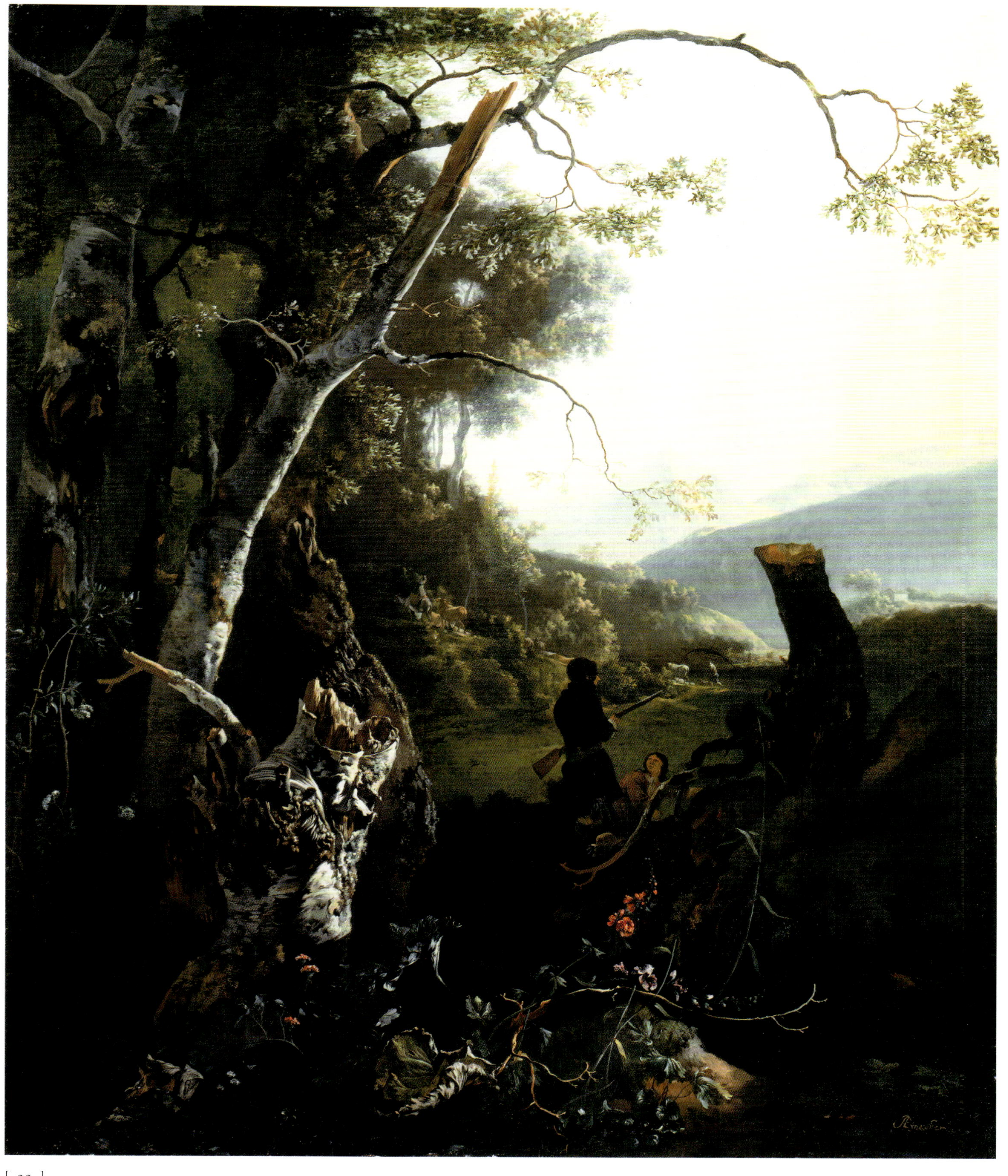

[33]

FLOODS, FIRES, AND OTHER DISASTERS

LUDOLF BACKHUYSEN
1630–1708

The son of a scribe, Backhuysen (also spelled Bakhuyzen or Backhuisen) trained as a clerk in the German town of Emden before moving to Amsterdam in 1649 to join the Bartolotti trading company, where his fine handwriting soon attracted notice.[1] Examples of the masterful calligraphy he produced throughout his life are preserved in the Kupferstichkabinett, Dresden, the Rijksprentenkabinet, Amsterdam, and the British Museum, London. A related activity was Backhuysen's production of intricate pen drawings, primarily of marine subjects on prepared canvas, panel, and parchment. These works were probably inspired by pen drawings made by Willem van de Velde II (1633–1707) in the 1650s. During the early part of his career, Backhuysen apparently thought of himself primarily as a calligrapher, for he did not join the painters' guild in Amsterdam until 1663, after which he rapidly attracted major commissions. With the move to England in 1672 of Willem van de Velde II and his father Willem I (1611–93), Backhuysen became the leading marine painter in the Netherlands. His international fame was so great that Peter the Great, czar of Russia, visited his studio and reportedly took drawing lessons from him. Other admirers included Cosimo II de' Medici, grand duke of Tuscany, and Frederick I of Prussia, elector of Saxony.

Houbraken's extensive account of the artist states that Backhuysen learned marine painting from Hendrick Dubbels (1620/21–1676?) and Allart van Everdingen (q.v.).[2] Backhuysen's early, more monochromatic works also show the influence of Simon de Vlieger (q.v.). Later paintings, made after 1665, are much brighter in color and more daringly dramatic in design and in their representation of weather conditions. While Backhuysen's subjects were often based upon actual battles or events of his time, his intention was not precise historical documentation but rather glorification of the Dutch nation and of Amsterdam's mercantile might. At the age of seventy-one, he took up etching for the first time in a series of views of the river IJ and the sea (*D'Y stroom en zeegezichten*), whose title page shows the Maid of Amsterdam in a triumphal chariot.

NOTES

1. Biographical information on Backhuysen is based on A. K. Wheelock Jr.'s account of his life in Wheelock 1995, 14, and on B. P. J Broos's essay in *Dictionary of Art* 1996, 3:84–86.

2. Houbraken 1718–21, 2 (1721):236–44.

[34]

Ships in Distress off a Rocky Coast, 1667

Inscriptions: on rock at lower center, *LBackh / 1667*

Oil on canvas, 114.3 × 167.3 cm (45 × 65⅞ in.)

Ailsa Mellon Bruce Fund, National Gallery of Art, Washington, D.C., 1985.29.1

References: Sutton 1986, 306; Goedde 1986, 142; Goedde 1989, 177, 202–204, fig. 161; Minneapolis/Toledo/Los Angeles 1990–91, no. 4; Walsh 1991a, repr.; Wheelock 1995, 14–18.

In this large and exceptionally dramatic scene, three large cargo vessels flying Dutch flags battle rough water and high winds that have swept them dangerously near a rocky coast.[1] The extreme peril of their situation is indicated by the remains of a wrecked ship at the right foreground, whose sunken mast displays a ragged flag and whose cargo is tossing about in the waves. The site is apparently far from home, as suggested by the enormous rocks in the foreground that dwarf the endangered ships—an ominous contrast to the familiar beaches and dunes of the Dutch shoreline.[2] Eroded by wind and water, these natural ruins take on a strangely forbidding aspect, for the one at the far left recalls a shouting face in profile, while the boulder beside it rises like a hand as if to warn off the approaching vessels. Similarly irregular shapes are reiterated in the boiling clouds beyond, which become almost tangibly solid presences as they pass through tones from pale golden-pink and gray at the upper left to near-black in the center. Backhuysen has made the pull and power of the water alarmingly real by adding airborne droplets flicked from a brush loaded with lead white paint.[3] In the midst of the gale, the gilded wooden lions attached to the bows of the vessels in the foreground seem to roar in response to the plunging of their crafts.

A precedent for this scene, painted by an artist of the previous generation, is Simon de Vlieger's (q.v.) *Ships in Distress on a Rocky Coast* of about 1645 (Fig. 130), which features a similar interplay between menacing rocks and storm clouds, although sky and sea are more distinctly separated by a continuous horizon.[4] Beyond the rocks in De Vlieger's painting are foundering ships, a lifeboat, and several sailors making their way onto the rocky shore. In the Washington painting, in which all elements of the scene are enlarged so that their relationships become more dynamic, the storm-tossed sailors continue struggling to save their vessels and themselves despite the threat of impending destruction. The ship in the center with foresheet reefed remains under human control, while the men on board the ship at the right,

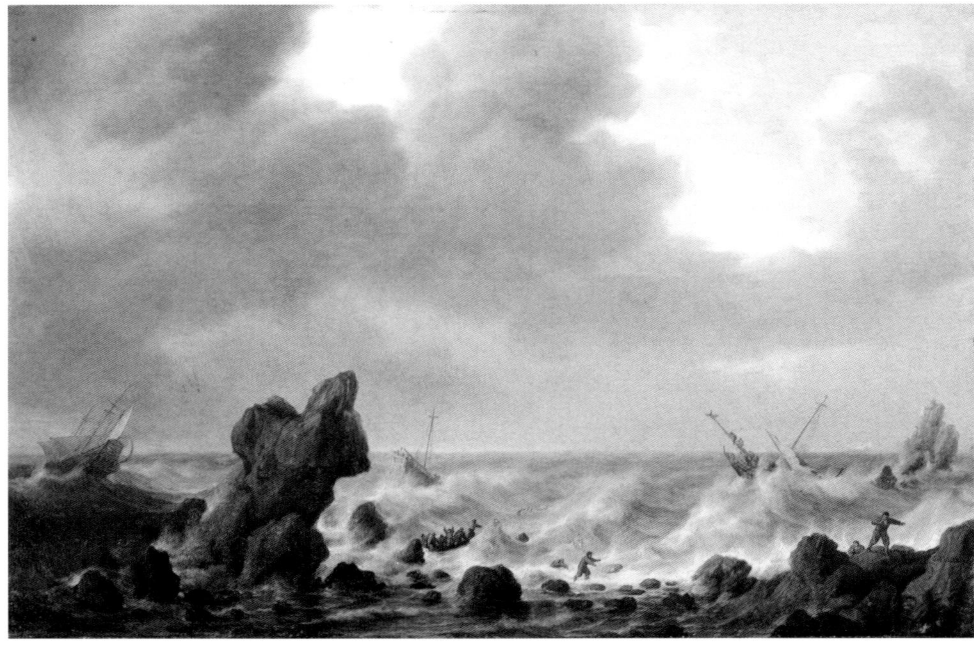

Fig. 130. Simon de Vlieger, *Ships in Distress on a Rocky Coast*, c. 1645, oil on panel, Fogg Art Museum, Harvard University Art Museums, Cambridge, Massachusetts

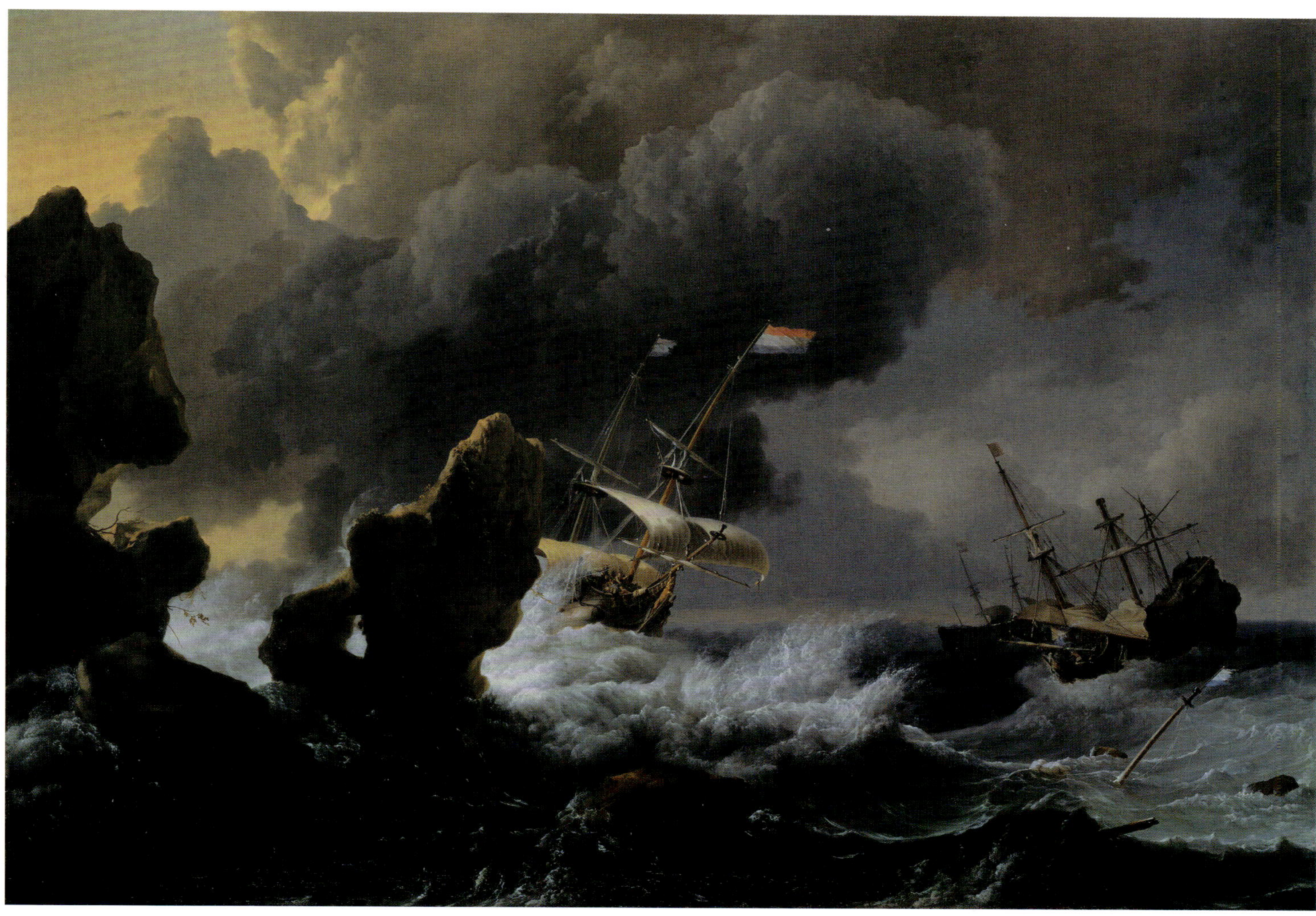

whose rear mast has broken off, have dropped the sails and sawed off the top section of the mainmast to prevent it from snapping.[5] Although the danger of collision between these rapidly approaching ships clearly exists, the brightening sky at the upper left and the sailors' concentrated actions imply that they may yet escape disaster.[6]

In a nation whose citizens were closely involved with the sea, marine painting became a popular artistic specialty, although shipwreck scenes (not surprisingly) were produced rather infrequently. Nonetheless, marine tempests with endangered vessels appear often in Netherlandish paintings and prints from the sixteenth century on. L. O. Goedde has explored their rhetorical parallels with tempest themes in Christian and classical literature, in which storm-tossed boats may allude to such concepts as the Ship of State or the turbulent voyage of human life in its quest for salvation.[7] While it seems likely that the depiction of brave Dutch sailors navigating dangerous, distant seas had particular interest for viewers of this period, the sheer visceral excitement of this scene (no less powerful today) seems sufficient reason for its existence. Dutch artists also produced memorable depictions of domestic landscapes menaced by floods from broken dikes (Cats. 36–38), but marine paintings such as Backhuysen's yield an even higher level of dramatic tension by showing ships and men caught between land and sea in a way that makes solid ground appear as much a menace as churning water.

NOTES

1. These three-masted ships can be identified as the new type of cargo vessel known as the *fluit* ("flute") that the Dutch invented at Hoorn in the 1590s to haul bulky freight such as timber, hemp, and tar. Fluits made possible the development of the great Dutch maritime empire, for their round sterns, broad bottoms, and small decks allowed them to be sailed with a much smaller crew than traditional merchant ships required. G. S. Keyes in Minneapolis/Toledo/Los Angeles 1990–91, 41–42.

2. A. K. Wheelock Jr. has suggested that these ships may have been following a trade route to or from Scandinavia or the Baltic—major thoroughfares for the transport of grain and lumber whose coastlines had the kinds of cliffs and rocky shores seen in this painting. Wheelock 1995, 16.

3. Wheelock 1995, 18.

4. A date of c. 1645 has been suggested by J. Kelch and G. S. Keyes for a similar scene by De Vlieger (Alfred Bader Collection, Milwaukee): *Ship in Distress off a Rocky Coast*. Minneapolis/Toledo/Los Angeles 1990–91, 186–88, no. 46, repr.

5. Wheelock 1995, 15.

6. While Wheelock believes that Backhuysen meant to create the impression that the men will prevail against the forces of nature (Wheelock 1995, 15), Goedde is of the opinion that few of these sailors will survive collision with the cliffs (Goedde 1986, 142).

7. Goedde 1986 and Goedde 1989.

ESAIAS VAN DE VELDE
1587–1630

The numerous Dutch artists named Van de Velde, also represented in this exhibition by Esaias's second cousin Jan van de Velde II (q.v.), included painters, draftsmen, and printmakers. Esaias was the son and possibly the pupil of Hans van de Velde (1552–1609), a Protestant art dealer who settled in Amsterdam in 1585, having fled the religious turmoil of Antwerp.[1] Esaias may also have studied in Amsterdam with Gillis van Conninxloo (1544–1607) and David Vinckboons (1576–before 1633). In 1609, the year of his father's death and the signing of the Twelve Year Truce with the Spanish, Esaias moved to Haarlem, where he married Katelyna Maertens, with whom he would have four children. In 1612 he joined the Haarlem guild, the same year as Willem Buytewech (q.v.) and Hercules Segers (q.v.). The teacher of Jan van Goyen (q.v.) in Haarlem, Esaias van de Velde moved by 1618 to The Hague, where he spent the remainder of his career. Although he also produced genre scenes and a few narratives, his most influential contributions, both as a painter and printmaker, were his innovative naturalistic landscapes, whose directness of vision and straightforward techniques depart strongly from the ornamental linear grace of the previous mannerist generation.

NOTE

1. For biographical material on Esaias van de Velde, see J. G. C. A. Briels in Keyes 1984, 20–26; P. C. Sutton's biographical essay in Amsterdam/Boston/Philadelphia 1987–88, 497; and I. Haberland's account of the Van de Velde families in *Dictionary of Art* 32 (1996):137–40.

[35]

Repairing the Broken Dike on the River Lek by Vianen, 1624

Inscriptions: center foreground, *Esyas vanden Velde fecit.* Below the image, *Den tienden Ianuary vierentwintich Iaer / En sestienhondert, nae Godts zoon geboren waer / De Leck door hooge vloet en ijsgangh soo aen parste, / Vijanen, dat den Dyck daer tegen over barste. / Dit maeckten bij de Vaert een gat soo wyt en diep, / Dat over al het landt van 't water onder Liep, / Tot binnen Amsterdam, daer t'op de Straeten woelde, / En eyndelyck door t'Y, in Zuyder-Zee wech spoelde. / Het Gadts gelegentheyt, en hoet met Rijs en Aerdt, / Door Kloek beleyt en Volck gestopt is met der vaerdt / Wert hier perfeckt vertoont, Esyas vanden Velde / Dit tot gedachtenis nae t'Leven ons bestelde. A. door den gebroken dijk B. het dorp C. den dom tot Utrecht D. het vinger-*

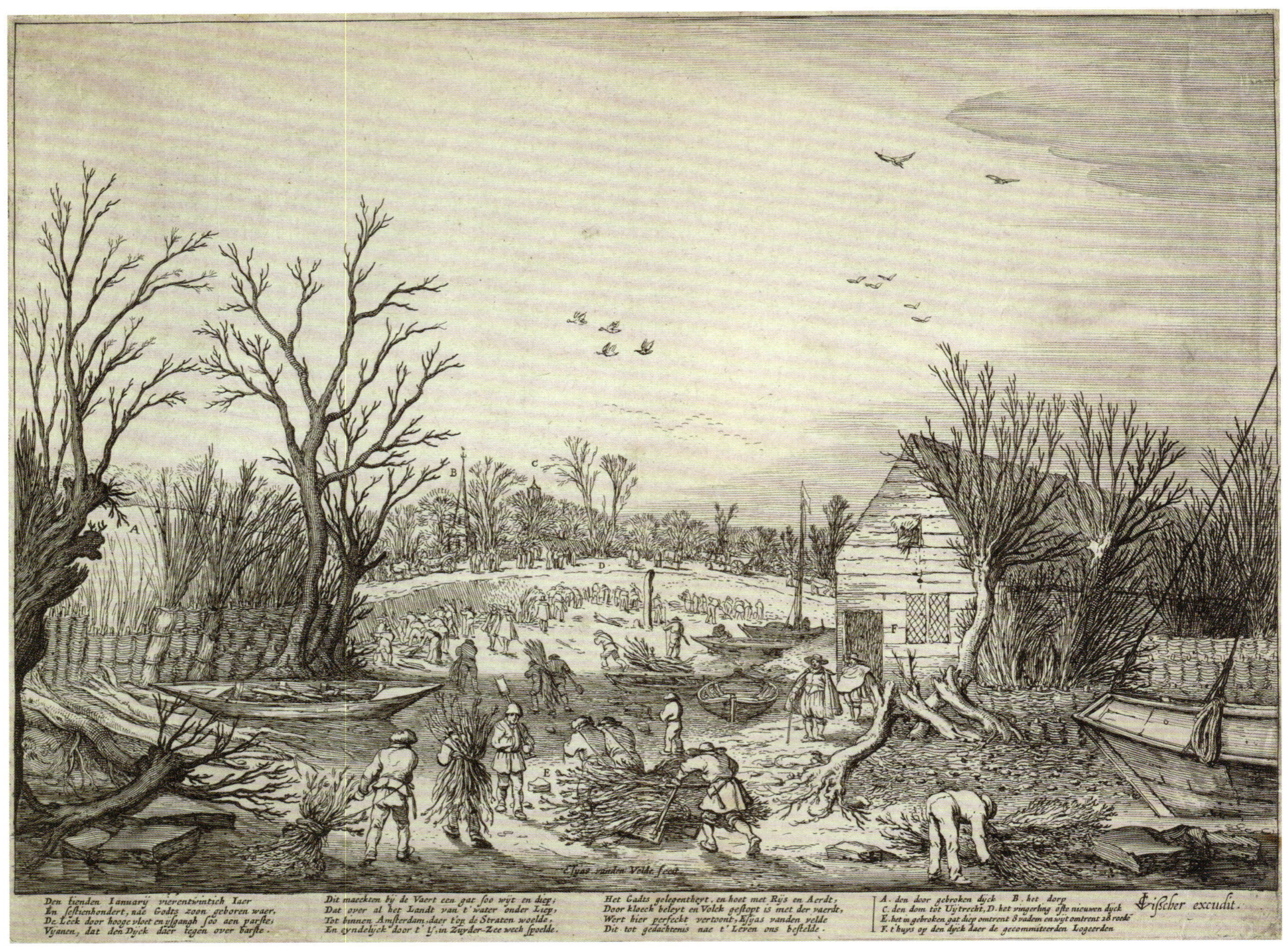

ling ofte nieuwen dijck E. het in gebroken gat diep omtrent 8 vadem en wyt omtrent 28 voede F. t'huys op den dyck daer de gecommiteerden Logeerden. CJ (in ligature) *Visscher excudit*

(On the tenth of January 1624 in the year of our Lord, the Lek River at Vianen was flooded so high because of ice breaking up that the dike there burst. This breach was so strong and made a hole so wide and deep that water flooded over all of the land, below Liep and as far as Amsterdam, whose streets churned with water. And likewise the water washed through the IJ and into the Zuyder-Zee. [This is] the hole's position showing how the flood was stopped with twigs and earth by wise policy and brave folk. This scene is perfectly represented by Esaias van de Velde, who made it from life to record the event. A. the breached dike. B. the village. C. the cathedral in Utrecht. D. the foundations of the new dike. E. the broken opening in the old dike, about 8 fathoms deep and about 18 rods [decameters] across. F. the superintendent's house on the dike. C.J. [Claes Jansz.] Visscher publisher.)

Etching and engraving, 282 × 391 mm (11⅛ × 15⅜ in.); state iii/v

Courtesy of the Fogg Art Museum, Harvard University Art Museums, Cambridge, Massachusetts, Light-Outerbridge Collection, Anonymous Fund for the Acquisition of Prints Older than 150 Years, M24769

References: Freedberg 1980, 29–30, fig. 24; Keyes 1984, 315–16, no. E2, pl. 65; Hollstein 32 (1988):245, no. 3; Cambridge 1992, 34–35, fig. 22; Amsterdam/Dordrecht/Rotterdam 2000, 120; Buisman 2000, 358–59.

The Dutch produced printed broadsheets such as this one to document noteworthy contemporary events or accidents such as explosions, fires (Cats. 40 and 41), and floods (Cats. 36 and 37), or even strange occurrences believed to be portents; for example, the stranding of whales along the coastline.[1] Accordingly, Van de Velde's print depicts the aftermath of the Great Flood of 1624, which happened in the middle of an uncommonly hard winter that had produced exceptionally heavy snowfall and river ice. On the night of 10 January at the village of Vianen in South Holland, the River Lek, swollen by melting ice, burst its dike (one of the most vital in the entire country) and flooded miles of countryside as far north as Amsterdam, whose streets reportedly churned with water.[2]

As is customary in broadsheets, a panoramic view of the site is combined with a descriptive text below it, followed by a lettered list that draws attention to significant points of interest in the scene. Here, for example, letter A indicates the breached dike; B, the village; C, the cathedral spire in nearby Utrecht; D (in the center), the foundations of the new dike; E, the broken opening in the old dike; and F, the dike superintendent's house, which was located on the dike itself. The rhymed description explains what caused the accident, the extent of the flood, and the actions taken by the local citizens who filled in the gap, bringing to their task twigs and earth and great courage.

The collecting and transport of bundles of sticks for this purpose constitute the major actions in the foreground, between the two sides of the broken dike, beyond which a crowd of small figures can be seen constructing the new section of dike at the center of the scene. Trees and church spires further in the distance place this cleanup and construction effort in the context of a complete local landscape, whose bare trees and sky vividly evoke the chill of early January. Van de Velde's sharp cropping of the composition at left and right as well as his plain, rather scratchy line impart a convincing reportorial directness to a scene made, as the caption testifies, from life ("nae t'Leven").

The rowboats and sailboats grounded throughout this scene are reminders of the ubiquitous presence of water in the Dutch landscape, which, as S. Schama has argued, constituted a kind of "flood society" that relied less upon the traditions of social dependence established elsewhere in Europe by vassal lords than on notions of reciprocity for physical safety as demanded by the dike reeve and other guardians of the water.[3] Thus, while this print depicts a devastated landscape, scattered with the refuse of broken walls and trees, its primary message involves retrieval and renewal, made possible by everyone's dedication to working together for the common good.

NOTES

1. On the use of Dutch broadsheets in the seventeenth century, see Van Deursen 1991, 134–52. German broadsheets of the same period are discussed in Coupe 1966 and in Harms 1980.

2. Buisman 2000, 355.

3. Schama 1987, 40.

ROELANT ROGHMAN

1627–92

Great nephew of Roelandt Savery (1576–1639) and brother of the printmaker Geertruydt Roghman (1625–before December 1657), Roelant Roghman was, according to Houbraken, a friend of Rembrandt, with whom he may have studied in Amsterdam.[1] Little is known, however, about his biography, and none of his paintings are dated. A painter, draftsman, and etcher, Roghman produced imaginative forest scenes and mountain landscapes, as well as topographically correct drawings of castles and villages. Among these works is a group of 241 chalk drawings, made in 1646 and 1647, of castles and country villas in the provinces of Holland, Utrecht, and Gelderland.[2] A number of these scenes depict ruined medieval buildings. He also collaborated with his sister Geertruydt on a series of landscape prints entitled *Plaisante landschappen* (Pleasant landscapes), which can be related to the print series of local sites produced during the early years of the century by Willem Buytewech (q.v.) and Jan van de Velde (q.v.), among others.

NOTES

1. Houbraken 1718–21, 1 (1718):174. For biographical material on Roghman, see P. C. Sutton in Amsterdam/Boston/Philadelphia 1987–88, 435; F. J. Duparc in Cambridge/Montreal 1988, 184; and N. van de Kamp's essay in *Dictionary of Art* 1996, 26:543–44.

2. An exhibition of Roghman's castle drawings was held at the Rijksmusem, Amsterdam, in 1989. Complete publication of the castle drawings was issued in two volumes as Van der Wyck and Kloek 1990.

[36]

The Bursting of the Dike outside of Amsterdam, 1651

(four scenes on one plate)

Inscriptions: above and within each scene, the names of places,

Upper scene, top center, *Den doorgebrooken Dyck bÿ Jaaphannes* (The breached dike at Jaaphannes); over the horizon at left, *Raerdorp ... Duerckerdam*; over the horizon at right, *Jaaphannes ... Diemen*

Center scene, top center, *Den doorgebrooken Dyck bÿ Houtewael* (The breached dike at Houtewael); over the horizon at left, *Durckerdam*; over the horizon at right, *Diemer-meer*; bottom center, *Roelant Roghman fecit*

Lower left scene, top, *Het doorbreeken vanden Dyck bÿ Houtewael op Sondach den 5 Maart A. 1651* (The breaching of the dike at Houtewael on Sunday 5 March in the year 1651); over the horizon at left, *Nieuwendam*

Lower right scene, top, *Aldus vertoonden hem 't gadt aan Jaaphannes* (Representing the hole in the dike at Jaaphannes)

At the bottom are legends pointing out aspects of each scene in letters A–L. *A. Het groote gadt omtreent de Bocht bÿ het Nieuwe diem wydt 30 Rodern diem 20. 25. c 30 voeten onder het ordinary water* (The big hole in the area of the bend near New Dike measuring 30 rods wide and a depth of 20, 25, or 30 feet under ordinary water [meaning the average water level for this area]). *B. Stucken van den Dyck* (Pieces of the dike). *C. Nieuw ghemaachte Dyck* (Newly constructed dike). *D. Nieuwe vaart* (The new passageway). *E. Herbergen bÿ de Bocht* (Inns at the bend of the water). *F. Het gadt inden Dyck van de Diemermeer, wydt omtrent 25 Roeden, diep onder het ghemeene winter-water 20 25. to 27 voeten* (The hole in the dike of the Diemermeer measuring 25 rods wide and, under the average winter water level in this area 20, 25, to 27 feet). *G. Het gadt by Houtewael wydt omtreent 18 Roeden. Diep onder het ghemeene water 20. 25. a 30 voeten* (The hole by Houtewael, width around 18 rods, underwater depth 20, 25, and 30 feet). *H. Huisen op den Dyck tussen beyde gaten* (Houses on the dike between the two holes). *I. Nieuw gemaakte Dam* (Newly constructed embankment). *K. Komeny voor 'arbeyds volck* (Arrival of the workers). *L. S. Antonis dyck bÿ Houtewael* (The St. Anthony's Dike at Houtewael)

Bottom, far right, *'Amsterdam by Lodewyck Spillebout Boeksvercooper inde Calverstraat* (Published in Amsterdam by Lodewyck Spillebout, bookseller in the Kalverstraat)

Etching, 421 × 515 mm (16¾ × 20⅜ in.); only state

Courtesy of the Fogg Art Museum, Harvard University Art Museums, Cambridge, Massachusetts, Light-Outerbridge Collection, Richard Norton Memorial Fund, M24646

References: Hind 1915–32, 4:35, no. 11; Bille 1960, 210; Beck 1966, 20, no. 3; Gottschalk 1977, 161–76; Hollstein 20 (1978):90, no. 39; Van der Wyck and Kloek 1990, 2:22–23, fig. 28; Berlin/Amsterdam/London 1991–92, 100, fig. 28b; Amsterdam 1993–94, 106–7, no. 50; Amsterdam/Paris 1998–99, 229 n. 6; Buisman 2000, 513–14; Amsterdam/Dordrecht/Rotterdam 2000, 146.

The district on the outskirts of Amsterdam along the Diemerdijk (the dike on the way to Diemen) was a popular site for country walks by city dwellers, including Rembrandt, who made numerous drawings and prints of this pleasant rural landscape.[1] Also known as the Sint Anthonis Dike (after the nearby St. Anthony Leper Hospital), the area also attracted visitors because of the taverns built along the dike at the hamlets of Houtewael and Jaaphannes, where the customers could enjoy fine views across the water of the IJ. On the night of 5–6 March 1651, high tides and strong winds from the northwest caused the dike to break in two places. This catastrophe was precipitated by the late winter flooding into the countryside in north Holland from the Diemermeer (dry since 1629 but suddenly under sixteen feet of water again), which damaged or destroyed low-lying villages, farms, and country houses, inundating the countryside all the way to the center of Amsterdam and even beyond.[2]

Roghman made his own careful study of the broken dike and its surroundings, as indicated by two very different preparatory drawings in Brussels and London, both oriented in the same direction as the print.[3] The meticulously thorough horizontal drawing in Brussels (Fig. 131) establishes most details of the wide scene at the top of the print, which depicts the beginnings of repair and reclamation activity at Jaaphannes. The British Museum's extraordinary sketch (Fig. 132), made for the bottom left image on the printed sheet, represents the artist's attempt to imagine what he could not have seen: the moment the dike gave way at Houtewael and the waters crashed through, menacing everyone in the vicinity. By freely applying watery ink with his brush, Roghman made the medium itself evoke the effect of a flood in progress. In the print, executed with more controlled technique and imagery, the tiny stranded figures who gesture for help from the top of the broken dike in the center have been omitted, but the people running for their lives on the segment at the far left have been retained.

In his use of a printed broadsheet format to convey the particulars of a natural disaster, Roghman was probably inspired, at least in part, by Esaias van de Velde's earlier depiction of the aftermath of the Great Flood at Vianen of 1624 (Cat. 35). But while Van de Velde concentrated on the human efforts involved in reclaiming the landscape for habitation, Roghman seems most interested in examining the profound alterations to the topography at different times, from the

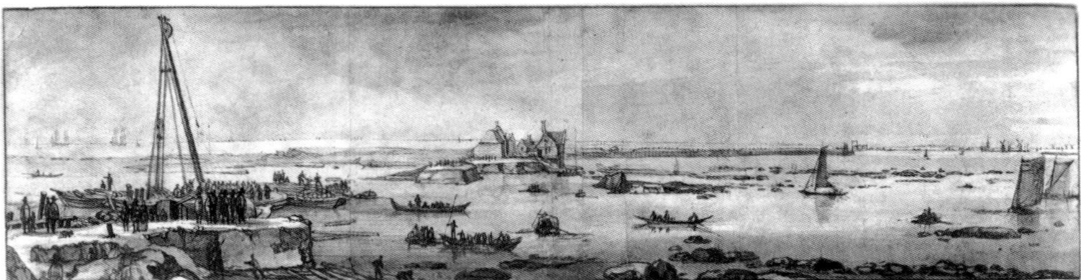

Fig. 131. Roelant Roghman, *Break in the Dike at Jaaphannes*, c. 1651, drawing. Koninklijke Musea voor Schone Kunsten, Brussels

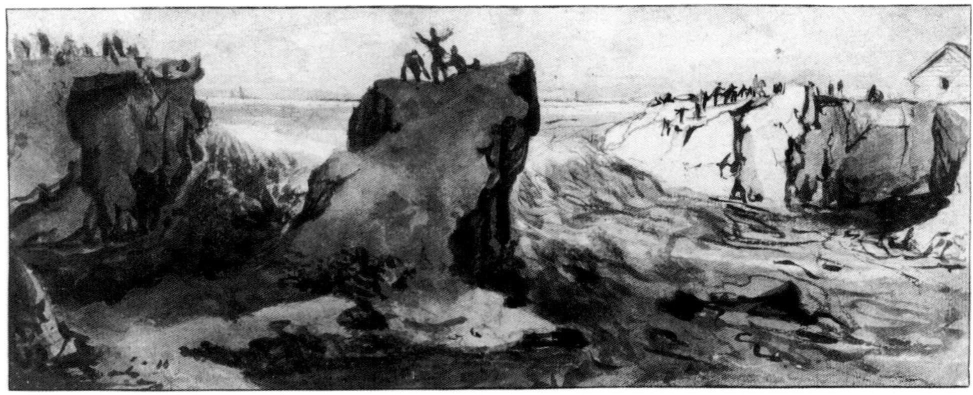

Fig. 132. Roelant Roghman, *The Broken Dike at Houtewael*, c. 1651, pen and wash drawing, British Museum, London

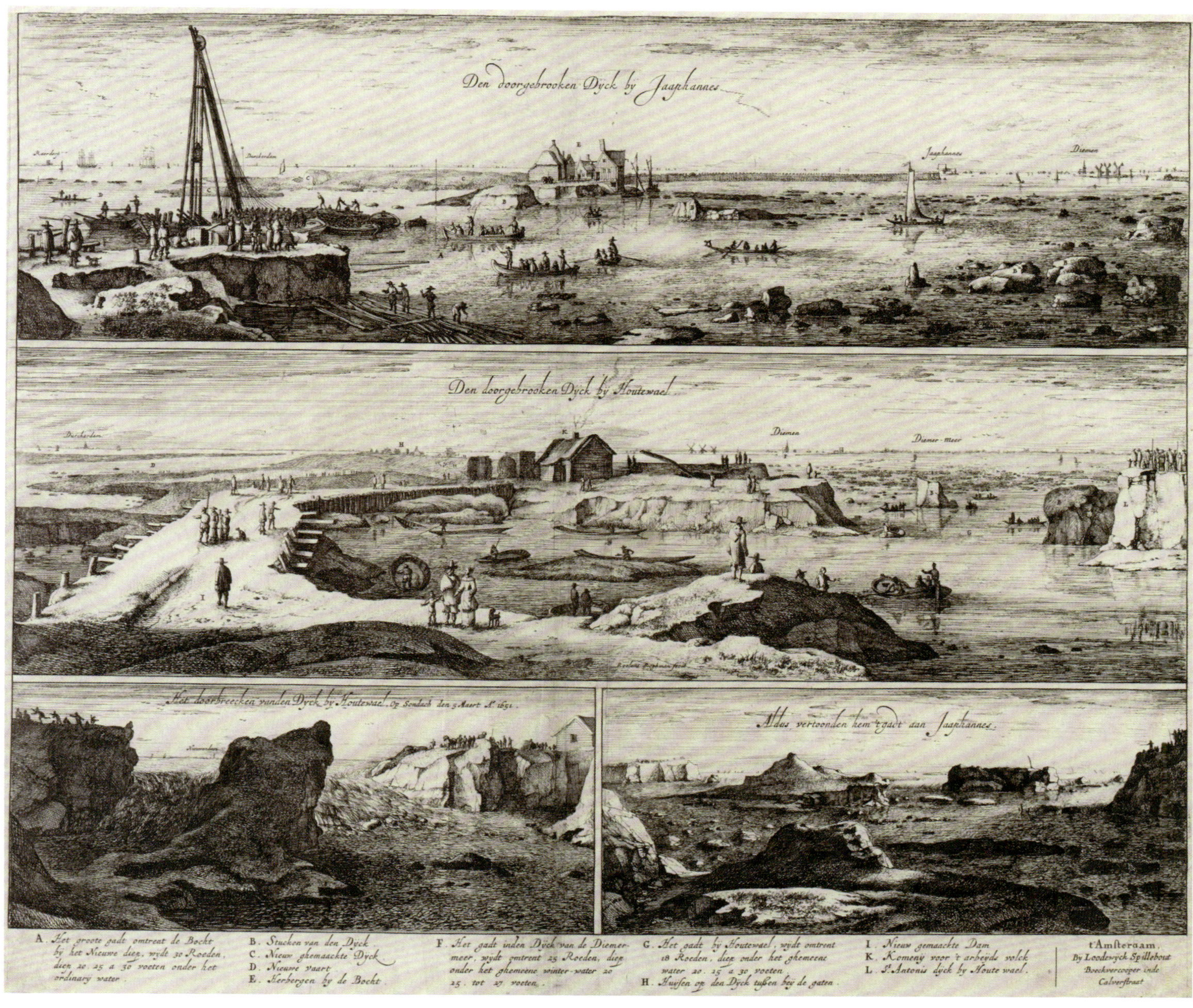

moment of the disaster through its aftermath. Taking unusually wide panoramic views in the top two scenes, he elevates the horizon for a high viewpoint that allows the observer to appreciate the full extent of the devastation. As indicated by the legend, the break at Houtewael was about 18 rods (63 meters) wide, while nearby Jaaphannes suffered an even larger breach of 30 rods (approximately 110 meters), with waters rising to depths of as much as 30 feet (11.4 meters).[4]

In the scene at the top, people in boats navigate the flooded countryside at Jaaphannes, where two breaks in the dike have stranded the cluster of taverns and taphouses in the center.[5] In the middle illustration, showing Houtewael, the artist makes a closer examination of the gap in the dike at the right, while representing the new construction at the left as observed by visitors. The lower zone brings the viewer still closer to the breaks at Houtewael (left) and Jaaphannes (right), but now as if the crisis were in the process of happening. With inundation, the integrity of the landscape becomes shattered into fragments whose disjunction is emphasized by Roghman's use of varied shapes and strong contrasts of light and shadow.

Roghman was not the only artist to depict this widely reported disaster and the reclamation activities that followed. Jan van Goyen (q.v.), who traveled from The Hague to observe the scene, made almost twenty sketches of the site,[6] while the Amsterdam artist Jan Asselijn (after 1610–52) produced paintings that show both the breaking of the dike (dated 1651, Staatliches Museum, Schwerin, inv. 2697) and its reconstruction during the summer of 1652 (dated 1652, Staatliche Museen, Berlin, no. 2/58). In addition, Pieter Nolpe (q.v.) produced an engraving (Cat. 37) after a painting by Willem Schellinks (q.v.; Fig. 69) that illustrates the rupture of the dike as a dramatic event in progress, as well as an etching, after J. Esselens and I. Colin, that incorporates two images representing the condition of the area after the accident.[7]

NOTES

1. For discussion of the district around Diemen, see Lugt 1915, 147; Schmitz 1990, 6–20; Mulder, Blok, and Van Reenen 1987; and especially Amsterdam/Paris 1998–99, 207–8 and 213–18.

2. The rupture of the Sint Anthonis Dike and the artists who represented it have been discussed in Bille 1960; Beck 1966; A. Chong in Amsterdam/Boston/Philadelphia 1987–88, 252–53; and in Buisman 2000, 513–15. Buisman's map of the areas that flooded in this early March disaster includes territory as far south as the vicinity of Antwerp and as far north as the vicinity of Groningen and Emden (Buisman 2000, 515).

3. Koninklijke Musea voor Schone Kunsten, Brussels (no. 2223) and British Museum, London (no. 1836-8-11-471). A. M. Hind was the first to connect the latter drawing with Roghman's print (Hind 1915–32, 4:35). See also Sumowski 1979–92, 10 (1992):5020, no. 2224.

4. Seventeenth-century measures, different from today's, used a foot of approximately 15 inches. On the difficulties of finding modern equivalents for these earlier units of measure, see Cat. 37, n. 1.

5. Amsterdam/Paris 1998–99, 216–17.

6. Van Goyen's drawings (leaves 166–84 in his sketchbook of 1650–51) are discussed in Beck 1966.

7. Repr. Hollstein 14 (1956):175; and Amsterdam/Boston/Philadelphia 1987–88, 253, fig. 2.

PIETER NOLPE
1613/14–1652/53

Nolpe was an Amsterdam etcher, engraver, and draftsman whose 319 known prints are all dated between 1637 and 1652. Most reproduce works by other artists such as Claes Moeyaert (q.v.), Willem van Nieulandt (q.v.), Simon de Vlieger (q.v.), and, as in the example catalogued here, Willem Schellinks (q.v.).[1] Aside from a small number of emblems and biblical illustrations he designed himself, Nolpe also produced engravings of contemporary historical events, including the parades honoring Marie de' Medici's ceremonial entrance into Amsterdam of 1638, after designs by Jan Martzen (c. 1607–after 1647), and the festivities of 1642 in honor of Queen Henrietta Maria of England, after a painting by Pieter Potter (1597/1601–1653).[2] Nolpe's varied output of prints also includes a series of beggars and peasants, after designs by Pieter Quast (1605/6–47).

NOTES

1. Nolpe's life and work were first investigated by C. M. Dozy in an 1897 article in *Oud Holland* (Dozy 1897, 24–50, 94–120, 139–58, and 220–44). For a recent discussion, see C. Shuckman's entry in *Dictionary of Art* 1996, 23:191.

2. Hollstein 14 (1956): nos. 86–94 and 161.

[37]

PIETER NOLPE, AFTER WILLEM SCHELLINKS

The Rupture of the St. Anthony's Dike, 1651

Inscriptions: title at bottom, *VERTONINGE ENDE NAE T'LEVEN AFGEBEELT, HET DOOR BREECKEN VANDE S'ANTHONIS DYCK BUYTEN AMSTERDAM.* (Presentation represented from life of the breaking of the St. Anthony's Dike outside Amsterdam.)

Text below title, *Veroorsaeckt door de hooge watervloet met een stercken Noord westen wint, op den 5. Martÿ, 1651 å In welcken het water 3 duÿmen hoger is bevonden, als het was, Inde seer bekende alderheÿligen Vloet Anno 1570 door / Welck het waeter, met sulcken force en gewelt is Ingestort, dat het in corten tÿt een diepte maeckte, van 30 voeten, mede nemende al het gene sÿnnen loop mocht hinderen, selfs de dÿck Vande diemer meer door brekende die / Daer door, sodanigh is ondergelopen dat het water (inde selve) wel 16 voeten hoge stondt, tot seer groote schade, vande Ingelanden, ende de omleggende. soo dat t'water over St. Anthonis Mart warmostraet en nieuwe dÿck liep.*

(The cause of the flood of high water was a strong northwest wind on the 5th of March, 1651, which made the water rise 3 duymen higher than it had ever risen before, even in the famous All Saints' Day Flood in the year 1570.[1] The water rushed in with such force and violence that in a short time it reached a depth of 30 feet, taking with it all former impediments to its course, especially the dike of the Diemermeer, which, in being broken through, created such a flood that the waters rose to a height of 16 feet causing very great damage to the lands in the polder and its surroundings, with water extending all the way to St. Anthony's Market [now Nieumarkt] Warmoesstraat and the new dike.)

Left of text, *A. t'Volck staende tussen de twee Braecke op den dÿck.* (People standing between the two breaks in the dike.); *B. Een stuck wt den dÿck gebrokt* (A piece out of the broken dike.); *C. Houte wael.* (Houtewael.); right of text, *Gemackt en gedruckt bÿ Pieter Nolpe tot Amsterdam en van W. Schellinks getekent.* (Made [i.e., etched] and published by Pieter Nolpe of Amsterdam and drawn by W. Schellinks.)

Etching on laid paper, 402 × 505 mm (15 13/16 × 19 7/8 in.); state ii/iii

Courtesy of the Herbert F. Johnson Museum of Art, Cornell University, Ithaca, New York, Gift of Professor Joseph Dallett, 99.079

References: Muller 1863–82, 2018; Atlas Van Stolk 2161, as cited in Van Rijn and Van Ommeren 1859–1933, 2 (1897):322–23; Hollstein 14 (1956):175, no. 208; Simoni 1985, 164–65; Amsterdam 1993–94, 106–7, no. 50.1; Ithaca 1999, 15, no. 11; Amsterdam/Dordrecht/Rotterdam 2000, 147.

This cataclysmic scene has the effect of being represented "nae t'leven" (from life), as the inscription declares, in every aspect of its arrangement, which places the observer in the very path of a torrent bursting through a broken dike. On either side of the cascade, which sweeps pieces of the dike along with it, desperate people call out and signal to each other across the gap. At the far right, a drowning is averted, as a man is dramatically pulled to safety at the top of the precipice. Throughout the scene, the printmaker's assured manipulation of line sets up effective contrasts between the diagonally rushing water, framed at left and right by the more densely etched segments of the broken barrier and above by the movement of a tumultuous sky, defined in sweeping, counter-diagonal hatchings. At the left background, smoke from a chimney in the village of Houtewael is blown horizontally toward the right, indicating the wind's velocity and direction. As the legend explains, this disaster, which occurred on 5 March 1651 and destroyed two segments of the St. Anthony's Dike outside Amsterdam, was precipitated by high northwesterly winds that caused the waters to rise even higher than they had during the terrible All Saints' Day Flood of 1570. In Amsterdam, whose nearby towers are visible at the center and right background of this scene, the waters swept all the way to St. Anthony's Market (now known as the Niewmarkt), where the Waag (weighing house) of 1488 still stands.

Nolpe's print, based upon a painting by Willem Schellinks (q.v.) now in the Amsterdams Historisch Museum (Fig. 69), follows its model closely but changes the positions of the figures at the right, especially the endangered man who has not yet climbed high enough to be saved. While both painting and print present a compelling interpretation of the disaster, it is clear that the artists have also applied their powers of invention to the composition. In comparison, Roelant Roghman's large etching of four scenes from the event (Cat. 36) probably had a more documentary intention, since his depictions concentrate primarily on topographical transformations to the landscape caused by the flooding. It was Nolpe's print, however, that copyists turned to for inspiration when breaks in the dike near Zutphen in 1784 and near

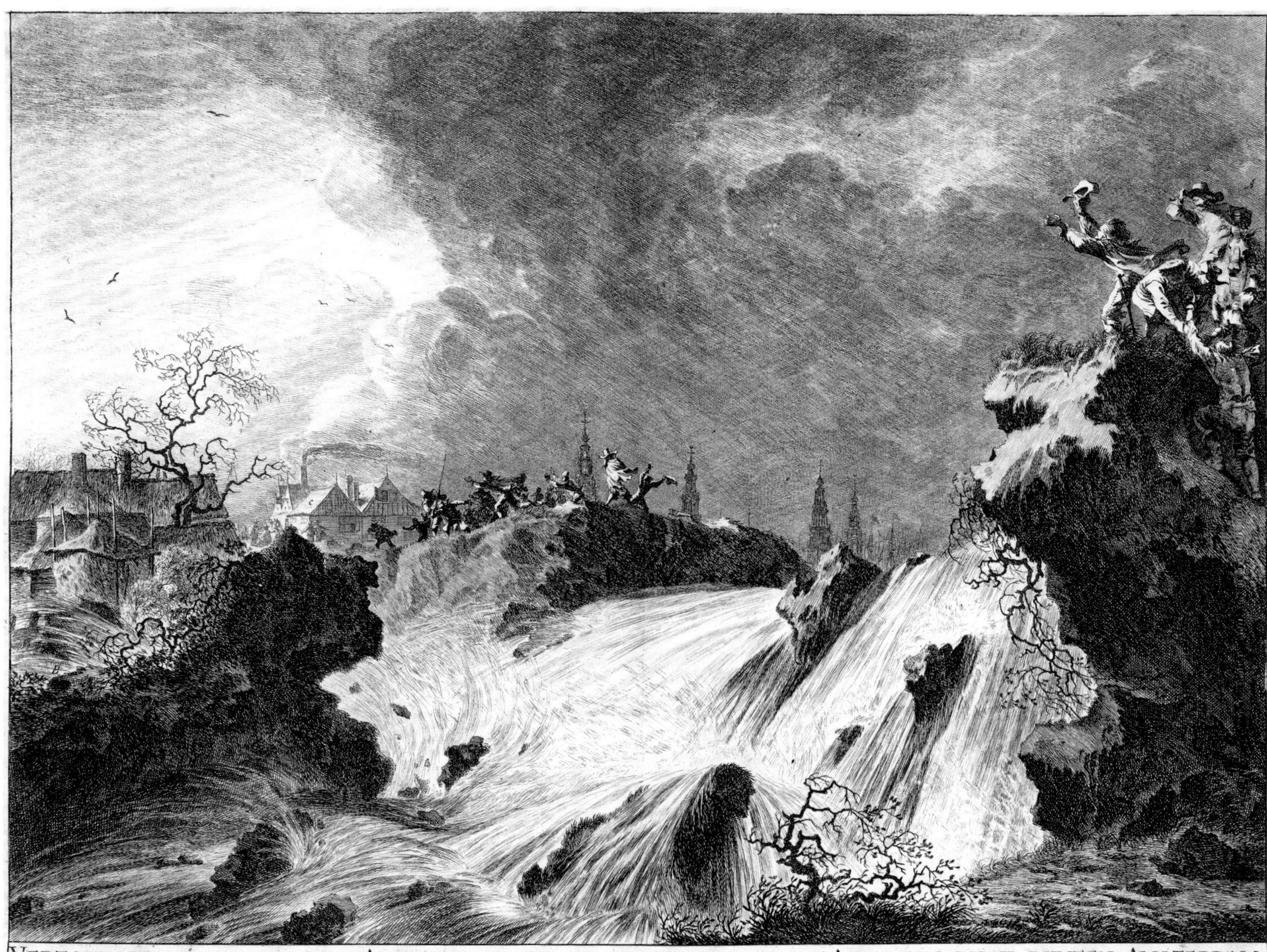

Bemmel in 1799 again stimulated the market for this kind of subject.[2]

NOTES

1. Translating seventeenth-century measures into modern ones is complicated by the fact that units were not then standardized by name or by exact number. Thus, an Amsterdam *voet*, or foot (equal to 11 duim or 38.3 centimeters or approximately 15 inches in today's terms) differed slightly from both a Prussian *Zoll* (12 to one foot equaling 31.4 cm) or a Parisian *pouche* (12 to one foot equaling 32.5 cm), with further variations in other parts of Europe. Accordingly (and assuming that the Amsterdam foot was the measure used), Nolpe's inscription states that the water rose approximately 7.7 cm. I am grateful to Erik Löffler for sharing with me the unpublished chart of measures used for reference at the RKD, The Hague.

2. Amsterdam/Dordrecht/Rotterdam 2000, 147. Nolpe also etched two plates with scenes of the disaster after I . Colin and J. Esselens, *The Dike at Jaaphannes and Houtweael after the Break of 1651*, repr. Amsterdam/Boston/Philadelphia 1987–88, 253, fig. 2.

ROMEYN DE HOOGHE
1645–1708

A political printmaker and book illustrator of exceptionally diverse talents, De Hooghe began making prints in the style of Nicolaes Berchem (q.v.) but went on to work, between 1670 and 1691, as a newspaper illustrator for the Amsterdam journal *Hollandsche Mercurius*.[1] Following the French invasion of the Netherlands in 1672, he produced memorable political caricatures of Louis XIV as well as stirring depictions of major events of the war, often combining contemporary and allegorical figures. His powerfully baroque style was used both for individual etchings and for illustrations in patriotic books, such as Abraham de Wicquefort's *Advis fidelle aux veritable Hollandois* … (Faithful advice to the true Dutch), published in 1673 (Cat. 39). An ardent royalist, De Hooghe made prints to glorify William III, stadtholder of the Dutch Republic who became king of England, as in the series that commemorates the joint coronation, in 1689, of William III and Mary Stuart and his designs for triumphal arches for William's entry into The Hague in 1691.[2]

By early 1687 De Hooghe had settled in Haarlem, where he became Commissioner of Justice; in the following year, he built a house and established a drawing school. In 1691 William III put him in charge of the German stone quarries at Lingen, the source of the stone used to build the royal hunting lodge Het Loo, for which De Hooghe was asked to design ponds and garden statuary. The same year he was appointed doctor of law at Harderwijk University. Between 1692 and 1694 De Hooghe was working in Alkmaar, where he made paintings for both the Grote Kerk and the town hall, among his other projects. Between 1701 and 1703 he was engaged in designing church windows for Zaandam and Hoorn. His murals for the Enkhuizen town hall (executed by other artists after his death) were designed in 1707. In addition to his artistic activities, De Hooghe authored his own political treatises, including *Spiegel van staat des vereenigde Nederlanden* (Mirror of the state of the United Netherlands, 1706–7), to which he contributed allegorical illustrations.

NOTES

1. De Hooghe's biography is recounted in Landwehr 1973, 15–16, and in M. J. C. Otten's biographical essay in *Dictionary of Art* 2000, 168–69. H. T. Wilson's Ph.D. dissertation on De Hooghe includes useful information on both the artist and his historical context (Wilson 1974).
2. Hollstein 9 (1949):125.

[38]

Dikes by Coevorden, 1673

Inscriptions: in trompe-l'oeil cartouche at the top, *Afbeelding. Hoedanig den Dyck, die door order van den Bisschop van Munster, / boven 't Huys te Laer, tot by Gramsbergen, door de Rivier de Vecht, met gro / te Kosten was geleÿt, om de stercke stadt Coeverden, door 't ophouden van / dat water, te doen verdrincken, op den eersten October, Å 1673, is door / gebrooken, en meest wegh gespoelt, waar door over 600 soldaten en / Boeren verdroncken zijn. Desen Dyck was meer als 2½ uur gaens lang / geweest, breedt, onder 30, en boven 8, passen, met verscheijde schansen / en Reduÿten, versterckt en doorgaens met pallissaden bezet: met / militie te voet en paerd, en 60,500 groote, als kleijne stucken Ca / non, voorzien: Hebbende de Stadt Coeverden, boven, over de / 40 roeden, en beneden, over 100 roeden, onder water gestaen.*

(Illustration. How the dike was laid at great cost by order of the bishop of Münster north of Huys te Laer all the way to Gramsbergen through the river Vecht in order to drown the brave city of Coevorden by holding back the water. On the first of October 1673 it broke and was largely swept away, drowning more than 600 soldiers and peasants. This dike, whose length took more than 2½ hours to travel, was less than 30 feet wide at its lower part and 8 feet tall and was fortified with various retrenchments and redoubts, provisioned with 60,500 small and large cannons, and strengthened with palisades throughout so that militia on foot and on horseback could cross it: The upper part of the city of Coevorden was submerged under 40 rods of water, and the lower part under 100 rods of water.)

At left,
VERKLARINGE DER CYFER GETALLEN IN DESE FIGURER ANGEWESEN
(Explanation of each of the scenes indicated by a number)

1. *Huys te gramsbergen.*
(A house at Gramsbergen.)
2. *Een stuck van den dyck met 2 reduyten.*
(A piece of the dike with two redoubts.)
3. *Neerstortent Canon en schans korven.*
(Nearby cannon and basket entrenchments.)
4. *Drie plaetse daer den Dyck is deur gebrooken.*
(Three places where the dike was breached.)
5. *de Caros met den oversten Stockmar.*
(The carriage with Officer Stockmar.)
6. *Neerstortende en wegh spoelende huysen.*
(Houses collapsing and being swept away.)
7. *Elendigh omkoomen van mensen en beesten.*
(Miserable deaths of men and animals.)
8. *Schepen daer Rabenhaupt met over lant is koomen zeijlen om t geen overig was van den dyck wegh te haelen.*
(Ships that Rabenhaupt is sailing overland in order to remove the remains of the dike.)
9. *de wegh na Zwol.* (The road to Zwolle.)
10. *Innemen der vijants reduiten.*
(Capturing of enemy redoubts.)
11. *Verdroncken Ruytery en soldaten.*
(Drowned riders and soldiers.)

At right,
OP COEVERDENS: Miraculeuse Verlossinge hoe wroet de Bisschop met sijn mÿter in het slÿck, / En stuwt he water op, om Coewerden te winnen? / Hÿ breeckt sijn hooge Eedt, Godt breeckt sijn Hoge Dÿck / Die sonder Godt begint, wat baet 'et te beginnen. / Bÿ Groeningen was 't Vÿer, nu 't water sonder vrucht. / Strÿdt, Bisschop, strÿdt, Bisschop, strÿdt niet meer, ofte strÿdt met Aerdt 'en Lucht. H. Selijns

(At Coevorden: Miraculous deliverance from the bishop, who dug with his miter in the mud / to let the waters rise in order to win Coevorden. He broke his solemn vow / so God broke his dike / that godlessly was begun / In Groningen fire had no success,[1] and here water also failed / Fight, bishop / Fight, bishop / Fight no more, or fight with earth and air. H. Selijns)

Bottom center,
uyt gegeven t Amsterdam by Marcus Doornick
(published in Amsterdam by Marcus Doornick)

Bottom right,
R. de Hooge fecit (R. de Hooge made it)[2]

Etching, 375 × 476 mm (14¾ × 18¾ in.) (sheet); state ii/ii[3]

Lent by the Metropolitan Museum of Art, New York, Harris Brisbane Dick Fund, 1947, 47.100.269

References: Van Rijn and Van Ommeren 1895–1933, 3 (1897):90, no. 2496; Landwehr 1973, 50, 73; Schama 1987, 277.

Storms with excessive rain or snow that caused water levels to rise accounted for most of the ruptured dikes and consequent flooding in the Dutch provinces during the seventeenth century, as illustrated in prints by Esaias van de Velde (Cat. 35), Roelant Roghman (Cat. 36), and Pieter Nolpe (Cat. 37). De Hooghe's large and compellingly dramatic scene documents a disaster in which bad weather was also a factor but which was precipitated by military maneuvers during the traumatic period known as the "Rampjaar" (Disaster Year) when the Dutch provinces were invaded by the armies of Louis XIV and his supporters.[4] Coevorden, an ancient fortified town strategically located at the border of Dutch and German territory on a major canal just north of the Vecht River, was a particular target for the enemy troops of the bishop of Münster, as was the castle at nearby Gramsbergen. Although Coevorden had fallen to the enemy in 1672 after a fourteen-day siege, it was recaptured under the command of Carel Rabenhaupt in December of that year. In a decision that would have unexpectedly fatal consequences for everyone concerned, the bishop ordered the building of a dike through the river Vecht wide enough to serve as a road-

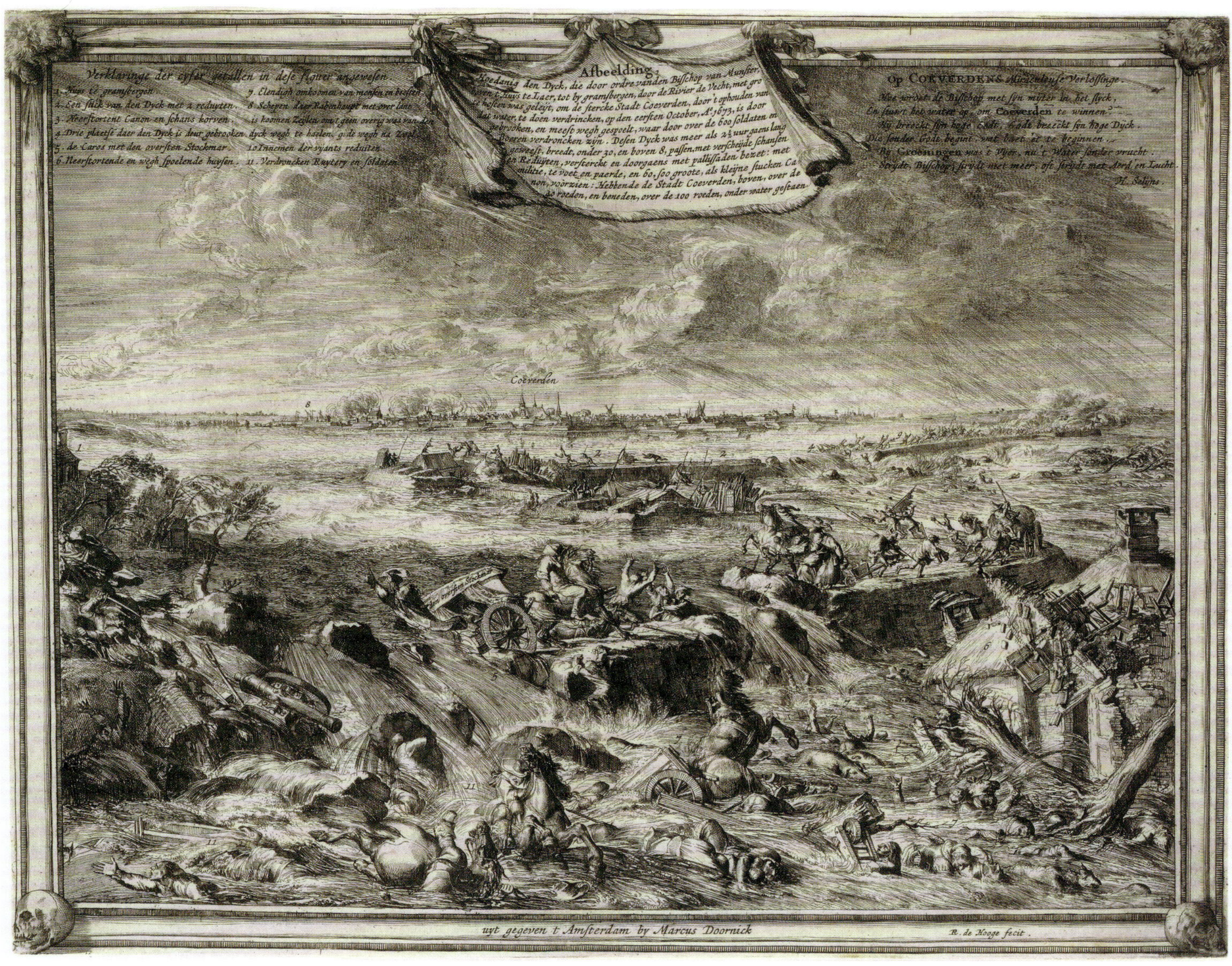

way for militia on horseback, with the intention of holding back water that would inundate Coevorden. Heavy rains fell on 27 September and again on 1 October, causing water levels to rise. On the night of 1–2 October, as the army of the bishop marched in, the dike collapsed in three places, admitting flood waters that swamped the invaders, drowning some six hundred soldiers and local country folk and engulfing both the upper and lower parts of the town.

De Hooghe's oversized print has an epic, even cinematic effect, as its uncommonly large, almost square pictorial field displays a vast open vista stretching from the drowning horses and people in the immediate foreground to the distant skyline of Coevorden on the horizon. Between the two, a terrifying series of incidents unfolds as farmhouses, trees, animals, and local inhabitants are swept away along with the invading soldiers, horses, cannons, and carriages. In the misery and terror of this scene, whose scope recalls the Deluge, the torrent that cascades violently through the broken dike becomes the common adversary of the Dutch and French alike, making the rising water something of a second invasion. At the right, a farmhouse collapses into the turbulent flood, its roof and walls shattering, as the road along the dike behind it disintegrates, sending panic-stricken men and horses to their deaths, along with pigs and sheep. The inevitability of losing all solid footing in a landscape that had been familiar and safe is captured throughout the scene, perhaps most vividly in the farmer at the right frantically driving his horse-drawn hay cart along the dike toward immanent disaster. De Hooghe's genius at staging the most exciting and compelling interpretation of historical events is also the product of his lively etching technique and his manipulation of a design whose space is very deep, yet whose major diagonals project out in the direction of the viewer, following the explosive trajectory of the flood waters.

Even the framing of this scene intensifies the drama of a cataclysm in progress, as De Hooghe surrounds his panorama with a narrow, illusionistic border like a picture frame whose corners are marked by emblematic heads: skulls facing outward at the bottom corners and, at the top, heads symbolizing the four winds (two at each corner) that face downward and inward so that they seem to be blowing currents of air into the scene. Between them, the cloth hanging in the center that forms the print's descriptive cartouche seems agitated by the same strong breeze that drives the distant clouds below and beyond it. As in other printed broadsheets of this kind (Cats. 35–37), a numbered list of points of interest in the scene below is included at the upper left to guide the viewer through the melee. A stirring poem signed by H. Selijns at the upper right makes the point that God and deliverance are on the side of the Dutch and that the enemy commander (the bishop of Münster), who has fruitlessly dug with his miter in the mud to build the dike, can now only battle with soil and air, having lost his troops.

NOTES

1. The unsuccessful siege of the city of Groningen in 1672 by the forces of the prince-elector of Cologne and the bishop of Münster was also depicted by De Hooghe in an etching (31 × 39.2 cm) published in Tobias van Domselaer's two-volume *Het ontroerde Nederlandt* (Netherlands in turmoil) of 1674/76.

2. I am greatly indebted to Erik Löffler for assistance in translating and interpreting the inscriptions on this print.

3. The entry describing this print in Van Rijn and Van Ommeren's companion volumes to the Atlas van Stolk suggest that it exists in two states, the second bearing the inscription. Van Rijn and Van Ommeren 1895–1933, 3(1897):90, no. 2496.

4. For discussion of the Coevorden flood, see Coert 1991 and Buisman 2000, 666.

[39]

The Destruction of Bodegraven and Zwammerdam, 28 December 1672, from *Abraham de Wicquefort's Advis fidelle aux veritable Hollandois touchant ce qui s'est passé dans les villages de Bodegrave & Swammerdam & les crautés inoüies, que les François y ont exerceés avec un mémoire de la dernière marche de l'armeé du roy de France en Brabant et en Flandre The Hague, 1673* (Faithful advice to the true Dutch, touching on events that happened in the villages of Bodegraven and Zwammerdam involving the incredible cruelties that the French perpetrated, with a remembrance of the last march of the army of the king of France in Brabant and in Flanders, The Hague, 1673), Amsterdam, 1673

Etching, 203 × 306 mm (8 × 12 in.) (image); 23 × 19 × 4 cm (9 1/16 × 7 1/2 × 1 9/16 in.) (book)

Lent by the Metropolitan Museum of Art, New York, The Elisha Whittelsey Collection, The Elisha Whittelsey Fund, 1963, 63.609.6

References: none

The author of this illustrated treatise, Abraham de Wicquefort (1606–82), was a native Dutchman who became a diplomatic envoy in France and Germany and was among the witnesses to the negotiations at the Congress of Westphalia that brought the end of the Thirty Years War (1618–48). Best known as a political theorist, he is credited with having written the earliest account of how diplomacy works: *L'ambassadeur et ses fonctions*, published in 1680–81 in The Hague and translated into English as *The Embassador and His Functions* in 1716.[1]

In 1673 De Wicquefort published an outraged response to events that had occurred in December of the previous year during the French invasion of the Dutch provinces. *Advis fidelle aux veritable Hollandois* (Faithful advice to the true Dutch) is an impassioned tract that he composed in order to inform his countrymen about the devastation and loss of life that the French had recently inflicted upon two neighboring Dutch towns, Bodegraven and Zwammerdam, located just north of Gouda. His book, which contains ten double-page illustrations by De Hooghe, helped rally the Dutch to William III's cause during the war with France that would last until 1678. The book's popularity was so great that it was reissued in three smaller (13 × 17 cm) volumes in 1674.

The destruction of Bodegraven and Zwammerdam occurred during Christmas week on 28 December 1672, when the French army under the command of the duke of Luxembourg pillaged and burned both undefended villages, raping the women and killing virtually every inhabitant including livestock. Even taking into account the possibility of exaggeration in *Advis fidelle*'s text and illustrations, the savagery of this assault was apparently extreme, for when William III visited Bodegraven on New Year's Eve, two days after the massacre, he reportedly found no more than three houses that had escaped total destruction; the dead lay unburied in the ruins of their homes, and only one baby was found alive.[2] Whether the violence was caused by the accumulated frustration of soldiers, prevented from marching toward their intended target of The Hague by unexpectedly thawing ice, or by excessive religious zeal against the Protestant Dutch is unknown.[3] In any case, De Wicquefort's text and De Hooghe's illustrations both evoke a situation of unrelenting annihilation and terror.

De Hooghe's ability to capture a complex contemporary event as if the viewer were actually witnessing it (see also Fig. 70 and Cat. 38) is displayed here in his staging of multiple incidents that show how the invaders used both water and fire to torture and kill individual villagers. At the center foreground, a soldier pushes a man through the softening ice as another pours icy water over him from a long-handled pail. Above them a baby is skewered on a spear in an incident that recalls the Massacre of the Innocents (Matthew 2:16–18). The ship at the left, from which a sailor is being pulled onto the ice, has been set afire, as has the inn at the right, whose top floors are engulfed in flames as its inhabitants attempt to flee soldiers bearing swords and guns. From the inn's signboard, several villagers have been hung like sides of meat, while prisoners with bound hands, including women stripped to the skin, are led away to execution. The terrified naked woman at the near right is surrounded by leering men on all sides, one vomiting on her as he douses her with freezing water from his hat. Throughout this scene, loss of control or restraint causes the atrocities to multiply, making the very fabric of civilization seem in the process of dissolution.

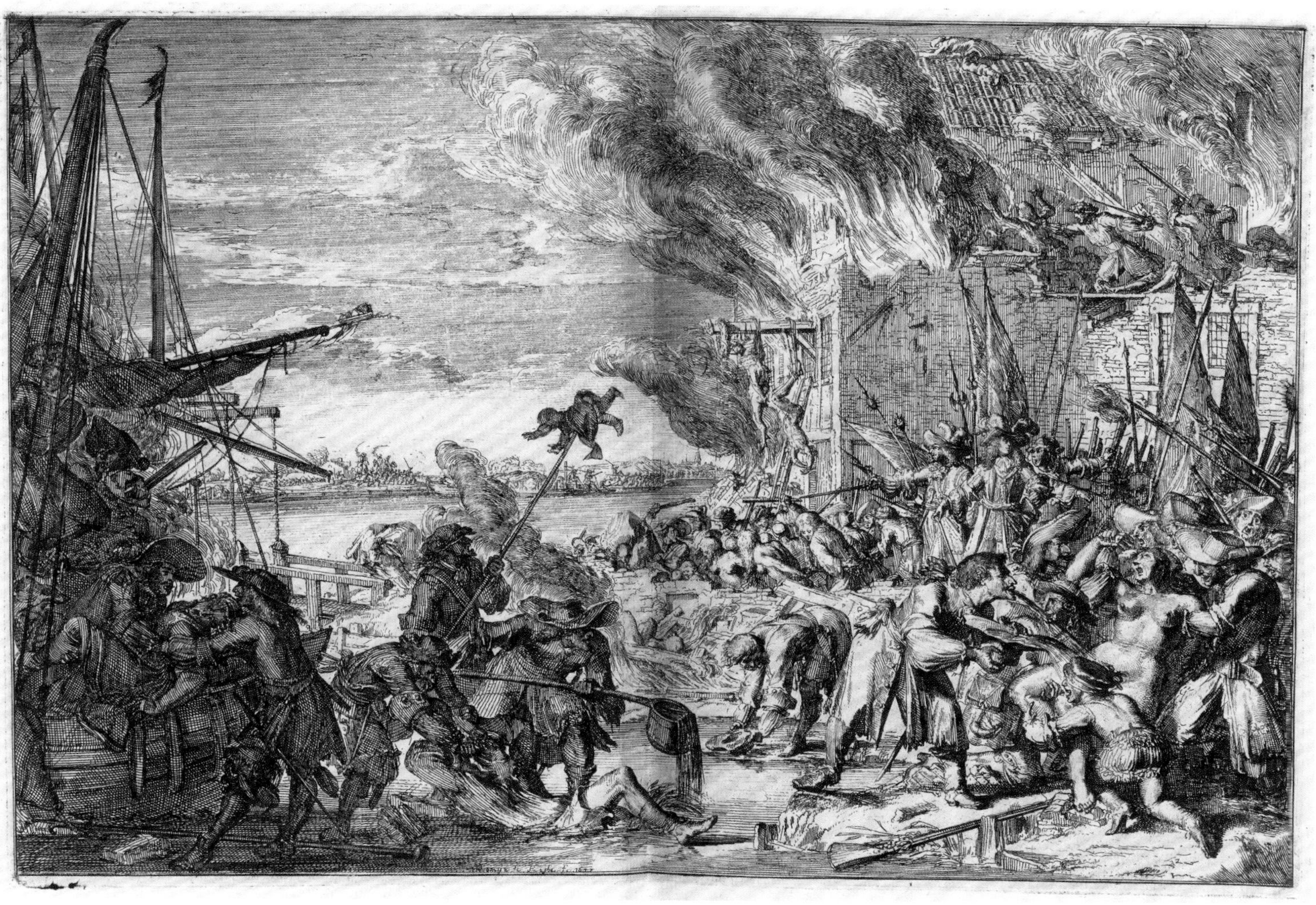

NOTES

1. De Wicquefort's influential book on diplomacy was written in prison, for like the great legal scholar Hugo Grotius, he was sentenced to life imprisonment in Castle Loevestein following the assassination of Johan de Witt, grand pensionary of the United Provinces, who had hired him as special secretary for French correspondence. He escaped in 1679. De Wicquefort's life and contributions to diplomacy are discussed in Berridge, Keens-Soper, and Otte 2001, 80–124.

2. Robb 1966, 1:269. Louis XIV's declaration of war against the Dutch in April 1672 was followed by the rapid conquest by his armies (and those of his allies the bishop of Münster and the archbishop of Cologne) of all the Dutch provinces with the exception of Holland and Utrecht, although the city of Utrecht had already been taken by the French. In July 1672, alarmed by the rapidity of the enemy advance, the Dutch opened the dikes, flooding the countryside from 's-Hertogenbosch to Amsterdam and sealing off the peninsula that includes most of the provinces of Holland and Utrecht.

3. By Christmas, the flooded landscape had frozen so that the duke of Luxembourg, commander of the French troops at Utrecht, was able to march his army westward on the ice with the intention of sacking The Hague. His soldiers set out with this expectation, but because of a thaw on 28 December, Luxembourg could not proceed and retreated with his army, allowing the French troops to vent their fury on the villages of Bodegraven and Zwammerdam. On the events leading up to this situation, see Trevelyan 1930, 311–17; Robb 1966, 1:265–69; and Wilson 1974, 159–65. De Wicquefort claimed that the background to the massacre was that the troops had been promised riches from sacking The Hague, but when their hopes were dashed, they took immediate revenge (De Wicquefort 1673, 48).

JAN DE BAEN
1633–1702

Orphaned at the age of three, Jan de Baen was taken in around 1645 by his uncle, the painter and magistrate Heinrich Piemans, who lived in Emden in East Friesland and was his first teacher of painting.[1] In 1646 De Baen was apprenticed to the Amsterdam portraitist and history painter Jacob Backer (1608–51), and in 1660 he moved to The Hague. There he married Maria de Koinderen, with whom he would have at least eight children, and soon became successful as a portraitist. Houbraken's account of his life also states that he worked for the court of Charles II in London, an undocumented service that probably occurred in the late 1660s.[2] Other distinguished clients included Johann Maurits of Nassau-Siegen, Frederick William, elector of Brandenburg, members of the stadtholder's family, and the directors of the Dutch East India

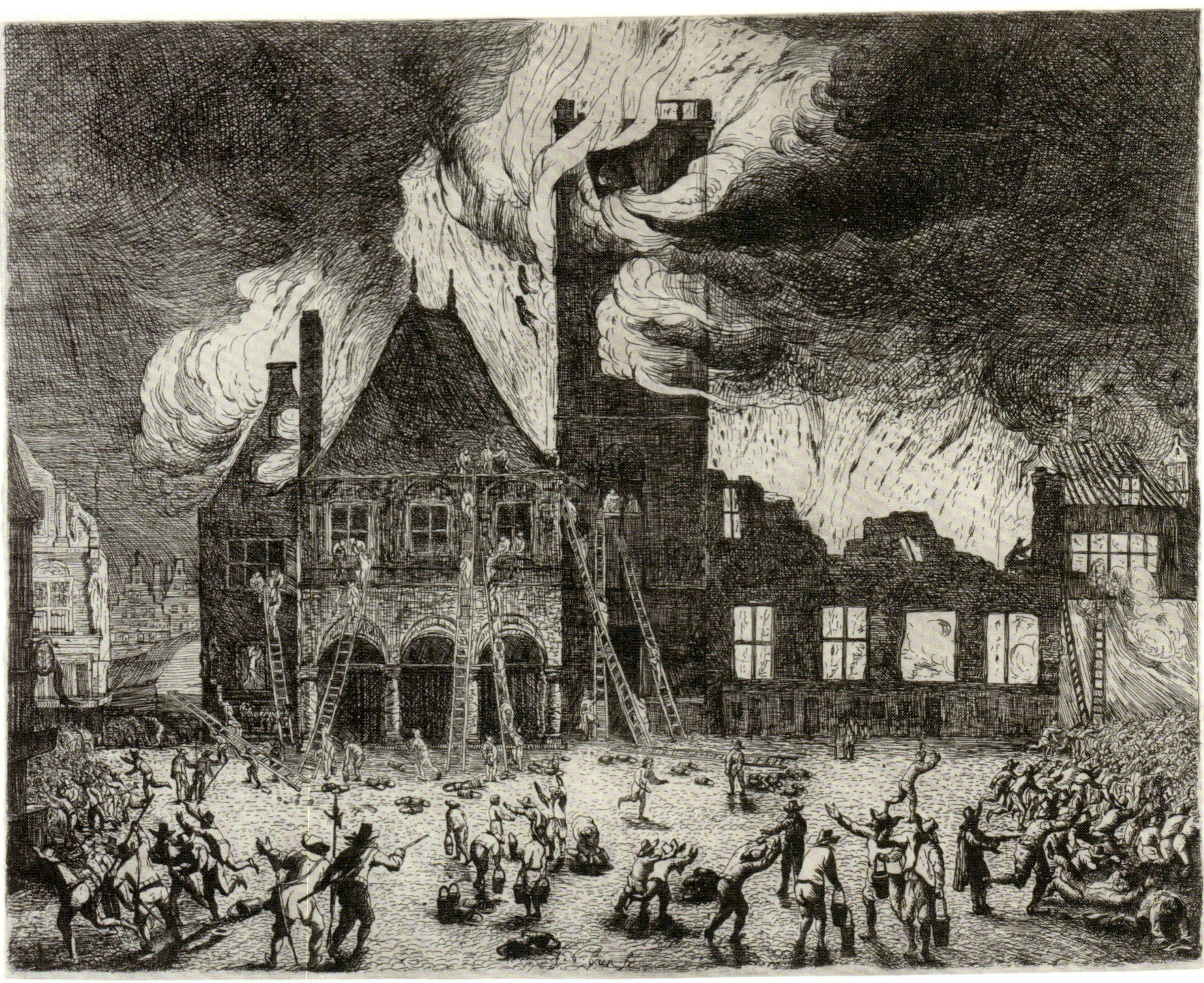

Company in Hoorn, whose group portrait of 1682 is in the Westfries Museum. De Baen's fashionable, life-size portraits, usually in half-length format, brought him not only a comfortable income but also a respected position in society. From 1660 on, he was a member of Pictura, the painters' confraternity in The Hague. In 1672 he became captain of The Hague civic guard and in 1699 was appointed regent of the city's drawing academy.

NOTES

1. Biographical information on De Baen is based upon R. E. O. Ekkart's essay in *Dictionary of Art* 1996, 3:42.

2. Houbraken 1718–21 (1753), 2:305.

[40]

Burning of the Town Hall, Amsterdam, 1652

Inscriptions: none

Etching, 261 × 338 mm (10¼ × 13 15/16 in.); state i/ii

Courtesy of the Fogg Art Museum, Harvard University Art Museums, Cambridge, Massachusetts, Light-Outerbridge Collection, Richard Norton Memorial Fund, M24443

References: Hollstein 1 (1949):64; Nash 1972, 247; Lawrence/New Haven/Austin 1983–84, 198–200, no. 57.

The original town hall of Amsterdam, built in 1395 on the Dam, was severely damaged by fire in 1421 and again in 1452, which necessitated restoration and additions to the main building, whose shaky spire would eventually be taken down in 1615. By the early seventeenth century, the historic but dilapidated structure had become far too small for the many political, judicial, and administrative functions it housed. In 1639 the burgomasters first made the proposal to the town council for a new town hall.[1]

This grand neoclassical structure, designed by Jacob van Campen (1595–1657), rose behind the site of the old building on the west side of the Dam between 1648 and 1655.

In the early hours of 7 July 1652, fire broke out in the Old Town Hall, soon reducing it to a ruin. Rembrandt's pen and wash drawing (Museum Het Rembrandthuis, Amsterdam, Fig. 75), whose inscription notes that he sketched the scene from the Weigh House two days after the event, shows the gutted structure with ladders still uselessly propped against the remains of its walls.[2] Jan de Baen's etching of the event is the only known work from his early years, and it remains an anomaly in an oeuvre that consists almost entirely of painted portraiture. Made in a reproductive medium that allows an image to be broadly disseminated, the print memorializes a building of great historic importance to the city of Amsterdam, while serving as the souvenir of a major civic accident, as would representations of the Delft gunpowder explosion made two years later by Herman Saftleven and Daniel Vosmaer (Cats. 41 and 42).[3]

Because of its nocturnal setting this conflagration has a frightening immediacy, for the flames that make visible the distinctive profile of the landmark building destroy it even as they reveal it. The progress of the fire is shown to be implacable. The wing at right—the location of the Discount Bank, which played a crucial role in Amsterdam's financial ascendancy—has been almost completely consumed, its shattered facade backlit by a raging inferno.[4] The tower in the center, site of the burgomasters' chamber where decisions affecting the entire Republic were made, is still intact, but smoke and flames pour from its windows. The original medieval core of the building at left, where the Courts of Justice were housed, has not yet ignited and is the focus of desperate men maneuvering ladders and bucket brigades. That their efforts are hopeless is indicated both by the enormity of the blaze and by the attitudes of the people in the illuminated square—some standing by helplessly, many more running from the intense heat. Not until the early 1670s did more effective means of fighting fires become available with the development of the pump and flexible fire hose by the Amsterdam fire master and architectural painter Jan van der Heyden (q.v.). His treatise describing the new system and vividly illustrating its advantages was published in 1690 (Cat. 46 and Figs. 76 and 135).

NOTES

1. On the need for building a new town hall, see Fremantle 1959, 24. As early as 1641, Pieter Saenredam (1597–1665) had made a detailed architectural portrait drawing that documents the appearance of the Old Town Hall (Rijksmuseum, Amsterdam), perhaps in response to discussions about building a new one. Some seventeen years after the fire, the drawing became the model for his painting *The Old Town Hall, Amsterdam*, dated 1657, which he sold to the city as a commemorative piece for display in the new town hall. It was installed there in 1658 but is now on loan to the Rijksmuseum, Amsterdam.

2. Jan Abrahamsz. Beerstraaten (1622–66) also drew the ruins after the fire (Amsterdams Historisch Museum, see Fig. 74) and made a painting of the same site from a different point of view (Rijksmuseum, Amsterdam, no. A 21; repr. Amsterdam/Toronto 1977, 203, no. 99). A drawing by Pieter de With (fl. 1650–60) also shows the ruins of the Town Hall (Herzog Anton Ulrich-Museum, Braunschweig, no. 363; repr. Sumowski 1979–92, 10 [1991]:5465). Another painting of the fire in progress by Gerrit Lundens (1622–c. 1683) is now in the Amsterdams Historisch Museum (repr. Amsterdam/Toronto 1977, 223, no. 119).

3. Hollstein notes the existence of a second state of De Baen's print dated 9 July 1652, two days after the event (Hollstein 1 [1949]:64), as also mentioned by L. Stone-Ferrier in Lawrence/New Haven/Austin 1983–84, 200.

4. For definition of the functions that took place in various sections of the old Town Hall, see Haak 1969, 232.

HERMAN SAFTLEVEN
1609–85

Brother of the peasant genre painter and allegorist Cornelis Saftleven (1607–81), Herman Saftleven was born in Rotterdam but had settled in Utrecht by around 1632. His marriage there to Anna van Vliet in 1633 was documented, as were the subsequent births of the couple's two sons and two daughters (Sara Saftleven was to become a flower painter). In 1659 Herman Saftleven became an official citizen of Utrecht and during the period between 1655 and 1657 served on several occasions as dean of the St. Luke's guild. In 1662 he took charge of arranging the sale of part of the collection of the earl of Arundel, whose widow, Lady Althea Talbot, was one of his patrons. Late in his career, beginning around 1680, he was commissioned to make watercolors of plants for the botanist Agnes Block (1629–1704) at her country estate, Vijverhof, on the Vecht River, near Utrecht. Saftleven was buried in the Buurkerk in Utrecht on 5 January 1684.[1]

Both a painter and a printmaker, Saftleven painted a few rustic barn interiors with his brother but became primarily a specialist in landscape, which he first painted and etched in Italianate styles influenced by Cornelis van Poelenburch (q.v.) and Jan Both (q.v.). After about 1645, perhaps under the influence of a trip to the eastern Dutch province of Gelderland, he shifted to native Dutch scenes. More than 1 200 landscape drawings by Saftleven are known, including topographical views of Utrecht and its monuments, as well as views of other parts of the Netherlands and the Rhine regions of Germany. Of particular interest are the drawings he made to record buildings damaged or destroyed in the hurricane or tornado that devastated Utrecht in 1674 (Cat. 48 and Fig. 138). Saftleven's practice of making documentary drawings served him well, for around 1682, some eight years after this storm, he sold to the city of Utrecht a series of twenty-two drawings he had made of the local churches before their destruction.

NOTE

1. Both of the Saftleven brothers have been the subjects of monographs by W. Schulz (for Cornelis, see Schulz 1978, and for Herman, see Schulz 1982). On Herman Saftleven's biography, see also Schulz in *Dictionary of Art* 1996, 27:517–19, and Amsterdam/Boston/Philadelphia 1987–88, 474–76.

[41]

View of Delft after the Explosion of the Gunpowder Arsenal on October 12, 1654, 1654

Inscriptions: across the top, *.De Stadt Delft. Al waer de H.M. heere Staten haer Magusijn. tooren op den Maendach voorde middach tussen tiennen en half Elf ueren Den 12 octob: 1654. is in de locht op ge Sprongen Als:.A.* (The city of Delft where the arsenal tower of the H[igh] and M[ighty] States [of Holland] exploded on Monday morning between the hours of ten and half past ten on October 12, 1654, as A)

Across the bottom: *.A. is dus daennigeh gadt ofte poel al waerden tooren gestaen heeft toen ick het tekende 13 voeten diep was ende vol / waters stont sinde op den 29 octob: niewen stil getekent. / .B. is de nieuwe kerk al waer de glaessen end een groot Gadt uit het dack geslagen was ende seer beschadicht doch / de wapens ende het Sepeltuer nich geen vande ornemente om sijn hoochheijts Gaft nietbeschadicht / .C. Is de oude Kerck al waer glaessen ende Mueren sijn wech geslagen Ick hebbe een Remerkabel dingen in dese Kerck gesien dat de / muer achter het Wapen vanden Admirael Tromp was wech gesprongen ende sijn wapen bliffen gangen ende niet beschadicht noch vanden Admirael Piet hein van gelicken niet beschadicht: / .D. de plaets al waer de Doellen heft gestaen en ook al water de meit vanden Doellen op* *den 27 octob: op dese plaets van onderen uit de steenen is / ge haelt ende met kleeren en al begraven datse soo mijserabel was getrackteert. / .E. De boomen van die op de Stadts Wallen staen sinde als niet ofte weinnich beschadicht Et.* (A. is the hole or pool 13 feel deep and full of water where the tower had stood when I drew it on 29 October new style. B. is the Nieuwe Kerk where the glass was destroyed and a large hole torn in the roof and was very damaged, but the coats of arms and the sepulchre and the ornament on his majesty's grave were not damaged. C. is the Oude Kerk where the glass and the walls were torn away. I saw a remarkable thing in this church that the wall behind the arms of Admiral Tromp was blown away but the arms were not damaged, also those of Admiral Piet Hein were similarly not damaged. D. is the place where the Militia Hall stood and also where the maid of the Militia Hall was pulled out fully clothed from under the stones on 27 October so miserable from having been buried. E. the trees which stand on the city walls were little or not at all damaged.)[1]

Black chalk, pen and brown ink, brush and brown wash on two sheets of paper, 249 × 749 mm (9 13/16 × 29½ in.)

Lent by the Metropolitan Museum of Art, New York, Purchase, Bequest of Helen Hay Whitney, by exchange, and the Mnuchin Foundation, Mr. & Mrs. David M. Tobey and Werner H. Kramarsky Gifts, 1995, 1995.197

References: Schulz 1982, 75, no. 617; Broos 1985, 114, 135, no. 7a; Logan 1996; Plomp 1996, 355–57; New York/London 2001, 486–87, no. 124.

Saftleven's extraordinary panoramic drawing, made on 29 October 1654, records this Utrecht artist's experience of one of the great accidental catastrophes of the seventeenth century: the explosion of a huge gunpowder depot in Delft, where some eighty or ninety thousand pounds of gunpowder had been left in storage since the Dutch wars with the Spanish (see also Cat. 42). The explosion, which occurred on the morning of Monday, 12 October 1654, laid waste a large sector in the northeast part of the city, killing hundreds of people including the celebrated Delft painter Carel Fabritius (1622–54). Saftleven's meticulous documentation of the event, which includes a title, explanatory texts, and a detailed illustration, is similar to contemporary printed broadsheets (Cats. 35–38), which combined images with texts in order to comment on events or issues of wide public interest. As C. Logan has pointed out, Saftleven, who had the apparently unique idea of using this distinctive documentary format for a drawing, may have produced his elaborate, large-scale illustration on speculation, hoping that it would serve a public commemorative function.[2] A related intention may stand behind Vermeer's celebrated horizontal, panoramic *View of Delft* (c. 1660, Mauritshuis, The Hague, no. 92), made only a few years later, in which the artist placed himself outside the city walls, looking north as if to bring back the intactness of the recently damaged city.[3] Taking an opposite point of view, from the northeast section of the city looking south, Saftleven's drawing maximizes the effects of the devastation.

The unusual breadth of Saftleven's vista, drawn on two horizontal sheets of paper attached at the center, suggests that it was made not on the site, but in the studio, as does the first part of the legend inscribed below, which notes that the artist drew the scene (past tense) on 29 October.[4] If Saftleven made preparatory sketches outdoors, none are known today; but even if such compositional aids were employed, the assurance of this complex production, which reveals no hesitations or corrections whatsoever, is astonishing. At almost seventy-five centimeters across, the image is slightly too wide to be taken in at one glance, forcing the viewer to scan the scene closely and sequentially from side to side. Guided by letters that mark points of special interest described in the text, one identifies ground zero (A) as the large pool of water (thirteen feet deep) in the center where the underground arsenal stood, beyond which stands the Nieuwe Kerk (New Church) (B), whose glass was destroyed and whose roof was badly damaged in the explosion. At the far right appears the Oude Kerk (Old Church) (C), which also lost its glass as well as parts of its walls. Between the two churches, the letter D identifies the site of the lost militia hall.

Interestingly, Saftleven also reminds the viewer of what was miraculously spared. Letter E at the far left draws attention to the trees along the town wall, which also escaped with little damage—a point the artist reiterates visually by contrasting them to the bare, burned remnants of trees at the far right. Also saved was the maid of the militia hall, who was pulled fully clothed from under the stones on 27 October, "miserable from having been buried" ("al begraven datse soo mijserabel was getrackeert"); the coats of arms and sepulchre in the Nieuwe Kerk on the grave of William the Silent (1533–84), founder of the Dutch Republic; and in the Oude Kerk, the coats of arms of two great Dutch admirals, Maarten Tromp (1597–1653) and Piet Hein (1588–1629). Such pointed patriotic references to the historic importance of Delft and its inhabitants suggest how strongly the damage to this particular city must have reverberated throughout the Dutch provinces, especially in the years following 1648, when national independence was finally established by the Treaty of Münster.

Seventeen days after the explosion, when Saftleven made this drawing, this site surely remained busy, if not with rescuers, then with salvage workers picking through the rubble, not to mention the curious visitors who reportedly flocked to Delft from within and even beyond the Dutch provinces.[5] Yet unlike paintings of this subject by Saftleven's contemporaries (Cat. 42), this scene is utterly devoid of people, though not of human presence. The silent and surprising emptiness and immobility of the ruined city generates much of the drawing's intense mood. Although the foreground area has been flattened by the explosion, the background is crowded with buildings (remnants of human effort and presence) whose shapes remain intact even though their roofs have been blown off and their inhabitants are now absent. As reported by Dirck van Bleyswijck, historian of the city of Delft, the blast (described as stronger than a hundred thousand cannon detonations in a city under attack) destroyed more than two hundred houses and deprived at least three hundred more of their roofs and windows, along with all the fragile glassware and porcelains inside.[6]

By using short, lively strokes of black chalk with brown wash—darker in the foreground and paler toward the background—Saftleven conveys his own seemingly spontaneous reaction to a view he observed directly from life. Yet at the same time, the unusual size of this drawing, the controlled beauty of the artist's draftsmanship, which includes subtle shadings of clouds in the sky, and the elegant precision of his calligraphy elevate the image to a more enduring commemoration.

NOTES

1. For translation of the inscriptions, see Logan 1996, 209 n. 2.

2. There is no evidence that Saftleven was commissioned to make the drawing for the municipality or for another patron; indeed it seems possible that the artist retained it during his lifetime. Recorded in the inventory of the collector Sybrand Feitama (1694–1758), it may have come into the collection of his father Isaac (d. 1709) as early as 1695, within ten years of Saftleven's death. Logan 1996, 209; Broos 1985, 114.

3. A. Chong and E. Haverkamp-Begemann in The Hague 1977, 246, no. 92.

4. Logan 1996, 205.

5. Among the visitors were Elizabeth, Queen of Bohemia, and the Amsterdam artist Gerbrand van

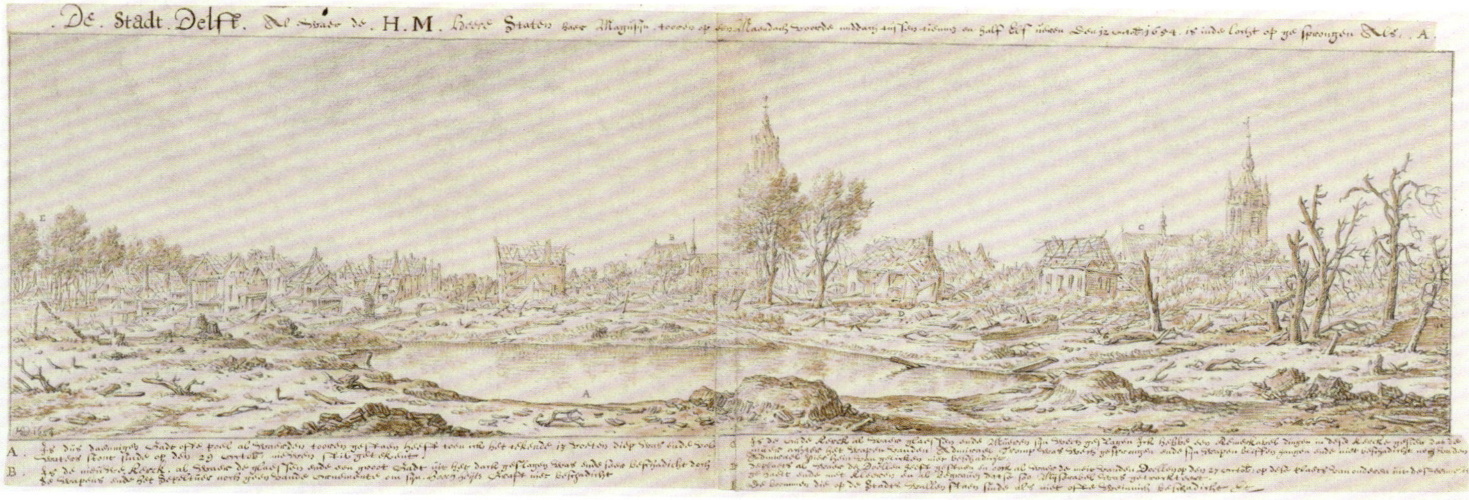

[41]

den Eeckhout (1621–1674), who had been hired to make a drawing (Kupferstichkabinett, Staatliche Museen, Berlin, inv. no. 12815) of the ruin site for the title page etching of a pamphlet by Jan Philipsz. Schabaeltje, *Historisch Verhael van het wonderlich en schrickelick opspringen van 't-Magasyn-huys, voor-gevallen op den 12 october 1654 binnen Delft* (A historical account of the wondrous and terrible explosion of the powder magazine which occurred on 12 October 1654 inside Delft). For discussion of both drawing and print, see M. Plomp's entry on the Berlin drawing in New York/London 2001, 470–71. See also D. H. A. C. Lokin in Delft 1996, 97–98, fig. 80, and 128 n. 14.

6. Van Bleyswijck 1667/80, 2:622–38.

DANIEL VOSMAER
1622–1669/70

Daniel Vosmaer, the son of a goldsmith, was baptized in Delft on 13 October 1622, and joined the St. Luke's guild in that city in 1650. His few known works are all landscapes and cityscapes. The Vosmaer family of artists and artisans also included Daniel's brother Nicolaes, a seascape painter (d. 1654), and his uncle Jacob (1584–1641), a specialist in flower painting.[1] Interestingly, the Vosmaer brothers apparently had connections to one of the most celebrated Delft artists, Carel Fabritius (1622–54). A series of documents dating from 1666 reveals that Daniel and Nicolaes Vosmaer had collaborated around 1652 with Fabritius on a painting, now lost, for which Fabritius contributed the preliminary drawing, Daniel the landscape, and Nicolaes the seascape.[2] By this time, although Daniel retained his citizenship in Delft, he was living in the town of Den Briel (Brielle), south of Rotterdam. On 23 August 1661 he had married Annetje Edwards de Neefe, a baker's widow, in the Grote Kerk. The couple had five children and apparently prospered, since both Daniel and his brother Abraham, also a resident of Den Briel, were able to derive substantial incomes from leases on the town's taxations of beer and wine.

Like his contemporary, Egbert van der Poel (q.v.), Daniel became known for his depictions of the so-called Delft Thunderclap, the massive explosion that occurred on the morning of 12 October 1654 in an armory where gunpowder from the Dutch war with the Spanish had been stored. This catastrophe destroyed a large section of Delft, killing Fabritius, among hundreds of others. Vosmaer painted depictions of the disaster and its immediate aftermath, as well as a number of more retrospective cityscapes with ruined buildings, shown as they came to look some time after the event had occurred. Both types of scenes are discussed here.

NOTES

1. Archival material about Vosmaer's family and life is from Albers and Van der Houwen 1996, 13, 19, nn. 14–18, and New York/London 2001, 421. An undated, unpaginated essay by Aart van der Houwen in the Gemeente Archief, Brielle ("De Brielse Schilder Daniel Vosmaer") reviews biographical data drawn from the town archives.

2. Obreen 1877–90, 5:167–69; Bredius 1915–22, 4 (1917):1437–38; Brown 1981, 52, 154–56 (doc. nos. 34–36); Montias 1982, 212–13; discussion of documents in New York/London 2001, 128–29 and 421.

[42]

Explosion of the Powder Magazine at Delft, 1654

Inscriptions: signed and dated, lower right corner, *den 12 October 1654 / Daniel Vosmaer*

Oil on panel, 73.7 × 104.1 cm (29 × 41 in.)

Wadsworth Atheneum Museum of Art, Hartford, Connecticut, The Ella Gallup Sumner and Mary Catlin Sumner Collection Fund, 1943.96

References: MacLaren 1960, 293–94; Donahue 1964, 20–21, fig. 2; Haverkamp-Begemann 1978, 199–200, no. 166; MacLaren/Brown 1991, 2:307 n. 2; New York/London 2001, 328 n. 5.

On the morning of Monday, 12 October 1654, shortly after 11:30, the ancient city of Delft was rocked by a deafening blast, as some eighty to ninety thousand tons of gunpowder that had remained in storage after the Dutch wars with the Spanish exploded in their hidden underground depot, located in the northeastern sector of the city (see also Cat. 41). Known as the Secreet van Hollandt, this munitions vault had been located since 1572 in the former Clarissenklooster or Convent of St. Clare. The so-called Delft Thunderclap (*Delftsche donderslag*) was heard all the way to the island of Texel, some seventy miles north of Delft, according to the town chronicler, Dirck van Bleyswijck, who wrote a vivid and extensive account of the disaster in the second volume of his history of Delft.[1] The explosion destroyed or damaged hundreds of houses, leveling the area bounded by the Singel to the east, the Verwersdijk to the west, the Geergweg to the north, and the Doelenstraat to the south and damaging other more distant structures throughout the city. Of the gunpowder depot itself, nothing remained but a deep pool of black water. This area would later be used as a horse market and it remains, even today, largely open and unbuilt upon.[2]

Among the hundreds of dead and wounded was the leading Delft painter, Carel Fabritius, who resided on the Doelenstraat. Brought from the wreckage alive, he succumbed to his injuries shortly thereafter, according to Van Bleyswijck, whose account also celebrated the rescue efforts and miraculous survival of those who were saved from the rubble. They seemed to emerge, in his words, "as if rising from the dead" ("... als uit de dood herrezen ..."): an eighty-year-old man, pulled out unharmed after thirty-six hours, and a baby holding an apple and still seated in her highchair after twenty-four hours under the ruins, who suffered only a slightly injured hand and thanked her rescuers with a friendly laugh.[3]

The Delft calamity, which transformed a section of the city into an instant ruin, attracted sympathetic and curious visitors from all over Europe, including Elizabeth Stuart, the widowed queen of Bohemia, and inspired the writing of numerous pamphlets and poems. Perhaps the most eloquent lines were penned by the dramatist Joost van den Vondel (1587–1679), who compared the scene of devastation to a churchyard full of bodies, noting how the gunpowder that had formerly protected the nation had now become, in a catastrophic instant, its enemy.[4] Indeed, it was not only the violence and unexpectedness of the disaster—whose cause was never explained—that captured the imagination of Vondel and others, but the fact that Delft was hallowed with such national historic importance. The original meeting place for the delegates of the Dutch provinces (States General), it was also the site of the assassination, in 1584, of William the Silent, leader of rebels, at the order of Philip II of Spain. The fatal bullet hole is still visible in the wall of the Prinsenhof, and Prince William's grave in the Nieuwe Kerk (New Church) remains one of the most important historic sites in the Dutch provinces.

Demand for depictions of the Delft explosion must have remained lively even years after the event, for Vosmaer made several versions of this composition, while his contemporary Egbert van der Poel (q.v.) produced more than twenty, including paintings that show the explosion in progress (Fig. 133).[5] Both artists selected a low viewpoint and panoramic horizontal format, taking a very similar vantage point from the northeast. Along the horizon can be seen the large towers of the Nieuwe Kerk at the far left, the Oude Kerk (Old Church) nearer the center of the scene, and between them the tower of the Town Hall. At the far right is the chapel of the St. Joris Gasthuis (St. George Hospital). In the Hartford painting, the pool of water at the right middle ground is probably the one that materialized at the site of the explosion itself, since it appears in other versions of the scene; the area around it has been almost flattened, and the trees broken off and burned bare.

An early work by Vosmaer, this example is executed in the broad, rather choppy brushstrokes and monochromatic brown and gray tones characteristic of his style of the 1650s—a manner of painting highly appropriate for this subject. In contrast to the jumble of fallen houses and twisted trees beyond, the more open foreground acts as a stagelike space, where selected figures act out the experience of the disaster. At the left, a man in a red cape stands alone with bent head beside a curved bridge. In the center, two men assist an injured woman. A boy runs toward them from the right, hands pressed over his ears as if the concussion of the blast were still ringing painfully in his head. Similar staffage was repeated in other paintings of this scene by both Van der Poel and Vosmaer, which raises the possibility that Van der Poel may have contributed the figures to Vosmaer's paintings.[6] It seems clear, in any case, that these artists developed something of a formula that could generate additional versions of the scene in response to continuing public demand.

For the painting in Hartford, Vosmaer used a closer vantage point than that seen in Van der Poel's versions of the event, so that the observer is brought nearer the scene and the vertical towers of the Oude Kerk and Nieuwe Kerk rise more emphatically above the shattered city.[7] Their apparent intactness, which contrasts so

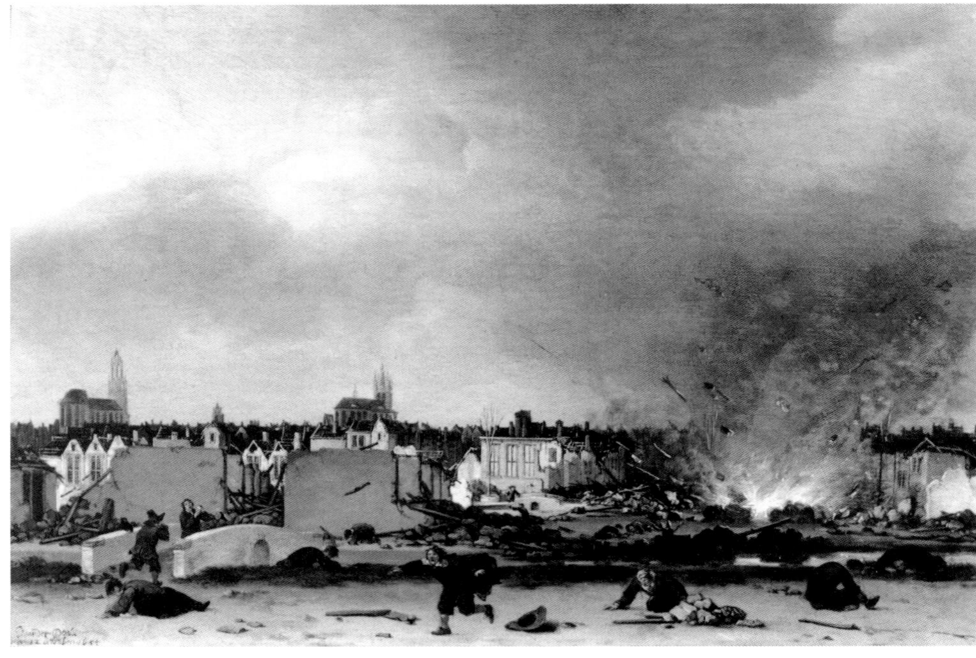

Fig. 133. Egbert van der Poel, *The Explosion of the Powder Magazine at Delft on Monday 12 October 1654*, oil on panel, Stedelijk Museum, Delft (on loan from the Rijksdienst Beeldende Kunst, The Hague)

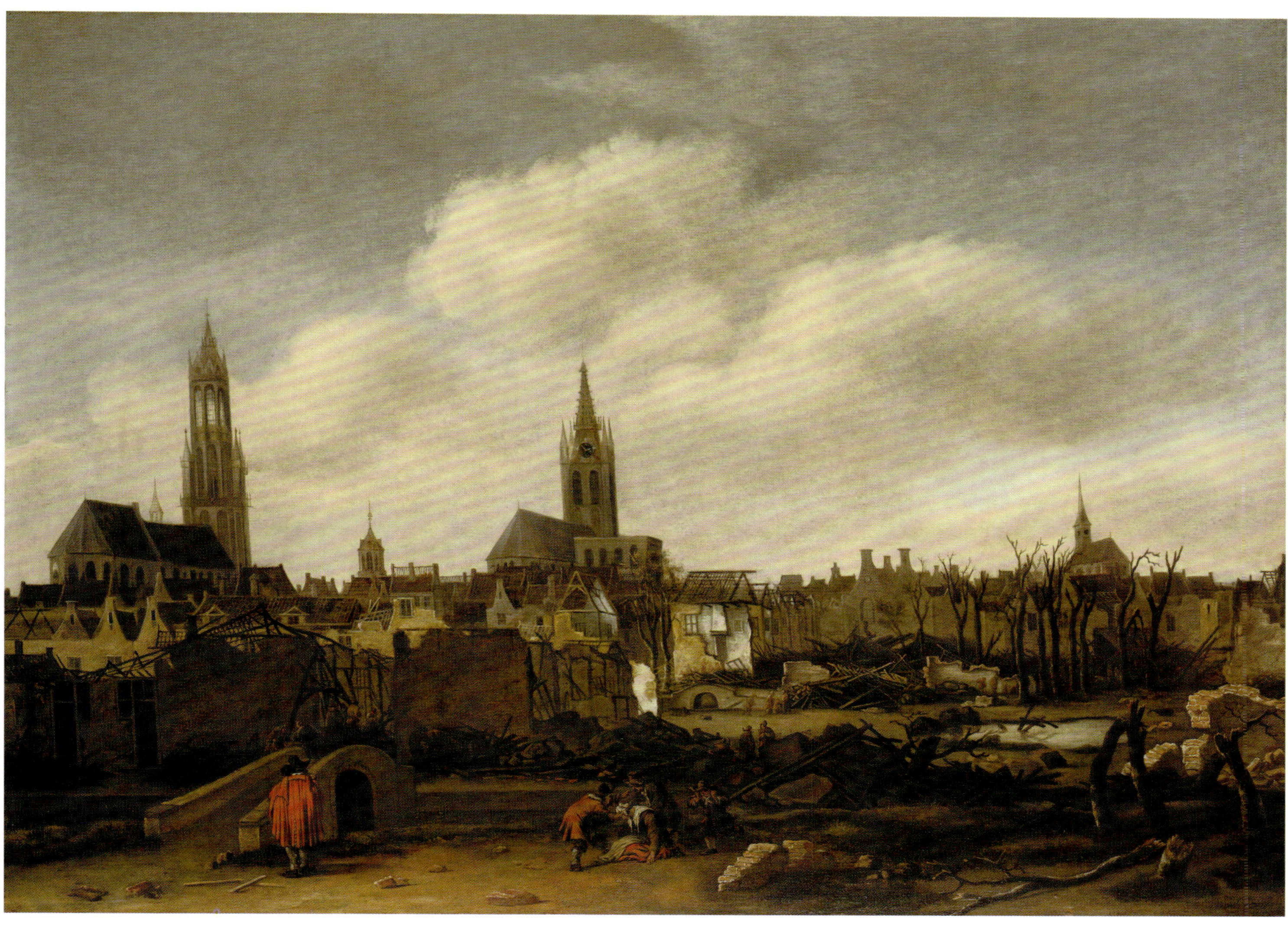

memorably with the wrecked roofs and walls all around, is belied by the account of a contemporary witness, Herman Saftleven, whose elaborate documentary drawing of the site, also reproduced here (Cat. 41), itemizes significant damage to both structures, including the loss of their stained glass. Nonetheless, the fact that the distinctive, instantly recognizable profiles of both churches were left standing—and more visible than ever before—must have evoked intense gratitude in the citizens of Delft, who were confronting a suddenly devastated city, inexplicably bombarded from within.

NOTES

1. Van Bleyswijck 1667–80, 2:622–33. See also MacLaren/Brown 1991, 1:306–9; Delft 1996, 94–96; and New York/London 2001, 326–27.

2. MacLaren/Brown 1991, 1:307.

3. "…zou zij haar redders uit dank een vriendlelijck lach gegeven hebben. Een van haar handjes was een weinig bezeerd; in het andere hield zig een appeltje vas om mee te spelen." Van Bleyswijck 1667–80, 2 (1680): 630. Quoted in Delft 1996, 128, n. 14. The astonishing story of the baby in the highchair was also reported in an unpaginated, undated Amsterdam pamphlet by Jan Philipsz. Schabaeltje: *Historisch Verhael van het wonderlich en schrickelick opspringen van 't-Magasyn-huys, voorgevallen op den 12 october 1654 binnen Delft* (A historical account of the wondrous and terrible explosion of the powder magazine, which occurred on 12 October 1654, inside Delft). Rembrandt's student Gerbrand van den Eeckhout (q.v.) included this incident in his pen and wash drawing of the aftermath of the explosion (Kupferstichkabinett, Staatliche Museen, Berlin, inv. no. 12815), made for the title page etching of the booklet. Both drawing and print are discussed and illustrated in M. Plomp's entry on the Berlin drawing in New York/London 2001, 470–71. See also D. H. A. C. Lokin in Delft 1996, 97–98, fig. 80, and 128 n. 14.

4. Vondel/Verwey 1986, 908, as quoted in Logan 1996, 205, and by M. Plomp in New York/London 2001, 486.

5. Versions of the scene by both artists are listed in MacLaren/Brown 1991, 1:307–8 n. 2. Van der Poel's extreme involvement with the subject may be explained by the fact that he lived so near the explosion site, next to Carel Fabritius in the Doelenstraat. One of his three young daughters may even have been killed in the blast, for her burial in the Nieuwe Kerk was recorded only two days later, on 14 October 1654.

6. The suggestion that Van der Poel painted the figures in Vosmaer's paintings is made in MacLaren/Brown 1991, 1:307–8 n. 4.

7. A very similar composition by Vosmaer (oil on panel, 72 × 97 cm) is in the Stedelijk Museum Het Prinsenhof, Delft , inv. no. PDS 107 (repr. Delft 1996, 97, fig. 79).

[43]

View of Delft after the Explosion of 1654, c. 1660–65

Inscription: traces of a signature at right corner

Oil on canvas, 67.6 × 55.6 cm (26⅝ × 21⅞ in.)

Philadelphia Museum of Art, John G. Johnson Collection, cat. no. 500

References: Hofstede de Groot 1 (1907):565, no. 317 (as de Hooch); Valentiner 1913, 96 and repr. 346 (as de Hooch); Brière-Misme 1927, vol. 10, 53–56 (as de Hooch); Valentiner 1926–27, 58 n. 2 (as Hendrik van der Burch?); Valentiner 1930, 28, repr., and 269 (as de Hooch); Valentiner 1932, 319 (as de Hooch); Donahue 1964, 23 and fig. 5 (as Vosmaer); Delft 1996, 98–99, fig. 81 (as Vosmaer).

This scene represents an area of ruined buildings and architectural remains in the northeastern sector of Delft: the site of the Delft Thunderclap, the cataclysmic explosion of a large gunpowder storage depot that unexpectedly blew up on the morning of 12 October 1654 (for further discussion of the event, see Cats. 41 and 42). To a viewer of this period, the ruins alone would probably have identified this city as Delft, for the accident was widely publicized throughout Europe and attracted many curious visitors. The well-dressed couple at the far left, strolling like tourists through the district, seem to be discussing the injured boy with a red cap, who is seated on a low mound of rubble. He has a bandage on his head and his arm in a sling as if he were recovering from the immediate aftereffects of the blast. Beside him, a small girl with her back to the viewer plays with a hoop, while two men stand in quiet discussion at the far right.

The scene as a whole, organized in a vertical format, builds effectively from foreground to background, beginning with an open, partially shadowed expanse of bare ground in the front to an area of low, truncated foundations and stairways in the middle ground, behind which broken walls appear in front of more-intact houses with damaged roofs. At the right background rises the large shape of Delft's Nieuwe Kerk (New Church), seen from the side and identifiable by its distinctive, three-level Gothic tower. An inscription on a documentary drawing made seventeen days after the event by Herman Saftleven (Cat. 41) reports that the explosion badly damaged this building, tearing a large hole in its roof and destroying its glass, but none of these losses are visible here.

Indeed, in contrast to Vosmaer's early depiction of the Delft explosion in Hartford (Cat. 42), in which the immediate aftermath of the event is pictured in an arid, blackened landscape from which all grass and foliage have been burned away, the Philadelphia painting presents a mellower, less devastated interpretation of the site, as it must have appeared some years after the disaster. The large trees at the left, although thinly foliated, are covered with leaves and silhouetted against a blue sky with white clouds, while grass has grown back on the ground and shrubbery around the broken walls. The shattered walls and foundations, bathed in softly filtered sunlight, stand out as distinct shapes, weathered to harmonious tones of brown and tan. Clearly this is a place that has been acted on by time as well as by circumstance. And yet the sightseers' response to the injured boy implies that the artist has depicted this corner of the city not long after its destruction. Such staffage, which was probably added to enliven the scene with an anecdotal reminder of what caused the ruins, appears to have been borrowed from Vosmaer's Delft contemporary Pieter de Hooch, who included an almost identical couple at the left in his *Family Portrait in a Courtyard* of about 1657–60 in the Akademie in Vienna.[1]

NOTE

1. Oil on canvas, 114 × 97 cm, Gemäldegalerie der Akademie der bildenden Künste, Vienna, inv. no. 715 (Sutton 1980, no. 24, color pl. III, facing p. 32). The little girl with the hoop is also very similar to a figure in De Hooch's *Woman Reading with a Child*, whose present location is unknown (Sutton 1980, no. 50, fig. 53). Most early scholars attributed the Philadelphia painting to De Hooch, as did Hofstede de Groot in the first volume of his lexikon of Dutch paintings, published in 1907 (Hofstede de Groot 1 [1907]:565), but W. R. Valentiner's first publication on De Hooch (but not his later ones) stated that the work "seems to me to be more likely by Hendrik van der Burch than Pieter De Hooch." Valentiner 1926–27, 58 n. 2.

[44]

View of a Dutch Village with a Ruined Wall, c. 1660–65

Oil on panel, 64.1 × 53 cm (25¼ × 20⅞ in.)

The Frances Lehman Loeb Art Center, Vassar College, Poughkeepsie, New York, Agnes Rindge Claflin Fund, 1962.2

References: Donahue 1964, 18, 24–25, fig. 1; Faison 1964, 231; Vassar College Art Gallery 1967, 18; Sutton 1986, 240, fig. 356; Delft 1996, 100; Liedtke 2000, 220, 221, fig. 276; New York/London 2001, 423–25, no. 87.

This unusual painting depicts a quiet, sun-dappled view of a Dutch village that features a dramatic contrast between foreground and background, established by differences in the scale and condition of the buildings in the two areas. In the background, rows of modest red-brick houses with triangular gables are set into the landscape in front of a low hill with a densely planted forest. In front of the houses, a screen of regularly spaced trees provides shade for a small park. Here, neatly laid-out squares of grass and shrubbery create a protected, civilized environment, where several pairs of the local inhabitants quietly converse, as a dog ambles into the scene at the far left. Other figures appear near the various house doorways and along the curving bridge at the right.

The intactness of this peaceful vista provides a striking foil for the immediate foreground, which is occupied by the looming shapes of a ruined house and its attached brick wall. The weathered surface of the wall seems virtually on the picture plane, so that its top, broken off at a diagonal emphasized by a continuous line of sunlight, forms a kind of inner frame for the tranquil townscape just beyond it, further emphasizing the village's atmosphere of protected seclusion.[1] The wall rises to the right to join the shattered section of a house, whose triangular roof still retains many of its red ceramic tiles, even though the whitewashed wall beneath it, also touched with soft sunlight, has been badly damaged. Vosmaer's choice of a vertical format for his painting emphasizes the tenacity of these damaged structures, which still stand as ascending shapes within the picture space, as does the tall, densely foliated tree rising over the ruined house at the right. The close juxtaposition of these highly contrasting motifs makes one question what might have caused the destruction of this building and, further, why the villagers have never repaired it.

Vosmaer's well-known depictions of the immediate and longer-range consequences of the Delft gunpowder explosion of 1654, two of which are discussed here (Cats. 42 and 43), would suggest that the Vassar painting also refers to the aftermath of this catastrophic event. That the broken walls appear sheared off, rather than crumbling and collapsing, and are nowhere overgrown with foliage implies that the event that transformed them must have been both sudden and shattering. Indeed, while the large tree in the foreground is intact, several of the ones in the park, although still green, appear to have been truncated to half

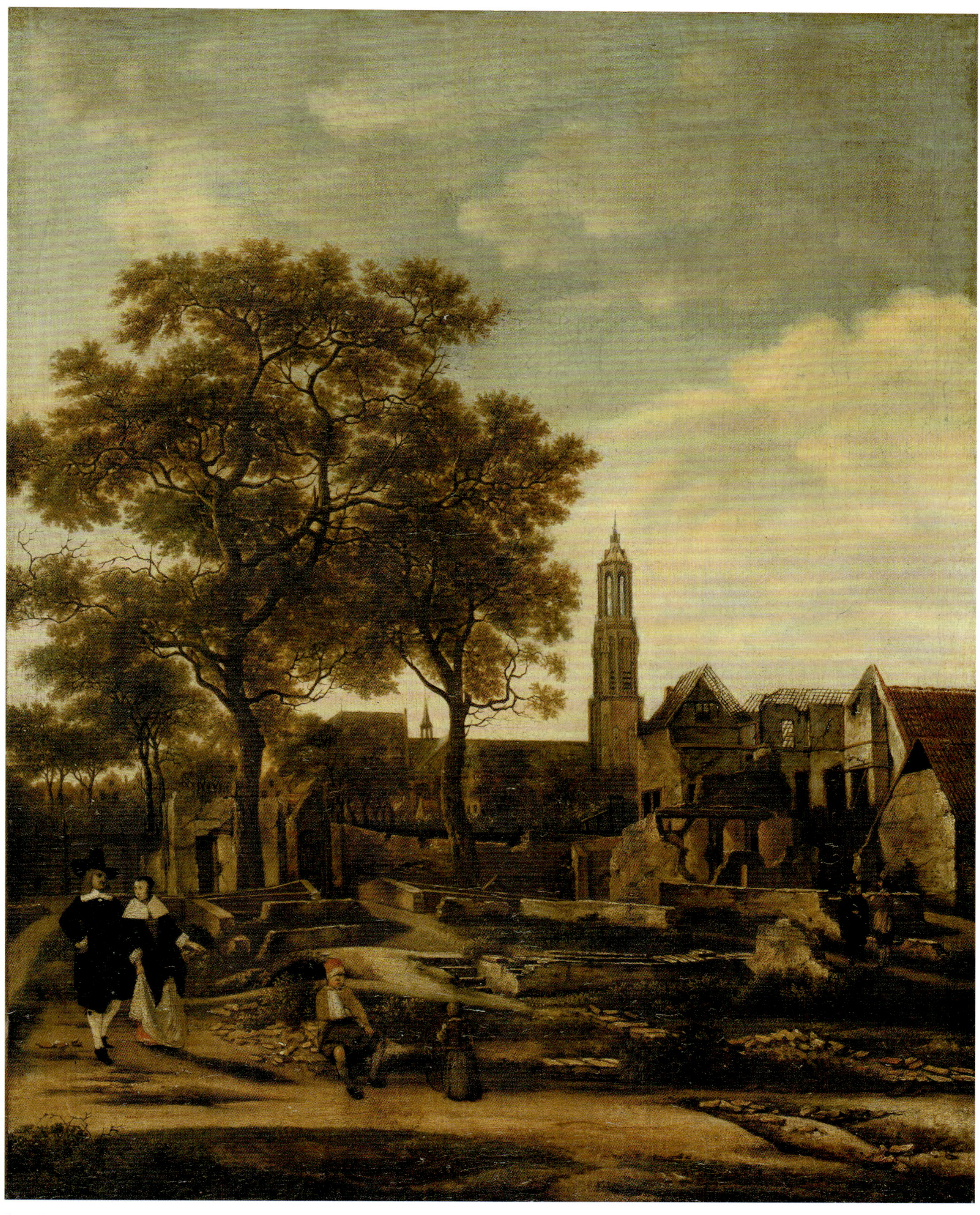

[43]

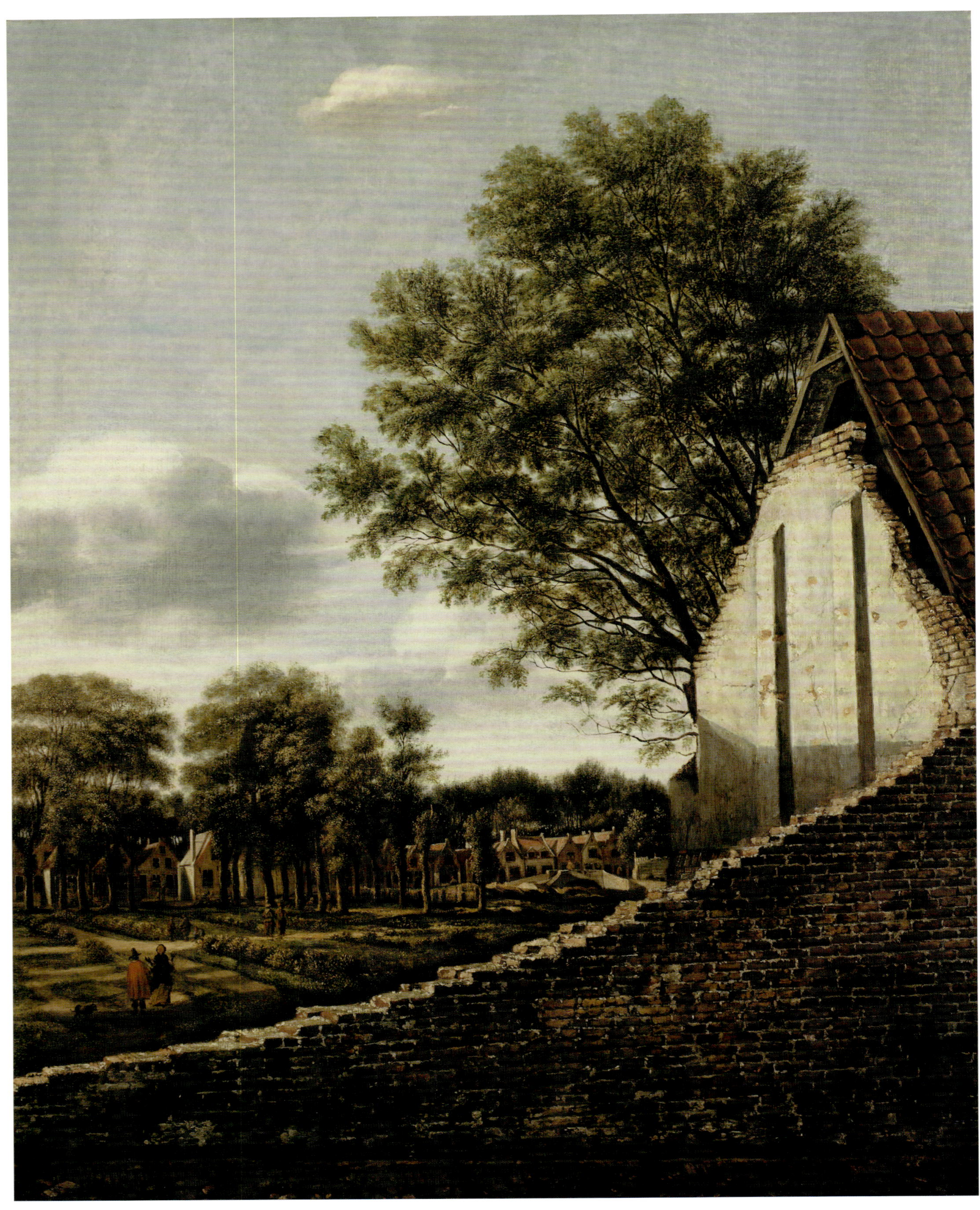

their original height. The close integration of these damaged motifs into the landscape as a whole, greatly assisted by a soft illumination that binds all parts of the scene, produces an effect of serenity, not violence. At the same time, the eye-catching irregularities of the broken wall have the effect of reminding the viewer, through contrast, that the small houses beyond the wall are whole and well cared for. A Delft citizen of this period might well have enjoyed remembering, from the safe vantage point of the present, how a recent local trauma had been survived and transcended. Something of the same sentiment may have inspired the widespread appreciation for various medieval ruins in the Dutch landscape that would have reminded viewers of this period of the Dutch triumph in the wars with the Spanish.

NOTE

1. Vosmaer often exploited such sunlit edges in his paintings as devices to clarify the structure of a composition or to distinguish its individual parts. Examples are the long, horizontal road in *View of Den Briel* in the Detroit Institute of Arts and the sunlit top of the jetty in *View of Delft* in the Ponce Art Museum, Puerto Rico—both of which traverse almost the entire width of the picture space. Donahue 1964, figs. 3 and 4.

EGBERT LIEVENSZ. VAN DER POEL 1621–64

Son of a goldsmith, Egbert van der Poel was baptized in the Oude Kerk in Delft on 9 March 1621.[1] His teacher is not known, but in 1650 he joined the Delft guild of St. Luke as a landscape painter. In 1651 he married Aeltgen Willems van Linschooten at Maassluis near Rotterdam. Baptismal records of his three daughters, born between 1651 and 1654, indicate that he continued to live in Delft. By the following year, he had settled in Rotterdam, where the baptism of a son was recorded in November 1655. Van der Poel was buried in Rotterdam on 18 June 1664.

Before 1654 Van der Poel concentrated on the kinds of peasant interiors painted by Rotterdam artists such as Cornelis Saftleven (1607–81) and Hendrick Martensz. Sorgh (1610/11–70) along with sketchy, rather monochromatic winter landscapes and canal and beach scenes. On 12 October 1654, however, an event occurred that profoundly marked his life and subsequent choice of subject matter: the explosion of Delft's huge underground storage depot for gunpowder (the "Delft Thunderclap") that left a large section of the city in ruins). Along with his fellow townsman Daniel Vosmaer (Cats. 42 and 43), Van der Poel repeatedly depicted the explosion and its aftermath even after moving from Delft to Rotterdam in 1655 (Fig. 133). During his late years, he painted related themes with nocturnal lighting effects such as fires (Fig. 73), festivals with flaming torches, and moonlit landscapes. Although Van der Poel is not widely known today, J. M. Montias listed him as the thirteenth out of the twenty most frequently recorded artists in Delft inventories.[2]

NOTES

1. Biographical material is from Goldschmidt 1922 and A. Rüger's account in New York/London 2001, 324. On Van der Poel's depictions of ruins, see Delft 1996, 94–96.

2. Montias 1982, 257, table 8.5.

[45]

Peasants Fleeing a Burning Barn, c. 1655

Inscriptions: signed lower left, *Eg van der Poel*

Oil on panel, 36.8 × 49.5 cm (14½ × 19½ in.)

The Detroit Institute of Arts, Founders Society Purchase, gift of James E. Scripps, by exchange, 1993.36

References: Milwaukee 1992, 134–35, no. 67, repr.; Keyes, Kuretsky, Rüger, and Wheelock 2004, 162–63, no. 67.

Depictions of fires were given a special designation in seventeenth-century Dutch inventories as *brandjes* (little fires), which indicates that the subject had considerable popularity and that

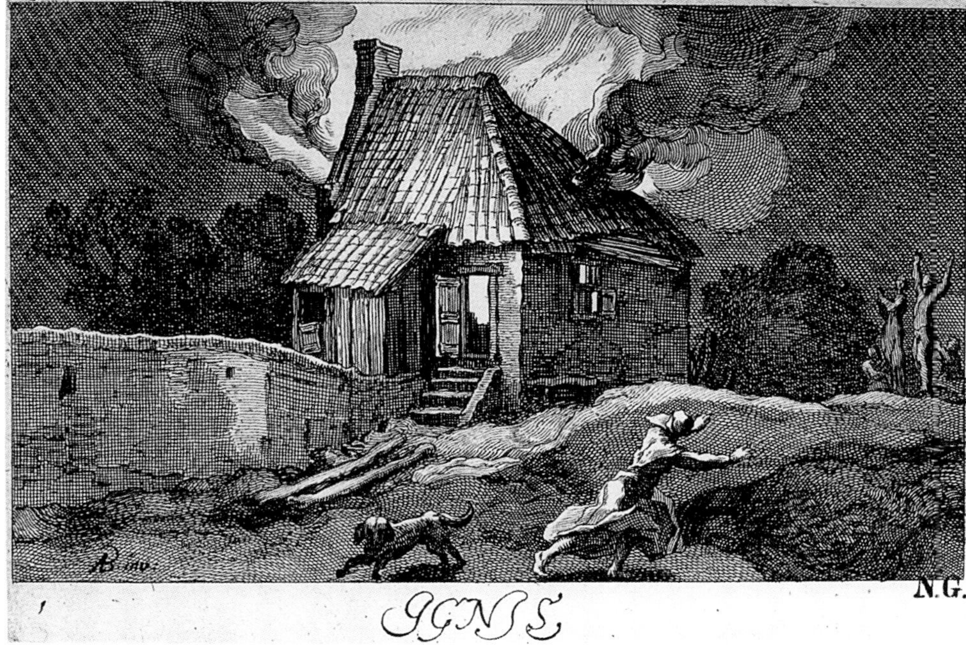

Fig. 134. Cornelis Bloemaert, *Ignis* (Fire), from *The Four Elements*, c. 1615–25, engraving, Prentenkabinet van de Universiteit Leiden

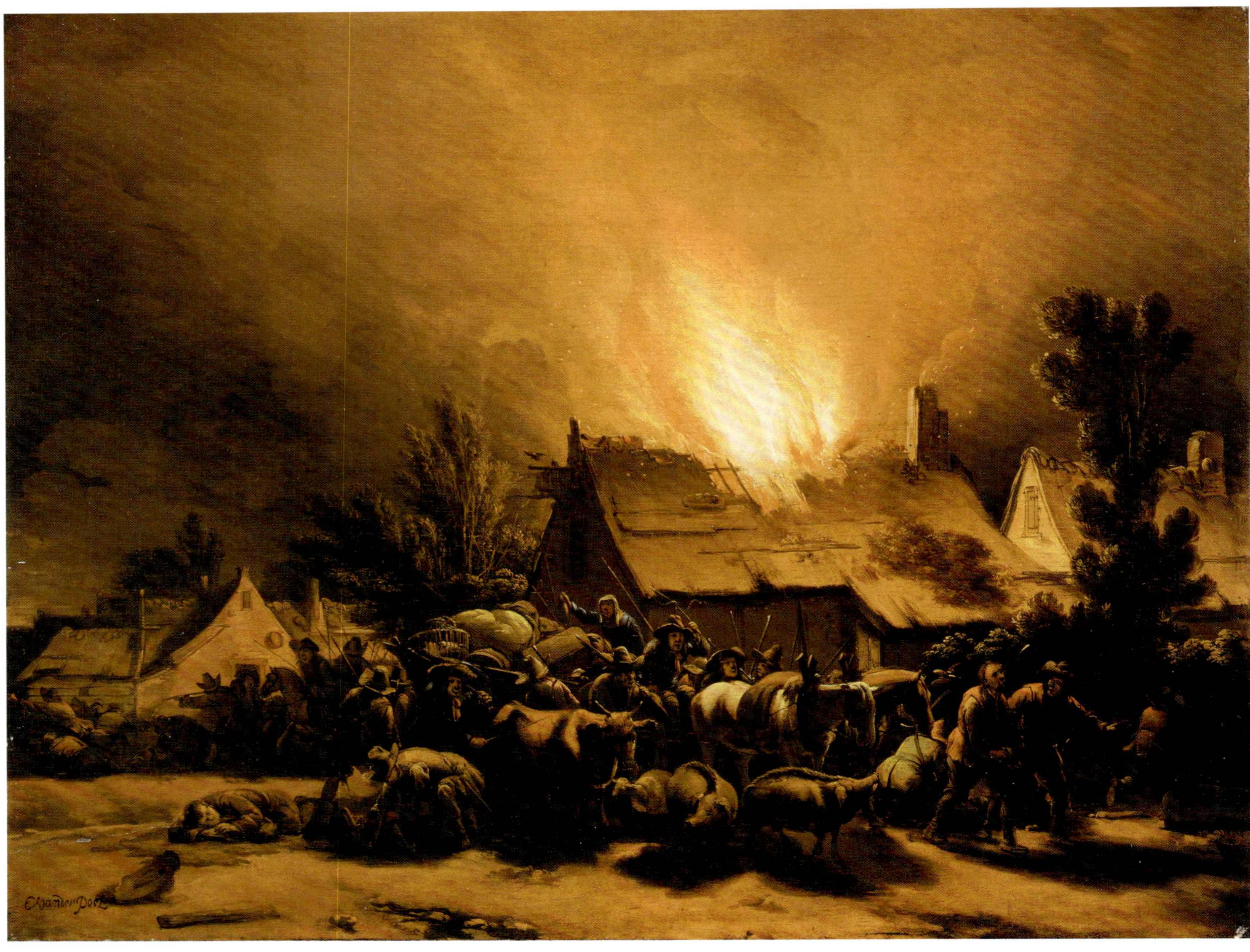

the artistic virtuosity needed to paint it was widely recognized.[1] Van der Poel was particularly singled out for his abilities in this area by Gerard van Spaan, whose history of the city of Rotterdam, published in 1698, praises him as "den besten Brantschilder van gansch Nederland" (the best fire painter in all of the Netherlands).[2] While other painters and printmakers tended to record conflagrations involving well-known civic buildings (Cat. 40 and Fig. 76), Van der Poel was often drawn to the destruction of anonymous rural structures such as barns or houses in local villages (see also Fig. 73).[3] Precedents for these images can be found in prints by Abraham Bloemaert's (q.v.) sons Frederick (q.v.) and Cornelis (1603–?1684) in which figures are seen fleeing from burning cottages whose thatched roofs have caught fire.[4] Cornelis Bloemaert's *Ignis* (Fire) from his *Four Elements* series of about 1615–25 is also a nocturnal scene (Fig. 134).

Van der Poel's interest in subjects involving accidental, life-threatening fire seems to have begun only after the devastating explosion of the Delft gunpowder magazine on 12 October 1654. Among the hundreds who died in the disaster was Van der Poel's next-door neighbor on the Doelenstraat, the painter Carel Fabritius (1622–54). It is also likely that one of Van der Poel's children was injured or killed in the blast, as suggested by a burial notice in the Nieuwe Kerk of 14 October 1654. While other Delft painters such as Daniel Vosmaer depicted the aftermath of this disaster, Van der Poel preferred to recreate the explosion as if it were actually happening: a flash of light, fallen or running figures, and instant, extensive destruction (Fig. 133).

The accident depicted in the Detroit painting is of much smaller scope, yet this nocturnal barn fire is so fierce that it has the effect of an explosion. The flames that burst through the wooden roof of the thatched structure eat away the top of the building while lighting up the intact façades of nearby houses. Wood and thatch buildings were especially vulnerable to fire, yet not until the early 1670s was effective firefighting equipment invented by Jan van der Heyden (q.v.), as described and illustrated in his treatise of 1690 (Cat. 46).[5] It is therefore not surprising that these figures flee rather than trying to fight the fire. A crowd of frightened figures and farm animals, including a pair of large hogs, escapes into the foreground as a man lies unconscious on the ground at the far left. At the right, a second injured figure is being helped to safety. Between them is a horse-drawn cart piled with goods rescued from the burning barn. Van der Poel's loose, powerfully assured brushwork allowed him to capture the solidity of the physical world and its potential for dissolution, while showing how fire casts the very fabric of ordinary life into chaos.

NOTES

1. M. Verhoef has made a study of night lighting effects in scenes illuminated by fire or moonlight in "'Brantjes' en 'Maneschijntjes' over lichteffecten in de nacht," in Rotterdam 1994–95, 125–32.

2. Van Spaan 1698, 422; quoted in M. Verhoef, "'Brantjes' en 'Maneschijntjes' over lichteffecten in de nacht," in Rotterdam 1994–95, 125–32. New York/London 2001, 326.

3. Other representations of fires by Van der Poel are *Burning House*, dated 1664, Staatliche Museen, Schwerin (inv. 504); *Fire in a Town Square*, Staatliche Kunstsammlungen, Karlsruhe (no. 258); *Burning Windmill*, dated 1662 (sold, Phillips, London, 16 April 1996, no. 46); and three depictions of burning barns, one dated 1658, private collection, Copenhagen (citation from photograph in the RKD, The Hague, and two in the Stedelijk Museum Het Prinsenhof in Delft (both on loan from the Rijksdienst Beeldende Kunst, The Hague inv. nos. NK2430 and NK2784). Van der Poel even turned to a related classical subject in *Aeneas Fleeing the Burning of Troy* (sold, Christie's, London, 7 July 1995, no. 290).

4. According to M. Roethlisberger, *Burning Cottage*, from Frederick Bloemaert's *Small Landscape* series (Roethlisberger 1993, 1:201, no. 255.6 and 2: fig. 378) was engraved after 1635, while Cornelis Bloemaert's *Ignis* from his series *The Four Elements* was engraved in the 1620s (Roethlisberger 1993, 1:230, no. 293, 2: fig. 429), after a drawing by Abraham Bloemaert of 1605–15 in Leiden. Repr. Leiden 1985, 50.

5. Jan van der Heyden, *Beschryving der niewlijks uitgevonden en geoctrojeerde slang-brand-spuiten*, published in Amsterdam in 1690, has recently been translated into English by L. S. Multhauf (Van der Heyden/Multhauf 1996).

JAN VAN DER HEYDEN
1637–1712

Painter, draftsman, printmaker, inventor, and engineer, Jan van der Heyden was one of the most remarkable figures of his time. The son of Mennonite parents, he moved with his family to Amsterdam from Gorkum (Gorinchem) in 1650. Van der Heyden's early training remains obscure, although it has been suggested that he may have studied the reverse technique of glass painting in Gorkum, perhaps continuing his studies with his elder brother, who made and sold mirrors.[1] In any case, Van der Heyden's artistic activities focused primarily on the depiction of townscapes, a thematic specialty to which he made major contributions. The extreme clarity of detail he achieved in rendering brickwork and other architectural motifs suggests that the artist may have used magnifying glasses, as well as lenses, mirrors, and a camera obscura. Few of his views appear to be literal records, however, for he seems to have preferred to evoke the distinctive character of various locales through selection and distillation. Van der Heyden also painted landscapes (two on glass) and, late in his career, a number of still lifes featuring exotic curiosities and scientific instruments. The figures in his paintings were sometimes added by other artists such as Adriaen van de Velde (q.v.).

Van der Heyden was active as a painter throughout his life, but his primary career—and the source of his great prosperity—was his activities as a municipal official and inventor-engineer. In 1670 he was appointed overseer of Amsterdam's street lighting, and in 1672 he and his brother Nicolaes became the joint fire chiefs of Amsterdam. These appointments relate to Jan's ingenuity as an inventor, for he developed a system of modern street lighting using square glass lanterns with safely contained oil lamps that remained in effect in Amsterdam until 1840. Between 1669 and 1671, he and his brother invented a novel approach to firefighting, using engines fitted with water pumps and long hoses capable of sucking water directly from the canals. The illustrated treatise he wrote with his son, Jan the Younger, remains the founding document for today's modern system of firefighting.[2] The etchings in this manual, based on meticulous preliminary drawings, are not only impressive feats of artistic virtuosity in themselves, but also provide records of buildings lost to fire and of industrial districts of Amsterdam not depicted in the townscapes of this period. As C. S. Ackley has noted, varied styles of execution suggest that several printmakers produced these illustrations.[3]

NOTES

1. For information on Van der Heyden's life, see Wagner 1971, 9–16, De Vries 1984, 108–12, and L. de Vries's biographical essay in *Dictionary of Art* 1996, 14:503–4.

2. The treatise, entitled *Beschryving der nieuwlyks uitgevonden en geoctrojeerde slang-brand-spuiten en haare wyze van brand-blussen, tegenwoording binnen Amsterdam in gebruik zijnde* (Description of the newly invented and patented hose fire engine and her ways of fighting fires, now used in Amsterdam), was published in Amsterdam in 1690.

3. Boston/St. Louis 1980/81, 302.

[46]

Rope and Tar Fire, Amsterdam, 24 June 1680, figure 8 (double page) from Jan van der Heyden and Jan van der Heyden the Younger, *Beschryving der nieuwlyks uitgevonden en geoctrojeerde slang-brand-spuiten en haare wyze van brand-blussen, tegenwoording binnen Amsterdam in gebruik zijnde* (Description of the newly invented and patented hose fire engine and her ways of fighting fires, now used in Amsterdam), Amsterdam, 1690

Etching, 329 × 253 mm (9½ × 12 15/16 in.) (platemark), 457 × 273 × 64 mm (18 × 10¾ × 2½ in.) (book)

Lent by the Metropolitan Museum of Art, New York, The Elisha Whittelsey Collection, The Elisha Whittelsey Fund, 1957, 57.567

References: Wagner 1970, 122, fig. 4, and 125; De Vries 1984, 88–90; Van der Heyden/Multhauf 1996, 50, 53–54, pl. 9.

Fire was a constant threat within the dense urban fabric of Amsterdam, whose closely sited buildings were framed in timber or made entirely of wood. A vagrant spark from a coal fire, a fallen candle, or a lightning strike could produce a conflagration that might reduce the most imposing structure to rubble, as did the 1652 fire that destroyed the city's Old Town Hall (Cat. 40).[1] Despite a network of canals that threaded channels of water throughout much of the city, even the most dedicated bucket brigades could not prevent incineration of entire blocks of houses. As Van der Heyden explains in his revolutionary firefighting manual of 1690 (see Van der Heyden biography

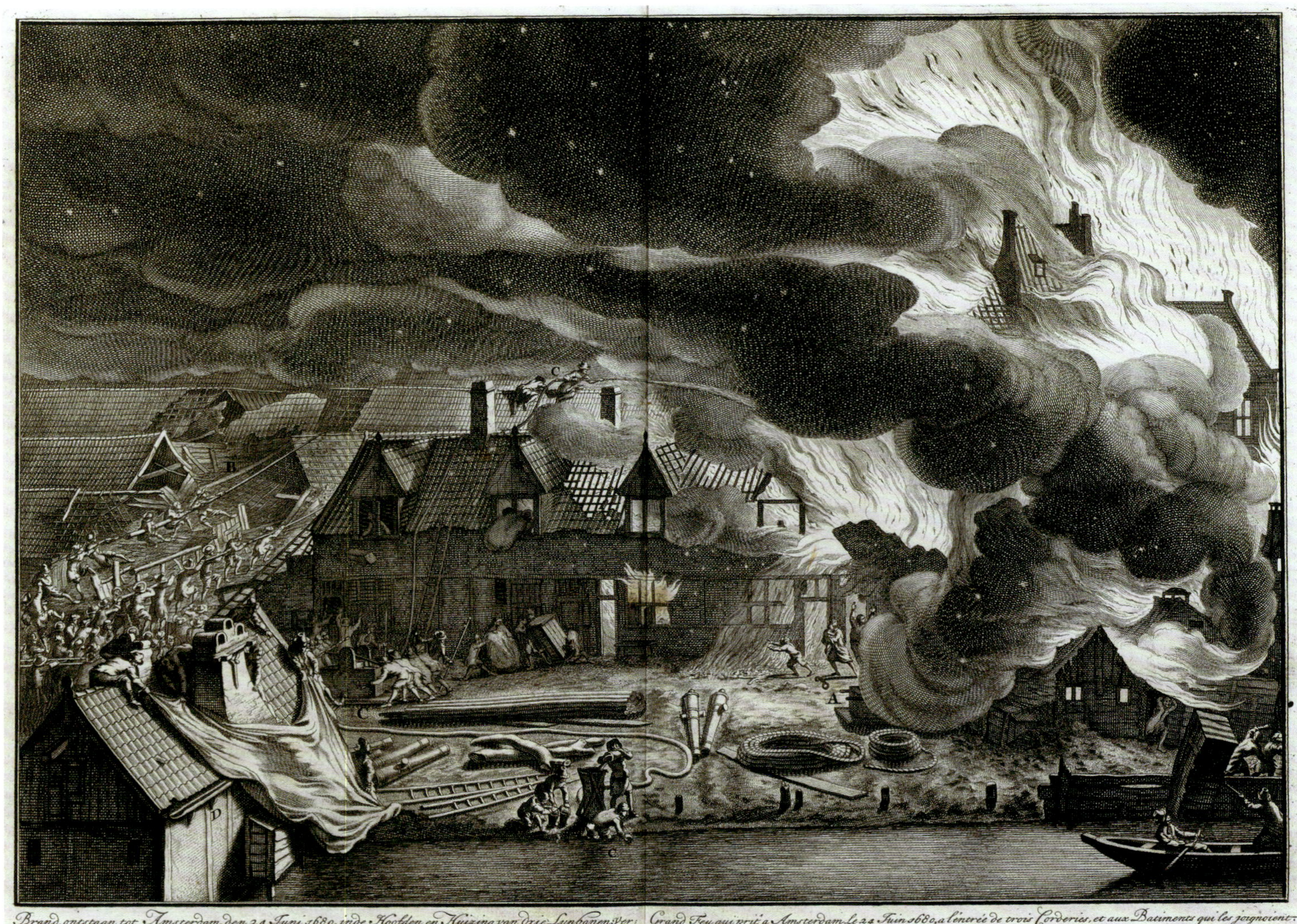

above), thirty-six rows of men would have to be lined up from water's edge to burning building (impossible in the city's narrow streets) to provide a volume of water comparable to what his recently invented fire hose could supply—and, even so, most of the water passed along in buckets would spill or leak away in the confusion of the event.[2] The new system with its light, maneuverable engines, suction pumps, and long, flexible pressure hoses made of leather allowed firefighters to work quickly in confined spaces and to direct long jets of water, even over distance, into the center of a fire. Van der Heyden vividly illustrated the contrast between the old and new approaches in a cutaway view of a burning house (Fig. 135) that shows the new equipment easily saturating the upper floors and the roof, as a few bucket carriers mill about uselessly at ground level at lower left.

The double-page illustration reproduced here shows a violent conflagration that ignited on 24 June 1680 between the Haarlemmer Tower and Zoutkeeten—an industrial district in the northeastern sector of Amsterdam near the harbor of Houthaven. This was a highly combustible area of the city, with sulfur refineries (left foreground, labeled D) and rows of small buildings containing tar and tarred rope. In his commentary, Van der Heyden notes that the fire broke out in three connected structures and rapidly raged out of control because untrained bystanders, believing that tar fires cannot be extinguished with water, ignored the fire engine that had been brought in by Nicolaes van der Heyden (letter A at the right). While attempting to make a cut-off for the fire, they wasted precious time deploying antiquated hooks, ladders, and tarpaulins (letter B at left), and only the arrival of reinforcements with additional engines and pressure hoses saved the district from devastation (letter C, foreground and middle ground). Van der Heyden used this near-catastrophe to demonstrate the limitations of outdated equipment and to argue that all parts of the city be supplied with his new invention.

In Van der Heyden's dramatic illustration, both buildings and figures are dwarfed by the

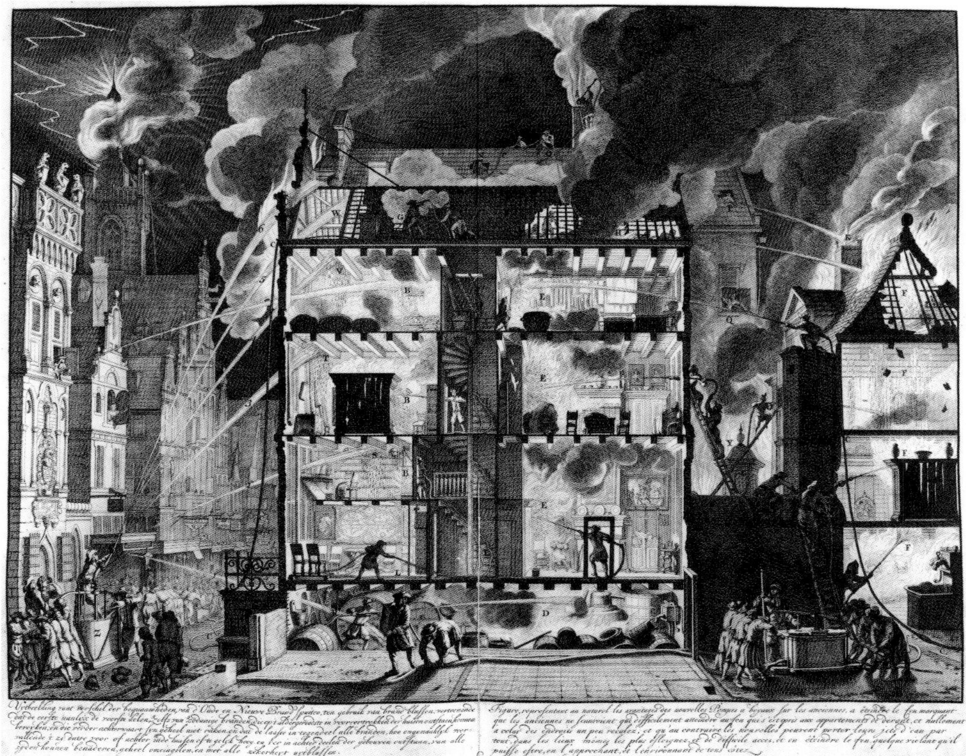

Fig. 135. Jan van der Heyden, *Demonstration of the old versus the new methods of firefighting*, from *Beschryving der nieuwlyks uitgevonden en geoctrojeerde slang-brand-spuiten* ..., Amsterdam, 1690, pl. 2, The Metropolitan Museum of Art, New York

explosive inferno at the far right which emits billowing clouds of black smoke that fill the scene and even seem to float through the picture plane into the viewer's space. As water from the canal in the immediate foreground is pumped in orderly fashion into long hoses, firemen climb the central building to direct pressure-driven jets of water into the center of the blaze. Meanwhile, the amateur volunteers at left, who attempt to cover the sulfur plant with a large tarpaulin, clamber ineffectually over the burning ropewalks beyond it—an area that would prove to be largely destroyed in the fire.[3]

NOTES

1. Van der Heyden also illustrated the destruction by fire of the old Amsterdam Town Hall as figure 3 in his manual on firefighting (see Fig. 76).

2. Van der Heyden 1690, pt. 1, chap. 1, 2; Van der Heyden/Multhauf 1996, 13.

3. The next illustration in the book (Van der Heyden 1690, pl. 9, and Van der Heyden/Multhauf 1996, 55, pl. 10) shows the same scene after the event, exposing the ruined area at left where the firebreak was unsuccessfully attempted, and juxtaposing it with the intact structures saved by the qualified firefighters.

[47]

Two Wooden Houses in the Goudsbloemstraat Burned 25 November 1682

Inscriptions: lower right, *J van der Heyde 1682*. on the gable of the house at left, *1654*

Brown and black ink, gray wash over black chalk on cream antique laid paper, 268 × 200 mm (10⁹⁄₁₆ × 7⅞ in.)

Courtesy of the Fogg Art Museum, Harvard University Art Museums, Cambridge, Massachusetts, Temporary Loan, TL38477

References: *Duits Quarterly* 1968; De Vries 1984, 93; Wagner 1970, 119 n. 19, 126–27, pl. 11.

This drawing, made eight years before the publication of Jan van der Heyden's firefighting manual of 1690 (see discussion under Cat. 46), demonstrates how carefully and precisely he prepared the book's etched illustrations. The drawing establishes almost all of the details found in the final print and is even oriented in the same direction. Probably a counterproof was taken from this sheet to assist in transferring the composition to the plate for printing.[1]

In the text of his book, Van der Heyden reports with his usual specificity that the blaze represented here, which broke out at 2:00 a.m. on the night of 25 November 1682, was caused by an alchemist's furnace that had become carbonized because of its continuous heat and had burned through the thin wall of two adjoining wooden houses.[2] Since the inhabitants of both buildings were asleep, further catastrophe was averted only by a passing official of municipal lanterns who sounded the alarm to summon the fire engines. The effectiveness of their rapid response is obvious in this illustration, because, despite some broken windows and fallen roof tiles, both structures still stand, as do the closely massed buildings beside and behind them. Only from the back of the houses, which Van der Heyden also sketched (Fig. 136), does the seriousness of the fire become fully evident.

At the front of the buildings, rescued residents (including two children) discuss the event or begin cleanup efforts, as a woman shakes a quilt from an upper window and a man rakes through a heap of roof tiles and rubble.[3] In effect, this scene reads as an almost-ruin, because only the

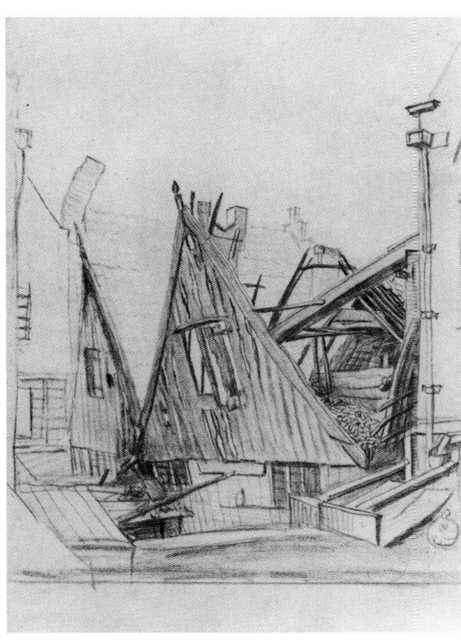

Fig. 136. Jan van der Heyden, *Wooden Houses, Goudsbloemstraat, Amsterdam (seen from the back), after the Fire of 25 November 1682*, black chalk drawing, Collection Frits Lugt, Institut Néerlandais, Paris

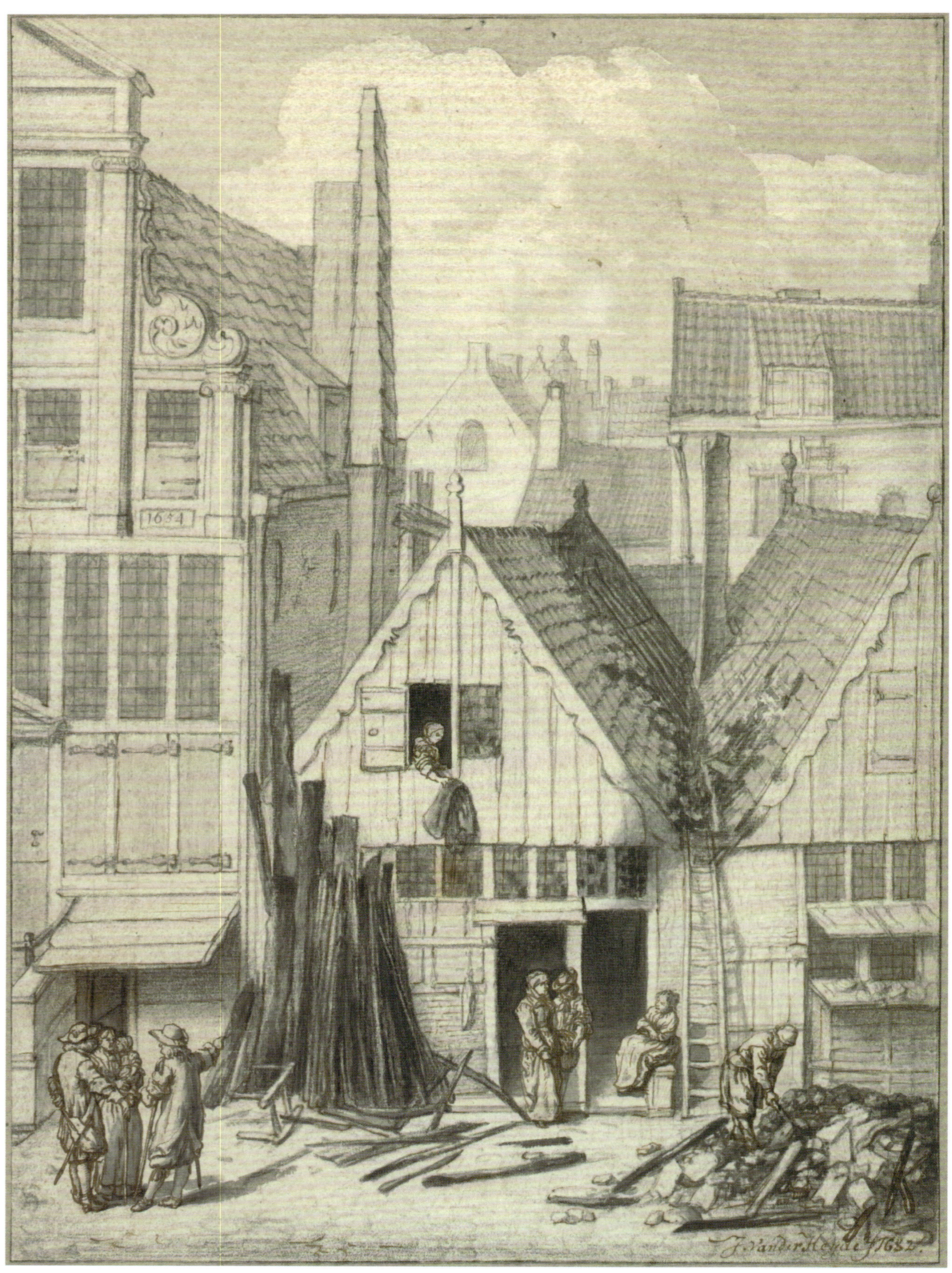
1654

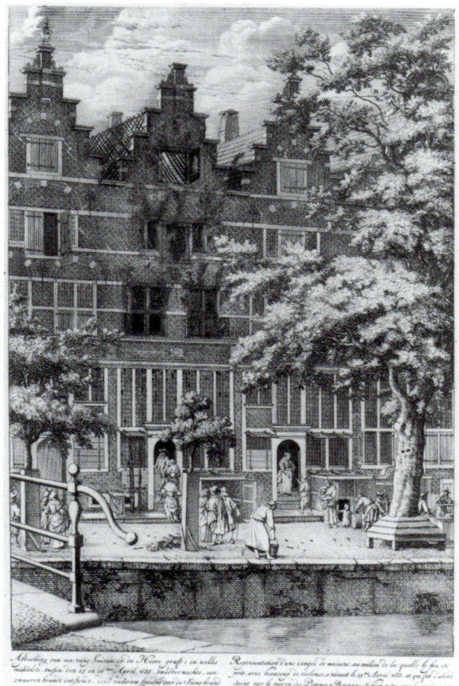

Fig. 137. Jan van der Heyden, *Houses on the Herengracht*, Amsterdam, *after the fire of 25–26 April 1683*, from *Beschryving der nieuwlyks uitgevonden en geoctrojeerde slang-brand-spuiten ...* Amsterdam, 1690, pl. 14, The Metropolitan Museum of Art, New York

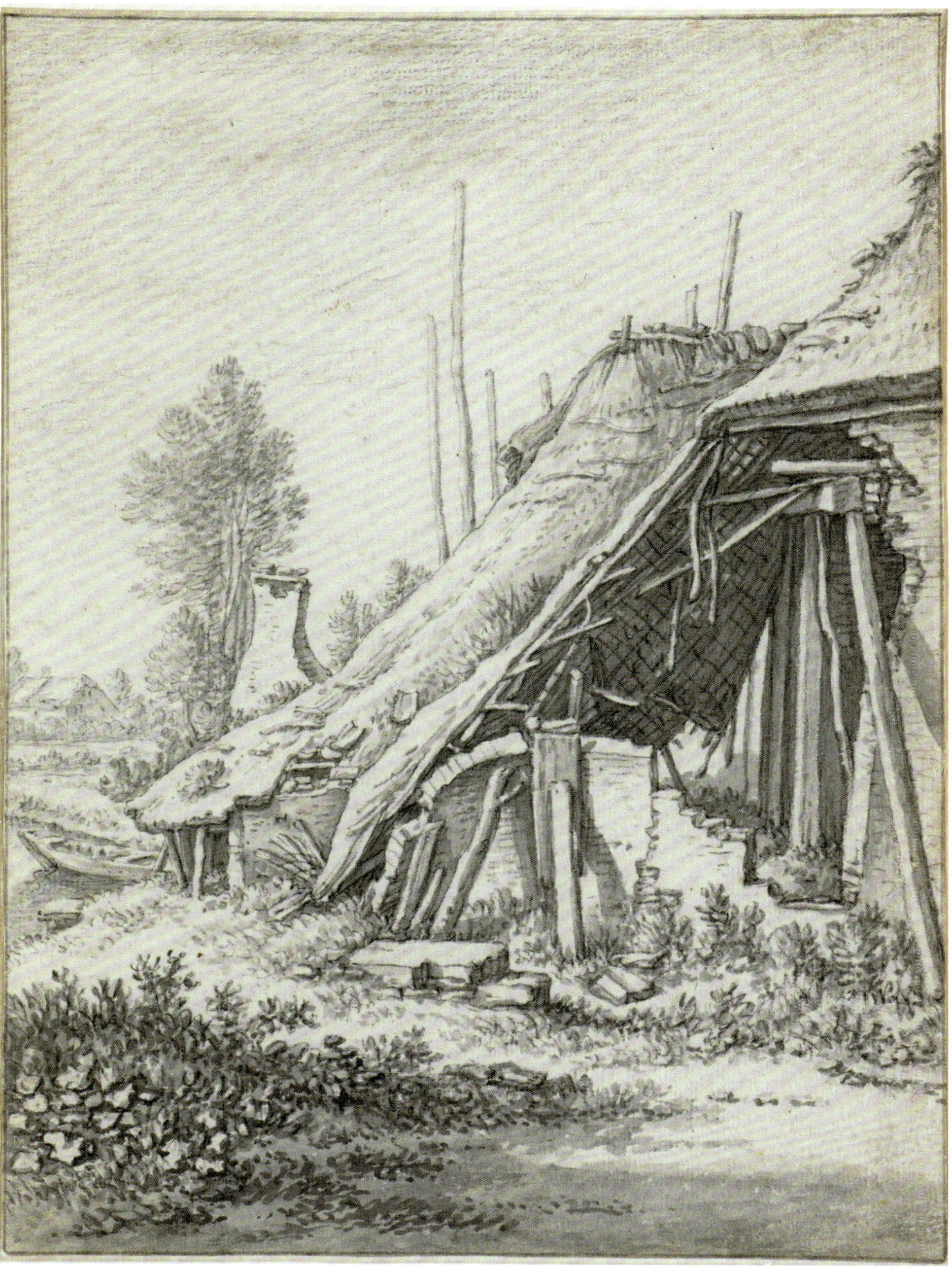

blackened timbers stacked against the facade in the center and a few missing tiles and windowpanes indicate damage that is largely out of sight.[4] Rising in a vertical format, Van der Heyden's drawing explores the lovely, intricate geometry of Amsterdam's tightly clustered gables and facades, reminding the viewer that rapid control of fire preserves much more than the single structure in which it begins. Thus a row of elegant townhouses in the Herengracht would also be saved in April 1683, even as the building in the center was gutted by fire (Fig. 137).

NOTES

1. The print is plate 12 in Van der Heyden 1690. See also Van der Heyden/Multhauf 1996, 67. Since printmaking reverses the direction of the image that is drawn on the etching plate, taking a counterproof from a preparatory drawing can help the artist see how the final composition will look and guide his drawing on the plate. The manner in which Van der Heyden prepared his plates is not altogether certain, for he apparently used separate drawings of the buildings, the firefighting apparatus, and the figures, beginning with free charcoal sketches of the damaged buildings and working through progressively more detailed and finished drawings in pen and ink. Wagner 1970, 119–20, and De Vries 1984, 95–99.

2. Van der Heyden 1690, pt. 2, chap. 4, 30–32; Van der Heyden/Multhauf 1996, 62–64.

3. The authorship of the staffage in Van der Heyden's works has often been debated. In some of his paintings and prints, it may have been contributed by other artists such as Jan van de Velde (q.v.), Jan van Vianen (1660–after 1676), or his son, Jan van der Heyden the Younger.

4. A second sketch of the back of the houses (Koninklijk Oudheidkundig Genootschap, Amsterdam) also shows extensive damage in the attic area. Repr. Wagner 1970, 130, pl. 12.

HERMAN SAFTLEVEN

[48]

Ruined Cottages in Apstede, near Utrecht, 1674

Inscriptions: verso, in brown ink, *Dit op dandersijde getekent van Herman Saft Leven is in Apstee Ao* (in ligature) *1674* (see below for translation)

Black chalk with brush and gray-green ink wash and touches of blue wash on cream laid paper with a watermark, 197 × 152 mm (7¾ × 6 in.)

The Frances Lehman Loeb Art Center, Vassar College, Poughkeepsie, New York, Purchase, Friends of the Frances Lehman Loeb Art Center Fund, 2002.15

References: Schulz 1982, 284, no. 589, repr., fig. 198, and probably also 283, no. 584-A.

With their steeply pitched, thatched roofs and very low walls, these rustic cottages represent the kinds of traditional farmhouses seen along the Amstel and Vecht rivers and known by the terms *langhuis* (longitudinal shape) or *stolp* (square shape), a distinction difficult to make here because this image is so sharply cropped at the right.[1] This abrupt segmentation dramatically accentuates the contrast between the structure at the right, whose shattered wall exposes its ruined interior, and the much less damaged roof and chimney of the house just behind it to the left. At the left background is a quiet vista with a waterway and a moored rowboat, beyond which is a distant house sheltered by trees. Soft touches of chalk and gray washes define the ground foliage in the immediate foreground, while faint touches of blue wash are visible in the water.

This small drawing is one of a group of fifty-two sketches, all approximately 20 by 15 centimeters in size and all inscribed on their versos: *Dit op dander sijde getekent van Herman Saft Leven is ... ao 1674* (Drawn on the other side by Herman Saftleven, this site is [name of place inserted] in the year 1674). The Vassar drawing represents Apstede, near the eastern Dutch city of Utrecht. This region of the Dutch provinces suffered grievously during the early 1670s, beginning with the invasion of the troops of Louis XIV, which overran the area on 23 June 1672 and occupied it until 23 November 1673. The French occupation of the province of Utrecht, noted in the verso inscriptions of several of Saftleven's "op dander sijde" drawings,[2] prompted an outpouring of prints, illustrated books, and propaganda sheets showing widespread mayhem, violence, and destruction of property. This devastation is evoked with horrifying vividness in Romeyn de Hooghe's illustrations for Abraham de Wicquefort's *Advis fidelle aux veritable hollandois*, published in Amsterdam in 1673 (Cat. 39 and Fig. 70). At the same time, Tobias van Domselaer published his account of the devastations of the Rampjaar (Disaster Year) in an illustrated treatise, *Het ontroerde Nederlandt* (The Netherlands in turmoil), whose two volumes appeared successively in 1674 and 1676 (see Fig. 15).[3]

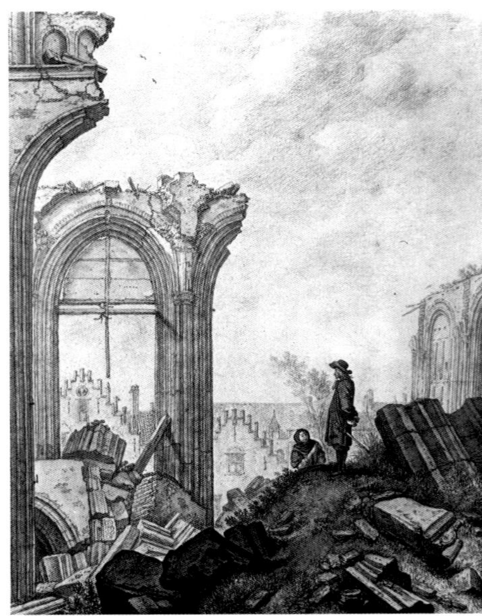

Fig. 138. Herman Saftleven, *The Nave of Utrecht Cathedral, Destroyed in the Storm of 1674*, black chalk and gray wash drawing, Gemeentearchief, Utrecht

Saftleven's rustic hut, hardly the kind of imposing estate illustrated in Van Domselaer's book, probably shows the ravages not of such intentional demolition, but rather of a second catastrophe—this one caused by nature—that followed almost immediately in the same area. On 1 August 1674, a violent storm developed in western Europe, originating in France, proceeding to the region around Brussels, and raging through Antwerp, Utrecht, and Amsterdam. The cyclone that struck Utrecht destroyed the tower and nave of its cathedral (Fig. 138) along with five additional church steeples and all but two of the windmills along the town wall, while severely damaging buildings and bridges in the surrounding areas.[4] Saftleven made himself the local documentarian of this catastrophe, and his drawings, most of which are now in the Gemeentearchief, Utrecht, evoke both the violence and the unpredictable path of the storm, which struck each building in a unique way, leaving untouched spots of peaceful landscape next to areas of utter devastation. A comparison of this image to Ruisdael's drawing of a collapsed farmhouse of about 1655 (Cat. 30) shows how differently time alone acts on such a structure.

NOTES

1. For discussion of the *langhuis* and *stolp* in Rembrandt's prints and drawings, see B. Bakker's useful essay in Washington 1990, 33–59.

2. Schulz 1982, nos. 629, 633, and 634.

3. As D. Cearfoss Mankin has discussed, Van Domselaer's second volume includes images of ruined castles and villas along the Vecht—some medieval, some classical in style—that were apparently destroyed because their owners had refused to pay taxes to the French invaders. Cearfoss Mankin 1996, chap. 1, 16–31.

4. Buisman 2000, 671–75. See also Den Tonkelaar 1980 and Utrecht 1974, the catalogue accompanying the exhibition *De dom in puin* (Cathedral in ruin) at the Centraal Museum, Utrecht.

TIME AND TRAVEL

JACQUES DE GHEYN II,
AFTER KAREL VAN MANDER

[49]

The Prodigal Son (Allegory of Idleness and Luxury), 1596

Inscriptions:

Left center, *K van Mandere inuen, Iacobus de geÿn sculptor et excu.* (Designed by K. van Mander, engraved and published by Jacques de Gheyn)

At left on rock, dedicatory inscription,
Illustrissimo & Generoso Comite a Solms
D/omi/no in Müntzenbergh & Sonnewalt,
D/omi/no sibi semper observantia colendo
Hoc opus Kaerlo de Mandere Inventu/m
Jacobus de Geijn sculptor dedicavit.
Anno S. M D XC VI

(By always regarding him with respect, Jacques de Gheyn, engraver, dedicates this work, designed by Karel van Mander, to the illustrious and noble Count of Solms, Lord of Müntzenberg and Sonnewalt. In the year of our Lord 1596)

Below the scene, four couplets,
Disce voluptati comes ut metanoea, merasque
Sub blando Meretrix nectat amore tricas;
Libertas abeat quo tàm speciosa benigni
Quae patris excusso quaeritur Imperio:
Dilapsum huc retulisse pedem ne culpa pudoris
Terreat, aut tanti quae subit ira Patris.
Tardus ut irasci, sic est ignoscere promptus
Quos videt admissi poenituisse mali. PHogerb:

(Learn how repentance is a companion to pleasure,
And how under the cloak of flattering love
A public woman heaps deceit upon deceit
Destroying precious freedom, which he seeks after having
Rejected the authority of his obliging father:
After having squandered everything,
Let him not be discouraged by shame to return
And confront the wrath of such a great father.
As slowly as he is inclined to become angry,
So quickly will he forgive those who repent the evil committed. PHogerb:)[1]

Engraving, 422 × 670 mm (16⅝ × 26⅜ in.) (platemark), 455 × 704 mm (17¹⁵⁄₁₆ × 27¹¹⁄₁₆ in.) (sheet), printed from two plates, sheets trimmed and joined at center; state i/iii

Museum of Fine Arts, Boston, Gift of the Print and Drawing Club, 1979.123

References: De Roever 1885, 268; E. Valentiner 1930, 51–52, pl. 32; Ter Laan 1939; Hollstein 7 (n.d.):185, no. 410; Rotterdam 1974, 21; Boston/St. Louis 1980–81, 21–25, no. 12; Van Regteren-Altena 1983, 1:48–49; Paris 1985, 109–10, no. 70, pl. 61; Los Angeles/Toledo/Sarasota/Austin/Baltimore 1988–89, no. 112; Filedt Kok 1990, 271–72, 387, no. 410; Amsterdam 1993–94a, 183, 372, no. 30; *The New Hollstein* 2000, 1:76–77.

This finely detailed, large-scale image, whose composition recalls Raphael's *School of Athens*, was printed on two plates so that its size approx-

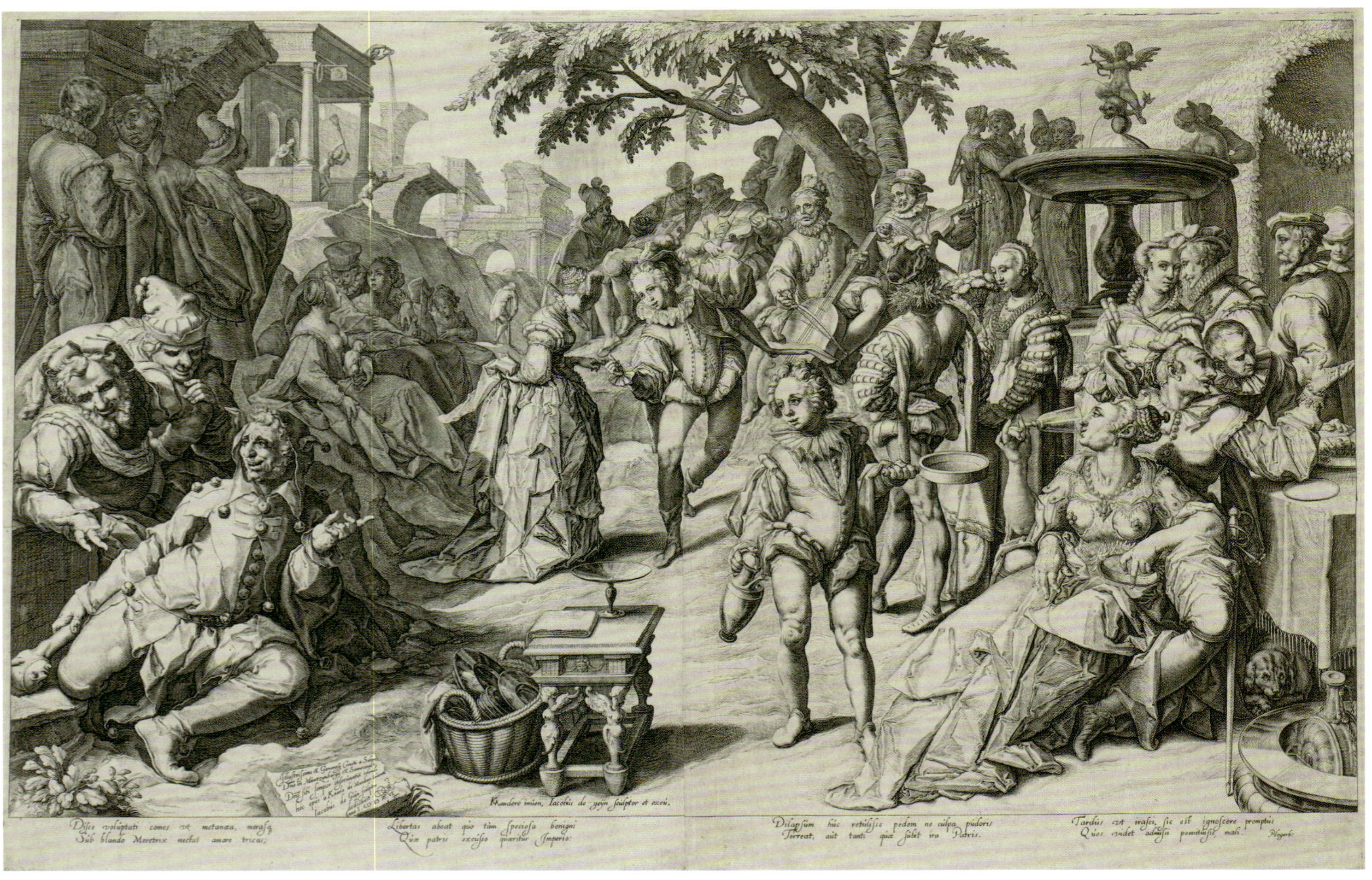

imates that of a painting.[2] Such a spacious pictorial field allowed the printmaker to dispose some three dozen elaborately dressed figures in a complex and visually rich arrangement that conveys the extravagance of the prodigal son's life of luxury before he squandered his inheritance and lost his virtue. One of Christ's parables on repentance (Luke 15:11–32), the story was frequently represented by Dutch printmakers and painters either as a banquet or celebration such as De Gheyn's or as the depiction of the young man's ensuing destitution and humiliation (Cat. 17) that finally sent him home to beg for his father's forgiveness. The inscription below this scene by the poet and doctor Pieter Hogerbeets (1542–99) is a warning that love and pleasure are seductive traps for the unwary sinner and reminds the viewer that the Father (meaning God) will forgive anyone who truly repents.[3] A second inscription on the block of stone at the lower left dedicates the print to Georg Eberhard, count of Solms and lord of Müntzenberg (1566–1602), one of the Dutch military leaders who commanded the states of Zeeland during the war with Spain—a struggle that would continue until the signing of the Twelve Year Truce in 1609, which marked the beginning of an independent Dutch Republic. Whether Eberhard commissioned the print himself or it was presented to him is unclear, but he was removed from his post in October 1596 following the disastrous surrender of the city of Hulst to Spanish troops.[4]

As in many mannerist prints and paintings, the seductive lure of the image itself seems more powerful than any admonitory message it contains. As A. W. Lowenthal has discussed, scenes of this kind often involve an interplay between constraint and license, since exceptional control and elegance of design are combined with sexually charged or licentious subject matter.[5] As a result, intriguing tensions develop within the image and within the beholder alike. In De Gheyn's print, every aspect of the scene is rendered in crisp, tightly controlled strokes of the burin defining complex but clearly delineated shapes that overlap while passing through shifting intensities of light and shadow. At the center of this dense visual matrix is the prodigal son, a stylish youth in a short doublet who tips his feathered hat, extending a graceful finger to lead his lavishly costumed partner in the dance. At the upper right, other couples flirt beside a fountain of love topped by a pissing cupid on a dolphin who aims his arrow toward the center of the scene.

Despite the prodigal son's elegance and decorum, other incidents in the foreground and background imply that he has placed himself in a morally dubious environment that can only corrupt him. At the left, snickering onlookers in fools' costume grin mockingly at the dancing couple, while a bejeweled woman at the right, her bodice cut out in circles to expose her breasts, drinks wine and lounges between the spread legs of her male companion. In the left background a young man, representing the prodigal son's future, is expelled from an inn or brothel by two women, as a third figure leans from the roof to empty a chamber pot over his fleeing form. Since the inn is perched beside a precipice, his fall into the ravine below seems inevitable. Here the final stage of dissolution and moral decay is illustrated by the small figure of a cripple limping on his crutches into the background. Behind him, the magnificent Roman buildings have fallen into ruin, injecting a further cautionary reminder about the hazards of luxury. During this period, as the Dutch struggle against Spanish dominion continued, the print's warning about pleasure and extravagant living would have been timely, especially as directed toward young people.

NOTES

1. Transcription and translation into English of the inscriptions on this print were made by G. Luijten in Amsterdam 1993–94a, 372.

2. De Gheyn never visited Italy, but he could have known Raphael's fresco of 1508–11 for the Stanza della Segnatura in the Vatican through an engraving published by Giorgio Ghisi (1520–82) in Antwerp (Amsterdam 1993–94a, 372 and n. 2). The impression of De Gheyn's engraving that is reproduced here, from the collection of the Museum of Fine Arts, Boston, is a fine and rare early impression that is in excellent condition, although a few millimeters from the center of the design were cropped when the sheets were trimmed and pasted together by an earlier owner.

3. The author of this inscription, Pieter Hogerbeets (1542–99), was a friend of Karel van Mander (1548–1606), the Dutch artist and art theorist who was the designer of this print. As C. S Ackley has noted (Boston/St. Louis 1980–81, 23), Van Mander himself would soon give similar advice to artists in his book of painting, *Het schilder-boeck*, published in Haarlem in 1604, in which young art students are warned about the dangers of such distractions. Van Mander/Miedema 1973, 1:77–78.

4. On Eberhard's biography, see Boston/St. Louis 1980–81, 23, and Paris 1985, 110 and n. 4.

5. On the polarity between license and restraint in Dutch mannerist painting, see Lowenthal 1986, 57–61.

JACOB PYNAS
1592/93–after 1650

Jacob Pynas and his brother Jan (1581/82–1631), who belonged to an aristocratic Roman Catholic Dutch family from Alkmaar, moved in 1690 to Amsterdam, where they were to become, along with their brother-in-law Jan Tengnagel (c. 1584/85–1635), painters of small-scale, finely worked narrative scenes from ancient history and the Bible.[1] These so-called Pre-Rembrandtist artists, a group that included Rembrandt's teacher, Pieter Lastman (1583–1633), were deeply influenced by Adam Elsheimer (1578–1610), a German artist working in Rome whose works were also copied and circulated by the Dutch printmaker Hendrick Goudt (1580/85–1648). Both Pynas brothers apparently spent time in Rome, Jacob from 1605 to about 1608. According to Houbraken, the young Rembrandt spent several months in Jacob Pynas's studio in Amsterdam after leaving Lastman's in 1622.[2] In 1631 Jacob became a citizen of Delft, joining the Delft guild of St. Luke in the following year, but in 1641 and 1643 was again in Amsterdam. The place and date of his death remain unknown. A gifted draftsman (Cat. 51) as well as a painter, Pynas, like the other Pre-Rembrandtists, concentrated on stories from the Old and New Testaments and from classical mythology, emphasizing the concrete physical and temporal context of each story by clarifying details of its setting and costume.

NOTES

1. Jacob Pynas as a painter was first discussed in Bauch 1936 and later by A. Tümpel in Sacramento 1974, 26–31, 67–78. For a summary of his biography and development, see A. Tümpel in *Dictionary of Art* 1996, 25:758–59.

2. Houbraken 1718–21, 1 (1718):214–15.

[50]
The Adoration of the Magi, 1617

Inscriptions: signed with monogram and dated lower right, *JP f 1617*

Oil on copper (mounted on masonite), 40.6 × 55.6 cm (16 × 21⅞ in.)

Wadsworth Atheneum Museum of Art, Hartford, Connecticut, The Ella Gallup Sumner and Mary Catlin Sumner Collection, 1959.103

References: Cunningham 1959; Murray 1959, 164, pl. 454; Oehler 1967, 153, fig. 8, 160; Haverkamp-Begemann 1969, 282; Montreal/Toronto 1969, no. 102; Held 1969, 386; Sacramento 1974, 68–69, no. 9; Haverkamp-

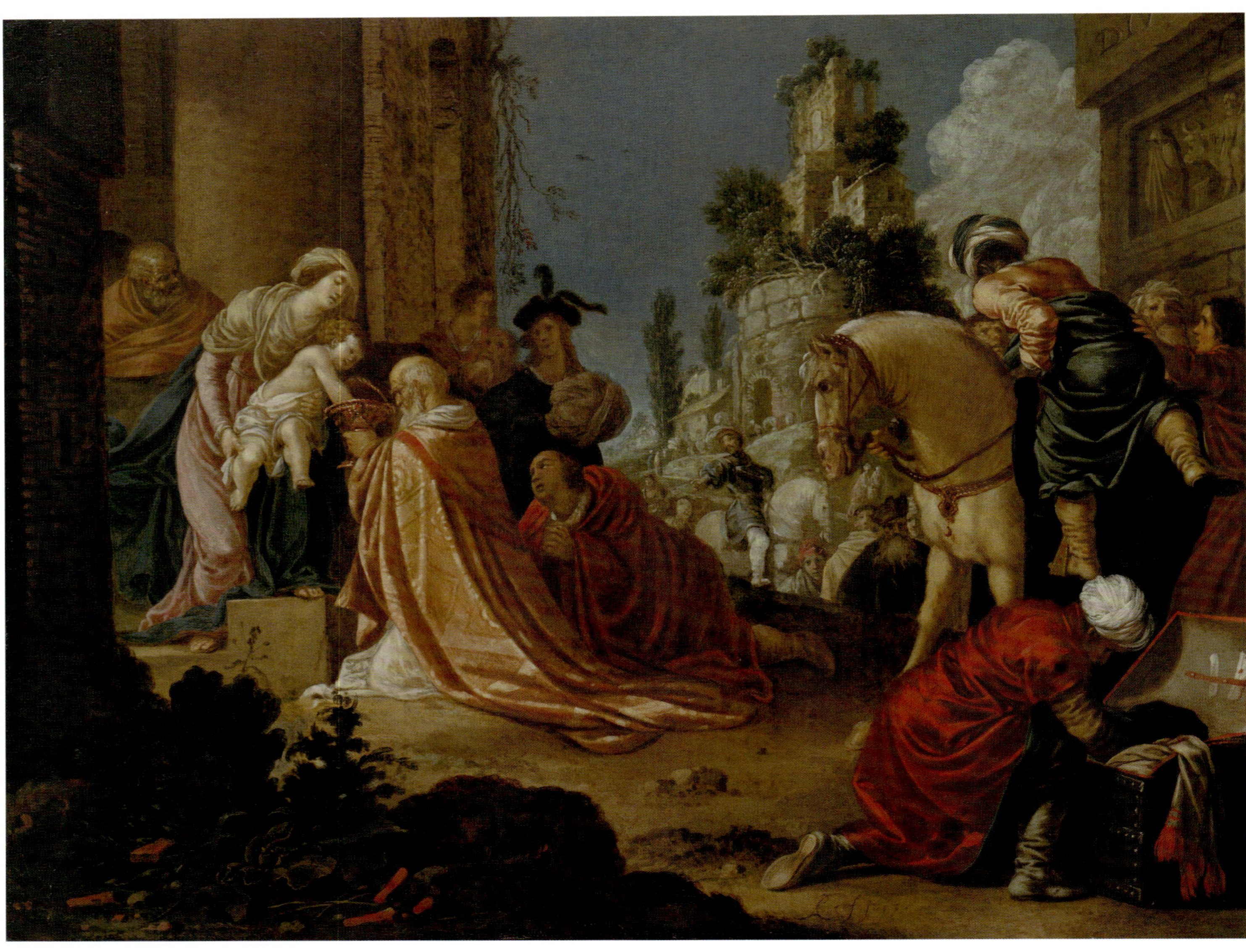

Begemann, 1978, 29, 175, no. 119, pl. 50; Washington/Detroit/Amsterdam 1980–81, 132–33, no. 23.

One of the most frequently depicted of all the New Testament stories (Matthew 2:1–12), the Adoration of the Magi is the tale of the three wise men, learned astrologers, who saw a rising star and journeyed to Jerusalem to ask: "Where is he who has been born king of the Jews? For we have seen his star in the East and have come to worship him." King Herod, greatly perturbed at their news, sent the Magi to Bethlehem, asking that they inform him of Christ's whereabouts. The Magi then followed the star, which led them to the place of Christ's birth, and there they saw the Christ child with his mother Mary and fell down and worshipped him. Out of their coffers of treasure, they made three offerings: gold, in recognition of his kingship; frankincense or incense, as a tribute to his divine priesthood; and myrrh (a resin for burying the dead), as a sign that he would die for humanity. The story thus represents the earliest recognition of Christ by those possessing worldly power. To emphasize that Jesus was worshipped by people of every age and race, the Magi came to be described in later legendary treatises as personifications of the three ages of man and of the three parts of the known world: Europe, Asia, and Africa.[1]

This lively and colorful scene, dated 1617, is one of Pynas's earliest known paintings yet is rendered with a degree of inventive assurance that suggests he was a thoroughly experienced artist by this time.[2] Typical of the Pre-Rembrandtists' approach to narration, this image has been freshly conceived in ways that emphasize the temporal and physical context of the Adoration as an event in progress, involving different stages of arrival and mingling major characters with accessory figures. At the forefront of the elegant retinue, winding its way up the hill to the site of the Nativity, is the African magus with a striped turban, seen from behind, who dismounts from his white horse at the far right. Closest to the viewer, at the right foreground, a servant in bright red with a white turban crouches to reach into an open trunk of goods to retrieve the Moorish horseman's offering.[3]

The Adoration itself appears more distantly in the middle ground at the left, beyond a shadowed repoussoir of foliage and fallen bits of masonry. Here an elderly bearded magus in a gold brocade cape kneels to offer a jeweled golden vessel to the lively infant, being held out to him as a kind of reciprocal human offering by Mary, who takes an unusual standing position here as Joseph hovers protectively behind mother and child.[4] Behind the old magus, a younger magus in red kneels deeply with devoutly clasped hands, his offering held in readiness by the young man with the plumed hat beside him. The importance of paying tribute by making offerings is underlined here by the Roman relief at the far right, whose pagan sacrificial scene, accompanied by the letters DIVO (to the god), alludes to the ancient religions that were superceded by Christianity.[5]

The smooth surface of the copper support on which Pynas painted this scene encouraged him to emphasize fine detail, both in the colorful costumes of the figures and in their fully developed setting. Most striking is the sunlit, architecturally framed vista at the center background, where a tower of ancient Roman ruins, partly overgrown with foliage, rises almost as high as the clouds on several levels, as if to declare that multiple layers of time exist within this ancient landscape. As in many other Dutch biblical scenes (Cats. 49, 53, 54, 56, 57, and 67), ruins are featured here in order to inject an aura of antiquity and foreignness into a scene that occurred in a distant time and place. Although the building in which this Nativity takes place is developed in less detail, it too is a massive Roman ruin. In this context, as in similar scenes of the Adoration of the Shepherds (Cat. 15), this motif alludes to the crumbling of the Old Order before the coming of Christ.

NOTES

1. On the story of the journey of the Magi and how it was amplified by post-biblical commentators, see Trexler 1997, esp. chap. 1. According to Trexler, St. Augustine (d. 430) was the first to suggest that the Magi represented the entire gentile world, while the Venerable Bede (d. 735) elaborated on this idea to connect them to the three parts of the world and was the first to name the magi: Melchior (the old and bearded one), Caspar (the beardless youth), and Balthasar (according to various texts, the dark-skinned and/or dark haired magus) (Trexler 1997, 38–39). In the fourteenth century, however, John of Hildesheim stated that Caspar was a young, black Ethiopian king (Kaplan 1985, 100).

2. According to the Wadsworth Atheneum catalogue (Haverkamp-Begemann 1978, 175), A. Tümpel's suggestion that the date may possibly be read as 1613 (Sacramento 1974, 68) cannot be sustained. A. Tümpel has identified Pynas's earliest firmly dated painting as *Nebuchadnezzar Restored to His Kingdom*, dated 1616, in the Alte Pinakothek, Munich. A. Tümpel in Sacramento 1974, 27.

3. The man unpacking the trunk is identified as one of the magi in the Wadsworth Atheneum's catalogue (Haverkamp-Begemann 1978, 175). It seems improbable, however, that anyone but a servant would be engaged in this task or that the second kneeling figure at the left would be not be one of the magi, an identification also made in Washington/Detroit/Amsterdam 1980–81, 132.

4. According to A. Tümpel, Pynas adapted this highly unusual, unseated pose from earlier depictions of the Sacra Conversazione. Washington/Detroit/Amsterdam 1980–81, 132, no. 23.

5. Haverkamp-Begemann 1978, 175, and A. Tümpel in Sacramento 1974, 68.

[51]

Landscape with the Calling of St. Peter, 1626

Inscriptions: lower left, *1626*

Pen and brown ink, border by the artist in pen and brown ink, 201 × 287 mm (7 15/16 × 11 5/16 in.)

Lent by the Metropolitan Museum of Art, New York, Rogers Fund, 1967, 67.147.1

References: Bean 1968–69; Sacramento 1974, 74–75, no. 12; Washington/Denver/Fort Worth 1977, 19, no. 16; Keyes 1974–80, 160, n. 27, fig. 3, and 163; Cambridge/Montreal 1988, 172–73, no. 66; Vienna/New York/Fort Worth 1993 and 1995, 48 and 49 n. 6; White and Crawley 1994, 293; Schatborn 1997, 6, fig. 7, and 23 n. 23

As in his earlier painting of the Adoration of the Magi (Cat. 50), Pynas locates his biblical narrative within an Italianate landscape in which the past is evoked by worn architectural vestiges of antiquity, built into the massive mountain at the right. Both the large bridge and the smaller, more distant house are constructed upon ancient arcades whose rising forms accentuate the steep rise of the mountain, only part of which extends into the picture space. Pynas's linear hatchings emphasize the shapes of rocks, trees—even clouds—with a firmness that recalls the work of slightly earlier Haarlem draftsmen and printmakers, such as Willem Buytewech (Cats. 2a and 2b) and Jan van de Velde (Cats. 3a–d). In contrast to the density and visual drama of the precipitous view to the right, the scene at the left opens into a peaceful, extended vista of lake and landscape within which various figures appear, walking in quiet conversation or maneuvering a boat toward the shore. Further in the distance are two men with a flock of sheep and a man driving a horse or donkey. Within the deeply shadowed foreground, the two principal figures loom as darker silhouettes at the left: Christ speaking persuasively to St. Peter, who is about to become one of his first apostles.

As A. Tümpel has pointed out, two very different Gospel accounts of the Calling of Peter exist.[1] In St. Luke's version, Christ, while preaching amid multitudes of people on the shore, asks the fisherman Peter, whose boat is moored nearby, to take him out onto the water so that he may more easily speak to the crowds from the boat. When Christ tells Peter, who had previously caught nothing, to put out his net, his boat miraculously fills with fish, as does the boat of a second fisherman. Peter falls to his knees in astonishment, and Christ tells him, "Be not afraid, henceforth you will catch men" (Luke 5:1–11).

Pynas has clearly taken his interpretation not from this frequently used source but from the Gospel of Matthew, which recounts that Jesus was walking beside the Lake of Galilee where he encountered two fisherman casting their net into the water: Simon, known as Peter, and his brother Andrew. When he asked them: "Come with me and I will make you fishers of men," they abandoned their nets and followed him (Matthew 4:18–20). In Pynas's drawing, Andrew can be seen in the boat moored at the far left, while Peter has disembarked and kneels on the shore with his arms opened wide to indicate his acceptance of Christ's words. In the sky above the two figures is a flock of birds in flight. Pynas may also have used other, seemingly natural aspects of the landscape to intensify the implications of this spiritual conversion. The huge rock beside Peter at the right recalls the words Christ would later speak to him: "Thou are Peter, and upon this rock I will build my church …" (Matthew 16:18); while the tiny flock of sheep on the distant shore behind Christ recall his role as the Good Shepherd who watches over humanity: "I am the good shepherd: the good shepherd giveth his life for the sheep" (John 10:11). Six years before he made the drawing in the Metropolitan Museum, Jacob Pynas had produced a freer sketch, dated 1620, of exactly the same composition, which reveals, by comparison, how controlled and clarified the later version really is.[2]

NOTES

1. A. Tümpel in Sacramento 1974, 74, in which the author points out that Jacob Pynas's brother Jan produced a painting (Schapiro Collection, London) based on Luke's account of the story that in turn became the source for a painting dated 1637 by Jacob Pynas, now in a private collection, Groningen (Sacramento 1974, 30, fig. 37).

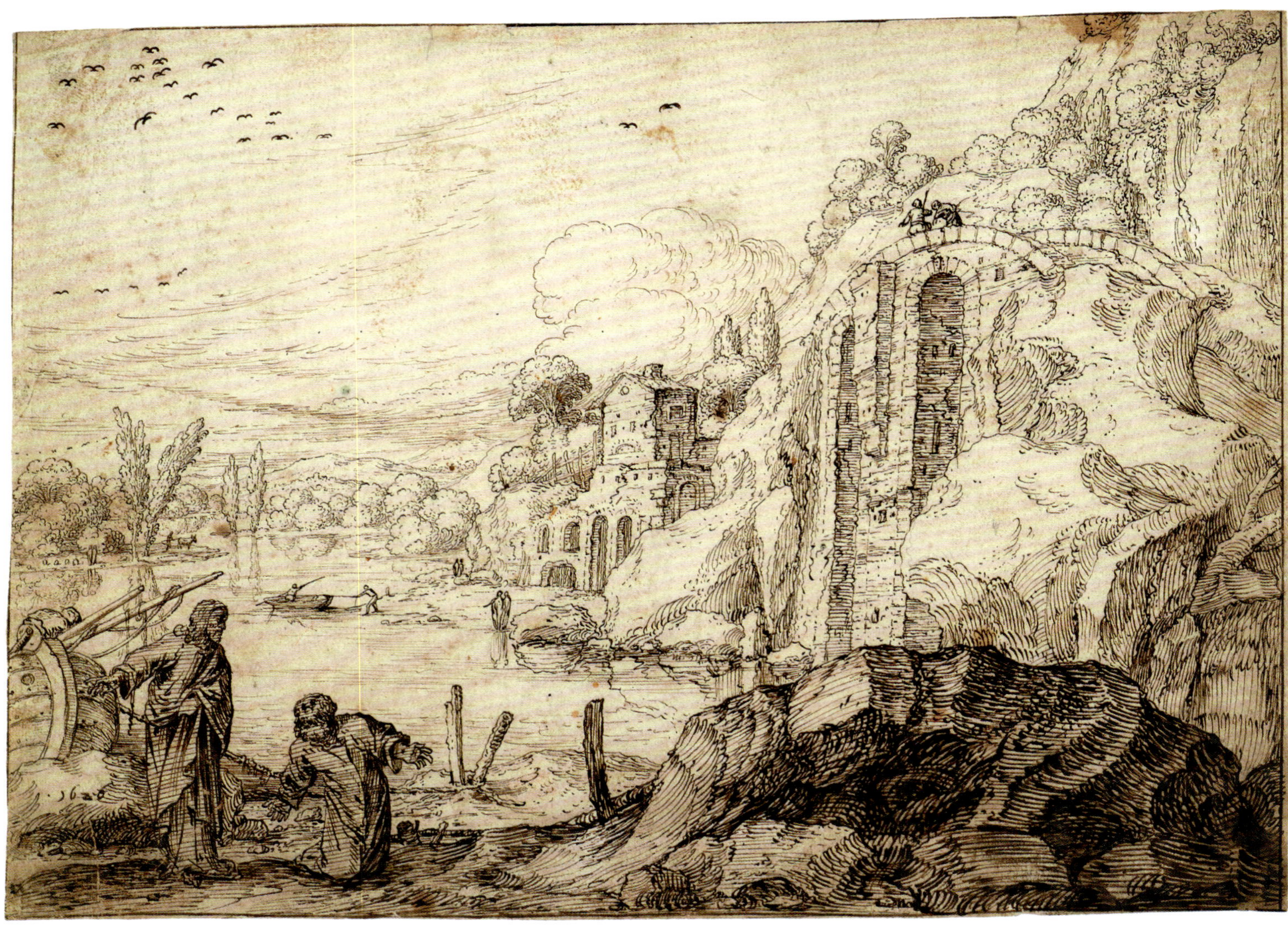

2. This unsigned drawing dated 1620 (190 × 283 mm, P. and N. de Boer Foundation, Amsterdam) is accepted by scholars as an autograph work by Pynas. Repr. Cambridge/Montreal 1988, 172, fig. 1.

BARTHOLOMEUS BREENBERGH
1598–1657

Born to a wealthy Protestant family in Deventer (his father was the town apothecary), Breenbergh was baptized in the Dutch Reformed Church on 13 November 1598.[1] He moved to Hoorn during his youth, but his artistic apprenticeship apparently took place in Amsterdam, as suggested by the fact that his early works show the strong influence of Pieter Lastman (1583–1633) and Jan Pynas (1581/82–1631). Documentary evidence places him in Amsterdam in 1619, but later that year he was in Rome, where he remained until 1629, working closely with Paulus Bril (1554–1626) and Cornelis van Poelenburch (q.v.). An important member of the first generation of Dutch Italianate landscapists, Breenbergh was one of the founders of the Schildersbent, a confraternity of Netherlandish artists working in Rome in which he was given the nickname of "Het Fret" (The Weasel).

While the majority of Breenbergh's approximately two hundred known drawings were made in Italy, most of his paintings date from the period following his return to Amsterdam in 1629, after which he married Rebecca Schellingwou. The most productive period of his career, the early 1630s, saw Breenbergh combining his recent experiences of the radiant light and hilly terrain of Italy with biblical and mythological narratives, inspired by the renewed influence of Lastman and the other Pre-Rembrandtists. Roman ruins are the setting for nearly all of Breenbergh's meticulously refined works, in which he skillfully integrates figures into expansive Italianate panoramas, often rich in detail. By distributing his light across the picture space rather than concentrating it in one area, he creates a convincing sense of space and perspective.[2]

Later in his career, beginning in the late 1640s, Breenbergh made approximately fifty etchings after his own drawings, showing ruins in the vicinity of Rome. In later life his productivity diminished, although the quality of his paintings remained high. Surprisingly, Breenbergh seems to have been quickly forgotten after his death, as few of his works are cited in seventeenth-century Dutch inventories and auction catalogues. His reputation rapidly regenerated in eighteenth-century France, however, when his name came to be considered virtually synonymous with Dutch Italianate landscape painting.

NOTES

1. Biographical material on Breenbergh is drawn from Roethlisberger 1981, 1–19; A. Chong's biography in Amsterdam/Boston/Philadelphia 1987–88, 283; and N. C. Sluijter-Seijffert's extensive biographical essay in *Dictionary of Art* 1996, 4:733–35.

2. Roethlisberger 1981, 7.

[52]

Landscape with Ruins, c. 1630

Inscriptions: traces of signature and date in the shadow of the rocks in front of the foundation and in the spandrel of the left-hand arch in the ruins and dated on the ruins, lower left, *B.... 16..*

Oil on panel, 30.9 × 54.9 cm (12⅛ × 21⅝ in.)

Lent by the Toledo Museum of Art, Purchased with funds from the Libbey Endowment, Gift of Edward Drummond Libbey, 65.170

References: Utrecht 1965, no. 27, fig. 28, and reprint, 1978, 81–82, no. 27; San Francisco/Toledo/Boston 1966–67, 112, no. 70; Wittman 1967, 475, pl. XV; Roethlisberger 1969, no. 96; Roethlisberger 1981, 58, no. 131 and fig. 131.

A painting of great delicacy of brushwork and color, especially its pale greens and blues, this landscape projects an extraordinary luminosity. It can be related to a number of other works painted shortly after Breenbergh's decade of residence in Italy, which ended in 1629 with his return to Amsterdam.[1] In the beauty of these landscapes, one senses that the artist's experience of the Italian terrain and atmosphere even intensified when he was no longer able to paint them from observation, as if the countryside and climate that were so different from that of his homeland had become increasingly vibrant in his memory. Painted on copper or panel, each of these scenes is a wide horizontal panorama with a zone of shadow all across the foreground, beyond which is a large sunlit ruin at left or right with a vista of faraway mountains at the opposite side. Although most of these works incorporate classical or biblical narratives, the Toledo painting is populated simply by grazing cows and goats and relaxed country people in conversation.

As M. Roethlisberger has suggested, the large, barrel-shaped ruin at the right, reddish brown in color, appears to be a creation of the artist's fantasy rather than a known structure, although it recalls a building in one of Gabrielle Perelle's (c. 1603–77) prints after Jan Asselijn (after 1610–1652), which identifies the ruin as the Temple of Marcus Cursus.[2] In Breenbergh's painting, it is monumental in scale, looming over the landscape; the ruin dwarfs the distant mountain at the far left and the fortified town in the middle ground, making the nearby figures and animals appear small and delicate. To the left of the ruin is a fountain with a standing sculpture of Venus silhouetted against the hills and sky far beyond. The small Cupid figure, pissing a stream of water into the basin below her, adds a humorous note that makes the ancient world seem alive in both past and present.

NOTES

1. Paintings with similar composition and coloring include Breenbergh's *Landscape with Atalanta and Hippomenes*, dated 1630, in the Staatliche

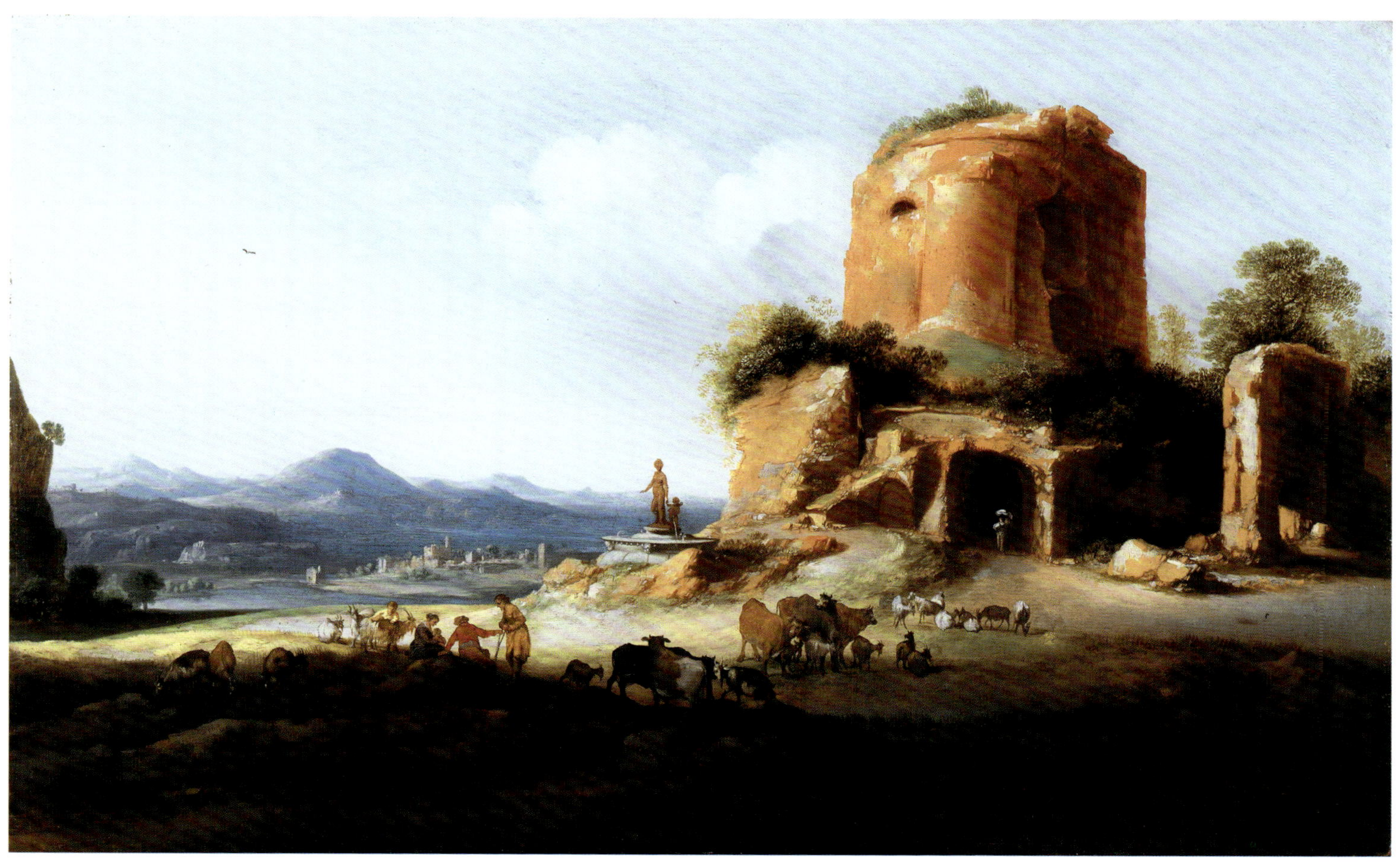

Kunstsammlungen, Kassel (no. 207); *Landscape with the Voyage of Eliezer and Rebecca*, dated 1630, Collection Mr. and Mrs. Michael Hornstein, Montreal; and *Landscape with Moses and Aaron Turning the Nile into Blood*, dated 1631, in the J. Paul Getty Museum, Los Angeles (no. 70.PB.14). Repr. Roethlisberger 1981, figs. 133–35.

2. Roethlisberger 1981, 58; repr. Steland-Stief 1971, pl. XXIV. Roethlisberger (ibid.) also notes that a similar structure appears in Breenbergh's undated *Landscape with Ruins* in the Fitzwilliam Museum, Cambridge, England (no. 432).

[53]

The Preaching of St. John the Baptist, 1634

(Poughkeepsie only)

Inscriptions: lower right, *B.B. f. A. 1634*

Oil on panel, 54.6 × 75.2 cm (21½ × 29⅝ in.)

Lent by the Metropolitan Museum of Art, New York, Purchase, Annenberg Foundation Gift, 1991, 1991.305

References: Hoet 1752–70, 1 (1752):125, no. 12, and 135, no. 15; Coral Gables 1951, no. 11; Bille 1961, 2:90–91, no. 26; Paris 1970–71, 29; Fuchs 1973, 80–81 n. 11 and pl. 10, no. 33; Salerno 1977–78, 1:239–41, 3:1000 n. 25; Roethlisberger 1981, 17 and 68, no. 165, fig. 165; Haak 1984, 144, fig. 298; New York 1985, 85, 88–89, no. 11; Vergara 1985, 408 and fig. 82; New York 1988, 24–25, 39, repr., no. 7; Montreal 1990, 98, no. 23; The Hague/San Francisco 1990–91, 197–99, no. 14.

One of Breenbergh's largest and most fully elaborated narrative paintings, *The Preaching of St. John the Baptist* combines an exceptionally diverse and colorful crowd of figures with an equally complex Italianate landscape.[1] The enormous colonnaded ruin that rises at the left middle ground appears to be based upon the Colosseum, whose circular amphitheater and towering shard of rubble appear in other depictions of the monument by Breenbergh (Cat. 55e).[2] Like other Dutch history paintings in which ancient ruins indicate the fall of the Old Dispensation at the commencement of the Christian era (Cats. 15, 50, and 54), this is also a scene about spiritual transformation. John the Baptist, who is considered to be the last prophet of the old era and the first saint of the new, was Christ's cousin, and his miraculous birth was also announced by an angel. It was he who prepared the world for the coming of Christ by preaching in the wilderness of Judea about the arrival of a Messiah and the importance of repentance, offering baptism in the River Jordan (John 1, Matthew 3, Luke 3). When Christ appeared among the multitudes to be baptized, John recognized him as the savior and declared: "Behold the Lamb of God who takes away the sin of the world" (John 1:29).

In Breenbergh's landscape John, wearing his traditional camel-skin garment, stands on a hillock at the right, speaking to the multitudes and pointing toward heaven with his right hand, while displaying a large crucifix in his left. In contrast to the simply dressed preacher, many of the figures around him are decked out in the most flamboyantly luxurious costumes, such as the stocky bearded man at the center in pink and blue satin bloomers and a broad-brimmed hat that virtually explodes with multicolored ostrich plumes.[3] At the right foreground, a young mother in a bright red dress and blue cape sits beside a basket of vegetables with her young child, a scene recalling images of the Virgin Mary with the young Christ child (Cat. 67). Throughout the crowd, people of diverse ages, types, and races are combined to suggest the extent and influence of John's preaching throughout the world. The presence of different tribes—such as the Pharisees and the Sadducees mentioned in the text—whom John chastised as "you brood of vipers" (Matthew 3:7, Luke 3:7–9)—may be represented here by the most elaborately attired figures, as the saint exhorts the rich and the proud to repent and be baptized.

Both the configuration of this landscape with its multiple levels of ground and its varied lighting help to clarify the story as a conversion narrative, for the scene has been artfully divided into contrasting areas of sunlight and shadow that imply a distinction between those who attend closely to John's sermon (in the light) and those who ignore him or remain oblivious to his message (in the dark). The figures in half-shadow on the hill in front of the ruins have apparently come out primarily to enjoy a country picnic, but those closer to John are absorbing and discussing his words. An effective counterpoint to this dense and colorful crowd is the empty, soaring landscape beyond, which rises to a mountain peak behind the small figure of the saint.

Very close in date to Breenbergh's painting is a large grisaille oil sketch of the same subject by Rembrandt, now in the Staatliche Museen, Berlin (Fig. 139), which may have been intended as the preparatory study for an etching that was never made.[4] While both artists place their

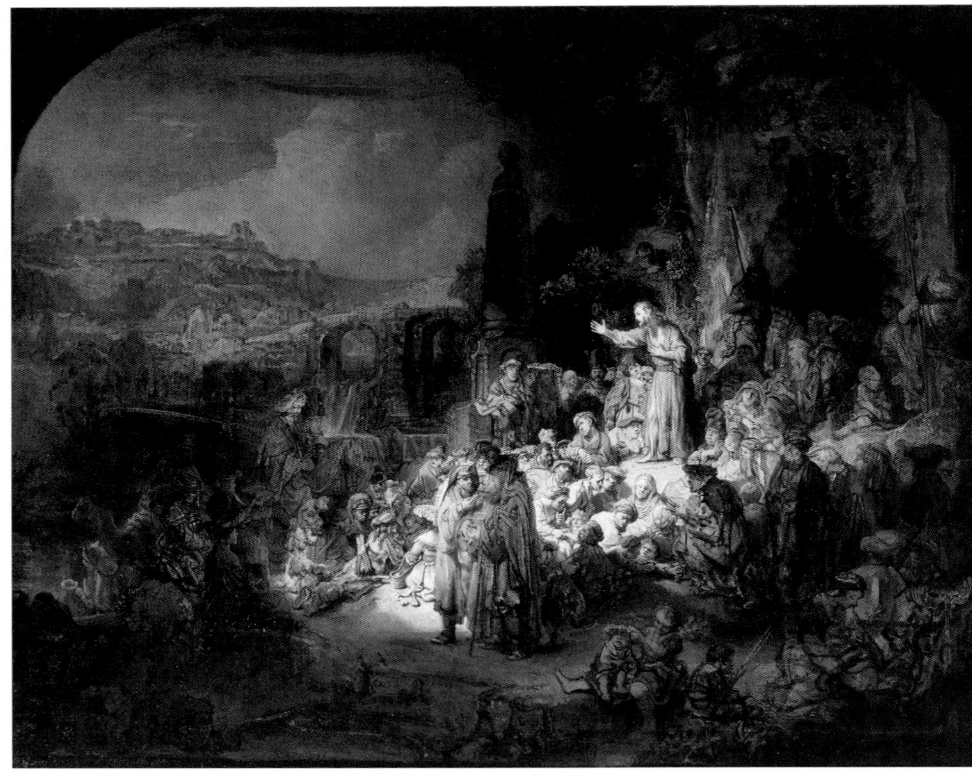

Fig. 139. Rembrandt, *The Preaching of John the Baptist*, c. 1634–36, oil on canvas, Staatliche Museen, Berlin

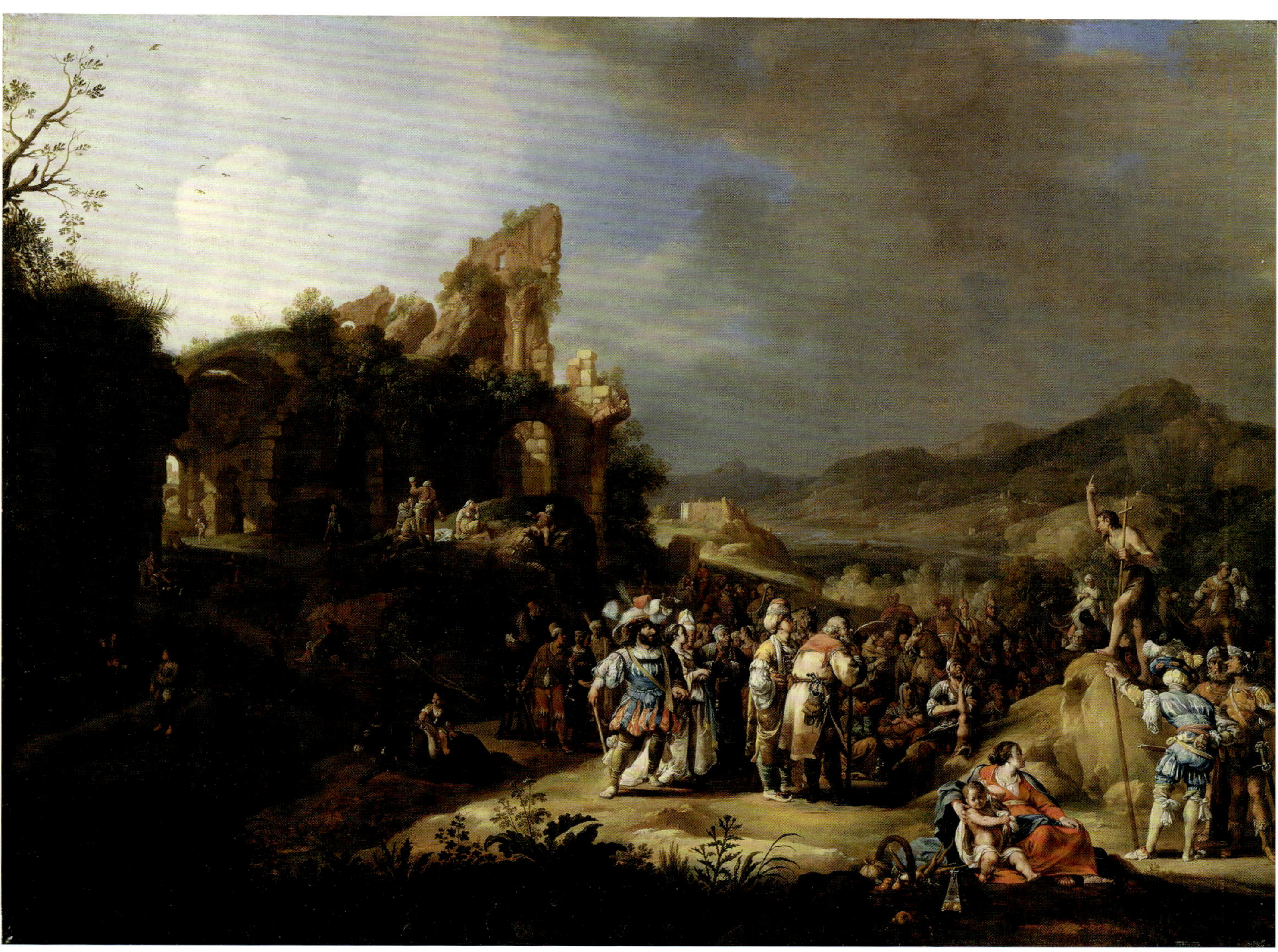

scenes in ancient settings and emphasize the diversity of the audience, Breenbergh's more colorful and polished presentation, with its emphasis on elaboration of detail, relates more closely to early seventeenth-century Dutch history painting by the so-called Pre-Rembrandtist artists such as Jacob Pynas (Cats. 50 and 51) and Claes Cornelisz. Moeyaert (Cats. 57 and 58).

For Breenbergh, who belonged to a Protestant family, and possibly for Rembrandt as well, the subject of John the Baptist preaching may have had special interest as a sacred precedent for the Reformation's emphasis on the Word.[5] Reformers such as Martin Luther taught that people must hear the gospel preached in order to be moved to faith, but during the Spanish dominion of the Netherlands, Protestant preaching was forbidden in the churches. Instead, the new doctrines were spread in the open air by "hedge preachers" who went out into the countryside, often attracting vast crowds to the fields outside the cities.[6]

NOTES

1. Breenbergh painted a second version of this subject with fewer figures and a less detailed setting (oil on panel, 103.5 × 146.2 cm) which is in the collection of Richard L. Feigen, New York, also the former owner of the Metropolitan Museum's painting. For discussion of both paintings with reproductions, see B. P. J. Broos in The Hague/San Francisco 1990–91, 197–202.

2. Aside from the print exhibited here, Breenbergh also made several drawings of the Colosseum, including two now in the Kupferstichkabinett, Dresden, and examples in the Staatliche Kunstsammlungen, Kassel, the Metropolitan Museum of Art, New York, the British Museum, London, and the Kupferstichkabinett, Berlin. Roethlisberger 1969, nos. 12, 44, 53, 82, 147, and 161.

3. B. P. J. Broos, who has found a close prototype for this figure in the elaborately dressed ensign in a woodcut by Hans Schäufelein and Josse de Negler of c. 1512–15, also cites an etching by Jacques Callot of c. 1622, *The Sermon of St. Amadeus*, from which Breenbergh borrowed the showily dressed standing man seen from behind at the far right. B. P. J. Broos in The Hague/San Francisco 1990–91, 202, figs. 4 and 5.

4. Scholars date Rembrandt's grisaille to about 1634, but the artist subsequently enlarged his painting from 38 × 52 cm to 62 × 80 cm and designed a frame for it in the 1650s, possibly for its new owner, Jan Six of Amsterdam. The Six family would retain the work until 1803. *Rembrandt Corpus* 3 (1989):84–85.

5. Rembrandt's religious affiliation has been the subject of debate, because his mother was Roman Catholic, while his father converted to Calvinism. His children, however, were all baptized in the Calvinist (Reformed) church. Schwartz 1985, 18–19, 300.

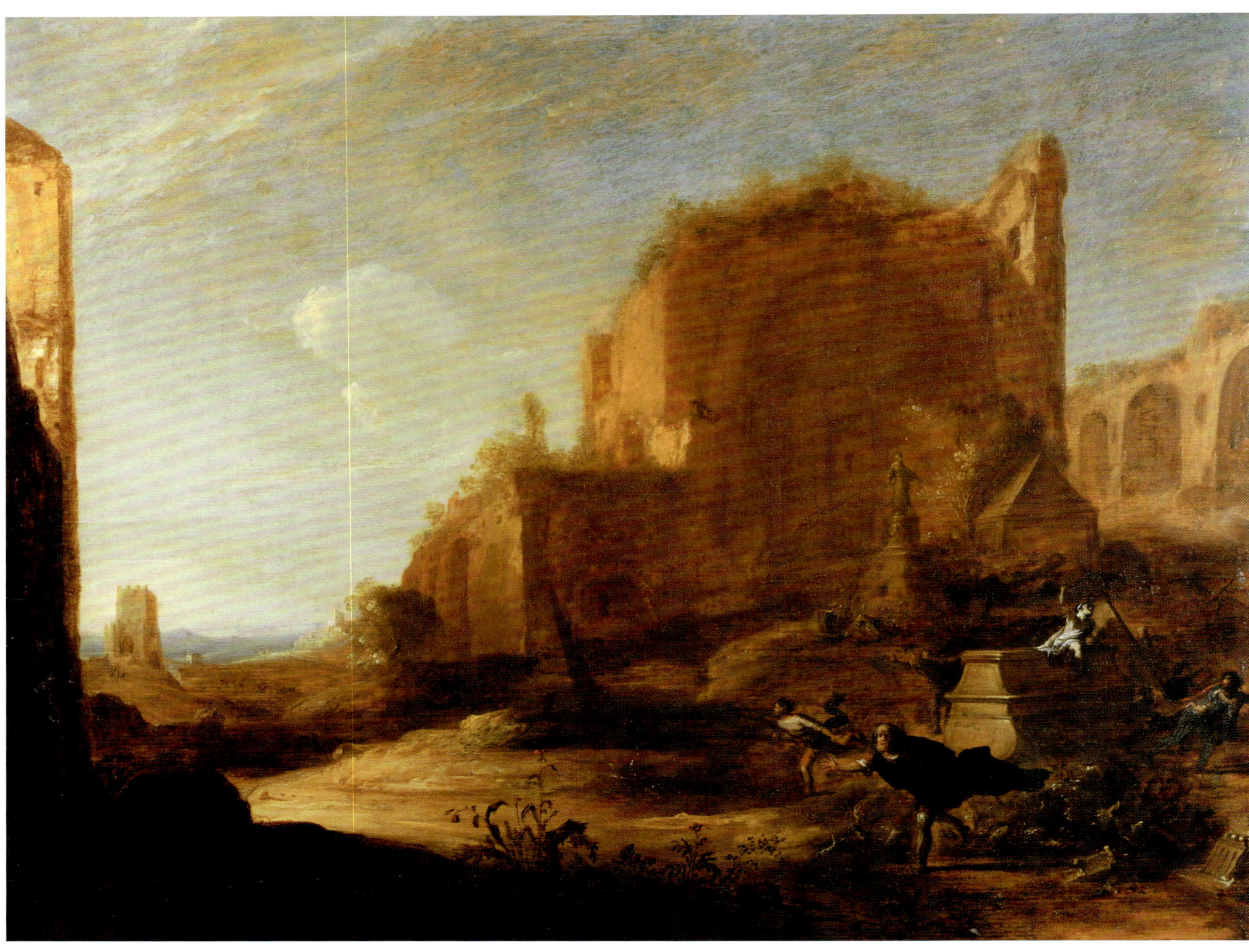

6. On Rembrandt's depictions of the preaching of Jesus and John in relation to Protestant hedge preaching of the sixteenth century, see Halewood 1982, 66–75.

[54]

Resurrection of Christ, 1639

Inscriptions: on side of tomb at right, *Bbreenbergh ... 1639*

Oil on panel, 41.1 × 54.2 cm (16⅕ × 21⅓ in.)

Collection Eugene Victor Thaw and Company, Inc., New York

References: Roethlisberger 1981, 77–78, no. 195.

Bright, early morning light fills this hilly Italian landscape, which is dominated by the massive forms of ancient ruins. At the left foreground, the darkly shadowed edge of a wall forms a repoussoir, framing a long vista, within which more distant structures emerge in the rising light. The golden-brown mountain of ruined masonry at the right, weathered and overgrown with foliage, has a soaring apse, largely obscured by shadow, and an extension at the left that identify it as the Temple of Venus and Roma in the Roman Forum. The adjacent barrel-vaulted structure at the far right clearly derives from the Basilica of Constantine and Maxentius.[1] Before the apse of the larger ruin are a pyramidal tomb and the statue of an unidentifiable male figure (more likely Christian than ancient Roman)[2] on a sculpted pedestal that has been further elevated on a stone base. He faces toward the right as if witnessing the extraordinary happening in which the small foreground figures are engaged.

From the lid of an opened sarcophagus climbs the tiny figure of a beardless Christ, emitting a small burst of supernatural radiance paler than the morning sunlight. As he frees himself from his loosening winding sheet and raises his arm in triumph, the seven figures around the tomb flee in all directions, their astonishment and fear most obvious in the man running toward the viewer whose face is distorted with terror. An exceptionally original interpretation of Christ's Resurrection, this painting may have been influenced by Rembrandt's etching *The Angel Appearing to the Shepherds* of 1634, in which the appearance of the angel announcing Christ's

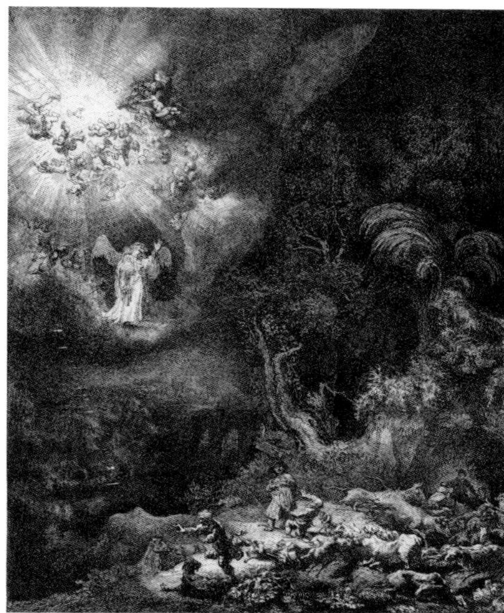

Fig. 140. Rembrandt, *The Angel Appearing to the Shepherds*, 1634, etching. Frances Lehman Loeb Art Center, Vassar College, Poughkeepsie, New York

birth under a radiant aura of heavenly light causes the astounded shepherd folk to run for their lives (Fig. 140).[3] Breenbergh, however, has de-emphasized the supernatural aspects of the Resurrection to a surprising extent, making it a rather small and inconspicuous moment within a much larger context of space and time. As in scenes of the Nativity and the Adoration that feature ancient ruins (Cats. 15 and 50), Christ's emergence signals the new era that will be built upon the crumbling foundations of the past. The manifestations of history loom so large in this landscape, however, that the appearance of this tiny, very human figure (whom one recognizes only secondarily) seems all the more momentous. Breenbergh was also able to capture a wide range of light modulations, combining broadly painted areas with more finely rendered details such as the flowering plants at the center foreground that contrast with the fallen rubble on either side.

NOTES

1. The ruins in this painting have been identified by M. Roethlisberger, who has drawn attention to Breenbergh's drawing in the Musée du Louvre, Paris (no. 22 557) that shows the same buildings from almost the same vantage point (Roethlisberger 1981, 77, no. 133, fig. 133).

2. According to E. d'Ambra (personal communication, August 2003, Vassar College), neither the ankle-length garment of this sculpted figure nor its gesture (arms opened on either side to imply recognition or revelation) suggests that it is Roman. Thus Breenbergh probably intended it to refer to impending Christian veneration of Jesus after his earthly death and spiritual resurrection.

3. In 1639, the year of Breenbergh's painting, Rembrandt painted his version of the Resurrection for the *Passion Cycle* (Alte Pinakothek, Munich, no. 397), an equally original interpretation, but one that is entirely opposite in effect. Here the main focus is the large angel surrounded by heavenly light who raises the lid of the tomb to bring forth a Lazarus-like Christ from the dead.

[55]

Six prints from *Verscheÿden vervallen gebouwē— … romen* (Various ruined buildings within and without Rome), 1639/40 (from a series of seventeen numbered prints)

Inscriptions: title page, *Verscheÿden vervallen gebouwē— soo binnen als buyten Romen. Geteykent en Ghe-ets door Bartholomaus Breenbergh Schilder. Gedaen in 't Jaer 1640*

(Various ruined buildings in and outside Rome, drawn and etched by Bartholomaus Breenbergh, painter. Done in the year 1640.)

Etchings; early states; mounted in one frame: top row, 1, 2, and 6; bottom row, 3, 10, and 13

a. *Title Page (Verscheÿden vervallen gebouwē—)* (no. 1), dated 1640; 100 × 62 mm (3⁵⁄₁₆ × 2⁷⁄₁₆ in.) (platemark); 102 × 63 mm (4 × 2½ in.) (sheet)

b. *Calidarium of the Hot Springs of Diocletian* (no. 2); 97 × 61 mm (3¹³⁄₁₆ × 2⅜ in.) (platemark); 100 × 64 mm (3¹⁵⁄₁₆ × 2½ in.) (sheet)

c. *The Villa of the Emperors in Rome* (no. 6), dated 1640; 100 × 61 mm (3¹⁵⁄₁₆ × 2⅜ in.) (platemark); 103 × 63 mm (4¹⁄₁₆ × 2½ in.) (sheet)

d. *Ruins of St. Lorenzo Vecchio near Bolsena* (no. 3); 91 × 64 mm (3⁹⁄₁₆ × 2½ in.) (platemark); 93 × 66 mm (3⅝ × 2⅝ in.) (sheet)

e. *Ruins of the Colosseum* (no. 10); 102 × 63 mm (4 × 2½ in.) (platemark); 106 × 66 mm (4³⁄₁₆ × 2⅝ in.) (sheet)

f. *The Hot Springs of Caracalla* (no. 13), dated 1639; 102 × 62 mm (4 × 2⁷⁄₁₆ in.) (platemark); 105 × 66 mm (4⅛ × 2⅝ in.) (sheet)

Print Collection, The Miriam and Ira D. Wallach Division of Art, Prints and Photographs, The New York Public Library, Astor, Lenox and Tilden Foundations

References: Hollstein 3 (1949):206; Freedberg 1980, 62–63, fig. 109; Boston/St. Louis 1980–81, 173–74.

Netherlandish artists recorded Roman ruins beginning in the sixteenth century, a period that also saw the beginning of print series of ancient sites with the publication in 1551 of Hieronymus Cock's (c. 1510–70) *Praecipuae aliquot Romanae antiquitatis ruinarum monumenta* … (see Fig. 3). Willem van Nieulandt II's (q.v.) cycle entitled *Varia Antiquitates Romana, sive Ruine* of 1618 was another important precursor for Breenbergh's suite of prints, which includes sheets dated both 1639 and 1640.[1]

The seventeen small etchings in this cycle, all in a vertical format, include a title page, dated 1640 (Breenbergh 1, Cat. 55a), that describes the scenes to follow as "fallen buildings" (*vervallen gebouwē—*) located inside and outside Rome. It is likely that Breenbergh based the prints, six of which are reproduced here, on drawings he had made a decade earlier in Italy. He probably intended them for sale to armchair tourists but also used them as a convenient storehouse of motifs for his later Italianate scenes. In any case, the decision to present such large structures in miniature scale and to render them in fine, delicate lines results in an unusual intimacy and spontaneity of effect, especially as most scenes include tiny figures casually making their way through the rubble. The series includes representative examples of villas, palaces, bridges, aqueducts, baths or hot springs, and churches, along with one very untraditional view of the Colosseum.[2]

In this daringly original image (Breenbergh 10, Cat. 55e), the artist places the most recognizable feature of the monument—its colossal cylinder of repeating, multistoried arches—in the background. Delineating this area very lightly, he overlaps it almost completely with a densely etched, deeply bitten architectural remnant (one arch and four crumbling uprights) that rises boldly above the foreground debris. A minute view through the arch discloses a distant vertical shard of masonry. As a whole, this small image therefore encapsulates the most fundamental qualities of ruins: fragmentation, irregularity, instability, and the framing of unexpected vistas.

Within the context of the entire series, each print acquires added interest when compared with scenes that display different shapes or a different interplay of solids and voids—even when the same kind of site is represented. For example, the shambling rise of the ruins of

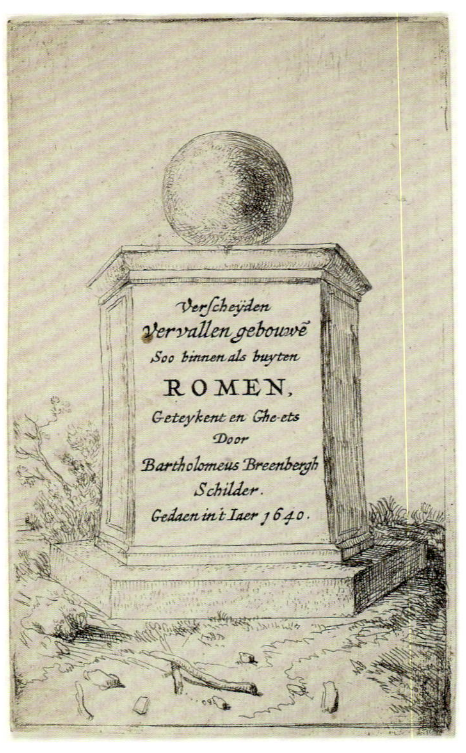

[55a]

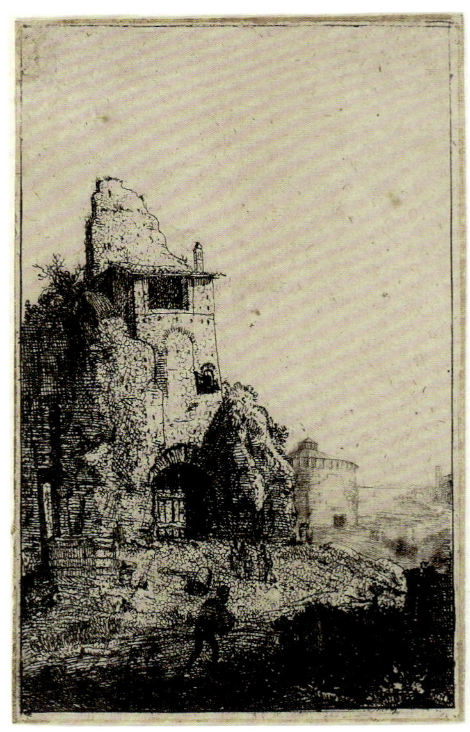

[55b]

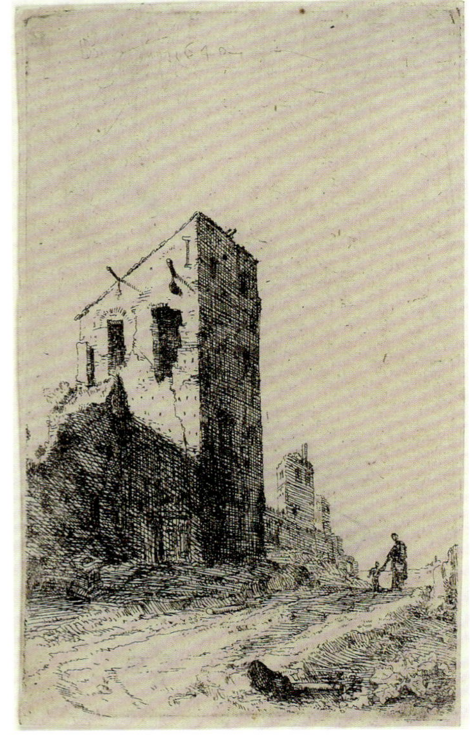

[55c]

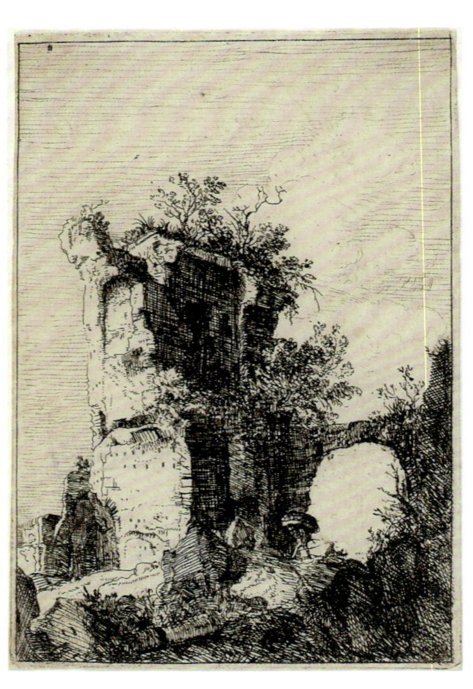

[55d]

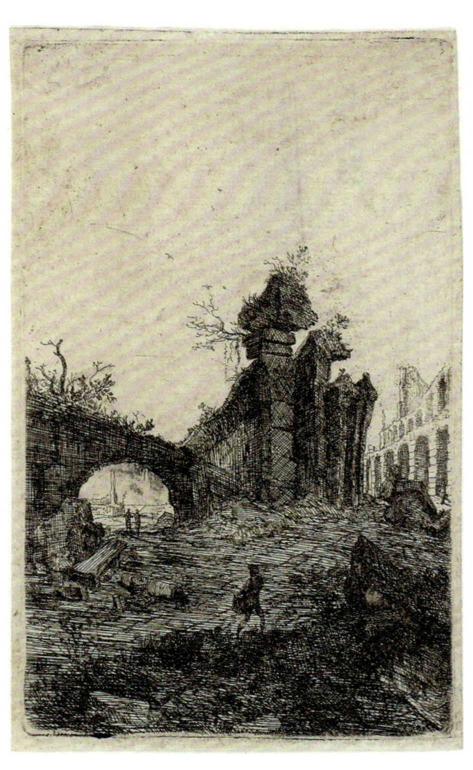

[55e]

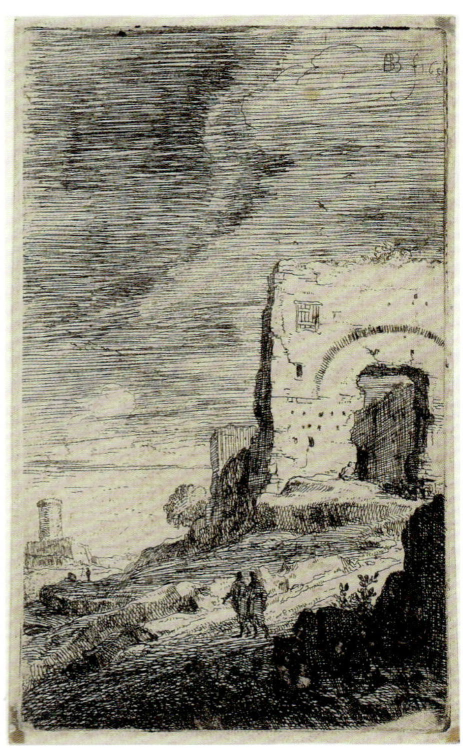

[55f]

Diocletian's Calidarium (Breenbergh 2, Cat. 55b) is set in contrast to the flatter, more massive facade of the Baths of Caracalla, seen under a darkening sky (Breenbergh 13, Cat. 55f, dated 1639). The extreme irregularity of the overgrown remains of the church of S. Lorenzo Vecchio near Bolsena (Breenbergh 3, Cat. 55d) makes this building appear a kind of abstract sculpture when compared to a section of the Palatine Palace (Breenbergh 6, Cat. 55c, 1640), whose vertical sides and slanting top remain intact.[3] Setting the viewpoint of each scene at ground level allowed Breenbergh to suggest the size of the ruined structures, thereby creating a memorable polarity between the bulk of each monument and the diminutive scale of its printed representation.

NOTES

1. Jan Gossaert (c. 1478–1532) made drawings of ancient ruins and sculptures for Philip of Burgundy, only four of which are known today, but many of Maerten van Heemskerck's (1498–1574) Roman drawings are preserved, including two sketchbooks in the Staatliche Museen, Kupferstichkabinett, Berlin (Veldman 1993). Cock also produced a second print series of Roman ruins in 1562 entitled *Operum antiquorum Romanorum* ... Other Dutch printmakers who took up this theme in the seventeenth century include Carel de Hooch (c. 1590–1638), Herman van Swanevelt (q.v.), and Jan Gerritsz. van Bronkhorst (c. 1603–before 1661), whose prints were based on designs by Cornelis van Poelenburch (q.v.).

2. The preparatory drawing for this print, dated 1639, is in the Kupferstichkabinett, Dresden (repr. Roethlisberger 1969, 47, no. 147). Two other drawings of the Colosseum by Breenbergh are in the Staatliche Kunsthalle, Kassel (no. 5062) and the British Museum, London (repr. Roethlisberger 1969, nos. 12 and 82).

3. I am indebted to Eve d'Ambra for discussion about Roman buildings in Breenbergh's series.

WILLEM VAN NIEULANDT II
1584–1635

Willem van Nieulandt II, a Flemish/Dutch painter and draftsman best known for his depictions of ancient ruins, was born in Antwerp, but in his early youth moved with his family to Amsterdam, where he became a pupil of Jacob Savery (1545–1602).[1] In 1601–2 he traveled to Rome, where he lived with his uncle and teacher Willem van Nieulandt I (1560–1626), with whom he has often been confused because of close similarities in the styles of the two artists as well as their names: in Italy, both were known as Guglielmo Terranuova. Van Nieulandt II's second teacher in Italy was the gifted and influential Flemish landscapist Paulus Bril (1554–1626), who also produced Roman townscapes with ancient ruins.

In 1604, Van Nieulandt returned to Antwerp, where he became a master in the guild of St. Luke. In 1606, however, he returned to Amsterdam, where he married Anna Hustaert, with whom he had several children. In 1628 his daughter Catherine married the still-life painter Adriaen van Utrecht (1599–1651). Interestingly, Van Nieulandt was also active as a playwright and rhetorician, with six known tragedies and an elaborate didactic poem to his credit.[2] The strongly emotional emphasis of his biblical narratives, which reflect the influence of the Amsterdam Pre-Rembrandtists, must also be connected to his own involvement as a dramatist. Willem van Nieulandt II's 115 known etchings, which were based on the drawings he made in Rome, catalogue many of the best-known Roman ruin sites; for example, his series of 1618 entitled *Varia Antiquitates Romana, sive Ruine*.[3] Such architectural records served as very useful aides-mémoire after he had resettled in northern Europe, as for the painting reproduced here, which features a variation on the Temple of Minerva Medica.

NOTES

1. Biographical material is based on H. Devissher's entry in *Dictionary of Art* 1996. 23:123–24, and on Welu 1979–80, 3–6. The basic study of both the Willem van Nieulandts was published in 1911 by G. J. Hoogewerff in *Oud Holland* (Hoogewerff 1911).

2. Van Nieulandt's literary production is discussed in Van den Branden 1875 (cited in Welu 1979–80, 6) and in Keersmaekers 1957.

3. Hollstein 14 (1956):162–67.

[56]
Laban Searching for His Idols, 1630

Inscriptions: lower right corner, *Guil. van Nieuwlandt 1630*

Oil on panel, 82.5 × 100.3 cm (32½ × 39½ in.)

Worcester Art Museum, Worcester, Massachusetts, Charlotte E.W. Buffington Fund, 1980.7

References: Welu 1979–80, 2–7.

The source for this Old Testament narrative, Genesis 31:17–55, recounts events that took place after Jacob's departure from Mesopotamia for Canaan with all his servants, flocks, and household possessions. Accompanied by his wives Leah and Rachel, daughter of his uncle Laban, Jacob was unaware that this baggage included Laban's idols, or household gods. Rachel had stolen them on his behalf because

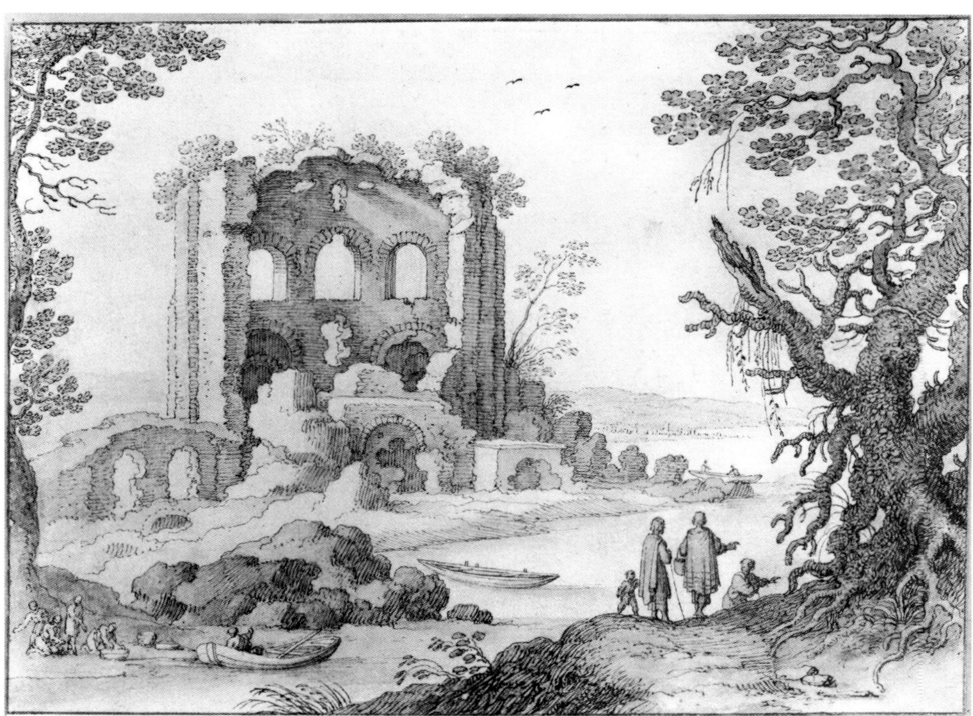

Fig. 141. Willem van Nieulandt II, *Landscape with the Temple of Minerva Medica, Rome*, before 1630, pen and brown wash drawing, Collection Frits Lugt, Institut Néerlandais, Paris

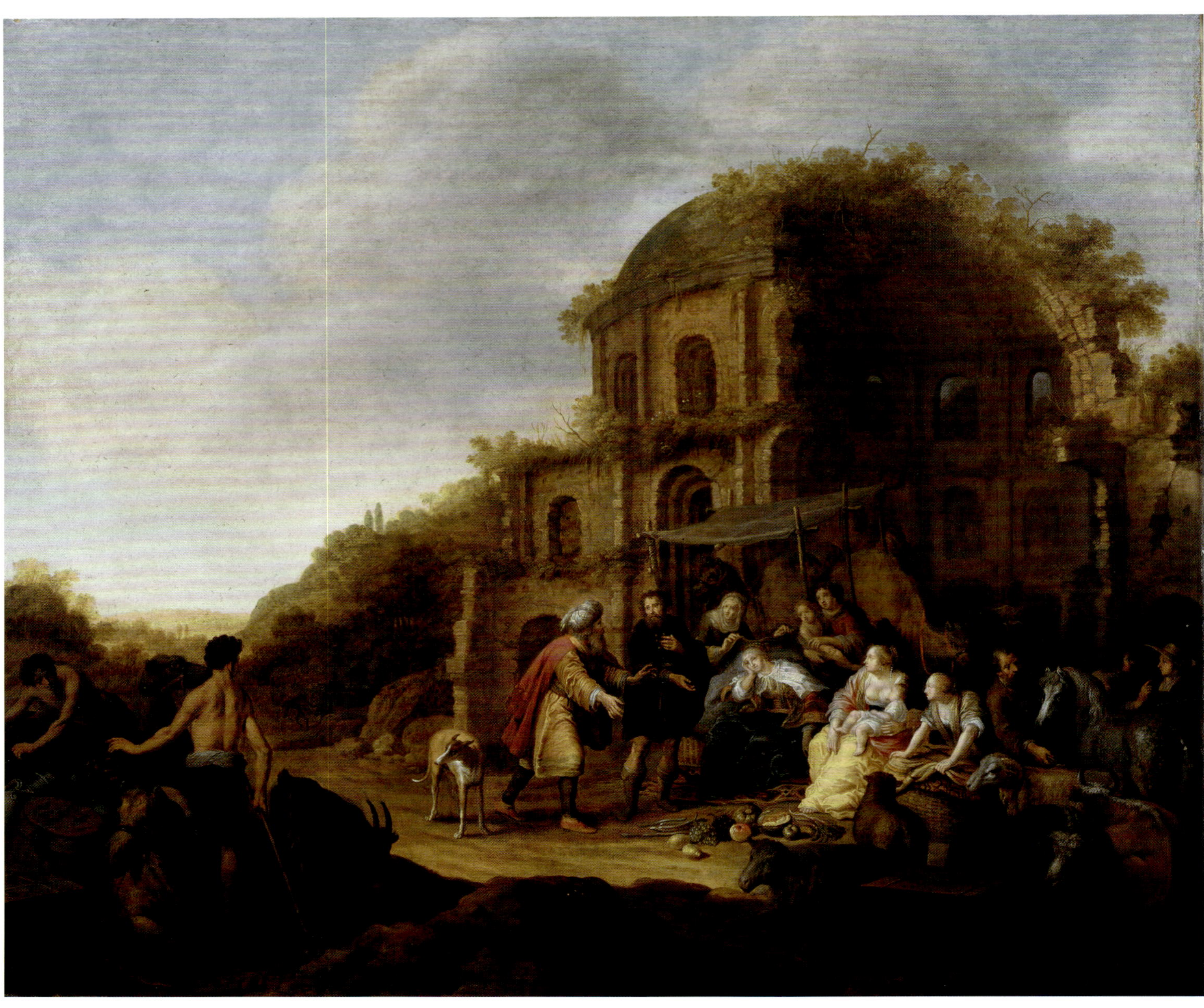

Laban had repeatedly cheated Jacob of his rightful wages and property during his twenty years of service. Possession of the household gods, according to ancient custom, assured a man's claim to his property, along with leadership of his family.[1] When Laban pursued Jacob and demanded his property, Jacob innocently invited him to make his own search for his belongings. But Rachel had cleverly secreted the idols in the camel's saddle on which she sat, warning her father that she could not rise to greet him because "... the custom of women is upon me" (Genesis 31:35). Because Old Testament law prohibited men from touching a menstruating woman or anything she had touched until it had been purified, her ruse was successful.

Van Nieulandt has presented his story as if it were a theatrical performance, disposing his cast of characters before the compelling backdrop of a ruin based on a well-known Roman monument that had come to be known by the seventeenth century as the Temple of Minerva Medica. This domed, decagonal structure on the via Giovanni Gelotti, originally called the Nymphaeum Hortorum Licinianorum, was part of a complex of Roman buildings erected during the reign of Emperor P. Lucinius Gallienus (A.D. 253–68). Van Nieulandt also recorded it in both a drawing (Fig. 141) and a print.[2] Half-shattered, weathered, and overgrown with foliage in this painting, the ruined temple indicates that the scene happened in the distant past in a faraway place—a device commonly used by Dutch history painters.

Here, Laban, wearing a turban and a rich golden costume with a red cape, gestures insistently to Jacob, who stands between him and his daughter, eloquently indicating her drooping demeanor as she slumps weakly with her head propped on her hand. Within the shadowed foreground at the left, Laban's servants conduct a search of the saddlebags, while the women of the household protectively encircle Rachel. A striking addition to the scene is the colorful still life of ripe fruits and vegetables on the ground in front of Rachel—perhaps, as in Dutch family portraits, an allusion to the fertility of Laban's household as emphasized by the fact that Rachel is of childbearing age and two of the other women hold young children. Since an important aspect of the dispute between Jacob and Laban had concerned the fair division of Laban's flocks (Genesis 30:29–43), sheep, goats, and cows (not to mention camels) also play a significant role here.

In his choice and interpretation of this story, Van Nieulandt was clearly influenced by the group of history painters working in Amsterdam during the first half of the century (later classified as the "Pre-Rembrandtists") whose detailed treatment of Old Testament narratives often explored familial relationships or conflicts. Such subjects had great appeal in the highly domestic, middle-class society of the Dutch provinces.[3] As J. A. Welu has pointed out, Van Nieulandt's interest in the themes of distrust and deception that are central to the story of Laban and Rachel parallel his concentration on subjects of human conflict in his theatrical writings.[4]

NOTES

1. These images, representing the household gods and used for divination, were known collectively as the teraphim and were probably similar to the Lares and Penates in a Roman household.

2. For discussion of this structure and Van Nieulandt's representations of it, see Brussels/Rotterdam/Paris/Berne 1968–69, 1:111–12, and Welu 1979–80, 5–6 and fig. 5. Van Nieulandt's engraving belongs to his print series *Monumenta haec et venerandae antiquitatis romanae vestigial*. Hollstein 14 (1956):164–65, no. 19, repr.

3. The major prototype for this scene—though lacking its emphasis on ruins—is Pieter Lastman's (c. 1583–1633) *Laban and Rachel*, dated 1622, in the Musée Municipal, Boulogne-sur-Mer, no. 147. Claes Cornelisz. Moeyaert (q.v.), working slightly later, also addressed this narrative in his painting dated 1647, now in the Detroit Institute of Arts, no. 57.17.

4. Welu 1979–80, 3.

CLAES CORNELISZ. MOEYAERT
c. 1590/91–1655

Moeyaert was the most prolific and one of the most internationally famous of the Amsterdam history painters who had such strong influence on Rembrandt's early work—hence their subsequent (and rather awkward) art-historical designation as "Pre-Rembrandtists." Born into a patrician Roman Catholic family that had fled Amsterdam during the religious conflicts in the late sixteenth century, Moeyaert returned to the city with his family at the age of fourteen.[1] His teacher is unknown, but his landscapes, occupied by dramatically gesturing figures acting out biblical and mythological narratives, reveal the influences of Adam Elsheimer (1578–1610), Pieter Lastman (1583–1663), and Jan (1583/84–1631) and Jacob Pynas (q.v.). Although his works often include Roman ruins, no visit to Italy was ever recorded.

As a leading Roman Catholic artist in Amsterdam, Moeyaert received numerous commissions from clerics such as Sibrandus Sextius, the priest of the Begijnhof, and Hendrickje Jansdr. Coppiers, the mother superior of the Catholic orphanage. In 1650 he painted three altarpieces for the chapel of the Begijnhof. In 1638 he participated in the design of the triumphal arches welcoming the entry of Marie de' Medici to Amsterdam. That Moeyaert achieved considerable international fame is indicated by the fact that Christian IV of Denmark commissioned him in 1639 to paint two large pendant historical themes (completed in 1643) for Kronborg Castle, Elsinor.

A talented animal painter, Moeyaert gave cattle, horses, and sheep prominent roles in his narrative paintings and etchings, of which approximately twenty-five are known. Most date from before 1624, and they include pure landscapes as well as historical subjects. His etched illustrations of sea battles for David Pietersz. De Vries's *Various Voyages in Four Parts of the World* appeared in 1655. In addition to working as an artist, Moeyaert was active in local theatrical productions, creating stage decorations for the Amsterdam theater (Schouburgh) in 1639 and 1640 and serving on its board of directors. His pupils included Salomon Koninck (1609–56), Jan Baptist Weenix (q.v.), and Nicolaes Berchem (q.v.).

NOTE

1. Biographical information on Moeyaert and his family is adapted from A. Tümpel's monograph on the artist (Tümpel 1974) and from her essay in *Dictionary of Art* 1996, 21:780–91.

[57]
The Meeting of Jacob and Joseph in Egypt, c. 1636

Inscriptions: none

Oil on canvas, 137.2 × 164.5 cm (54 × 64¾ in.)

Bowdoin College Museum of Art, Brunswick, Maine, Museum purchase, Florence C. Quinby Fund in Memory of Henry Cole Quinby, Class of 1916, 1970.041

References: Tümpel 1974, 103–4, fig. 141, and 253, no. 55; Sacramento 1974, 84–85, no. 16.

The Dutch public's appreciation for Old Testament subjects can be related to the fact that so many of these narratives involve human quandaries in which individuals undergo tests of their virtue or faith. Familial situations such as conflicts about inheritance, estrangements, and reconciliations also resonated with this intensely domestic society. Moreover, a nation that had only recently succeeded in establishing its own "promised land" found compelling historical precedent in the Israelites' quest for a safe and prosperous homeland.[1] Joseph's reunion with his father, Jacob, which Moeyaert painted twice, brings together a number of these narrative strands, while allowing the artist to explore an emotional confrontation within a fully elaborated setting.[2] Moeyaert's experience with the Amsterdam theater served him well in his interpretation of this dramatic story.

As recounted in chapters 37–46 of Genesis, Joseph, his elderly father's favorite son, was sold into slavery by his eleven jealous brothers. Having been taken to Egypt, he became pharoah's viceroy because of his ability to prophesy and interpret dreams. Joseph's prediction of seven years of plenty followed by seven years of famine made it possible for the Egyptians to stockpile food. When the famine arrived, and Joseph's brothers came to buy grain, he tested them with various trials, eventually revealing his identity and persuading them to bring his father to Egypt to live, along with themselves, their families, and their flocks and herds. Moeyaert has depicted the moment when Joseph arrives by chariot in Goshen for the meeting with his father: "… and he presented himself unto him; and he fell on his neck, and wept on his neck a good while" (Genesis 46:29).

By structuring this scene with two separate groups of figures at left and right and elaborating it with numerous details, Moeyaert was able to show that the meeting of this long-separated father and son is an event that will also reunite

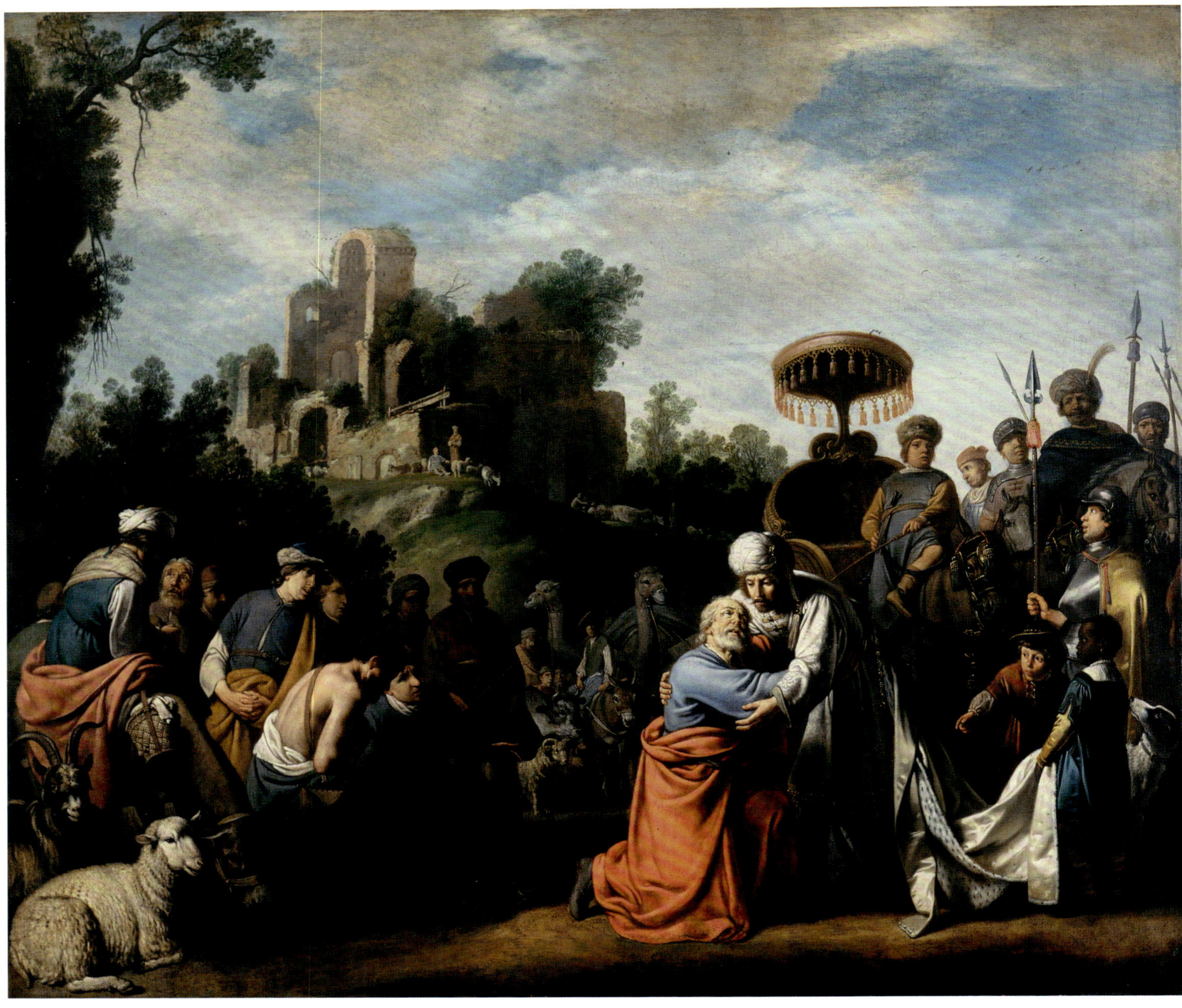

an entire fractured family. At the right, Jacob, wearing an eye-catching red cloak, kneels as his son Joseph reaches out to embrace him. Joseph's immense wealth is emphasized by his golden chariot and an impressive retinue that includes mounted soldiers with spears and two young pages, one light- and one dark-skinned, who are responsible for handling their master's ermine-lined train. At left are the plainly dressed herdsmen, representing Joseph's brothers, who have repented their terrible deed and look on remorsefully. Moeyaert's talents as an animal painter are vividly displayed throughout this scene, especially in the gathering of camels and other beasts waiting patiently between and behind the two figure groups.

A secondary but significant focus of this scene is the complex of Roman ruins on the hill in the background. Such ancient architectural remains (even geographically incongruous ones) appear frequently in Dutch history paintings to indicate that the story took place in the distant past. In his depiction of an earlier incident from the story of Jacob (Cat. 56), Willem van Nieulandt included a Roman site he could have studied on the spot. Moeyaert's ruin was probably his own invention, however, since there is no evidence that the artist ever visited Italy.

NOTES

1. On the Dutch identification with the Jews, see Schama 1987, 93–125.

2. A more horizontal version of the subject by Moeyaert, dated 1628, is in the Hamburger Kunsthalle (panel, 77.4 × 163 cm), inv. no. 702.

[58]

The Herd, 1638

Inscriptions: lower right, *Cl M fec/1638/2*

Etching, 119 × 195 mm (4 11/16 × 7 11/16 in.) (platemark), 126 × 204 mm (4 15/16 × 8 1/16 in.) (sheet); state ii/ii

Museum of Fine Arts, Boston, William A. Sargent Fund, 50.285

References: Hollstein 14 (1956):58; Tümpel 1974, 104, pl. 142; Boston/St. Louis 1980–81, 126–27, no. 79; London 1986, 195, no. 88.

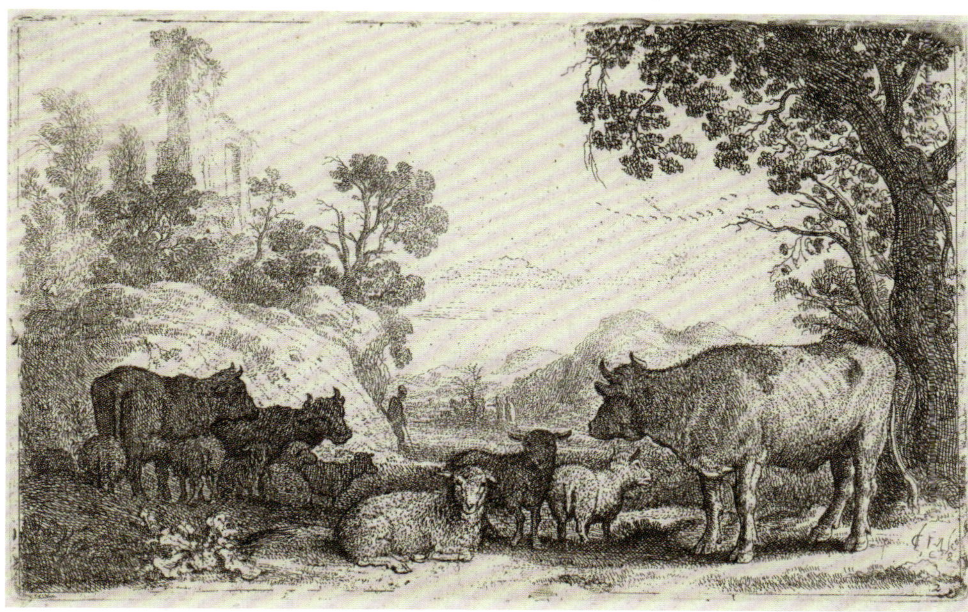

Moeyaert's affection for animals and his sensitivity to the character of different breeds is well displayed in this untraditional pastoral scene, in which the herdsman has been reduced to a small anonymous figure in the middle ground leaning on his staff and gazing off into the distance. At his back rises a rocky hill topped by trees and the fragment of a classical or medieval building. By adding a second coulisse, or framing device, in the large tree at the right and yet another in the distant mountains, Moeyaert creates a stagelike foreground area, a reminder that he was also active as a set designer. His actors are not human beings, however, but an engagingly individualized herd of cattle and sheep, whose shapes and positions are subtly coordinated with landscape forms beside and behind them. The large beasts at left and right face inward, framing the mountains that dip toward the horizon far in the distance. At the center foreground, two sheep—one illuminated and one in shadow—look curiously out at the viewer. In comparison to more refined bucolic scenes by artists such as Karel Dujardin (Cat. 64) or Nicolaes Berchem (Cat. 66), Moeyaert's print has a charmingly straightforward simplicity in that the animals are neither idealized nor engaged in any action. They simply stand or sit, motionless and quiet, fitting comfortably into the landscape.

Moeyaert's etching technique contributes much to the seemingly artless effect of this scene. Rather than elegantly drawn contours or complex hatching intended to recreate textures, he employs a delicate stippled touch throughout much of the print, reserving dark cross-hatching for areas in shadow. Yet the sophistication of his handling of the medium is evident in the bull at right, whose body is placed at a transition between light and shadow that Moeyaert articulates with complete assurance by shifting the shape and density of his strokes. As C. S. Ackley has observed, the delicately furry masses of stipple and hairy broken touches in this etching tend to dissolve any effect of line in favor of a tonal, almost painterly softness.[1]

The Herd has a companion piece in the same format, also dated 1638, which includes another ruin on a hill and some of the same animals (Fig. 142). In this print, however, the direction of the scene is reversed toward the foreground, where a plain, rather elderly herdsman stands among his animals, more of which are now gazing benevolently out of the picture space. As A. Tümpel has noted, both prints can be related to Moeyaert's painting of Jacob and Rachel (c. 1638, present location unknown), a narrative in which animals play an important role.[2]

NOTES

1. Boston/St. Louis 1980–81, 126.

2. This painting was at Galerie Müllenmeister, Solingen, in 1969. Tümpel 1974, 104, fig. 142.

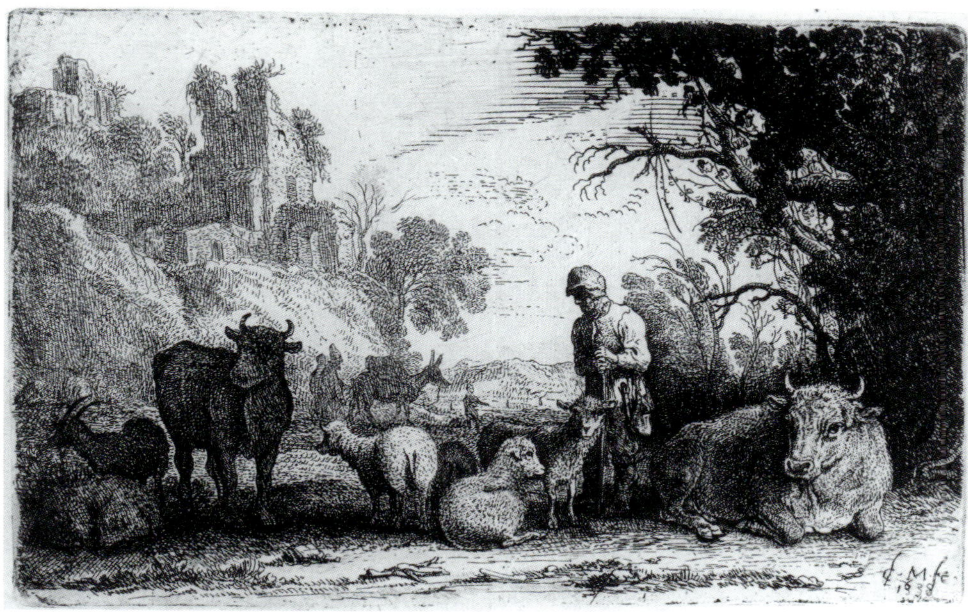

Fig. 142. Claes Cornelisz. Moeyaert, *The Herdsman (Shepherd with Cattle)*, 1638, etching. Rijksprentenkabinet, Rijksmuseum, Amsterdam

HERMAN VAN SWANEVELT (attr.)
c. 1600–1655

Swanevelt's birth date is not known, although Houbraken states that he came from Woerden near Rotterdam.[1] His birth date was probably near 1600, as his earliest known work is a drawing of Paris inscribed *HvS a Paris: 1623/24 October* (Herzog Anton Ulrich-Museum, Braunschweig).[2] Between 1629 and 1641, he was in Rome, where he was given the nickname "Heremyt" (Hermit) by the confraternity of Netherlandish artists known as the Schildersbent or Bentvueghels (Flock of Birds). Swanevelt's style, which parallels that of the early Claude Lorrain (1600–1682), links the first generation of Dutch Italianate landscapists such as Cornelis van Poelenburch (q.v.) and Bartholomeus Breenbergh (q.v.), by whom he was strongly influenced, with the more monumental effects of the second generation of artists, such as Jan Both (q.v.) and Nicolaes Berchem (q.v.). Much admired in Italy, he received major commissions for the Vatican, for the Buen Retiro Palace in Madrid, and for the collection of Cardinal Antonio Barberini.

After his years in Rome, Swanevelt settled in Paris, where he married in 1644. A member of the Académie Royale de Peinture et de Sculpture, he contributed to the decoration of the Cabinet de l'Amour for the Hôtel Lambert, along with Jan Asselijn (after 1610–1652). Swanevelt was a fine draftsman and a prolific printmaker who produced at least 117 etchings showing views of Rome and its surroundings, many featuring ruins. Some were made in Rome, but many appeared during the last years of his life in Paris, when most of his earlier prints were reissued.[3]

NOTES

1. Houbraken 1718–21, 2 (1719):352.
2. On Herman van Swanevelt's biography, see the biographical essay by L. Bos in *Dictionary of Art* 1996, 30:60–61; and P. Schatborn in Amsterdam 2001, 77–83.
3. On Herman van Swanevelt's prints, see Blume 1994.

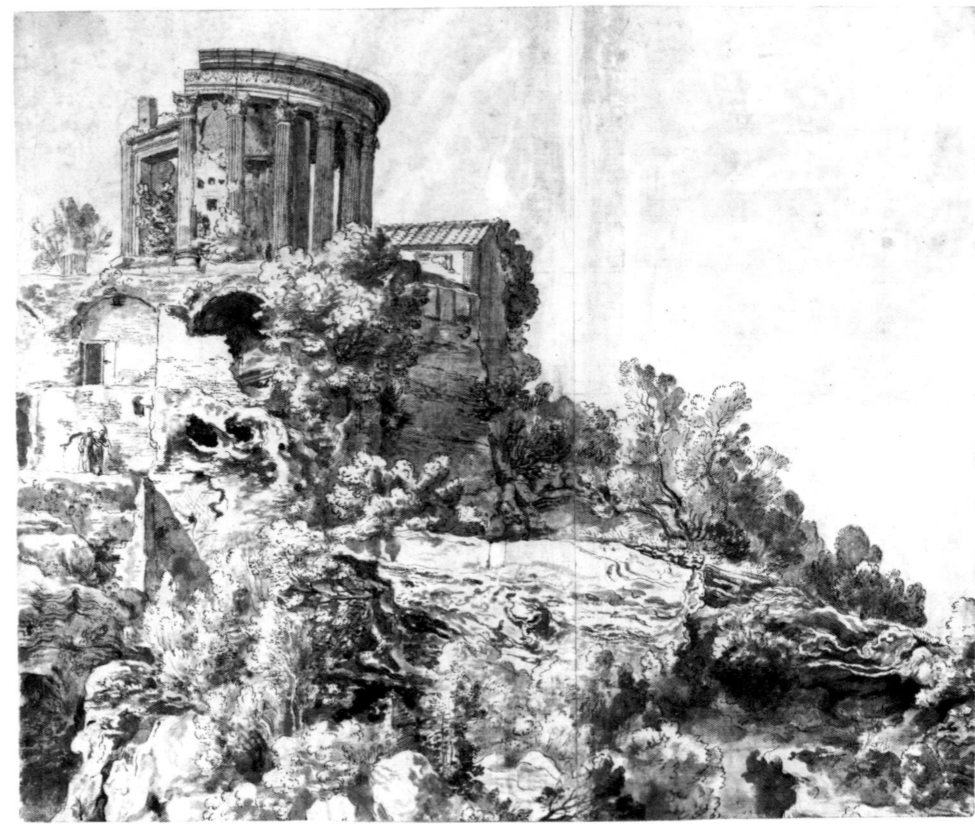

[59] recto

[59]

View of Tivoli (recto) *View of the Ponte Nomentano and View of the Roman Campagna* (verso), c. 1630–40

(Poughkeepsie and Louisville only)

Inscriptions: none.

Pen and brown ink, brown wash, touches of opaque white, over faint traces of black chalk, on paper; framing line in brown ink; extraneous spots of brown and green oil paint on the recto, 399 × 481 mm (15¾ × 18 in.)

The Pierpont Morgan Library, New York, Purchased by Pierpont Morgan, 1910, Acc. no. III,212

References: Fairfax Murray 1905–12, 3: nos. 212–14, repr. (cited here and in all following citations as Bartholomeus Breenbergh); New York 1953, no. 62; Philadelphia/Detroit 1960–61, no. 11; Ann Arbor 1964, no. 25, pl. 14; Scott 1968, 306; New York 1968–69, no. 2, repr.; Roethlisberger 1969, nos. 18–19, both repr., and under no. 163; Van Regteren-Altena 1971, 537; Paris/Antwerp/London/New York 1979–80, no. 72, repr.; Cambridge/Montreal 1988, no. 16, repr.; Montreal 1990, 31, fig. 13.

Tivoli, twenty miles northeast of Rome, was the vacation retreat of Roman emperors, poets, and philosophers including Augustus, Hadrian, and Horace. Among its villas and gardens, the round Temple of the Sibyl—also known as the Temple of Vesta—remains one of the most dramatic of all ruin sites, perched on ancient foundations upon a high precipice thickly overgrown with vegetation. From the ravine below, spray from the Aniene Falls rises to cool the air on even the hottest summer days. Built in the first century B.C., the graceful circular temple attracted the attention of numerous Netherlandish artists (see also Cats. 3b and 65), who recorded its distinctive peristyle of fluted Corinthean columns made of the travertine that was quarried near Tivoli.[1] This large drawing captures the building and its site with unusual completeness and accuracy, from the finely sculpted capitals (ten of the original eighteen columns remain) to the richly detailed frieze of ox heads supporting decorative swags of flowers and fruit and the stonework (*opus incertum*) facing its concrete cella.[2] Immediately to the right is a rectangular building with a tiled roof and engaged Ionic columns: another first-century B.C. Roman temple known as the Temple of Hercules that in the seventeenth century functioned as the Christian church of S. Giorgio.[3]

As in most representations of this site, the ruins of the round temple at Tivoli are viewed here from below, impressively silhouetted against the sky. Artists have depicted the monument from a variety of vantage points that have made it appear to be larger or smaller and more or less ruined, as seen in an early seventeenth-century example by Paulus Bril (1554–1626), in which it is dwarfed by the massive ravine but appears almost intact (Fig. 143). In the New York drawing, the temple is closer to the viewer but seen from an angle that allows both the regularity of its design and the irregularity of its incomplete shape to be simultaneously appreciated. The bold composition of this drawing, in which the diagonal wedge of the rocky hillside and its architectural crown occupy two-thirds of the picture space, is accentuated by deep brown washes of ink, whose contrast with the page evokes brilliant southern sunlight. While the steep approach to the temple makes it appear at first glance tantalizingly inaccessible, two small figures appear halfway up the hill at the far left, while several carpets have been hung informally from the low wall between the two buildings.

Two sketchbook sheets were pasted together to make this large drawing, which may have been trimmed at the right, as the seam is not centered. On the verso, the seam separates two distinct scenes that are vertically oriented, bottom to bottom, in opposite directions. At the top is a carefully detailed drawing of the Ponte Nomentano, the ancient fortified bridge across the Aniene River outside Porta Pia that the artist would have seen every time he traveled to or from Tivoli along the Via Nomentano.[4] A tiny sketch near the top edge seems to have been a preliminary notation for the second drawing on the lower half of the page, which shows a view of the Roman campagna featuring a small building (possibly a wayside chapel) over an ancient vaulted foundation that appears partly ruined.

The traditional attribution of this well-known sheet to Bartholomeus Breenbergh (q.v.) was based on its similarities to his many pen and wash drawings of Roman landscapes with ruins, including Tivoli and its round temple.[5] Yet recent scholars have also expressed doubts, especially because Breenbergh usually signed his large-scale drawings. Following a suggestion made by M. Royalton-Kisch, J. S. Turner, who finds Breenbergh's fully documented drawings bolder in their light-dark contrasts and less insistent in treatment of detail, has proposed Herman van Swanevelt, who was in Rome between 1629 and 1641 and who was strongly influenced by Breenbergh. Turner argues that the shimmery fragmentation of surface, feathery trees, and handling of tonality in Swanevelt's drawings seem very close to those of the New York drawing and notes that his nickname "Hermit" in the confraternity of Dutch artists in Rome was based on his habit of going off on his own to make sketches of ruins.[6]

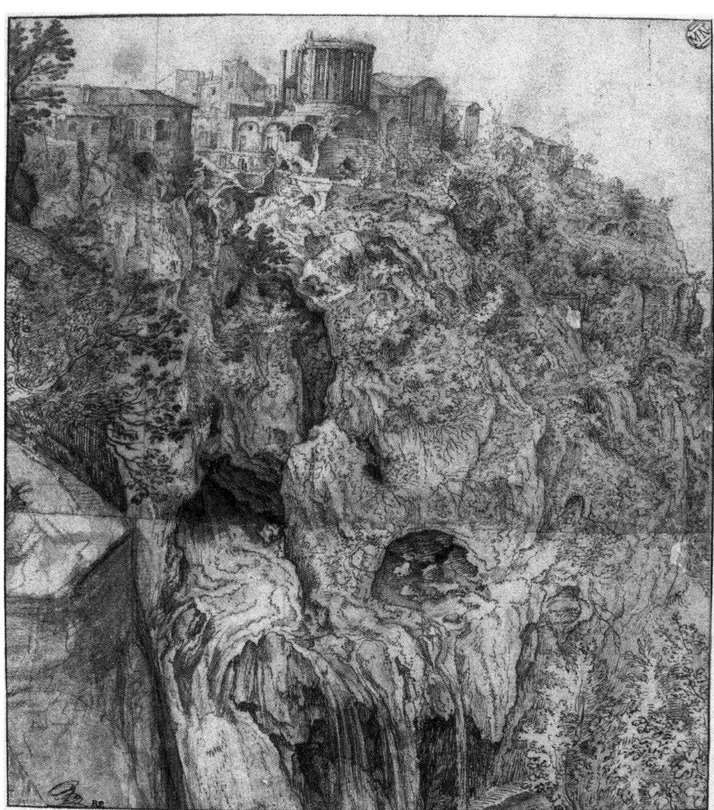

Fig. 143. Paulus Bril, *Tivoli and the Temple of the Sibyl*, c. 1600–1610, black chalk, graphite, and brush in brown and blue drawing, Cabinet des Arts Graphiques, Musée du Louvre, Paris

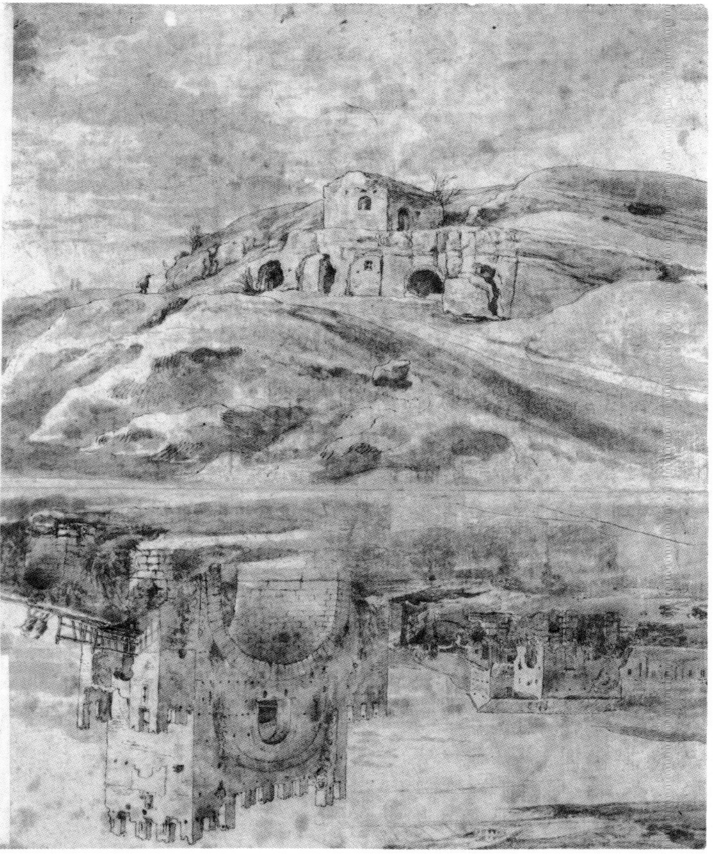

[59] verso

NOTES

1. A variety of views of the round temple at Tivoli by other Netherlandish draftsmen is illustrated in Amsterdam 2001, 34, 35, 37, 62, 63, 69, 139, and 198.

2. On the site and architectural details of the Temple of the Sibyl at Tivoli, see Hanfmann 1964, 64, and Boëthius and Ward-Perkins 1970, 137 and pl. 83.

3. F. Stampfle, who notes that S. Giorgio was used as a church until 1884, cites a Piranesi etching that shows a complete view of the structure (F. Stampfle in Paris/Antwerp/London/New York 1979–80, 94).

4. For discussion of the buildings on the verso of the drawing, see F. Stampfle in Paris/Antwerp/London/New York 1979–80, 94.

5. Breenbergh's *View of the Temple of the Sibyl, Tivoli* in the Crocker Art Gallery, Sacramento, California (no. 144-21), is signed and dated 1627 (Roethlisberger 1969, 36, no. 88, repr.). Roethlisberger also catalogued (no. 89) as "Poelenburgh (?)" a very similar unsigned and undated view of the temple that is now in the Kupferstichkabinett, Dresden (no. 2437, as Breenbergh).

6. More complete discussion of the attribution of this drawing will appear in J. S.Turner's forthcoming catalogue of Dutch drawings in the collection of the Pierpont Morgan Library. Her catalogue entry, which I am grateful to have seen, states that M. Royalton-Kisch first suggested the Swanevelt attribution to her in conversation, an opinion subsequently endorsed in a letter she received from P. Schatborn. Turner finds the closest comparison to the Morgan drawing to be Swanevelt's *Hillside with Vegetation* in the Institut Néerlandais, Paris (inv. no. 4771, repr. in Amsterdam 2001, 80, fig. E).

SIMON DE VLIEGER
1600/1601–53

Primarily a specialist in marine painting, Simon de Vlieger was also an accomplished draftsman, etcher, and designer of tapestries and stained glass.[1] A native of Rotterdam, he has not been documented with a particular teacher. In 1627 he married Anna Gerridts van Willige and in 1634 moved to Delft, where he joined the guild of St. Luke. By 1638 he had become a resident of Amsterdam, where he was invited to join artists designing decorations for Marie de' Medici's triumphal entry into the city. He became a citizen of that city in 1643. De Vlieger's marine paintings, which show the early influence of Jan Porcellis (c. 1580–1632), also include depictions of fleets approaching imaginary coastal scenes inspired by Adam Willaerts (1577–1664) and representations of shipwrecks in stormy weather. Along with a few paintings of forest scenes and approximately twenty etchings of diverse subjects such as villages, beaches, and animals, he produced numerous drawings of wooded landscapes and two drawings of the ruins of Rijnsburg Abbey near Leiden (see Cats. 5 and 11).[2]

Another aspect of De Vlieger successful career was his lucrative official commissions, including tapestry designs for the city magistrate of Delft in 1640–41; paintings for the organ shutters in the St. Laurenskerk, Rotterdam, in 1642; and designs for stained-glass windows for the Nieuwe Kerk, Amsterdam, in 1648. Among his many pupils were the celebrated marine painters Willem van de Velde the Younger (1633–1707) and Jan van de Cappelle (1626–79), as well as the still-life and marine painter Abraham van Beyeren (q.v.).

NOTES

1. Information on De Vlieger's life and career is based on essays by G. S. Keyes in Minneapolis/Toledo/Los Angeles 1990–91, 184–91, 263–64, and in *Dictionary of Art* 1996, 32:671–73.

2. De Vlieger's chalk and wash drawings of Rijnsburg Abbey in the collection of the Courtauld Institute, London (Witt Bequest 1952, no. 3355) and in the National Gallery of Scotland, Edinburgh (no. D1132) have both been dated to the 1630s (New York/London 1986, 156–57).

[60]
The Inn in the Ruins, c. 1640–50

Inscriptions: lower right, *S. de V*

Etching, drypoint, and engraving, 189 × 280 mm (7 7/16 × 11 in.) (platemark); state iv/v

Davison Art Center, Wesleyan University, Middletown, Connecticut, inv. 39-01-206

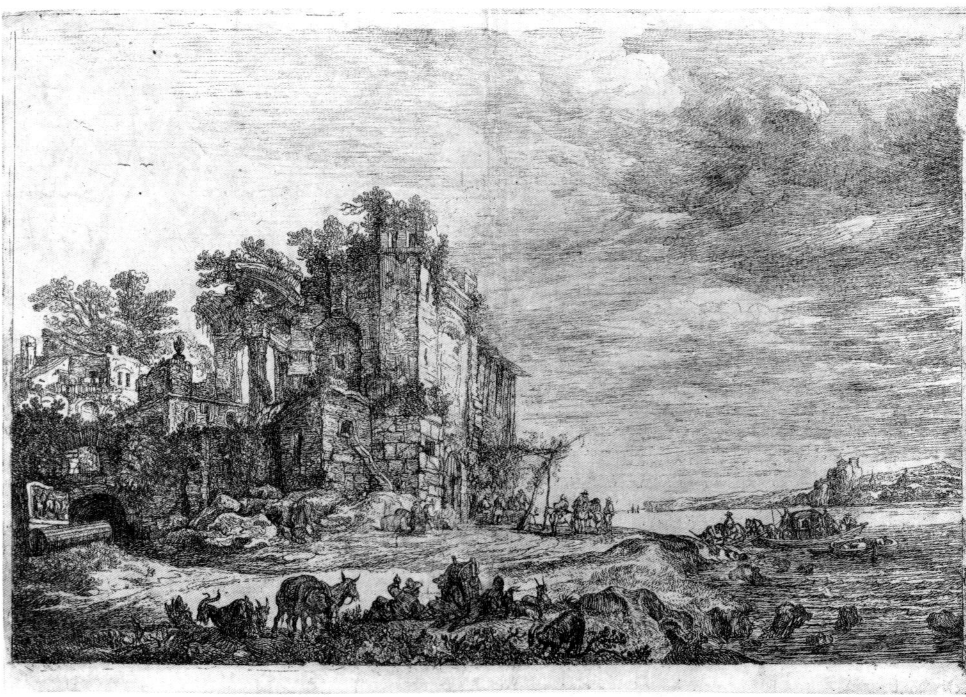

Fig. 144. Simon de Vlieger, *The Inn in the Ruins*, c. 1640–50, etching, drypoint, and engraving, state i/v, Kupferstichkabinett, Staatliche Museen, Berlin

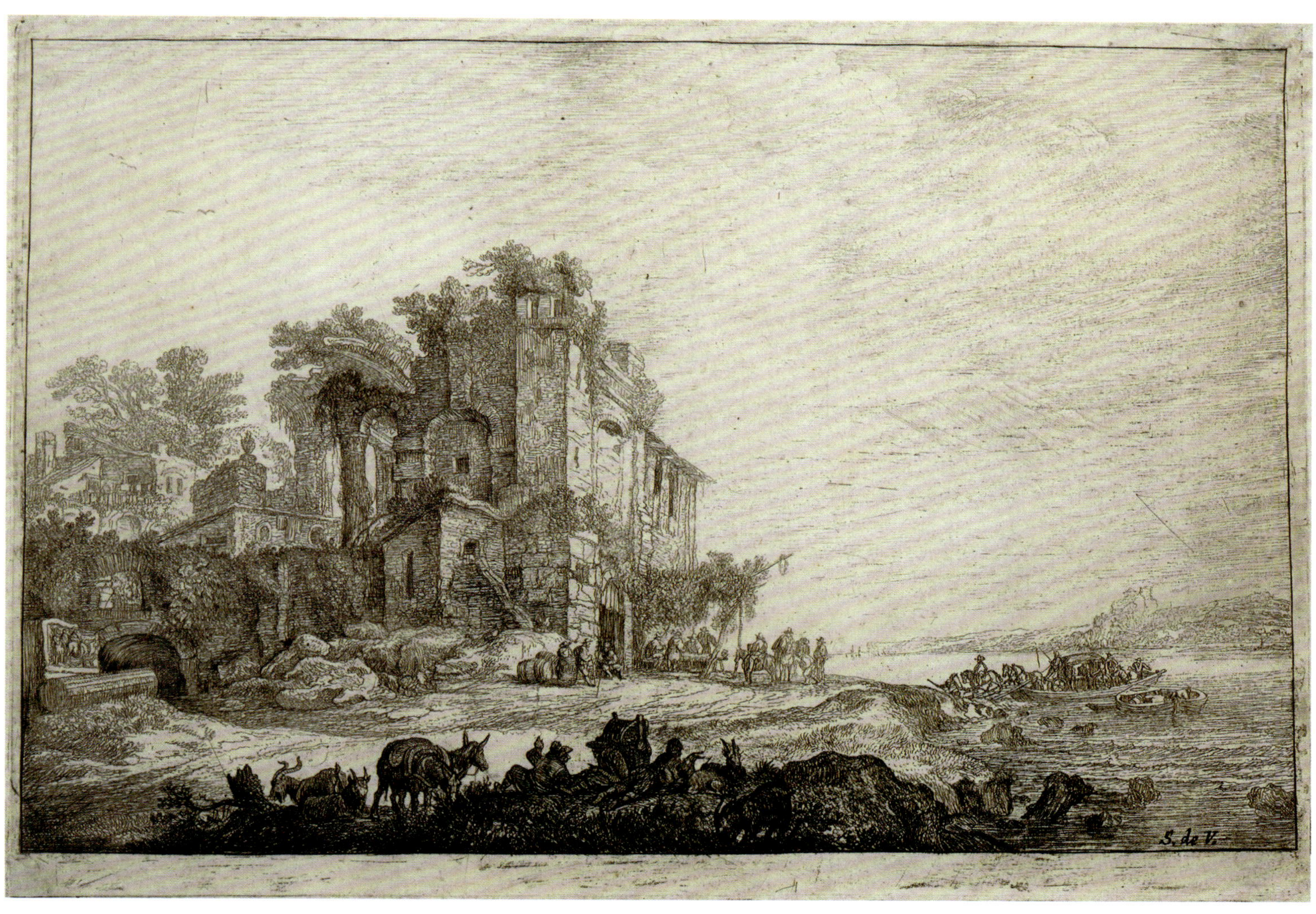

References: De Groot 1979, 111; Boston/St. Louis 1980–81, 181, no. 121; Hollstein 41 (1992):126–27.

There is no evidence that Simon de Vlieger ever saw Italy. Yet this impressively complex landscape features the kinds of motifs often used by Dutch Italianate artists such as Jan Both (q.v.) and Jan Baptist Weenix (q.v.). In the immediate foreground, a herdsman with a flock of goats and two travelers with a pack horse appear within the densely hatched zone that marks the immediate foreground. The figures are at rest, reclining and apparently conversing about the large, partially ruined architectural complex that rises beyond them to dominate the scene. This clearly imaginary structure, which seems to grow out of the land, is seen from the low viewpoint of the onlookers, and it appears to have been constructed section by section (but also alternatively ruined and repaired) over the course of centuries. Like many ancient buildings, especially Roman ones, it has been partly adapted for modern purposes. Its tall right side, weathered but intact, displays a garland on a pole that identifies it as an inn for travelers and passersby. Under the attached arbor, men have gathered at an outdoor table as horsemen approach, and a horse-drawn coach is about to be off-loaded from the ferry at the far right. In contrast to the more medieval right half of the building, the left side consists of weathered classical columns and the fragment of a tall Roman archway or barrel vault. A fragment of a Roman relief sculpture and the section of a large fluted column appear on the ground at the far left.

The blend of Italian and Dutch motifs in this scene makes it an intriguing combination of past and present and of the foreign and the familiar, especially because waterways with flat-bottomed ferryboats were such a common sight in the Dutch landscape.[1] De Vlieger's expertise as a marine painter is also evident in his assured delineation of the strongly foreshortened dinghy and the ripples of water lapping the shore. Early states of the print (Fig. 144) include a heavily overcast sky whose low, moisture-laden clouds seem to have migrated to this site from northern Europe. Perhaps for this reason, the artist burnished them out in the third state, a change that allows the mass of the ruin to stand out more strongly against the sky. In this good impression of the fourth state, very delicate traces of clouds evoke the shifting breezes and dampness of the atmosphere.[2]

NOTES

1. See, for example, Esaias van de Velde, *The Ferryboat*, dated 1622, Rjksmuseum, Amsterdam, no. A 1293; repr. Amsterdam/Boston/Philadelphia 1987–88, pl. 27.

2. The signature was added in the fourth state, in which a right-angle scratch above the horizon at right also appears. The signature was removed in the fifth state.

JAN BOTH
c. 1615–52

One of the most influential and versatile of the Dutch Italianate painters, Jan Both painted and etched landscapes of the Italian *campagna* that present a rare combination of imagined settings (very few of his sites are identifiable) with naturalistic lighting and detail. He was born in Utrecht around 1618, the son of the glass painter Dirck Both. According to Sandrart, both Jan and his brother Andries (c. 1612–41) became students of Abraham Bloemaert (q.v.) and then traveled through France to Italy.[1] Documents place them together in 1638 in Rome, where both came under the influence of Pieter van Laer (1599–?1642). In 1639 Jan was commissioned, along with Nicolas Poussin (1594–1665) and Herman van Swanevelt (1600–1655), among others, to paint pastoral and historical landscapes for Philip IV's Buen Retiro in Madrid. Three years later, the brothers traveled together to Venice, but after the drowning of Andries on 23 March 1641, Jan returned to Utrecht, where he is documented in 1646 and 1649. In 1649 he was elected to office in the St. Luke's guild. A second aspect of Jan Both's career was his collaboration with other artists, primarily figure or animal painters, including Nicolas Knüpfer (c. 1603–55), Cornelis van Poelenburch (q.v.), Jan Baptist Weenix (q.v.), and Pieter Saenredam (1597–1665).

Unlike many Dutch Italianate painters, Both rarely included mythological or religious figures in his works, preferring instead to use peasants, shepherds, and motifs from everyday life.[2] Classical ruins appear only occasionally in his landscapes. The bulk of Both's oeuvre is composed of views of the Roman countryside and forests based on studies he made in Italy. There are many problems of dating and attribution, because only a few of the approximately three hundred paintings ascribed to him are dated. Artists who were strongly influenced by Both's warm, golden lighting include Aelbert Cuyp (q.v.), Nicolaes Berchem (q.v.), and Adam Pynacker (q.v.).

NOTES

1. Sandrart 1675, 1:185, as cited in Burke 1976, 35. Biographical information is based on Burke 1976, 34–36, and L. Trezzani's essay in *Dictionary of Art* 1996, 4:485–89.
2. J. D. Burke has suggested that Both's work is closer to the naturalistically conceived Italianate landscapes of the Utrecht painter Carel de Hooch (active 1633–38) than to the more idealized scenes by Cornelis van Poelenburch (q.v.) and Bartholomeus Breenbergh (q.v.). Burke 1976, 43.

[61]

Landscape with Ruins and Two Cows at the Waterside, c. 1640–50

Inscriptions: none

Etching, 200 × 276 mm (7⅞ × 10⅞ in.) (platemark), 217 × 290 mm (8$^{9}/_{16}$ × 11$^{7}/_{16}$ in.) (sheet); state ii or iii/vi

Museum of Fine Arts, Boston, Gift of Miss Ellen T. Bullard, 25.1142

References: Hollstein 3 (1949):160–61, no. 8; Burke 1976, 199, 305–6; De Groot 1979, 114; Boston/St. Louis 1980–81, 176–77, no. 118.

In the foreground of this mountainous Italian landscape, two large cows and two men, reminiscent of the peasants found in works by Pieter van Laer (1599–?1642), pause on the road beside a quiet pond. Behind them another traveler can be seen making his way up the hill, where the scene rises to a dramatic crest with ancient ruins. A mountain at the right background and a diagonal mass of cloud complete the viewer's exhilarating experience of ascending in stages beyond down-to-earth everyday experience. It is easy to understand why Italianate landscapes became so popular with Dutch viewers, who were accustomed to seeing their peasants and cows in a flat, often rainy countryside.

This etching belongs to a series of four horizontal prints depicting scenes in the vicinity of Rome; Roman ruins are featured in three of the four.[1] Although Both usually invented his settings, which can seldom be identified, the large, fragmentary structures in the background of this scene may represent a particular site, possibly near Tivoli, they reappear in the artist's painting entitled *Buildings at the Edge of a Lake* in the National Gallery of Scotland, Edinburgh (Fig. 145), and again in a print and two drawings by Bartholomeus Breenbergh (q.v.).[2] C. S. Ackley, who dates Both's etching to the late 1640s after his return from Italy, has suggested that the print may have been based upon the Edinburgh painting, since it employs the same composition in reverse.[3]

Comparison of the two, in which different figures appear, reveals how artists use the techniques peculiar to painting and printmaking to achieve similar effects. In the painting, modulations of color and brushwork evoke the golden,

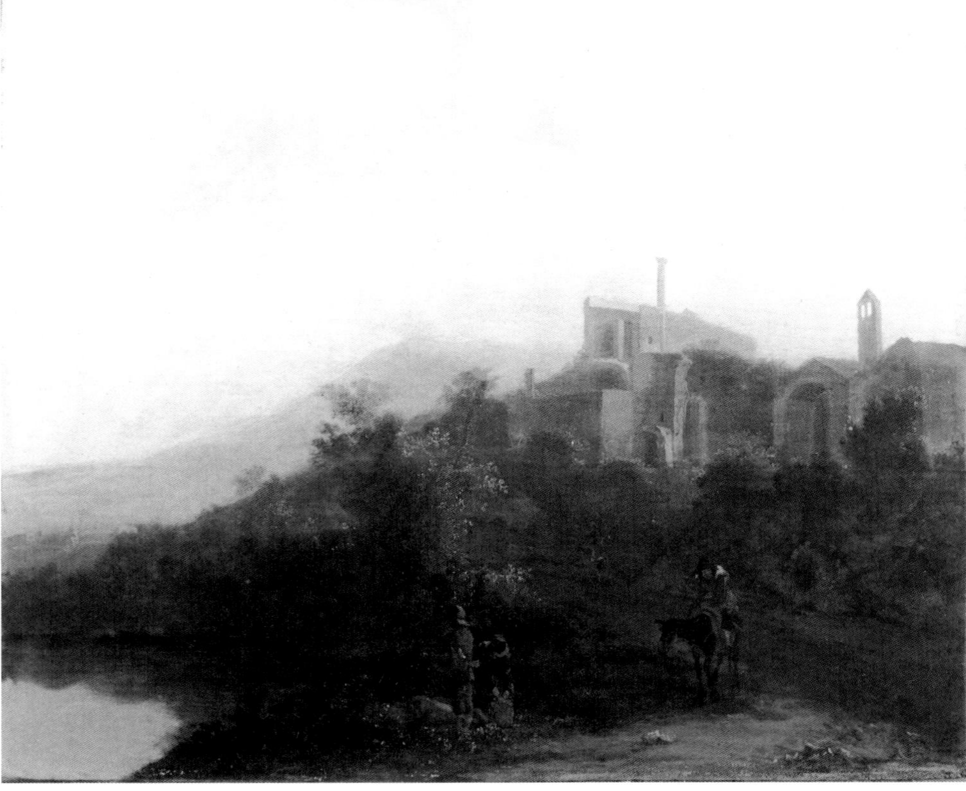

Fig. 145. Jan Both, *Buildings at the Edge of a Lake*, c. 1640–45, oil on canvas, National Gallery of Scotland, Edinburgh

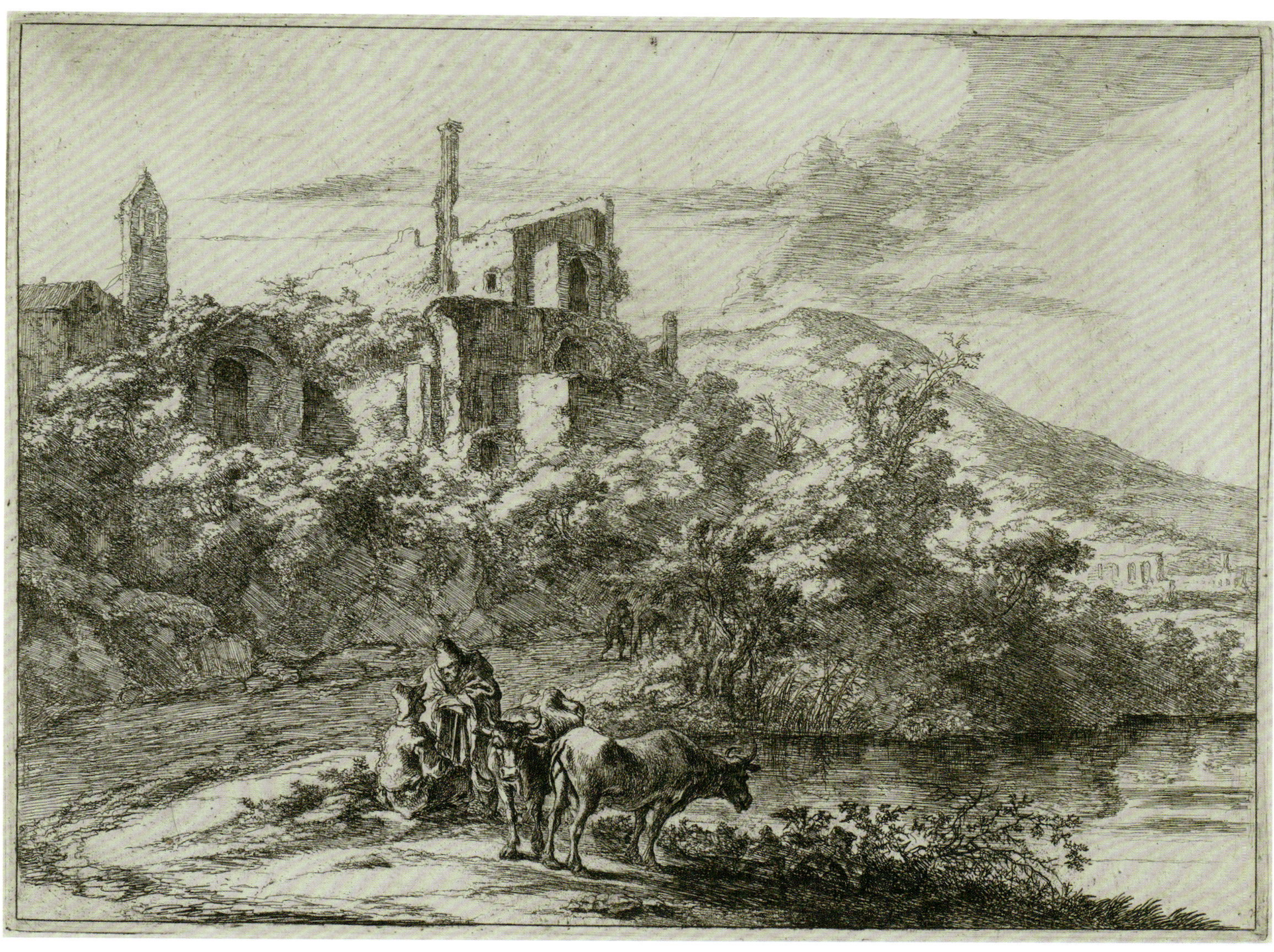

form-dissolving Italian illumination for which Both became famous. To the printmaker, who works only with black lines on a white page, direction and density of stroke become paramount, as in this radiant image, in which repetition of open, slanting, parallel lines, reiterated in all spatial zones from the foreground foliage to the distant mountain, evokes the lowness of the sun's rays and the translucency of shadows.[4] The overall design is no less controlled, as the artist has effectively balanced rising and falling diagonals in a way that makes the scene appear poised in place and time: between near and far, between present and past.

NOTES

1. J. D. Burke and C. S. Ackley have expressed the opinion, however, that two of the four prints (Hollstein 9 and 10) are by another hand and were added to the series by an early publisher. Burke 1976, 287; Ackley in Boston/St. Louis 1980–81, 176.

2. Breenbergh's print is reproduced in Hollstein 3 (n.d.):207, no. 16. One of the Breenbergh drawings, which shows the same ruins (in reverse) as those in Both's print, is in the Musée Condé, Chantilly (repr. Roethlisberger 1969, no. 52, fig. 52), while the other, whose authenticity is doubted by M. Roethlisberger, is in the Musée du Louvre, Paris (Roethlisberger 1969, 30, under no. 52). Both Roethlisberger and F. Lugt (who finds the Louvre drawing authentic) state that the ruins it depicts are near Tivoli (Lugt 1929–33, 1 [1929]: no. 173, repr.). J. D. Burke, on the other hand, has suggested that the ruins in Both's painting in Edinburgh may represent the remains of the Baths of Albano near Rome (Burke 1976, 306).

3. Ackley in Boston/St. Louis 1980–81, 176.

4. This point is made in Ackley's insightful discussion of the print, which also points out Both's use of passages of bitten, granular tone, which, combined with areas of fine, scribbled line, helps the artist avoid contour drawing, so that broader patterns of light and shadow can emerge. Ackley in Boston/St. Louis 1980–81, 176.

JAN DE BISSCHOP

[62]

Panoramic View of Rome (on two sheets), c. 1650

(Sarasota only)

Inscriptions: on the lower half of the verso of part 1 (see below), the artist inscribed in brown ink the names of the monuments depicted on the recto (from left to right), *Horti Medicei; S. Trinità de' Monti; Palatium Pontifi / cis in Quirinali; Mons Pincius olim Collis hortulorum; Capitolium; Columna Antonini; Aventinus; il Giesù; Pantheon / hod. La Rotonda; S. Andrea della Valle; S. Agnese; S. Maria del' Anima.*

On the upper right of the verso of part 2 (see below), the artist inscribed in brown ink, *Gesicht*

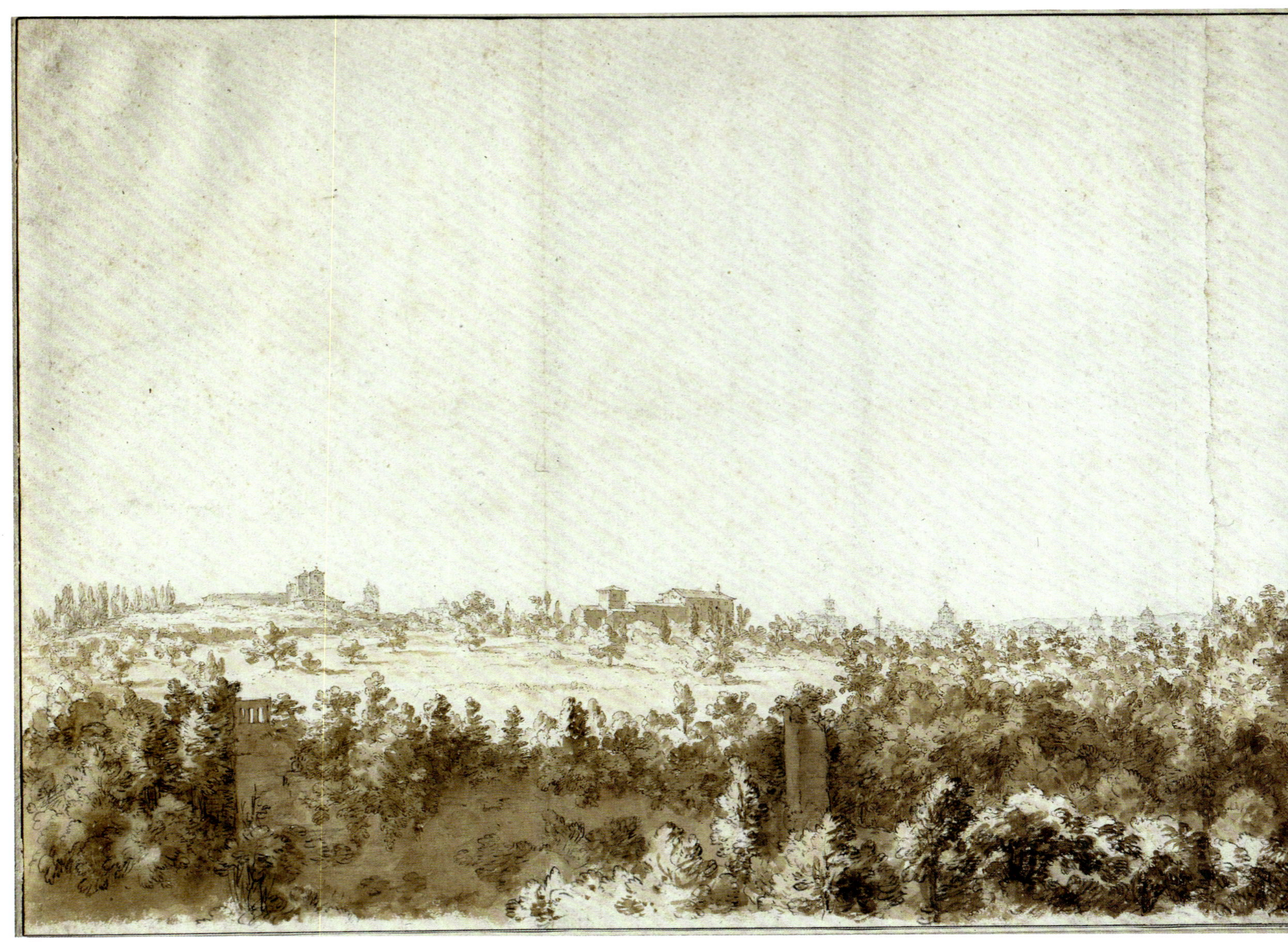

van Romen buyten Porta del popolo. Across the lower half in brown ink, he inscribed the names of the monuments depicted on the recto (from left to right): *Monte Mario; S. Maria in Valli / cella vulgo La Chiesa Nova; Palatium / Sfortia*[e]*; S. Maria del popolo; Porta del popolo seu Flaminia; Montes … Vaticani; S. Gio.Batt*[a] *. de' Fiorentini; Castel S. Agnolo seu / Moles Adriani; S. Spirito in Sassia; Palatium Columnensium; Santo Officio; Tiberis; S. Pietro in Vaticano; Prata Quintia vulgo sed rectius Neroniana; Belvedere.*

Pen and brown ink, brown, reddish-brown, and blue-gray washes over preliminary indications in black chalk, framing line in brown ink. Executed on two sheets (whose join is visible just left of center), this drawing was subsequently cut to the right of the join and divided into two equal parts, probably in or before the eighteenth century.

Part 1 (left), 355 × 500 mm (14 × 19⅝ in.)
Part 2 (right), 352 × 502 mm (13 13/16 × 19¾ in.)

The Pierpont Morgan Library, New York, Purchased as the Gift of the Fellows, Acc. no. 1968.6:1–2

References: Oberlin 1963, no. 14; Berckenhagen 1969, 25, repr. (detail), 26; Morgan Library Acquisitions 1969, 131; Van Gelder 1971, 209, fig. 32 (detail); Morgan Library Fellows Report 1973, 100–101, 109; Berlin 1974, under no. 19; New York 1974, no. 43, repr; Poughkeepsie 1976, 58–60, no. 43, repr; New York 1976–77, unpaginated; Paris/Antwerp/London/New York 1979–80, no. 118, repr; Held 1981, 176–77; New York 1981, no. 85, repr.; Colenbrander 1985, 109; Cambridge/Montreal 1988, 66–67, no. 9, repr.; Schapelhouman 1990, 320, 323 n. 15; Amsterdam 1992, no. 14, repr.; Zwollo 1999, fig. 3; Amsterdam 2001, 198, 213 n. 6.

Wide, panoramic drawings on two sheets such as this one are rare, although a similar format was employed by Herman Saftleven for his view of the destruction of Delft after the catastrophic gunpowder explosion of 1654 (Cat. 41).[1] The two drawings could hardly be more different

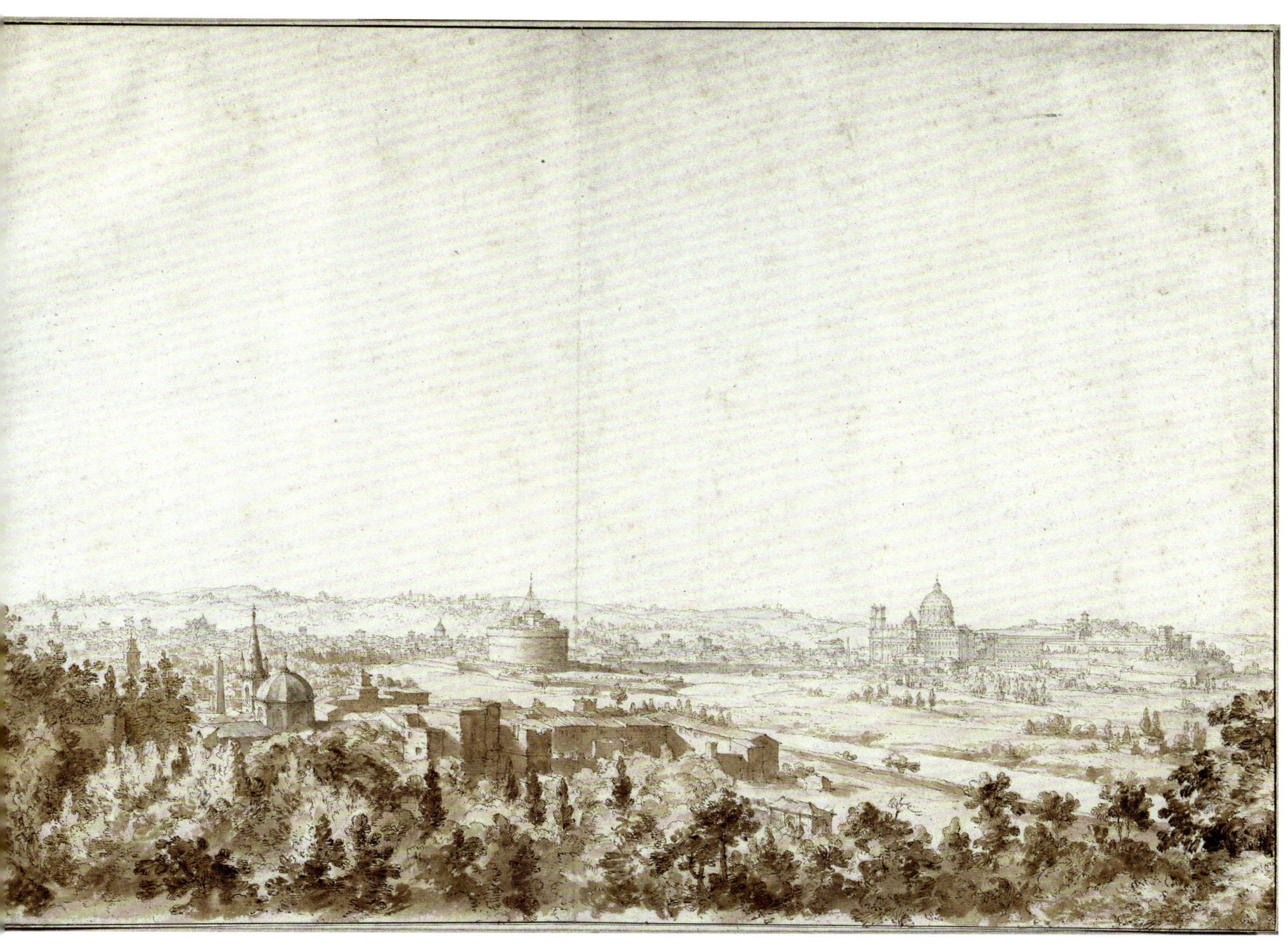

in intention and effect, however, since De Bisschop's Roman vista surveys a sunlit scene that has endured for centuries and whose foreground is defined by a continuous band of luxuriant foliage. Within it are fragments of ancient buildings and beyond it is a long line of celebrated monuments and sites, beginning with the Medici gardens at the far left and ending at the far right with St. Peter's and the Vatican. All are carefully identified in the artist's hand on the backs of the two sheets. Since the viewer cannot take in the entire panorama at a single glance and must examine the monuments one by one, the drawing offers a delightful visual excursion that also includes (from left to right): the double towers of Santa Trinità de' Monti, the Palazzo Senatorio, the Column of Marcus Aurelius, the Gesù, the Pantheon (identifiable by its low dome), the churches of S. Andrea della Valle and S. Agnese, the larger Church of S. Maria del Populo, and the bulky cylinder of the Castel Sant'Angelo with its crenellated top.

Whether De Bisschop ever went to Italy has been debated, for no documentary evidence of such a trip has ever been found, and it does not seem possible that this landscape was made directly on the spot. Indeed, as J. S. Held has pointed out, in reality there is no vantage point from which this particular vista can be seen (today or in the seventeenth century). The artist apparently added the long line of trees and bushes across the foreground to mask an incongruity of viewpoints in the two sheets: the one on the left was drawn from a considerably lower angle than the sheet on the right.[2] Another curious aspect of this image is that it shows a view of St. Peter's with Bernini's south tower still in place, although the structure had been removed in 1646. De Bisschop was only eighteen years of age in that year, and (assuming he did make an Italian visit) it seems unlikely that he could have produced such a complex and accomplished drawing so early in his career. More likely is the possibility that he worked from an earlier drawing or print (or a combination of prototypes) made in Italy during the period when Bernini's tower was under construction (1642–46).[3] Another composite drawing with an identical panoramic view was made by Theodoor Matham (1605–76) on three sheets, two of which are in the Rijksprentenkabinet, Amsterdam, and one in the Archiefdienst voor Kennemerland, Haarlem.[4] Since Matham's drawing does not include Bernini's tower, however, it is unlikely it was De Bisschop's source. Probably both artists had access to an earlier version of this composition.

Even if De Bisschop never saw Rome with his own eyes and assembled his panorama from views recorded by earlier artists, this spectacular drawing captures the excitement of arriving at a place whose display of famous historic structures of varied shapes, sizes, and ages is unmatched anywhere else in the world. Even more remarkable was the artist's decision to set these powerful monuments well back within a broad vista of open terrain, making them smaller in scale and paler in tone than the fragments of ruins and the dense growth of foliage in the immediate foreground. As a result, the Eternal City seems to rise in the distant sunlight like a vision made real, as it surely appeared to visitors of this period from northern Europe—or to the many Dutch viewers back home who found their way to Rome through art alone.

NOTES

1. Only inscriptions in the hand of the artist himself are reproduced here. Additional notations by later artists or collectors are listed by F. Stampfle in Paris/Antwerp/London/New York 1979–80, 141, and in J. S. Turner's forthcoming catalogue of the Dutch drawings in the collection of the Pierpont Morgan Library. I am greatly indebted to her for allowing me to consult the draft of her entry, upon which much of my discussion of the drawing is based.

2. Held 1981, 176–77.

3. Jacob van der Ulft (1621–89), who often based his works upon De Bisschop's, made two undated copies after the Morgan Library's drawing (Musée du Louvre, Paris, and the De Grez Collection, Musées Royaux des Beaux-Arts, Brussels), in which the different perspectives of the two sides of the scene are even more apparent. But in neither of these drawings does Bernini's tower appear. Stampfle in Paris/Antwerp/London/New York 1979–80, 141.

4. In her entry on De Bisschop's drawing in her forthcoming catalogue of the Dutch drawings in the Pierpont Morgan Library, J. S. Turner points out that the Rijksprentenkabinet, Amsterdam, acquired two of the sheets of Matham's three-part drawing in 1900 (central section) and in 1909 (left section) but that the missing right section was only discovered quite recently by A. Zwollo in the Archiefdienst voor Kennemerland, Haarlem (Cf. Zwollo 1999, fig. 2). M. Schapelhouman has dated the Amsterdam drawings to c. 1660 but stated that they may have been made earlier, during Matham's visit to Rome in 1633–37 (Schapelhouman 1990, 320, 323 n. 15).

WILLEM SCHELLINKS (attr.)
1623–78

A widely traveled artist, Willem Schellinks was active as a painter, printmaker, and poet in Amsterdam, where he began as a topographical draftsman, making drawings in black chalk and gray wash of Amsterdam houses and their architectural details.[1] In 1646 Schellinks and Lambert Doomer (q.v.) journeyed together through France, as recorded in Schellinks's diary and in drawings by both artists.[2] Under the influence of contemporary landscapists such as Jan Both (q.v.) and Jan Asselijn (after 1610–1652), Schellinks produced Italianate drawings and paintings during the late 1640s, even before visiting Italy in the early 1660s. Between 1661 and 1665, he traveled to France, England, Malta, Germany, and Italy, acting as tutor to the young son of an Amsterdam merchant. That Schellinks concentrated on topographical scenes during this trip is partly explained by the fact that Laurens van der Hem, a wealthy Amsterdam art collector with a special interest in topographical images, helped finance the journey as well as a large atlas by Johannes Blaeu. The so-called *Atlas van der Hem* (see also Fig. 126), also known as the *Atlas Prince Eugene* (Nationalbibliothek, Vienna), includes 120 pages of Schellinks's drawings, many enlarged from his recent travel sketches.

Schellinks also produced paintings of dramatic contemporary events such as *The Burning of the English Fleet at the Battle of Medway of 1667* (private collection, on loan to the Rijksmuseum, Amsterdam) and *The Breach in the St. Anthonis Dike near Houtewael* (Amsterdams Historisch Museum; Fig. 69), the latter recorded in an engraving by Pieter Nolpe (Cat. 37). In 1667 Schellinks married Maria Neus, widow of the Amsterdam printmaker Dancker Danckerts (1634–66).

NOTES

1. On Willem Schellinks's biography, see the essay by P. Mens in *Dictionary of Art* 1996, 28:73–74.

2. Van den Berg 1942, 1–31.

[63]

Ruins of an Aqueduct with a House Built into One End, c. 1655–65

Inscription: on the verso, in graphite at upper right corner, *33*; at lower left, *37*; at lower left corner, partially trimmed away, *C. Polenburg*

Point of brush and gray and brown wash, 203 × 290 mm (8 × 11 7/16 in.)

The Pierpont Morgan Library, New York, Purchased by Pierpont Morgan, 1910, Acc. no. I,116

References: Fairfax Murray 1905–12, 1: no. 116, repr. (as Cornelis Poelenburch); Ann Arbor 1964, no. 51, pl. 14.

The refitting of Roman ruins for new uses in later periods (see also Cat. 60) is well illustrated in this brush drawing, which shows the remains of a Roman aqueduct. Rising at the right foreground to the very top of the horizontal page, the arched structure recedes into depth, becoming increasingly filled in with masonry, but also progressively paler and more translucent in tone until it ends in the rectangular house built into it at the far left. Nearest the viewer, deeper and more detailed touches of warm brown wash define the aqueduct's building blocks, whose monumental scale is indicated by a small figure walking under the largest arch. The adjacent doorway, which also shows evidence of later construction, casts an arched patch of sunlight onto the wall beside it. Throughout this scene, the imposing forms of this ancient water carrier appear softened both by the play of sunlight and shadow on its weathered walls and by the foliage sprouting between the massive stones and along the top of the structure.

Traditionally attributed to Cornelis van Poelenburch (q.v.), this fine drawing has elicited a variety of other opinions about its authorship, including the suggestion of Jan Asselijn (after 1610–1652), who spent a decade in Rome between about 1635 and 1645 and may have been Schellinks's teacher.[1] J. S. Turner's recent reattribution of the work to Willem Schellinks is based upon its similarities to drawings at Windsor Castle and at the Museum Boijmans Van Beuningen, Rotterdam, that feature similar foliage and brushwork and are signed or inscribed with Schellinks's name.[2] The difficulties of establishing both the authorship and the date of this drawing are complicated by the fact that Schellinks apparently depicted Roman views even before he went to Italy in the early 1660s by making copies after Asselijn.[3] That Dutch artists depicted Roman ruins not only by observing them directly but by copying prints and drawings underlines the powerful attraction these motifs had for northern European artists and viewers.

NOTES

1. The museum files note that both F. Lugt and P. Schatborn related *Ruins of an Aqueduct* to Asselijn, as did A. Zwollo, who proposed Asselijn or Pieter van Bloemen (1657–1720).

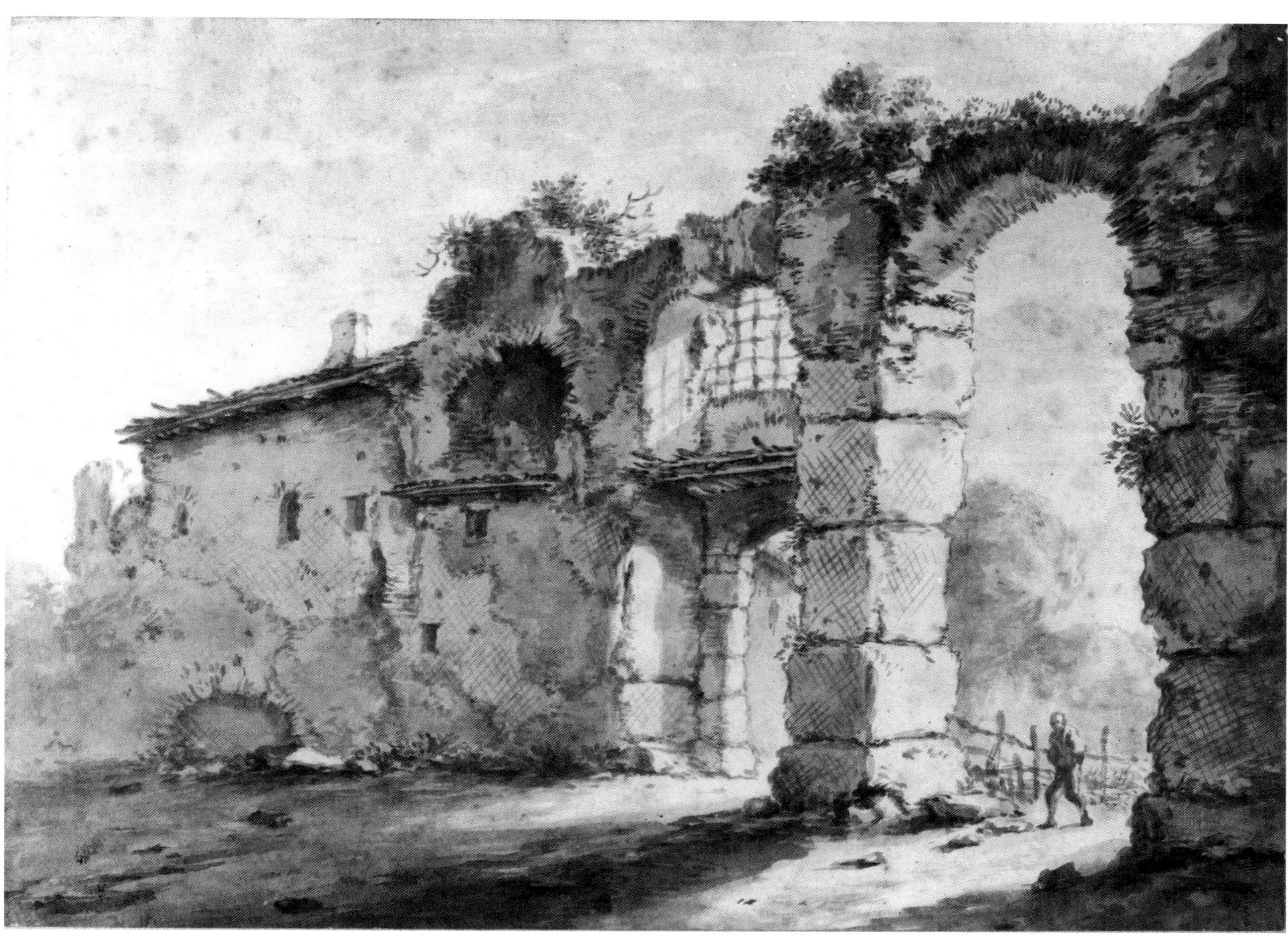

[63]

2. I am indebted to J. S. Turner for sharing with me the drafts of her catalogue entries for her forthcoming catalogue of Dutch drawings at the Pierpont Morgan Library, in which she offers full discussion of the varied opinions about the attributions and the dating of this work. In arguing in favor of an attribution to Schellinks, Turner cites his *View of the Grotto of the Nymph Egeria* (Museum Boijmans Van Beuningen, Rotterdam, inv. no. 2967-289) and *Interior of Roman Ruins-the Colosseum, Rome?* (Royal Library, Windsor Castle, inv. no. 6301).

3. A. Steland-Stief, who states that Schellinks copied Asselijn's Roman views, cites two drawings by Schellinks that bear old inscriptions *na Asselin* and *na zijn meester Asselin* (Steland-Stief 1986, 90, 99–100). For this citation, my thanks to J. S. Turner.

KAREL DUJARDIN
1626–78

Baptized in Amsterdam's Lutheran Church on 27 September 1626, Dujardin studied in Haarlem with the Italianate landscape painter Nicolaes Berchem (q.v.) According to Houbraken, he was Berchem's most gifted pupil.[1] In 1650 Dujardin (who may have traveled to Italy during the late 1640s) married Suzanne van Royen in Lyons, a city often used by Netherlandish artists as a stopover on trips to or from Italy. Documents of the same year place him in Amsterdam. By September 1652 he was living on the Rozengracht, where he apparently remained until about 1655. In October 1656, Dujardin was listed as a founding member of Pictura, the recently established painters' confraternity in The Hague, whose records list his name again in 1657 and 1658. By May 1659, however, he was back in Amsterdam, where he painted a portrait (dated 1669, Rijksmuseum, Amsterdam) of the governors of the Amsterdam House of Correction. He apparently continued to live in that city until 1674 or 1675.

Dujardin sailed from Texel Island on his second trip to Italy in 1675, with a stop along the way in Tangier, and spent the remainder of his life in Rome and Venice. The society of Netherlandish artists in Rome (the Schildersbent, or Flock of Birds), which had a custom of nicknaming its members, gave Dujardin the nickname of "Bokkebaart" (Goat's Beard or Goatee). He was buried in Venice on 9 October 1678. A gifted draftsman and printmaker as well as a painter, Dujardin specialized primarily in brilliantly illuminated Italianate landscapes, similar to those of his teacher, but he also painted por-

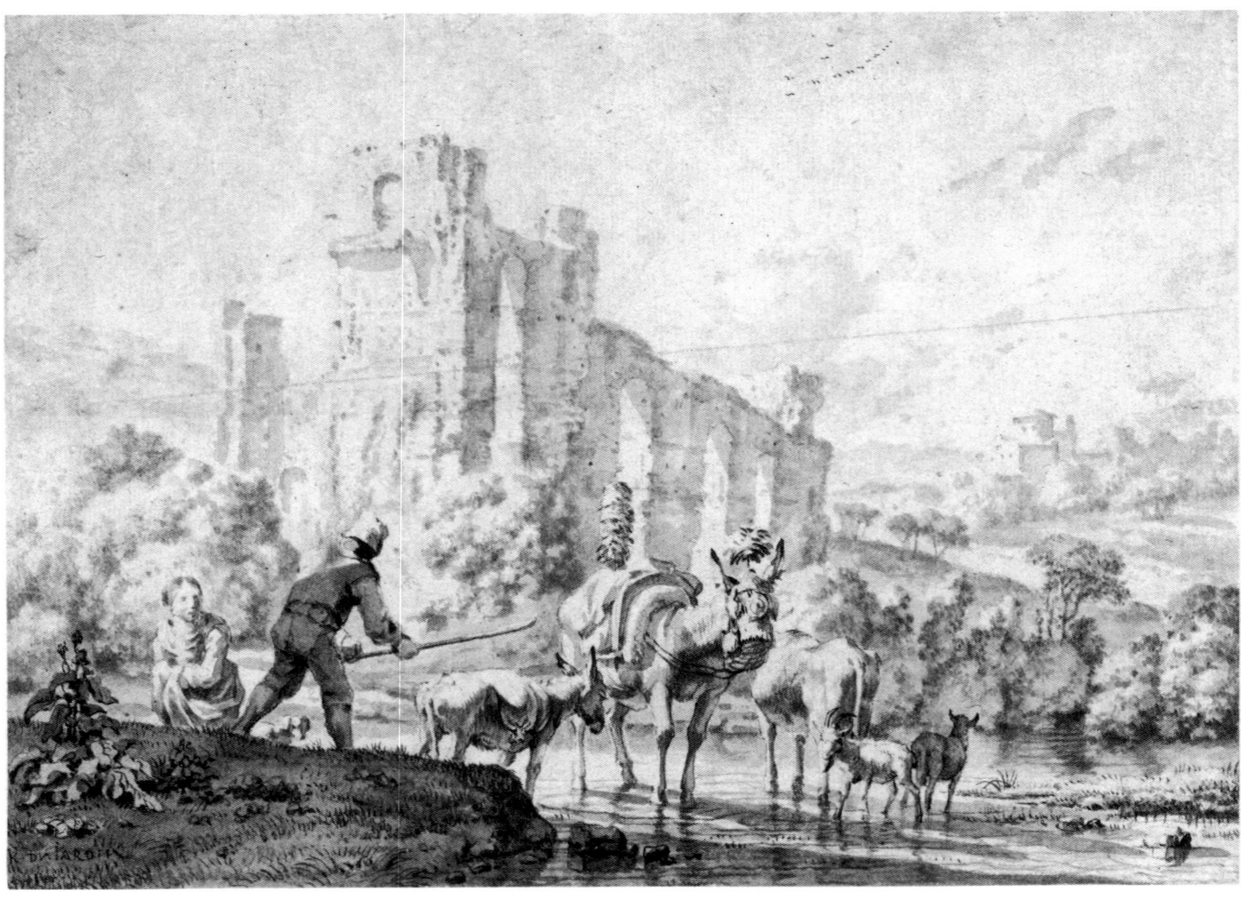

traits, Italian street scenes, and, after around 1658, a number of history paintings. In his works, gradations of light and shadow are handled with particular delicacy.

NOTE

1. Houbraken 1718–21, 3 (1721):56. Archival sources on Dujardin are listed in Kilian 1993, appendix A: 202–40 and 207, docs. 38 and 39.

[64]

Muleteer and Shepherdess with Animals at a Stream, c. 1660

(Poughkeepsie and Louisville only)

Inscriptions: lower left corner in brush and black ink, *K. DV. IARDIN*

Point of brush, black and gray washes, over slight indications of black chalk, on paper, 137 × 197 mm (5 7/16 × 7¾ in.)

The Pierpont Morgan Library, New York, Purchased by Pierpont Morgan, 1910, Acc. no. I,142

References: London 1883, no. 177; Fairfax Murray 1905–12, 1: no. 142, repr.; Brochhagen 1958, 47, no. 90; Ann Arbor 1964, no. 33, pl. 18; Paris/Antwerp/London/New York 1979–80, 133, no. 110, repr.; Cambridge/Montreal 1988, no. 46; Amsterdam 1989, no. 15.

Aqueducts such as the one in this drawing appear frequently in Dutch Italianate views of the Roman campagna (see also Cats. 63 and 69). Indeed, they were among the most eye-catching ancient structures in the Italian countryside, combining sophistication of engineering with architectural grace. Only a small part of Rome's extensive aqueduct system was built above ground, the great majority consisting of channels of stone or terracotta pipe built just under the ground, but at least thirty miles of these distinctively arched conduits could be seen crossing valleys in the vicinity of Rome.[1] With the disintegration of the Roman Empire in the fifth century A.D. these and other large-scale structures could no longer be maintained and gradually fell into ruin. To seventeenth-century artists, however, the old Roman aqueducts remained all the more powerful as monumental visual presences from antiquity. In their nonfunctional state, they appear as elevated passages to nowhere, their soaring spans truncated by time.

Dujardin may have intended that the large aqueduct receding into the background of this landscape act as a temporal and expressive counterpoint to the natural waterway in the foreground, where a muleteer and shepherdess with their dog encourage several farm animals to enter the shallow stream. With delicate but firm touches of the brush, the artist brings to life the varied shapes and sizes of this small group of creatures (two mules, a goat, a sheep, and a cow), which seem as much bathed in the luminously transparent atmosphere as in the water itself. Although the larger of the two mules with blinkers and panniers is very similar to one of the animals in Dujardin's etching *Two Mules*, this composition seems to have been intended to stand on its own, not to serve as the preparatory study for a print.[2] Dujardin dated few of his drawings, making his chronology difficult to establish, but K. Brochhagen has suggested a date of about 1660 for the New York drawing on the basis of its similarities to

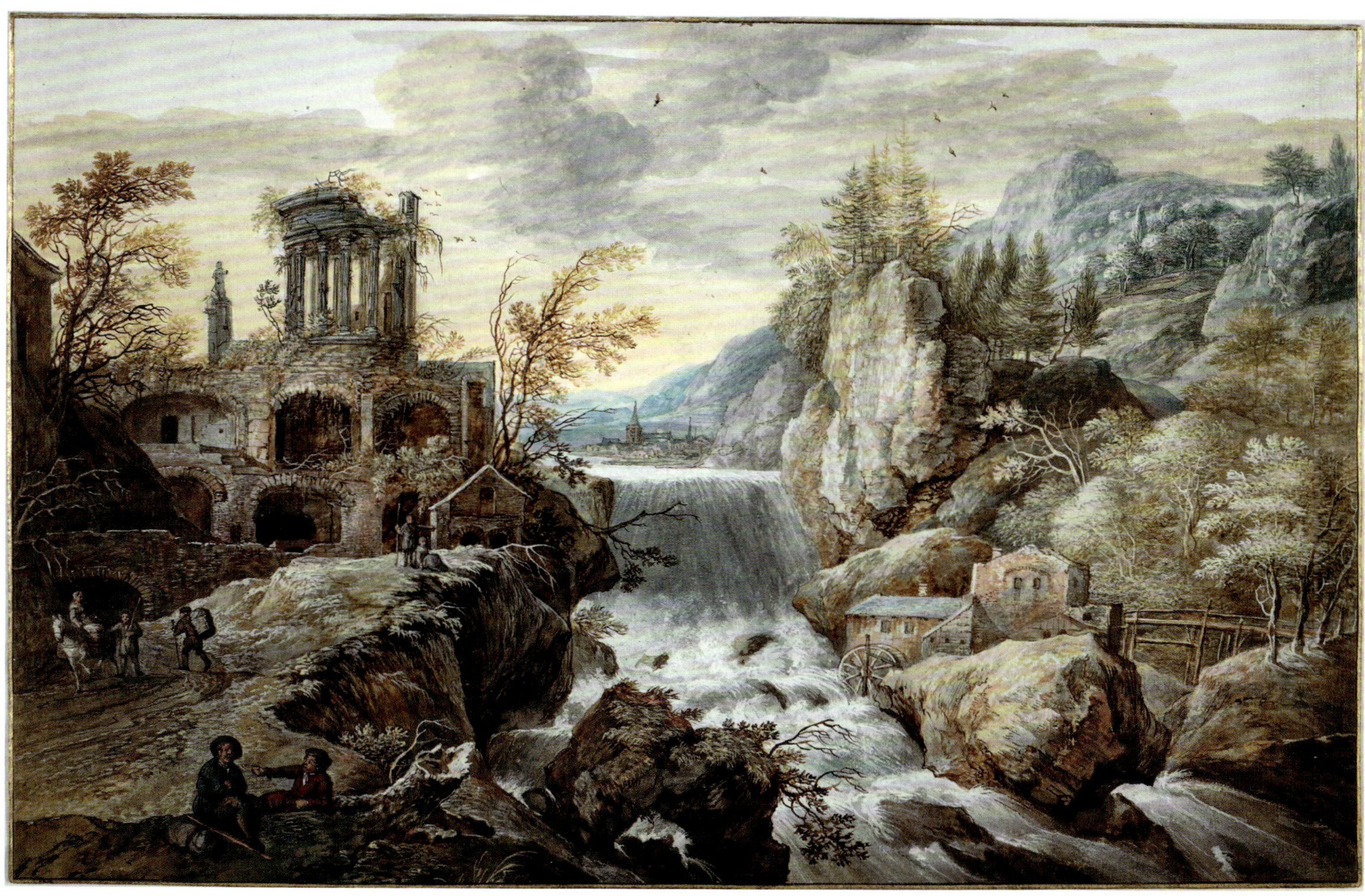

a dated landscape painting by Dujardin, now in Antwerp, of 1660.[3]

NOTES

1. On Roman aqueducts and their history, see Hodge 2002, Aicher 1995, and Ashby 1935.

2. The etching *Two Mules* is reproduced as Hollstein 6 (n.d.):28, no. 2. F. Stampfle has also related to the New York drawing Dujardin's black chalk drawing of these small, sturdy beasts of burden that is now in the Rijksprentenkabinet, Amsterdam, inv. no. A102 (Paris/Antwerp/London/New York 1979–80, 134). J. S. Turner, who generously allowed me to consult the entry on Dujardin from her forthcoming catalogue of Dutch drawings at the Pierpont Morgan Library, also draws attention to two mules that appear in a second black chalk drawing by Dujardin in the Rijksprentenkabinet, Amsterdam (inv. no. RP-T-1881-A-102). Repr. Amsterdam 2001, 155, fig. D.

3. Koninklijk Museum voor Schone Kunsten, Antwerp, inv. no. 668. Brochhagen 1958, 47, no. 190.

GERRIT BATTEM
1636–84

Born in Rotterdam, Gerrit Battem was the nephew of two well-known landscape specialists: Philips Koninck (1619–88) and Abraham Furnerius (1628–54), who may have been his teacher.[1] In 1667 Battem married Margaretha Scheffer and by the following year was registered as a resident of Utrecht. There he came under the influence of the dramatic Alpine landscapes of Roelandt Savery (1576–1639), who had been active in Utrecht from 1619 to 1639. Battem himself probably never saw the Alps, although he may have traveled through the mountainous countryside along the Rhine.

A number of oil paintings by Battem are known, and one early etching, dated 1658, but he is best known for his detailed, highly finished compositions in gouache. These include the biblical scenes painted during his early years and, after about 1665, winter scenes and brilliantly colored landscapes with forests, villages, and canals, as well as composite fantasy scenes such as the painting illustrated here.

NOTE

1. Biographical material on Battem is based upon Saur/Künstler-Lexikon 1992, 7 (1993):483–84. H. Verbeek wrote a thesis on the artist for the University of Leiden in 1983 (Verbeek 1983).

[65]

Landscape with a Waterfall and the Temple of the Sibyl, c. 1670–79

Inscriptions: none

Gouache, watercolor, and brown ink on cream antique laid paper, 244 × 380 mm (9⅝ × 14 15/16 in.)

Courtesy of the Fogg Art Museum, Harvard University Art Museums, Cambridge, Massachusetts, loan from Maida and George Abrams, 25.1998.80

References: Verbeek 1983, no. Lg 9; Amsterdam/Vienna/New York/Cambridge 1991–92, 178–79, no. 80.

The ruins of ancient buildings were often freely appropriated, rearranged, or relocated to suit an artist's fancy, but rarely to the extent seen in Battem's vivid landscape. In his hands, ruins that recall the round Temple of the Sibyl at Tivoli (see also Cats. 3b and 59) materialize in an utterly whimsical way beside a roaring northern waterfall. As W. W. Robinson has observed, Battem often depicted rough Alpine scenery with gigantic boulders, mountains, and fir trees, motifs that appear in paintings by Roelandt Savery (1576–1639), who had spent time in the Tyrolian Alps (see Fig. 21), and in prints after the drawings made by Pieter Bruegel the Elder (c. 1525–69) on his way to northern Italy.[1] Absorbing foreign scenery through artistic intermediaries rather than through his own empirical experience seems to have stimulated Battem's creative response to it. The same phenomenon is evident in the landscapes of his more famous contemporary Jacob van Ruisdael (q.v.), whose Scandinavian landscapes with waterfalls, dating from the 1660s and 1670s, may also have been known to Battem.[2]

In this painting, the passage of time is emphasized not only by the ruin, which is raised on a foundation of massive ancient arcades and silhouetted against the sky, but also by the unstoppable motion of the waterfall, whose plunge from the river above begins next to the ruin, splitting the landscape into two parts. The stone water mill at the lower right, dwarfed by the monumental boulder beside it, is another motif associated with transience.[3] Although Battem has used a horizontal format for his landscape, the scene builds vertically on both sides, which are quite different in effect. In contrast to the dramatic emphasis on tumbling water, rocks, and mountains on the right, the quieter left side, painted in darker colors, emphasizes human beings and their works, as various travelers walk or rest on the road leading to the ruined temple.[4]

Battem's choice of medium served his intentions well, for gouache (also called body color) is an opaque watercolor whose pigments, bound with glue, emphasize solidity of forms. Less softly luminous than watercolor, it has a brighter, sharper effect, especially because it employs white pigment for the definition of lighter tones. The advantages are obvious in this landscape, whose waterfall tumbles so forcefully through its rocky passage that it seems to have eroded the left bank on which the temple and its foundations are precipitously perched.

NOTES

1. The waterfall and strongly silhouetted tree at the left derive from an engraving after Bruegel that shows the falls of the Aniene River at Tivoli, but the remainder of the composition, including the temple, seems to be based on another source. Verbeek 1983, no. Lg 9 (cited by W. W. Robinson in Amsterdam/Vienna/New York/Cambridge 1991–92, 178). *Prospectus Tyburtinus* (View of Tivoli), c. 1555–56, by Johannes and Lucas van Doetecum after Bruegel, is reproduced in New York 2001, 124, no. 24.

2. Ruisdael's landscapes with waterfalls and huge boulders, whose imagery often derives from paintings and drawings by Allart van Everdingen (q.v.), are discussed in Slive 2001, 153–248.

3. In his discussion of Ruisdael's paintings of mills, S. Slive cites emblem no. 55 in Sebastián de Covarrubias Orozco's *Emblemas Morales* (Madrid, 1619), whose commentary reads: "The good of this transitory life, / Which flows like a river, / Are at one moment on the water wheel, / which goes up full and falls down empty." Slive 2001, 130.

4. Similar compositional arrangements appear in other works by Battem, indicating that he had a tendency to produce variants of the same designs. For examples, see W. W. Robinson in Amsterdam/Vienna/New York/Cambridge 1991–92, 178.

NICOLAES BERCHEM
1620–83

Son of the still-life painter Pieter Claesz. (c. 1597–1660), Nicolaes Berchem was a versatile, prolific, and highly successful painter, etcher, and draftsman.[1] Aside from Italianate landscapes, Mediterranean harbors, histories, and allegories, he also depicted Dutch scenes, including winter and night scenes, hunts, and battles. According to the records of the St. Luke's guild in Haarlem, Berchem first studied with his father. Houbraken claims that he also studied with an unusually large number of teachers: Jan van Goyen (q.v.), Claes Moeyaert (q.v.), Pieter de Grebber (c. 1600–1653), and Jan Wils (c. 1610–60).[2] Berchem joined the Haarlem guild of St. Luke in 1642; his pupils would include such major Dutch artists as Karel Dujardin (q.v.) and Pieter de Hooch (1629–84). In 1650 he traveled with Jacob van Ruisdael (q.v.) to Westphalia, where both artists made drawings of Castle Bentheim, among other sites in the area. Although usually classified as a Dutch Italianate artist of the second generation, Berchem has never actually been documented in Italy. If he did make this journey, it probably took place during the 1650s; only after mid-century did he begin concentrating on Italianate scenes. In 1677 he moved to Amsterdam, where he died in 1693.

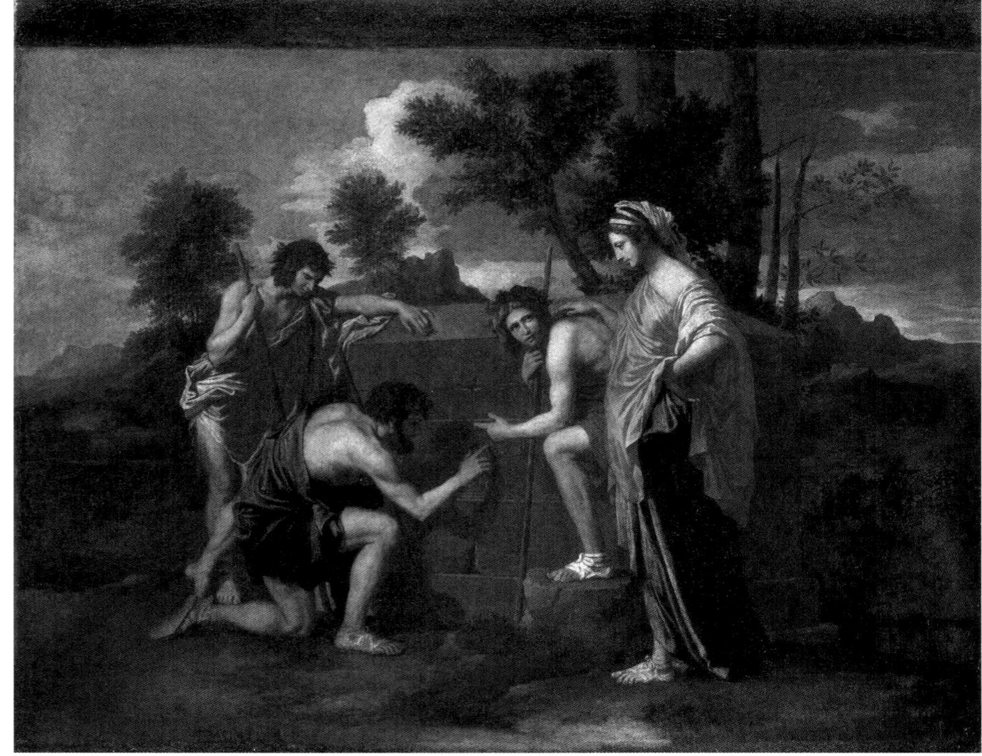

Fig. 146. Nicolas Poussin, *Et in Arcadia Ego*, c. 1635–36, oil on canvas, Musée du Louvre, Paris

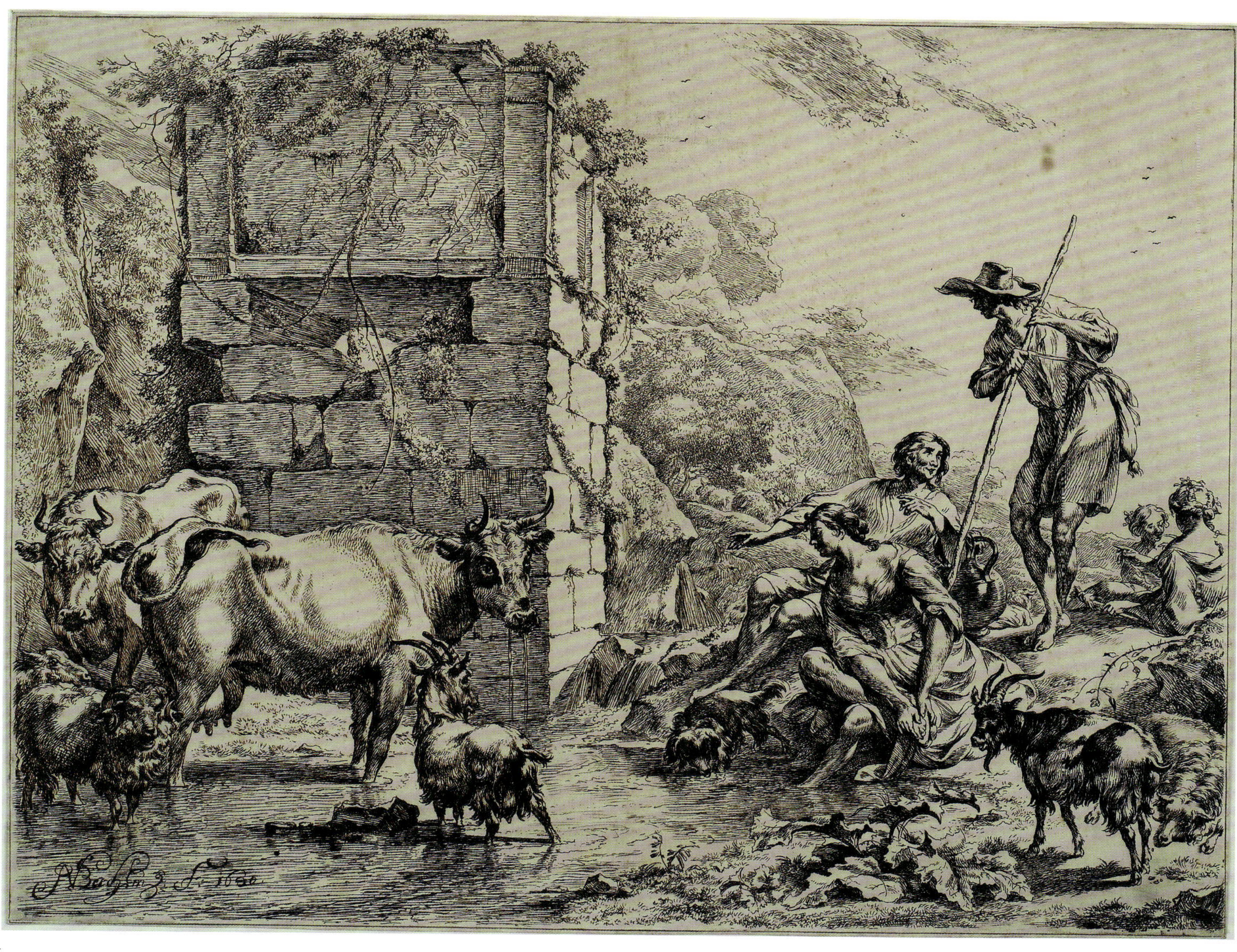

Berchem often used identifiable sites such as the Temple of the Sibyl or the waterfalls at Tivoli and frequently incorporated ancient ruins into his landscapes. His popular pastoral scenes with lively figures and Italianate lighting often place such strong emphasis on shepherds, shepherdesses, and herdsmen that they could be considered bucolic genre scenes. The arcadian quality of such idealized paintings and prints made him popular not only with the Dutch public of his own time, but also with eighteenth-century artists and collectors who found his elegant, picturesque works highly compatible with Rococo taste.[3]

NOTES

1. Bibliographical information is based on P. C. Sutton's essay in Amsterdam/Boston/Philadelphia 1987–88, 262, and J. Kilian's essay in *Dictionary of Art* 1996, 3:757–60.

2. Houbraken 1718–21 (1753), 2 (1718):109–14, as cited in Slive 1995, 241, and J. Kilian in *Dictionary of Art* 1996, 3:757.

3. Significantly, I. von Sick entitled her 1930 monograph on Berchem *Nicolaes Berchem: Ein Vorläufer des Rokoko.*

[66]

The Resting Herd, from a series of five animal prints, 1680

Inscriptions: lower left, *N.Berghem f. 1680*

Etching, 283 × 377 mm (11⅛ × 14⅞ in.); state ii/viii

Print Collection, The Miriam and Ira D. Wallach Division of Art, Prints and Photographs, The New York Public Library, Astor, Lenox and Tilden Foundations

References: Lugt 1927, pl. III, no. 5; Hollstein 1 (1949):249; Boston/St. Louis 1980–81, 292–93, no. 205.

Approximately 60 prints by Berchem are known, the earliest of which date from the mid-1640s and focus on peasant herdsmen or horsemen, rendered in a strongly tonal way by meshes of closely crosshatched lines. This example, which is dated 1680, has a different, more decorative effect.[1] The artist's gracefully calligraphic touch as well as his idealization of rustic figures relate this Italianate scene to the taste for pastoral imagery (literally, imagery pertaining to shepherds), which remained popular with the Dutch public throughout the seventeenth century in poetry, drama, and the visual arts.[2] Scenes of this type, whose origin can be traced to Roman poetry such as Virgil's *Bucolics*, transport the viewer into an ideal, timeless realm, where life is easy, harmonious, and unrestrained. The warmth and light of Italian settings with their poetic vestiges of the past allowed artists to evoke the ancient origins of a theme that shows figures and animals in an idyllic realm safe from the corruptive effects of civilization (see also Cats. 61, 68, and 69).

In Berchem's etching, young shepherdesses and herdsmen have paused for rest and conversation at the edge of a watering place fed by a little waterfall. At the right, these elegantly garbed rural figures are grouped against the rising form of a mountain and an open sunlit sky. The more enclosed left side, where cows and goats stand quietly in the water, is dominated by the large block of a crumbling stone sarcophagus, overgrown with vines and topped by the relief of a warrior on horseback attacking a fallen foe. One is reminded of Nicolas Poussin's (1594–1665) well-known pastoral painting of about 1635 entitled *Et in Arcadia Ego* (Fig. 146), in which young shepherds and shepherdesses pause before a tomb whose inscription reminds them that death is present even in Arcadia ("and in Arcadia so am I").[3] In Berchem's print, the seated herdsman at the right gestures toward the time-worn monument and turns as if to discuss it with his standing companion. Yet in the context of these contented figures and animals (no artist depicted goats more gracefully than Berchem), the tomb and the warlike subject of the relief do not seem threatening intrusions. Instead, their presence intensifies the harmonious enjoyment of nature experienced by the inhabitants of this landscape.

NOTES

1. Berchem's print has a careful and complete preparatory drawing, dated 1679 (pen and wash, 28.2 × 38.2 cm) and now in the Petit Palais, Paris, whose composition is reversed in the etching. Repr. Lugt 1927, 10, no. 5, pl. III.

2. For a discussion of Dutch pastoral imagery and its development, see Kettering 1983. Dutch pastoral poetry and painting of this period were also stimulated by the taste, in a rapidly urbanizing society, for country houses and rural estates, where people could retreat to enjoy idyllic natural surroundings outside cities; for example, Jacob Cats's estate Sorgvliet (Care's Flight) near The Hague.

3. Poussin's earlier version of *Et in Arcadia Ego*, in the collection of the duke of Devonshire, Chatsworth, dates from c. 1630, and the second version, in the Musée du Louvre, Paris, from c. 1635–36. Both are discussed and illustrated in E. Panofsky's classic essay on Poussin and the elegiac tradition. Panofsky 1955, figs. 91 and 92. See also Jan Asselijn's (after 1610–1652) painting of herdsmen at a watering place with a similar tomb (Muzeum Narodowe w Warszawie, Warsaw, no. Wil 1072): Steland-Stief 1971, pl. xxxv, no. 175.

CORNELIS VAN POELENBURCH
1594/95–1667

One of the most internationally celebrated of the Dutch Italianate painters, Poelenburch had important patrons throughout his career, including Cosimo II de' Medici; the grand duke of Tuscany; Frederick V, the elector palatine; Prince Frederick Henry of Orange; and King Charles I of England, whom he served as court painter between 1637 and 1641.[1] Baron van Wittenhorst, the leading collector in Poelenburch's native city of Utrecht, owned fifty-five of his paintings, and Peter Paul Rubens (1577–1640), who visited his workshop in 1627, also owned several of his works.

A student in Abraham Bloemaert's (q.v.) large workshop, Poelenburch also had contact with the Amsterdam Pre-Rembrandtists Jan (1581/82–1631) and Jacob Pynas (q.v.). In 1617 he moved to Rome, where he was one of the founders of the Schildersbent, the Netherlandish confraternity of artists, who gave him the nickname "Satiro" (Satyr), either because he sometimes included such mythological figures in the small-scale Italianate landscapes that made his reputation or perhaps because of his great fondness for women.[2] An admirer of Raphael, Poelenburch was also strongly drawn to the work of the Flemish landscapist Paulus Bril (1554–1626), who may have been his mentor in Italy.

By 1625, when Poelenburch moved back to Utrecht, he was already becoming very well known. In 1627 the States of Utrecht gave one of his paintings to Amalia van Solms, wife of the Dutch Stadtholder Frederick Henry, probably to mark her husband's installation as stadtholder to the province of Utrecht in November 1626.[3] In 1629 the artist married the daughter of a notary and clerk, Jacomina van Steenre, with whom he had four children, and he soon became one of the most productive and prosperous Dutch landscapists, with a large studio of his own. He served as head (*hooftman*) of the Utrecht painters' guild in 1656 and as its dean in 1657, 1658, and 1664.

After his return from Italy, Poelenburch's paintings continued to show strong Italian influence, with mountainous settings and warm Mediterranean light. His treatment of light is particularly striking, for sometimes his landscapes are rear-lit with the foreground in shadow; at other times, penetrating light permeates the entire scene.[4] Roman ruins and classical fragments play a major role both in Poelenburch's highly refined, polished paintings (usually on panel or copper) and in the many drawings he made of the Roman countryside.

NOTES

1. On Poelenburch's biography, see N. Sluijter-Seijffert's essay in *Dictionary of Art* 1996, 25:65–68 and M. J. Bok's essay in Baltimore/San Francisco 1997–98, 387–88. Ambiguities about Poelenburch's exact date of birth are discussed in Bok 1984.

2. The latter suggestion was made in written communication to this author by N. Sluijter-Seijffert, who notes that the nicknames given to members of the Schildersbent usually referred to the artists' personal characteristics.

3. I am indebted for this idea to N. Sluijter-Seijffert (written communication to author, June 2004), who credits it to E. D. Nieuwenhuis, author of a 2001 dissertation on Paulus Moreelse for the University of Leiden.

4. J. Spicer in Baltimore/San Francisco 1997–98, 41.

[67]
The Rest on the Flight into Egypt, c. 1650–60

Inscriptions: on stone at lower right, *C. P.*

Oil on copper, 23.8 × 26 cm (9⅜ × 10¼ in.)

The Frances Lehman Loeb Art Center, Vassar College, Poughkeepsie, New York, Purchase, The Betsy Mudge Wilson, Class of 1956 Memorial Fund, 1965.9

References: Sluijter-Seijffert 1984, 106, 140–43, pl. 10.

The Holy Family's flight into Egypt, recounted in the Gospel of Matthew (Matthew 2:13–23), took place after the three Magi had paid tribute to the infant Christ in Bethlehem (Cat. 50). When King Herod ordered that all the children of Bethlehem be slaughtered, hoping that the newborn Jesus would be slain among them, an angel appeared to Joseph in a dream and told him to flee with Mary and the child into Egypt. Medieval apocryphal treatises such as the Apocrypha to the New Testament and Jacobus de Voragine's *The Golden Legend* elaborated on this basic narrative by inventing a picturesque incident from the early part of the journey that came to be known as the Rest on the Flight. During the late fifteenth and early sixteenth

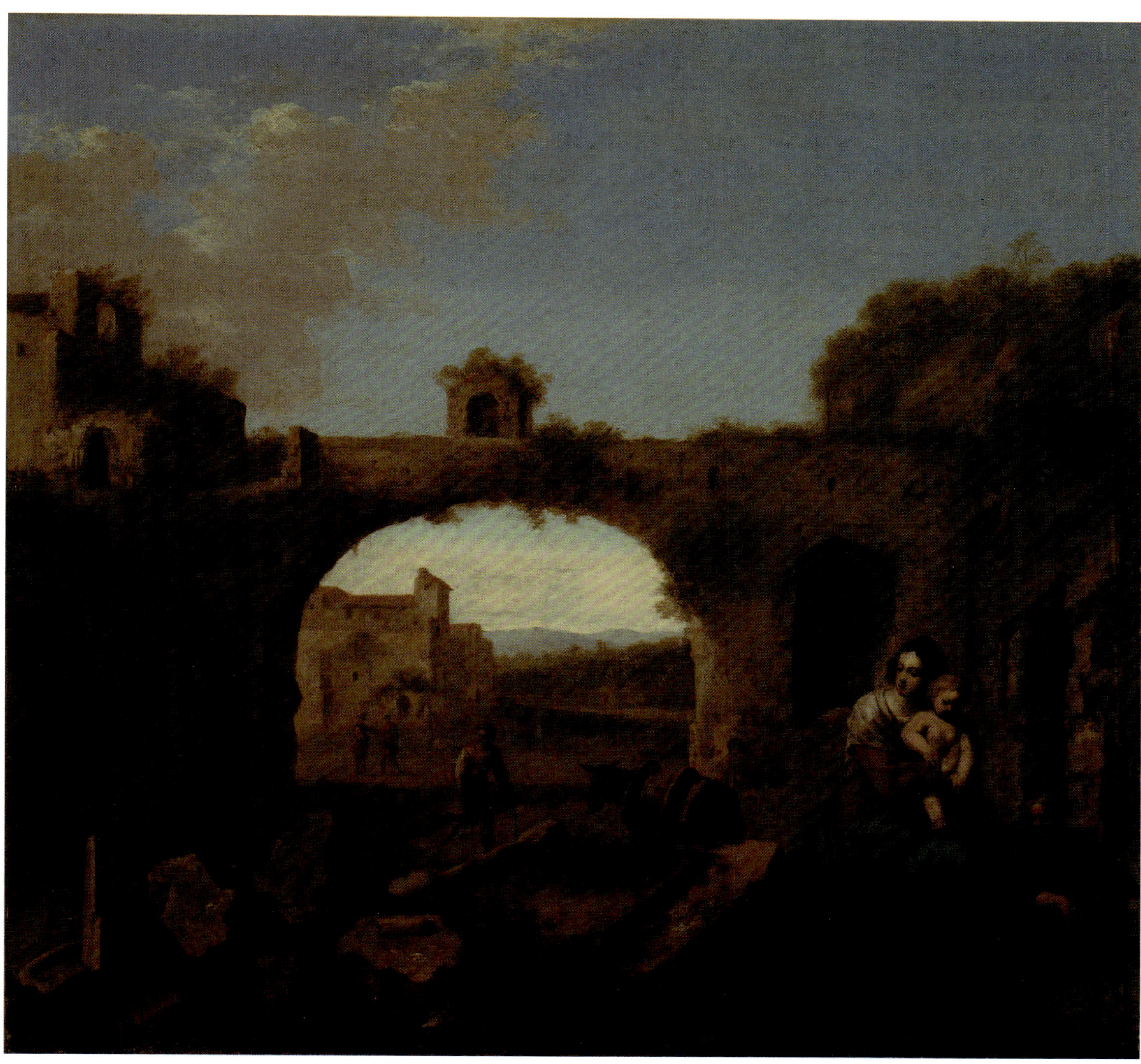

centuries—a period of rapidly developing interest in landscape—Netherlandish painters seized upon this subject because it allowed them to develop a new, down-to-earth interpretation of the Holy Family relaxing in the Flemish countryside.[1]

Poelenburch, on the other hand, has relocated the scene to the Roman campagna, as did the majority of his contemporaries, who used the antiquity of this setting to evoke the distant past. In Vassar's small painting, Mary, holding the Christ child in her arms, is seated informally at the far right, with Joseph behind them on a lower level of ground. All across the immediate foreground are the broken remains of large antique cornices, column drums, and sculptured capitals, which, in this context, can be understood as a reference to the fall of the Old Order with the coming of Christ. Beside these monumental ancient shapes, the small figures pause before resuming their journey. Behind them and near the center of the scene, the ass waits, bearing an empty saddle and facing toward the distant landscape. By boldly framing this vista with a Roman archway or aqueduct, the artist was able to incorporate into the scene implications of both the past and the future.

This popular subject had considerable appeal for a domestic Dutch society, which placed a high premium on family life, especially parental

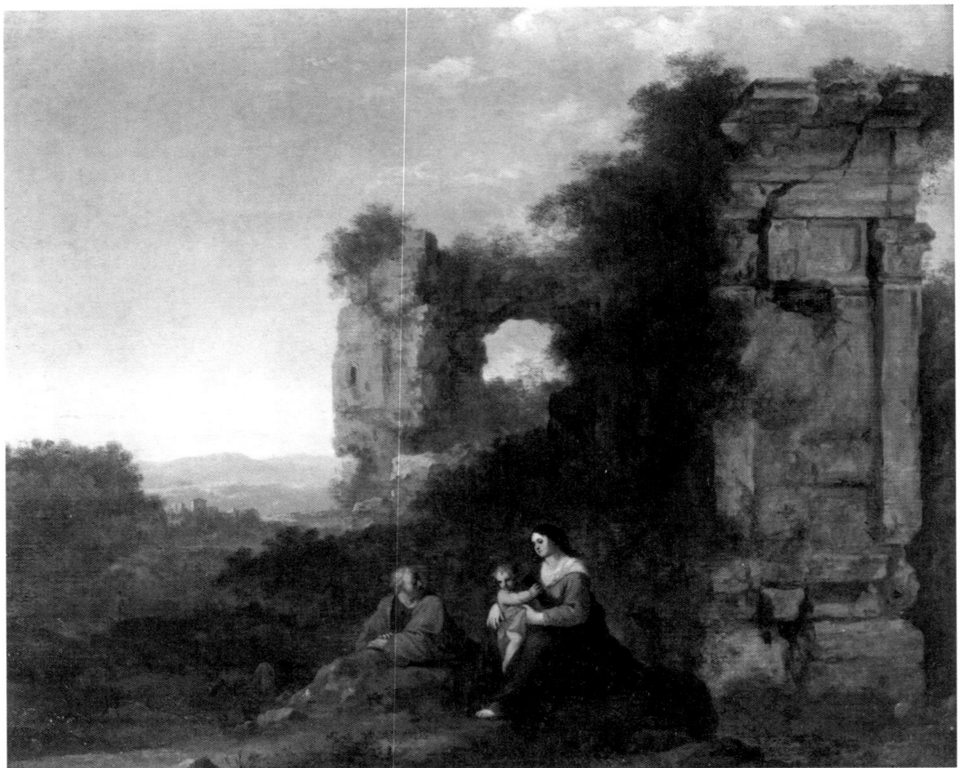

Fig. 147. Cornelis van Poelenburch, *The Rest on the Flight into Egypt*, c. 1640, oil on panel, Museum of Fine Arts, Boston

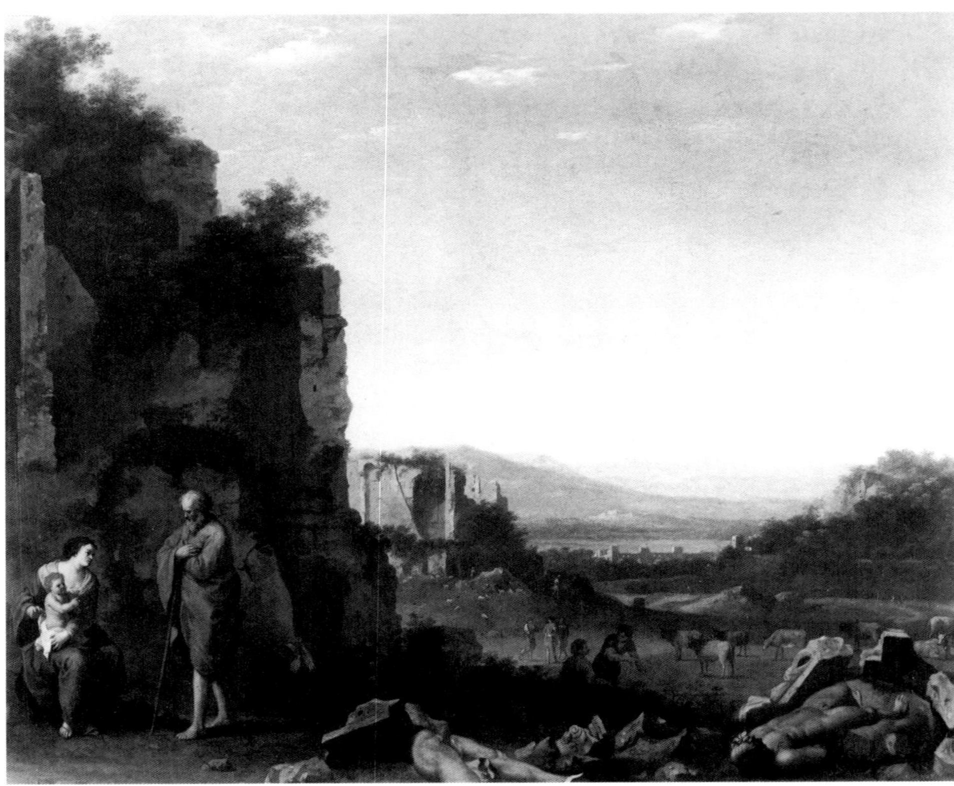

Fig. 148. Cornelis van Poelenburch, *The Rest on the Flight into Egypt*, c. 1630–40, oil on copper, Courtesy of the Fogg Art Museum, Harvard University Art Museums, Cambridge, Massachusetts

care of children. At least nine versions of the subject by Poelenburch exist, including two others in American collections. In the painting at the Museum of Fine Arts, Boston (Fig. 147), the Holy Family is centered in the foreground, with the landscape receding into the distance at the left; behind the figure rise the overgrown remains of a Roman building with pilasters and a frieze, perhaps the ruin of a triumphal arch. A larger and more elaborated Rest on the Flight at the Fogg Art Museum, Cambridge, Massachusetts (Fig. 148), devotes more of the picture space to a landscape vista with ruins based on the Hippodrome in the eastern part of the Palatine and includes shepherds and their flocks, along with more detailed remnants of fallen Roman sculpture in the foreground.[2] Vassar's painting, probably the latest of the three, has been dated about 1659 by W. Stechow and to the decade of the 1650s by N. Sluijter-Seijffert.[3]

NOTES

1. See, for example, Gerard David (c. 1460–1523), *The Rest on the Flight into Egypt*, c. 1510, in the National Gallery of Art, Washington, D.C., no. 1973.1.43; repr. Hand and Wolff 1986, 65.

2. On the setting of the Cambridge version, see Amsterdam/Boston/Philadelphia 1987–88, 433, and Montreal 1990, 168. Both works are on panel. The dimensions of the Boston painting are 22.9 × 30.5 cm and of the Cambridge painting, 33 × 43.2 cm. The motif of pagan sculptures that collapse like fallen idols as the Holy Family passes by them has a long history in manuscript illumination and early Netherlandish panel painting, as in Melchior Broederlam's *Flight into Egypt* of c. 1399, from the right wing of the *Retable de Champmol*, Musée de la Ville, Dijon.

3. Letter of 11 December 1966 from W. Stechow to T. J. McCormick, director of the (then-named) Vassar College Art Gallery (museum files, Frances Lehman Loeb Art Center, Vassar College). Stechow based his opinion upon the painting's similarities to Poelenburch's *Diana and Nymphs* in the Statens Museum for Kunst, Copenhapen, which is dated 1659. N. Sluijter-Seijffert (written communication to the author, June 2004) believes that the paucity of dated works by Poelenburch makes a more exact dating untenable.

JAN BAPTIST WEENIX
1621–60/61

An exceptionally versatile artist, Jan Baptist Weenix is best known for his views of the Italian campagna, many containing real or imagined ruins, but he also painted genre scenes, animals, portraits, still lifes, and exotic seaports. According to Houbraken, who based his account on the firsthand report of Weenix's son Jan (c. 1642–1719), Jan Baptist was the son of Jan Jansz. Weines, an Amsterdam architect, and studied first with Jan Micker (c. 1598–1664) in Amsterdam, next with Abraham Bloemaert (q.v.) in Utrecht, and finally with Claes Moeyaert (q.v.) in Amsterdam.[1] In 1639 he married Josijntje de Hondecoeter, daughter of the landscape painter Gillis Claesz. de Hondecoeter (c. 1580–1638), and the couple settled in Amsterdam.

On 30 October 1642, Weenix, a Roman Catholic, traveled to Italy, unable to persuade his Protestant wife to join him, according to Houbraken. In Rome he became a member of the Netherlandish artists' confraternity known as the Schildersbent where he was nicknamed "Ratel" (Rattle) in reference to his speech impediment. During his years in Italy, Weenix attracted the patronage of Cardinal Giovanni Battista Pamphili, who became Pope Innocent X in 1644.[2] Perhaps in homage to his illustrious benefactor, he signed his paintings Gio[vanni] Batt[ista] Weenix even after his return to Amsterdam in 1647. In 1649 he was elected to office in the painters' college in Amsterdam along with Cornelis Poelenburch (q.v.) and Jan Both (q.v.). His one documented pupil was his son, Jan Weenix (1642–1719), who became famous for his paintings of hunting trophies. In 1657 Weenix moved to the Huys ter Mey, an old mansion near Utrecht, where, according to Houbraken, he died at the early age of thirty-nine in bankruptcy. On 25 April 1659 a public auction was held at which more than a hundred paintings from his estate were sold.

Most of Weenix's landscapes feature architectural elements or classical ruins, often combined with robust peasants and frequently employing a characteristic arrangement of figures against an architectural repoussoir, balanced by a landscape vista. Like other Dutch Italianate painters of this period, such as Jan Asselijn (after 1610–1652), Nicolaes Berchem (q.v.), and Jan Both (q.v.), Weenix's works reveal his appreciation for the clear, warm light of Italy.

NOTES

1. Houbraken 1718–21, 2 (1719):77–83, 3 (1721): 113, 131. Biographical and archival material on Jan Baptist Weenix is reviewed by M. J. Bok in Baltimore/San Francisco 1997–98, 390–91, 440, and in J. Kilian's essay in *Dictionary of Art* 1996, 33:24–26.

2. C. S. Schloss has argued, however, that Weenix probably worked instead for Innocent's X's nephew, Cardinal Camillo Pamphili, because the artist left Rome the same time the Cardinal was exiled. Schloss 1983, as cited in Amsterdam/Boston/Philadelphia 1987–88, 520.

[68]

Figures among Ruins in the Roman Campagna, c. 1650–55

Inscriptions: none

Oil on canvas, 124.5 × 119.4 cm (49 × 47 in.)

Wadsworth Atheneum Museum of Art, Hartford, Connecticut, The Ella Gallup Sumner and Mary Catlin Sumner Collection Fund, 1926.294

References: Austin 1939; Stechow 1948, 188, 197, fig. 5; San Francisco/Toledo/Boston 1966–67, 120–21, no. 78; New York 1968–69, no. 57, pl. 51; Paris 1970–71, under no. 228; Ginnings 1970, 137; Haverkamp-Begemann 1978, 64, pl. 69 and 201–2, no. 169; Sutton 1990, 355, figs. 130–35; Utrecht/Frankfurt am Main/Luxembourg 1993, 269 n. 12.

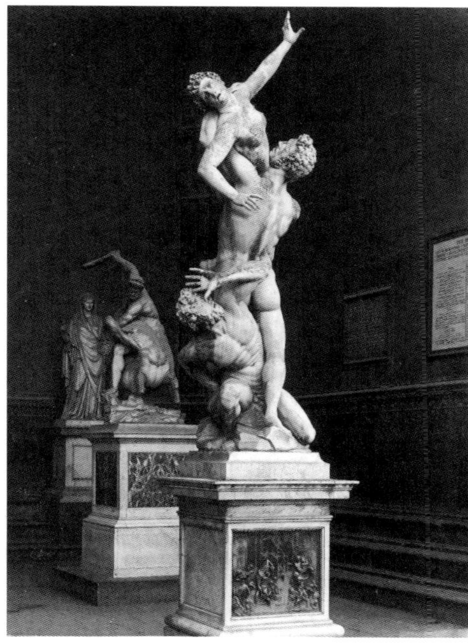

Fig. 149. Giovanni Bologna, *Rape of the Sabine Women*, 1583, marble, Loggia dei Lanzi, Florence

The condition of this fine painting has suffered, but it is the largest and in many respects the most complex in a sequence of Italianate genre-landscapes that Weenix painted between 1647 and 1658. In each, the artist shows a woman seated beside the ruins of an ancient temple, balanced by a vista of the Roman campagna.[1] In the Hartford painting, the distinctive plateau of Monte Cavo in the Alban Hills outside Rome rises in the distance, softened by atmospheric perspective. The setting as a whole is an imaginative composite, however, as it incorporates structures from the Roman Forum near the Palatine Hill: the ruins of the rectangular triumphal arch (Arco di Gione), constructed by Constantine in the early fourth century, and the nearby church of San Giorgio in Velabro, whose temple front and twelfth-century Romanesque campanile are clearly visible at the right.[2] Throughout this scene, Weenix uses architecture to imply multiple layers of history, for the graceful Doric columns and lintels that mark the remains of a classical building at the left foreground appear to be from the sixteenth century, suggesting that even more recent monuments are not immune to erosion.[3] This point is underscored by the presence of a large sculpture elevated on a high base at the upper left: Giovanni Bologna's (1529–1608) *Rape of the Sabine Women* (Fig. 149). Weenix transforms this famous Renaissance monument, still intact today, into another ruin, showing two of the figures in the piece with broken-off arms so that the sculpture becomes a kind of fictive antiquity.[4]

Within this ancient landscape, banded with alternating zones of sunlight and shadow, are well-dressed shepherds and travelers who seem to belong to the present as much as the past. A still-life grouping at the immediate right includes a traveler's hat, a ceramic jug, and a knapsack, while a mass of overgrown rubble at the left forms a dark repoussoir, slightly dwarfing the scene beyond it. Beyond it, figures and animals sprawl casually on the ground. At the left foreground, a buxom woman under a parasol is observed by the youth beside her as she teaches a spaniel to sit up on its hind legs while holding a morsel of food on its nose. Such depictions of canine discipline and self control, deriving from Plutarch's (c. 45–120) *Moralia*, can also be found in Dutch emblems and family portraits as allusions to *leer-sucht* (willingness to learn), which the Dutch considered the most important prerequisite for raising well-behaved children.[5] Whether Weenix intended his painting to have a moralizing implication is uncertain, but his placement of the woman and boy directly under Bologna's erotic abduction scene was probably not fortuitous. The youth, who

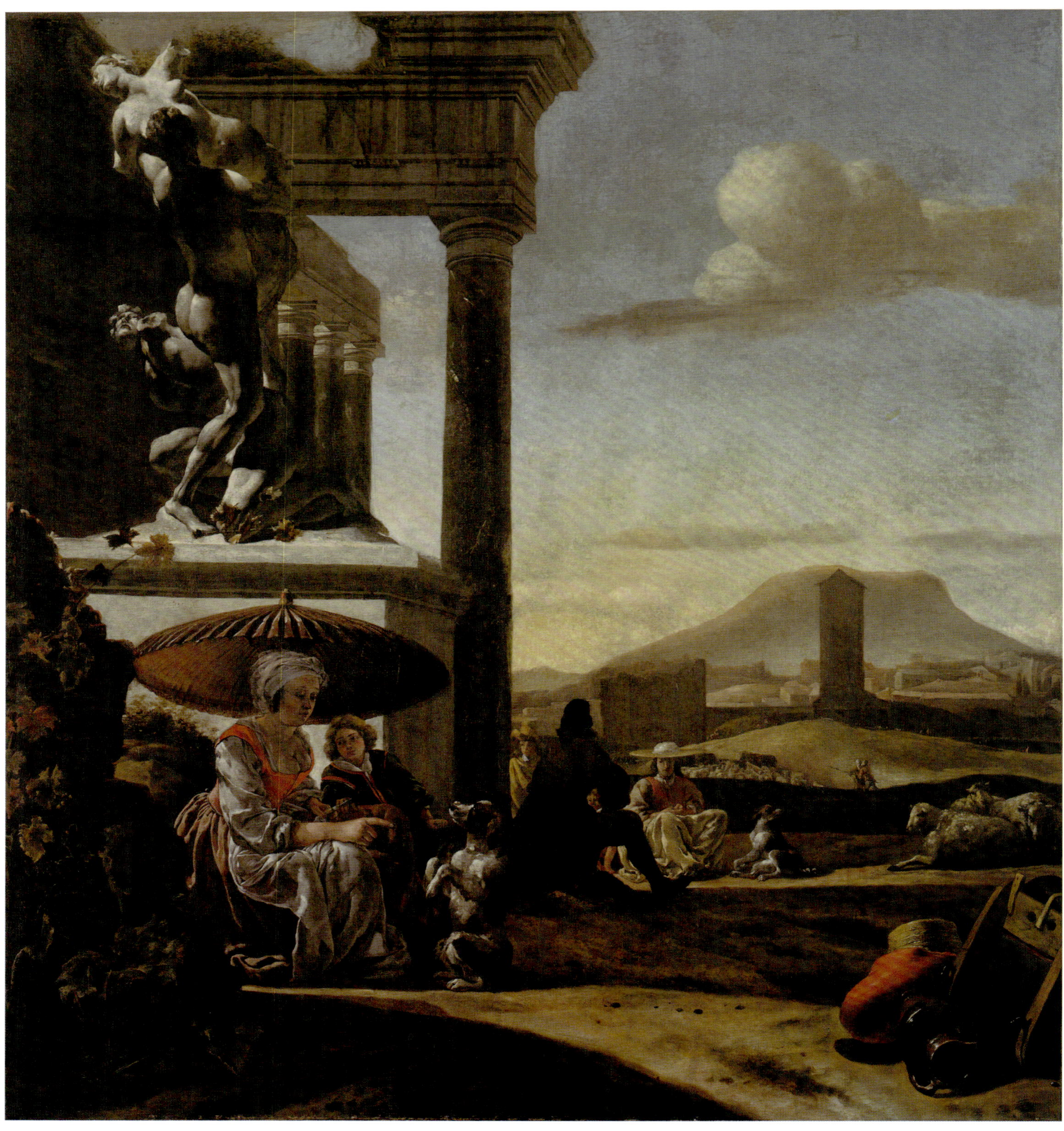

[68]

seems of an age between childhood and adulthood, gazes wistfully at the provocatively dressed woman (not at the obedient dog) as if aware of the challenge that longing poses to self-control.

NOTES

1. *Landscape with Rider and Ruins*, The Hermitage, St. Petersburg, is dated 1647 (repr. Blankert 1978, 176–77, no. 96). *The Rest on the Flight* in the Philadelphia Museum of Art and the similarly composed *Italian Peasants and Ruins* in the Detroit Institute of Arts have both been dated c. 1647–50 by P. C. Sutton (Sutton 1990, 354, fig. 130 and fig. 130–3). *The Sleeping Shepherdess* in the National Gallery of Ireland, Dublin (no. 511), dates from c. 1656–57, according to L. F. Orr (Baltimore/San Francisco 1997–98, 354, fig. 1), while *Peasant Family in a Roman Landscape*, Mauritshuis, The Hague, is dated 1658 (repr. Sutton 1990, 354, figs. 130–32).

2. The buildings in the Hartford painting have been identified by E. Williams, who credits her information to I. Q. van Regteren-Altena (verbal communication to author, Cambridge, Massachusetts, July 2003); and E. Williams in New York 1968–69, no. 57.

3. Williams in New York 1968–69, no. 57.

4. A variant of the same ruined sculpture, seen from a slightly different viewpoint, appears in Weenix's *Italian Landscape with Boy and Dog* (panel, 74.4 × 59 cm), which was in the London art trade in 1995 (sold, London, Bonhams Knightsbridge, 7 June 1995, no. 153). Photo RKD, The Hague. Weenix's son Jan also included a similar sculptural group in his *Merrymakers in an Italian Landscape* in the Musée des Beaux-Arts de Brest (Haverkamp-Begemann 1978, 202).

5. The origin of this idea in Plutarch's theory of education, as derived from Aristotle, is explicated fully in Bedaux 1990. P. C. Sutton discussed Weenix's dogs as references to good training or discipline in his analysis of Weenix's *Rest on the Flight* in the Philadelphia Museum of Art (Sutton 1990, 354–55).

ADRIAEN VAN DE VELDE
1636–72

Adriaen van de Velde was the son and the younger brother of two well-known marine painters: Willem van de Velde I (1611–93) and Willem van de Velde II (1633–1717). According to Houbraken, his father was his first teacher in Amsterdam, but because he showed no inclination for marine painting, he was sent to Haarlem to work with the landscape specialist Jan Wijnants (c. 1635–84).[1] On 5 April 1657 he married Maria Ouderkerk in Amsterdam, where he continued to be recorded regularly until his death in 1672. More than Wijnants, it was Paulus Potter (1625–54) who became a major influence on Adriaen van de Velde's landscapes and depictions of farm animals, along with Philips Wouwerman (1619–68) and Nicolaes Berchem (q.v.). There is no evidence that the artist ever traveled to Italy, although many of his finest paintings and drawings are Italianate landscapes with herders and animals. In addition, he painted local scenes that include beaches, forests, and winter landscapes, as well as a small group of historical and religious paintings and at least one genre piece.

A versatile draftsman, Van de Velde made twenty-eight etchings, most of which depict farm animals, and numerous drawings that include sketches from life of landscapes and animals and drawings of nudes and figures made after studio models. His preparatory studies for paintings are of particular interest because they reveal the multiple stages of his working process, beginning with outlines for an overall design and chalk studies for major figures or animals and ending with finely finished, highly detailed drawings of an entire composition.[2] He also contributed staffage to the works of contemporaries including Jacob van Ruisdael (q.v.), Meindert Hobbema (1638–1709), and Jan van der Heyden (q.v.).

NOTES

1. Houbraken 1718–21, 3 (1721):90–91. Biographical material on Adriaen van de Velde is based on A. Chong's essay in Amsterdam/Boston/Philadelphia 1987–88, 492, and on W. W. Robinson's biography of the artist in *Dictionary of Art* 1996, 32:144–46.

2. On Adriaen van de Velde's preparatory drawings, see Robinson 1979.

[69]

Pastoral Landscape with Ruins, 1664

Inscription: lower center, *A. v. Velde f. 1664*

Oil on canvas, 67 × 78.4 cm (26⅜ × 30¾ in.)

The Art Institute of Chicago, Sidney A. Kent Fund, acc. no. 1894.1024

References: Smith 1829–42, 5:211–12, no. 126; Hofstede de Groot 4 (1907):511–12, no. 185; Bille 1961, 57–58, 124, no. 235; Robinson 1979, 19; Montreal 1990, 188–90, no. 61, color repr.

A number of Adriaen van de Velde's finest landscapes represent the countryside around Rome, even though there is no evidence that he ever crossed the Alps or saw Italy, except through the works of Dutch Italianate contemporaries such as Karel Dujardin (q.v.).[1] Dujardin's drawing *Muleteer and Shepherdess with Animals at a Stream* of about 1660 (Cat. 64) presents a similar scene with a male and female herder and their animals before the soaring remains of an ancient bridge or aqueduct. Such settings also appear in narrative paintings by Cornelis van Poelenburch (Cat. 67), who was in Italy between 1617 and 1625. Van de Velde's painting emphasizes the ruins by allowing their dark shapes to be projected in *contre-jour* effect against a bright blue sky with puffy cumulus clouds. Emissaries from the distant past, these architectural fragments seem partly merged with the hilly landscape both in their shapes and in their overgrowth of vines and foliage. The uppermost arch, placed just at the point where the slanting profile of architecture crosses that of the horizon, helps focus attention on the figures and animals relaxing in a sunny spot below.

In his biography of Van de Velde, written in the early eighteenth century, Houbraken commented that "he zealously drew and painted cows, bulls, sheep and landscapes and carried his equipment each day out to the countryside—a practice that he maintained until the end of his life once per week."[2] This observation seems plausible, at least with respect to the animals in this painting, whose appearance and down-to-earth attitudes suggest that the artist observed them from life in some Dutch field or farmyard.[3] More than the idealized pastoral types often seen in Italianate landscapes (Cats. 52, 61, 64, and 66), this man and woman also seem to be everyday country folk, especially the herder, who leans familiarly with legs crossed against his white horse, his arm thrown affectionately over the animal's back. As the man looks into the picture space, perhaps toward his

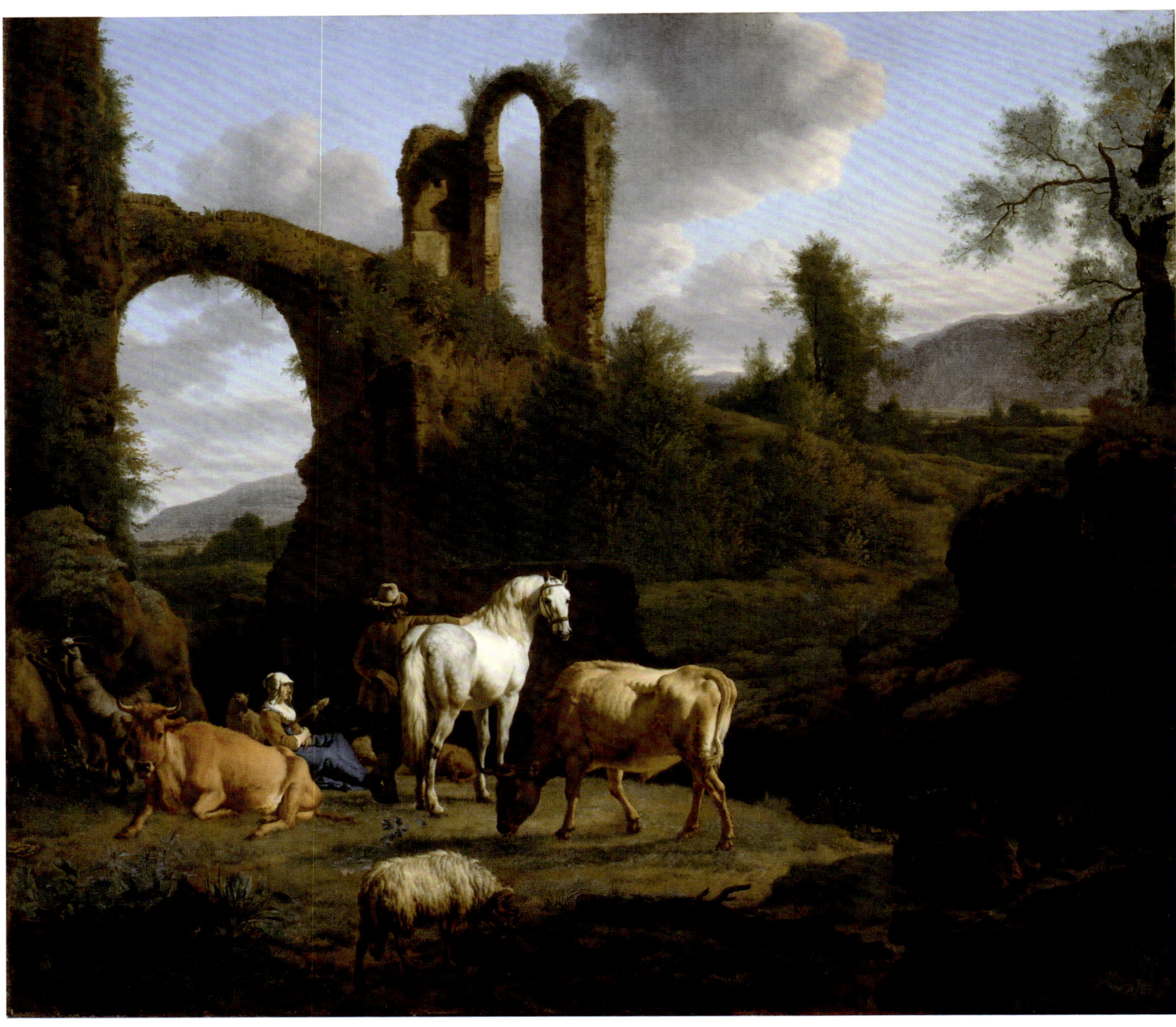

female companion, the horse turns its head to gaze at the viewer, enhancing the immediacy of the scene.

As W. W. Robinson has demonstrated, Van de Velde was in the habit of making careful preparatory studies for his paintings: in this case, the pen and gray wash drawing *Shepherd and Shepherdess with Cattle near a Stream* in the Teylers Museum, Haarlem (Fig. 150).[4] Although the ruins and a number of the same animals are repeated in both works, there are also significant changes, such as the addition in the painting of the white horse and the shift from a vertical to a slightly more horizontal format that puts greater emphasis on spatial recession. Hofstede de Groot suggested that the Chicago landscape was originally half of a pair, since it was sold in early auctions of two distinguished Amsterdam collections (the Gerrit Braamcamp sale of 1771 and the J. Gildemeester sale of 1800) with another landscape of similar size (oil on canvas, 66.1 × 79.1 cm, Royal Collection, Windsor Castle), which is also signed and dated 1664.[5]

NOTES

1. Scholars have tended to assume that Dujardin made a trip to Italy early in his career (J. Kilian in *Dictionary of Art* 1996, 9:380), but his presence there cannot be documented until 1675.

2. Houbraken 1718–21, 3 (1721):90–91. Cited by A. Chong in Amsterdam/Boston/Philadelphia 1987–88, 492.

3. F. J. Duparc points out (Montreal 1990, 190 and nn. 4–6) that Van de Velde must have made individual livestock studies, because some of the animals in the Chicago painting appear in other works by him, such as the horse (*Wooded Landscape with Cattle*, Pushkin

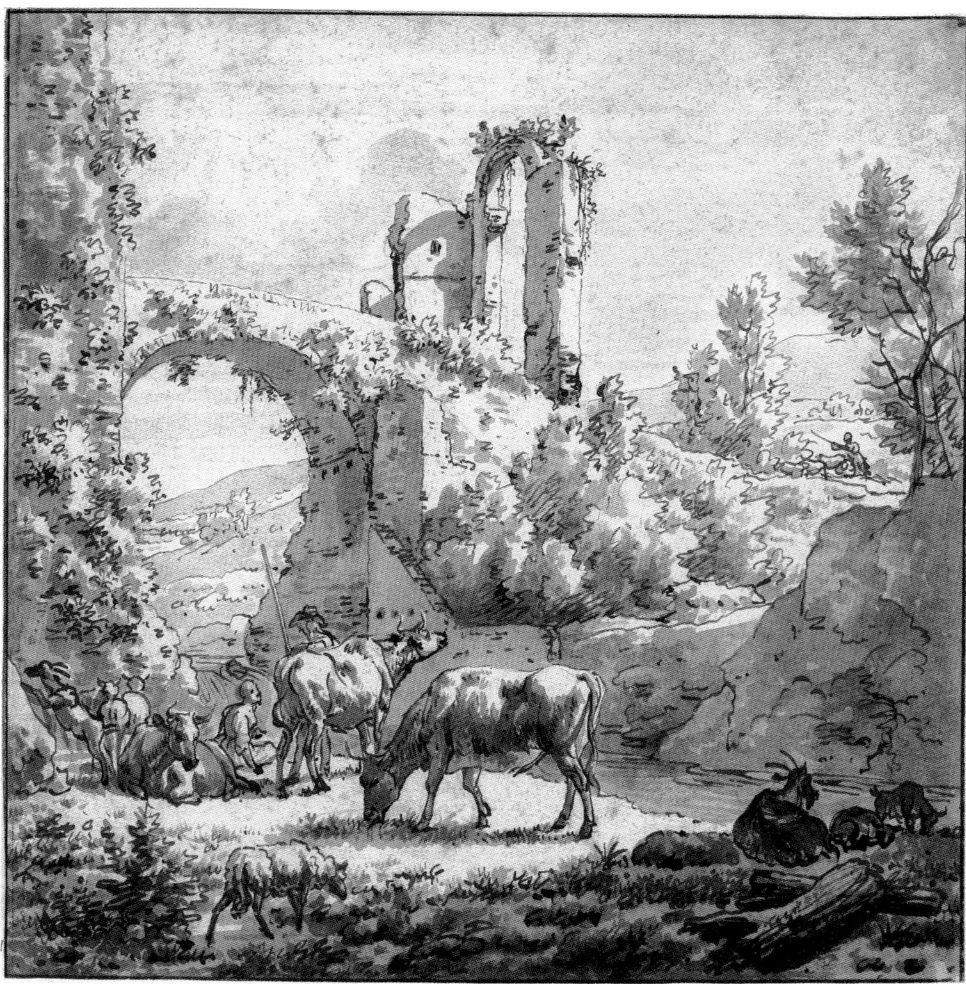

Fig. 150. Adriaen van de Velde, *Shepherd and Shepherdess with Cattle near a Stream*, c. 1664, pen and gray wash drawing, Teylers Museum, Haarlem

State Museum of Fine Arts, Moscow, oil on canvas, 34 × 31 cm, inv. 3252) and the resting cow on the left which appears in reverse in *Cattle and Sheep under Trees*, dated 1668 (Queen's Collection, Buckingham Palace, oil on panel, 37.8 × 42.9 cm, inv. 1481) and again in a similar landscape in The Mauritshuis, The Hague (oil on panel, 29 × 35.5 cm, inv. 197).

4. Robinson 1979, 19, no. B-5.

5. The possibility of a pendant, first suggested by Hofstede de Groot 4 (1907):511, was also noted by F. J. Duparc in Montreal 1990, 190. But according to C. White, writing on the painting in the Queen's collection: "… this does not agree with the companion picture described in the Braamcamp catalogue." White 1982, 130, no. 204, repr. 175.

JAN VAN DER HEYDEN

[70]

Ideal Landscape with Romanesque Church, c. 1665–67

Inscriptions: on small pyramid, illegible signature; on stone at right, *J V Heyde* (spurious)

Oil on panel, 40.6 × 46.2 cm (16 × 18 3/16 in.)

Philadelphia Museum of Art, John G. Johnson Collection, 1917, cat. 595

References: Roberts 1897, 2:237; Hofstede de Groot 8 (1907):409, no. 281; Grant 1908, 147; Valentiner 1913, 2:135; Wagner 1971, 103, no. 158; Sweeny 1972, 45–46, 312, fig. 595; Sutton 1992, 84–85, fig. 1.

Even in his Dutch townscapes, in which every brick seems rendered with perfect completeness of detail, Van der Heyden practiced an art of omission, idealizing his scenes by editing away any hint of the dirt, congestion, or crime found in major seventeenth-century cities such as Amsterdam.[1] It is therefore not surprising that the artist produced a number of architectural fantasies, which scholars have dated to the later 1660s.[2] While depictions of imaginary architecture had been rendered by earlier Netherlandish painters and printmakers such as Hans Vredeman de Vries (1527–after 1604) and Bartholomeus van Bassen (c. 1590–1652), Van der Heyden brought new naturalism to the theme by combining buildings with landscape in plausible outdoor illumination. In his works, the raking light that brings out the texture of a wall or the varied shapes of very disparate structures also helps to join them in unexpected visual harmonies. That these paintings appear so unified and believable testifies to the artist's architectural approach to building a composition, for his solidly constructed designs often juxtapose classical and medieval as well as foreign and local edifices—both imagined and real, both intact and ruined.

Within the shadowed foreground of this scene, a large segment of a broken classical cornice lies on the ground. Beyond are the remains of a medieval brick wall or castle foundation whose blind arches are framed in stone voussoirs. Seated upon an adjacent lower wall is a shepherd playing his pipe to a flock of sheep gathered at a small pond. The monumental scale of these ancient architectural remains is accentuated by the smallness of the figure, who sits near a pyramidal stone structure—half in shadow, half in sunlight—that may represent the base of a lost obelisk. At the right, within the long vista leading to a mountainous background, are a horseman and other figures along with a distant village church.[3] Within the sunlight the dominant structures in this landscape rise: the remains of a magnificent Renaissance tomb, overgrown with vines at the top, which overlaps a large Romanesque church above and behind it at the left.

In his choice of buildings, Van der Heyden has combined structures built in different historical eras and standing in different states of preservation. The Romanesque church, Ottonian in plan, has a Netherlandish step-gable at its western entrance, while the Renaissance tomb displays Michelangelesque pilasters and segmented arches decorated with stone urns and sculptural details. Van der Heyden, who had never been to Italy, might have studied such motifs in prints or architectural pattern books such as Vredeman de Vries's *Variae architecturae formae*, published in Antwerp in 1601.[4] As L. de Vries has observed,

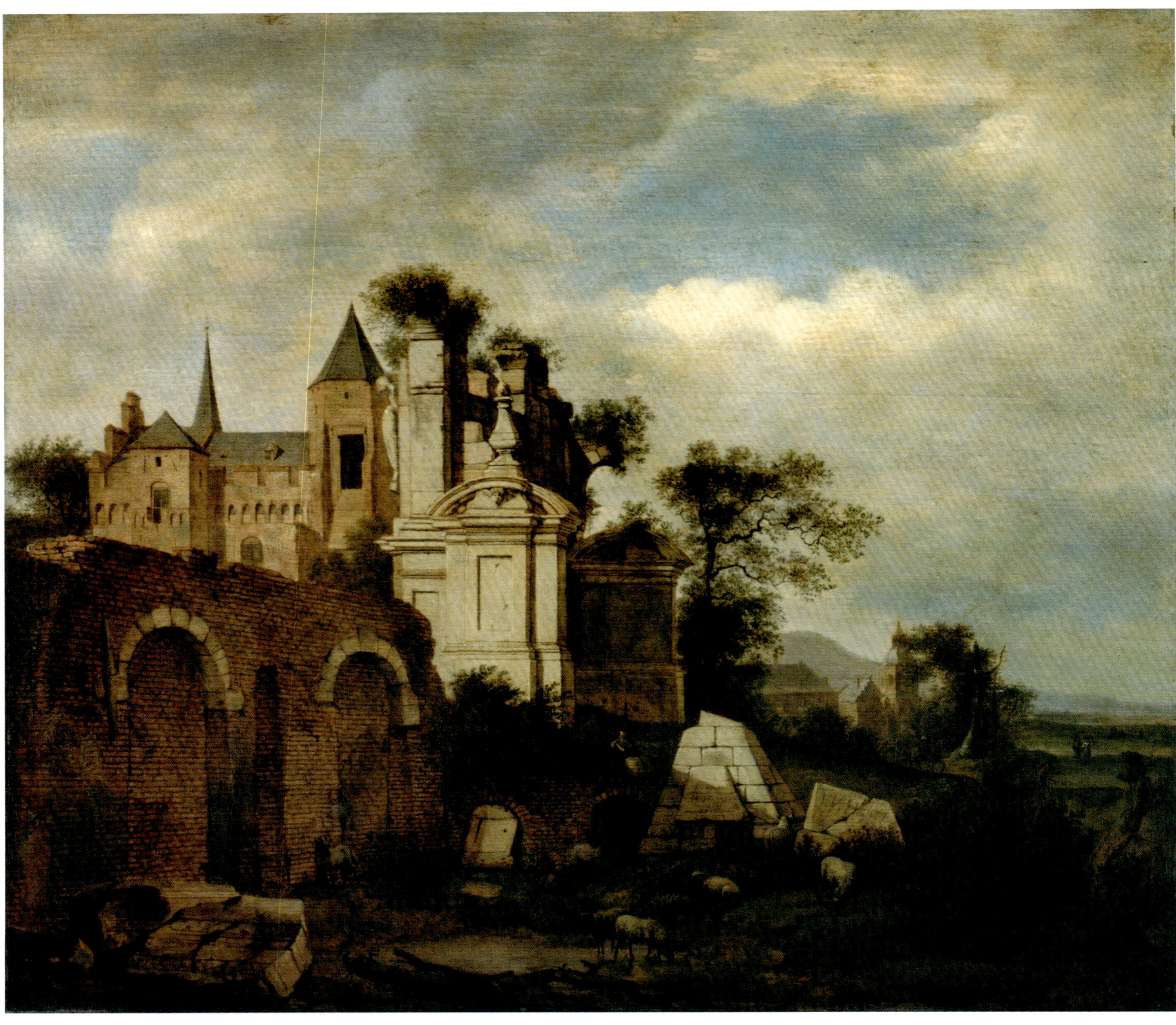

[70]

Van der Heyden often juxtaposed medieval and classicizing buildings that display contrasts between traditional and modern architecture. Indeed, he was active during a period when the Dutch were reviving French and Italian classicizing styles for new palaces and administrative buildings such as the Amsterdam Town Hall.[5] In the Philadelphia painting, however, the structure in classical style (a tomb at that) is in ruins. Thus this landscape with its piping shepherd seems reminiscent of an Italianate pastorale in which the buildings now perform the leading roles. Van der Heyden's interest in the irregularities of ruined structures is also illustrated in his undated depiction of an unidentified medieval Dutch castle and gateway in the Museum Boijmans Van Beuningen, Rotterdam (Fig. 151).

NOTES

1. Westermann 1996, 111.

2. Wagner 1971, 39. H. Wagner classified eight paintings specifically as "Phantasieansichen," but many other works by the artist, including the example discussed here, illustrate free combinations of different structures, sometimes including ruins. Wagner 1971, 93–94, nos. 116–23.

3. When the painting was sold with the Adriaen Hope collection in London in 1894, the sale catalogue noted "figures beautifully introduced by Adriaen van de Velde" (sale cat., Christie's, London, 30 June 1894, no. 29). Hofstede de Groot, however, believed that the figures were painted by Van der Heyden himself and further noted that a mediocre copy of the work from the collection of E. C. P. Hull was sold at J. T. Frere et al., London, 5 July 1907, no. 29, and again in London

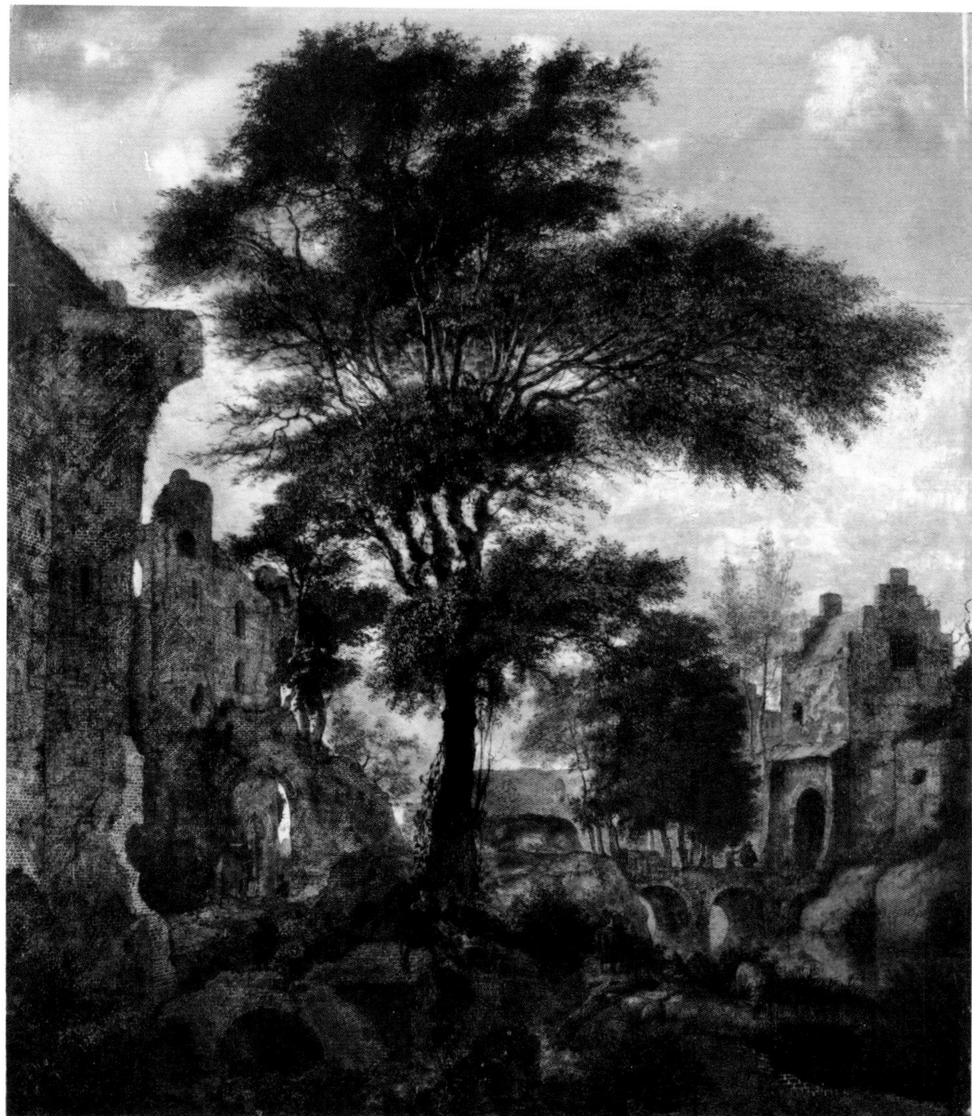

Fig. 151. Jan van der Heyden, *Medieval Castle Ruins and Gateway in the Woods*, 1665, oil on panel, Museum Boijmans Van Beuningen, Rotterdam

(place not specified) on 20 September 1911, no. 10. Hofstede de Groot 8 (1927):409, no. 281.

4. A facsimile of Vredeman de Vries's *Variae architecturae formae* (Antwerp, 1601) was published by Van Hoeve, Amsterdam, in 1979. I am indebted to Brian Lukacher for useful consultation on the architecture in this painting and for his reference to Hans Vredeman de Vries's pattern book.

5. De Vries 1984, 37–38. For example, Van der Heyden's *Fantasy Palace beside Three Canals* in the Virginia Museum of Fine Arts, Richmond, features a palace with classical pilasters and a cupola that recalls the new Amsterdam Town Hall, designed by Jacob van Campen (1595–1657) and erected on the Dam in Amsterdam between 1648 and 1655 (repr. De Vries 1984, 40, fig. 24).

FRANS POST
c. 1612–80

Brother of the well-known Dutch classical architect Pieter Post (1608–69), Frans Post was born about 1612 in Haarlem, where he probably studied with his father, a glass painter. As a landscape specialist, he may also have been influenced by his brother's early paintings, among which is a single known Italianate landscape with ruins.[1] In October 1636 Post was among the expedition of engineers, architects, scientists, poets, and artists who sailed to Brazil under the leadership of Prince Johan Maurits of Nassau-Siegen, governor-general of the recently established Dutch colony at Recife.[2] Because of disputes with the States General and the local church and planters, the Dutch settlement in northeast Brazil lasted only eight years, and Post returned home with other colonists in 1644. A decade later, the Portuguese would reestablish their control of the region. Post remained in Haarlem for the rest of his life, joining the St. Luke's guild in 1646 and serving as its officer in 1656–57 and in 1658. In 1650 he married Jannetje Bogaert, daughter of a schoolmaster, in Zantvoort, near Haarlem.

With Albert Eckhout (c. 1610–65/66), Post was among the first Europeans to directly observe and paint the New World. Yet although he spent eight years in Brazil, only six of his landscapes, all dated between 1637 and 1640, can be assigned to that period.[3] Four (Musée du Louvre, Paris) apparently belonged to a collection of some thirty paintings by Post that Johan Maurits presented to Louis XIV of France in 1679. Post continued to specialize in Brazilian and West Indian scenes even after his return to the Netherlands, painting for an enthusiastic clientele that included the Dutch stadtholder, Frederick Henry. In 1647 he produced the illustrations for two important publications: Caspar van Baerle's (Baerlaeus's) treatise on the administration of Johan Maurits in Brazil entitled *Rerum per octennium in Brazilia gestarum historia*, and Georg Marcgraf's wall map entitled *Braziliae qua parte partet Belgis*. Dated works by Post exist from almost every year between 1647 and 1669, but none from the last decade of his life are known, which suggests that he may have stopped painting. He was buried in the Grote Kerk in Haarlem on 17 February 1680.

NOTES

1. Bibliographical material on Frans Post is based on F. J. Duparc's essay in *Dictionary of Art* 1996 25:325–27. Pieter Post's *Landscape with Ruins* (private collection, The Hague) is illustrated in Montreal 1990, 42, fig. 22. For further discussion of Pieter Post's landscapes, see Gudlaugsson 1954 and Larsen 1962, 132 and 231.

2. On Johan Maurits's Brazilian expedition, see The Hague 1953 and Joppien 1979.

3. Of the six paintings that survive from Post's Brazilian period, four are in the Musée du Louvre, Paris, one is in the Rijksmuseum, Amsterdam, and the other in the collection of J. de Sousa-Leão, Rio de Janiero. See De Sousa-Leão 1973, figs. 1–6.

[71]
The Ruins of Olinda, c. 1665

Inscriptions: signed, lower center, *F. Post*

Oil on panel, 50.8 × 73.7 cm (20 × 29 in.)

Private collection

References: Guimarães 1957, 210, repr. 210; Larsen 1962, 30, no. 120; De Sousa-Leão 1973, 27, 109, no. 77, repr.; New York 1985, no. 9; The Hague 1991, 106–7, no. 30.

Frans Post continued painting the exotic scenery of the New World long after his eight years of residence (1636–44) in the Dutch colony in Brazil. While his later paintings of the 1650s and '60s tend to be imaginative elaborations of actual sites, they still convey the excitement of the artist's direct observation of this faraway land with its dark-skinned people and unfamiliar plant and animal life. This fine example displays Post's characteristic use of a wedge-shaped, deeply shadowed foreground area projecting silhouettes of palm fronds and other tropical foliage against the light while framing and directing attention to a sunlit panorama under a bright but cloud-filled sky. The same schema had been developed by Dutch landscapists during the first half of the seventeenth century for the representation of local scenery (Cat. 10). Post's paintings give this standard pictorial structure a startling new life, and they must have seemed both alien and oddly familiar to Dutch viewers of his time. The use of an empirically European style for such obviously foreign scenery not only reminds the observer of the Dutch occupation of distant parts of the world but also suggests how colonization involves taking possession of both the nature and culture of a region.[1]

The city of Olinda, former capital of Pernambuco, was an important center of the sugar trade on the northeast coast of Brazil. Its seizure by the Dutch from the Portuguese in 1630 marked the beginning of a period of ascendancy in Brazil that would end with a Portuguese victory in 1654.[2] Post produced numerous views of Olinda from different viewpoints, often varying or inventing the architectural details of major buildings in the area. The wide horizontal format of this painting allowed the artist to include two ruined structures: Carmo Cathedral (seen here at the left), which was destroyed after the Dutch capture of the city, and the sixteenth-century Jesuit church (seen here at the far right), whose roof was consumed by fire in 1631.[3] Post places special emphasis on the shell of the cathedral, overgrown with plants and brightly illuminated beyond the shadowed foreground foliage.

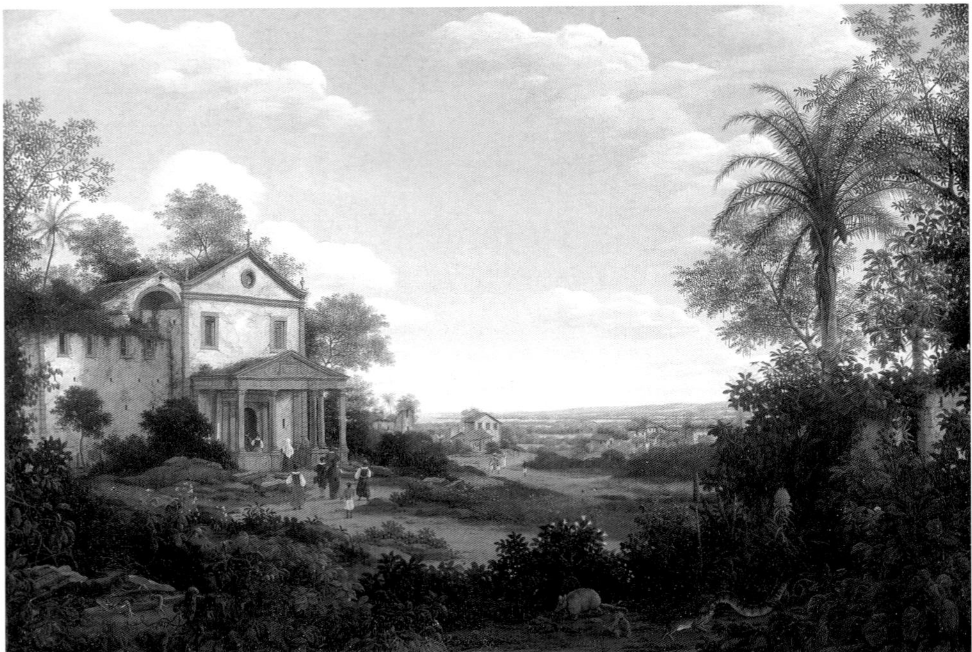

Fig. 152. Frans Post, *Brazilian Landscape*, 1665, oil on canvas, The Detroit Institute of Arts

Post's frequent displays of damaged or ruined Catholic churches within his tropical landscapes may have been partly inspired by early seventeenth-century prints made in his native city of Haarlem that feature castles or manor houses destroyed during the Dutch wars with the Spanish (Cats. 2a and 2b, 4, and 5). Like them, the ruins in Post's Brazilian settings may also have been intended to have political or patriotic significance, perhaps reminding viewers that Portuguese (Catholic) power crumbled during the occupation of this region by the Protestant Dutch, even though it would be established again in 1654.[4] While many of these scenes, such as *Brazilian Landscape* of 1665 in the Detroit Institute of Arts (Fig. 152), show native Brazilians entering a ruined church to worship, here the buildings seem empty, and the local inhabitants appear in relaxed conversation along the road to or from market.[5] Behind them, the land slopes down to a long vista that opens onto a blue river with distant mountains rising in the haze.

NOTES

1. As M. Westermann points out, the use of a European style for Dutch paintings of Brazil did, in effect, emphasize the occupied status of the territory both to its Dutch governors and to rival monarchs. She notes that paintings or tapestries made by the Dutch during their occupation of Brazil were given as important diplomatic gifts during the second half of the seventeenth century. Westermann 1996, 115–16. On representations of Brazil by Dutch artists, see Whitehead and Boeseman 1989.

2. The history of the Dutch colony in Brazil is reviewed in Boxer 1957.

3. For Post's paintings of Olinda that include ruined churches, see De Sousa-Leão 1973, nos. 47, 48, 78, 79, 80, 81, 86, 106, 123, 133, and 140.

4. This suggestion was made by H. Honour in Washington/Cleveland/Paris 1975–77, no. 80 (unpaginated).

5. De Sousa-Leão has identified the façade of the church in the Detroit painting as that of the church of the Jesuits in Olinda, with the addition of an elaborate Renaissance portico with pillars, classical urns, and a sculptured pediment. De Sousa-Leão 1973, 27 and 89.

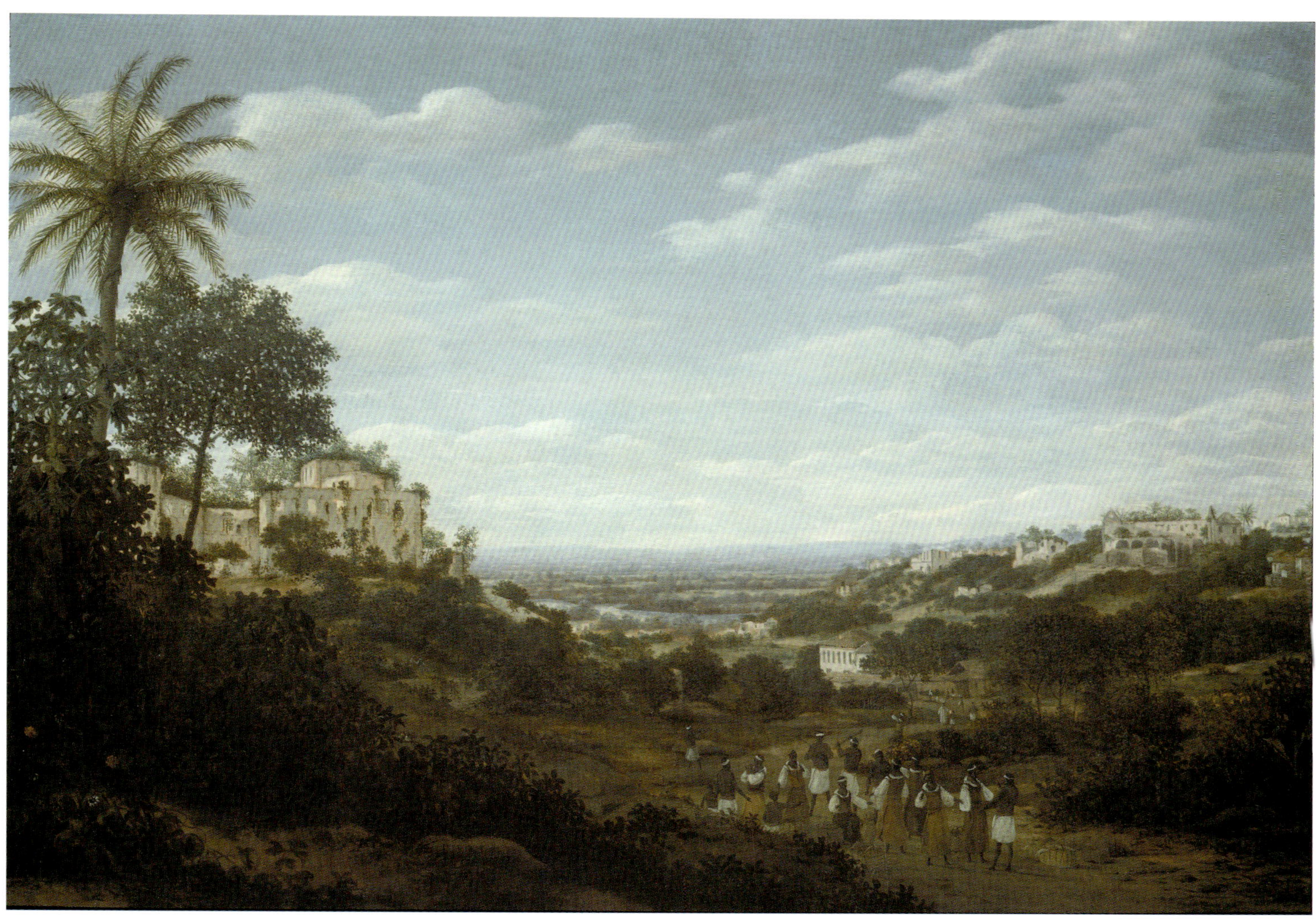

[71]

TIME AND TRANSFORMATION EMBODIED

FREDERICK BLOEMAERT
1614/17–90

Fourth son of the celebrated painter and draftsman Abraham Bloemaert (q.v.), Frederick was born in Utrecht and may have studied first with his father, for whom he often served as proxy in witnessing documents. Filippo Baldinucci, writing in the early eighteenth century, stated that Abraham first instructed some of his children in the use of the burin but observed that Frederick disliked engraving and gave it up later in his life.[1] Frederick probably received his most serious training as an engraver, however, from Crispijn van de Passe the Younger (b. 1597), who was working in Utrecht during the 1630s.

His career would be dedicated almost exclusively to producing prints (more than 380) after his father's drawings—more, by far, than any other artist engaged in reproducing Abraham's designs. In addition, it was Frederick who during the 1650s prepared his father's drawing book for students (*Tekenboek*) for publication. A devout Roman Catholic, who reportedly lived a quiet life and was unmarried at the time of his death, Frederick helped found and subsequently became regent of the Catholic Chamber of Charity (Aalmoezenierskamer) in Utrecht in 1674–75. His largest and most ambitious production was the engraved series he produced with his brother Cornelis, *Twelve Bishops and Prelates of Utrecht* (between c. 1626 and c. 1649).[2] Only three prints can be attributed to Frederick that are based on his own designs rather than those of his father; all are portraits of clergymen.[3]

NOTES

1. Baldinucci 1846, 596–610; cited in Roethlisberger (1993, 1:527–30), which fully surveys what is known of Frederick Bloemaert's biography.
2. Cf. Roethlisberger 1993, 1:281–88, nos. 431–42, 2: figs. 602–14.
3. Roethlisberger 1993, 1:529–30, nos. FB1–FB3, figs. FB1–FB3.

[72]

FREDERICK BLOEMAERT,
AFTER ABRAHAM BLOEMAERT

Landscape with a Hermit Praying, c. 1605 (design); after 1635 (engraving)

Inscriptions: in the lower margin, *O! verè felix, fugiens qui gaudia mundi / In sylvis vitam degree soliis amat; / Sic latitans soliq-Deo servire paratus / Continuis precibus regna superna petit / Abraham Bloemaert inven: Fred: Bloemaert sculp: et exc.*

(Oh truly happy is he who loves to spend his life in solitude in the woods, fleeing the pleasures of the world! Thus hiding away, ready to serve God, he seeks the supreme kingdom with continuous prayers. Invented [designed] by Abraham Bloemaert; engraved and published by Frederick Bloemaert)

Engraving, 254 × 191 mm (10 × 7½ in.) (sheet); only state

Lent by the Metropolitan Museum of Art, New York, The Elisha Whittelsey Collection, The Elisha Whittelsey Fund, 1949, 49.95.2772

References: Von Heinecken 1778–90, 3:31 (as *St. Francis*); Hollstein 2 (1949):93; New York 1973, no. 42; Roethlisberger 1993, 1:136–37, no. 89, 2: fig. 154; Gibson 2000, 154–55, fig. 107.

In this stunning image, to which M. Roethlisberger has assigned a date of about 1605 for Abraham Bloemaert's design and after 1635 for his son Frederick's engraving, the small figure of an anonymous saint kneels in prayer at the far right.[1] Before him is a cross propped up against a tree stump.[2] Behind him is his hermit's shack, tucked so closely into the trees that it is almost fused with them. Silhouetted against the light, the devout recluse is dwarfed by massive, twisted trunks and roots that grow around and out of a crumbling brick foundation. Because the figure is elevated and placed at some distance beyond the foreground, the viewer's eye is aligned with these densely convoluted shapes, which have been layered and turned in upon themselves as if to show how complicated the interactions between natural and human creations can become. The dramatic proliferation of forms that rise behind the hermit also helps to express the intensity of his devotions. A Latin inscription below the scene, whose graceful script reiterates the play of lines above it, describes the happiness of those who live alone in the woods, dedicating their solitude to constant prayer.

The theme of holy hermits, or penitent saints who retreat to nature to find closer union with God, became popular in the period around 1600, encouraged by Jesuit scholars such as Heribert Rosweyde (1569–1629), rector of the Jesuit church in Antwerp, whose monumental, nine-hundred-page *Vitae patrum* (a compilation of the lives of hermit saints), was published by the Plantin Press in Antwerp in 1615.[3] Abraham Bloemaert's initial series of fifty-two anchorites and anchoresses (*Sacra eremus ascetarum*), engraved and published in 1612 by Boëthius Adam Bolswert (c. 1580–1633), was apparently prepared for these texts, which were reissued by Rosweyde and Petrus Ribadineira in 1619 in a second, even larger edition of nearly sixteen hundred pages. Between about 1620 and 1630, Abraham designed a second series of eighty-one engravings of hermits (*Thebais sacra*) that was engraved after 1636 by Frederick, possibly as a sequel to the first set.[4] *Landscape with a Hermit Praying* is more than twice the size of these prints and greatly reduces the scale of the figure but should nonetheless be related to both hermit series. Abraham Bloemaert's series of landscape and farmhouse scenes, engraved by Bolswert in 1614, expresses a more secular praise of rural life as indicated by the text on its title page.[5]

NOTES

1. On the date of the print, see Roethlisberger 1993, 1:137.
2. For discussion of the solitary hermit St. Jerome and his association with the motif of the tree stump, see Kuretsky 1974. Two other similar images are Cats. 73 and 74.
3. M. Roethlisberger has thoroughly discussed the influence of the Antwerp Jesuits on Bloemaert (Rosweyde was also from Utrecht) and has closely analyzed the various editions and the order of prints within them. Roethlisberger 1993, 1:171–83, nos. 163–214, 2: figs. 262–317.
4. On the second hermit series, see Roethlisberger 1993, 1:355–67, nos. 577–657, 2: figs. 767–851.
5. This Latin inscription reads in translation: "Oh ever so happy and blessed by a good fate is he who may spend his years free from civic burdens, living safely under the roof of his shed! He is not perturbed by many diversions, his will does not waver in a heart beset by doubts, but glad for the work of his ancestors and with a serene spirit he gathers the yellow crop or the ripe fruits of the trees, or leads the large flocks to his pastures. What if a diligent wife assumes part of the work, oh ever so happy and blessed with a supreme fate is he!" (repr. and trans. in Roethlisberger 1993, 1:196–97, 2: fig. 349).

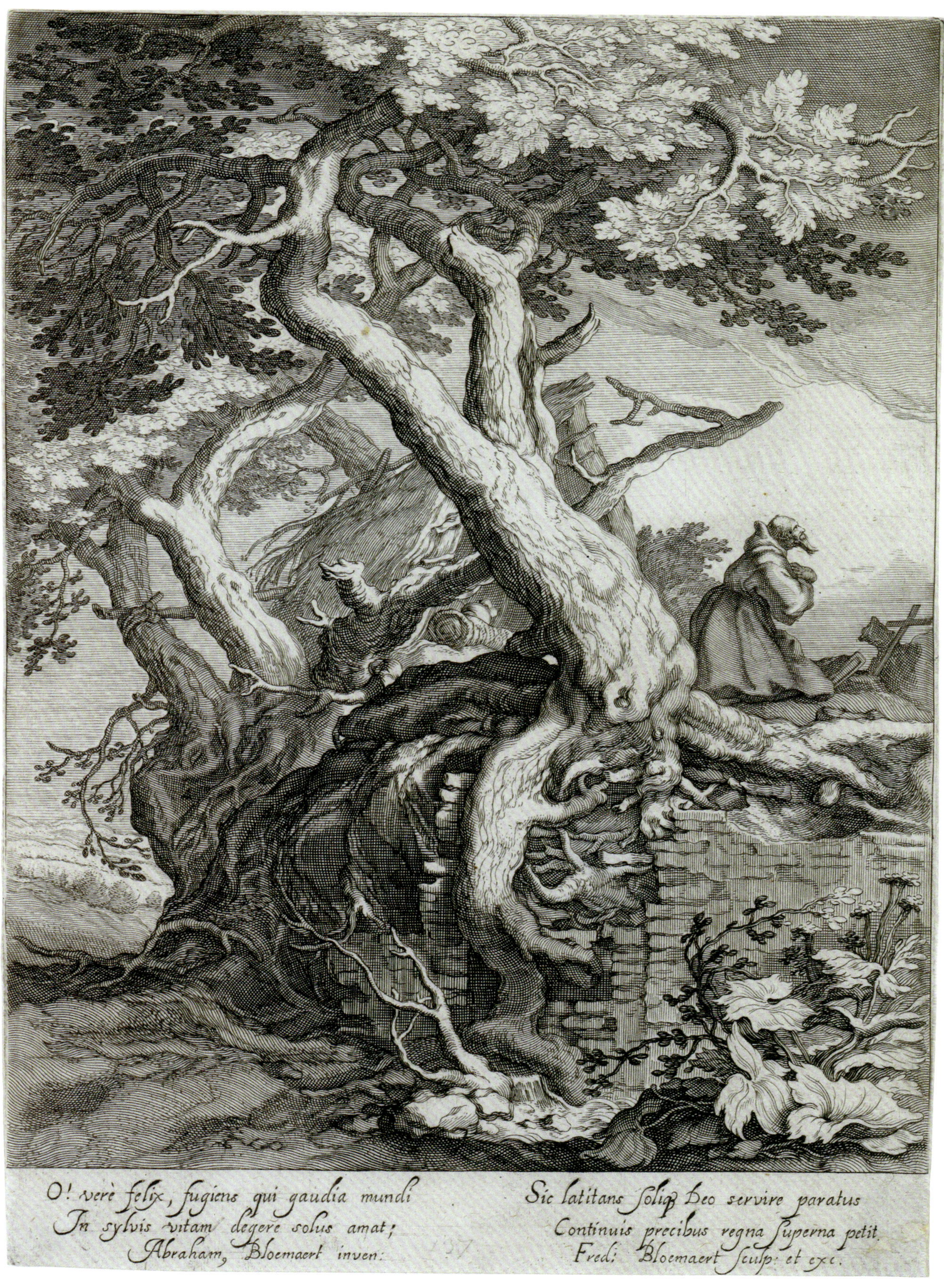
O! verè felix, fugiens qui gaudia mundi
In sylvis vitam degere solus amat;
Abraham, Bloemaert inven:
Sic latitans soliq; Deo servire paratus
Continuis precibus regna superna petit.
Fredi: Bloemaert sculp: et exc.

REMBRANDT HARMENSZ. VAN RIJN

[73]

St. Jerome with the Pollard Willow, 1648

Inscriptions: center foreground, *Rembrandt f. 1648*

Etching and drypoint, 180 × 135 mm (7⅛ × 5¼ in.) (platemark); state ii/ii

The Frances Lehman Loeb Art Center, Vassar College, Poughkeepsie, New York, Gift of Mrs. Felix M. Warburg and her Children, 1941.1.68

References: Hollstein 19 (1969):99, no. 103; Kuretsky 1974; Limouze 1995, 150–51, no. 57; London/Amsterdam 2000, 247–50, no. 59.

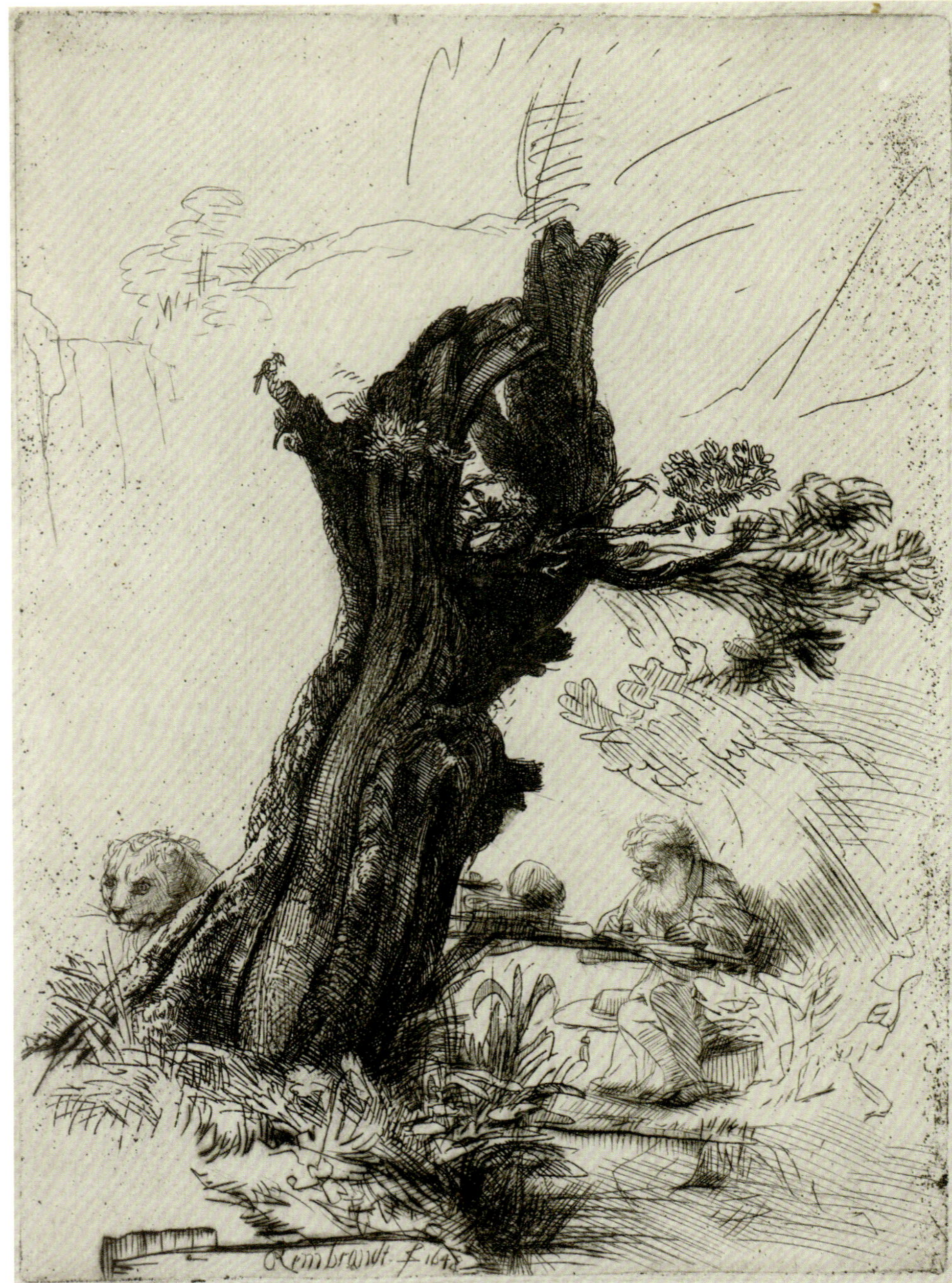

One of Rembrandt's most memorable images, this print employs a daring and artful interplay of the incomplete: a seemingly unfinished scene that focuses on a fragment. The ancient, densely etched willow stump in the center, blasted as if by lightning into two sections at the top, leans toward the right and puts out a leafy branch. Under this natural canopy sits an equally ancient St. Jerome peering through his pince-nez as he labors at an improvised desk attached to the tree stump. The lion from whose paw Jerome removed a thorn, according to legend, emerges from behind the tree like a large house cat. The patron saint of Renaissance humanists, Jerome was revered equally for his scholarship and his devoutness, for he became a hermit who dedicated his life to pious study. His careful translation of the Bible from Hebrew into Latin (the Vulgate) as well as his learned biblical commentaries opened the way to editions in all modern languages. Not surprisingly, Jerome was also the hero of Protestant reformers who advocated personal study of the Bible rather than church ritual as the way to God.

In Rembrandt's print, the skull and the crucifix on the saint's desk express the idea that Christian devotion is the means by which to transcend mortality. The old tree with its flowering branch, an image often associated with St. Jerome, conveys the same message, especially when understood as an analogy to the Tree of Death (originally the Tree of Life in the Garden of Eden until the Fall of Adam and Eve), from which the True Cross was believed to have been made.[1] That this natural ruin still sprouts a brave show of foliage in Rembrandt's print underlines associations between nature and resurrection that may even be present in similar scenes that do not specifically represent Jerome (Cats. 72 and 74).

One of the most surprising aspects of this etching is its shifting degree of finish, for the tree stump is rendered in such detail that the directions of growth of the rough bark and the smoother exposed wood beneath are easily visible, as is the tiny woodpecker perched at the upper left. The tree, the flowering branch, and areas of grass in the foreground are further heightened with drypoint accents. Yet St. Jerome and the lion are more sketchily rendered, while only a few lines evoke the ravine in the background. As S. Dickey has shown, Rembrandt made a number of seemingly incomplete etchings between 1643 and 1648. In these works, she argues, contrasting degrees of finish allow the image to function like an emblem, where a counterplay between different motifs is often used to promote reflection on their relationship.[2] Here, for example, the viewer cannot avoid associating the old man with the ancient tree, whose blooming branch illustrates the idea that age can bring a mellow blossoming to all living things.

NOTES

1. For discussion of this theological association, which is also mentioned in St. Jerome's writings, see Kuretsky 1974.

2. Dickey 1986. It should also be mentioned that scholars have expressed a variety of opinions about whether Rembrandt's print should be considered finished or unfinished, such as A. Hind, who called it "a tree study with St. Jerome thrown in" (Hind 1932, 106).

GERARD DOU
1613–75

Founder of the Dutch school of *fijnschilders* (painters who worked in a meticulously realistic style), Dou spent his entire life in the university town of Leiden, where he produced genre paintings, depictions of solitary religious figures, portraits, history paintings, and a few still lifes, executed in minute detail on small oak panels.[1] He was first trained as a glazier, the profession of his father, before he took up painting, beginning in 1628 with a three-year apprenticeship with Rembrandt. Dou was a founding member of the Leiden guild of St. Luke (established in 1648) and also served a high-ranking position in the local militia, evidence of his elevated social status. An indication of the enormous popularity of his paintings, which fetched unusually high prices, is the fact that several were included in a gift from the Dutch government to Charles II in 1660 to mark his accession to the English throne. Dou's clients also included Queen Christina of Sweden, Archduke Leopold Wilhelm, and Cosimo II de' Medici. In 1665, a time when exhibitions devoted to individual artists were extremely rare, John de Bye, a wealthy Leiden connoisseur, rented space in which to display twenty-seven of Dou's paintings.[2]

Dou's works are often strikingly illusionistic in their frequent use of trompe-l'oeil niche enframements and in their smooth, enamel-like finish and almost obsessive attention to detail. This dazzling technical virtuosity, which he applied to familiar domestic subjects and settings, explains both his popularity and its subsequent decline in the mid-nineteenth century, when his art came to be criticized for its seeming literalness. Beginning in the 1960s, however, new research on Dutch emblem literature by J. A. Emmens and E. de Jongh revealed that the diverse objects in seemingly realistic scenes such as Dou's may often be encoded with complex philosophical and emblematic allusions.[3] In response to the investigations of these scholars, a strong revival of interest in Dou and other Dutch *fijnschilders* has resulted in continuing research and several major exhibitions in recent years.[4]

NOTES

1. Bibliographical information is derived from R. Baer's entry in *Dictionary of Art* 1996, 9:192–95 and from A. K. Wheelock Jr.'s and R. Baer's essays in Washington/Dulwich/The Hague 2000–2001, 12–24, 26–52.

2. Washington/Dulwich/The Hague 2000–2001, 30.

3. An article by J. A. Emmens on the philosophical interpretation of Dou's (now-lost) genre triptych *The Lying-in Room* was the first of a number of his publications in this area (see Emmens 1963 and A. K. Wheelock Jr.'s discussion in Washington/Dulwich/The Hague 2000–2001, 17–18). E. de Jongh's fundamental publication of 1967 (*Zinne- en minnebeelden in der schilderkunst van de zeventiende eeuw*) was followed by numerous articles and two important exhibitions, the first devoted to genre painting, the second to genre prints. De Jongh 1967; Amsterdam 1976; Amsterdam 1997.

4. An exhibition of Leiden *fijnschilders* organized by E. J. Sluijter was held at the Stedelijk Museum "De Lakenhal," Leiden, in 1988 (Leiden 1988); the following year, P. Hecht's exhibition on Dutch *fijnschilders* opened at the Rijksmuseum (Amsterdam 1989–90). R. Baer's exhibition of 2000 at the National Gallery of Art, Washington, D.C., was devoted exclusively to Dou's paintings (Washington/Dulwich/The Hague 2000–2001).

[74]
The Hermit, 1670

Inscriptions: on book strap in center, *GDov 1670*; at top of right page in book, *GDov*

Oil on panel, 46 × 34.5 cm (18⅛ × 13⅝ in.)

Timken Collection, National Gallery of Art, Washington, D.C., 1960.6.8 (1560)

References: Hofstede de Groot 1 (1907):348, no. 19; Martin 1911, no. 11; Martin 1913, 6; Baer 1995; Wheelock 1995, 56–60; Washington/Dulwich/The Hague 2000–2001, 132–33, no. 34; Tokyo 2003, 140–41, no. 57.

Between 1635 and 1670, Dou painted at least eleven representations of devout hermits, a subject he probably learned from his teacher Rembrandt, whose 1648 etching *St. Jerome with the Pollard Willow* (Cat. 73) involves a similar juxtaposition of an ancient figure with the remains of a large tree stump.[1] Differences in medium aside, the two artists' approaches could hardly be more different. While Rembrandt explores the evocative possibilities of the incomplete in his style as well as his choice of central motif, Dou uses his meticulous brushwork to define and fix the most minute details and textures of figure and setting. Yet delicate modulations of soft light at the center of his scene, which gradually fades into surrounding shadow, prevent this painting from appearing rigid or labored.

With all his attention to fine detail, Dou has omitted attributes that would identify the hermit as any particular saint. Instead he explores the broader notion of earthly transience, which, this image suggests, can be overcome through Christian devotion. The bald, white-bearded hermit wearing a Franciscan habit kneels within a setting of crumbling brick arches that suggests the foundations of a cloister. His hands are clasped in prayer and rest upon a large Bible as he directs his pious gaze to the crucifix before him. As in Rembrandt's etching, the presence of the large tree stump with a sprouting top can be understood as a metaphor for Christ's resurrection on the wood of the cross—an association Dou emphasizes by pointedly juxtaposing tree and crucifix. Placing a human skull at the base of the crucifix allows the artist to emphasize the old hermit's mortality while referring to the legend that the tree from which the cross was fashioned grew from seeds that had sprouted in the skull of Adam.[2] Further reminders of transience in this scene are the horse's skull and the empty pitcher on the ground (beside which is a large canteen for water), the hourglass and tattered cloth on the table, and the extinguished lantern hanging from the tree.[3] The painting thus reminds the viewer that that all earthly things are subject to decay and death but also that death is necessary as a prelude for eternal life. The rosary that dangles from the hermit's belt displays another tiny skull at the end of its string of beads. Within such a thoroughly symbolic scene, the enormous, finely detailed thistle plant at the right foreground probably has meaning too, perhaps in this context as an allusion to the crown of thorns.[4]

In expressing the inevitability of time's passing, Dou's painting, like other kinds of vanitas images (Cats. 77–79) reminds viewers to make good use of their lives. The hermit provides a virtuous example, and the fact that so much of the red sand in his hourglass has yet to fall suggests that even at his advanced age, his time, well spent, will be sufficient. Dutch men and women of this period apparently used such paintings as springboards for reflection about their own lives, as suggested by a double portrait attributed to Dou in the Brooklyn Museum (Fig. 153). This couple is presented in an interior beside an open book, a lute, and a globe—objects suggestive of knowledge, pleasure, and worldliness. Behind them, below a crystal sphere

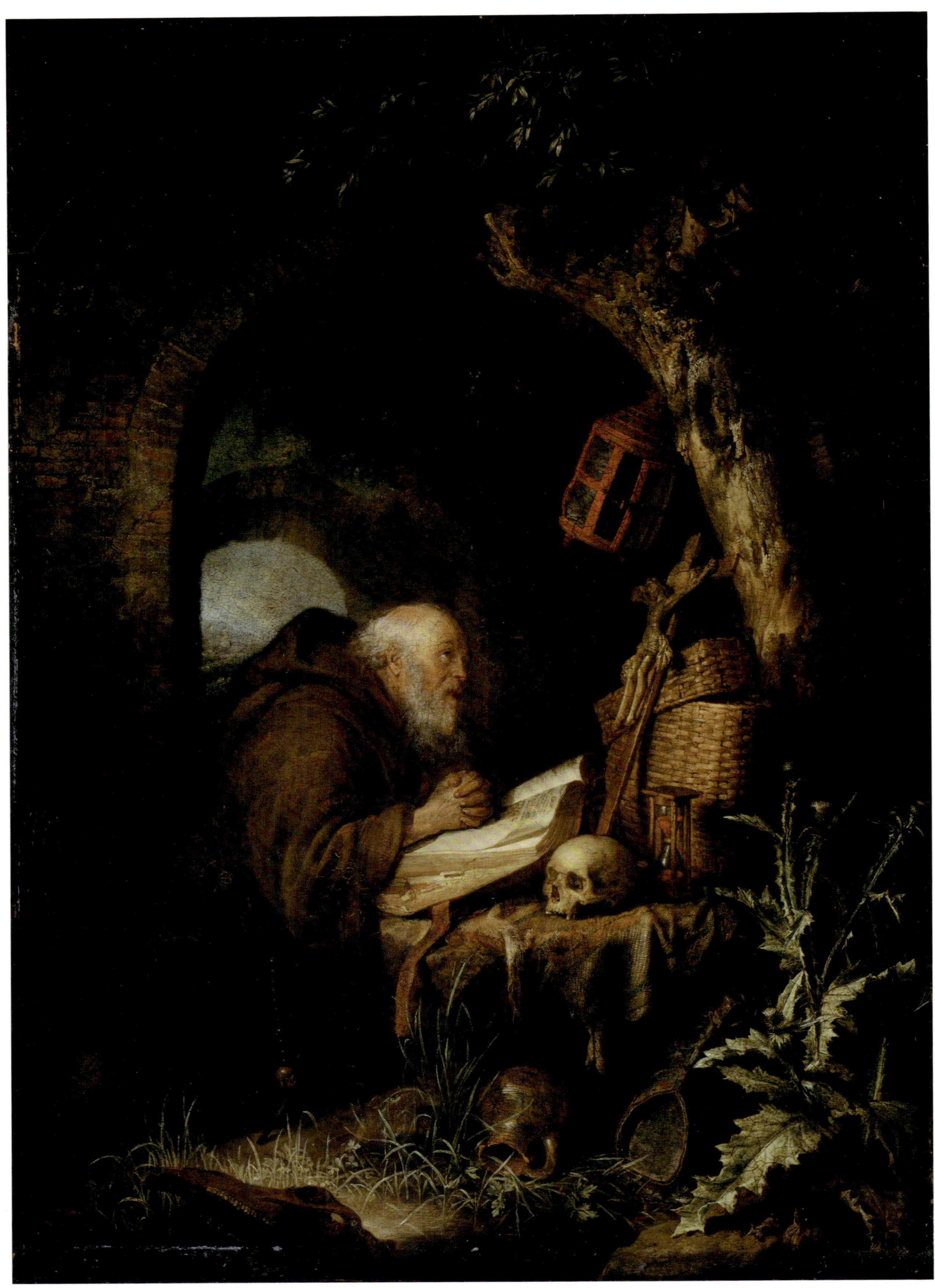

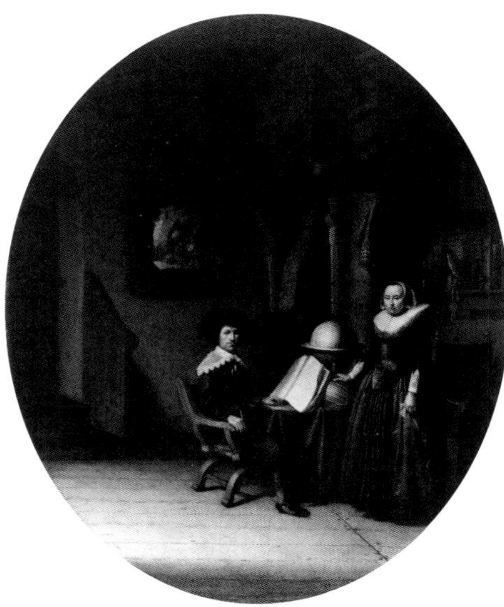

Fig. 153. Gerard Dou (attr.), *Portrait of the Burgomaster Hasselaar and His Wife*, oil on panel, Brooklyn Museum

symbolizing heaven, hangs a painting of a praying hermit within a ruin that is very similar to the work discussed here.[5]

NOTES

1. These painting are reproduced in W. Martin's monograph of 1911 (Martin 1911, nos. 5–11). Rembrandt's earliest depiction of this subject (now lost) was recorded in a print dated 1631 by Joris van Vliet (active c. 1631–35); Kuretsky 1974, 578.

2. See Kuretsky 1974 and Wheelock 1995, 58.

3. The empty basket against which the crucifix leans has also been interpreted as a prefiguration of Christ's empty tomb. London 1980, 15–17; cited in Wheelock 1995, 58 and 60 n. 4.

4. Different symbolic meanings for the thistle have been discussed by E. de Jongh, who notes that thistles were thought to be aphrodisiacs in antiquity and therefore came to be associated with sexuality and eroticism. By the Renaissance, he argues, this meaning had shifted, as indicated by the appearance of thistles in betrothal and marriage portraits, where they may allude to marital fidelity and devotion. E. de Jongh in Haarlem 1986, 126–27.

5. The association of this painting (which R. Baer rejects as a genuine Dou) with Dou's *Hermit* in the National Gallery of Art, Washington, D.C., was made by A. K. Wheelock Jr. (Washington 1995, 60, fig. 2).

ADRIAEN PIETERSZ. VAN DE VENNE
1589–1662

A painter, draftsman, book illustrator, and poet, Adriaen van de Venne was the son of Protestant parents who had fled to Delft because of religious persecution in the southern Netherlands.[1] Having first studied with a goldsmith in Leiden, Van de Venne became the pupil of the grisaille painter Hieronymus van Diest (active c. 1600) in The Hague but subsequently moved with his father and brother to Middelburg, where documents place him between 1614 (the date of his marriage to Elisabeth de Pours) and 1624. His early paintings show strong influence of Flemish artists such as Jan Bruegel the Elder (1568–1625), as, for example, *Fishing for Souls* (dated 1614; Rijksmuseum, Amsterdam), an allegory of the Protestant/Catholic conflict during the Dutch struggle for independence.

Aside from producing paintings, Van de Venne also worked as a print designer and book illustrator in Middelburg, collaborating with his brother Jan (d. 1625), a successful publisher and art dealer whose clients included the prolific and well-loved poet Jacob Cats. Many of Adriaen's illustrations were used in Cats's popular emblem books. Indeed, Adriaen remained Cats's chief illustrator until at least 1656, but he also produced several illustrated books of his own, including *Wys-mal* (Wise folly; 1634) and *Tafereel van de belacchende wereld* (Picture of the ridiculous world; 1635). By 1625 Van de Venne had moved to The Hague, where he registered in the guild of St. Luke, serving as its deacon in 1637. In 1656 he became one of the founders of Pictura, the local painters' confraternity. He also produced large printed portraits of the stadtholders, political prints and broadsheets, and an extraordinary album of miniatures (1625–26; British Museum, London) that may have been a gift to the new Stadtholder Frederick Henry from Frederick V of Bohemia, known as the Winter King.[2] His paintings of genre figures, both colored and grisaille, are often emblematic combinations of pictures and texts that further elucidate his response to the life of his time.

NOTES

1. Cornelis de Bie, writing in 1661 was the only early writer to provide commentary on Adriaen van de Venne (De Bie 1661, 234–36). For further biographical details, see M. Royalton-Kisch in *Dictionary of Art* 1996, 32:230–32.

2. Royalton-Kisch 1988.

[75]

Allegory of Poverty ("They are feeble legs that must carry poverty"), c. 1635

Inscriptions: on banderole at center and right foreground, *'t Sijn ellendige beenen die Armoe moete draege* (They are feeble legs that must carry poverty)

Oil on panel, 54.5 × 42.2 cm (21 7/16 × 16 5/8 in.)

Allen Memorial Art Museum, Oberlin College, Ohio, Mrs. F. F. Prentiss Fund, 1960, 60.94

References: Franken 1878, 56, no. 28 or 29 (incorrectly described as grisaille: "Illustration d'un proverbe. Grisaille. Musée de Gotha"); Schneider 1883, no. 228; Aldenhoven 1890, 28, no. 228; Wurzbach 1906–11, 2 (1910):759; Bol 1958, 131; Bernhard 1965, 130; Stechow 1967, 155, fig. 59; Nash 1972, fig. 79; Plokker 1984, 211–12 and n. 5 (Rotterdam grisaille version); Sutton 1986, 212; Wieseman n.d.

Adriaen van de Venne was responsible for some of the most remarkable images ever made of the homeless and destitute. Human ruins frequently appear in his paintings and prints: impoverished beggars, cripples, or wretched homeless folk, whose misshapen bodies and tattered garments reveal how profoundly adversity of circumstance can alter and transform the physical self. In the wake of the Eighty Years' War, poverty remained a grim reality in Europe, even within the prosperous Dutch Republic, whose cities outlawed itinerant and able-bodied street beggars while making municipal charity available to the infirm, the elderly, and others classified as the "deserving poor" (*rechten armer*).[1] The family in Van de Venne's painting would therefore have been regarded with wariness, if not outright disdain, by citizens comfortably connected to society by work and by permanent abodes such as the rustic cottage at the far right, where two men appear in conversation.

Above the low horizon rises the bizarre silhouette of a beggar, able-bodied but blind, being led by a white dog on a chain. He carries on his back an old woman, who in turn carries a child on hers. Fused into a single ragged shape, larger at the top, these tightly interlocked figures give compelling visual form to the heavy burden imposed by poverty. As the child squalls miserably at the top, the old woman clutches a bowl for alms and anxiously shakes a beggar's clapper (*Lazarusklep*) to attract donations. Beside the blind man, whose trousers are frayed through at the knees and whose wooden shoes are stuffed

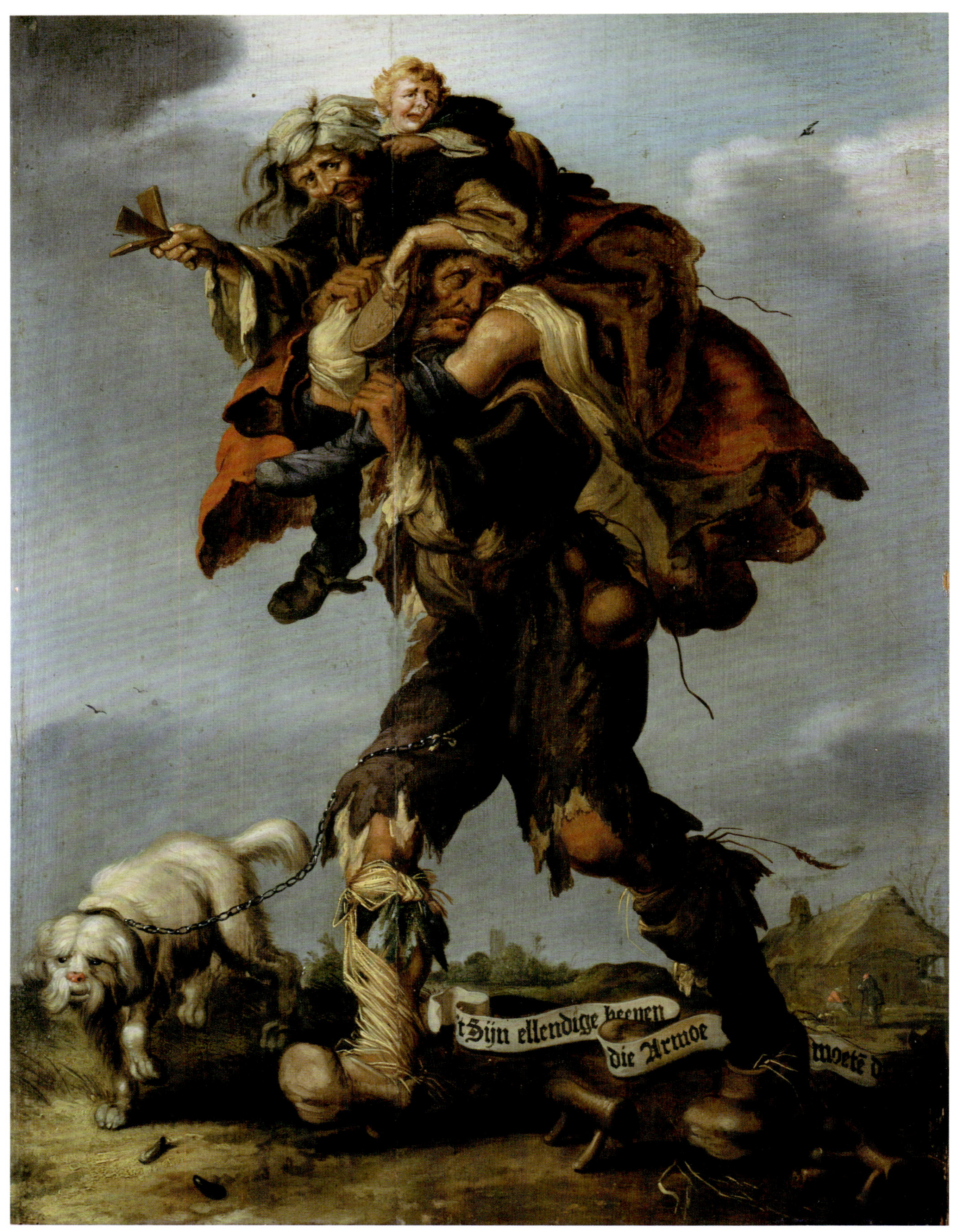
't Zijn ellendige beenen
die Armoe

with straw, are a pair of discarded hand cleats, used by the lame to help propel themselves along the ground.[2] Between the man's striding legs, which frame a view of a distant village, a lettered scroll unfurls to display the motto: "'t Sijn ellendige beenen die Armoe moete draege" (They are feeble legs that must carry poverty).

While Van de Venne has defined the condition of poverty with great specificity, he avoids sentimentality, approaching his subject with mordant humor. As in the popular emblem books of this period, his juxtaposition of image and text encourages the viewer/reader to contemplate the relationship between the two in order to extract a morsel of homey wisdom spiced with wit. The ironic aspect of Van de Venne's painting would have been obvious to seventeenth-century viewers who saw it beside its original companion piece, *Allegory of Wealth* (Fig. 154; location unknown).[3] In the pendant, an elegant, dandyish young man carries on his back a fashionable young lady who spills wine and carelessly scatters gold coins. Here the background dwelling becomes a castle, while the ground is strewn with the kind of party and gaming equipment used by the wealthy: a mask, balls, and a badminton racket. The banderole comments amusingly on the idea that being rich is a burden that only the strong can carry: "Het sijn stercke beene die Weelde konne drage" (They are strong legs that can carry wealth).[4]

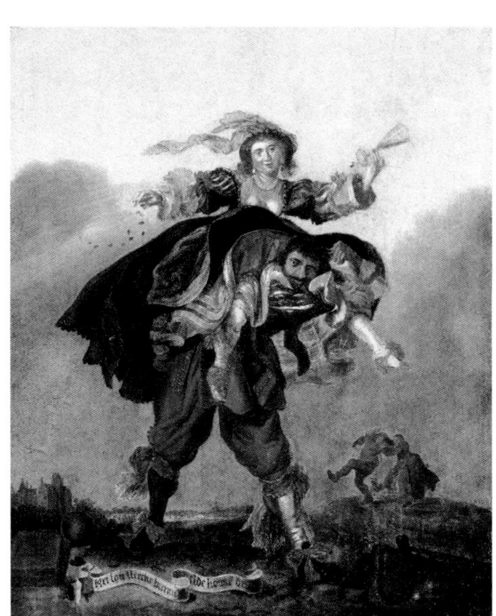

Fig. 154. Adriaen van de Venne, *Allegory of Wealth* ("They are strong legs that can carry wealth"), c. 1635, oil on panel, location unknown

NOTES

1. In the Dutch provinces, public almshouses were established to offer assistance to those unable to care for themselves, but such aid was restricted to town residents deemed deserving of help. Stringent ordinances prohibited able-bodied vagrants from being accommodated in charitable guesthouses for more than three days. For discussion of Dutch poor laws and municipal charitable practices, see Muller 1985, esp. 72–89.

2. M. Wieseman (n.d., n. 3) points out that the same cripples' cleats appear in Pieter Bruegel the Elder's *Battle between Carnival and Lent* (Kunsthistorisches Museum, Vienna) and *Crippled Beggars* (Musée du Louvre, Paris).

3. Both *Allegory of Poverty* and *Allegory of Wealth* were formerly in the collection of the dukes of Saxe-Coburg-Gotha and were on view at Schloss Friedenstein, Gotha, in 1885 and 1890 (Aldenhoven 1890, nos. 227 and 228). *Allegory of Wealth* (identified as formerly Aldenhoven 1890, no. 227) was sold at Christie's, New York, 1 November 1989, no. 67. For discussion of copies after both compositions, see Stechow 1967, 55; Plokker 1984, 212 n. 7, and 215–16 n. 3; and Wieseman n.d., n. 4. Another version of the Oberlin composition, rendered in grisaille rather than color, is in the Museum Boijmans Van Beuningen, Rotterdam (panel, 60 × 92 cm, no. 2194); the location of its pendant is unknown.

4. A version of *Allegory of Wealth* was engraved for Cats's popular book *Spiegel van den ouden ende nieuwen tijdt* (Mirror of the old and the new time), The Hague, 1632 (repr. Plokker 1984, 215, fig. 87a). Van de Venne also painted colored rich/poor pendants entitled respectively *Armoe soeckt list* (Poverty leads to cunning) and *Rijkdom soecht weelde* (Wealth leads to luxury), now in a private collection (repr. Bol 1989, 86–87, figs. 76 and 77).

CORNELIS VISSCHER
1629–58

Little is known about Cornelis Visscher's life, but this virtuoso printmaker, who often made etchings and engravings after works by other artists, was probably born in Haarlem. There he studied with Pieter Soutman (c. 1580–1657), who was among the artists hired to make reproductive prints after Rubens's designs in Antwerp. By mid-century, Visscher was serving in a similar capacity for his teacher, for whom he engraved historical portraits that Soutman designed and published. In 1653 Visscher became a member of the Haarlem artists' guild, but in 1655 he moved to Amsterdam, where he spent the rest of his short life (he died at the age of twenty-eight). A prolific printmaker and draftsman, Visscher can be credited with some two hundred engravings, primarily portraits and genre scenes of his own design (many with inscriptions) and numerous chalk drawings on vellum that include both portraits and scenes from everyday life.[1] Although Visscher's works are not well known today, except to specialists, his prints were often copied during and after his own time, and he was so greatly admired in the eighteenth century that both the historian Arnold Houbraken and the print publisher Pierre-François Basan called him the ideal model for young apprentices to follow.[2]

NOTES

1. Biographical information on Cornelis Visscher is based on Waller 1974, 17, and on E. de Jongh in Amsterdam 1997, 318–19.

2. Houbraken 1718–21, 3 (1721):77, and Basan 1767, 2:535. Cited in Amsterdam 1997, 320 nn. 4 and 5.

[76]
Rat-Catcher, 1655

Inscriptions: upper right on paper attached to wall, *C. Visscher inv et sculp. 1655* (designed and engraved by C. Visscher)

Below print,
Fele fugas mures! magnis si furibus arces exiguos fures, furor est. me respice vilis si modo numus adest mures felesque fugabo. Clement de Jonghe excudit (You drive rats away with a cat. It is folly to use big blackguards to try to keep little blackguards at a distance. Behold my cheap wares; if there's money I'll drive off both rats and cats. Published by Clement de Jongh)[1]

Engraving, 377 × 318 mm (14 13/16 × 12 1/2 in.); state iv/vi

Courtesy of the Fogg Art Museum, Harvard University Art Museums, Cambridge, Massachusetts, Gift of William Gray from the Collection of Francis Calley Gray, G3935

References: Wurzbach 1906–11, 2 (1910):796; Lawrence/New Haven/Austin 1983–84, 76–78, no. 14; Hollstein 40 (1992):59–62, no. 50; Amsterdam 1997, 318–20. Amsterdam/London 2000–2001, 123, fig. b.

The beggars and rat-catchers who appear in Dutch art often present a similarly bizarre or disheveled appearance (Cat. 75) that can make both appear to be society's rejects. Rat-catchers, however, were self-employed professionals whose door-to-door visits offered a paid service that was vital during a period in which vermin were ubiquitous.[2] The ratsbane or arsenic used by exterminators was a controlled substance, sold only to a limited number of people who

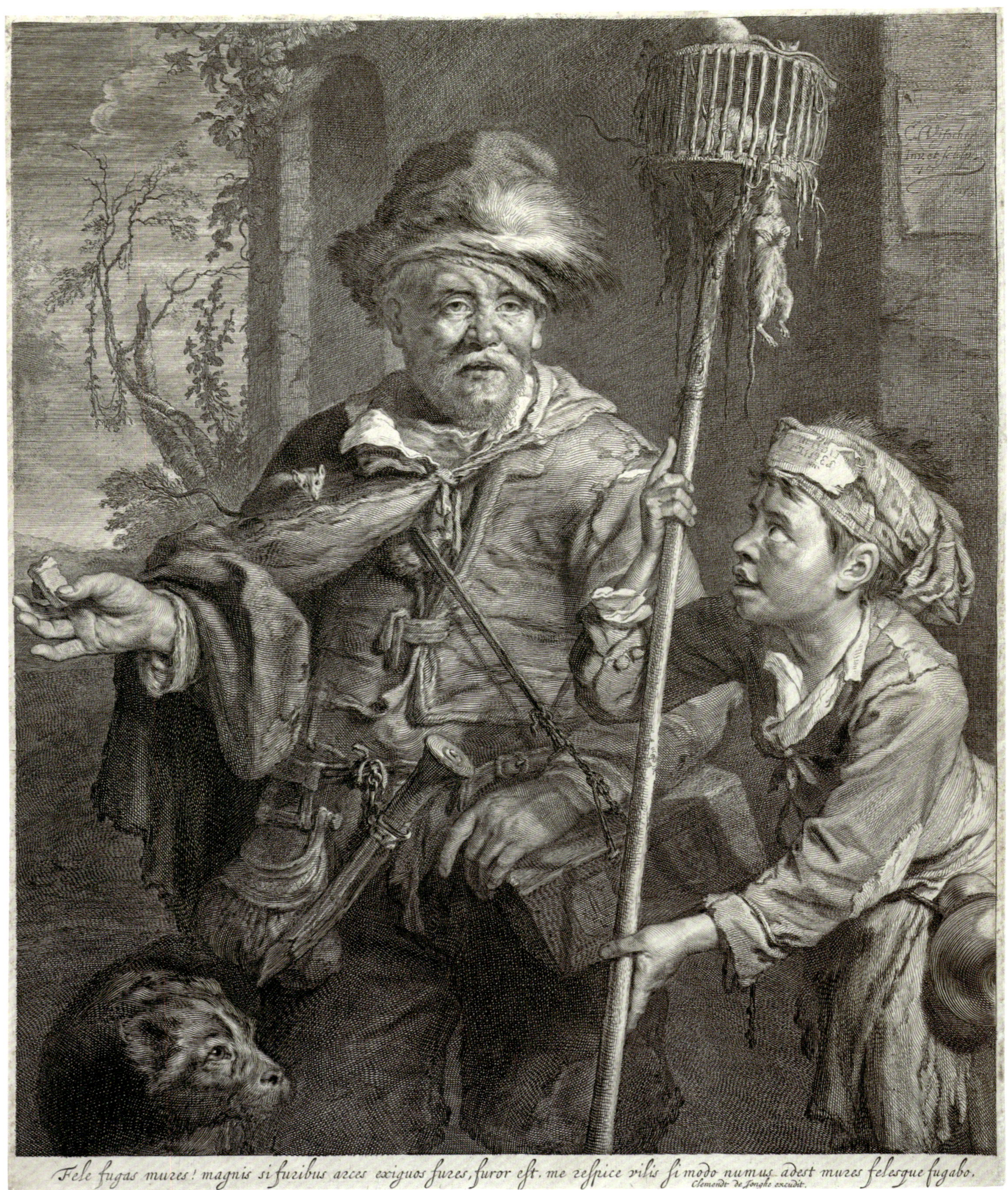
Fele fugas mures! magnis si furibus arces exiguos fures, furor est. me respice vilis si modo numus adest mures felesque fugabo.
Clemendt de Jonghe excudit.

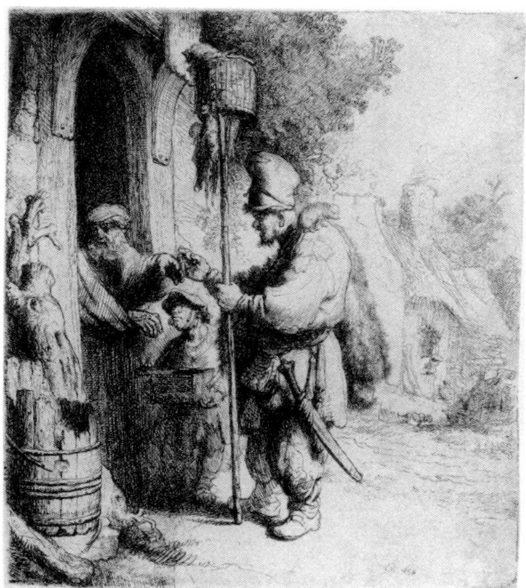

Fig. 155. Rembrandt, *The Ratcatcher*, 1632, etching and burin, Museum of Fine Arts, Boston

needed city permits to buy or sell it.[3] The wooden box carried by the rat-catcher in this print displays the coats of arms of Haarlem and Amsterdam, the two cities in which Cornelis Visscher was active. Such a box probably would have contained either rat poison or perhaps the small domesticated ferrets used to kill rats.[4] Accompanied by his dog, the rat-catcher has a pointed spade at his belt that was used to dig into burrows of rats' nests.[5] He displays a tablet of poison to the viewer, as his assistant holds up a long pole topped by a basket from which several dead rats hang. Live vermin on top of it and within it provide a before-and-after demonstration of the treatment's effectiveness.

The same contrast of dead and living is seen at the left background, where dead and living trees are intertwined above the rat-catcher's extended hand, while the anonymous building behind the figures appears to have fallen partly into ruin.[6] The rat-catcher's fur hat and fine costume also show the effects of time and wear, as does the man himself, who is vigorous but clearly elderly in comparison to his lively young assistant. Although Visscher presents a more dignified interpretation of the subject, his print must have been partly inspired by Rembrandt's well-known etching *The Ratcatcher* of 1632 (Fig. 155), in which a more outlandish, tattered figure offers his wares at a doorway, beside which is a ruined barrel and a dead tree. Visscher probably borrowed from Rembrandt an engaging detail common to both prints: the tamed rat that rides like a trusting mascot at the shoulder of both exterminators.

NOTES

1. Translation by E. de Jongh in Amsterdam 1997, 320 n. 9.

2. Epidemics of the plague were common in this period, but its origin in the fleas carried by rats was not yet known, even though domestic creatures such as cats, dogs, and pigs were slaughtered during plague years—including the year 1655, the date of Visscher's print. The text included in his print ("I'll drive off rats and cats ...") may refer to this extensive extermination of small animals during plague outbreaks (Amsterdam 1997, 320 n. 9).

3. Amsterdam 1997, 319–20.

4. At least two late nineteenth-century accounts of the profession of rat catching and its equipment were written in England: Barkley 1896 and Matthews 1898, cited by L. Stone-Ferrier in Lawrence/New Haven/Austin 1983–84, 78 nn. 2 and 3. On the use of ferrets, see Matthews 1898, 17.

5. Barkley 1896, 23.

6. L. Stone-Ferrier compares this section of the print to Roemer Visscher's emblem (in *Sinnepoppen*, 1614) that juxtaposes dead and living trees under the motto "Keus baert angst" (Choice causes worry). She suggests that the emblem's cautionary message about choosing wisely in life between flourishing and barren alternatives may relate to a warning in this print to be cautious about dealing with tradesmen such as the rat catcher. Lawrence/New Haven/Austin 1983–84, 76, figs. 10 and 78.

JAN SAENREDAM,
AFTER ABRAHAM BLOEMAERT

[77]

Vanitas, c. 1605

Inscriptions: on the crumpled piece of paper in chancery cursive calligraphy, *Hospes an non huc? / Nài, curru lydio. / Joan. Saenredam sculp. Robbertus de Baudous. Excudebat. Ablommaert Pinx.* (A guest to this place, no? Yes, on the funeral [Lydian] chariot. Engraved by Jan Saenredam, published by Robertus de Baudous, painted by A. Bloemaert)

Surrounding the image, *FORTE LOCUS DABITUR CONTRA OMNIA CAETERA TUTUS; NULLA SED ARX TUTA EST MORTIS AB IMPERIO. SIVE SUMUS SCEPTRO INSIGNES, SIVE ARVA LIGONE PERFODIMUS, ΘΑΝÁΤΩ, ΠÁΝΤ ЄΣ ΟΦЄΙΛÓΜЄΘΑ, / R. lubbaeus* At the bottom, (*ἕκαστοι*) *ΘΝΑΤÀ ΜЄΜΝÁΣΘΩ ΠЄΡΙΣΤЄ́ΛΛΩΝ ΜЄ́ΛΗ: Pindarus* (A place safe from all other things may be given to us; but no fortress is safe from the reign of death; whether we are famous by merit of the scepter or plow the earth with the hoe, all of us must pay death its due.—R. Lubbaeus. Each should remember that he stretches out mortal limbs—Pindar)[1]

Engraving, 374 × 319 mm (14¾ × 12 9/16 in.) (platemark), 375 × 320 mm (14¾ × 12⅝ in.) (sheet), state ii/ii

Museum of Fine Arts, Boston, Harvey D. Parker Collection, P7354

References: Bartsch 1803–21, 3:30; Van der Blom 1970, 41; Braunschweig 1978, 173; Berlin 1979, no. 87; Münster/Baden-Baden 1979–80, 194; Hollstein 23 (1980):83, no. 110; Bartsch (Illustrated) 4 (1980):339; De Meyere 1981, 174; Naumann 1981, 1: fig. 134; Bergamo 1981, 66, repr.; Roethlisberger 1991, 20–23; Roethlisberger 1993, 1:101–3, no. 55; 2: fig. 101; Worthen 1993, 282–97, fig. 193; Amsterdam 1993–94a, 550–51, no. 221.2.

As M. Roethlisberger has discussed, it is likely that Saenredam's intricate engraving reproduces a lost painting by Abraham Bloemaert that Karel Van Mander admiringly cited in 1604 as being in the collection of their mutual friend Jacques Razet: "Skull with other increments, very well executed and colored."[2] Roethlisberger cites a Bloemaert panel that was sold in several late eighteenth-century sales, where it was described as if it had a painted grisaille frame, and he suggests that Van Mander's comment may have been sparked by a striking chromatic contrast in the painting between a colored center and a monochromatic frame.[3]

In most prints, everything is "en grisaille," so to speak, unless the image has been printed in color or coloring has been added subsequently.[4] Yet this engraving also displays an effective contrast between the central image and frame, which consists of a complexly figured, outer field with a narrower inner zone that contains Greek and Latin inscriptions on all sides. These remind the viewer, in the words of Richard Lubbaeus (rector of the Latin School at Bergen op Zoom), that no fortress is safe from the reign of death and that those who rule with the scepter and those who plow the earth with a hoe must both give death its due.[5] At left and right in the outer frame are bundles of picks and shovels for digging graves, along with carpenters' tools for making coffins and trumpets and flaming torches as allusions to the brevity of fame, or possibly to the Last Judgment. At the top, flanked by flaming oil lamps and resting on the long carrying bars and ropes used to lower it into the grave, is a coffin covered by a cloth that displays three coats of arms. The one in the center is that of the St. Luke's guild of artists; a crossed pen and burin have been added,

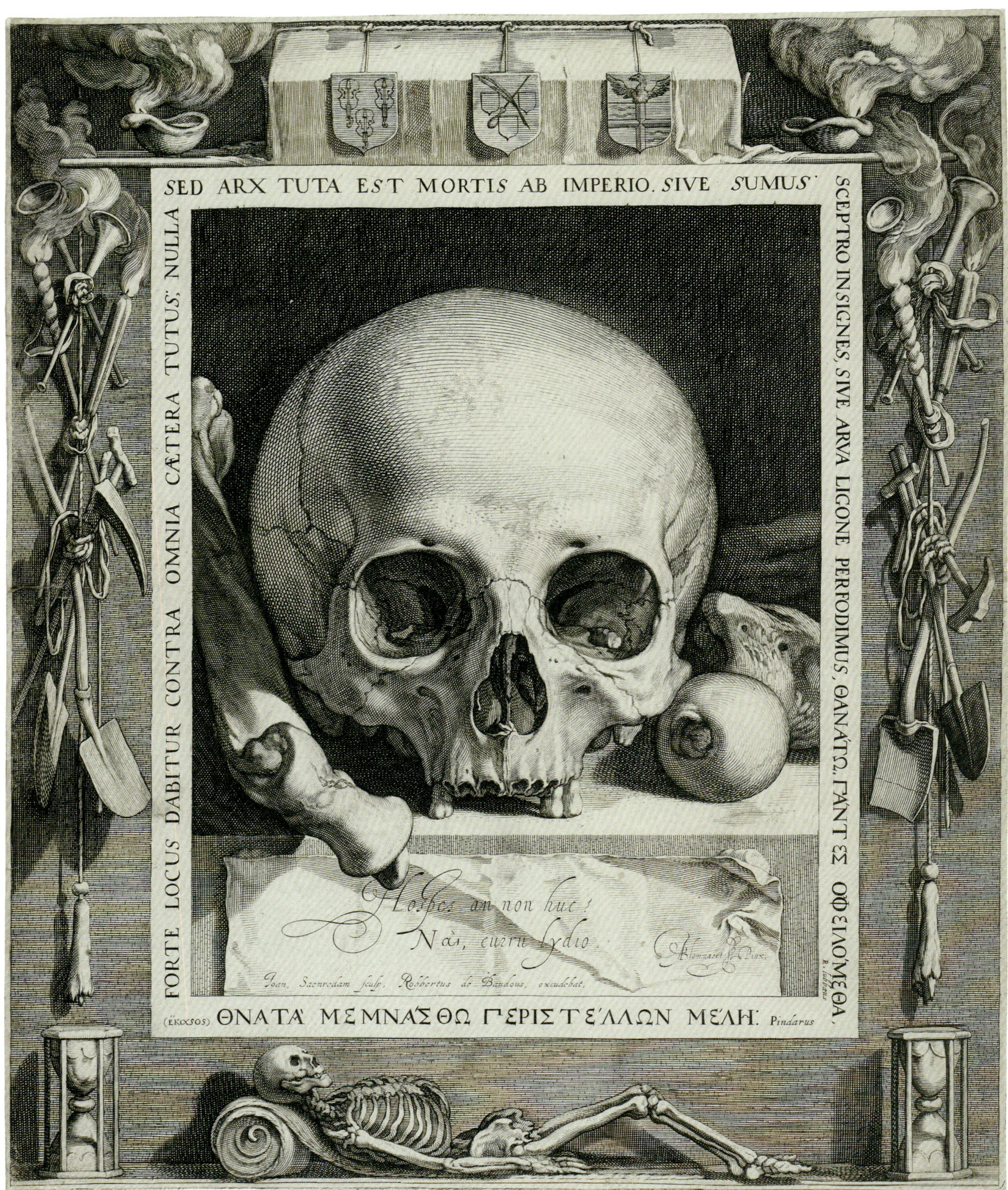
SED ARX TUTA EST MORTIS AB IMPERIO. SIVE SUMUS
SCEPTRO INSIGNES, SIVE ARVA LIGONE PERFODIMUS, ΘΑΝΑΤΩ ΠΑΝΤΕΣ ΟΦΕΙΛΟΜΕΘΑ.
FORTE LOCUS DABITUR CONTRA OMNIA CÆTERA TUTUS; NULLA
ΘΝΑΤΑ ΜΕΜΝΑΣΘΩ ΠΕΡΙΣΤΕΛΛΩΝ ΜΕΛΗ. Pindarus

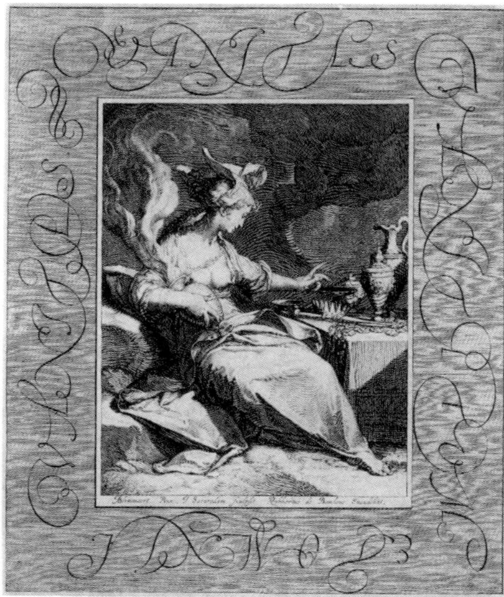

Fig. 156. Jan Saenredam after Abraham Bloemaert, *Vanitas*, c. 1605, engraving, Rijksprentenkabinet, Rijksmuseum, Amsterdam

suggesting that the deceased is an engraver and that the print as a whole may be understood as a vanitas image that relates specifically to art.[6] In the bottom section of the outer frame, placed between two hourglasses, is a reclining skeleton, whose elevated knees and head create an eerily animated effect. Here the adjacent inscription, from Pindar, reads: "Each should remember that he stretches out mortal limbs."

The extraordinary visual power of the central image of a skull, humerus, and thighbone resting on a slab is generated partly by scale contrasts with the outer frame, which make these human remain appear to loom dramatically in their confined space. Indeed, the image also functions as a sophisticated trompe l'oeil, since the bone at left appears to project into the viewer's world, while casting its long shadow onto the crumpled paper attached to the slab within the picture space. Here, graceful cursive calligraphy entreats the viewer: "Won't you be a guest in this place?" (i.e., join the deceased in death), below which is the affirmative answer: "Yes, I will, but on the Lydian chariot," meaning the slow, funeral chariot.[7] The starkly frontal position of the skull creates an intense confrontation with the viewer, who must gaze directly into its cavernous eye sockets. Saenredam's mastery of lighting effects is nowhere more evident than in this remarkable image, in which shifts in the direction and density of his hatchings bring out the contrast between solids and voids, emphasizing how death leaves behind only the empty shell of the living person.

According to A. N. Worthen, who has discovered the preparatory drawing for this engraving,[8] another vanitas print by Jan Saenredam after Bloemaert should be considered its companion piece. Of almost identical size it also incorporates a frame, in this case decorated with sweeping calligraphic inscriptions ("Vanitas Vanitatum et Omnia Vanitas," or "Vanity of vanities, all is vanity"; Fig. 156).[9] Placing the two prints side by side makes the death's head loom even larger, for the pendant depicts a graceful, full-length female figure who points to objects denoting power and wealth on the table beside her, as smoke, rising from the urn she holds, forms dark clouds above and behind her.

NOTES

1. Inscriptions on this print are transcribed and translated in Roethlisberger 1993, 1:102, Worthen 1993, 286–87, and Amsterdam 1993–94a, 550.

2. Van Mander/Miedema 1994–99, 1 (1994):449, fol. 296v, lines 42–45, cited in Roethlisberger 1993, 1:101.

3. According to Roethlisberger, there is evidence that this panel corresponded closely in size to the central portion of Saenredam's print, as indicated in Amsterdam sales catalogues of 1788 (25.4 × 20.3 cm), 1797 (26.7 × 20.3 cm), and 1800 (25.4 × 21.6 cm)—the second and third of which mention that it had a vanitas frame (Roethlisberger 1993, 1:101). He also discusses and illustrates a canvas (45.4 × 32.2 cm, art trade, Valls, London, 1990) that has a similar but not identical composition and includes the same Latin inscription found in the print, but does not have a frame. Roethlisberger 1993, 1:105, no. 57; 2: fig. 105.

4. The 2002 exhibition at the Baltimore Museum of Art curated by S. Dackerman provides an excellent survey of this practice in northern Renaissance and baroque prints. See Baltimore 2002.

5. On the translation and interpretation of the print's inscriptions and their relationship to its imagery, see Roethlisberger 1993, 1:102 and Worthen 1993, 286–87.

6. Roethlisberger notes that the escutcheon of the St. Luke's guild was displayed when the guild buried impoverished artists and that the unidentified shields at left and right may either refer to the deceased's parents or may allude respectively to music (three inverted violins) and to art (an eagle as the bird of Apollo). Roethlisberger 1993, 1:102.

7. In this context, Roethlisberger cites Erasmus's *Adagia* (no. 2277), which specifies that Lydian chariots were slower in races than Greek ones. Roethlisberger 1993, 1:103.

8. Worthen 1993, 289 fig. 193, British Library, London, Ms. dept. Add. 5259, no. 204.

9. Hollstein 23 (1980):85, no. 112; Worthen 1993, 264, repr., and 286.

N. L. PESCHIER

active 1659–61

Nothing is known about Peschier beyond the fact that six signed and dated paintings, all of superb quality, are known from the period between 1659 and 1661.[1] Indeed, even his nationality has been disputed, for although his vanitas still lifes can be related to paintings by Leiden artists such as David Bailly (q.v.), neither the Leiden municipal archives nor the records of the town's St. Luke's guild reveal any trace of him.[2] Peschier's rather broad technique and the French inscriptions that sometimes appear in his paintings have suggested to certain scholars that he may have been either a French artist working in the Netherlands or a Dutch artist active in France.[3]

NOTES

1. Victoria and Albert Museum, London (66.6 × 88.8 cm, signed and dated 1659); Rijksmuseum, Amsterdam (57 × 70 cm, signed and dated 1660); Montreal Museum of Art (70 × 89 cm, signed and dated 1660); collection Fritz Lugt, Institut Néerlandais, Paris (89.3 × 103.5 cm, signed and dated 1661). All four are illustrated in Sutton 1990. Another signed and dated vanitas of 1661 that was in the art trade in 1965 (Brod, London, 89.5 × 103.5 cm) includes a skull, dead birds, prints, a document, and a tin lamp. Photo RKD, The Hague.

2. P. Sutton reports that this search was undertaken in 1980 by P. M. J. de Baer. Sutton 1990, 233.

3. Sutton 1990, 233, and Faré 1962, 1:111.

[78]

Vanitas, 1661

Inscriptions: lower left, *N vs Le Peschier Fecit 1661*

Oil on canvas, 82 × 103.5 cm (31½ × 40 in.)

Philadelphia Museum of Art, The Henry P. McIlhenny Collection in Memory of Frances P. McIlhenny, 1986-26-287

References: Sutton 1990, 233–37.

In still life, whose dominant motifs are inanimate, the artist may express the notion of time both by the choice of motifs and by their arrangement. Accordingly, Peschier has grouped his collection of diverse, overlapping objects at the edge of a table, using a powerfully irregular design that makes them seem precariously poised, verging on imbalance. This effect is intensified by the fact that the tabletop is illuminated at the left and covered by a dark cloth at the right, while modulations

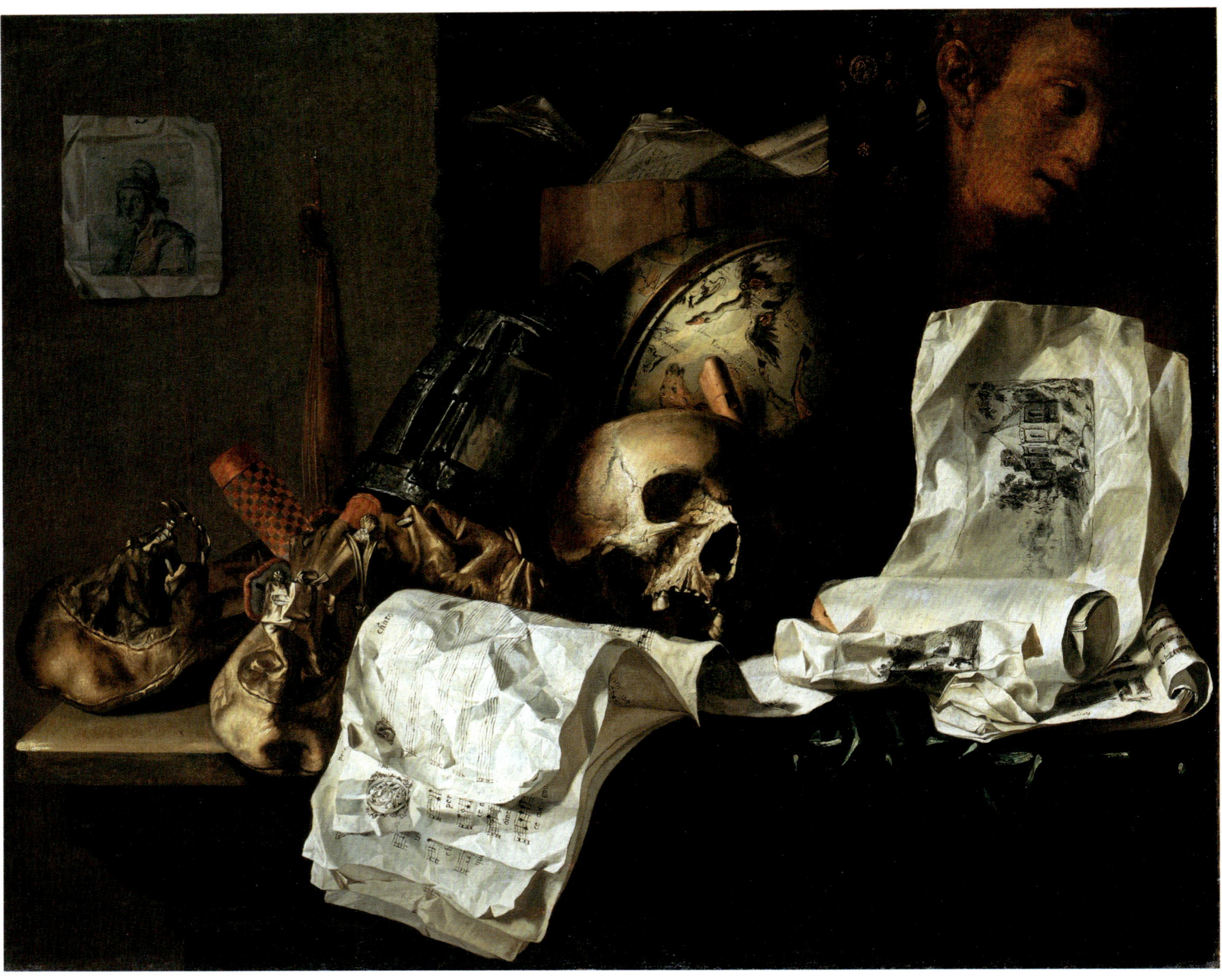

in lighting brighten the crumpled pages in the foreground and cast other parts of the scene into shadow. The human skull in the center—half-lighted, half-shadowed—identifies this painting as the popular subject type to which the Dutch applied the term vanitas. Such images encouraged meditation on temporality and the evanescence of earthly life as described in Ecclesiastes 1:2: "Vanity of vanities, saith the Preacher, vanity of vanities; all is vanity." Variations on this theme appear in two other works in this catalogue (Cats. 77 and 79), which include some of the same motifs.

In the foreground of Peschier's painting, under the jaw of the skull and illusionistically overlapping the table edge, is a worn book of music, which, like the recorder behind the skull and the violin on the wall at the left, embodies evanescence: music as an art of fading sounds. At the right is an equally well-thumbed collection of prints. The one at the top, clearly visible, displays a landscape with a church (Fig. 157) from part two of the 1616 series entitled *Amoenissimae aliquot regiunculae et / antiquorum monumentorum ruinae* … (Various most pleasant landscapes and ruins of ancient monuments) by Jan van de Velde II (Cat. 3). Other papers, probably documents, have been stuffed into the cylindrical container in the background, before which is a celestial globe whose curving shape repeats that of the skull.[1] While terrestrial globes in Dutch paintings often symbolize worldliness, celestial ones can suggest the idea of heaven. Here the visible figures of the constellations also encourage the viewer to see this object as another locus of artistic representation, along with the pen and wash drawing of a peasant, tacked to the wall at the upper left, and the terra-cotta bust of a young man at the upper right, whose head is inclined, poignantly, at exactly the same angle as the skull.[2] A large, extinguished oil lantern and two worn money bags at the left complete this grouping of objects, which may also have been intended to refer to the various kinds of human existence: the life of wealth and power (*vita practica*, indicated by the money bags and documents), the life of contemplation (*vita contemplativa*, sug-

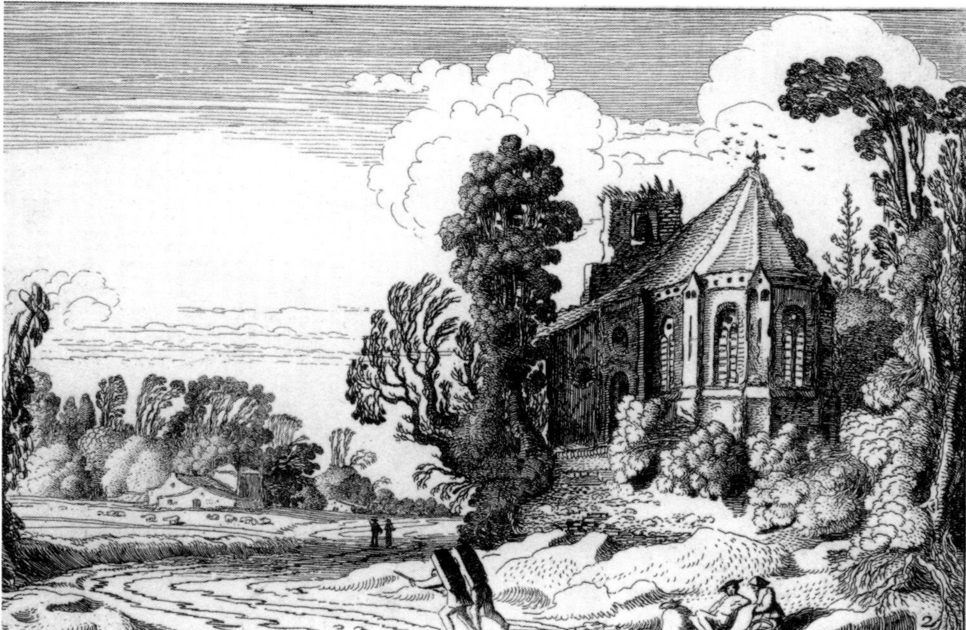

Fig. 157. Jan van de Velde II, *Landscape with Church*, 1616, etching from *Amoenissimae aliquot regiunculae*, part 2, 1616, Museum of Fine Arts, Boston

gested by the globe and other works of art), and the life of pleasure (*vita voluptaria*, commonly symbolized by musical instruments).[3]

It should be noted that vanitas still lifes are always oxymorons, in a sense, because they present objects that symbolize transience while giving them permanence through their painted representation. In images such as Peschier's that incorporate depictions of other works of art, the observer confronts an interpretive quandary. Are we to look to art as a means of transcending the limitations of earthly life or to recognize that artists and their works are also mortal?

NOTES

1. The decorated black tube to the right of the globe may be a carrying case for rolled documents or, as Sutton proposes with hesitation, a baton. Sutton 1990, 233.

2. As Sutton has pointed out, the globe clearly displays several of the constellations of the Northern Hemisphere—Lyrae, Cygnus, and Pegasus—while the drawing is in the style of the Haarlem artists Adriaen van Ostade (1610–85) and Cornelis Dusart (1660–1704); Sutton 1990, 233.

3. Based upon Hadrianus Junius's sixteenth-century commentary on the Judgment of Paris, I. Bergström used these three categories to interpret the objects in Dutch vanitas still lifes. Bergström 1956, 154 and 307 n. 2; cited in Sutton 1990, 234 and 237 n. 14.

DAVID BAILLY
1584–1657

Son of a Flemish fencing master who had emigrated to Leiden, David Bailly studied portraiture in Amsterdam with Cornelis van der Voort (1576–1624), after which he embarked on a period of travel to Germany and Italy, visiting Hamburg, Venice, and Rome, as well as several German courts on his way home.[1] By 1613 he was back in Leiden, where he produced portrait paintings and drawings that include representations of professors and students at the University of Leiden and of fellow artists such as Jan Pynas (1581/82–1631) and Crispijn van de Passe the Younger (c. 1597–c. 1670). In 1642, at the age of fifty-eight, he married Agneta van Swanenburgh, daughter of a Leiden notary, and in 1648 helped found the Leiden St. Luke's guild. He became dean of the guild in 1649.

Equally gifted as a portraitist and still-life painter, Bailly contributed substantially to the popularity of vanitas subjects in Leiden by developing a new pictorial type fusing portraiture with complex arrangements of objects intended to evoke transience and temporality. The most elaborate of his vanitas portraits is *Self-Portrait with Vanitas Still Life*, signed and dated 1651, in the Stedelijk Museum "De Lakenhal," Leiden (Fig. 158). Among his pupils were his nephews, vanitas still-life painters Harmen (1612–after 1655) and Pieter van Steenwijck (c. 1615–after 1654).

NOTE

1. On Bailly's life and art, see Bruyn 1951; Popper-Voskuil 1973; and J. Bruyn's essay in *Dictionary of Art* 1996, 3:77–78.

[79]

Vanitas Still Life with Portrait, c. 1650

Inscriptions: signed in the middle on the edge of the book, ... *de gijn / .. CXXIX*

Oil on canvas, 94.6 × 116.2 cm (37¼ × 45¾ in.)

Courtesy of the Herbert F. Johnson Museum of Art, Cornell University, Ithaca, New York, Gift of Mr. and Mrs. Louis V. Keeler, Class of 1911, by exchange, 86.006

References: Leiden 1970, 11–13, no. 13 (as Jacques de Gheyn III); Albany/Buffalo/Syracuse/Ithaca/Rochester/Utica 1991, 50–53, no. 4 (as David Bailly); Johnson Museum Handbook 1998, 118 (as Bailly); Erickson 2000, 318–19, 320, fig. 109 (as Bailly).

This complex still life/portrait can be classified among what the Dutch called vanitas subjects: images that encourage meditation on the transience of human life and the evanescence of worldly possessions and concerns (see Cats. 77 and 78). F. W. Robinson has pointed out that this painting, once attributed to Jacques de Gheyn III (c. 1595–1641), appears rather to be the work of David Bailly, whose more elaborate *Self-Portrait with Vanitas Still Life* of 1651 is very similar in size (89.5 × 122 cm), format, concept, and style (Fig. 158).[1] Both paintings feature a figure in half length who displays a painted portrait to the viewer and sits or stands beside a tabletop. And in both, the tabletop is covered with a profusion of diverse objects that evoke the notion of transience: watches, hourglasses, human skulls, fragile flowers, long-handled pipes, and burning candles or wicks (whose smoke dissipates in the air), along with wine glasses, books, and musical instruments (whose sounds inevitably fade into silence) as allusions to the ephemerality of worldly pleasure. Above the tables in both scenes float several gleaming soap bubbles. In the painting in Ithaca, the tiny reflection of the artist at his easel in the upper half of the hourglass—a motif that appears in other Dutch still lifes—serves as a kind of signature that comments on the artist's virtuosity, while also acknowledging that the

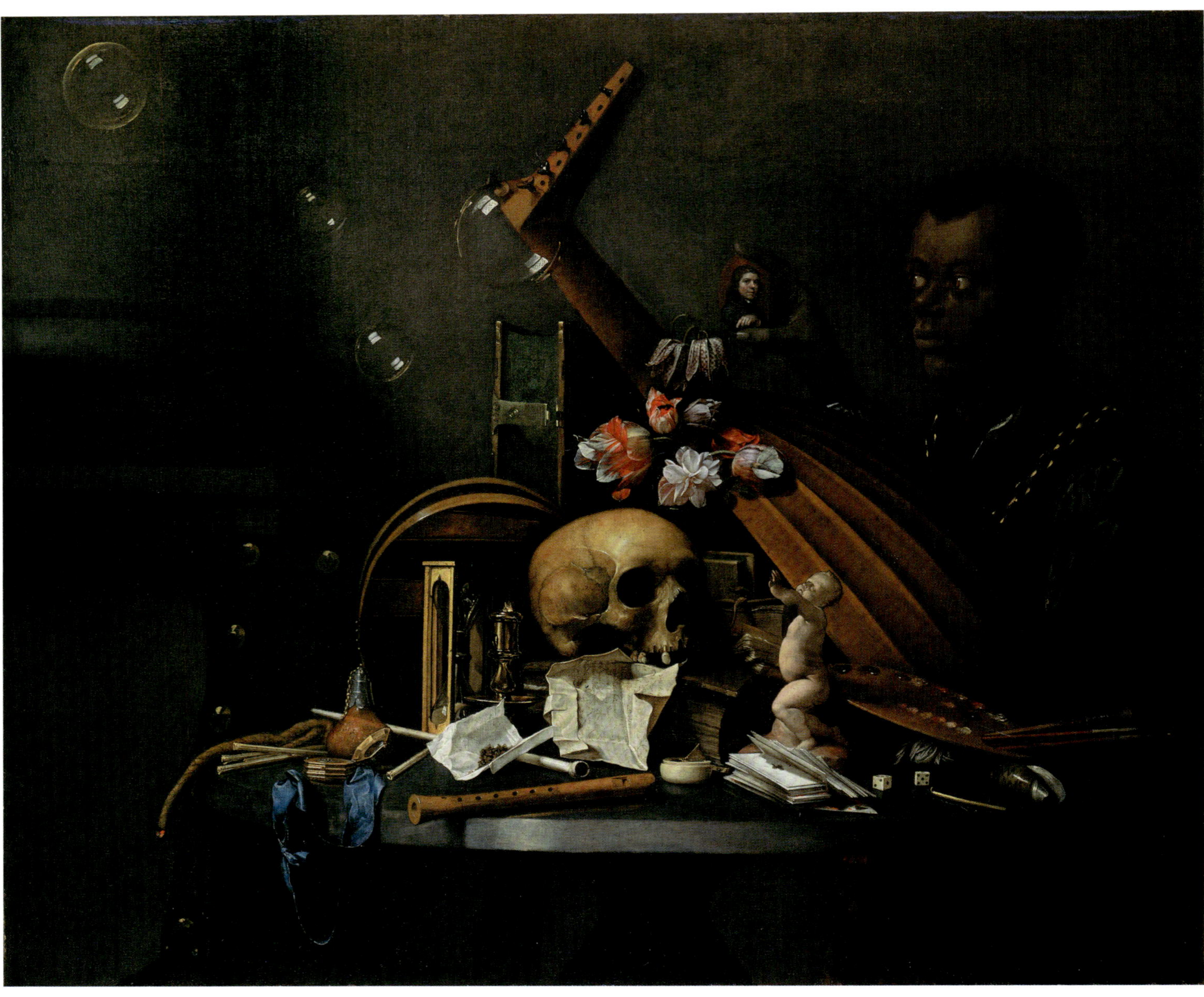

painter himself is part of the temporal process to which all living things are subject.[2]

In the painting in the Johnson Museum, the dark-skinned youth holds up a small portrait miniature of a man wearing a satin jacket and a gold chain, which in this context probably refers to a servant's loyalty to his master.[3] Such figures of servants or pages appear occasionally in elegant genre scenes or portraits, representing people of color who were brought to the Netherlands from Africa and the East and West Indies by the extensive Dutch trading fleet.[4] In medieval and Renaissance art, dark-skinned figures sometimes represented St. Maurice (Mauritius), the third-century Arabian knight from Thebes whose name was sometimes shortened to Maurus (meaning Moor or Negro in Latin).[5] In making this connection, M. L. Wurfbain has raised the intriguing possibility that the miniature displayed by this young man may portray Maurits Huygens (1595–1642), older brother of Constantijn Huygens and godson of Prince Maurits of Orange, whose portrait by Rembrandt (1632, Hamburger Kunsthalle) he finds very similar to the miniature in this painting.[6]

Vanitas still lifes usually make a point of showing the beauty and preciousness of things of this world to emphasize how easily the senses are enticed by them. This painting is no exception, for the pyramidal grouping of objects on the oval tabletop seems to invite the observer to reach for the deck of cards and the dice or to pick up the crumpled letter and try to read its illegible message. The artist has also juxtaposed or compared related kinds of objects such as the pocket watch with its blue ribbon at the left and the small round sundial in the center or the skull above it and the glossy tropical shell at the far right. The pear-shaped, metal-capped powder horn, seen beside the matches and smoldering rope at the left, is visually reiterated and revised in the elongated hourglass beside it. Such a high level of artistic virtuosity draws attention to the image itself as a crafted object whose success in capturing the transient physical world in paint shows how art can transcend the limitations of mortality.[7] As in Bailly's *Self-Portrait with a Vanitas Still Life*, this scene makes repeated references to art not only in its display of the portrait miniature but also in the palette and brushes on the table and the small sculpture of a lively putto, who raises his arm as if warding off the death's head before him.[8]

NOTES

1. Robinson in Johnson Museum Handbook 1998, 188, and correspondence of 2003, in which he noted that the files of the Johnson Museum at Cornell University also include mention of Pieter van Roerstraten (1629/30–1700) and Peter Sion (d. 1695) and that the photograph of this painting is filed in the RKD, The Hague, with reproductions of works attributed to David Bailly. An apparently false signature (*de gijn*) and date of 1629 are inscribed on the book in the center. According to the 1970 catalogue of the exhibition *IJdelheid der Ijdelheden* at the Lakenhal, Leiden, in which the painting was attributed to Jacques de Gheyn III, it can also be related to the works of Jacob Walscapelle (1644–1727), Hendrick Andriessen (1607–55), and Pieter van der Willigen (1635–94); Cf. Leiden 1970, 11.

2. C. Brusati has explored the use of reflected self-portraits in Dutch still-life painting in Brusati 1990–91.

3. Chains of honor, bestowed by rulers on subjects who had served them well, were worn as tokens of loyalty, as in Anthony van Dyck's *Self-Portrait with a Sunflower* (c. 1633, collection of the Duke of Westminister, Eaton Hall, Cheshire), in which the artist points to the chain that binds him to Charles I; and in Rembrandt's *Aristotle Contemplating the Bust of Homer* (1653, Metropolitan Museum of Art, New York, no. 61.198), in which the philosopher's gold chain, according to J. Held, represents the decoration bestowed on him by Alexander the Great (Held 1991, 46–55). M. D. Carroll has offered an alternative reading of the chain in this painting as an allusion to the Neoplatonic concept of the "golden chain of Homer," which symbolizes the divine order of the universe and the hierarchy of creation that allows man to ascend to the divine through art (Carroll 1984, 48–50).

4. Frans Hals's *Family Portrait in a Landscape* (c. 1648, Thyssen-Bornemisza Collection, Madrid, no. 124) includes a young black page, for example, as does Hendrik van den Burgh's *The Game of Cards* (c. 1660, The Detroit Institute of Arts, no. 29.2).

5. Bernen and Bernen 1973, 182. See, for example, Matthias Grünewald, *The Meeting of Sts. Erasmus and Maurice* (c. 1520–22, Alte Pinakothek, Munich, no. 1044).

6. M. Wurfbain in Leiden 1970, 12–13. Rembrandt's portrait of Maurits Huygens was painted as the companion piece to the portrait of his friend Jacques de Gheyn III, now in the Dulwich Art Gallery, London (no. 99). For discussion of both portraits and their sitters, see *Rembrandt Corpus* 2 (1986): nos. A56 and A57.

7. J. B. Hochstrasser convincingly analyzes allusions to time in relation to artists' craft or painting practice in "*Goede Dingen Willen Tijd Hebben*: Time as Meditation on Painting in Dutch Still Life of the seventeenth century," Heck and Lippincott 2002, 117–35. My thanks to Celeste Brusati for this reference, which reached me just as this volume was going to press.

8. As B. Barryte has pointed out, the inclusion of this sculptural motif intensifies the painting's self-referential emphasis on art, while the juxtaposition of an exuberant child with a death's head (an image originating in the fifteenth century) underlines the central vanitas theme of the piece. Barryte in Albany/Buffalo/Syracuse/Ithaca/Rochester/Utica 1991, 53 and 129 n. 15. See also Janson 1937.

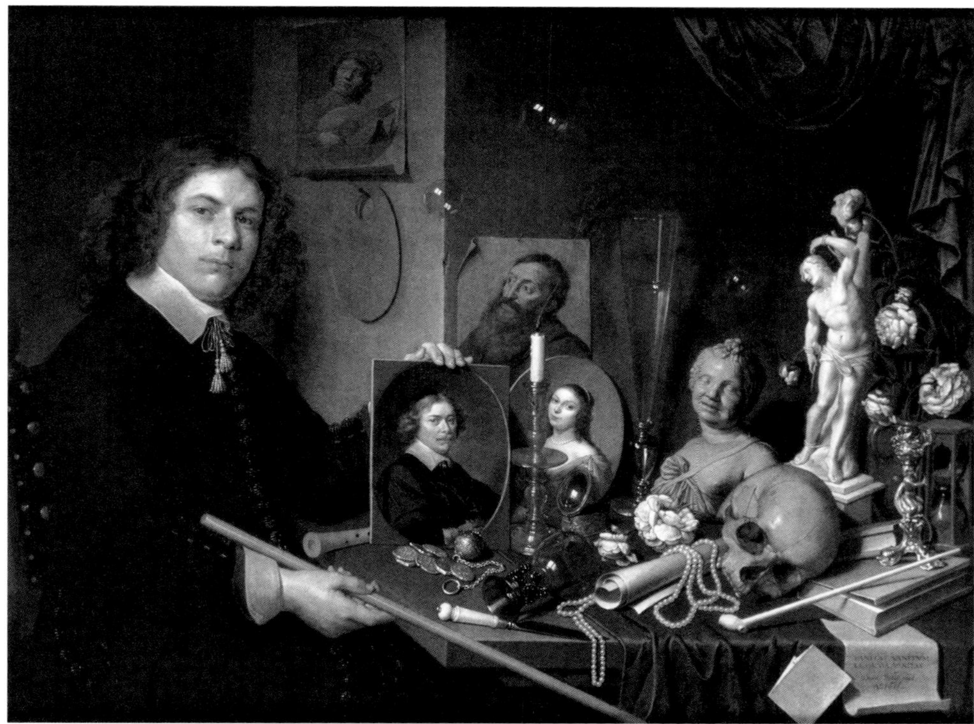

Fig. 158. David Bailly, *Self-Portrait with Vanitas Still Life*, 1651, oil on panel, Stedelijk Museum "De Lakenhal," Leiden

ABRAHAM VAN BEYEREN
1620/21–90

Van Beyeren was one of the finest of all Dutch still-life painters, yet little is known of his life, including the name of his teacher. Indeed, his art seems to have been largely ignored during his lifetime, since he was not included in Arnold Houbraken's fundamental lexicon of Netherlandish painters (*De groote schouburgh*), published in Amsterdam between 1718 and 1721. Sale records also reveal that his pictures fetched low prices, while records of payments demanded by tradesmen suggest that the artist suffered considerable financial hardship.[1]

It is possible that Van Beyeren's frequent moves from city to city were flights from creditors.[2] By 1639 he was living in Leiden, where he married Emerentia Staecke. In 1640 he joined the painters' guild in The Hague where his second marriage, to Anna van Queborn, was recorded in 1647. Through this marriage, he became a relative of Pieter de Putter (before 1600–1659), the fish painter whose work influenced Van Beyeren's monochrome fish still lifes of the 1640s. In 1656 the artist became one of the founding members of the new artists' confraternity in The Hague (Pictura), but by 15 October 1657 he had moved and was registered in the Delft guild. In 1663 he returned to The Hague and rejoined Pictura but from 1669 to 1674 is documented in Amsterdam. His membership in the Alkmaar guild was recorded in 1674. Between 1675 and 1677 he lived in Gouda, but in 1678 he moved to Overschie where he died in 1690.

Unlike most Dutch painters, Van Beyeren did not specialize in one subject. His freely rendered seascapes are close in style to the works of Jan van Goyen (q.v.), whom he probably knew in The Hague. Apart from fish still lifes, he also painted fruit and flower pieces, elaborate banquet and game pieces influenced by Jan Davidsz. de Heem (1606–83/84), and more modest but beautifully painted kitchen pieces.

NOTES

1. Bredius 1915–22, 1(1915):1166. Cited in Bergström 1956, 229 and 312 n. 3.

2. For further archival information, see Bredius 1915–22, 1 (1915):1165–72.

[80]

Preparations for a Meal, 1664

Inscriptions: upper right, *AVB* (in monogram) *f 1664*

Oil on canvas, 80.6 × 68.6 cm (31¾ × 27 in.)

The Detroit Institute of Arts, Founders Society Purchase, 35.21

References: Indianapolis 1937, no. 5; Detroit 1970, 17; Sullivan 1979, 65, fig. 2; Albany 2002, 40–41, no. 6; Keyes, Kuretsky, Rüger, and Wheelock 2004, 26–27, no. 7.

The new artistic specialty of still-life painting that developed in the Dutch provinces in the seventeenth century fostered close scrutiny of the physical world, encompassing everything from the most elegant and costly objects and foodstuffs to the most mundane. As in landscapes of this period, familiar things are often shown with new sharpness and specificity, especially when unexpected visual contrasts inform the viewer more deeply about the nature of what is represented. Like a landscape, a still-life painting that implies temporal process or physical transformation can give even utterly immobile objects a powerful presence.

Van Beyeren's still life displays various foodstuffs and kitchen and drinking utensils on a weathered stone pedestal with a scroll design in relief. Dominating this thoughtfully balanced grouping of objects are two diagonally placed turkeys that form reciprocal shapes at left and right, illustrating the process of food preparation. At the right, a partially plucked bird rests on its back on a velvet drapery with its head and neck falling limply over the fabric-covered table edge. In the left background, a second fowl, skinned and eviscerated, hangs by the neck from the top of an arched doorway with its glistening organ meats (heart, liver, and lungs) exposed to the viewer. Displaying both the external and internal characteristics of the game emphasizes its freshness, as in the oysters, whose roughly textured shells are opened to the reveal the soft, succulent delicacy within or the bright Seville orange, whose intact exterior is juxtaposed with sparkling cut wedges. In a number of Dutch still lifes, fragmentation or evisceration offers an intriguing or pungent visual experience that can engage the viewer with the physical world even more deeply, as also seen in Jan Baptist Weenix's *Farm Interior with a Dead Swine* in the Victoria and Albert Museum, London (Fig. 159).[1]

In Van Beyeren's grouping of objects, assured brushwork displays the artist's uncanny ability to capture the most subtle visual harmonies, as evident in his repetition of warm orange tones in the birds, the orange, and the redware ceramic pitcher or in his paralleling of the similar shapes of the wide-mouthed brass mortar with the transparent, serpent-stemmed Venetian wineglass at the far right.[2] Such repetitions, found again in the reiteration of the curving claw of the foreground turkey in the curved handle of the wine pitcher immediately above it, help unify this strikingly asymmetrical design which is structured around intricate balancing of horizontal, vertical, and diagonal accents.

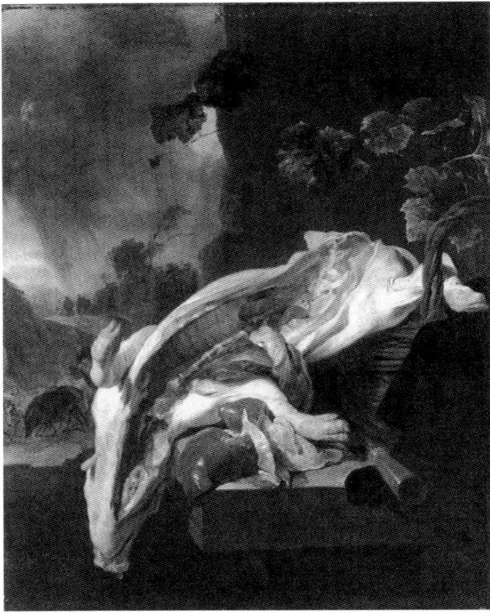

Fig. 159. Jan Baptiste Weenix, *Farm Interior with a Dead Swine*, c. 1650–55, oil on canvas, Victoria and Albert Museum, London

The origin of Van Beyeren's still life can be traced in part to mid-sixteenth-century arrangements of food (including entrails and offal) by Netherlandish artists such as Pieter Aertsen (1508/9–75), whose *Kitchen with Christ in the House of Mary and Martha* (versions of 1552, Kunsthistorisches Museum, Vienna, and of 1553, Museum Boijmans Van Beuningen, Rotterdam) combine an elaborate foreground still life with a background religious incident perhaps to indicate that one must pass through the earthly domain of the flesh (the Dutch word for meat is "fleisch") and of material concerns before reaching the spiritual realm.[3] Although kitchen pieces with raw meats and vegetables were occasionally painted by seventeenth-century Rotterdam artists such as Hendrick Maertensz. Sorgh (1610/11–70) and Pieter de Bloot (1601–58), Van Beyeren's painting in Detroit is primarily a melding of two more common Dutch still-life types: the breakfast piece and the game piece.[4] The breakfast piece, developed before 1650, characteristically includes wineglasses, table utensils, and selected foods such as oysters, fruit, bread, or nuts arranged on a tabletop and painted in a rather monochrome tonality. Game pieces, produced after mid-century, are showier, more colorful groupings featuring trophies of the hunt that frequently include both hanging and recumbent birds.[5] By convincingly blending these two types and adding kitchen motifs, Van Beyeren presents his two birds at transitional stages between freshly caught game and food for the table.

NOTES

1. It should be noted, of course, that a Dutch viewer would not have found unusual the sight of recognizable birds or animals being prepared for cooking (unlike many present-day Americans accustomed to supermarket packaging). Nonetheless, "re-presenting" lifeless creatures this vividly might startle an observer of any period. One is also reminded in this context of Rembrandt's two paintings of slaughtered oxen (Glasgow Art Gallery, c. 1638, and Musée du Louvre Paris, 1655). K. Craig sees in these paintings of eviscerated beasts implications of Christ's crucifixion and ties their central motifs to the story of the Prodigal Son, in which the slaughtered ox that signals the prodigal's return home has been understood as an allegory of Christ's forgiveness of sinners. (Craig 1983a).

2. D. R. Barnes has identified the type of ceramic in Van Beyeren's painting, while P. G. Rose has commented on how such meats were spiced and cooked (Albany 2002, 40).

3. The interpretation of Aertsen's kitchen pieces with background religious narratives has been the subject of considerable art-historical research, including articles by A. Grosjean (Grosjean 1974) and K. Craig (Craig 1983) and articles by K. Moxey, W. Kloek, R. Falkenburg, E. M. Kavaler, and H. Buijs in volume 40 of *Nederlands kunsthistorisch jaarboek* (1989)—an issue devoted entirely to the artist.

4. Seventeenth-century kitchen pieces occasionally retain the sixteenth-century practice of placing a religious scene in the background, as in as Pieter de Bloot's *Kitchen Still Life with Christ in the House of Mary and Martha*, Liechtenstein Collection, Vaduz (repr. in R. James, "Van 'boerenhuysen' en 'stilstaende dinghen,'" in Rotterdam 1994–95, 133–41).

5. For material on both still-life types, see Bergström 1956, chaps. 2, 3, and 7, and Sullivan 1984.

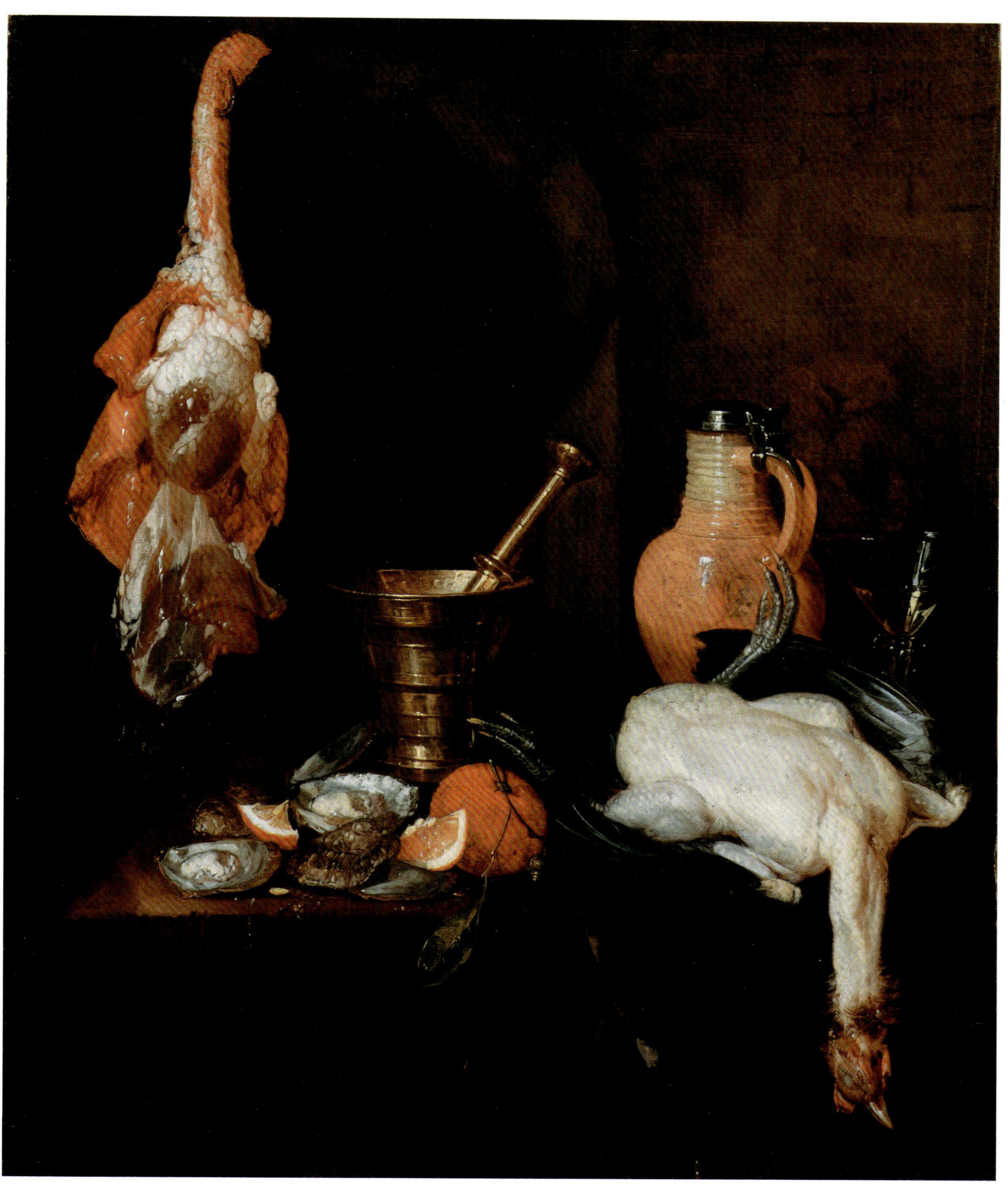

GERARD DE LAIRESSE
1640–1711

Gerard de Lairesse, the "Dutch Poussin," was the son and student of the Liège painter Renier de Lairesse (1597–1667). Having fled to Utrecht following an unhappy love affair in 1664, he moved to Amsterdam in 1665 or 1666, where he acquired citizenship in 1667.[1] There he soon found close connections with a group of artists, writers, and admirers of French culture who were members of a society (Nil Volentibus Arduum, or "nothing voluntary is difficult"), founded by Andries Pels (1631–81). Lairesse illustrated Pels's plays and acted as the society's engraver, while beginning an extremely successful career as both a printmaker and a painter. An artist who worked in an idealized classicizing style and often took his subjects from Ovid and Virgil as well as the Bible, Lairesse's work appealed to wealthy Amsterdam collectors, for whom he executed decorative allegorical cycles, ceilings, and grisailles for elegant townhouses along the Herengracht. He also contributed decorations to royal residences such as Het Loo and the Mauritshuis in The Hague. When the landscape painter Johannes Glauber (1646–1726) arrived in Amsterdam in 1684, the two artists collaborated on large classical landscapes with figures and ruins, such as the decorations for the house of the merchant Jacob de Flines (now in the Rijksmuseum, Amsterdam). Lairesse's fame brought him many major civic commissions, including the decoration of the new Amsterdam theater (1685–90) and seven large canvasses of about 1688 for the Council Room of the Binnenhof in The Hague.

In 1690 syphilis deprived Lairesse of his sight (its ravages were already evident by 1665, as indicated in Rembrandt's haunting portrait of him in the Metropolitan Museum of Art, New York). With the termination of his career as a painter, he concentrated on art theory and became a successful lecturer on art. His talks were issued by his sons in book form in 1701 as *Grondlegginge der teekenkunst* (Principles of design) and in a much larger volume of 1707 entitled *Het groot schilderboek* (The great book of painters), which was translated and reissued in numerous editions throughout Europe during the eighteenth century.

NOTE

1. Biographical information on Lairesse is based on De Vries 1998, 4–8, and on A. Roy's essay in *Dictionary of Art* 1996, 18:650–53.

[81]

The Dissection of a Uterus with Fetus, part 4, no. 56 from Govert Bidloo, *Ontleding des menschelyken lichaams* (Dissection of the human body): *by de Weduwe van Joannes van Someren, de Erfgenaamen van Joannes van Dyk, Hendrik en de Weduwe van Dirk Boom,* Amsterdam, 1690, with illustrations by Gerard de Lairesse,[1] 1690

Etching, 813 × 533 mm (32 × 21 in.) (overall, open)

Department of Printing and Graphic Arts, The Houghton Library, Harvard College Library, Cambridge, Massachusetts, Typ. 632.90.211 (Poughkeepsie); History of Medicine Division, National Library of Medicine, National Institutes of Health, Bethesda, Maryland (Sarasota and Louisville)

References: Bidloo 1685/90, pt. 4: no. 56; Ottawa 1996, 34–35, 183–86, fig. 10.

Dissection of the human body involves a process of deliberate destruction, as the physical self is invaded, fragmented, and ultimately transformed through the anatomist's sequential explorations. Only by delving beneath the surface and demolishing the body's structures can their configuration and organization be seen, recorded, and understood. Gerard de Lairesse's stunning illustrations for Govert Bidloo's treatise on anatomy are major works by an artist whose admiration for idealized classical art led him to paint, draw, and engrave impressive theatrical tableaux that emphasize the perfection of wholeness. Indeed, in his writings, Lairesse repeatedly disdained deformed or ruined things. His theoretical treatise on art, published in 1701, protests artists' use of picturesque depictions of damaged or irregular motifs such as twisted trees, ruined buildings, and crippled beggars.[2] That this particular artist produced illustrations of anatomized bodies is therefore of considerable interest.

According to Bidloo's introduction, Lairesse made his drawings through observation of the actual dissections.[3] He was not responsible for the unsigned engravings, however, having largely given up printmaking during this period, and the identity of the engraver remains uncertain.[4] The book's series of 106 illustrations opens with full-length, front-and-back views of a man and woman, shown as intact, classicizing nudes standing in contrapposto. The highly detailed prints proceed, following Bidloo's text, to reveal the structural and circulatory organization and the varied material textures of the human body, meticulously charting distinctions between male and female anatomy. Working through his cadavers from skin and hair to skeleton, the anatomist moves from part to part, beginning with the head, delineating muscles and bones, along with the organs, glands and vascular system. Lenses for magnification would clearly have been needed to draw many of the illustrations. In each, Lairesse's uncanny ability to preserve a sense of the whole while simultaneously fragmenting it to disclose its underlying formations produced images of extraordinary visual power. While the scientific accuracy of the Bidloo treatise has been challenged, the beauty of Lairesse's illustrations has always been recognized—so much so that they were notoriously plagiarized by the English anatomist William Cowper (1666–1709/10) for his *Anatomy of Humane Bodies*, published in Oxford in 1698.[5]

As this illustration of a dissected uterus demonstrates, the seventeenth century was a period of intense scientific interest in gynecology and embryology, which involved study of all aspects of the reproductive anatomy of males and females and included research on fetal development.[6] Here the corpse of a woman is seen at an angle, closely framed within the picture space, foreshortened, and cropped on all sides so that it is abstracted yet still perfectly recognizable. Although the head, arms, and legs are outside the picture space and a drapery covers the neck and shoulder, the breasts and pubic area remain visible. Between them, skin, fatty tissue, and muscle have been peeled back in layers and folded aside to reveal within the uterus a fetus of approximately eight months, which, as the text on the facing page points out, would have shifted within a few weeks to the head-down position that precedes birth. To the left is the large detached placenta (fanlike in shape) with its dense overlays of blood vessels and, above it, a loop of the intestine displaying smaller veins.[7] As in printed broadsheets and books of this period that record floods and fires (Cats. 35, 38, and 46), small letters throughout the image refer the viewer to descriptive legends on the facing page.

As a scientific illustration, Lairesse's depiction offers an informative account of major features of the female reproductive system. Yet it reads as more than a dispassionate anatomical diagram, perhaps because it was made by an artist who was not a scientist himself and who was accustomed to making images that tell stories and convey emotions. Delicate and varied

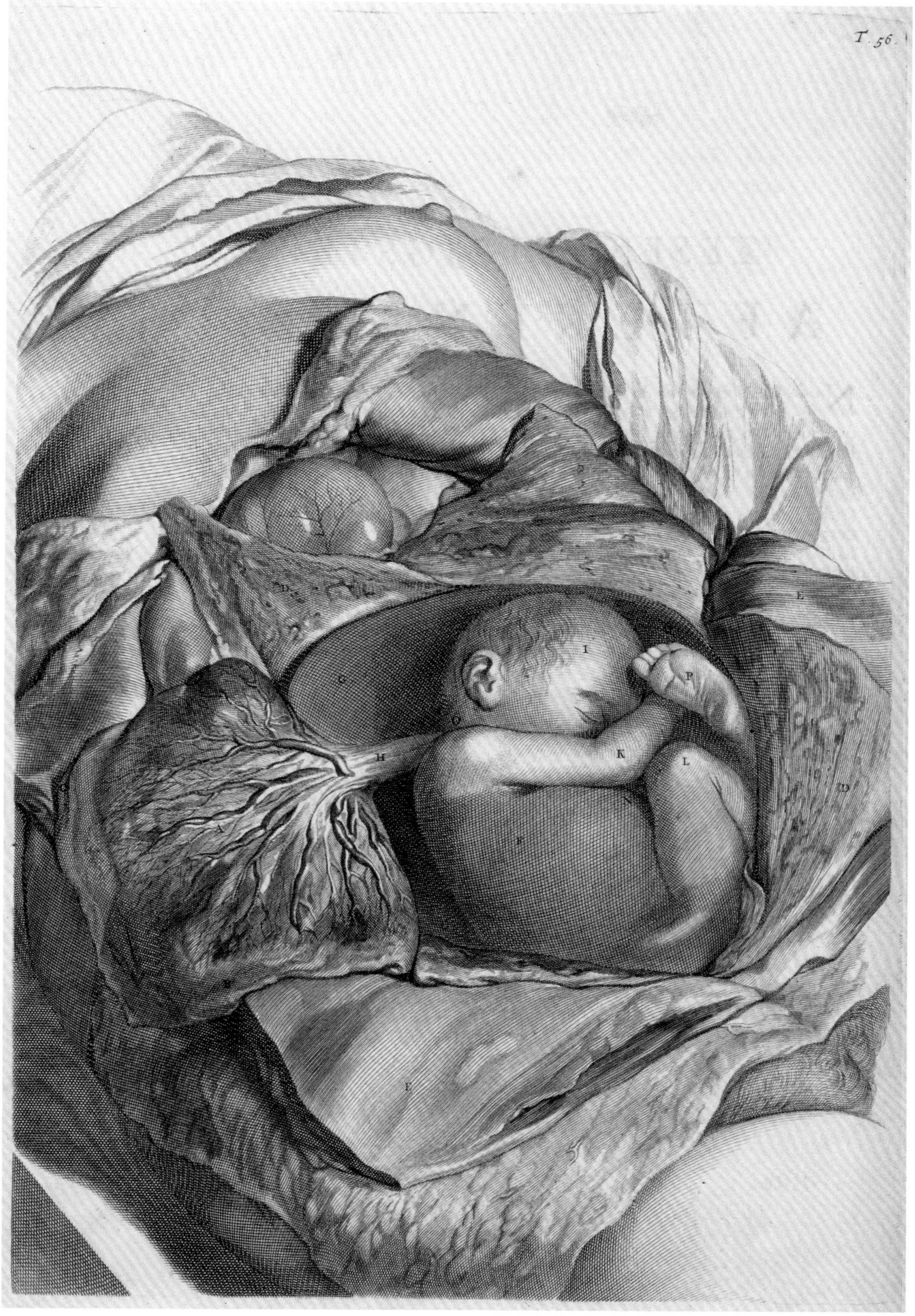

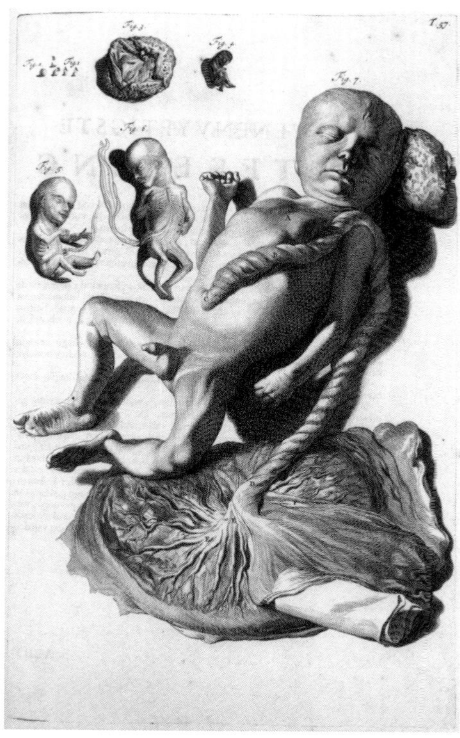

Fig. 160. Gerard de Lairesse, *A Stillborn Fœtus* from Govert Bidloo, *Ontleding des menschelyken lichaams*, Amsterdam, 1690, pt. 4, no. 57, Department of Printing and Graphic Arts, The Houghton Library, Harvard College Library, Cambridge, Massachusetts

shading produces vivid effects of three-dimensionality while capturing distinctions among varied kinds of bodily substance such as skin, hair, and striated muscle tissue. By showing the fetus within the larger context of the mother's body, Lairesse's illustration evokes a poignant connection between the two that transcends their anatomical relationship. Within the ruined body of the mother, the intact form of the unborn child seems to sleep in its uterine container, still enclosed and protected even as the process of dissection exposes it to view. On the following page (Fig. 160), the image of the eight-month fetus lying next to its placenta might almost remind a modern viewer of a fallen flier beside a deflated parachute. This page (in contrast to subsequent illustrations that show the fetus anatomized) charts the most primal stages of human growth and transformation, from ovum through embryo and from three days to eight months, culminating here in a human organism that is whole, though no longer alive.

The author of this study, Govert (Godefridi) Bidloo (1649–1713), belonged to a prominent Mennonite family in Amsterdam (his nephew Lambert Bidloo was the physician who attended Peter the Great during his stay in the Netherlands and later became director of Moscow's first medical school). Like Lairesse, Govert Bidloo was involved in theatrical activities as a young man, writing poems and plays for the Amsterdam theater. Around 1670 he served an apprenticeship with the Amsterdam surgeon (and father of the still-life painter Rachel Ruysch [1664–1750]) Frederick Ruysch (1638–1731), later receiving his doctorate from the University of Franeker in 1682. In 1688 he became professor at the Theatrum Anatomicum in The Hague, where he attended the Dutch stadtholder, William of Orange, subsequently following him to England in 1688–89, when he came to the throne as King William III. In 1694 he became professor of Anatomy at Leiden University, but he returned to London in 1701 to care for William during his final illness.[8]

NOTES

1. Bidloo's book first appeared in Amsterdam in a Latin edition of 1685 entitled *Anatomia humani corporis*. It was apparently so popular that it was reissued five years later, in a Dutch edition entitled *Ontleding des menschelyken lichaams*. The two editions are identically laid out with the same illustrations designed by Gerard de Lairesse.

2. In the 1738 English version of Lairessse's *Het groot schilderboek* (The great book of painters), published in 1707, the Dutch term *schilderachtig*, which can mean "worthy of being pictured," is translated as "painter-like" or "designer-like," as in his title of book V, chapter XV: "Of the word painter-like against ruins and beggars"; or the title of chapter XVII: "Of things deformed and broken falsely called painter-like" (Lairesse 1738, 338). On the interpretation of this term and concept in the seventeenth century, see Bakker 1995 and the essay herein by W. S. Gibson.

3. The first page of Bidloo's unpaginated introduction states that the illustrations in the book were drawn from life: "naar het leven getekend."

4. The engraver of the signed title page, Abraham Blooteling (1640–90) may have made the anatomical plates, but other reproductive engravers such as Pieter van Gunst (1659–1724) have also been proposed. For a summary of this question, see Ottawa 1996, 186. Lairesse's wash drawings, now in the library of the Faculté de Médecine, Université de Paris, have been thoroughly discussed in Dumaître 1982.

5. The first to attack the treatise for inaccuracies was Bidloo's teacher, the Amsterdam anatomist Frederick Ruysch, who made his own studies of fetuses, as discussed in Hansen 1996. Other physicians also criticized the brevity of the text and the scientific clarity of some of the illustrations. Dumaître 1982, 33–37, and Ottawa 1996, 185.

6. It should be noted, however, that northern Italian physicians did the fundamental research on embryology and gynecology, particularly the Paduan anatomist Fabricius ab Aquapendente, who published *De formato foetu* in 1600. On this and other references to the early medical literature, see Ottawa 1996, 34 n.72.

7. For medical consultation on this illustration and its relationship to current understanding of anatomy, I am indebted to Dr. John Rodman and Dr. Robert Post.

8. For biographical material on Govert Bidloo, see Rotterdam 1974, no. 10, and Ottawa 1996, 183–84.

NICOLAES MAES
1634–93

Born in Dordrecht, where he had his earliest drawing lessons, Maes was the son of a well-to-do merchant.[1] Between about 1648/50 and 1653, he became a pupil in Rembrandt's studio in Amsterdam. He later moved back to Dordrecht, where he painted a few biblical subjects in the style of his teacher while developing his own innovative approaches to genre painting. Maes's domestic subjects include lace makers, milkmaids, and old women in prayer or dozing over Bibles. In an extraordinary group of paintings representing eavesdroppers, he invented a new form of moralizing domestic drama, placing his figures in complex, multilevel spatial environments.[2] These works would deeply influence the Delft genre painters Johannes Vermeer (1632–75) and Pieter de Hooch (1629–84).

In Dordrecht, Maes also began his long and productive career as a painter of portraits, a subject that became his sole specialty after about 1660—primarily pendant portraits, but also single portraits and a few group portraits of children and families. The hundreds of portraits Maes painted after his move to Amsterdam in 1673 under the influence of Anthony van Dyck (1599–1641) display increasingly colorful and elaborate costumes and often incorporate imaginary garden settings.

NOTES

1. Biographical material on Maes is based on W. W. Robinson's essay in *Dictionary of Art* 2000, 201–4.

2. On Maes's paintings of eavesdroppers, see Robinson 1987 and Hollander 2002, 103–11.

[82]
Family Portrait, c. 1660

Inscriptions: traces of effaced signature and date 166(0?) on balustrade

Oil on canvas, 110 × 147 cm (43¼ × 57¾ in.)

Private collection

References: Hofstede de Groot 6 (1916): 597, 554a (as Maes); Valentiner 1924, 51, pl. 56 (as Maes); Sumowski 1983, 3:1964, no. 43, 1968–69, repr. (as Maes, c. 1657/58); Kuretsky 1997, 71, 81 n. 73, 104, fig. 3-26 (as Maes); Krempel 2000, 366, no. F 1, figs. 424–25 (as "Cornelis Bisschop, zugeschreiben").

This well-dressed family presenting themselves for posterity offers something of a testimonial to the importance of domestic bonds in the Dutch Republic, where family, rather than court or church, became the central organizing

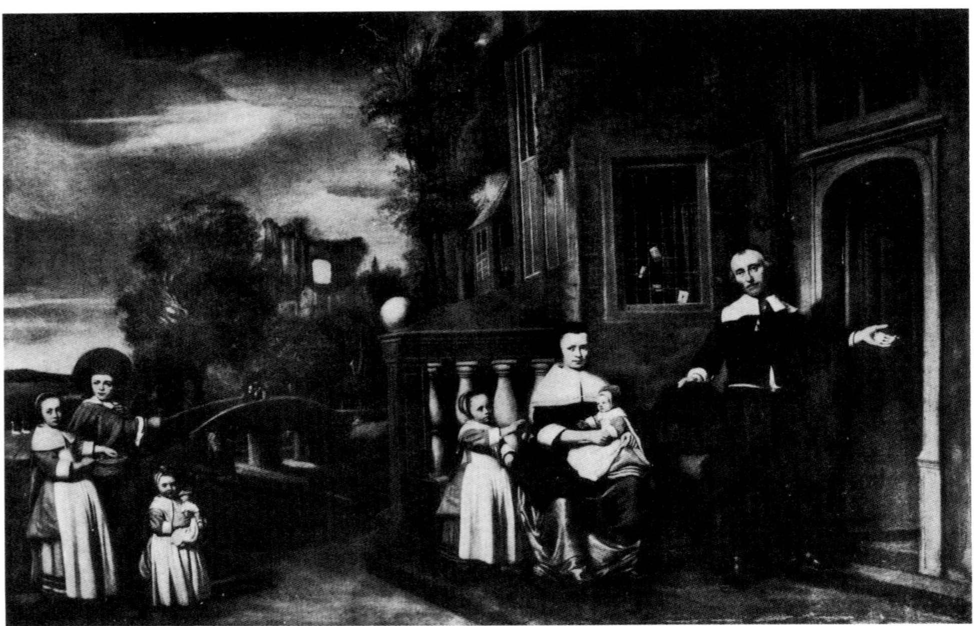

Fig. 161. Nicolaes Maes, *Family Portrait in a Landscape* (original state), oil on canvas, location unknown

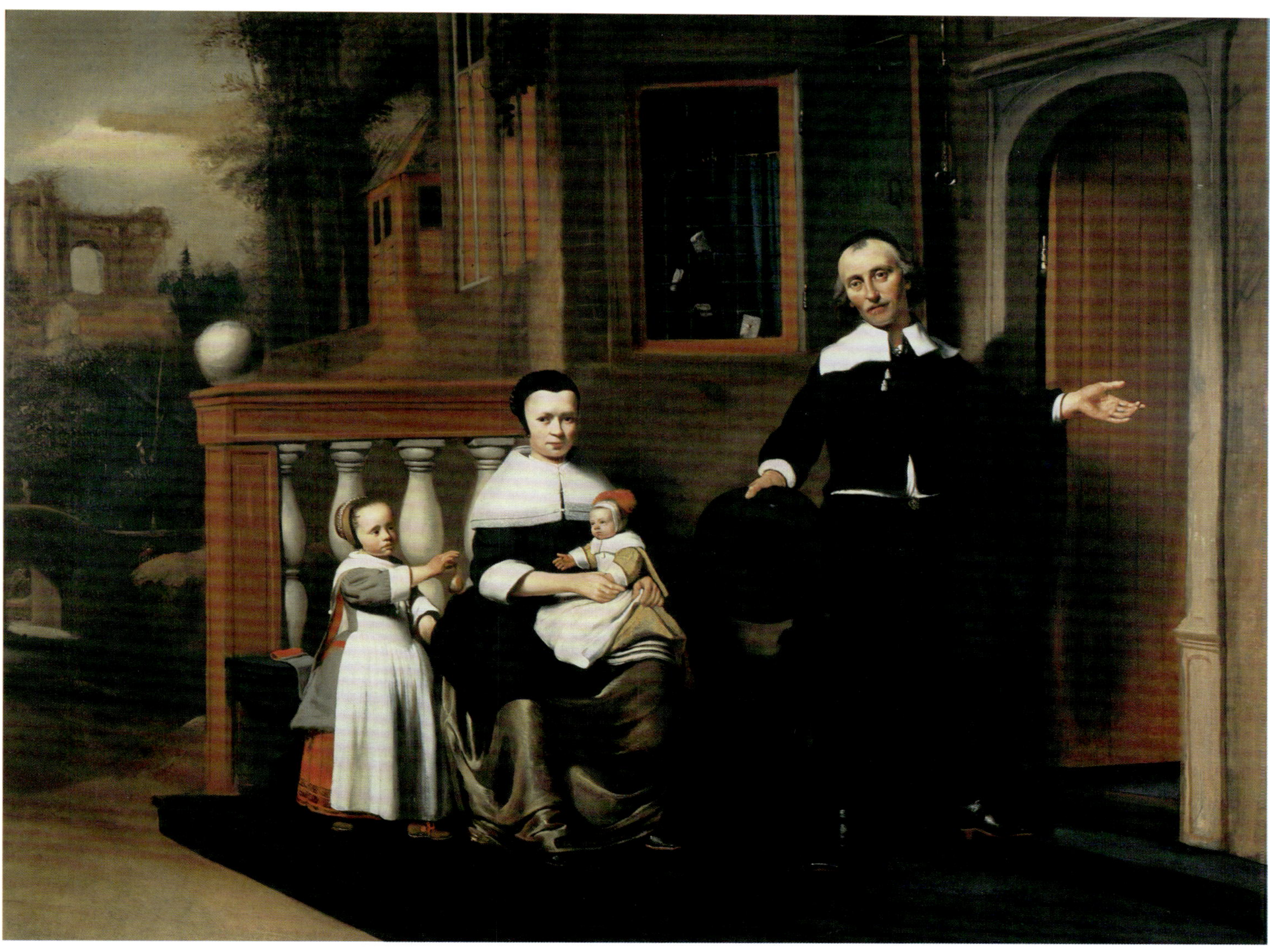

unit of society. Yet instead of showing his sitters within a household interior as so many Dutch portraitists did, here the artist has placed them outdoors, at the exterior entranceway to their home, which is emphasized by a large balustrade topped by a decorative stone ball. As E. de Jongh has discussed, pillars or balustrades with stone spheres were commonly employed in seventeenth-century Dutch portraits as allusions to the virtues of wisdom, patience, and steadfastness or to peace of mind.[1] The composure of this family and the subtle interactions among husband, wife, and children define a harmonious group of people who are also shown as individuals. The seated mother, centered within the family and placed at her husband's right hand, holds her appealingly doll-like baby on her lap, as the young daughter at left playfully offers a piece of brightly colored fruit to the lively infant. At right stands the paterfamilias, who gestures proudly (hat in hand) toward his wife and children while gazing directly at the viewer. His other hand, illuminated and framed within the open doorway, draws attention to the entrance of his home, underscoring the importance of the unseen interior beyond the threshold where family life is experienced.[2] Even his feet help connect outside with inside, for they point in different directions, the left foot lifted onto the raised sill as if he were about to enter the house. A further link between exterior and interior worlds is the window between the two adult figures whose grid of framed panes acts as a message board into which several pieces of mail have been tucked.[3]

Although the building represented here is probably an artistic invention, it is clearly meant to evoke the kinds of country houses or villas that became popular with well-to-do Dutch citizens as places of retreat and refreshment away from the business of city life. In an increasingly urbanized nation, such rural retreats (which ranged from modest to ostentatious) offered the benefits of quiet surroundings, purer air and water, and time for recreation and meditative communion with nature.[4] Relating to this pleasure in country life was the taste for pastoral imagery that emerged in Dutch art, drama, and poetry of this period.[5] *Hofdichten*, or country house poems, which derive from ancient pastoral poetry such as Virgil's *Bucolics*, praise nature as an idyllic realm safe from civilization's ills.[6]

The well-kept house in this painting seems even more stable and more solidly built because of its contrast to the large ruin that rises from the trees at the left background. Dutch portraits sometimes include vanitas motifs such as skulls or hourglasses as reminders of the brevity of earthly existence. Ruins can have similar associations, although in family portraits, the motif could also convey alternative meanings: an allusion to the long lineage of the family or a record of a visit to a particular site (see Fig. 22). When the ruin is Italianate, it may refer to a sitter's classical learning or connections to Italy, or act as a device to place individuals or families within a pastoral setting.[7] For example, a large family portrait (Fig. 23) by the Haarlem artist Herman Mijndertsz. Doncker (c. 1620–after 1656) presents an elaborately dressed group before a hilly Italianate landscape, which displays major tourist sites in and around Rome: the Temple of the Sibyl at Tivoli on the hilltop at left, a section of the Colosseum in the center, and one of the bridges over the Tiber at right.[8] In the portrait exhibited here, the unidentified medieval ruin appears to be Dutch rather than Italian, which suggests that the artist intended to connect this family to its own past—dynastically, nationalistically, or both.

Any discussion of this painting must also take into account the fact that it was once almost twice its present size (136 × 207 cm, Fig. 161). Valentiner's illustration of the painting in his 1924 monograph on Maes shows a much wider composition with a more complete view of the ruin including a hump-backed bridge that forms an interval between the family group at the right and a second group of three children standing together in the left foreground.[9] An adolescent boy gestures toward the bridge, as a girl beside him balances a basket on her hip and a smaller child holds a doll. Behind them is a body of water with two white swans. This fracture of what would appear to be the same family may indicate that the children at left are no longer living, for in a period of intermittent outbreaks of the plague and other disease mortality was high and portraiture offered a means of trying to transcend it.

The traditional attribution of this work to Nicolaes Maes has been cited in most of the recent art-historical literature, although W. W. Robinson (written communication, 2004) has expressed doubts, while L. Krempel's study of 2000 on the dated paintings of Maes ascribed the work to the gifted Dordrecht genre painter and portraitist Cornelis Bisschop (1630–74), who was a follower of Maes.[10] Having recently examined the painting, Krempel has stated (written communication, 2004) that he now believes that the painting is by Maes, as he finds similarities between it and the signed and dated *Family Portrait* by this artist in the North Carolina Museum of Art, Raleigh.

NOTES

1. Cf. De Jongh 1993.
2. For discussion of the use and implications of threshold settings in the works of Rembrandt and his contemporaries, see Kuretsky 1997.
3. A similar window-frame mail-receiver appears in *A Woman Peeling Apples* (Rijksmuseum, Amsterdam, no. 514) by Cornelis Bisschop (1630–74), who was a close follower of Maes in Dordrecht. Repr. Bernt 1969–70, 1: no. 113. Open cupboards or cabinet doors that hold mail in a similar way also appear in illusionistic Dutch still-life paintings such as Cornelis Norbetus Gijsbrechts's (active 1657–75) *Open Cupboard Door* of 1665 in the Fresno Metropolitan Museum, California. Repr. Denver/Newark 2001–2, 23, fig. 23.
4. For discussion of Dutch country houses and villas in the seventeenth century, see Van der Wijck 1972, Van der Wijck 1982, and Cearfoss Mankin 1996 (to which I am indebted for the previous two references).
5. Dutch pastoral imagery in art and literature is thoroughly discussed in Kettering 1983.
6. Country house poetry and its origins are the subject of Van Veen 1985.
7. Ruins as indicators of long dynastic lineage sometimes appear in aristocratic portraits such as Aelbert Cuyp's *Portrait of Michiel and Cornelis Pompe van Meedevoort with their Tutor* of c. 1652–53 in The Metropolitan Museum of Art, New York (repr. Washington/London/Amsterdam 2002, 151). Gerrit Pietersz. de Jongh's *Family before the Chapel of Our Lady (Capel van ons Lieve Vrouw), Heiloo* (1630, oil on panel, Rijksmuseum Het Catharijnconvent, Utrecht) shows the group before a major pilgrimage site: the ruins of the Roman Catholic Chapel of Our Lady at Heiloo (Fig. 22). Associations with Italy are emphasized in Bartholomeus Breenbergh's *Portrait Group in a Landscape with Ruins* of 1634, whose present location is unknown. Repr. Roethlisberger 1981, no. 169.
8. Doncker produced both single and family portraits with ruins as well as families in pastoral garb. See Laarmann 2000, esp. figs 11, 13, and 17 and nos. 15, 19, 23, and 38.
9. Valentiner 1924, 51. The location of the missing half of the portrait remains unknown, but Krempel noted that the left section (81.2 × 57.1 cm) was sold at Christie's, London, on 21 July 1972, no. 49, and that the painting in its complete state appeared in an auction at Kleinberger, Paris, on 17/18 June 1913, no. 57 (Krempel 2000, 366).
10. Krempel 2000, 366, no. F1. 4.

Bibliography

Van der Aa 1852–78
J. van der Aa, *Biografisch woordenboek der Nederlanden*, 7 vols., Haarlem, 1852–78.

Aalbers 1987
J. Aalbers, "Geboorte en geld: Adel in Gelderland, Utrecht en Holland tijdens de eerste helft van de 18de eeuw," in J. Aalbers and M. Prak, ed., *De bloem der natie: Adel en patriciaat in de Noordelijke Nederlanden*, Meppel and Amsterdam, 1987, 56–78.

Adams 1994
A. J. Adams, "Competing Communities in the 'Great Bog of Europe': Identity and Seventeenth Century Dutch Landscape Painting," in W. J. T. Mitchell, ed., *Landscape and Power*, Chicago, 1994, 35–76.

Aicher 1995
P. J. Aicher, *Guide to the Aqueducts of Ancient Rome*, Wauconda, Illinois, 1995.

Aikema 1996
B. Aikema, *Jacopo Bassano and His Public: Moralizing Pictures in an Age of Reform, ca. 1535–1600*, Princeton, New Jersey, 1996.

Albany 2002
Matters of Taste: Food and Drink in Seventeenth Century Art and Life (D. R. Barnes and P. G. Rose), Albany Institute of History and Art, New York, 2002.

Albany/Buffalo/Syracuse/Ithaca/Rochester/Utica 1991
In Medusa's Gaze: Still Life Paintings from Upstate New York Museums (B. Barryte with essay by N. Bryson), Albany Institute of History and Art, New York, Albright-Knox Art Gallery, Buffalo; Everson Museum of Art, Syracuse, New York; Herbert F. Johnson Museum of Art, Cornell University, Ithaca, New York; Memorial Art Gallery of the University of Rochester, New York; and Munson-Williams-Proctor Institute Museum of Art, Utica, New York, 1991.

Albers and Van der Houwen 1966
M. Albers and A. van der Houwen, "Daniel Vosmaer en het Gezicht op Den Briel," *Brielse Mare* 6, no. 1 (April 1966): 6–20.

Aldenhoven 1890
C. Aldenhoven, *Katalog der Herzoglichen Gemäldegalerie, Gotha*, Gotha, 1890 (new ed., 1895).

Allan 1983
A. J. Allan, *De ruïne van Brederode*, Nederlandse Kastelen, pt. 48, Overloon, 1983.

Allen 1987
E. J. Allen, *The Life and Art of Pieter Molyn*, PhD diss., University of Maryland, 1987.

Alpers 1983
S. Alpers, *The Art of Describing: Dutch Art of the Seventeenth Century*, Chicago, 1983.

Alpers 1990
——, *Rembrandt's Enterprise: The Studio and the Market*, Chicago, 1990 (1st ed., 1988).

Altena 2000
P. Altena, "Wandelaar op grond van de historie: Mr Johannes In de Betouw (1732–1820) en zijn Nijmegen," *Jaarboek Numaga* 49 (2000): 9–15.

Ampzing 1628
S. Ampzing, *Beschrijvinge ende lof der Stad Haerlem in Holland*, Haarlem, 1628.

Amsterdam 1955
De triompf van het manïerisme: De Europese stijl van Michelangelo tot El Greco (R. van Luttervelt et.al.), Rijksmuseum, Amsterdam, 1955.

Amsterdam 1956
Exposition de dessins et eaux-fortes de Rembrandt et de son entourage, Bernard Houthakker, Amsterdam, 1956.

Amsterdam 1964
De Verzameling van Bernard Houthakker (J. W. Niemeijer), Rijksprentenkabinet, Rijksmuseum, Amsterdam, 1964.

Amsterdam 1967
Hercules Seghers (K. G. Boon and J. Verbeek), Rijksmuseum, Amsterdam, 1967.

Amsterdam 1971
Master Drawings Exhibited by Bernard Houthakker, Bernard Houthakker C.V., Amsterdam, 1971.

Amsterdam 1976
Tot lering en vermaak: Betekenissen van Hollandse genrevoorstellingen uit de zeventiende eeuw (E. de Jongh), Rijksmuseum, Amsterdam, 1976.

Amsterdam 1981
Jan van Goyen, 1596–1656: Conquest of Space, K. & V. Waterman, Amsterdam, 1981.

Amsterdam 1986
Art before the Iconoclasm: Northern Netherlandish Art 1525–1580/De eeuw van de beeldenstorm (W. th. Kloek, W. Halsema-Kubes, and R. J. Baarsen), Rijksmuseum, Amsterdam, 1986.

Amsterdam 1988
De prentschat van Michiel Hinloopen: Een reconstructie van de eerste openbare papierkunstverzameling in Nederland (J. van der Waals), Rijksmuseum, Amsterdam, 1988.

Amsterdam 1988–89
Jan Lievens, 1607–1674: Prenten en tekeningen (P. Schatborn), Rembrandthuis, Amsterdam, 1988–89.

Amsterdam 1989
De verzameling van mr. Carel Vosmaer (1826–1888), The Hague (ed. J. F. Heijbroek), Rijksprentenkabinet, Rijksmuseum, Amsterdam, 1989.

Amsterdam 1989–90
De Hollandse fijnschilders van Gerard Dou tot Adriaen van der Werff (P. Hecht), Rijksmuseum, Amsterdam, 1989–90.

Amsterdam 1992
Episcopius: Jan de Bisschop (1628–1971), advocaat en tekenaar/Lawyer and Draughtsman (R. E. Jellema and M. Plomp), Rembrandthuis, Amsterdam, 1992.

Amsterdam 1993–94
Nederland naar 't leven: Landschapsprenten uit de Gouden Eeuw (B. Bakker and H. Leeflang), Rembrandthuis, Amsterdam, 1993–94.

Amsterdam 1993–94a
Dawn of the Golden Age: Northern Netherlandish Art, 1580–1620 (G. Luijten, A. van Suchtelen, R. Baarsen, W. Kloek, and M. Schapelhouman), Rijksmuseum, Amsterdam, 1993–94.

Amsterdam 1997
Mirror of Everyday Life: Genre Prints in the Netherlands, 1550–1700 (E. de Jongh and G. Luijten), Rijksmuseum, Amsterdam, 1997.

Amsterdam 2001
Drawn to Warmth: 17th-Century Dutch Artists in Italy (P. Schatborn, with an essay by J. Verberne), Rijksprentenkabinet, Rijksmuseum, Amsterdam, 2001.

Amsterdam/Boston/Philadelphia 1987–88
Masters of 17th-Century Dutch Landscape Painting (P. C. Sutton et. al.), Rijksmuseum, Amsterdam; Museum of Fine Arts, Boston; Philadelphia Museum of Art, 1987–88.

Amsterdam/Cleveland 1992
Chiaroscuro Woodcuts: Hendrick Goltzius and His Time (N. Bialler), Rijksprentenkabinet, Rijksmuseum, Amsterdam; and Cleveland Museum of Art, 1992.

Amsterdam/Cleveland 1999–2000
Still-Life Painting from the Netherlands, 1550–1720 (A. Chong and W. Kloek), Rijksmuseum, Amsterdam; and Cleveland Museum of Art, 1999–2000.

Amsterdam/Dordrecht/Rotterdam 2000
Geschiedenis in Beeld (J. Beijerman-Schols, J. F. Heijbroek, E. M. L. van der Maas, J. C. Nix, and E. F. van der Wolde), Rijksmuseum, Amsterdam; Dordrechts Museum; and Historisch Museum, Rotterdam, 2000.

Amsterdam/London 2000–2001
Rembrandt the Printmaker (E. Hinderding, G. Luijten, and M. Royalton-Kisch), Rijksmuseum, Amsterdam; and British Museum, London, 2000–2001.

Amsterdam/New York/Toledo 2003–4
Hendrick Goltzius (1558–1617): Drawings, Prints and Paintings (H. Leeflang and G. Luijten with contributions by H. Leeflang, M. Schapelhouman, N. Orenstein, G. Luijten, M. C. Plomp, and L. W. Nichols.), Rijksmuseum, Amsterdam; Metropolitan Museum of Art, New York; and Toledo Museum of Art, Ohio, 2003–4.

Amsterdam/Paris 1998–99
Landscapes of Rembrandt: His Favorite Walks (B. Bakker, M. van Berghe-Gerbaud, E. Schmitz, and J. Peeters), Gemeentearchief, Amsterdam; and Fondation Custodia, Institut Néerlandais, Paris, 1998–99.

Amsterdam/Toronto 1977
Opkomst en bloei van het Noordnederlandse stadsgezicht in de 17de eeuw/The Dutch Cityscape in the 17th Century and Its Sources (B. Haak, R. J. Wattenmaker, and B. Bakker), Amsterdams Historisch Museum; and Art Gallery of Ontario, Toronto, 1977.

Amsterdam/Vienna/New York/Cambridge 1991–92
Seventeenth-Century Dutch Drawings: A Selection from the Maida and George Abrams Collection (cat. by W. W. Robinson and intro. by P. Schatborn), Rijksprentenkabinet, Rijksmuseum, Amsterdam; Graphische Sammlung Albertina, Vienna; The Pierpont Morgan Library, New York; and Fogg Art Museum, Harvard University, Cambridge, Massachusetts, 1991–92.

Ann Arbor 1964
Italy through Dutch Eyes (W. Stechow), University of Michigan Museum of Art, Ann Arbor, 1964.

Armstrong 1990
C. M. Armstrong, *The Moralizing Prints of Cornelis Anthonisz.*, Princeton, New Jersey, 1990.

Ashby 1935
T. Ashby, *The Aqueducts of Ancient Rome*, Oxford, 1935.

Ashton, Slive, and Davies 1982
P. S. Ashton, S. Slive, and A. I. Davies, "Jacob van Ruisdael's Trees," *Arnoldia* 42 (1982): 2–31.

Augustine/Cutler 1955
St. Augustine, *Confessions and Enchiridion*, trans. and ed. A. C. Cutler, Library of Christian Classics 7, Philadelphia, 1955.

Austin 1939
A. E. Austin Jr., "Hartford Reports the Year's Purchases," *Art News* 38 (14 October 1939): 9.

Baer 1973
C. O. Baer, *Landscape Drawings*, New York, 1973.

Baer 1995
R. Baer, "Image of Devotion: Dou's 'Hermit Praying,'" *Minneapolis Institute of Arts Bulletin* 67 (1995): 22–33.

Bakker 1995
B. Bakker, "*Schilderachtig*: Discussions of a Seventeenth-Century Term and Concept," *Simiolus* 23 (1995): 147–62.

Bakker 1996
——, "Oud maar niet lelijk: Oude gebouwen in de Hollandse beeldende kunst van de zeventiende eeuw," in H. Hendrix and R. Schenkeveld-van der Dussen, eds., *Oud en lelijk: Ouderdom in de cultuur van de Renaissance*, Utrecht Renaissance Studies 3, Amsterdam, 1996, 37–55.

Baldinucci 1681–1728
F. Baldinucci, *Delle notizie dei professori del disegno da Cimabue in qua*, 6 vols., Florence, 1681–1728.

Baldinucci 1846
——, *Cominciamento e progresso dell'arte dell'intagliare in rame*, Florence, 1846.

Baldwin 1985
R. W. Baldwin, "'On earth we are beggars, as Christ himself was': The Protestant Background of Rembrandt's Imagery of Poverty, Disability, and Begging," *Konsthistorisk tidskrift* 54 (1985): 122–35.

Baltimore 2002
Painted Prints: The Revelation of Color in Northern Renaissance and Baroque Engravings, Etchings and Woodcuts (S. Dackerman), Baltimore Museum of Art, 2002.

Baltimore/San Francisco 1997–98
Masters of Light: Dutch Painters in Utrecht during the Age of Light (J. A. Spicer and L. F. Orr), Walters Art Gallery, Baltimore; and Fine Arts Museums of San Francisco, 1997–98.

Bandmann 1970
G. Bandmann, "Höhle und Säule auf Darstellungen Mariens mit dem Kinde," *Festschrift für Gert von der Osten*, Cologne, 1970, 130–48.

Baridon 1985
M. Baridon, "Ruins as a Mental Construct," *Journal of Garden History* 5 (1985): 84–96.

Barkley 1896
H. C. Barkley, *Studies in the Art of Rat-Catching*, London, 1896.

Barlow 2000
R. S. Barlow, *The Vanishing American Outhouse: A History of Country Plumbing*, New York, 2000.

Bartsch 1803–21
A. Bartsch, *Le peintre graveur*, 21 vols., Vienna, 1803–21 (new ed., Leipzig, 1845–70; suppl. by R. Weigel, Leipzig, 1843).

Bartsch (Illustrated)
——, *The Illustrated Bartsch*, ed. W. Strauss, New York, 1978–.

Basan 1767
F. Basan, *Dictionnaire des graveurs anciens et modernes depuis l'origine de la gravure*, Paris, 1767.

Basel 1987
Im Lichte Hollands (P. ten Doesschate Chu), Kunstmuseum, Basel, 1987.

Basel/Tübingen 1990
Frans Post, 1612–1680 (T. Kellein and U.-B. Frei), Kunsthalle, Basel; and Kunsthalle, Tübingen, 1990.

Bassano 1992
Jacopo Bassano e l'incisione: La fortuna dell'arte bassanesca nella grafica di riproduzione dal XVI al XIX secolo (ed. E. Pan), Museo Civico, Bassano, 1992.

Bauch 1936
K. Bauch, "Beiträge zum Werk der Vorläufer Rembrandts: Die Gemälde des Jakob Pynas," *Oud Holland* 53 (1936): 79–88.

Bean 1968–69
J. Bean, "Report of the Department of Drawings," *The Metropolitan Museum of Art Bulletin* 27 (1968–69): 85–87.

Beck 1966
H.-U. Beck, "Jan van Goyen am Deichbruch von Houtewael (1651)," *Oud Holland* 81 (1966): 20–33.

Beck 1972–73
——, *Jan van Goyen, 1596–1656*, 2 vols., Amsterdam, 1972–73.

Beck 1987
——, *Jan van Goyen, 1596–1656: Ein Oeuvreverzeichnis, III (Ergänzungen)*, Doornspijk, 1987.

Beck 1990
——, "Der unbekannte Zeichnungssammler Lugt 2986 b identiziert: Jacob Helmolt in Haarlem," *Oud Holland* 104 (1990): 372–78.

Beckett 1970
R. B. Beckett, ed., *John Constable's Discourses*, Ipswich, 1970.

Bedaux 1982
J. B. Bedaux, "Beelden van 'leersucht' en tucht: Opvoedingsmetaforen in de Nederlandse schilderkunst van de zeventiende eeuw," *Nederlands kunsthistorisch jaarboek* 33 (1982): 49–74.

Bedaux 1990
——, "Discipline for Innocence: Metaphors for Education in Seventeenth-Century Dutch Painting," in J. B. Bedaux, *The Reality of Symbols: Studies in the Iconology of Netherlandish Art, 1400–1800*, Maarssen, 1990, 109–60.

Beek et al. 1975
M. Beek et al., *Victor de Stuers: Holland op zijn smalst; Ingeleid en toegelicht door een werkgroep van het Kunsthistorisch Instituut der Universiteit van Amsterdam, bestaande uit M. Beek et al.*, Bussum, 1975.

Beening 1963
T. J. Beening, *Het landschap in de Nederlandse letterkunde van de Renaissance*, PhD diss., Universiteit te Nijmegen, 1963.

Bell 1947
A. E. Bell, *Christian Huygens and the Development of Science in the Seventeenth Century*, London, 1947.

Benesch 1928
O. Benesch, ed., *Die Zeichnungen der niederländischen Schulen des XV. und XVI. Jahrhunderts*, Beschreibender Katalog der Handzeichnungen in der Graphische Sammlung Albertina 2, Vienna, 1928.

Benjamin 1999
W. Benjamin, *The Arcades Project*, trans. H. Eiland and K. McLaughlin, Cambridge, Massachusetts, and London, 1999, esp. pt. C, 82–100.

Berckenhagen 1969
E. Berckenhagen, "Zeichnungen von Nicolas Poussin und seinem Kreis in der Kunstbibliothek Berlin," *Berliner Museen*, n.s. 19, no. 1 (1969): 24–33.

Van den Berg 1942
H. van den Berg, "Willem Schellinks en Lambert Doomer in Frankrijk," *Oudheidkundig jaarboek* 11 (1942): 1–31.

Van Berge-Gerbaud 1997
M. van Berge-Gerbaud, *Rembrandt et son école: Dessins de la collection Frits Lugt: Fondation Custodia, Paris*, Paris, 1997.

Bergamo 1981
Vanitas (A. Veca), Lorenzelli Gallery, Bergamo, 1981.

Bergström 1956
I. Bergström, *Dutch Still-Life Painting in the Seventeenth Century*, trans. C. Hedström and G. Taylor, London, 1956.

Berlin 1921
Katalog Kaiser-Friedrich Museum, Berlin, Berlin, 1921.

Berlin 1974
Die holländischen Landschaftszeichnungen, 1600–1740 (W. Schulz), Staatliche Museen Preussischer Kulturbesitz, Berlin, 1974.

Berlin 1975
Vom späten Mittelalter bis zu Jacques Louis David: Neuerworbene und neubestimmte Zeichnungen im Berliner Kupferstichkabinett (F. Anzelewsky et. al.), Staatliche Museen Preussischer Kulturbesitz, Berlin, 1975.

Berlin 1979
Manierismus in Holland um 1600: Kupferstiche Holzschnitte und Zeichnungen aus dem Berliner Kupferstichkabinett (H. Mielke), Berlin-Dahlem Museum, 1979.

Berlin/Amsterdam/London 1991–92
Rembrandt: De Meester en zijn Werkplaats; Tekeningen en Etsen (H. Bevers, P. Schatborn, and B. Welzel), Altes Museum, Berlin; Rijksmuseum, Amsterdam; and National Gallery, London, 1991–92 (English ed., *Rembrandt: The Master and His Workshop: Drawings and Etchings*, New Haven, Connecticut, 1991).

Bernen and Bernen 1973
S. Bernen and R. Bernen, *A Guide to Myth & Religion in European Painting, 1270–1700: The Stories as the Artist Knew Them*, New York, 1973.

Bernhard 1965
M. Bernhard, *Verlorene Werke der Malerei: In Deutschland in der Zeit von 1939 bis 1945 zerstörte und verschollene Gemälde aus Museen und Galerien*, Munich, 1965.

Bernt 1969–70
W. Bernt, *The Netherlandish Painters of the Seventeenth Century*, 3 vols., London, 1969–70.

Berridge, Keens-Soper, and Otto 2001
G. R. Berridge, M. Keens-Soper, and T. G. Otto, eds., *Diplomatic Theory from Machiavelli to Kissinger*, New York, 2001.

Bidloo 1685/90
G. Bidloo, *Anatomia humani corporis*, with illustrations after Gerard de Lairesse, Amsterdam, 1685 (Dutch ed., *Ontleding des menschelyken lichaams*, Amsterdam 1690).

De Bie 1661
C. de Bie, *Het gulden cabinet van de edele vry schilder-const*, Antwerp, 1661 (reprint, with an intro. by G. Lemmens, Soest, 1971).

Bierens de Haan and Jas 2000
J. C. Bierens de Haan and J. R. Jas, "Ruïnes en kasteelresten," in *Geldersche kasteelen: Tot defensie en eene plaissante wooninge; Architectuur, interieurs, tuinen*, Zwolle, 2000, 59–69, 167.

De Bièvre 1988
E. de Bièvre, "Violence and Virtue: History and Art in the City of Haarlem," *Art History* 11, no. 3 (1988): 303–34.

Bille 1960
C. Bille, "Een dijkdoorbraak te Amsterdam ruim 400 jaar geleden," *Maanblad Amstelodamum* 47 (1960): 204–11.

Bille 1961
——, *De Tempel der Kunst: of, Het Kabinet van den Heer Braamcamp*, 2 vols., Amsterdam, 1961.

Birmingham et al. 1957–58
An Exhibition of Dutch, Flemish and German Paintings from the Collection of Walter P. Chrysler, The Birmingham Museum of Art, Alabama, et. al., 1957–58.

De Bisschop 1668–69
J. de Bisschop, *Signorum veterum icones*, 2 vols., Amsterdam, 1668–69.

De Bisschop 1671
——, *Paradigmata graphices variorum artificum*, Amsterdam, 1671.

Blanc 1869
C. Blanc, "Galerie Delessert, part 1," *Gazette des beaux-arts*, 2nd ser., pt. 1 (1869): 105–27.

Blankert 1978
A. Blankert, with contributions by R. Ruurs and W. L. van de Watering, *Vermeer of Delft: Complete Edition of the Paintings*, Oxford, 1978 (1st Dutch ed., *Johannes Vermeer van Delft, 1632–1675*, Utrecht, 1975).

Van Bleyswijck 1667–80
D. van Bleyswijck, *Beschryvinge der Stadt Delft*, 2 vols., Delft, 1667–80.

Van der Blom 1970
N. van der Blom, "Een epigram op een Vanitas van Bloemaert," *Hermeneus* (September–October 1970): 41f.

Blume 1994
A. C. Blume, "Herman Swanevelt and His Prints," *Oud Holland* 108 (1994): 1–13.

Bock 1930
E. Bock, *Geschichte der graphische Kunst von ihren Anfängen bis zur Gegenwart*, Berlin, 1930.

Bock and Rosenberg 1930
E. Bock and J. Rosenberg, *Die niederländischen Meister: Beschreibendes Verzeichnis sämtlicher Zeichnungen; Staatlichen Museen zu Berlin, Die Zeichnungen alter Meister im Kupferstichkabinett*, 2 vols., Berlin, 1930.

Von Bode 1913
W. von Bode (intro.), *Catalogue of the Collection of Pictures and Bronzes in the Possession of Sir Otto Beit*, London, 1913.

Boëthius and Ward-Perkins 1970
A. Boëthius and J. B. Ward-Perkins, *Etruscan and Roman Architecture*, Harmondsworth, 1970.

Bok 1984
M. J. Bok, "The Date of Cornelis van Poelenburch's Birth," *Hoogsteder-Naumann Mercury*, no. 2 (1984): 9–11.

Bok 1996
——, "Laying Claims to Nobility in the Dutch Republic: Epitaphs, True and False." *Simiolus* 24 (1996): 209–26.

Bol 1958
L. J. Bol, "Een Middelburgse Brueghel-groep, VIII: Adriaen Pietersz. van de Venne, schilder en teyckenaar; B. Haagse periode, 1625–1662," *Oud Holland* 73 (1958): 128–47.

Bol 1989
——, *Adriaen Pietersz. van de Venne: Painter and Draughtsman*, Doornspijk, 1989.

Bollebakker 1998
H. Bollebakker, "De noodklok over kasteel Nederhemert," *Heemschut* 75, no. 5 (October 1998): 25–32.

Bolten 1994
J. Bolten, ed., "Ruïne van Rijnsburg in prent en tekening, 1600–1800," *Delineavit et Sculpsit*, no. 13 (September 1994): 1–122.

Bolten 1998
J. Bolten, "The Beginnings of Abraham Bloemaert's Artistic Career," *Master Drawings* 36 (1998): 17–25.

Bonn 1960–61
Rheinische Landschaften und Städtebilder, 1600–1850 (F. Goldkuhle), Rheinisches Landesmuseum, Bonn, 1960–61.

Boon 1978
K. G. Boon, *Netherlandish Drawings of the 15th and 16th Centuries: Catalogue of the Dutch and Flemish Drawings in the Rijksprentenkabinet, Rijksmuseum, Amsterdam*, 2 vols., The Hague, 1978.

Boorstin 1983
D. Boorstin, *The Discoveries*, New York, 1983.

Bordeaux 1990
L'or & l'ombre: Catalogue critique et raisonné des peintures hollandaises du dix-septième et du dix-huitième siècles conservées au Musée des Beaux-Arts de Bordeaux (O. Le Bihan), Musée des Beaux-Arts de Bordeaux, 1990.

Van Borsselen 1613
P. van Borsselen, *Den Binckhorst*, Amsterdam, 1613.

Bos and Krop 1993
E. P. Bos and H. A. Krop, eds., *Franco Burgersdijk (1590–1635): Neo-Aristotelianism in Leiden*, Amsterdam and Atlanta, 1993.

Boston/St. Louis 1980–81
Printmaking in the Age of Rembrandt (C. S. Ackley), Museum of Fine Arts, Boston; St. Louis Art Museum, 1980–81.

Boström 1949
K. Boström, "David Baillys stilleben," *Konsthistorisk tidskrift* 18 (1949): 99–110.

Boxer 1957
C. R. Boxer, *The Dutch in Brazil, 1624–1654*, Oxford, 1957.

Van den Brand 2003
P. van den Brand, "De bezieling van het ontwerp … een kwestie van informatie en interactie," *Belvedere* 7, no. 19 (October 2003), suppl.

Van den Branden 1875
F. J. van den Branden, *Willem van Nieuwelandt: Kunstschilder en dichter, 1584–1635*, Ghent, 1875.

Braunschweig 1978
Die Sprache der Bilder: Realität und Bedeutung in der niederländischen Malerei des 17. Jahrhunderts (R. Klessmann et. al.), Herzog Anton Ulrich-Museum, Braunschweig, 1978.

Braunschweig 1979
Jan Lievens: Ein Maler im Schatten Rembrandts (ed. R. Klessmann), Herzog Anton Ulrich-Museum, Braunschweig, 1979.

Braunschweig 1991
Jacob Isaaksz. van Ruisdael: Wasserfall mit Wachtturm; Eine werkmonographische Austelling (J. Luckhardt), Herzog Anton Ulrich-Museum, Braunschweig, 1991.

Brearley 1919
H. C. Brearley, *Time Telling through the Ages*, New York, 1919.

Bredius 1915–22
A. Bredius, *Künstler-Inventare: Urkunden zur Geschichte der höllandischen Kunst des 16., 17., und 18. Jahrhunderts*, 8 vols., The Hague, 1915–22.

Brière-Misme 1927
C. Brière-Misme, "Tableaux inédits ou peu connus de Pieter de Hooch," *Gazette des beaux-arts* 10 (1927): 51–79, 258–86, and 15 (1927): 361–80.

Briganti, Trezzani, and Laureati 1983
G. Briganti, L. Trezzani, and L. Laureati, eds., *Painters of Everyday Life in 17th-Century Rome*, Rome, 1983.

Brochhagen 1958
K. Brochhagen, *Karel Dujardin: Ein Beitrag zum Italianismus in Holland im 17. Jahrhundert*, Cologne, 1958.

Brom 1957
G. Brom, *Schilderkunst en litteratuur in de 16e en 17e eeuw*, Utrecht, 1957.

Brookner 2001
A. Brookner, *Romanticism and Its Discontents*, London, 2001.

Broos 1985
B. P. J. Broos, "Notitie der teekeningen van Sybrand Feitama, II: Verkocht, verhandeld,

verëerd, geruild en overgedaan," *Oud Holland* 99 (1985): 110–54.

Broos 1987
——, "Notitie der teekeningen van Sybrand Feitama, III: De verzameling van Sybrand I Feitama (1620–1701) en van Isaac Feitama (1666–1709)," *Oud Holland* 101 (1987): 171–213.

Brown 1981
C. Brown, *Carel Fabritius: Complete Edition with a Catalogue Raisonné*, Oxford, 1981.

Brown 2001
D. B. Brown, *Romanticism*, London, 2001.

Brown 2003
P. A. Brown, *Better a Shrew Than a Sheep: Women, Drama, and the Culture of the Jest in Early Modern England*, Ithaca, New York, and London, 2003.

De Brune 1624
J. de Brune, *Emblemata of zinne-werck*, Amsterdam, 1624.

Brusati 1990–91
C. Brusati, "Stilled Lives: Self-Portraiture and Self-Reflection in Seventeenth-Century Netherlandish Still-Life Painting," *Simiolus* 10 (1990–91): 168–82.

Brusati 1995
——, *Artifice and Illusion: The Art and Life of Samuel van Hoogstraten*, Chicago, 1995.

Brussels/Rome 1995
Fiamminghi a Roma: Artistes des Pays-Bas et de la principauté de Liège à Rome à la Renaissance (A.-C. de Liedekerke), Palais des Beaux-Arts, Brussels; and Palazzo delle Esposizioni, Rome, 1995.

Brussels/Rotterdam/Paris/Berne 1968–69
Dessin de paysagistes hollandais du XVIIe siècle de la collection particulière conservée à l'Institut Néerlandais de Paris (C. van Hasselt), 2 vols., Bibliothèque Albert Ier, Brussels; Museum Boijmans Van Beuningen, Rotterdam; Institut Néerlandais, Paris; and Musée des Beaux-Arts, Berne, 1968–69.

Bruyn 1951
J. Bruyn, "David Bailly: 'Fort bon peintre en pourtraicts et en vie coye,'" *Oud Holland* 66 (1951): 148–64.

Bruyn 1987–88
——, "Toward a Scriptural Reading of Seventeenth-Century Dutch Landscape Paintings," in Amsterdam/Boston/Philadelphia 1987–88, 84–120.

Buijsen 1993
E. Buijsen, *The Sketchbook of Jan van Goyen from the Bredius-Kronig Collection*, The Hague, 1993.

Buisman 2000
J. Buisman, *Duizend jaar weer, wind en water in de Lage Landen: Deel 4, 1575–1675*, Franeker, 2000.

Burchard 1917
L. Burchard, *Die holländische Radierer vor Rembrandt*, Berlin, 1917.

Burger 1988
A. C. M. Burger, *Het Kasteel van Egmond: Een schets van de ontwikkeling van het 'Slot op den Hoef,'* Schoorl, 1988.

Burke 1976
J. Burke, *Jan Both: Paintings, Drawings, and Prints*, Outstanding Dissertations in the Fine Arts, New York, 1976.

Burnet/Willey 1691/1965
The Sacred Theory of the Earth by Thomas Burnet (intro. by B. Willey), London, 1965 (modern reprint of 1691 ed. of Burnet's book; 1st ed., London, 1681).

Burtt 1954
E. A. Burtt, *The Metaphysical Foundations of Modern Science*, New York, 1954.

Bussum 1975
Amsterdam Historisch: Een stadsgeschiedenis aan de hand van de collectie van het Amsterdams Historisch Museum, Bussum, 1975.

Cambridge 1958
Drawings from the Collection of Curtis O. Baer (A. Mongan), Fogg Art Museum, Harvard University, Cambridge, Massachusetts, 1958.

Cambridge 1992
The Made Landscape: City and Country in Seventeenth-Century Dutch Prints (K. H. Nguyen), Harvard University Art Museums, Cambridge, Massachusetts, 1992.

Cambridge/Montreal 1988
Landscape in Perspective: Drawings by Rembrandt and His Contemporaries (F. J. Duparc), Arthur M. Sackler Museum, Harvard University, Cambridge, Massachusetts; and Montreal Museum of Fine Arts, 1988.

Capetown 1952
Seventeenth Century Dutch Painting, National Gallery of South Africa, Capetown, 1952.

Carroll 1984
M. D. Carroll, "Rembrandt's Aristotle: Exemplary Beholder," *Artibus et historiae* 5, no. 10 (1984): 35–56.

Cats 1632
J. Cats, *Spiegel van den ouden en nieuwen tijdt*, The Hague, 1632 (reprint, Amsterdam, 1968).

Cats 1655
——, *Hof-gedachten*, Amsterdam 1655.

Cats 1657
——, *S'werelts begin, midden, eijnde, besloten in den Trou-ringh*, Amsterdam, 1657.

Cats 1700
——, *Alle de wercken*, Amsterdam, 1700.

Cats/Luijten 1996
——, *Sinne- en minnebeelden*, ed. and with commentaries by H. Luijten, 3 vols., The Hague, 1996.

Cats/Vieu-Kuik 1980
J. Cats, *Het Spaens-heydinnetje*, ed. H. J. Vieu-Kuik, The Hague, 1980.

Cearfoss Mankin 1996
D. Cearfoss Mankin, *Dutch Seventeenth-Century Images of Classicizing Palaces and Villas inside The Netherlands*, PhD diss., University of Kansas, 1996.

Chapel Hill/Chicago 1993
Graven Images: The Rise of Professional Printmakers in Antwerp and Haarlem, 1540–1640 (T. A. Riggs and L. Silver), Ackland Art Museum, University of North Carolina at Chapel Hill; and Mary and Leigh Block Gallery, Northwestern University, Chicago, 1993.

Chapel Hill/Ithaca/Worcester 1999
Fresh Woods and Pastures New: Seventeenth-Century Dutch Landscape Drawings from the Peck Collection (F. W. Robinson and S. Peck, with contributions by T. Laurentius and D. Kushel), Ackland Art Museum, The University of North Carolina at Chapel Hill; Herbert F. Johnson Museum of Art, Cornell University, Ithaca, New York; and Worcester Art Museum, Massachusetts, 1999.

Chong 1991
A. Chong, "New Dated Works from Aelbert Cuyp's Early Career," *Burlington Magazine* 133 (September–December 1991): 606–12.

Chong 1992
——, "Aelbert Cuyp and the Meaning of Landscape," PhD diss., New York University, 1992.

Cincinnati 1941
Exhibition of Prints of the Fifteenth, Sixteenth, Seventeenth and Eighteenth Centuries from the Collection of Herbert Greer French, Cincinnati Art Museum, 1941.

Cincinnati 1993
Six Centuries of Master Prints: Treasures from the Herbert Greer French Collection (ed. K. L. Spangenberg), Cincinnati Art Museum, 1993.

Cipolla 1967
C. M. Cipolla, *Clocks and Culture, 1300–1700*, London, 1967.

Cleveland 1982
European Paintings of the 16th, 17th, and 18th Centuries, Cleveland Museum of Art Catalogue of Paintings 3, Cleveland, 1982.

Cobouw 1997
"Kastelenstichting tegen herbouw Nijmeegse burcht," *Cobouw* 141, no. 44 (6 March 1997): 3.

Coert 1991
G. A. Coert, "De Munsterse inundatie bij Coevorden in 1673," *Ons Waardeel* (1991): 222.

Cohen 1994
H. F. Cohen, *The Scientific Revolution: A Historiographical Inquiry*, Chicago, 1994.

Colenbrander 1985
H. Colenbrander, "Una veduta di Jan de Bisschop della chiesa dei SS. Cosma e Damiano a Roma," *Mededelingen van het Nederlands Instituut te Rome*, n.s. 11, no. 46 (1985): 107–19.

Collins 1953
L. C. Collins, *Hercules Seghers*, Chicago, 1953.

Cologne 1981
Wort & Bild (H. Raupp), Belgisches Haus, Cologne, 1981.

Coral Gables 1951
Dutch Old Masters, The University of Miami Art Gallery, Coral Gables, Florida, 1951.

Coupe 1966
W. A. Coupe, *The German Illustrated Broadsheet in the Seventeenth Century: Historical and Iconographical Studies*, 2 vols., Baden-Baden, 1966.

Craig 1983
——, "Pars Ergo Marthae Transit: Pieter Aertsen's 'Inverted' Paintings of *Christ in the House of Mary and Martha*," *Oud Holland* 97 (1983): 25–39.

Craig 1983a
K. Craig, "Rembrandt and *The Slaughtered Ox*," *Journal of the Warburg and Courtauld Institutes* 46 (1983): 25–39.

Crew 1978
P. Crew, *Calvinist Preaching and Iconoclasm in The Netherlands, 1554–69*, Cambridge, England, 1978.

Croiset van Uchelen 1976
A. R. A. Croiset van Uchelen, "Dutch Writing-Masters and the 'Prix de la Plume Couronnée," *Querendo* 6 (1976): 319–46.

Cundall 1891
F. Cundall, *The Landscape and Pastoral Painters of Holland: Ruisdael, Hobbema, Cuijp, Potter*, London, 1891.

Cunningham 1959
C. C. Cunningham, "Jacob Pynas's Adoration of the Magi," *Wadsworth Atheneum Bulletin* (Winter 1959): 10–13.

Daniel 1981
S. H. Daniel, "Seventeenth-Century Scholastic Treatments of Time," *Journal of the History of Ideas* 42, no. 4 (October–December 1981): 587–606.

Davies 1992
A. I. Davies, *Jan van Kessel (1641–1680)*, Doornspijk, 1992.

Davies 2001
——, *Allart van Everdingen*, Soest, 2001.

Davies 1988
D. Davies, "The Evocative Symbolism of Trees," in D. Cosgrove and S. Daniels, eds., *The Iconography of Landscape: Essays on the Symbolic Representation, Design and Use of Past Environments*, Cambridge, England, 1988, 32–42.

Davis 1884
C. Davis, *A Description of the Works of Art Forming the Collection of Alfred de Rothschild*, 2 vols., London, 1884.

Delbanco 1928
G. Delbanco, *Der Maler Abraham Bloemaert (1564–1651)*, Strassbourg, 1928.

Delft 1996
Delft Masters: Vermeer's Contemporaries; Illusionism through Light and Space (M. C. C. Kersten and D. H. A. C. Lokin), Stedelijk Museum Het Prinsenhof, Delft, 1996.

Denslagen 1987
W. F. Denslagen, *Omstreden herstel: Kritiek op het restaureren van monumenten; Een thema uit de architectuurgeschiedenis van Engeland, Frankrijk, Duitsland en Nederland (1779–1953)*, The Hague, 1987.

Denslagen 1997
——, "Architectura Renovata: Een inleiding op het themanummer over het Valkhof te Nijmegen." *Bulletin KNOB* 96 (1997): 81–83.

Denslagen 2004
——, *Romantisch modernisme: Nostalgie in de monumentenzorg*, Amsterdam, 2004.

Denver/Newark 2001–2
Art and Home. Dutch Interiors in the Age of Rembrandt (M. Westermann with S. Willemijn Fock, E. J. Sluijter, and H. P. Chapman), Denver Art Museum; and The Newark Museum, 2001–2.

Derrida 1991
J. Derrida, "From 'Des Tours de Babel' [1985]" in P. Kamuf, ed. and intro., *A Derrida Reader: Between the Blinds*, New York, 1991, 243–53.

Des Chene 2001
D. Des Chene, *Spirits and Clocks. Machine and Organism in Descartes*, Ithaca, New York, and London, 2001.

Descartes/AT 1964–76
R. Descartes, *Oeuvres de Descartes*, 12 vols., ed. A. Adam and P. Tannery, rev. ed., Paris, 1964–76.

Detroit 1970
Paintings in the Detroit Institute of Arts: Checklist of the Paintings Acquired before May, 1970, Detroit, 1970.

Van Deursen 1991
A. T. van Deursen, *Plain Lives in a Golden Age: Popular Culture, Religion, and Society in Seventeenth-Century Holland*, Cambridge, England, 1991.

Dickey 1986
S. S. Dickey, "'Judicious Negligence': Rembrandt Transforms an Emblematic Convention," *Art Bulletin* 68 (1986): 253–62.

Dictionary of Art 1996
The Dictionary of Art, ed. J. S. Turner, New York, 1996.

Dictionary of Art 2000
From Rembrandt to Vermeer: 17th-Century Dutch Artists, ed. J. S. Turner, Grove Dictionary of Art, New York, 2000.

Dieren 1937
Tentoonstelling van belangrijke 16e en 17e eeuwsche Hollandsche schilderijen (D. Katz), Dieren bij Arnhem, 1937.

Dohrn-van Rossum 1996
G. Dohrn-van Rossum, *History of the Hour: Clocks and Modern Temporal Orders*, Chicago and London, 1996.

Van Domselaer 1674–76
T. van Domselaer, *Het ontroerde Nederland: Door de wapenen des konings van Vrankryk dat*

is een waarachtigh verhaal van den Fransen, Engelsen, Keulsen, en Munstersen oorlogh, tegen de Vereenigde Nederlanden, 2 vols., Amsterdam, 1674 and 1676.

Donahue 1964
S. Donahue, "Daniel Vosmaer," *Vassar Journal of Undergraduate Studies* 19 (December 1964): 18–27.

Donahue 1966
——, "The Rest on the Flight into Egypt by Cornelis van Poelenburgh," *Fogg Art Museum, Harvard University: Acquisitions, 1965*, Cambridge, Massachusetts, 1966, 155–60.

Dordrecht 1976
Het Huis te Merwede, Gemeentearchief, Dordrecht, 1976.

Dordrecht 1977–78
Aelbert Cuyp en zijn familie: Schilders te Dordrecht (W. Veerman, J. M. de Groot, and J. G. van Gelder), Dordrechts Museum, 1977–78.

Dordrecht/Leeuwarden 1988
Meesterlijk vee: Nederlandse veeschilders 1600–1900 (C. Boschma, J. M. de Groot, G. Jansen, J. W. M. de Jong, and F. Grijzenhout), Dordrechts Museum; and Fries Museum, Leeuwarden, 1988.

Dozy 1888–90
C. M. Dozy, "Nalezing op F. Muller's Catalogus van Nederlandsche Historieprenten," in F. D. O. Obreen, *Archief voor Nederlandsche Kunstgeschiedenis*, Rotterdam, pt. 7, 1888–90.

Dozy 1897
——, "Pieter Nolpe," *Oud Holland* 15 (1897): 24–50, 94–120, 139–58, 220–44.

Duits Quarterly 1968
"Firefighting in Amsterdam in the Seventeenth Century," *Duits Quarterly*, no. 12 (1968): 10–16.

Dulwich 2002
Inspired by Italy: Dutch Landscape Painting 1600–1700 (L. B. Harwood), Dulwich Picture Gallery, 2002.

Dumaître 1982
P. Dumaître, *La curieuse destinée des planches anatomiques de Gérard de Lairesse*, Amsterdam, 1982.

Dumas 1991
C. Dumas, *Haagse Stadsgezichten: Topografische schilderijen van het Haags Historisch Museum*, Zwolle, 1991.

Düsseldorf 1953
Niederrheinansichten holländischer Künstler des 17. Jahrhunderts (H. Dattenberg), Kunstmuseum, Düsseldorf, 1953.

Eckerling 1977
L. Eckerling, "Isaack van Ostade," MA thesis, University of California at Los Angeles, 1977.

Eckerling Kaufman 1995
L. Eckerling Kaufman, *Isaak van Ostade, 1621–1649*, PhD diss., 2 vols., University of California at Los Angeles, 1995.

Egger 1931–32
H. Egger, *Römische Veduten: Handzeichnungen aus dem XV–XVII Jahrhundert zur Topographie der Stadt Rom*, 2 vols., Vienna, 1931–32.

Ekamper 2003
P. Ekamper et al., *Bevolkingsatlas van Nederland: Demografische ontwikkelingen van 1850 tot heden*, The Hague, 2003.

Emmens 1963
J. A. Emmens, "Natuur, Onderwijzing en Oefening: Bij een drieluik van Gerrit Dou," in J. Bruyn et al., eds., *Album Discipulorum J. G. van Gelder*, Utrecht, 1963, 125–36.

Enkhuizen 1990
Portret van Enkhuizen in de Gouden Eeuw (R. E. O. Ekkart), Zuiderzeemuseum, Enkhuizen, 1990.

Erickson 2000
P. Erickson, "Good for Harry, England and St. George: British National Identity and the Emergence of White Self Fashioning," in P. Erickson and C. Hulse, eds., *Early Modern Visual Culture: Representation, Race and Empire in Renaissance England*, Philadelphia, 2000, 315–45.

Ertz 1979
K. Ertz, *Jan Brueghel der Ältere (1568–1625): Die Gemälde mit kritischem Oeuvrekatalog*, Cologne, 1979.

Esmeijer 1977
A. Esmeijer, "Cloudscapes in Theory and Practice," *Simiolus* 9 (1977): 123–49.

Fairfax Murray 1905–12
C. Fairfax Murray, *Collection of Drawings by the Old Masters formed by C. Fairfax Murray (J. Pierpont Morgan Collection)*, 4 vols., London, 1905–12.

Faison 1964
S. L. Faison, *Art Tours and Detours in New York State: A Handbook to More Than 75 Outstanding Museums and Historic Landmarks in the Empire State outside of New York City*, New York, 1964.

Falkenburg 1996
R. L. Falkenburg, "'Schilderachtig weer' bij Jan van Goyen," in *Jan van Goyen*. (C. Vogelaar, with E. Buijsen, E. J. Sluijter, R. L. Falkenburg, and E. M. Gifford), Stedelijk Museum De Lakenhal, Leiden, 1996, 60–69.

Falkenburg 1997
——, "Onweer bij Jan van Goyen," *Nederlands kunsthistorisch jaarboek* 48 (1997); published Zwolle, 1998, 117–61.

Faré 1962
M. Faré, *La nature morte en France: Son histoire et son evolution du XVIIe au XXe siècle*, 2 vols., Geneva, 1962.

Feinblatt 1949
E. Feinblatt, "Note on Paintings by Bartholomeus Breenbergh," *Art Quarterly* 12 (1949): 266–71.

Feitama II, NdT + number
Refers to Fritz Lugt's typed copy (at the RKD) after the manuscript (also at the RKD) of Feitama II, Notitie der Teekeningen. See below.

Feitama II, Notitie der Teekeningen
Sybrand Feitama II. Notitie der Teekeningen uit de oudste en latere aanteekeningen, sedert de jaren 1685 en 1690, tot 1746, somtyds met volle zekerheid, somtyds naar de beste gissinge, of naar myn geheugen, opgemaakt. The manuscript of the *Notitie* at the RKD is an annotated inventory of the drawings Sybrand II (1694–1758), his grandfather Sybrand I (1620–1701), and his father Isaac (1666–1709) acquired and in some cases includes references to their subsequent history.

Filedt Kok 1990
J. P. Fieldt Kok, "Jacques de Gheyn II: Engraver, Designer and Publisher I, II," *Print Quarterly* 7 (1990): 248–81, 370–96.

Follinus 1613
H. Follinus, *Simonides, ofte memorie kunst*, Sandtvoort, 1613.

De la Fontaine Verwey 1976
H. de la Fontaine Verwey, "The Golden Age of Dutch Calligraphy," *Litterae textuales* 4 (1976): 69–78.

Francis 1959
H. S. Francis, "Dutch Drawings," *The Bulletin of the Cleveland Museum of Art* 46, no. 3 (March 1959): 39–43.

Franits 1993
W. E. Franits, *Paragons of Virtue: Women and Domesticity in Seventeenth-Century Dutch Art*, Cambridge, England, 1993 (paperback ed., 1995).

Franits 1997
W. E. Franits, ed., *Looking at Seventeenth-Century Dutch Art: Realism Reconsidered*, Cambridge, England, 1997.

Franken 1878
D. Franken, *Adriaen van de Venne*, Amsterdam and Paris, 1878.

Franken and Van der Kellen 1883 (rev. 1968)
D. Franken and J. van der Kellen, *L'oeuvre de Jan van de Velde, graveur hollandais, 1593–1641*, Amsterdam, 1883 (rev. ed., 1968).

Fraser, Haber, and Müller 1972
J. T. Fraser, F. C. Haber, and G. H. Müller, eds., *The Study of Time: Proceedings of the First Conference on the International Study of Time, Oberwohlfach (Black Forest), West Germany*, Berlin, Heidelberg, and New York, 1972.

Freedberg 1980
——, *Dutch Landscape Prints of the Seventeenth Century*, London, 1980.

Freedberg 1982
——, "The Hidden God: Image and Interdiction in the Netherlands in the 16th Century," *Art History* 5 (1982): 133–53.

Freedberg 1988
D. Freedberg, *Iconoclasm and Painting in the Revolt of the Netherlands, 1566–1609*, New York, 1988.

Freedberg 2002
——, *The Eye of the Lynx: Galileo, His Friends, and the Beginnings of Modern Science*, Chicago, 2002.

Freedberg, Burnstock, and Phenix 1984
D. Freedberg, A. Burnstock, and A. Phenix. "Paintings of Prints? Experiens Sillemans and the Origins of the *Grisaille* Sea-Piece: Notes on a Rediscovered Technique," *Print Quarterly* 1 (1984): 148–88.

Fremantle 1959
K. Fremantle, *The Baroque Town Hall of Amsterdam*, Utrecht, 1959.

Friedländer 1967–76
M. J. Friedländer, *Early Netherlandish Painting*, 14 vols., Leiden, 1967–76.

Fromentin 1876/1960
E. Fromentin, *The Masters of Past Time*, ed. H. Gerson, New York and Garden City, New Jersey, 1960 (original ed., *Les maîtres d'autrefois*, Paris, 1876).

Fuchs 1973
R. H. Fuchs, "Rembrandt en Italiaanse kunst: Opmerkingen over een verhouding," in O. von Simson and J. Kelch, eds., *Neue Beiträge zur Rembrandt-Forschung*, Berlin, 1973, 75–82.

Gabucci 2001
A. Gabucci, *The Colosseum*, trans. M. Becker, Los Angeles, 2001.

Van Gelder 1933
J. G. van Gelder, *Jan van de Velde, 1593–1641: Teekenaar-schilder*, The Hague, 1933.

Van Gelder 1938
——, "De memorie van Rembrandt's prenten in het bezit van Valerius Röver," *Oud Holland* 55, no. 1 (1938): 1–16.

Van Gelder 1971
——, "Jan de Bisschop, 1628–1671," *Oud Holland* 86 (1971): 201–59.

Van Gelder and Joost 1985
J. G. van Gelder and I. Joost, *Jan de Bisschop and His Icones and Paradigmata: Classical Antiquities and Italian Drawings for Artistic Instruction in Seventeenth Century Holland*, 2 vols., Doornspijk, 1985.

Gerzi 1971
T. Gerzi, *Netherlandish Drawings in the Budapest Museum: Sixteenth-Century Drawings*, 2 vols., Amsterdam and New York, 1971.

Gibson 2000
W. S. Gibson, *Pleasant Places: The Rustic Landscape from Bruegel to Ruisdael*, Berkeley, California, Los Angeles, and London, 2000.

Giezen-Nieuwenhuys 1987
H. W. M. Giezen-Nieuwenhuys, *Nederlandse duiventillen: Historische duifhuizen geschilderd en beschreven*, Zutphen, 1987.

Giltay 1980
J. Giltay, "De tekeningen van Jacob van Ruisdael," *Oud Holland* 94, nos. 2–3 (1980): 141–208.

Ginnings 1970
R. J. Ginnings, *The Art of Jan Baptist Weenix and Jan Weenix*, PhD diss., University of Delaware, 1970.

Ginsberg 1970
R. Ginsberg, "The Aesthetics of Ruins," *Bucknell Review* 18, no. 3 (Winter 1970): 89–102.

Glasbergen and Leenheer 1974
J. B. Glasbergen and S. H. C. Leenheer, *Duizend jaar Rijnsburg*, Leiden, 1974.

Glasbergen and Van Regteren Altena 1965
W. Glasbergen and H. H. van Regteren Altena, "De Abdij van Rijnsburg: Opgravingen in 1960/61 en 1963/64 (Voorlopige mededeling)," *Leids jaarboekje* 57 (1965): 144–57.

Goedde 1986
L. O. Goedde, "Convention, Realism, and the Interpretation of Dutch and Flemish Tempest Painting," *Simiolus* 16 (1986): 139–49.

Goedde 1989
——, *Tempest and Shipwreck in Dutch and Flemish Art: Convention, Rhetoric, and Interpretation*, University Park, Pennsylvania, 1989.

Goeree 1668
W. Goeree, *Inleiding tot de algemeene teycken-konst*, Middelburg, 1668 (2nd ed., Amsterdam, 1697; 3rd ed. [replica], Soest, 1974).

Goldschmidt 1922
A. Goldschmidt, "Egbert van der Poel und Adriaen van der Poel," *Oud Holland* 40 (1922): 57–66.

Gorissen 1959
F. Gorissen, "Die Burgen im Reich Nimwegen ausserhalb der Stadt Nimwegen," *Beiträge zur niederrheinischen Burgenkunde, Niederrheinisches Jahrbuch* (ed. A. Mock) 4 (1959): 105–68.

Gosschalk 1866
J. Gosschalk, "De ruïne van het kasteel Brederode ten behoeve van naaischolen," *De Nederlandsche spectator* 10, no. 9 (July 1866): 230–31.

Gottschalk 1977
M. K. E. Gottschalk, *Stormvloeden en rivieroverstromingen in Nederland*, pt. 3, Assen and Amsterdam, 1977.

Grant 1908
J. K. Grant, "Mr. John G. Johnson's Collection of Pictures in Philadelphia: Part IV," *Connoisseur* 22, no. 8 (1908): 141–52.

Graves 1913–15
A. Graves, *A Century of Loan Exhibitions, 1813–1912*, 5 vols., London, 1913–15.

Greenwich 1999
The Story of Time (ed. K. Lippencott), Royal Observatory Greenwich, in association with the National Maritime Museum, Greenwich, England, 1999.

Greenwich/Dublin 2003–4
Love Letters: Dutch Genre Paintings in the Age of Vermeer (P. C. Sutton, L. Vergara, and A. J. Adams, with J. Kilian and M. E. Wieseman), Bruce Museum of Arts and Science, Greenwich, Connecticut; and National Gallery of Ireland, Dublin, 2003–4.

Grelle 1987
A. Grelle, *Vestigi delle antichità di Roma … et altri luoghi: Momenti dell'elaborazione di un'immagine*, Rome, 1987.

Grisebach 1974
L. Grisebach, *Willem Kalf: 1619–1693*, Berlin, 1974.

De Groot 1979
I. de Groot, *Etchings by the Dutch Masters of the Seventeenth Century*, Maarssen, 1979.

Grosjean 1974
A. Grosjean, "Toward an Interpretation of Pieter Aertsen's Profane Iconography," *Konsthistorisk tidskrift* 43 (1974): 121–43.

Grotius 1714
H. Grotius, *Van de Outheid der Batavische, nu Hollandsche Republyk*, Amsterdam, 1714.

Grotius 1801–3
——, *Parallelon Republicarum liber tertius: De moribus ingenioque populorum Atheniensium, Romanorum, Batavorum, Vergelijking der gemeenbesten*, Haarlem, 1801–3.

Gudlaugsson 1954
S. J. Gudlaugsson, "Aanvullingen omtrent Pieter Post's werkzaamheid als schilder," *Oud Holland* 69 (1954): 59–70.

Guimarães 1957
A. Guimarães, "Na Holanda com Frans Post," *Revista do Instituto Histórico Geográphico Brasileiro* 235 (1957): 85–295.

Haak 1969
B. Haak, *Rembrandt: His Life, His Work, His Time*, New York, 1969.

Haak 1984
——, *The Golden Age: Dutch Painters of the Seventeenth Century*, London, 1984.

Haarlem 1986
Portretten van echt en trouw: Huwelijk en gezin in de Nederlandse kunst van de zeventiende eeuw (E. de Jongh), Frans Halsmuseum, Haarlem, 1986.

Haarlem 2002
Jacob van Ruisdael: De revolutie van het Hollandse landschap (M. Sitt and P. Biesboer, eds., with K. Müller), Frans Halsmuseum, Haarlem, 2002.

Haeger 1986
B. Haeger, "The Prodigal Son in 16th and 17th Century Netherlandish Art: Depictions of the Parable and the Evolution of a Catholic Image," *Simiolus* 16 (1986): 128–38.

Haeger 1988
——, "Philips Galle's Engravings after Maarten van Heemskerck's Parable of the Prodigal Son," *Oud Holland* 102, no. 2 (1988): 127–40.

The Hague 1953
Maurits de Braziliaan (A. B. de Vries, J. de Sousa-Leão, and W. Y. van Balen), The Mauritshuis, The Hague, 1953.

The Hague 1976
Jan van der Heyden (1637–1712): Kunstenaar en uitvinder, Koninklijke Bibliotheek, The Hague, 1976.

The Hague 1977
The Royal Cabinet of Paintings: Illustrated General Catalogue (E. Haverkamp-Begemann and A. Chong), Mauritshuis, The Hague, 1977.

The Hague 1980
Hollandse schilderkunst: Landschappen 17de eeuw (F. J. Duparc), Mauritshuis, The Hague, 1980.

The Hague 1991
The Hoogsteder Exhibition of Dutch Landscapes (P. Huys Janssen and P. C. Sutton), Hoogsteder & Hoogsteder, The Hague, 1991.

The Hague/Cambridge 1981–82
Jacob van Ruisdael (S. Slive), Mauritshuis, The Hague; and Fogg Art Museum, Harvard University, Cambridge, Massachusetts, 1981–82.

The Hague/San Francisco 1990–91
Great Dutch Paintings from America (B. P. J. Broos, with contributions by E. Buijsen, S. D. Kuretsky, W. Liedtke, L. F. Orr, J. Roding, and P. C. Sutton), Mauritshuis, The Hague; Fine Arts Museums of San Francisco, 1990–91.

Haitsma Mulier 1993
E. O. G. Haitsma Mulier, "De eerste Hollandse stadtsbeschrijvingen uit de zeventiende eeuw," *De Zeventiende Eeuw* 7 (1993): 97–116.

Halbwachs 1992
M. Halbwachs, *On Collective Memory*, ed. and trans. L. A. Coster, Chicago, 1992.

Halewood 1982
W. H. Halewood, *Six Subjects of Reformation Art: A Preface to Rembrandt*, Toronto, Buffalo, and London, 1982.

Hamann 1936
R. Hamann, "Hagars Abschied bei Rembrandt und im Rembrandt-Kreise," *Marburger Jahrbuch für Kunstwissenschaft* 8–9 (1936): 471–578.

Hamilton 1980
Man and Nature: A View of the Seventeenth Century (G. T. Scott), Art Gallery of Hamilton, Ontario, 1980.

Hamon 1992
P. Hamon, *Expositions, Literature and Architecture in Nineteenth-Century France* (trans. K. Sainson-Frank and L. Maguire) Berkeley, Los Angeles, Oxford, 1992, 53–93.

Hand and Wolff 1986
J. O. Hand and M. Wolff, *Early Netherlandish Paintings*, The Collections of the National Gallery of Art, Systematic Catalogue, Washington, DC, 1986.

Hanfmann 1964
G. M. A. Hanfmann, *Roman Art: A Modern Survey of the Art of Imperial Rome*, Greenwich, Connecticut, 1964.

Hannema 1955
D. Hannema, *Catalogue of the H.E. ten Cate Collection*, 2 vols., Rotterdam, 1955.

Hanover/Hartford/Boston 1973–74
One Hundred Master Drawings from New England Private Collections (F. W. Robinson), Hopkins Center Art Gallery, Dartmouth College, Hanover, New Hampshire; Wadsworth Atheneum, Hartford, Connecticut; and Museum of Fine Arts, Boston, 1973–74.

Hanover/Wellesley/Providence/Storrs 1969
Selections from the Collection of Dutch Drawings of Maida and George Abrams. A Loan Exhibition (F. W. Robinson), Hopkins Center, Dartmouth College, Hanover, New Hampshire; Jewett Arts Center, Wellesley College, Massachusetts; Rhode Island School of Design Museum, Providence; and Museum of Art, The University of Connecticut, Storrs, 1969.

Hansen 1996
J. V. Hansen, "Resurrecting Death: Anatomical Art in the Cabinet of Dr. Frederick Ruysch," *The Art Bulletin* 78, no. 4 (1996): 663–79.

Harms 1980
W. Harms, ed., *Deutsche Illustrierte Flugblätter des 16. und 17. Jahrhunderts*, 4 vols., Munich, 1980.

Hartford 1948
The Life of Christ, Wadsworth Atheneum, Hartford, Connecticut, 1948.

Hartford/Sarasota 1958
A. Everett Austin Jr.: A Director's Taste and Achievement, Wadsworth Atheneum, Hartford, Connecticut; and John and Mable Ringling Museum of Art, Sarasota, Florida, 1958.

Harwood 1988
L. B. Harwood, *Adam Pijnacker, c. 1620–1673*, Doornspijk, 1988.

Haskell 1980
F. Haskell, *Patrons and Painters: A Study in the Relations between Italian Art and Society in the Age of the Baroque*, New Haven, Connecticut, and London, 1980.

Haverkamp-Begemann 1959
E. Haverkamp-Begemann, *Willem Buytewech*, Amsterdam, 1959.

Haverkamp-Begemann 1969
——, "Rembrandt und seine Schule zur Austellung in Kanada," *Kunstchronik* 22 (1969): 281–308.

Haverkamp-Begemann 1973
——, *Hercules Segers: The Complete Etchings*, intro. by K. G. Boon and suppl. on Johannes Ruischer by E. Trautschold, Amsterdam, 1973.

Haverkamp-Begemann 1978
E. Haverkamp-Begemann, ed., *Wadsworth Atheneum Paintings: Catalogue I. The Netherlands and the German-Speaking Countries; Fifteenth–Nineteenth Centuries*, Hartford, Connecticut, 1978.

Hecht 1986
P. Hecht "The Debate on Symbol and Meaning in Dutch Seventeenth-Century Art: An Appeal to Common Sense," *Simiolus* 16 (1986): 173–87.

Heck and Lippincott 2002
C. Heck and K. Lippincott, eds., *Symbols of Time in the History of Art from Late Antiquity to the XXth Century*, Turnhout, 2002.

Heckscher 1958
W. S. Heckscher, *Rembrandt's Anatomy of Dr. Nicolaas Tulp*, New York, 1958.

Von Heinecken 1778–90
K. von Heinecken, *Dictionnaire des artistes dont nous avons des estampes*, Leipzig, 1778–90.

Held 1969
J. S. Held, "Die Ausstellung 'Rembrandt and His Pupils' in Montreal und Toronto," *Pantheon* 27 (1969): 384–89.

Held 1981
——, "European Drawings, 1375–1825, at the Morgan Library," review of *European Drawings, 1375–1825*, by C. D. Denison and H. B. Mules, *Master Drawings* 19, no. 2 (1981): 172–77.

Held 1991
——, "Rembrandt's Aristotle," in *Rembrandt Studies*, Princeton, New Jersey, 1991, 17–58.

's-Hertogenbosch/Heino/Haarlem 1984
Herinneringen aan Italië: Kunst en toerisme in de 18de eeuw (essay by R. de Leeuw), Noordbrabants Museum, 's-Hertogenbosch; Kasteel Het Nijenhuis, Heino; and Frans Halsmuseum, Haarlem, 1984.

Hetzler 1988
F. M. Hetzler, "Causality: Ruin Time and Ruins," *Leonardo* 21, no. 1 (1988): 51–55.

Van der Heyden 1690
J. van der Heyden and J. van der Heyden the Younger, *Beschryving der nieuwlyks uitgevonden en geoctrojeerde slang-brand-spuiten en hare wyze van brand-blussen, tegenwoordig binnen Amsterdam in gebruik zijnde*, Amsterdam, 1690 (2nd ed., 1735).

Van der Heyden/Multhauf 1996
J. van der Heyden, *A Description of Fire Engines with Water Hoses and the Method of Fighting Fires Now Used in Amsterdam* (trans. and intro. by L. S. Multhauf), Canton, Massachusetts, 1996.

Hielkema 2000
H. Hielkema, "Kasteel Nederhemert krijgt z'n restauratie," *Trouw* (25 November 2000): 33.

Hind 1915–32
A. Hind, *Catalogue of Drawings by Dutch and Flemish Artists Preserved in the Department of Prints and Drawings in the British Museum*, 5 vols., London, 1915–32.

Hind 1932
——, *Rembrandt, Being the Substance of the Charles Eliot Norton Lectures Delivered before Harvard University 1930–31*, Oxford and London, 1932.

Hirschmann 1919
O. Hirschmann, *Hendrick Goltzius*, Meister der Graphik 7, Leipzig, 1919.

Hirschmann 1976
——, *Verzeichnis des Graphischen Werk von Hendrick Goltzius*, Braunschweig, 1976.

Hodge 2002
A. T. Hodge, *Roman Aqueducts and Water Supply*, London, 2002.

Hodges 1985
D. L. Hodges, *Renaissance Fictions of Anatomy*, Amherst, Massachusetts, 1985.

Hoet 1752–70
G. Hoet, *Catalogus of naamlyst van schilderyen, met derzelver pryzen*, 3 vols., The Hague, 1752–70.

Hofstede de Groot 1907–28
C. Hofstede de Groot, *Beschreibendes und kritisches Verzeichnis der Werke der hervorragendsten holländischen Maler des XVII. Jahrhunderts*, 10 vols., Esslingen/Paris, 1907–28.

Hofstede de Groot 1907–27/1976
C. Hofstede de Groot, with the assistance of W. R. Valentiner, *A Catalogue Raisonné of the Works of the Most Eminent Dutch Painters of the Seventeenth Century*, 8 vols., London, 1907–27 [translation of German ed.] (facsimile ed. of English trans., 10 pts. in 3 vols., Cambridge, England, and Teaneck, New Jersey, 1976).

Hollander 2002
M. Hollander, *An Entrance for the Eyes: Space and Meaning in Seventeenth-Century Dutch Art*, Berkeley, California, Los Angeles, and London, 2002.

Hollstein
F. W. H. Hollstein, *Dutch and Flemish Etchings, Engravings and Woodcuts, ca. 1450–1700*, Amsterdam, [1949]– (for citations to revised volumes of Hollstein, see under *The New Hollstein*.)

Holman 1991–92
B. L. Holman, "Goltzius' *Great Hercules*: Mythology, Art, and Politics," *Nederlands kunsthistorisch jaarboek* 42–43 (1991–92): 397–412.

Holmes 1930
J. Holmes, "The Cuyps in America," *Art in America and Elsewhere* 18 (June 1930): 164–85.

Honig 1996
E. Honig, "Country Folk and City Business: A Print Series by Jan van de Velde," *Art Bulletin* 78, no. 3 (1996): 511–26.

Hoogewerff 1911
G. I. Hoogewerff, "De beide Willems van Nieuwlandt, oom en neef," *Oud Holland* 29 (1911): 57–61.

Hoogstraten 1678
S. van Hoogstraten, *Inleyding tot de hooge schoole der schilderkonst: Anders de zichtbare werelt*, Rotterdam, 1678 (reprint, [Soest], 1969).

Horace/Bennett 1914/67
Horace, *The Odes and Epodes*, trans. C. E. Bennett, Loeb Classical Library, Cambridge, Massachusetts, and London, 1914.

Houbraken 1718–21
A. Houbraken, *De groote schouburgh der Nederlantsche konstschilders en schilderessen*, 3 vols., Amsterdam, 1718–21 (2nd printing, Amsterdam, 1753).

Huffel 1921
N. G. van Huffel, *Cornelis Ploos van Amstel Jacob Corneliszoon, en zijne medewerkers en tijdgenoten: Historische schets van de techniek der hollandsche prentteekeningen gemaakt in de tweede helft der 18de eeuw*, Utrecht, 1921.

Huygens 1673
C. Huygens, *Horologium oscillatorium sive de motu pendulorum ad horologia aptato demonstrationes geometricae*, Paris, 1673.

Huygens/Blackwell 1986
Christiaan Huygens: The Pendulum Clock, or, Geometrical Demonstrations Concerning the Motion of Pendula as Applied to Clocks, intro. by H. J. M. Bos, trans and with notes by R. J. Blackwell, Ames, Iowa, 1986.

Huygens/Worp 1892
C. Huygens, "Batava Tempe," in J. A. Worp, ed., *Gedichten*, vol. 1, Groningen, 1892.

Indianapolis 1937
Dutch Paintings of the Seventeenth Century, John Herron Art Institute, Indianapolis, 1937.

Ithaca 1999
Reflections to Astound: Seventeenth-Century Dutch Prints from a Private Collection (J. B. Dallett and A. C. Weislogel), Herbert F. Johnson Museum of Art, Cornell University, Ithaca, New York, 1999.

Janson 1937
H. Janson, "The Putto with the Death's Head," *Art Bulletin* 19 (1937): 423–49.

Janssen, Kylstra-Wielinga, and Olde Meierink 1996
H. L. Janssen, J. M. M. Kylstra-Wielinga, and B. Olde Meierink, eds., *1000 jaar kastelen in Nederland: Functie en vorm door de eeuwen heen*, Utrecht, 1996.

Joachim 1959
H. Joachim, "Jacob de Gheyn's *Three Gypsies*, Pen and Ink, Chicago Art Institute," *The Art Institute of Chicago Quarterly* 53 (1959): 22.

Johnson Museum Handbook 1998
Herbert F. Johnson Museum of Art: A Handbook of the Collection, Cornell University, Ithaca, New York, 1998.

De Jong 2000
E. de Jong, "Projectontwikkelaar houdt kantoor in kasteel," *Cobouw* 144, no. 34 (18 February 2000): 3.

De Jongh 1967
E. de Jongh, *Zinne- en minnebeelden in de schilderkunst van de zeventiende eeuw*, Amsterdam, 1967.

De Jongh 1973
——, "'t Gotsche krulligh mal," *Nederlands kunsthistorisch jaarboek* 24 (1973): 85–145.

De Jongh 1974
——, "Grape Symbolism in Paintings of the 16th and 17th Centuries," *Simiolus* 7 (1974): 166–91.

De Jongh 1993
——, "Bij de balustrade, met gerust gemoed: De implicaties van een architonisch motief in de zeventiende-eeuwse portretkunst," *Oud Holland* 107, no. 1 (1993): 123–36.

De Jongh 1997
——, "Realism and Seeming Realism in Seventeenth-Century Dutch Painting," in W. Franits, ed., *Looking at Seventeenth-Century Dutch Art: Realism Reconsidered*, Cambridge, England, 1997.

Joppien 1979
R. Joppien, "The Dutch Vision of Brazil: Johan Maurits and His Artists," in E. van den Bogaaert, ed., *Johan Maurits van Nassau-Siegen, 1604–1679: A Humanist Prince in Europe and Brazil; Essays on the Tercentenary of His Death*, The Hague, 1979.

Josi 1821
C. Josi, *Collection d'imitations de dessins d'après les principaux maîtres hollandais et flamands, commencée par C. Ploos van Amstel, continuée et portée au nombre de cent morceaux …*, 2 vols., London, 1821.

Judson 1959
J. R. Judson, *Gerrit van Honthorst*, The Hague, 1959.

Judson 1973
——, *The Drawings of Jacob de Gheyn II*, New York, 1973.

Junius 1638
F. Junius, *The Painting of the Ancients*, London, 1638 (1st Dutch ed., 1641; facsimile reprint, Westmead, Farnborough, Hants., England, 1972).

Kalf 1917
J. Kalf, ed., *Grondbeginselen en voorschriften voor het behoud, de herstelling en de uitbreiding van oude bouwwerken*, Leiden, 1917.

Kampinga 1980
H. Kampinga, *De opvattingen over onze oudere vaderlandsche geschiedenis bij de Hollandsche historici der XVIe en XVIIe eeuw (vermeerderd met een register van personen door E.O.G. Haitsma Mulier)*, Utrecht, 1980.

Kaplan 1985
P. H. D. Kaplan, *The Rise of the Black Magus in Western Art*, Ann Arbor, Michigan, 1985.

Karstkarel 1978
P. Karstkarel, "Margareta de Heer en haar 'Stukjes,'" *Tableau* 1 (1978): 36–39.

Keersmaekers 1957
A. A. Keersmaekers, *De dichter Guilliam van Nieuwelandt en de senecaans klassieke tragedie in de Zuidelijke Nederlanden*, Ghent, 1957.

Van der Kellen 1867–73
J. P. van der Kellen, *Le peintre-graveur hollandais et flamand*, 2 vols., Utrecht, 1867–73.

Van der Kellen 1908
——, *Belangrijke prenten in Amsterdam*, Amsterdam, 1908.

Kettering 1983
A. Kettering, *The Dutch Arcadia: Pastoral Art and Its Audience in the Golden Age*, Montclair, New Jersey, 1983.

Kettering 1988
——, *Drawings from the Ter Borch Studio Estate*, The Hague, 1988.

Keyes 1974–80
G. S. Keyes, "Jacob Pynas as a Draughtsman," *Bulletin–Musées royaux des beaux-arts de Belgique/Brussels* 1–3 (1974–80): 147–70.

Keyes 1984
——, *Esaias van de Velde (1587–1630)*, Doornspijk, 1984.

Keyes 1986
——, "Department of Paintings," in *The Art of Collecting: Acquisitions at the Minneapolis Institute of Arts, 1980–1985*, Minneapolis, 1986, 56–66.

Keyes, Kuretsky, Rüger, and Wheelock 2004
Masters of Dutch Painting: The Detroit Institute of Arts (G. S. Keyes, S. D. Kuretsky, A. Rüger, and A. K. Wheelock Jr.), Detroit and London, 2004.

De Keyser 1943–44
P. de Keyser, "De Schrijfmeester Jan vanden Velde (1568–1623) en zijn beteekenis als schrijfkunstenaar," *De Gulden passer*, n.s., 21–22 (1943–44): 225–60.

Kilian 1993
J. M. Kilian, *Karel Dujardin*, PhD diss., Institute of Fine Arts, New York University, 1993.

De Klerk 1982
E. A. de Klerk, "*De Teecken-Const*: Een 17de eeuws Nederlands traktaatje" [with summary in English], *Oud Holland* 96 (1982): 16–60.

Kloek 1993
W. T. Kloek, "Northern Netherlandish Art," in Amsterdam 1993–94, 15–111.

Knuttel 1927
J. A. N. Knuttel, "Bauw-heers wel-leven," *Tijdschrift voor Nederlandsche taal- en letterkunde* 46 (1927): 180–85.

Knuttel 1962
G. Knuttel, *Adriaen Brouwer: The Master and His Work*, The Hague, 1962.

Koerner 1993
J. L. Koerner, *The Moment of Self-Portraiture in German Renaissance Art*, Chicago, 1993.

Kok 1996
M. Kok, "Het herstel van kasteel De Haar te Haarzuilens," *Bulletin KNOB* 95 (1996): 42–53.

Krautheimer 1980
R. Krautheimer, *Rome: Profile of a City, 312–1308*, Princeton, New Jersey, 1980.

Krefeld 1938
Deutsche Landschaften und Städtebilder in der niederländischen Kunst des 16. bis 18. Jahrhunderts, Kaiser Wilhelm Museum, Krefeld, 1938.

Krempel 2000
L. Krempel, *Studien zu den datierten Gemälden des Nicolaes Maes (1634–1693)*, Petersberg, 2000.

Kuipers-Verbuijs 1993
M. Kuipers-Verbuijs, *Middeleeuwse ruïnes in Nederland: Hun verleden, heden en toekomst*, final paper, Vrije Universiteit, Amsterdam, 1993.

Kuretsky 1974
S. D. Kuretsky, "Rembrandt's Tree Stump: An Iconographic Attribute of St. Jerome," *Art Bulletin* 61 (1974): 571–80.

Kuretsky 1994
——, "Worldly Creation in Rembrandt's *Landscape with Three Trees*," *Artibus et historiae* 15, no. 30 (1994): 157–91.

Kuretsky 1997
——, "Rembrandt at the Threshold," *Rembrandt, Rubens and the Art of Their Time: Recent Perspectives*, Papers in Art History from the Pennsylvania State University 11, College Park, 1997, 61–105.

Ter Laan 1939
K. ter Laan, *Woordenboek van de Nederlandse geschiedenis*, n.p., 1939.

Laarmann 2000
F. Laarmann, "Herman Meindertsz. Doncker—Ein origineller Künstler zweiten Ranges," *Oud Holland* 114, no. 1 (2000): 7–52.

Lacuelle-van der Kerk 1951
H. J. Lacuelle-van der Kerk, *De Haarlemse drukkers en boekverkopers van 1540–1600*, The Hague, 1951.

Lairesse 1701
G. de Lairesse, *Grondlegginge der teekenkunst*, Amsterdam, 1701.

Lairesse 1707
——, *Het groot schilderboek*, Amsterdam 1707.

Lairesse 1738
——, *The Art of Painting*, trans. J. F. Fritsch, London, 1738 (English ed. of Lairesse 1707).

Lairesse 1740
——, *Groot schilderboek*, 2 vols., 2nd ed., enlarged, Amsterdam, 1740 (reprint, Doornspijk, 1969).

Lairesse 1817
——, *A Treatise on the Art of Painting in All of Its Branches*, rev., corrected, and accompanied by an essay by W. M. Craig, 2 vols., London, 1817.

Lanciani 1897
R. Lanciani, *The Ruins and Excavations of Ancient Rome: A Companion Book for Students and Travelers*, Boston and New York, 1897.

Lanciani 1903
——, *The Destruction of Ancient Rome: A Sketch of the History of the Monuments*, New York, 1903.

Landes 1983
D. S. Landes, *Revolution in Time: Clocks and the Making of the Modern World*, Cambridge, Massachusetts, and London, 1983.

Landwehr 1973
J. Landwehr, *Romeyn de Hooghe the Etcher: Contemporary Portrayal of Europe, 1662–1707*, Leiden and Dobbs Ferry, New York, 1973.

Langereis 2001
S. Langereis, *Geschiedenis als ambacht: Oudheidkunde in de Gouden Eeuw; Arnoldus Buchelius en Petrus Schriverius*, Hiversum, 2001.

Larsen 1962
E. Larsen, *Frans Post, interprète du Brésil*, Amsterdam and Rio de Janiero, 1962.

Lawrence/New Haven/Austin 1983–84
Dutch Prints of Daily Life: Mirrors of Life or Masks of Morals? (L. A. Stone-Ferrier), Spencer Museum of Art, University of Kansas, Lawrence; Yale University Art Gallery, New Haven, Connecticut; and Huntington Gallery, University of Texas at Austin, 1983–84.

Leeflang 1997
H. Leeflang, "Dutch Landscape: The Urban View; Haarlem and Its Environs in Literature and Art, 15th–17th Century," *Nederlands kunsthistorisch jaarboek* 48 (1997): 52–115.

Van Leeuwen 1995
A. J. C. van Leeuwen, *De maakbaarheid van het verleden: P J.H. Cuypers als restauratiearchitect, 1850–1918*, Zeist, 1995.

Van Leeuwen 1685
S. van Leeuwen, *Batavia illustrata*, Amsterdam, 1685.

Van Leeuwen 1994
W. van Leeuwen, "Pittoreske bouwvallige architectuur versus gerestaureerde monumenten in het werk van P. J. H. Cuypers." C. van Eck, J. van den Eynde, and W. van Leeuwen, *Het schilderachtige: Studie over het schilderachtige in de Nederlandse kunsttheorie en architectuur, 1650–1900*, Amsterdam, 1994, 106–16.

Van Leeuwen and Pantus 1997
W. van Leeuwen and W.-J. Pantus, "Het Nijmeegs Valkhof als monument in het spanningsveld tussen vernieuwing en conservering," *Bulletin KNOB* 96 (1997): 84–102.

Leiden 1970
IJdelheid der Ijdelheden: Hollandse Vanitasvoorstellingen uit de zeventiende eeuw (M. Wurfbain and I. Bergström), Stedelijk Museum "De Lakenhal," Leiden, 1970.

Leiden 1986
Old Master Drawings from the Print Room of the University of Leiden (ed. J. Bolten), Prentenkabinet der Rijksuniversiteit Leiden, 1986.

Leiden 1988
Leidse fijnschilders: Van Gerrit Dou tot Frans van Mieris de Jongh, 1630–1760 (ed. E. J. Sluijter et. al.), Stedelijk Museum "De Lakenhal," Leiden, 1988.

Leiden 1996
Jan van Goyen (C. Vogelaar et. al.), Stedelijk Museum "De Lakenhal," Leiden, 1996.

Lemmens 1984
G. Lemmens, ed., *Het Valkhof te Nijmegen*, Nijmegen, 1984 (2nd, corrected ed. of exh. cat. Nijmeegs Museum "Commanderie van St. Jan," Nijmegen, 1980).

Lesger and Noordegraaf 1995
C. Lesger and L. Noordegraaf, eds., *Entrepreneurs and Entrepreneurship in the Modern Times: Merchants and Industrialists within the Orbit of the Dutch Staple Market*, The Hague, 1995.

Van Leusden 1961
W. van Leusden, *The Etchings of Hercules Seghers and the Problems of His Graphic Technique*, Utrecht, 1961.

Levesque 1994
C. Levesque, *Journey through Landscape in Seventeenth-Century Holland: The Haarlem Print Series and Dutch Identity*, University Park, Pennsylvania, 1994.

Levesque 1997
——, "Landscape, Politics and the Prosperous Peace," *Nederlands kunsthistorisch jaarboek* 48 (1997): 223–57.

Levine 1984
D. A. Levine, *The Art of the Bamboccianti*, PhD diss., Princeton University, 1984.

Levine 1988
——, "The Roman Limekilns of the Bamboccianti," *Art Bulletin* 70 (1988): 569–89.

Liedtke 2000
W. A. Liedtke, *A View of Delft: Vermeer and His Contemporaries*, Zwolle, 2000.

Limouze 1995
D. Limouze, *The Felix M. Warburg Print Collection: A Legacy of Discernment* (intro., catalogue, and essay by D. Limouze and essay by S. D. Kuretsky), The Frances Lehman Loeb Art Center, Vassar College, Poughkeepsie, New York, 1995.

Lipschitz 1988
S. Lipschitz, *Selected Works: The Minneapolis Institute of Arts*, Minneapolis, 1988.

Löffler 2000
E. P. Löffler, "De Ruïne van de Abdij te Rijnsburg in Fantasiegezichten," *Genootschap Oud Rijnsburg. Jaarboekje 2000*: 42–51.

Löffler 2001
——, "Kasteel De Waardenburg door Roelant Savery: Een reconstructie," *Delineavit et Sculpsit*, no. 23 (July 2001): 1–5.

Löffler 2002
——, "De ruïnes van kasteel Rossum en kasteel Brederode geïdentificeerd op werken van Roelant Savery en enkele tijdgenoten," *Delineavit et Sculpsit* 25 (September 2002): 7–16.

Logan 1996
C. Logan, "Recording the News: Herman Saftleven's *View of Delft after the Explosion of the Gunpowder Arsenal in 1654*," *Metropolitan Museum Journal* 31 (1996): 203–10.

London 1883
Exhibition of Etchings of Renier Zeeman and Karel Du Jardin with Illustrative Drawings, Burlington Fine Arts Club, London, 1883.

London 1974
Garantiert echt, Arcade Gallery, London, 1974.

London 1980
Ten Paintings by Gerard Dou, 1613–1675, David Carrit Ltd., London, 1980.

London 1986
Dutch Landscape: The Early Years; Haarlem and Amsterdam, 1590–1650 (C. Brown), National Gallery, London, 1986.

London 2001
Spectacular Bodies: The Art and Science of the Human Body in the Renaissance (M. Kemp and M. Wallace), Hayward Gallery, London, 2001.

London 2002
Inspired by Italy: Dutch Landscape Painting, 1600–1700 (L. B. Harwood), Dulwich Picture Gallery, London, 2002.

London/Amsterdam 2000
Rembrandt the Printmaker (E. Hinterding, G. Luijten, and M. Royalton-Kisch), British Museum, London; and Rijksmuseum, Amsterdam, 2000.

London/Birmingham/Leeds 1962
Old Master Drawings from the Collection of Mr. C. R. Rudolf, Arts Council, London; Birmingham Museum and Art Gallery; and Leeds City Art Gallery, 1962.

London/Paris/Cambridge 2002–3
Bruegel to Rembrandt: Dutch and Flemish Drawings from the Maida and George Abrams Collection (W. W. Robinson, with an essay by M. Royalton-Kisch), British Museum, London; Institut Néerlandais, Paris; and Fogg Art Museum, Cambridge, Massachusetts, 2002–3.

Los Angeles 1992
Goltzius and the Classical Tradition (G. Harcourt), Los Angeles County Museum of Art, Los Angeles, 1992.

Los Angeles 1997–98
Irresistible Decay: Ruins Reclaimed; The Getty Research Center for the History of Art and the Humanities (M. S. Roth, C. Lyons, and C. Merewether), The Getty Center, Los Angeles, 1997–98.

Los Angeles/Toledo/Sarasota/Austin/Baltimore 1988–89
Mannerist Prints: International Style in the Sixteenth Century (B. Davis), Los Angeles County Museum of Art; Toledo Museum of Art; John and Mable Ringling Museum of Art, Sarasota, Florida; Arthur M. Huntington Art Gallery, University of Texas, Austin; and The Baltimore Museum of Art, 1988–89.

Lowenthal 1986
A. W. Lowenthal, *Joachim Wtewael and Dutch Mannerism*, Doornspijk, 1986.

Lugt 1915
F. Lugt, *Wandelingen met Rembrandt in en om Amsterdam*, Amsterdam, 1915 (reprinted in German trans. as *Mit Rembrandt in Amsterdam*, Berlin, 1920).

Lugt 1927
——, *Inventaire général des dessins dans les collections publiques de France: Les dessins des Écoles du Nord de la collection Dutuit au Musée des Beaux-Arts de la Ville de Paris (Petit Palais)*, Paris, 1927.

Lugt 1929–33
——, *École hollandaise: Inventaire général des Écoles du Nord au Musée du Louvre*, 3 vols., Paris, 1929–33.

Lugt 1950
——, *École Nationale Supérieure des Beaux-Arts: Inventaire général des dessins des écoles du Nord*, Paris, 1950.

Luyken 1711
J. Luyken, *De bykorf des gemoeds*, Amsterdam, 1711.

Lydius 1668
J. Lydius, *'t Verheerlikt Nederland*, Amsterdam, 1668.

Macauley 1966
R. Macauley, *The Pleasure of Ruins*, New York, 1966.

MacLaren 1960
N. MacLaren, *The Dutch School*, National Gallery Catalogues, London, 1960.

MacLaren/Brown 1991
N. MacLaren and C. Brown, *The Dutch School, 1600–1900*, 2 vols., National Gallery Catalogues, London, 1991.

Maleuve 1999
D. Maleuve, *Museum Memories, History, Technology, Art*, Stanford, 1999.

Manchester 1965
Between Renaissance and Baroque: European Art, 1520–1600 (intro. by F. G. Grossman), City of Manchester Art Gallery, 1965.

Van Mander 1604
K. van Mander, *Het schilder-boeck. Den grondt der edel vry schilder-const*, Haarlem, 1604.

Van Mander/Miedema 1973
——, *Den grondt der edel vry schilder-const*, trans. and with a commentary by H. Miedema, 2 vols., Utrecht, 1973.

Van Mander/Miedema 1994–99
——, *Karel van Mander: The Lives of the Illustrious Netherlandish and German Painters, from the First Edition of the Schilder-Boeck (1603–04)*, ed. H. Miedema, 6 vols., Doornspijk, 1994–99.

De Marly 1970
D. de Marly, "A Note on the Metropolitan Fortune Teller," *Burlington Magazine* 113, no. 807 (1970): 388.

Martin 1911
W. Martin, *Gérard Dou: Sa vie et son oeuvre*, trans. L. Dimier, Paris, 1911.

Martin 1913
——, *Gerard Dou: Des Meisters Gemälde*, Stuttgart and Berlin, 1913.

Matthews 1898
I. Matthews, *Full Revelations of a Professional Ratcatcher*, Manchester, 1898.

Mazur-Contamine 1994
H. E. C. Mazur-Contamine,"Goltzius' Seven Oval Chiaroscuro Woodcuts—a Reinterpretation," *Delineavit and Sculpsit* 12 (April 1994): 1–45.

Meertens 1942
P. J. Meertens, *De loof van den boer: De boer in de Noord- en Zuidnederlandsche letterkunde van de Middeleeuwen tot heden*, deel 1, *Van de Middeleeuwen tot 1880*, Amsterdam, 1942.

Melion 1989
W. Melion, "Karel van Mander's 'Life of Goltzius': Defining the Paradigm of Protean Virtuosity in Haarlem around 1600," *Studies in the History of Art* 27 (1989): 113–33.

Melion 1992
——, "Memory and the Kinship of Writing and Picturing in the Early Seventeenth-Century Netherlands," *Word and Image* 8, no. 1 (January–March 1992): 48–70.

Melion 1993
——,"Theory and Practice: Reproductive Engravings in the Sixteenth Century Netherlands," in L. Silver and T. Riggs, eds., *Graven Images: The Rise of Professional Printmakers in Antwerp and Haarlem*, Evanston, Illinois, 1993.

Melion 1995
——, "*Memorabilia aliquot strenuitatis exempla:* The thematics of artisinal value in Hendrick Goltzius' *Roman Heroes*," *Modern Language Notes* 110 (1995): 1090–1134.

De Meyere 1981
J. de Meyere, "An Early Painting by Abraham Bloemaert," *Tableau* 4 (1981): 173–77.

Middelkoop 1994
N. Middelkoop, *De anatomische les van Dr. Deijman*, Amsterdams Historisch Museum, Amsterdam, 1994.

Mielke 1980
H. Mielke, review of *Netherlandish Drawings of the Fifteenth and Sixteenth Centuries*, by K. G. Boon, *Simiolus* 11 (1980): 39–50.

Milham 1923
W. I. Milham, *Time and Timekeepers*, New York, 1923.

Miller 1982
D. Miller, "Jan Victors: An Old Testament Subject in the Indianapolis Museum of Art," *Perceptions* 2 (1982): 22–29.

Milwaukee 1992
Leonart Bramer, 1596–1674: Painter of the Night (F. F. Hofrichter et. al.), Haggerty Museum of Art, Marquette University, Milwaukee, 1992.

Minneapolis/Toledo/Los Angeles 1990–91
Mirror of Empire: Dutch Marine Art of the Seventeenth Century (G. S. Keyes et. al.), Minneapolis Institute of Arts; Toledo Museum of Art; and Los Angeles County Museum of Art, 1990–91.

Montias 1982
J. M. Montias, *Arts and Artisans in Delft: A Socio-Economic Study of the Seventeenth Century*, Princeton, New Jersey, 1982.

Montias 2003
——, "How Notaries and Other Scribes Recorded Works of Art in Seventeenth-Century Sales and Inventories," *Simiolus* 30, no. 3/4 (2003): 217–35.

Montreal 1990
Italian Recollections: Dutch Painters of the Golden Age (F. J. Duparc and L. L. Graif), Montreal Museum of Fine Arts, 1990.

Montreal/Toronto 1969
Rembrandt and His Pupils (D. G. Carter and J. Bruyn), Montreal Museum of Fine Arts; and Art Gallery of Ontario, Toronto, 1969.

Morath 1996
W. Morath, *Zum Verständnis der Radierungen von Hercules Segers: Bildgeschichte und Formbegriff*, Hildesheim, 1996.

Morgan Library Acquisitions 1969
Pierpont Morgan Library: A Review of Acquisitions, 1949–1968, New York, 1969.

Morgan Library Fellows Report 1973
Fellows Report: Pierpont Morgan Library 16 (1973).

Moxey 1977
K. Moxey, *Pieter Aertsen, Joachim Beuckelaer, and the Rise of Secular Painting in the Context of the Reformation*, New York and London, 1977.

Muizelaar and Phillips 2003
K. Muizelaar and D. Phillips, *Picturing Men and Women in the Dutch Golden Age: Paintings and People in Historical Perspective*, New Haven, Connecticut, and London, 2003.

Mulder, Blok, and Van Reenen 1987
J. Mulder, H. Blok, and K. van Reenen, *Diemen buyten Amsterdam*, Amsterdam, 1987.

Mules 1985
H. B. Mules, "Dutch Drawings of the Seventeenth Century in the Metropolitan Museum of Art," *The Metropolitan Museum of Art Bulletin* 42 (Spring 1985): 3–56.

Müller 1927
C. Müller, "Abraham Bloemaert als Landschaftsmaler," *Oud Holland* 44 (1927): 193–208.

Müller 1949
H. P. Müller, *Die Ruine in der deutschen und niederländischen Malerei des 15. und 16. Jahrhunderts*, diss., University of Heidelberg, 1949.

Muller 1863–82
F. Muller, *Beredeneerde beschrijving van Nederlandse historieplaten, zinneprenten en historische kaarten*, Amsterdam, 1863–82 (reprint, Amsterdam, 1970).

Muller 1985
S. D. Muller, *Charity in the Dutch Republic: Pictures of Rich and Poor for Charitable Institutions*, Ann Arbor, Michigan, 1985.

Münster/Baden-Baden 1979–80
Stilleben in Europa (U. Bernsmeier, C. Klemm, J. Lammers, G. Langemeyer, and G. Luther), Westfälisches Landesmuseum für Kunst und Kulturgeschichte, Münster; and Staatliche Kunsthalle, Baden-Baden, 1979–80.

Murray 1959
P. Murray and L. Murray, *Dictionary of Art and Artists*, New York, 1959.

Nash 1972
J. M. Nash, *The Age of Rembrandt and Vermeer: Dutch Painting in the Seventeenth Century*, New York, Chicago, and San Francisco, 1972.

Naumann 1981
O. Naumann, *Frans van Mieris the Elder (1635–1681)*, 2 vols., Doornspijk, 1981.

Nederduytschen Helicon 1610
Nederduytschen Helicon: Eygentlijck wesende der Maetdicht beminders Lust-toneel, Haarlem, 1610.

Nelson 1979
L. Nelson Jr., "The Uses of Time in Poetry," in *Baroque Lyric Poetry*, New York, 1979, part 2, chap. 1.

New Brunswick 1983
Haarlem: The Seventeenth Century (F. F. Hofrichter), The Jane Voorhees Zimmerli Art Museum, Rutgers, the State University of New Jersey, New Brunswick, 1983.

The New Hollstein 2000
J. P. Filedt Kok and M. Leesberg, *The De Gheyn Family: The New Hollstein; Dutch & Flemish Etchings, Engravings and Woodcuts, 1450–1700*, ed. G. Luijten, 2 vols., Rotterdam, 2000.

New York 1953
Landscape Drawings and Water-Colors: Brueghel to Cézanne, The Pierpont Morgan Library, New York, 1953.

New York 1968–69
Gods and Heroes: Baroque Images of Antiquity (E. Williams), Wildenstein and Co., New York, 1968–69.

New York 1973
Abraham Bloemaert 1564–1651: Prints and Drawings, Metropolitan Museum of Art, New York, 1973.

New York 1974
Major Acquisitions of the Pierpont Morgan Library, 1924–1974, New York, 1974.

New York 1976–77
Roman Artists of the Seventeenth Century: Drawings and Prints (checklist by J. Bean and M. L. Myers), Metropolitan Museum of Art, New York, 1976–77.

New York 1981
European Drawings, 1375–1825 (cat. by C. D. Denison and H. B. Mules, with the assistance of J. V. Shoaf), The Pierpont Morgan Library, New York, 1981.

New York 1985
The Golden Ambiance: Dutch Landscape Painting in the Seventeenth Century (W. A. Liedtke), Minskoff Cultural Center, New York, 1985.

New York 1985a
Landscape Painting in Rome, 1595–1675, Richard Feigen & Co., New York, 1985.

New York 1988
Dutch and Flemish Paintings from New York Private Collections (A. J. Adams with E. Haverkamp-Begemann), National Academy of Design, New York, 1988.

New York 2001
Pieter Bruegel the Elder: Drawings and Prints (ed. N. Orenstein), Metropolitan Museum of Art, 2001.

New York 2002
The Thaw Collection: Master Drawings and Oil Sketches; Acquisitions since 1994 (C. E. Pierce, E. V. Thaw, J. S. Turner, W. M. Griswold, et. al.), The Pierpont Morgan Library, New York, 2002.

New York/London 1986
The Northern Landscape: Flemish, Dutch and British Drawings from the Courtauld Collections (D. Farr and W. Bradford), The Drawing Center, New York; and The Courtauld Institute Galleries, London, 1986.

New York/London 2001
Vermeer and the Delft School (W. A. Liedtke with M. C. Plomp and A. Rüger), Metropolitan Museum of Art, New York; and National Gallery, London, 2001.

New York/Paris 1977–78
Rembrandt and His Century: Dutch Drawings of the Seventeenth Century from the Collection of Fritz Lugt, Institut Néerlandais, Paris (C. van Hasselt), The Pierpont Morgan Library, New York; and Institut Néerlandais, Paris, 1977–78.

Nicolson 1956
B. Nicolson, "The Rijksmuseum *Incredulity* and Terbrugghen's Chronology," *Burlington Magazine* 98 (1956): 103–10.

Nieuw Nederl. biog. woordenboek 1911–37
Nieuw Nederlandsch biografisch woordenboek, 10 vols. Leiden, 1911–37.

Nijmegen 1997
Vervallen verleden: De ruïne in de Nederlandse teken- en schilderkunst (M. Kuipers-Verbuijs and A. G. Schulte), Nijmeegs Museum "Commanderie van St. Jan," Nijmegen, 1997.

Van Nispen tot Sevenaer 1995
E. O. M. van Nispen tot Sevenaer, "Monumentenzorg en oorlogsschade [text of a speech given in 1946]," *Monumenten en oorlogstijd: Jaarboek monumentenzorg* (1995): 32–48.

NRC Handelsblad 1996
"Nijmegen zonder burcht is tandeloos gebit langs de Waal: Vereniging wil het Valkhof terug," *NRC handelsblad* (27 March 1996): 2.

Oberlin 1963
Youthful Works by Great Artists, catalogue in *Allen Memorial Art Museum Bulletin, Oberlin College* 20, no. 3 (1963).

Obreen 1877–90
F. D. O. Obreen, *Archief voor Nederlandsche Kunstgeschiedenis*, 7 vols., Rotterdam, 1877–90.

Oehler 1967
L. Oehler, "Zu einingen Bildern aus Elsheimers Umkreis," *Städel-Jahrbuch*, n.F. 1 (1967): 148–70.

Olde Meierink et al. (ed.) 1995
B. Olde Meijerink, et al., ed., *Kastelen en ridderhofsteden in Utrecht*, Utrecht, 1995.

D'Onofrio 1968
C. d'Onofrio, *Roma nel Seicento*, Rome, 1968.

Orenstein 1995
N. Orenstein, "Prints and the Politics of the Publisher: The Case of Hendrick Hondius," *Simiolus* 23 (1995): 240–50.

Orenstein 1996
——, *Hendrick Hondius and the Business of Prints in Seventeenth-Century Holland*, Rotterdam, 1996.

Orlers 1642
J. J. Orlers, *Beschrijvinge der stad Leyden*, Leiden, 1642.

Orr 2000
L. F. Orr, "Another Masterpiece for the Dutch Collection," *Fine Arts: M. H. de Young*

Museum; California Palace of the Legion of Honor (Spring 2000): 7–8.

Von der Osten 1964
G. von der Osten, "Der Blick in die Geburtshöhle," *Kölner Domblatt* 23–24 (1964): 341–58.

Ottawa 1996
The Ingenious Machine of Nature: Four Centuries of Art and Anatomy (M. Cazort, M. Kornell, and K. B. Roberts), National Gallery of Canada, Ottawa, 1996.

Ovid/Innes 1955
Ovid, *Metamorphoses*, trans. M. M. Innes, Baltimore, 1955.

Pagels 1988
E. Pagels, *Adam, Eve, and the Serpent*, New York, 1988.

Panofsky 1955
E. Panofsky, "Poussin and the Elegiac Tradition," in *Meaning in the Visual Arts*, Garden City, New York, 1955, 295–320.

Panofsky 1958
——, *Early Netherlandish Painting: Its Origins and Character*, 2 vols., Cambridge, Massachusetts, 1958 (2nd ed., 1971).

Panofsky 1962
——, "Father Time," in E. Panofsky, *Studies in Iconology: Humanistic Themes in the Art of the Renaissance*, New York, 1962 (1st ed., 1939), 69–94.

Parente 1987
J. A. Parente Jr., *Religious Drama and the Humanist Tradition: Christian Theater in Germany and in the Netherlands, 1500–1680*, Leiden, New York, Copenhagen, and Cologne, 1987.

Paris 1970–71
Le siècle de Rembrandt: Tableaux hollandais des collections publiques françaises, Musée du Petit Palais, Paris, 1970–71.

Paris 1985
Le héraut du dix-septième siècle: Dessins et gravures de Jacques de Gheyn II et III de la Fondation Custodia collection Frits Lugt (C. van Hasselt and M. van Berge-Gerbaud), Institut Néerlandais, Paris, 1985.

Paris/Antwerp/London/New York 1979–80
Rubens and Rembrandt in Their Century: Flemish and Dutch Drawings of the 17th Century from the Pierpont Morgan Library (F. Stampfle), Institut Néerlandais, Paris; Koninklijk Museum voor Schone Kunsten, Antwerp; British Museum, London; and The Pierpont Morgan Library, New York, 1979–80.

Parthey 1863–64
G. Parthey, *Deutscher Bildersaal: Verzeichnis der in Deutschland vorhandenen Ölbilder verstorbener Maler aller Schulen*, 2 vols., Berlin, 1863–64.

Persels and Ganim 2004
J. Persels and R. Ganim, eds., *Fecal Matters in Early Modern Literature and Art: Studies in Scatology*, Studies in European Cultural Transition 21, Aldershot, Hampshire, England, and Burlington, Vermont, 2004.

Philadelphia/Detroit 1960–61
The Ruins of Rome, The University Museum, University of Pennsylvania, Philadelphia; and The Detroit Institute of Arts, 1960–61.

Plokker 1984
A. Plokker, *Adriaen van de Venne (1589–1662): De grisailles met spreukbanden*, Leuven and Amersfoort, 1984.

Plomp 1996
M. C. Plomp, "Langs de wallen van Delft: Een stadswandeling via zeventiende-eeuwse gezichten," *Antiek* 30 (March 1996): 348–61.

Plomp 1997
——, *The Dutch Drawings in the Teyler Museum*, vol. 2, *Artists Born between 1575 and 1630*, Haarlem, Ghent, and Doornspijk, 1997.

Pollmann 1999
J. Pollmann, *Religious Choice in the Dutch Republic: The Reformation of Arnoldus Buchelius*, Manchester, 1999.

Popper-Voskuil 1973
N. Popper-Voskuil, "Self-Portraiture and Vanitas Still-Life Painting in 17th Century Holland in Reference to David Bailly's Vanitas Oeuvre," *Pantheon* 31 (1973): 58–74.

Poughkeepsie 1976
Seventeenth Century Dutch Landscape Drawings and Selected Prints from American Collections (C. O. Baer with S. D. Kuretsky), Vassar College Art Gallery, Poughkeepsie, New York, 1976.

Poughkeepsie/Chicago/Pittsburgh/Athens 1999–2002
Landscapes of Retrospection: The Magoon Collection of British Drawings and Prints, 1739–1860 (B. Lukacher, F. Consagra, and S. Smiles), The Frances Lehman Loeb Art Center, Vassar College; Poughkeepsie, New York; The David and Alfred Smart Museum of Art, University of Chicago; The Heinz Architectural Center, Carnegie Museum of Art, Pittsburgh; and Georgia Museum of Art, University of Georgia, Athens, 1999–2002.

Priem 1997
R. Priem, "The 'Most Excellent Collection' of Lucretia Johanna van Winter: The Years 1809–22, with a Catalogue of the Works Purchased," *Simiolus* 25, nos. 2–3 (1997): 103–235.

Provoost and Wilkins 1995
M. Provoost and C. Wilkins, *Re-arch: Nieuwe ontwerpen voor oude gebouwen*, Rotterdam, 1995.

Puyvelde 1944
L. Puyvelde, *The Dutch Drawings in the Collection of His Majesty the King at Windsor Castle*, London and New York, 1944.

Rademaker 1725
A. Rademaker, *Kabinet van Nederlandsche outheden en gezichten*, 2 parts, Amsterdam, 1725 (reprint, Haarlem, 1975).

Rademaker 1732
——, *Rhijnlands fraaiste gezichten, vertoonende deszelfs lustplaatsen, heerenhuizen en dorpen*, Amsterdam, 1732.

Reallexikon 1937–
Reallexikon zur deutschen Kunstgeschichte, ed. O. Schmitt et. al., Stuttgart-Waldsee, 1937–.

Redford 1888
G. Redford, *A History of Sales of Pictures and Other Works of Art*, 2 vols., London, 1888.

Van Regteren-Altena 1935
I. Q. van Regteren-Altena, *Jacques de Gheyn: An Introduction to the Study of His Drawings*, Amsterdam, 1935.

Van Regteren-Altena 1971
——, "Marcel Roethlisberger, 'Bartholomeus Breenbergh, Handzeichnungen,'" *Art Bulletin* 53 (December 1971): 536–38.

Van Regteren-Altena 1983
——, *Jacques de Gheyn: Three Generations*, 3 vols., The Hague and Boston, 1983.

Reiss 1975
S. Reiss, *Aelbert Cuyp*, Boston, 1975.

Rembrandt Corpus
J. Bruyn et al., *A Corpus of Rembrandt Paintings*, 3 vols. to date, The Hague, Boston, and London, 1982–.

Renaud 1940
J. G. N. Renaud, "De iconografie van het slot te Egmond," *Maandblad voor beeldende kunsten* 17 (1940): 338–345.

Renaud 1942
——, "Oudheidkundige onderzoekingen in en om Rotterdam, III, Spangen," *Rotterdamsch jaarboekje* 10 (1942): 141–51.

Van Reyen 1965
P. E. van Reyen, *Middeleeuwse kastelen in Nederland*, Bussum, 1965.

Reznicek 1961
E. K. J. Reznicek, *Die Zeichnungen von Hendrick Goltzius*, 2 vols., Utrecht, 1961.

Reznicek 1986
——, "Hendrick Goltzius and His Conception of Landscape," in, *Dutch Landscape: The Early Years; Haarlem and Amsterdam, 1590–1650* (ed. C. Brown) National Gallery, London, 1986, 57–62.

Ribton-Turner 1972
C. J. Ribton-Turner, *A History of Vagrants and Vagrancy and Beggars and Begging*, Montclair, New Jersey, 1972.

Riggs 1977
T. A. Riggs, *Hieronymus Cock: Printmaker and Publisher*, New York and London, 1977.

Van Rijn and Kernkamp 1910
G. van Rijn and G. W. Kernkamp, *Nederlandsche historieprenten (1550–1900): Platen-atlas*, Amsterdam, 1910.

Van Rijn and Van Ommeren 1895–1933
G. van Rijn and C. van Ommeren, *Atlas van Stolk: Katalogus der historie-, spot-, en zinneprenten betrekkelijk de geschiedenis van Nederland verzameld*, 10 vols., Amsterdam, 1895–1933. (A catalogue of the Atlas van Stolk, a collection of prints and emblems relating to the history of the Netherlands [Historisch Museum, Rotterdam)] formed by Abraham van Stolk [1814–96] and his descendants.)

Robb 1966
N. A. Robb, *William of Orange: A Personal Portrait*, 2 vols., London, Melbourne, and Toronto, 1966.

Roberts 1897
W. Roberts, *Memorials of Christie's: A Record of Art Sales from 1766 to 1896*, London, 1897.

Robinson 1979
W. W. Robinson, "Preparatory Drawings by Adriaen van de Velde," *Master Drawings* 17 (1979): 3–23.

Robinson 1987
——, "The Eavesdroppers and Related Paintings by Nicolaes Maes," in "Holländische Genremalerei im 17. Jahrhunderts, Symposium, Berlin 1984," special issue, *Jahrbuch Preussischer Kulturbesitz*, no. 4 (1987): 283–313.

Robinson and Wilson 1980
F. W. Robinson and W. Wilson, *John and Mable Ringling Museum of Art: Catalogue of the Flemish and Dutch Paintings, 1400–1900*, Sarasota, Florida, 1980.

Roesler-Friedenthal and Nathan 2003
A. Roesler-Friedenthal and J. Nathan, eds., *The Enduring Instant: Time and the Spectator in the Visual Arts; A Section of the XXXth International Congress of the History of Art, London*, Berlin, 2003.

Roethelisberger 1968
M. Roethlisberger, *Claude Lorrain: The Drawings*, 2 vols., Berkeley, California, and Los Angeles, 1968.

Roethlisberger 1969
——, *Bartholomeus Breenbergh: Handzeichnungen*, Berlin, 1969.

Roethlisberger 1981
——, *Bartholomeus Breenbergh: The Paintings*, Berlin and New York, 1981.

Roethlisberger 1991
——, "Abraham Bloemaert's Vanitas Representations," *Delineavit et Sculpsit* 5 (1991): 20–27.

Roethlisberger 1991a
——, "Les tableaux des Bloemaert dans les collections publiques françaises," *La revue du Louvre et des Musées de France* 2 (1991): 62–70.

Roethlisberger 1993
——, *Abraham Bloemaert and His Sons: Paintings and Prints*, 2 vols., Doornspijk, 1993.

Roethlisberger 2000
——, "Abraham Bloemaert: Recent Additions to His Paintings," *Artibus et historiae*, no. 41 (2000): 151–69.

De Roever 1885
N. de Roever, "Jan Harmensz. Muller," *Oud Holland* 3 (1885): 266–76.

Rosenberg 1928
J. Rosenberg, *Jacob van Ruisdael*, Berlin, 1928.

Rotterdam 1954
Hercules Seghers (E. Haverkamp-Begemann), Museum Boijmans Van Beuningen, Rotterdam, 1954.

Rotterdam 1974
Denkers, dichters en mannen van de wetenschap XVe–XVIIe eeuw (R. Aldèr), Prentenkabinet, Museum Boijmans Van Beuningen, Rotterdam, 1974.

Rotterdam 1994–95
Rotterdamse meesters uit de Gouden Eeuw (F. Scholten et. al.), Rotterdam Historisch Museum, 1994; published Zwolle, 1995.

Rotterdam/Paris 1974–75
Willem Buytewech 1591–1624 (E. Haverkamp-Begemann), Museum Boijmans Van Beuningen, Rotterdam; and Institut Néerlandais, Paris, 1974–75.

Rotterdam/Washington 1986
Jacques de Gheyn II, 1565–1629, als tekenaar, Museum Boijmans Van Beuningen, Rotterdam; and National Gallery of Art, Washington, DC, 1986

Rowlands 1979
J. Rowlands, *Hercules Segers*, New York, 1979.

Royalton-Kisch 1988
M. Royalton-Kisch, *Adriaen van de Venne's Album*, London 1988.

Ruby 1999
L. W. Ruby, *Paul Bril: The Drawings*, Antwerp, 1999.

Sacramento 1974
The Pre-Rembrandtists (A. Tümpel with essay by C. Tümpel), Crocker Art Museum, Sacramento, California, 1974.

Salerno 1977–78
L. Salerno, *Landscape Painters of the Seventeenth Century in Rome / Pittori di paesaggio del Seicento a Roma*, 3 vols., Rome, 1977–78.

Sandrart 1675
J. von Sandrart, *Teutsche Akademie der edlen Bau-, Bild- und Mahlerey-Künste*, 2 vols., Nuremberg, 1675.

San Francisco/Toledo/Boston 1966–67
The Age of Rembrandt (intro. by H. Gerson), California Palace of the Legion of Honor, San Francisco; Toledo Museum of Art; and Museum of Fine Arts, Boston, 1966–67.

Saunders and O'Malley/Vesalius 1950
J. B. de C. M. Saunders and C. D. O'Malley, *The Illustrations from the Works of Andreas Vesalius of Brussels*, Cleveland, 1950.

Saur/Künstler-Lexikon 1992
K. G. Saur, ed., *Allgemeines Künstlerlexikon: Die bildenden Künstler aller Zeiten und Völker*, Munich, 1992–.

Schabaeltje 1654
J. P. Schabaeltje, *Historisch verhael van het wonderlich en schrickelick opspringen van 't-*

Magasyn-huys, voor-gevallen op den 12 october 1654 binnen Delft, Amsterdam, [1654].

Schama 1987
S. Schama, *The Embarrassment of Riches: An Interpretation of Dutch Culture in the Golden Age*, New York, 1987.

Schapelhouman 1990
M. Schapelhouman, "Splinters van een Kabinet: Losse notities over enkele zeventiende-eeuwse tekeningen," *Bulletin van het Rijksmuseum* 38, no. 4 (1990): 314–23.

Schatborn 1974
P. Schatborn, review of *Lambert Doomer: Sämtliche Zeichnungen*, by W. Schulz, *Simiolus* 9 (1974): 48–55.

Schatborn 1997
——, "Tekeningen van de gebroeders Jan en Jacob Pynas. II. Jacob Pynas," *Bulletin van het Rijksmuseum* 45, no. 1 (1997): 3–25.

Schepers 1976
J. Schepers, *Haus und Hof westfälischer Bauern*, Münster, 1960 (3rd ed., 1976).

Schiller 1971–72
G. Schiller, *Iconography of Christian Art*, 2 vols., Greenwich, Connecticut, 1971–72.

Schloss 1983
C. S. Schloss, "A Note on Jan Baptist Weenix' Patronage in Rome," in *Essays in Northern Art Presented to Egbert Haverkamp-Begemann on His Sixtieth Birthday*, Doornspijk, 1983, 237–38.

Schmitz 1990
E. Schmitz, "Rembrandt in Diemen," *De kroniek van het Rembrandthuis* 42, no. 1–2 (1990): 6–20.

Schnackenburg 1981
B. Schnackenburg, *Adriaen van Ostade, Isack van Ostade: Zeichnungen und Aquarelle*, 2 vols., Hamburg, 1981.

Schneider 1932/73
H. Schneider, *Jan Lievens, sein Leben und seine Werke*, Haarlem, 1932 (reprinted with a supplement by R. E. O. Ekkart, Amsterdam, 1973).

Schneider 1883
H. J. Schneider, *Katalog der Herzoglichen Gemäldegalerie, Gotha*, Gotha, 1883.

Schotel 1851
G. D. J., Schotel, *De Abdij van Rijnsburg*, The Hague, 1851.

Schrevelius 1647
T. Schrevelius, *Harlemum*, Haarlem, 1647.

Schulte et al. 1997
A. G. Schulte, ed., *Ruïnes in Nederland*, with contributions by M. J. Kuipers-Verbuijs, H. Klomp, N. C. M. Maes, J. Michaels, A. G. Schulte, A. de Vries, and R. J. Wielinga, Zwolle, 1997.

Schulz 1971
W. Schulz, "Doomer and Savery," *Master Drawings* 9 (1971): 253–59.

Schulz 1972
——, *Lambert Doomer, 1624–1700: Leben und Werke*, 2 vols., Berlin, 1972.

Schulz 1974
——, *Lambert Doomer: Sämtliche Zeichnungen*, Berlin and New York, 1974.

Schulz 1978
——, *Cornelis Saftleven, 1607–1681; Leben und Werke, mit einem kritischen Katalog der Gemälde und Zeichnungen*, Berlin and New York, 1978.

Schulz 1982
——, *Herman Saftleven, 1609–1685: Leben und Werke, mit einem kritischen Katalog der Gemälde und Zeichnungen*, Berlin and New York, 1982.

Schwartz 1966–67
G. Schwartz, "Saenredam, Huygens, and the Utrecht Bull," *Simiolus* 1 (1966–67): 69–93.

Schwartz 1985
——, *Rembrandt, His Life, His Paintings*, New York, 1985.

Schwartz and Bok 1990
G. Schwartz and M. J. Bok, *Pieter Saenredam: The Painter and His Time*, Marssen and The Hague, 1990.

Scott 1968
J. A. Scott, "Gods and Heroes: Baroque Images of Antiquity," *Archaeology* 21 (October 1968): 306–7.

Scott 1987
M. A. Scott, *Dutch, Flemish, and German Paintings in the Cincinnati Art Museum: Fifteenth through Eighteenth Centuries*, Cincinnati, 1987.

Scriverius 1623
P. Scriverius, "Laure-Cranz voor Laurens Coster van Haerlem, eerste vinder vande boek-druckery," in S. Ampzing, *Beschryvinge ende lof der Stad Haerlem in Holland*, Haarlem, 1623.

Segel 1974
H. B. Segel, *The Baroque Poem: A Comparative Survey*, New York, 1974.

Von Sick 1930
I. von Sick, *Nicolaes Berchem: Ein Vorläufer des Rokoko*, Berlin, 1930.

Simon 1930
K. E. Simon, *Jacob van Ruisdael*, Berlin, 1930.

Simon 1958
M. Simon, *Claes Jansz. Visscher*, PhD diss., Freiberg im Breisgau, 1958.

Simoni 1985
A. E. C. Simoni, "Terra incognita: The Beudeker Collection in the Map Library of the British Library," *The British Library Journal* 2 (1985): 143–73.

Sliggers 1979
B. C. Sliggers, *Dagelijckse aentekeningen van Vincent Laurensz. van der Vinne: Reisjournaal van een Haarlems schilder, 1652–1655*, Haarlem, 1979.

Slive 1953
S. Slive, *Rembrandt and His Critics, 1630–1730*, The Hague, 1953 (reprint, New York, 1988).

Slive 1988
——, "The Manor Kostverloren: Vicissitudes of a Seventeenth-Century Landscape Motif," in R. E. Fleischer and S. S. Munshower, eds., *The Age of Rembrandt: Studies in Seventeenth-Century Dutch Painting; Papers in Art History from the Pennsylvania State University III*, University Park, Pennsylvania, 1988, 132–68.

Slive 1995
——, *Dutch Painting, 1600–1800*, New Haven, Connecticut, and London, 1995.

Slive 2001
——, *Jacob van Ruisdael: A Complete Catalogue of His Paintings, Drawings and Etchings*, New Haven, Connecticut, and London, 2001.

Sluijter-Seijffert 1984
N. Sluijter-Seijffert, *Cornelis van Poelenburgh (ca. 1593–1667)*, PhD diss., Rijksuniversiteit, Leiden, 1984.

Smith 1829–42
J. A. Smith, *A Catalogue Raisonné of the Works of the Most Eminent Dutch, Flemish and French Painters*, 9 vols., London, 1829, and supplement, 1842.

Smith 1982
D. R. Smith, *Masks of Wedlock: Seventeenth-Century Dutch Marriage Portraiture*, Ann Arbor, Michigan, 1982.

Sobel and Andrewes 1998
D. Sobel and W. J. H. Andrewes, *The Illustrated Longitude*, New York, 1998.

De Sousa-Leão 1973
J. de Sousa-Leão, *Frans Post, 1612–1680*, Amsterdam, 1973.

Van Spaan 1698
G. van Spaan, *Beschrijvinge der stad Rotterdam: En eenige omleggende dorpen*, Rotterdam, 1698.

Spicer 1970
J. Spicer, "The 'naer het leven' Drawings: By Pieter Bruegel or Roelandt Savery?" *Master Drawings* 8 (1970): 3–30.

Spicer 1983
——, "'De Koe voor d'aerde statt': The Origin of the Dutch Cattle Piece," in A.-M. Logan, ed., *Essays in Northern European Art Presented to Egbert Haverkamp-Begemann on His Sixtieth Birthday*, Doornspijk, 1983, 251–56.

Springer 1910–12
J. Springer, *Die Radierungen des Hercules Seghers*, Berlin, 3 vols. 1910–12.

St. Petersburg, Florida 2001
Abraham Bloemaert and His Time (J. Hardin, with essays by M. Roethlisberger and S. Metzler), Museum of Fine Arts, St. Petersburg, Florida, 2001.

Stampfle 1991
F. Stampfle, with the assistance of R. S. Kraemer and J. S. Turner *Netherlandish Drawings of the Fifteenth and Sixteenth Centuries and Flemish Drawings of the Seventeenth and Eighteenth Centuries in The Pierpont Morgan Library*, Princeton, New Jersey, 1991.

Stechow 1938
W. Stechow, "Die 'Pellekussenpoort' bei Utrecht auf Bildern von J. van Goyen und S. van Ruisdael," *Oud Holland* 55 (1938): 202–8.

Stechow 1940–41
——, "The Myth of Philemon and Baucis in Art," *Journal of the Warburg and Courtauld Institutes* 4 (1940–41): 103–13.

Stechow 1948
——, "Jan Baptist Weenix," *Art Quarterly* 11, no. 3 (1948): 181–99.

Stechow 1966
——, *Dutch Landscape Painting of the Seventeenth Century*, London, 1966.

Stechow 1967
——, *Catalogue of European and American Paintings and Sculpture in the Allen Memorial Art Museum, Oberlin College*, Oberlin, Ohio, 1967.

Steland 1989
A. C. Steland, *Die Zeichnungen des Jan Asselijn*, Fridingen, 1989.

Steland-Stief 1971
A. C. Steland-Stief, *Jan Asselijn, nach 1610 bis 1652*, Amsterdam, 1971.

Steland-Stief 1986
——, "Zu Willem Schellinks' Entwicklung als Zeichner: Die Zeichnungen der Frankreichreise von 1646 und die Ausbildung zum Italianisten in der Nachfolge des Jan Asselijn," *Niederdeutsche Beiträge zur Kunstgeschichte* 25 (1986): 79–108.

Stokhuyzen 1962
F. Stokhuyzen, *The Dutch Windmill*, trans. C. Dikshoorn, Bussum, 1962.

Van Stolk 1895–1931
A. van Stolk, *Atlas van Stolk: Catalogus der historie-, spot- en zinneprenten betrekkelijk de geschiedenis van Nederland verzameld*, 11 vols., Amsterdam, 1895–1931.

Strauss 1977
W. Strauss, *Hendrik Goltzius, 1558–1617: The Complete Engravings and Woodcuts*, 2 vols., New York, 1977.

Strengholt 1977
L. Strengholt, *De dichter van Bauw-heers wel-leven: Pieter Janssoon Schaghen; Een oud literair vraagstuk opgelost*, Bijdragen tot de Nederlandse taal- en letterkunden 5, Leiden, 1977.

Struik 1981
D. J. Struik, *The Land of Stevin and Huygens: A Sketch of Science and Technology in the Dutch Republic during the Golden Century*, Dordrecht, Boston, and London, 1981.

De Stuers 1873
V. E. L. de Stuers, "Holland op zijn smalst," *De gids* 37, no. 3 (November 1873): 320–403.

De Stuers 1875
——, *Da Capo: Een woord over regeering, kunst en oude monumenten*, The Hague, 1875.

De Stuers 1879
——, *De ruïne van Brederode*, Haarlem, 1879.

Sullivan 1979
S. A. Sullivan, "Jan Baptiste Weenix: Still Life with a Dead Swan," *Bulletin of the Detroit Institute of Arts* 57 (1979): 64–71.

Sullivan 1984
——, *The Dutch Gamepiece*, Montclair, New Jersey, 1984.

Sumowski 1979–92
W. Sumowski, *Drawings of the Rembrandt School*, 10 vols., New York, 1979–92.

Sumowski 1983
——, *Die Gemälde der Rembrandt Schüler*, 5 vols., Landau/Pfalz, 1983.

Sutton 1986
P. C. Sutton, *A Guide to Dutch Art in America*, Washington, DC, 1986.

Sutton 1990
——, *Northern European Paintings in the Philadelphia Museum of Art from the Sixteenth through the Nineteenth Century*, Philadelphia, 1990.

Sutton 1992
——, *Dutch and Flemish Seventeenth-Century Paintings: The Harold Samuel Collection*, Cambridge, England, 1992.

Sweeny 1972
B. Sweeny, *The John G. Johnson Collection: Catalogue of Flemish and Dutch Paintings*, Philadelphia, 1972.

Sweerts 1698–1700
H. Sweerts, *Koddige en ernstige opschriften, of luyffens, wagens, glazen, uithangborden, en andere tafereelen*, 4 vols., 3rd ed., Amsterdam, 1698–1700.

Temminck 1972
J. J. Temminck, "Het Haarlem van de 16de Eeuw," in *Man Sagh Haerlem bestormen … Catalogus ter gelegenheid van herdenking van het beleg van Haarlem*, Haarlem, 1972, 5–14.

Temminck 1995
J. J. Temminck, ed., *Huis ter Kleef: Het enige kasteel van Haarlem*, Haarlem, 1995.

Temminck Groll 1988
C. L. Temminck Groll, "Het Valkhof te Nijmegen en het herbouwen van verdwenen monumenten," *ARTillerie* 6, no. 1 (October 1988): 19–33.

Thieme-Becker
U. Thieme and F. Becker, *Allgemeines Lexikon der bildenden Künstler*, 37 vols., Leipzig, 1907–50.

Tillema 1973
J. A. C. Tillema, "Victor de Stuers en de Sint Jan van Den Bosch," *Bulletin KNOB* 72, no. 4 (September 1973): 117–30.

Tokyo 2003
Renburanto to renburantoha: seisho shinwa monogatari / Rembrandt and the Rembrandt School: The Bible, Mythology and Ancient

History (A. Kofuku), National Museum of Western Art, Tokyo, 2003.

Tokyo/Kyoto 1976
Masterpieces of World Art from American Museums, Toyko-Kyoto National Museum, 1976.

Den Tonkelaar 1980
J. F. den Tonkelaar, "Het middenschip van de Dom vernietigd door een tornado? De Stormramp van 1 augustus 1674, meteorlogisch verklaard," *Jaarboek Oud-Utrecht* (1980): 95–109.

Toulmin and Goodfield 1965
S. Toulmin and J. Goodfield, *The Discovery of Time*, London, 1965.

Trevelyan 1930
M. C. Trevelyan, *William the Third and the Defence of Holland, 1672–4*, London, New York, and Toronto, 1930.

Trexler 1997
R. C. Trexler, *The Journey of the Magi: Meaning in the History of a Christian Story*, Princeton, New Jersey, 1997.

Tümpel 1974
A. Tümpel, "Claes Cornelisz. Moeyaert" and "Claesz Cornelisz. Moeyaert (Fortsetzung): Katalog der Gemälde" *Oud Holland* 88, nos. 1/2 (1974): 1–163 and no. 4 (1974): 245–90.

Utrecht 1961
Catalogue Raisonné of the Works by Pieter Jansz. Saenredam (P. T. A. Swillens and I. Q. van Regteren Altena), Centraal Museum, Utrecht, 1961.

Utrecht 1965
Nederlandse 17de-eeuwse Italianiserende Lanschapschilders (A. Blankert), Centraal Museum, Utrecht, 1965 (reprint, Soest, 1978).

Utrecht 1974
De Dom in puin, 1 augustus 1674: Herman Saftleven tekent de stormschade in de stad Utrecht, Centraal Museum, Utrecht, 1974.

Utrecht 1997
Bedevaarten in Nederland (C. Staal and M. Wingens), Museum Catharijneconvent, Utrecht, 1997.

Utrecht/Frankfurt am Main/Luxembourg 1993
Het gedroomde land: Pastorale schilderkunst in de Gouden Eeuw (P. van den Brink et. al.), Centraal Museum, Utrecht; Schirn Kunsthalle, Frankfurt am Main; and Musée National d'Histoire et d'Art, Luxembourg, 1993.

E. Valentiner 1930
E. Valentiner, *Karel van Mander als Maler*, Strassburg, 1930.

Valentiner 1913
W. R. Valentiner, *A Catalogue of a Collection of Paintings and Some Art Objects*, vol. 2, *Flemish and Dutch Paintings: John G. Johnson Collection*, Philadelphia, 1913.

Valentiner 1924
——, *Nicolaes Maes*, Stuttgart, Berlin, and Leipzig, 1924.

Valentiner 1926–27
——, "Pieter de Hooch," parts 1 and 2, *Art in America* 15, no. 1 (December 1926): 45–64: 15, and no. 2 (February 1927): 67–77.

Valentiner 1930
——, *Pieter de Hooch: The Master's Paintings*, New York, 1930.

Valentiner 1932
——, "Zum 30 Geburtstag Jan Vermeers, Oktober 1932: Vermeer und die Meister der holländischen Genremalerei," *Pantheon* 10 (1932): 305–24.

Vancouver 1957
Rembrandt to van Gogh, Vancouver Art Gallery, 1957.

Varriano 2004
J. Varriano, "Claude in the *Campagna*," *Plein Air Magazine* 1 (2004): 30–33.

Vassar College Art Gallery 1967
Vassar College Art Gallery: Selections from the Permanent Collection, New York, 1967.

Van Veen 1985
P. A. F. van Veen, *De soeticheydt des buyten-levens, verghselschaft met de boucken: Het hofdicht als tak van een georgische litteratuur*, Utrecht, 1985.

Van Veen/Orgel 1979
O. van Veen, with intro. and notes by S. Orgel, *Horatii Emblemata: Antwerp 1612*, New York and London, 1979.

Vekeman and Muller Hofstede 1984
H. Vekeman and J. Muller Hofstede, eds., *Wort und Bild in der niederländischen Kunst und Literatur des 16. und 17. Jahrhunderts*, Erftstadt, 1984.

Veldman 1974
I. M. Veldman, "Maarten van Heemskerck and Hadrianus Junius: The Relationship between a Painter and a Humanist," *Simiolus* 7, no.1 (1974): 35–54.

Veldman 1977
——, *Maarten van Heemskerck and Dutch Humanism in the Sixteenth Century*, Maarssen, 1977.

Veldman 1993
——, "Maarten van Heemskerck in Italy," *Nederlands kunsthistorisch jaarboek* 44 (1993): 125–41.

Verbeek 1983
H. Verbeek, *Gerrit Battem constrijck schilder, 1636–1684*, thesis, University of Leiden, 1983.

Vergara 1985
L. Vergara, "New York: Roman Landscapes at Feigen," *Burlington Magazine* 127 (1985): 405.

Vermeule 1956
C. Vermeule, "The Dal Pozz-Albani Drawings of Classical Antiquities: Notes on Their Content and Arrangement," *Art Bulletin* 30 (1956): 31–46.

Vermeulen 1928
E. A. J. Vermeulen, *Handboek tot de geschiedenis der Nederlandsche bouwkunst*, 3 vols., The Hague, 1928.

Vienna/New York/Fort Worth 1993 and 1995
Die Landschaft im Jahrhundert Rembrandts: Niederländische Zeichnungen des 17. Jahrhunderts der Graphischen Sammlung Albertina (M. Bisanz-Prakken), 1993 (English ed., *Drawings from the Albertina: Landscape in the Age of Rembrandt*, The Drawing Center, New York; and The Kimball Art Museum, Fort Worth, Texas, 1995).

Vienna/Salzburg 1986
Die Niederländer in Italien (R. Trnek), Akademie der Bildenden Künste, Vienna; and Residenzgalerie, Salzburg, 1986.

Virgil/Fairclough 1974
Virgil, trans. H. R. Fairclough, 2 vols., rev. ed., Loeb Classical Library, Cambridge, Massachusetts, and London, 1974.

Visscher 1614/1949
R. Visscher, *Sinnepoppen*, Amsterdam and Middelburg, 1614 (modern reprint with commentary by L. Brummel, The Hague, 1949).

Vondel 1930
J. van den Vondel, *De volledige werken van Joost van den Vondel*, vol. 5, ed. H. C. Diferee, Utrecht, 1930.

Vondel/Verwey 1986
J. van den Vondel, *Volledige dichtwerken en oorspronklijk proza*, ed. A. Verwey, Amsterdam, 1986.

De Vries 1984
L. de Vries, *Jan van der Heyden*, Amsterdam, 1984.

De Vries 1998
——, *Gerard de Lairesse: An Artist between Stage and Studio*, Amsterdam, 1998.

De Vries 2003
——, "Written Paintings: Real and Imaginary Works of Art in De Lairesse's *Schilderboeck*," *Visual Resources* 19, no. 4 (2003): 307–20.

De Vries 1915
R. W. P. de Vries, *Cornelis Ploos van Amstel et ses élèves: Essai d'une iconographie*, Amsterdam, 1915.

Van Vriesland 1939
V. E. van Vriesland, ed., *Spiegel van de Nederlandsche poëzie door alle eeuwen*, Amsterdam, 1939.

Wagner 1970
H. Wagner, "Jan van der Weyden als Zeichner," *Jahrbuch der Berliner Museen* 12 (1970): 111–50.

Wagner 1971
——, *Jan van der Heyden, 1637–1712*, Amsterdam and Haarlem, 1971.

Walford 1991
E. J. Walford, *Jacob van Ruisdael and the Perception of Landscape*, New Haven, Connecticut, and London, 1991.

Waller 1974
F. G. Waller, *Biographisch woordenboek van Noord-Nederlandsche graveurs*, Amsterdam 1974 (reprint of 1938 ed.).

Walsh 1991
J. Walsh, "Skies and Reality in Dutch Landscape," in D. Freedberg and J. de Vries eds., *Art in History, History in Art*, Chicago, 1991, 95–118.

Walsh 1991a
——, "Los Angeles—Dutch Marine Art," review of Minneapolis/Toledo/Los Angeles 1990–91, *Burlington Magazine* 133 (September 1991): 645–46.

Washington 1990
Rembrandt's Landscapes: Drawings and Prints (C. Schneider with contributions by B. Bakker, N. A. Ash, and S. Fletcher), National Gallery of Art, Washington, DC, 1990.

Washington and elsewhere 1985–87
Master Drawings from Titian to Picasso: The Curtis O. Baer Collection (E. Zafran), National Gallery of Art, Washington, DC; Indianapolis Museum of Art; The John and Mable Ringling Museum of Art, Sarasota, Florida; High Museum of Art, Atlanta; Walters Art Gallery, Baltimore; and Frederick S. Wight Art Gallery, University of California at Los Angeles, 1985–87.

Washington/Cleveland/Paris 1975–77
The European Vision of America (H. Honour), National Gallery of Art, Washington, DC; and Cleveland Museum of Art, 1975–76 (French ed., *L'Amérique vue par l'Europe*, Grand Palais, Paris, 1976–77).

Washington/Denver/Fort Worth 1977
Seventeenth Century Dutch Drawings from American Collections: A Loan Exhibition (F. W. Robinson), National Gallery of Art, Washington, DC; Denver Art Museum; and Kimbell Art Museum, Fort Worth, Texas, 1977.

Washington/Detroit/Amsterdam 1980–81
Gods, Saints, and Heroes: Dutch Painting in the Age of Rembrandt (A. Blankert, C. Brown, S. D. Kuretsky, B. Brenninkmeyer-de Rooij, E. J. Sluijter, D. P. Snoep, P. van Thiel, A. Tümpel, C. Tümpel, and A. K. Wheelock Jr.), National Gallery of Art, Washington, DC; Detroit Institute of Arts; and Rijksmuseum, Amsterdam, 1980–81.

Washington/Dulwich/The Hague 2000–2001
Gerrit Dou 1613–1675: Master Painter in the Age of Rembrandt (R. Baer, with contributions by A. K. Wheelock Jr. and A. Boersma), National Gallery of Art, Washington, DC; Dulwich Picture Gallery, London; and Mauritshuis, The Hague, 2000–2001.

Washington/London/Amsterdam 2002
Aelbert Cuyp (A. K. Wheelock Jr., A. Chong, and A. Rüger), National Gallery of Art, Washington, DC; National Gallery, London; and Rijksmuseum, Amsterdam, 2002.

Webster and Ford 1933
J. Webster and J. Ford, *Plays*, G. B. Harrison, ed., Everyman's Library 899, London and New York, 1933.

Weiss 1969
R. Weiss, *The Renaissance Discovery of Classical Antiquity*, Oxford, 1969.

Welu 1979–80
J. A. Welu, "Willem van Nieulandt the Younger: Staging an Old Testament Theme," *The Worcester Art Museum Journal* 3 (1979–80): 2–7.

Westermann 1996
M. Westermann, *A Worldly Art: The Dutch Republic, 1585–1718*, New York, 1996.

Westermann 1997
——, *The Amusements of Jan Steen: Comic Painting in the Seventeenth Century*, Studies in Netherlandish Art and Cultural History 1, Zwolle, 1997.

Weve 1997
W. F. Weve, *De kaart figuratief van Delft*, Rijswijk, 1997.

Wheelock 1995
A. K. Wheelock Jr., *Dutch Paintings of the Seventeenth Century*, Collections of the National Gallery of Art Systematic Catalogue, New York and Oxford, 1995.

White 1969
C. White, *Rembrandt as an Etcher: A Study of the Artist at Work*, 2 vols., University Park, Pennsylvania, 1969.

White 1982
——, *The Dutch Pictures in the Collection of Her Majesty the Queen*, Cambridge, England, 1982.

White 1987
——, *Peter Paul Rubens: Man and Artist*, New Haven, Connecticut, and London, 1987.

White and Crawley 1994
C. White and C. Crawley, *The Dutch and Flemish Drawings of the Fifteenth to the Early Nineteenth Centuries in the Collection of Her Majesty the Queen at Windsor Castle*, Cambridge, England, 1994.

Whitehead and Boeseman 1989
P. J. P. Whitehead and M. Boeseman, *A Portrait of Dutch 17th Century Brazil: Animals, Plants, and People by the Artists of Johan Maurits of Nassau*, Amsterdam, Oxford, and New York, 1989.

De Wicquefort 1673
A. de Wicquefort, *Advis fidelle aux veritable Hollandois touchant ce qui s'est passé dans les villages de Bodegrave & Swammerdam & les crautés inoüies, que les François y ont exerceés avec un mémoire de la dernière marche de l'armeé du roy de France en Brabant et en Flandre*, The Hague, 1673.

Widerkehr 1993
L. Widerkehr, "Jacob Matham Goltzij Privignus: Jacob Matham graveur et ses rapports avec Hendrick Goltzius," in *Goltzius Studies: Hendrick Goltzius (1558–1617)*, Nederlands Kunsthistorisch

Jaarboek 42–43 (1991–92), Zwolle, 1993, 219–60.

Wiegand 1971
W. Wiegand, *Ruisdael Studien: Ein Versuch zur Ikonographie der Landschaftmalerei*, diss., Hamburg, 1971.

Wieseman n.d.
M. E. Wieseman, "Adriaen Pietersz. van de Venne," www.oberlin.edu/allenart/collection/venne.html.

Van der Wijck 1972
H. W. M. van der Wijck, "Country-Houses in the Northern Netherlands: The Way of Life of a Calvinistic Patriciate," *Apollo* 96 (November 1972): 406–15.

Van der Wijck 1982
——, *De Nederlandse buitenplaats: Aspecten van ontwikkeling, bescherming en herstel*, Alphen aan den Rijn, 1982.

Wijn 1982
J. W. Wijn, *Het beleg van Haarlem*, The Hague, 1982 (1st ed., 1943).

Williamstown/Sarasota 1994–95
A Golden Harvest: Paintings by Adam Pynacker (L. B. Harwood), The Sterling and Francine Clark Institute of Arts, Williamstown, Massachusetts; and John and Mable Ringling Museum of Art, Sarasota, Florida, 1994–95.

Wilmer 1980
C. C. S. Wilmer, *Utrecht betekend: Vier eeuwen tekeningen en aquarellen uit de topographische atlas van het Gemeentearchief*, The Hague, 1980.

Wilson 1974
H. T. Wilson, *The Art of Romeyn de Hooghe: An Atlas of European Late Baroque Culture*, PhD diss., Harvard University, 1974.

Wittman 1967
O. Wittman, "The Golden Age in the Netherlands," *Apollo* 86 no. 2 (December 1967): 466–78.

Wolfson 1961
H. A. Wolfson, *The Philosophy of Spinoza*, Cleveland, 1961 (1st ed., 1934), chap. 9, "Duration, Time and Eternity."

Woodward 2001
C. Woodward, *In Ruins*, New York, 2001.

Worthen 1993
A. N. Worthen, "Calligraphic Inscriptions on Dutch Mannerist Prints," in *Goltzius Studies: Hendrick Goltzius (1558–1617), Nederlands Kunsthistorisch Jaarboek* 42–43 (1991–92), Zwolle, 1993, 261–306.

Wright 1981
C. Wright, *A Golden Age of Painting: Dutch, Flemish, German Paintings: Sixteenth–Seventeenth Centuries, from the Collection of the Sarah Campbell Blaffer Foundation; Catalogue*, San Antonio, Texas, 1981.

Wurzbach 1906–11
A. von Wurzbach, *Niederländisches Künstler-Lexikon*, 3 vols., Vienna and Leipzig, 1906–11

Van der Wyck and Kloek 1990
H. M. W. van der Wyck and W. T. Kloek with J. W. Niemeijer, *De kasteeltekeningen van Roelant Roghman*, 2 vols., Alphen aan den Rijn, 1990.

Yoder 1988
J. G. Yoder, *Unrolling Time: Christiaan Huygens and the Mathematization of Nature*, Cambridge, England, 1988 (reprint, 1990).

Zimmerman 1989
R. Zimmerman, *Künstliche Ruinen: Studien zu ihrer Bedeutung und Form*, Wiesbaden, 1989.

Zucker 1961
P. Zucker, "Ruins—An Aesthetic Hybrid," *Journal of Aesthetics and Art Criticism* 20, no. 3 (Winter 1961): 119–30.

Zucker 1968
——, *Fascination of Decay: Ruins: Relic, Symbol, Ornament*, Ridgewood, New Jersey, 1968.

Zwollo 1999
A. Zwollo, "De romeinse panoramas van Jan de Bisschop en Theodoor Matham," *Oud Holland* 113, nos. 1–2 (1999): 45–52.

List of Artists (*with catalogue numbers*)

Photograph Credits

The publishers wish to thank the museums, galleries, libraries, and private collectors named in the illustration captions for permitting the reproduction of works in their collections and for supplying photographs. Additional information regarding copyrights and credits is provided below:

© The Art Institute of Chicago, Cat. nos. 27, 69; Figs. 110, 128

Bayerische Staatsgemäldesammlungen, Alte Pinakothek, Munich, Fig. 71

© The Trustees of the British Museum, Figs. 32, 33, 35, 37, 38, 49, 119, 132, 142, 156

Biblioteque royale de Belgique, Brussels, Fig. 65

© Centraal Museum, Utrecht, Fig. 25

© Christie's Images Limited, Fig. 154

© The Cleveland Museum of Art, Cat. nos. 21, 32

Collection Frits Lugt, Institut Néederlandais, Paris, Figs. 47, 114, 136, 141

Courtauld Institute of Art Gallery, London, Fig. 14

The Currier Gallery of Art, Manchester, New Hampshire, Fig. 59

© The Detroit Institute of Arts, Cat. nos. 11, 25, 45, 80; Figs. 11, 152

Courtesy of the Fogg Art Museum, Harvard University Art Museums © 2004 President and Fellows of Harvard College, Cambridge, Cat. nos. 1, 9, 16, 18, 28, 35, 36, 40, 47, 65, 76; Figs. 28, 124, 130, 147

Gemäldegalerie, Staatliche Museen zu Berlin, Germany (Bildarchiv Preussischer Kulturbesitz/Art Resource, NY), Fig. 139

Gemeente Musea Delft, Collectie Stedelijk Museum Het Prinsenhof, on loan from Instituut Collectie Nederland, Fig. 133

Research Library, The Getty Research Institute, Los Angeles (84-B31171), Fig. 30

© The J. Paul Getty Museum, Fig. 87

Courtesy of the Herbert F. Johnson Museum of Art, Cornell University, Cat. nos. 37, 79

Herzog Anton Ulrich-Museum Braunschweig, Kuntsmuseum des Landes Niedersachsen, Figs. 57, 68

Department of Printing and Graphic Arts, Houghton Library, Harvard College Library: Typ 632.24.240 (B), Fig. 12; Typ 632.34.501, Fig. 20; Typ 632.90.211, Fig. 160

Department of Rare Books, Houghton Library, Harvard College Library: *54-1437, Fig. 5; Emb 17.11*, Fig. 13; Neth 3407.1*, Fig. 110; Neth 3147.20*, Figs. 112, 113, 117; Neth 3310.7*, Fig. 120

Kupferstichkabinett, Staatliche Museen zu Berlin, Germany (Bildarchiv Preussischer Kulturbesitz/Art Resource NY), Figs. 6, 50, 56, 79, 144

Leiden University Library, (ms. Hug. 9 fol. 18r), Fig. 31

Louvre, Paris, France (Réunion des Musées Nationaux/Art Resource, NY), Figs. 84, 86, 143, 146

© The Metropolitan Museum of Art, New York, Cat. nos. 19, 20, 26, 38, 39, 41, 46, 51, 53, 72; Figs. 1, 135, 137

© Museum Catharijneconvent, Fig. 22

© 2004 Museum of Fine Arts, Boston, Cat. nos. 2a-b, 3a-d, 49, 58, 61, 77; Figs. 3, 42, 148, 155, 157

© Board of Trustees, National Gallery of Art, Washington, DC, Cat. nos. 13, 34, 74; Figs. 19, 66, 67, 70, 76, 85

© The National Gallery of Scotland, Edinburgh, Fig. 145

Norton Simon Foundation, Fig. 21

RDK neg. L70314, 4373, Fig. 161

© Rijksmueum-Stitchting, Amsterdam, Figs. 8, 16, 36, 39, 40, 41, 43, 44, 45, 46, 48, 58, 61, 62, 63, 81, 83, 90, 111, 125, 142, 156

The Royal Collection © 2004, Her Majesty Queen Elizabeth II, Figs. 64, 78, 89

The Royal Pump Rooms, Royal Leamington Spa, Warwickshire, Fig. 122

Courtesy of Smithsonian Institution Libraries, Washington, DC, Fig. 129

Utrecht University Library, Fig. 15

© V&A Images, Victoria and Albert Museum, London, Figs. 34, 159

Specific photographer acknowledgements are as follows:

Jörg P. Anders, Figs. 6, 56, 139, 144

Richard Carafelli, Cat. nos. 13, 74

Bill Finney, Fig. 59

Ruben de Heer, Fig. 22

Kallsen Katya, Cat. nos. 9, 16, 18, 36

B. P. Keiser, Figs. 57, 68

Erik Löffler 2004, Fig. 102

G. J. Luijendijk, Fig. 108b

Allen Macintyre, Cat. nos. 1, 28, 35, 40, 47, 75; Fig. 124

R. J. Phil, Cat. 60

Chip Porter and Michael Macauley, Cat. nos. 17, 23, 44, 48, 67, 73; Figs. 7, 82, 116, 134, 138, 140

SMK Foto, Figs. 72, 123

Rick Stafford, Fig. 130

Malcolm Varon, Cat. nos. 19, 26, 41, 51

Joseph Zehavi 2004, Cat. nos. 30, 62

This book was composed in Janson, a typeface based upon seventeenth-century Dutch oldstyle letterforms attributed to the Hungarian punchcutter Nicholas Kis.